D0870128

CRITICAL PERSPECTIVES ON MEDIA AND SOCIETY

THE GUILFORD COMMUNICATION SERIES

Editors

Theodore L. Glasser
Department of Communication, Stanford University

Howard E. Sypher
Department of Communication Studies, University of Kansas

Advisory Board

Charles Berger	**Peter Monge**	**Michael Schudson**
James Carey	**Barbara O'Keefe**	**Ellen Wartella**

CRITICAL PERSPECTIVES ON MEDIA AND SOCIETY
Robert K. Avery and David Eason, *Editors*

THE JOURNALISM OF OUTRAGE: INVESTIGATIVE REPORTING
AND AGENDA BUILDING IN AMERICA
David L. Protess, Fay Lomax Cook, Jack C. Doppelt, James S. Ettema,
Margaret T. Gordon, Donna R. Leff, and Peter Miller

MASS MEDIA AND POLITICAL TRANSITION: THE HONG KONG
PRESS IN CHINA'S ORBIT
Chin-Chuan Lee and Joseph Man Chan

STUDYING INTERPERSONAL INTERACTION
Barbara M. Montgomery and Steve Duck, *Editors*

VOICES OF CHINA: THE INTERPLAY OF POLITICS AND
JOURNALISM
Chin-Chuan Lee, *Editor*

COMMUNICATION AND CONTROL: NETWORKS AND THE NEW
ECONOMIES OF COMMUNICATION
G. J. Mulgan

CASE STUDIES IN ORGANIZATIONAL COMMUNICATION
Beverly Davenport Sypher, *Editor*

CRITICAL PERSPECTIVES

ON
MEDIA AND SOCIETY

Editors

ROBERT K. AVERY
DAVID EASON
University of Utah

THE GUILFORD PRESS
New York   London

© 1991 Speech Communication Association
(excluding Editor's Introduction)
5105 Backlick Road
Annandale, VA 22003

Published by The Guilford Press
A Division of Guilford Publications, Inc.
72 Spring Street, New York, NY 10012

Printed in the United States of America

This book is printed on acid-free paper.

Last digit is print number: 9 8 7 6 5 4 3 2 1

Library of Congress Cataloging-in-Publication Data

Critical studies in mass communication / edited by Robert K. Avery,
David Eason.
    p.   cm. — (The Guilford communication series)
    Selected articles from the journal Critical studies in mass
communication.
    Includes bibliographical references and index.
    ISBN 0-89862-315-4 (hardcover). — ISBN 0-89862-289-1 (pbk.)
    1. Mass media criticism.   I. Avery, Robert K.   II. Eason, David.
III. Series.
P96.C76C73   1991
302.23—dc20   91-22126
                                                            CIP

To the memory of our parents
Scott and Alice
Lester and Nell

Contributors

Steve Barkin, College of Journalism, University of Maryland, College Park, Maryland

Douglas Birkhead, Department of Communication, University of Utah, Salt Lake City, Utah

Richard Campbell, Communication Department, University of Michigan, Ann Arbor, Michigan

James W. Carey, College of Communication, University of Illinois at Urbana-Champaign, Urbana, Illinois

Celeste Michelle Condit, Department of Speech Communication, University of Georgia, Athens, Georgia

Caren Deming, Media Arts Department, University of Arizona, Tucson, Arizona

James Ettema, Department of Communication Studies, Northwestern University, Evanston, Illinois

John Fiske, Department of Communication Arts, University of Wisconsin at Madison, Madison, Wisconsin

Theodore Glasser, Department of Communication, Stanford University, Stanford, California

Herman Gray, Department of Sociology, Northeastern University, Boston, Massachusetts

Lawrence Grossberg, Department of Speech Communication, University of Illinois at Urbana-Champaign, Urbana, Illinois

Michael Gurevitch, College of Journalism, University of Maryland, College Park, Maryland

Stuart Hall, Department of Sociology, The Open University, Milton Keynes, England

Robert Horwitz, Department of Communication, University of California at San Diego, La Jolla, California

Elizabeth Long, Department of Sociology, Rice University, Houston, Texas

Denis McQuail, Department of Communication, University of Amsterdam, Amsterdam, The Netherlands

Horace Newcomb, Department of Radio, Television, Film, University of Texas, Austin, Texas

Michael Schudson, Department of Communication, University of California at San Diego, La Jolla, California

Lynn Spigel, Department of Communication Arts, University of Wisconsin, Madison, Wisconsin

Linda Steiner, Department of Journalism and Media, Rutgers University, New Brunswick, New Jersey

Contents

PART II   THE APPLICATION OF CRITICAL APPROACHES

CRITICAL PERSPECTIVES ON MEDIA AND SOCIETY

Introduction

ROBERT K. AVERY, DAVID EASON

The essays in this volume were first published in the journal *Critical Studies in Mass Communication* from 1984 to 1989, the first six years of its existence. Those were years when varied theoretical and methodological perspectives were asserting themselves as "critical studies" within communication. The journal reflected these currents even as it, in turn, gave shape to them within the broader framework of the field.

The appearance of *CSMC* in March of 1984 has been singled out as clear evidence of a dramatic upheaval within our discipline. William Brown (1985) observed that the authorization of the journal represented the legitimation of rhetorical study of media content. Similarly, Gronbeck and Coder (1985, p. 380) concluded that the arrival of *CSMC* "explicitly recognizes the importance of humanistic, scholarly reflection upon the products and processes of mass mediated discourse." But the new journal's timely appearance was as much a product of chance as it was a carefully planned publication venue.

Restlessness within the Mass Communication Division of the Speech Communication Association had resulted in a formal proposal for a new mass communication journal as early as 1979. While the absence of serious mass communication criticism had been accurately identified by Samuel Becker's commissioned analysis of eighteen journals which served as important publication outlets for media researchers, this omission was not perceived as being any more serious than the lack of lengthy theoretical pieces or the paucity of well-conceived experimental studies. The very term "critical studies" was more a carry-over from other proposals before the Publications Board at the time than an editorial mandate for the newly emerging scholarly tradition.

With the benefit of hindsight, it can be concluded that both the timing and title for the new journal were most fortuitous. *CSMC* appeared during a period of intense change within the academy, and it afforded a forum for new voices, ideas, and approaches. But the journal was never permitted to become the mouthpiece of any one critical perspective. Indeed, the first "Editor's Note"

3

set forth the commitment which guided *CSMC* through its first six years of publication. Attempting to specify a single definition of "critical studies" was determined to be both unrealistic and unproductive for the good of the field. Rather, the journal was committed to a pluralistic ideal, and attempted to provide a forum for what W. J. T. Mitchell described as "dialectical pluralism." In Mitchell's words, that meant pluralism which "is not content with mere diversity but insists on pushing divergent theories and practices toward confrontation and dialogue" (1982, p. 613).

Critical Studies in Mass Communication was by no means the first scholarly journal to make this commitment. But positioned as an integral part of SCA's respected serials publication program, the new journal served an important pedagogical function for the field. Work that would have been submitted previously to European journals or American-based publication outlets which operated on the fringes of mainstream communication research began finding its way to *CSMC*'s editorial office. The appearance of this serious scholarship within an SCA journal did contribute to its legitimation and encouraged a broader readership than it had enjoyed before. And by defining "critical" in the widest possible sense, many scholars who had not contributed to the dialogue became actively involved. Suddenly, a whole range of research which formerly was considered outside of one's scholarly purview became central to the emerging debate within communication academic circles.

During the six years that *CSMC* was housed at the University of Utah, the journal promoted debate on a broad range of topics. This was accomplished in part by the grouping of articles with invited responses and by a thematically oriented "Review and Criticism" section. Only a small sampling of these issues could be represented here.

The studies selected for this volume continue to map out paths to critical engagement with some of the central issues raised by the relationship of media and society. They connect those issues to the lives of those who have thought about them previously—our varied intellectual traditions—and to that vast territory of diverse lives we mark with the phrase "everyday life." Sometimes these connections are made through historical reflection on the development of social and cultural theory, others through an analysis of the technology, still others through a study of media professionals. A major focus of these essays is the relationship of the media text to its audience. Sometimes this problem is explored through a textual analysis that specifies diverse relations with the audience and other times through the analysis of traces of the audience as found in interviews, surveys, or popular magazines.

The first section of this book features broad conceptual articles that link research traditions to the context of "culture," a term that continues to hold much power in discussions of the relationship of media and society. Dennis McQuail refigures the uses and gratifications tradition, one of the major social scientific approaches to audience studies since World War II, on a cultural model. James Carey, in an essay that responded to two other *CSMC* essays, assesses the importance of the Progressive tradition in American politics and social science as a legacy for understanding contemporary culture. Michael Schudson, writing within the spirit of the tradition Carey discusses, assesses the implications of the new study of popular culture for teaching and research within the humanities. The new valorization of popular culture, Schudson argues, raises difficult questions for humanistic education. Horace Newcomb, a media critic trained in literary studies, works some of the textual territory mapped by Schudson in seeking to provide a theorization for the different "readings" viewers construct of television programs.

Probably no thinker had greater influence on critical studies in the 1980s in this country than Stuart Hall, whose work in England at the Centre for Contemporary Cultural Studies at Birmingham University and more recently at the Open University, stimulated much interest in cultural studies. Hall's variant of cultural studies developed through a confrontation with French structuralism and in the essay included here, he engages the thinking of Marxist philosopher Louis Althusser for post-structuralist purposes. Elizabeth Long takes Hall's Birmingham school as a point of departure in a discussion of feminism and cultural studies. Lastly, Lawrence Grossberg analyzes some of the interpretive strategies of Marxist cultural analysis.

The second section offers studies of specific media, institutions, genres, shows, and audiences. Robert Horwitz analyzes the social organization of technology in an analysis of the consequences of the divestiture of AT&T. Theodore Glasser and James Ettema use interviews with investigative reporters to interpret the role of the news media in legitimating the moral order. Douglas Birkhead discusses the moral dimension of reporting in another context, examining the problem of ethics within the news media as a problem grounded in morality as a mode of reality construction.

The media text is analyzed in a number of studies. Caren Deming examines the police melodrama *Hill Street Blues* as a narrative text that mixes televisual, filmic, and literary forms while attracting an audience broader than the affluent urban viewers for whom the show was made. Richard Campbell also situates the problem of the media text within the context of its middle class audience in an analysis of *60 Minutes*. And in a complementary argument Herman Gray studies representations of black success and failure as a reflection of a dominant ideology that offers explanations that transform class and race issues into personal solutions.

Against the tradition of reading the audience in the text, a number of studies assert the priority of the audience. Steve Barkin and Michael Gurevitch interrelate survey research and content analysis of news of unemployment to consider a number of models of the audience-text relationship before concluding that the text is an empty vessel the audience fills up with its own meanings. Although less relativistic about the media text, Linda Steiner looks at reader "uses" of particular incidents and events in dominant media as they are reflected in an oppositional text, the "No Comment" page of *Ms.* magazine.

The attempt to account for the diversity of audience uses also led to new ways of analyzing the texts. In an influential essay, John Fiske argues that while media texts carry the dominant ideology of a society, they also should be examined as open texts that offer opportunity to resist the dominant meanings. In a critique of Fiske, Celeste Michelle Condit counters that Fiske and others who argue for the openness of media texts are too optimistic, and they fail to adequately describe the rhetorical constraints that make the construction of some interpretations easier than others.

Lynn Spigel takes an imaginative approach to understanding the audience, looking for traces of the historical audience of the 1950s in the women's magazines that advised readers on how to situate the television set and organize their life around it. Spigel argues that in such descriptions and advice, the magazines mapped out a domestic economy for the reception of television studies.

These essays show how the media continue to be a significant site for talking about the nature of culture in the United States. In the production and consumption of media texts, we continue to talk about who, and how, we are now.

REFERENCES

Brown, W. R. (1985). Mass media and society: The development of critical perspectives. In T. W. Benson (Ed.), *Speech communication in the twentieth century* (pp. 196–220). Carbondale: IL: Southern Illinois University Press.

Gronbeck, B. E., & Coder, E. (1985). Proceedings of the 1985 Iowa symposium and conference on television criticism: Public and academic responsibility. *Critical Studies in Mass Communication*, 2, 380–406.

Mitchell, W. J. T. (1982). *Critical Inquiry* and the ideology of pluralism. *Critical Inquiry*, 8, 609–618.

THEORETICAL APPROACHES
TO CRITICAL STUDY

1 Reflections on Uses and Gratifications Research

DENIS McQUAIL

HISTORICAL PERSPECTIVE

This tradition of research has been the object of a good deal of denigration as well as advocacy. It started life in the early 1940s as a fairly simple and straightforward attempt to learn more about the basis of appeal of popular radio programs and about the connection between the attraction to certain kinds of media content and other features of personality and social circumstances. Happily without the name with which it is now irrevocably saddled, it was one of several lines of advance in the new branch of social science concerned with mass communication. Its origins and underpinnings included: a simple wish to know more about the audience; an awareness of the importance of individual differences in accounting for the audience experience; a still fresh wonderment at the power of popular media to hold and involve their audiences; and an attachment to the case study as an appropriate tool and an aid to psychological modes of explanation.

There was enough work accomplished by the time that Klapper (1960) put together his review of research to allow an overview which still bears reading. There had also been some development of theory and method, as the exploratory case study gave way to the more systematic collection of numerical data and to the testing of hypotheses by statistical methods. The early research was quite diverse, although as it developed, there was some bias towards television and towards the child audience. This may simply reflect the circumstances of the time, when television was becoming established on both sides of the Atlantic and was being perceived as the new threat or promise in the socializing of young children. An additional factor, however, is probably a view of television as a continuous and undifferentiated use of time by children which was more amenable to analysis according to broad categories of type of content than was either book or film. Both film-going and reading had also largely ceded their "social problem" character to the new medium and were looked at almost benignly. By the time television came to be investigated in any large scale way during the 1950s and early 1960s (e.g., Himmelweit et al., 1958;

9

Schramm et al., 1961), the method of "uses and gratifications" research was sufficiently developed for it to be used as an instrument for investigating this large, undifferentiated, allocation of time by children. The appeal of the approach was its potential for differentiating within an otherwise seemingly featureless field of media behavior and providing variables of attention to television, beyond that of sheer amount, which could be related to possible causes of "addiction" or to the consequences of over-indulgence.

It is interesting to recall how broadly defined and diverse this field of research was at least until the early 1960s. It covered: inquiries into the allocation of time to different media; relations between media use and other uses of time; relations between media use and indicators of social adjustment and relationships; perceptions of the functions of different media or content types; and reasons for attending to media. It would be hard to distinguish much that is now placed within the "tradition" from other kinds of media research. The common strand was, nevertheless, a concern with the "function" of media, in its several senses, but especially the question of the kind and the strength of motive for media use and the links between such motives and the rest of experience.

1960 as a Turning Point

The decade of the 1960s has been treated as a watershed in respect of more than one feature of mass communication research and, however exaggerated this picture or distorted by hindsight, there are some reasons for so regarding it. Firstly, it was a time when communication research appeared to "take off" once more, certainly in Europe, as the social sciences became better established and discovered post-war energy and direction. Even in the United States, there seemed to occur a new beginning after the golden age of communication research whose passing was mourned by Berelson (1959). Secondly, there was a coming to terms with the accumulating evidence about media effect or the lack of it. Thirdly, there was the fact of television as a new medium of seemingly immense appeal, if not effect. Fourthly, although later in the decade of the 1960s, there was a growing tendency in the social sciences to react against "positivist" methods and concepts and against functionalism in its several variants. The favored modes of thinking were more "social-critical," interpretative, anti-scientistic, ethnographic, phenomenologistic. The particular turning point for uses and gratifications research seemed to follow the (rather obscure) publication of an important article by Elihu Katz in 1959, which provided a manifesto of a kind and a number of key slogans and terms. Thus:

> . . . less attention [should be paid] to what media do to people and more to what people do with the media. Such an approach assumes that even the most potent of mass media content cannot ordinarily influence an individual who has no 'use' for it in the social and psychological context in which he lives. The 'uses' approach assumes that people's values, their interests, their asso-

ciations, their social roles, are pre-potent and that people selectively 'fashion' what they see and hear to these interests. (Katz, 1959, p. 2)

While the thoughts expressed in this vein, belonging more generally to the "rediscovery of people," were very important for the blossoming of more research on media use (especially in connection with the re-assessment of media effects), the development was running counter to the stream of critical theory and research of the later 1960s.

Revival and Redefinition of the "Uses" Tradition

While early conceptions of the process of media effect had a place for a notion of audience response as a type of independent effect (Klapper had considered media gratifications almost exclusively in this light), researchers now turned to the possibility of using a motive or a satisfaction as an intervening variable in its own right. This was guided in part by the early use of indicators of interest as a relevant way of categorizing an audience (Lazarsfeld et al., 1944), and by the accumulation of evidence that audience choice and reaction were always selective in systematic ways. Thus, one of the innovations in the search for better concepts and methods of inquiry in relation to media effect was to take more account of the kind and strength of motivation of the relevant public. The guiding thought was that effects would be more likely to occur where a corresponding or relevant motive existed on the part of the receiver (e.g., Blumler & McQuail, 1968). In turn, this had a place in the development of theory and research concerning the active or "obstinate" audience (Bauer, 1964) and of interactive, in place of one-way, models of media influence. The rise of television has increased the demand for research into audiences that would go beyond head-counting and reach some more qualitative accounting of the audience and help relate program provision to various audience demands by ways other than pure market forces (Emmett, 1968/69). More "qualitative" audience research could be seen as a "half-way house" between the collection of "ratings" and the ultimate delivery of evidence about the longer-term social effects of the new medium, allowing some provisional evaluation of what might be going on.

The advance and then retreat of positivism and functionalism concerned uses and gratifications research especially during the late 1960s and early 1970s for a number of reasons. Firstly, most of the research involved was inescapably cast in the functionalist mold. The theory and research described by Klapper (1960) already presupposed a distinct functionalist framework in which media use is likely to be interpreted as a means of adjustment to, or reaction in, a system of connected personal relations or a wider social context. Moreover, the concepts and methods typical of the research were essentially individualist, psychologistic and had a strong leaning towards the "variable analysis" which had been an early target for more holistically-minded sociologists (e.g., Blumer, 1956) and historically-minded media theorists (e.g.,

Smythe, 1954). What came to be viewed, by the early 1970s, as typical of the tradition was a) functionalist in conception; b) individualist in method of data collection; and c) lending itself to multivariate statistical analysis. It embodied the methodological advances of the period with the demonic characteristics which became, increasingly, an object of disdain by the "critically" minded; that is, positivism, scientism, determinism, value-neutrality, and conservatism. There is more to be said of this, but first attention should be given to one additional strand in the complex of problems in which this research tradition has landed itself.

USES AND GRATIFICATIONS AND THE STUDY OF POPULAR CULTURE

Somewhat ironically, the main point of Katz' 1959 article was to suggest that the "uses" approach could help build a bridge to the humanistic tradition of popular culture. One source of the approach had been the New School of Social Research at Columbia University, with a measure of influence from the original Frankfurt School and having a mixture of sociopolitical, psychological and cultural concerns. There were thus historical and circumstantial as well as methodological grounds for Katz' suggestion. However, the various strands mentioned had tended to separate, and elsewhere they had barely come together. In Britain, for instance, the analysis of (mainly written) cultural forms had largely been carried out by academics applying somewhat elitist values mixed with social and political concerns. The influence of Q. D. and F. R. Leavis from the 1930s onward led to a greater (though still somewhat disdainful) attention to the popular arts, which eventually did bloom into a new school of socio-cultural analysis, with Raymond Williams, Richard Hoggart and Stuart Hall as prominent representatives and pioneers. Even so, the separation between the "culturalist" examining "texts" and the social scientist looking at audiences tended to persist. Again, there is another potentially long story and it is sufficient for now to say that Katz' call for a rapprochement based on the typical methods of "uses" research and of the analysis of texts and cultural forms, within a broadly humanistic program did seem to have some potential. It seemed, in particular, to offer an exit from the sterile debate between critics of mass culture and its defenders (cf. Rosenberg & White, 1957) and allow in evidence some representation of the voice of the "consumer." The new research approach would be a way of giving people a voice in cultural matters much as surveys had done in relation to political and social issues. It might even offer a way of testing the proposition of some sociologists and critics of mass culture that mass media served to perpetuate capitalist society. An early version of this view is to be found in the work of a pioneer in "uses" research: "Psychologically the effect (of escapist fiction) is distraction from somewhat habitual anxieties. Sociologically, the effect is to reduce the violence of assault on the existing social structure by cooling the discontent of underprivileged groups. The reading of anything at all which takes the reader's mind from his [sic] troubles has this cooling effect" (Waples et al., 1940, p. 123). In a similar vein, Irving Howe later described mass culture as filling the leisure hours of industrial workers, providing "relief from work monotony without making the return to work too unbearable" (Howe, 1957, p. 497).

It can be said at this point that Katz' call for a bridge-building was never really taken up, if it was ever heard and taken seriously. Certainly it did not lead to any notable bridge-building and was pushed aside by the greater attraction, to social scientists, of seemingly powerful data analysis techniques and, to humanists, of new literary-critical theory and method. Literary-cultural concerns were led even further away from positivism and functionalism, which came to be associated with manipulation and conservatism. Thus, the ground which had seemed so fertile for the development of humanistic "uses" research proved rather sour. The two main strands of relevant work were even further apart. The reasons are well analysed from the "cultural" side by Carey and Kreiling (1974), but ten years after their analysis and suggestion for an accommodation, there seems little progress to report.

What Went On?

The substance of the post-1960s renascence of uses and gratifications research, which still continues, can only be summarily characterized by a few key references. The account given here cannot pretend to be either full or unbiased, given the participation of the present writer in some of the work. However, an essential aspect of the tradition is its diversity and lack of coordination or of a common program. The wide currency and convenience of the shorthand label "uses and gratifications," the targeting of fairly coherent critiques by single authors, the use of the term "functionalist" as a blanket description, have all tended to exaggerate the degree to which the approach shares an identity and common philosophical and scientific basis. What we now see as evidence is a series of projects, which can be classified under a few broad headings. Firstly, there have been many studies of children and media, especially: Schramm (1961); Riley and Riley (1951); Maccoby (1954); Himmelweit and Oppenheim (1958); Furu (1971); Noble (1975); Greenberg (1974); various, mainly European, researches collected by Brown (1976); ongoing work in Sweden (e.g., Hedinsson, 1981; and Johnsson-Smaragdi, 1983). Secondly, there has been a good deal of attention to political communication and media gratifications. This is well-reviewed by McLeod and Becker (1981) and may be thought to begin with the work of Blumler and McQuail (1968). Thirdly, there have been numerous studies of particular forms and the basis of their appeal, including: McQuail et al. (1972), Mendelsohn (1964), Levy (1978), Tannenbaum (1980), and many others. Fourthly, there have been studies of media and wider social integration, the most significant being that of Katz et al. (1973). Fifthly, there have been studies of information-seeking and of the more cognitive aspects of media use: Atkin (1972), Kline et al. (1974), and Kippax & Murray (1980). Finally, we can distinguish a set of contributions to the development of theory and the formation of models. Some of these are to be found in Blumler and Katz (1974), and more recent examples include Blumler (1979) and Windahl (1981).

Criticism

The diversity mentioned earlier refers to theory, methods, aims and the kinds of media content studied. No common model, set of procedures or purposes informs the tradition, despite the attempts of Katz, Blumler and Gurevitch (1974) to give some shape to the assumptions that have guided "uses" research and to assess the state of the art. Ten years after that rendering of account there is probably no greater unity and there is some reason to look back on the direction taken by the revived tradition. Criticism of the approach has been lucidly and not infrequently expressed, notably by Chaney (1972), Elliott (1974), Carey and Kreiling (1974), and Swanson (1977). There have been three main lines of attack or sources of dislike: one relating to its theoretical underpinnings and associated method; another to its social and political implications; a third to its model of man and its way of handling cultural phenomena. The main theoretical charge is that it is essentially lacking in theory and such theory that it has is inadequate and confused. The common element of many studies seems to be a certain way of devising lists of verbal statements about media or media content which are labelled, variously, as "use," "gratification," "motivation," "satisfaction," "need," etc., implying distinctions and a conceptual status which cannot be validated. If there is a theory, according to critics, it is pure tautology moving from measured satisfaction back to an imputed need or forwards from a need to a use and gratification, with no independent way of measuring need, or even any coherent theory of needs, and certainly no way of determining the direction of influence between measured "need" and media use. The lack of theory is said to lead to a misuse of empirical method, to the extent that verbal statements or aggregate statistics derived from responses to verbal statements are reified to become new constructs supposed to stand for the gratifications offered by media content. At times these new constructs are seen merely as reflections of social class or other background variables and when used instead of the latter, they are likely to by mystifying and distorting.

 The social and political objections advanced from a perspective of critical theory rest mainly on the view that the incurable functionalism of the method ties the researcher to a conservative model of a social system in which all adjustment is for the best and which ends up portraying all kinds of media content as helping individuals to adjust. The method, as typically practiced, can only increase the chances of manipulation, since it adduces psychological and social reasons why people like what they get which can easily be turned to support the view that people get what they like, thus blunting any possible critical edge in the application of new knowledge which comes from the research.

The "cultural" objection has several grounds but, most centrally, exception is taken to the utilitarianism and behaviorism of the whole underlying model, in which cultural "behavior" is treated as both determined and instrumental and rarely as "consummatory" or an end in itself. The version of the meaning of cultural consumption as derived from statements or recognitions of statements by individuals is regarded as a poor substitute for an overall view in which the ritual nature of culture is recognized along with its great diversity of meanings. There is also a wider reluctance to accept a value-free and mathematical treatment of matters which should be seen as evaluative and qualitative and not amendable to sociological categorization. From a cultural point of view there seems to be no recognition, or use, of any kind of aesthetic theory.

While there has been no systematic demolition job on the results of uses and gratifications research, as distinct from its theory (except, selectively, by Elliott, 1974), there has been disappointment over the yield of findings which might add up to an explanation of media choice or which clearly show the part played by media in the process of effects. There is, seemingly, very little predictive power in any current index of motivation, in respect of effects. In his early review of the field, Klapper (1960) had already pointed to inconsistencies and low explanatory power in the first batch of studies. For the most part, the evidence we have still comprises certain consistent patterns linking one "gratification" with another and some gratifications with either social background variables or media use, or both. Perhaps this line of criticism is not taken very far because of its rather general application to mass communication research.

THE CENTRAL POINT OF THE TRADITION

The point of summarizing criticism is not to offer a new defense and assessment, but to consider the possibilities for future work, taking account of objections which deserve to be taken seriously. Before doing so, it is worth re-asserting the importance of the broad questions with which this tradition has always been concerned. It derives from a conviction that what is central for mass communication is not message-making or sending and not even the messages themselves, but the choice, reception and manner of response of the audience. In turn, an attention to the audience requires a sensitivity to the full range of meanings of that experience and thus to its diversity and fragility. It also means accepting that making, sending, choosing and responding to media messages involves a set of understandings which are, up to a point, shared by "makers" and "receivers" and which are usually both complex and unspoken. Thus diversity, ambiguity and even some mystery are to be expected on the "side" of production and content as well as on the "side" of reception. This is to underline the impossibility of artificially separating the question of audience experience from the sources of that experience in content itself. Nor can it be separated from aspects of the context in which the experience takes place—where, with whom, under what circumstances, through which channel. It may appear from these remarks that a true study of the media experience has to be about everything—society, culture, human behavior—and, for this reason, it is unlikely to be theoretically satisfying to everyone. Underlying the controversies of this kind of research is a pull in several directions: towards society as "first cause;" towards cultural content as the true determinant of response; or towards explanations to be found in individual behavior and personality.

It is worth being reminded of some of the relative success of the research tradition as it has been practiced, partly to redress the balance, partly to account for the appeal of the line of work. One apparent success has been to express, in differentiated verbal formulas, which are widely recognizable and available for consistent use, key elements of the image or dominant associations of specific media cultural products and kinds of media experience. The verbal expressions show some stability across cultures and over time and yet the methods used are sensitive enough to record differences in the perception of similar kinds of material. Information of this kind is often open to interpretation in terms of differences of plot, style or format and it does seem that cultural analysis and audience analysis can be mutually enriching. The research has also identified and given names and definitions to a set of "functions" of media-cultural experience which help to make sense of the innumerable details of audience reaction. These possibilities lend themselves, further, to making comparisons between media and between different audience groups which would otherwise be impossible.

We have, thus, the basic terms for discourse about media content and experience which have been discovered, drawn together and ordered by empirical procedures, rather than invented or put forward as concepts. This means that some form of three-way exchange is possible between the makers of culture, the audience and social scientists. This may be more a potential than an actuality, but the existence of something like a common terminology has been demonstrated (Himmelweit et al., 1980) and it is a necessary precondition for talking sensibly about the audience experience. Without this accomplishment, it would be difficult to approach the central issue of whether content "produces particular values and patterns of behavior amongst its devotees or do its devotees become devotees because of the values and behavioral tendencies they already possess" (Klapper, 1960, p. 190).

While the achievement in respect of explanation and interrelation of different kinds of evidence about people and their media use has been modest, it is not wholly lacking. There are too many, albeit scattered, indications of clarifying or meaningful associations between expectations from, and ideas about, media and other relevant indications of choice to doubt that approaches to media, as expressed in the terms developed by this tradition (and there is really no alternative source except introspection and invention) are not independently influential. In other words, on some occasions at least, prior experience, behavior, tendencies and values shape attention and response, and it would be untenable to claim otherwise and unreasonable to claim total agnosticism. Uses and gratifications research has added to the concepts and instruments of research a valid status. Thus, *something* can usually be identified as standing for a differentiated view of content and experience of its reception which is not simply the idiosyncratic outlook of one individual, nor simply a secondary expression of a personality trait, or a surrogate for a location in an organization or a society, or merely a description of the item of content itself. It is, or can be, independent in the statistical sense of being open to use as a separate variable with some explanatory power of its own. It is also independent, in the semantic sense, in being conceptually different from these other similar or related things which have been named. The problem, of course, lies not with this claim itself (although it is not uncontested), but with what to do if one accepts it, since it is almost impossible to find an acceptable name for this *thing*. There are too many names for it and the choice of any one presupposes a theoretical schema which can take the researcher into deep waters. Uses and gratifications researchers have found something by empirical investigation, they know some of its properties and uses, but they do not really know what it is. If this *is* the case, it gives some support to criticism of the approach as the poorer for its lack of theoretical foundation.

A Readjustment of View

There are several ways of coming to terms with the problems encountered in the progress of this research tradition, if one accepts the continued value of the enterprise, and it would be out of keeping with the spirit of this tradition to present any single blueprint for survival and prosperity. There are those who would not accept that serious problems have been encountered, beyond what is the normal result of academic competition, fundamental theoretical divergences and the inevitably slow growth of scientific knowledge. To the present writer, however, it seems that there are grounds for disappointment in the history of the tradition to date and that the research in the main direction being currently taken is not very likely to deliver all of its early promise. This refers especially to the understanding of cultural experience and to the explanation of variations which might be of relevance for social-cultural policy. Thus, one of the original aims of the research was to shed light on both "cultural-gaps" and "knowledge-gaps" in society and suggest ways of reducing them. This may no longer seem a very urgent goal in an era of media abundance, media deregulation and cultural relativism, but the facts of communication inequality are barely changed and the theoretical interest of the associated questions remains high. By contrast, although the fruits may still lie just beyond our grasp, the work that continues to be done does seem to have a potential for clarifying the process of media effect.

The tradition of uses and gratifications research has thus seemed to reveal an inescapable bias: despite its diversity it tends towards what can most conveniently be called a "dominant paradigm," however overworked and tendentious that phrase has become. This paradigm or model is no secret and is to be read from the "state of the art" assessment by Katz et al. (1974). It involves: a view of media consumption as a logical and sequential process of need-satisfaction and tension-reduction, relating the social-psychological environment to media use; a set of assumptions about the audience (notably its activity, rationality, resistance to influence, capacity for reporting about itself); and a recommendation to value-relativism on the part of the investigator. This basic paradigm has organized much work and continues to lend itself to further elaboration and application in research (Palmgreen, 1984). It is in fact more flexible than it sounds and can provide a powerful framework for looking at media in a wider social and cultural context. Yet it is also, not inconsistently, imperialistic, perhaps too powerful and tending to develop Moloch-like characteristics in the sacrifices which it demands from its devotees. These sacrifices are mostly in the form of a narrowing of vision and a submission to the ever-growing machine of data-collection and elaborate statistical analysis of numbers formed from much less substantial qualities.

While admitting an element of exaggeration in this picture, it does not seem very useful now to worry about the main component parts of the paradigm, although each merits critical attention, but better to consider whether there is really any alternative. In passing, it may be remarked that the components of the framework most in need of critical attention have to do with the "activity" assumption and the concept of "use," "gratification," "function," etc. There are many questions about the meaning of "activity," about the degree of activity that has to be present to sustain the program of empirical work, about how much of whatever kind of activity really exists in given audience situations. The dispute about the nature of the central concept has already been discussed, without resolution, but it does appear that the main choice lies between three (not mutually exclusive) possibilities: a concept of need related to the current circumstances of the audience member; a description or "image" of the key features of media content or the media experience; a satisfaction or gratification obtained or expected. Each of these has a different conceptual status, whichever word is chosen, and each has some place in the work typical of the research tradition. The suggestion which follows, although it involves a radical departure from the dominant model, would not, if adopted, render all work until now and all current debate redundant. It would, however, introduce some new concepts and change the balance of discussion. It would also move the model- (or road) building to a new site.

AN ALTERNATIVE BYWAY

If there is a broad highway in the development of uses and gratifications research, it can be characterized by an elaboration of models, by its statistical methods and its theory for relating social and cultural experience "forward" to media use and its later consequences and back again to experience. I worked on some sections of the road and travelled some way along it, by adapting a "uses" approach to the study of political campaign effects and by trying to establish connections between social background and media use (McQuail et al., 1972). The suggestion which follows is for a return to the bridge-building between the social sciences and the humanities, urged by Katz, but never really achieved. Broadly, it may be described as involving a "cultural-empirical" approach, using some of the concepts and advances of "main-road" work, but with some new concepts added and all within a new framework or model. A good many of the new elements are untried and the proposal has, consequently, a very tentative character.

The uses and gratifications "main road" approach has tended towards utilitarianism and determinism, treating "consumption" of media content of all kinds as having a place or purpose in larger schemes of individual need-gratification. A cultural approach would be much more likely to consider "consumption" of culture as an end in itself (the "consummatory" view urged by Carey and Kreiling, 1974) and, in any case, requiring an understanding in its own right and not only as a stage in some behavioral process of adjustment. Attention should thus be concentrated on the making of choices and on the meaningful encounter with cultural products. Towards this end, a distinction will have to be made between the more "cultural" kinds of content and the more informational kinds—between affectual/imaginative and cognitive spheres. This kind of distinction is often made for practical reasons, but most uses and gratifications theory adopts fundamentally the same model for all kinds of imputed need and media use, partly because different kinds of content can serve the same function, partly because the underlying process is held to be the same.

The first model suggested is intended to deal with the "non-cognitive" area, with audience use of fiction, amusement, drama or spectacle, which appeals to the imagination or seeks to provide various kinds of pleasure at the time of use, and has no consciously intended application afterwards in the rest of life. It seems advisable to take some account of the built-in purpose of media content, as well as the purpose formed by the audience member, although this practice has seemed to fall victim to an exclusive policy of "taking the audience point of view." Moreover, if cultural experience is to be considered according to its functionality or utility in a more or less behavioral model, it is reasonable to suppose that some kinds of media fare will be less amenable to this kind of treatment than some others. Indeed, it may be necessary to treat some media experiences not only neutrally in this respect, but as if according to a *counter-behavioral* stance. This is an important feature of the alternative conceptual framework sketched below.

The key proposition (it is no more) on which the following rests is that cultural experience (what happens at the time of attention to media) be treated as a generalized process of involvement, arousal or "capture." To the observer there is little to see except varying degrees of rapt attention and to the participant, the most salient aspect of the experience is an awareness of "being lost" in something, "involved," "carried away," "caught up," "taken out of oneself," or simply "excited" or "thrilled." There are conventional variations of expression for this according to the kind of content—whether comedy, tragedy, adventure, romance, etc.—but there seems to be an underlying similarity of what is meant by these kinds of expression and what is experienced in terms of mental and physiological reaction. The precise nature of this generalized sensation lies outside the scope of this essay and probably of the social sciences, but if it is so pronounced and familiar a phenomenon as presupposed here, we should not be denied the chance to include it in a conception of media use. Although our primary interest is in the giving of meaning to this fundamental general experience, we do need some concept of what it is. The evidence of its existence is mostly of a commonsense kind, but there is research and theory to support the contention. It seems that a measurable factor of general "arousal" in relation to television, at least, does exist and correlates with motivation to continue attending to media (Tannenbaum & Zillman, 1975; Tannenbaum, 1980). There is no reason why this should not also be true of other media. It also seems from studies of audience evaluations of media content that there is a general factor of liking, which is closely connected with the attribution of a quality of being "absorbing," involving or exciting (Himmelweit et al., 1980). The rather scarce work that has been done in this area does at least seem to justify the proposition advanced above.

To go beyond the fact of this sense experience and relate it with its typical content, we can propose that the essence of this general sensation is to *free* the spectator/reader/listener mentally from the immediate constraints and/or dullness of daily life and enable him or her to *enter into* new experiences (vicariously) which would not otherwise be available (except by use of the imagination). The media-cultural experience is thus potentially a powerful aid to, or substitute for, the imagination, enabling a person to enjoy a variety of emotional experiences and mental states—involving joy, anger, sexual excitement, sadness, curiosity, etc. We can identify with people and share the illusion of living in interesting situations or observe it all, with inside knowledge, from a privileged position and one of physical and emotional security. Many of these processes have been described or presumed by writers about culture since the time of Aristotle, although rather little has found its way into the models of uses and gratifications research. There is no need or space here to enlarge on this tradition, except to emphasize the most vital point that whenever we are "caught up" or "captured" in a drama, story or spectacle, we are, by definition, also cut off, not only from the constraints of the moment and a less interesting reality, but also from our own past and future. Consequently, there is likely to be a positive *dissociation* from social circumstances and future consequences. This is often part of the conscious purpose and pleasure of "exposure" to cultural experience—we do want to be somewhere or someone else, with no thought for the future. Insofar as this is true, it does undermine a major premise of the mainstream uses and gratifications model, which holds that media use is often a direct reflection of premedia experience and in some underlying way is structured as to its amount and kind by the rest of experience. The implication of what has just been written is that, if there is a relation, it may well be of a contradictory or quite unpredictable kind. In the view advanced here, the essence of audience "activity" is a process of self-liberation, however temporary, from everyday self and surroundings. Consequently, there is no obvious way to make causal connections between media experience and behavior.

There are some important practical consequences of all this for a revision of the dominant model of the process of mass media use. First of all, as noted above, we should treat affective/imaginative content separately from cognitive content, since the arousal-involvement factor is either less relevant or of a different kind. In Himmelweit's (1980) study of audience judgment, the most "highly rated" of the television programs assessed was "The News" and "absorbing" was one of the terms applied to it "very much," but it was only one of five "stylistic attributes" applied, rather than a single main criterion, as it was for other popular fictional programs. Secondly, the generalized "arousal" factor should not be included in the lists of gratifications or satisfactions and should be treated on another level, as a prior condition of attention or for what it is, as a general factor, which finds several more specific forms of expression, according to the individual or the content concerned.

Further elaboration is needed in order to cope with these "second order" concepts. In a "culturalist" model it is appropriate to use the concept of culture itself and it can be used in two senses. Firstly, "culture" in the collective sense as the body of objects and practices which pertains to, or is available to, a given group or public, or subset of society. It is in this sense, for instance, that the term "taste culture" (Lewis, 1980) has been used—to indicate a more or less structured set of preferences. A member of the media public can only choose from, or have ideas about, what is available physically or is accessible and familiar by reason of a collective situation and provision. Cultural differentiation is an important element in the model of media use because it is a directing or constraining factor in choice. It may have much to do with class and social position, but more generally it has to do with closeness and familiarity, more so probably than with individual competence, skill, or any "need" for culture.

The second relevant sense of culture is that of individual "taste." Again an old term, disregarded in the "dominant paradigm," perhaps because of its vagueness and its connotation (and denotation) of a subjective state of mind and of the making of value judgments. But it is probably no more imprecise than other functionalist terms and subjective choice and assessment is central to the old as well as the proposed new model. Cultural taste provides the key to selection amongst what is offered by the (collective) culture and is essentially arbitrary and unaccountable. If it were accountable it would explain the differences of preference for genres, themes and authors. It is evidently not entirely random, but the regularities that do appear, such as gender differences in choice as between, for example, "adventure" and "romance" are really an aspect of collective cultural distribution which makes the former less accessible to girls from an early age and steers them towards "romance." While "taste" relates to choice of content and habits of use, it is usual and perhaps only possible to describe it in terms of content. Media content (and most cultural production) is constructed according to a knowledge of tastes and likely preferences, and has some built-in appeal to a sector of the potential public.

There is one further element in the scheme of things which provides a bridge to the dominant behavioral model described above, helping to characterize and differentiate the vicarious experience and emotion offered by culture more finely and objectively than does the concept of taste. This element is *content*. Thus, affective media content can be differentiated according to the specific experience offered and gained. In practice, such gratifications, assuming the experience to be wanted, are hard to identify except by general types of content—much as in taste specification of basic themes, plots and genres. A given genre or type of content normally promises and gives a set of experiences of a predictable kind, which might have to do with curiosity about human situations, or laughter, or sex, or tension and release, or mystery, or wonder and so on. These (and others) are the satisfactions which people claim to expect or receive from the media and which are to be found both in descriptions of cultural (media) content and in lists and typologies of media gratifications. There is a necessary place in a culturalist model for the reflection on (and anticipation of) emotions, thoughts and sensations evoked by the cultural experience. There remains, nevertheless, a difficulty, familiar to uses and gratifications researchers, of distinguishing between the general and the particular, and between expectation and satisfaction.

TWO MODELS

Little more need be said before setting out the main terms and their sequence of a model of cultural (affective) experience (Figure 1). One may point out that "general expectation of involvement," "taste" and "satisfaction" can easily be

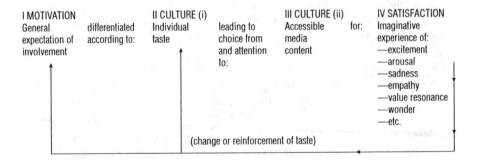

FIGURE 1. A Cultural Model.

associated with different things and thus be used as orientations towards, or descriptions of, several different things: a theme; a genre or type; a medium or channel; an actual media experience (specific film, television viewing, reading a particular book); an author or performer; a particular work. The situation in this respect is not very different from the case of conventional uses and gratifications research, where "gratifications," etc., are used to differentiate media and types of content. In both the cultural and the "uses" model, we can also use the same terms to characterize people. This should not lead to confusion, since quite different statements are involved. For example, it is quite different to say that someone has a taste for thrillers than to say that someone's "need for escape" is met by thrillers. In general, the lexicon of terms in a developed cultural model would depend on and say more about the specific content than about people and circumstances. Finally, the model, as drawn in Figure 1, is also sequential, since the general inclination to seek cultural experience precedes actual involvement, as does the pattern of taste. Actual media experience does lead to some awareness and reflection on what has happened, with some consequences for future cultural choice, and other more immediate consequences depending on the specific content and the degree of satisfaction obtained.

It is neither possible, nor really necessary, to give a full account of what an equivalent cognitive model (Figure 2) would look like, because of limitations of space and time and because such a model would not deviate too sharply from relevant components in the dominant paradigm. However, there are important differences of conceptualization from the cultural model. Firstly, the arousal/involvement factor would be replaced by a general factor of interest/curiosity. In turn, this would divide according to a set of interests, which are equivalent to cultural tastes and, in a similar way, a mixture of the arbitrary and the socially or culturally given in a particular environment. Thus some people are interested in football for reasons which are mysterious to some others, yet there are regularities in the aggregate distribution of interest in football, which show it to go with some other characteristics. As with "culture," information is variably available or accessible according to social posi-

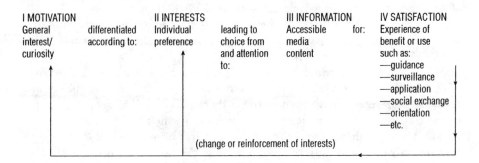

FIGURE 2. A Cognitive Model.

tion. Finally, there are specific gains or satisfactions which can be accounted for, much as in the uses and gratifications tradition, as uses and benefits, such as: helping in decisions and choices; opinion formation; providing subjects for conversation, etc. On the whole, one would expect more certainty of relationship between prior experience, information choices and satisfactions obtained. The key difference from the previous model (and at the same time, the factor which links this model to the dominant paradigm) is the absence of that *disconnection* between ordinary life and the moment or cultural experience. The motivating factor is one of connection and extension rather than disconnection.

CONCLUSION

It is early to assess the prospects for such an approach, or its implications for the research tradition as a whole. It needs itself to be tried out empirically, either in the collection of new data, or in reworking existing data, since there could be a considerable overlap between the kind of work generated by such a cultural model and what has been done already. At some points it clearly challenges the established tradition, at others it might be supportive or supplementary. The most fundamental challenge is to the notion of a direct causal connection between background circumstances, cultural choice and the "effects" of cultural experience. In effect, this model resurrects the notion of "escape" as a dominant motive for media use and emphasizes discontinuities, although the "escape" may well be subjectively perceived in a positive light— thus as escape into a better world (of the imagination). An example of the potential complexities of this model, which might baffle practitioners of causal analysis is offered by Zillman's (1980) suggestion that, contrary to the thesis of the school of "cultivation analysis" (e.g., Gerbner et al., 1976), it is not "scary" television which leads to a scary world view, but the experience of actual worry and anxiety which leads people to watch "scary" television precisely because it fictionally heightens fear and tension and then releases it. It is the second part of this process which, according to Zillman, might be sought out for its positive benefits. This is a simple enough proposition, but the chance of testing it by content analysis and surveys is virtually zero.

On the positive side, the framework suggested here may, by reviving the notion of "taste" and the value judgments which go with that concept, add to the refinement and accuracy of description of content and improve our understanding of individual differences. It can also help to increase sensitivity to essentially "cultural" attributes. The notion of "taste" (and, on the cognitive side, "interests") may also help to clarify the nature of the central concept of the tradition (use, gratification, motive, etc.) which has proved virtually impossible to pin down. On the one hand, it offers one other possible meaning, perhaps only compounding the problem by so doing. On the other hand, the separation of a generalized "drive" or "set," as motivational factor, from its specific manifestations in taste, choice and satisfaction may open the way to a more consistent treatment (or multiple treatment) of the second order concept.

In the end, one has to make a rather important choice as to whether one really wants to know most about *culture* (its origin, production, meaning and use), or about *people* in audiences (their identity, attributes, reasons for being there), or about individual *behavior* (kind, frequency, causes, consequences, interconnections), or about *society* and the working of the media within it. It is unlikely that any one paradigm or model can serve all four purposes and the one sketched here has most relevance for the first. The main thrust of the uses and gratifications tradition has been towards the construction of a major highway which serves to link all four purposes in one investigative enterprise. Real highways do facilitate very long, fast, journeys by large vehicles (research teams), but they also change the landscape they traverse, have restricted views and stimulate travel for its own sake or that of the vehicle. By comparison, the byway mapped out for reaching one rather limited goal of knowledge might be slow and winding, but should enable one to see more on the way and keep one generally in closer contact with nature.

REFERENCES

Atkin, C. K. (1972) Anticipated communication and mass-mediated information seeking. *Public Opinion Quarterly, 36*, 188–199.

Bauer, R. A. (1964). The obstinate audience. *American Psychologist, 19*, 319–328.

Berelson, B. (1959). The state of communication research. *Public Opinion Quarterly, 23*, 1–6.

Blumer, H. (1956). Sociological analysis and the "variable". *American Sociological Review, 21*, 683–690.

Blumler, J. G. (1979). The role of theory in uses and gratifications studies. *Communication Research, 6*, 9–36.

Blumler, J. G., & Katz, E. (Eds.). (1974). *The uses of mass communications*. London and Beverly Hills: Sage.

Blumler, J. G., & McQuail, D. (1968). *Television in politics*. London: Faber.

Brown, J. R. (Ed.). (1976). *Children and television*. London: Collier Macmillan.

Carey, J. W., & Kreiling, A. L. (1974). Popular culture and uses and gratifications. In J. G. Blumler & E. Katz. (Eds.), *The uses of mass communication* (pp. 225–248). London and Beverly Hills: Sage.

Chaney, D. (1972). *Processes of mass communication*. London: Macmillan.

Elliott, P. (1974). Uses and gratifications research: A critique and a sociological alternative. In J. G. Blumler & E. Katz. (Eds.), *The uses of mass communication* (pp. 249–268). London and Beverly Hills: Sage.

Emmett, B. (1968/69). A new role for research in broadcasting. *Public Opinion Quarterly, 32*, 654–665.

Furu, T. (1971). *The functions of television for children and adolescents*. Tokyo: Sophia University.

Gerbner, G., & Gross, L. (1976). Living with television: The violence profile. *Journal of Communication, 26*(2), 173–199.

Greenberg, B. G. (1976). Gratifications of television viewing and their correlates for British children. In J. G. Blumler & E. Katz. (Eds.). *The uses of mass communication* (pp. 71–92). London and Beverly Hills: Sage.

Hedinsson, E. (1981). *Television, family and society*. Stockholm: Almquist & Wiksel.

Himmelweit, H. T., Oppenheim, A. N., & Vince, P. (1958). *Television and the child*. London: Oxford University Press.

Himmelweit, H. T., Swift, B., & Jaeger, M. E. (1980). The audience as critic: A conceptual analysis of television entertainment. In P. H. Tannenbaum. (Ed.), *The entertainment functions of television* (pp. 67–97). Hillsdale, NJ: LEA.

Howe, I. (1957). Notes on mass culture. In M. Rosenberg & D. M. White. (Eds.), *Mass culture: The popular arts in America* (pp. 496–503). New York: Free Press.

Johnsson-Smaragdi, U. (1983). *TV use and social interaction in adolescence*. Stockholm: Almquist & Wiksel.

Katz, E. (1959). Mass communication research and the study of culture. *Studies in Public Communication, 2*, 1–6.

Katz, E., Blumler, J. G., & Gurevitch, M. (1974). Utilization of mass communication by the individual. In J. G. Blumler & E. Katz. (Eds.), *The uses of mass communications* (pp. 19–32). London and Beverly Hills: Sage.

Katz, E., Gurevitch, M., & Haas, H. (1973). On the use of mass media for important things. *American Sociological Review, 38*, 164–181.

Klapper, J. T. (1960). *The effects of mass communication*. Glencoe: Free Press.

Kippax, S., & Murray, J. P. (1980). Using the mass media: Need gratification and perceived utility. *Communication Research, 7*, 335–360.

Kline, G., Miller, P. V., & Morrison, A. J. (1974). Adolescents and family planning information. In J. G. Blumler & E. Katz. (Eds.), *The uses of mass communications* (pp. 113–136). London and Beverly Hills: Sage.

Lazarsfeld, P. F., Berelson, B., & Gaudet, H. (1944). *The people's choice*. New York: Duell, Sloan & Pearce.

Levy, M. R. (1978). The audience experience with television news. *Journalism Monographs, 55*.

Lewis, G. H. (1980). Taste cultures and their composition. In E. Katz & T. Szescko. (Eds.), *Mass media and social change* (pp. 201–207). Beverly Hills and London: Sage.

Maccoby, E. (1954). Why do children watch television? *Public Opinion Quarterly, 18*, 239–244.

McLeod, J., & Becker, L. B. (1981). The uses and gratifications approach. In D. Nimmo & R. R. Saunders (Eds.), *Handbook of political communication* (pp. 67–100). Beverly Hills and London: Sage.

McQuail, D., Blumler, J. G., & Brown, J. R. (1972). The television audience: A revised perspective. In D. McQuail. (Ed.), *Sociology of mass communications* (pp. 135–165). Harmondsworth: Penguin.

Mendelsohn, H. (1964). Listening to radio. In L. A. Dexter & D. M. White. (Eds.), *People, society and mass communications* (pp. 239–269). Glencoe: Free Press.

Noble, G. (1975). *Children in front of the small screen*. London: Constable.

Palmgreen, P. (1984). Uses and gratifications: A theoretical perspective. In R. N. Bostrom. (Ed.), *Communication Yearbook 8*. Beverly Hills: Sage.

Rosenberg, B., & White, D. M. (Eds.). (1957). *Mass culture*. Glencoe: Free Press.

Riley, M. W., & Riley, J. W. (1951). A sociological approach to communications research. *Public Opinion Quarterly, 15*, 444–460.

Schramm, W., Lyle, J., & Parker, E. B. (1961). *Television in the lives of our children.* Stanford: Stanford University Press.

Smythe, D. W. (1954). Some observations on communication theory. *Audiovisual Communication Review, 12,* 24–37.

Swanson, D. L. (1977). The uses and misuses of uses and gratifications. *Human Communication Research, 3,* 214–221.

Tannenbaum, P. H., & Zillman, D. (1975). Emotional arousal in the facilitation of aggression through communication. In L. Berkowitz (Ed.). *Advances in experimental social psychology* (Vol. 8, pp. 149–192). New York: Academic Press.

Tannenbaum, P. H. (1980). *The entertainment functions of television.* Hillsdale, NJ: LEA.

Waples, D., Berelson, B., & Bradshaw, F. R. (1940). *What reading does to people.* Chicago: University of Chicago Press.

Windahl, S. (1981). Uses and gratifications at the crossroads. In G. C. Wilhoit & H. de Bock (Eds.), *Mass communication review yearbook* (pp. 174–185). Beverly Hills: Sage.

Zillman, D. (1980). The anatomy of suspense. In P. H. Tannenbaum (Ed.), *The entertainment functions of television* (pp. 133–163). Hillsdale, NJ: LEA.

2 Communications and the Progressives

JAMES W. CAREY

The late Max Schachtman, a battle-scarred, Trotskyite veteran of radical politics, remarked to me over an argumentative dinner during the Vietnam War that in his experience whenever three members of the Left gathered the results were four political parties and five newspapers. Similarly, John Dewey observed in *Liberalism and Social Action* (1935, pp. 90–91) that, in the political struggles of the 1930s, liberals were "divided in outlook and endeavor while reactionaries" were "held together by a community of interest and ties of custom. . . ."

I thought of these two comments when reading the splendid essays by Peters (1989) and Sproule (1989). While I admire their work, these two pieces are an open invitation to the destructive denominationalism and factionalism that is endemic to progressive politics, intellectual or otherwise. At the outset, then, let me say I identify myself with these essays—their outlook, tendencies, and many of their arguments. I conceive intellectual work to be the formation of broad communities of overlapping consensus, and I wish to highlight only those differences in outlook that really do make a difference. Among the central tendencies in these essays that I wish to further are the following: (1) placing the problem of democracy—economic, political, cultural—squarely at the center of analysis; (2) relying upon American traditions of thought and analysis particularly at a time when we are overwhelmed by vocabularies and intellectual styles developed elsewhere, vocabularies and styles that do not travel the Atlantic easily and, when washed up on these shores, obscure as much as they clarify; (3) the attempt to find vitality in and direction from the progressive intellectuals who wrote earlier in this century; and (4) the historical form of the analysis and, though unevenly realized, the historicist style of interpretation. Both Peters and Sproule raise large, complex issues that are fateful for the future of a progressive intellectual life, and nothing I subsequently say is meant to detract from their achievements.

The subject of both of these essays is the progressive movement and the outlooks upon the media fostered within that movement. Professor Peters focuses on the contradictory attitudes through which an early generation of progressive scholars dealt with the national media that emerged during the 1890s. He provides a complex though generally faithful rendering of the work of John Dewey, Charles Cooley, Robert Park, Josiah Royce, and Walter Lippmann. His is a consistently informing essay that will do much to awaken interest in a group who laid down much of the modern understanding of the media.

Professor Sproule wishes to resurrect and revivify propaganda analysis, which was one element in the late phase of the progressive movement. He laments that the history of communication research has been written by the empirical social scientists who invented the view that propaganda had powerful social effects in order that they might have a position to dismantle. The myth of the magic bullet not only distorted what propaganda analysis was about, it also legitimated a different form of research and a different role for social scientists in the apparatus of government and rule. This tamed and domesticated research turned analysis away from the progressive agenda and produced a far less useful body of intellectual work. As things stand now, the only alternative to the social science effects tradition is, in his view, European critical theory—a theory weighed down by an arcane and impenetrable vocabulary, a disconnection from American experience, and a class formulation that evacuates the democratic tradition within which the propaganda analysts worked.

I generally agree with Professor Sproule's arguments and would pretty much endorse the first half of his essay, at least through the section on Harold Lasswell. I agree that there is much to be recovered from the tradition of muckraking and the propaganda analysis that grew out of it. I also think the field made the wrong turn when it focused the evidential questions on the effects of media on attitudes and behavior. Moreover, the "effects tradition" did carry with it an elitist conception of democracy and involved what I have called elsewhere, stealing from Kenneth Burke, a "bureaucratization of the imaginative" and the transformation of scholars from a prophetic to a priestly caste. Unfortunately, as in most things, the victors write the history, and the thin and schematic understanding of communication research which resulted has artificially closed down important options. Finally, I too believe we need to return to extended case studies of propaganda, although I hope it would include more than analyses of right-wing ideology.

Despite such agreement, I also believe that one must state significant differences openly and honestly, though with an eye toward reconciliation. While both of these essays are historical, they are historically very thin. As a result, they lack a palpable and sensuous grasp of the problems that both arrested and defeated progressive intellectuals. They are, in short, often one-dimensional treatments of many-dimensional problems and thinkers.

John Peters errs in undervaluing the early progressive thinkers; Michael Sproule errs in overvaluing a later generation. John Dewey, who wrote for 70 years and spans the entire progressive movement, comes in for dismissive treatment at the hands of both—a liberal pietist for Peters, a "straight thinker" for Sproule. Dewey, of course, is one of my heroes, not for any one book or article but for an extended lifetime of courageous public and intellectual service. More importantly, their dismissal of Dewey bespeaks a failure to grasp adequately the central problems within the progressive movement. Finally, there are problems of language and style. Peters writes as an ironist, and irony is, as Denis Donaghue has suggested, the language of nomads. Peters uses some postmodernist jargon to detach and distance himself from his subjects, and doing so allows him a stance of unearned superiority toward the very thinkers he wishes us to take seriously. If Peters establishes ironic distance, Sproule effaces all distance by embracing his subjects; he tries to convince us that the propaganda analysts secured an unassailable moral outlook from which to dissolve the political problems of the 1930s. Peters draws away while Sproule draws near to the progressive intellectuals, but neither achieves the correct critical distance.

To elucidate adequately both the agreements and the disagreements would require a detailed history of at least two significant decades—the 1890s and 1930s—and the close analysis of a number of key texts. Not having the space to do so, I will, instead, simply retell the story Peters and Sproule have laid out—but in my own language and with my own emphasis. I will have to do this more or less spontaneously, though I will be drawing, here and there, upon my own published work.

THE VOCABULARY OF SOCIAL ANALYSIS

Let me begin by picking up on the postmodernist language that Peters uses to frame his essay. Recent postmodernist work has described, if not celebrated, the "death of the social" and the "disappearance of society." Jean Baudrillard, for example, has described the death of the social as the disappearance of social life in the form of lived experience and the possibility of the textual representation of that experience. It also entails the loss of any sense of being part of a social unit that could be called society as a totality. All we have left are hyper-real representations of society.

Baudrillard is describing what Robert Park and other sociologists of his day used to call, in less spectacular language, a period of social disorganization. Park did not think social disorganization was a property of any one peculiarly fated period of history but was a recurrent episode in the natural history of social life. Periods of disorganization occurred when established habits, customs, manners, and institutions evaporated and/or broke down, when the coordinates of individual identity became obsolete, when the social order went opaque and defied our attempts to represent our experience to ourselves or to others or to form an adequate image of society as a whole. However, social disorganization is a temporary phenomenon, like swings in the business cycle. Eventually, the massive facticity of society reasserts itself, institutions reimpose themselves, a new social order is brought out of temporary social chaos.

I do not wish to overdraw the comparison, but in many ways the 1890s were similar to our own times: a period of intense epistemological crisis and rupture. The crisis was brought about by an unprecedented increase in the sheer scale of society. Society was experienced as a vast collection of unknown and unknowable forces that had to be made into "a knowable society," to use the apt phrase of Raymond Williams. In this crisis of social and self-representation (Who am I? What is the nature of the world I inhabit?), communication or mass communication was seized upon as both satan and savior: the means of solving the crisis that was also the source of the crisis. Communication had enlarged the scale of society, brought distant and unknowable forces to bear on community life, and made democracy radically problematic. Yet communication also offered the hope of transcending the community and reconstituting society and democracy on an enlarged scale. John Dewey, Charles Cooley, Robert Park, Josiah Royce, and, to a lesser degree, Walter Lippmann struggled to draw out of chaos both a knowable society and a democratic community.

However, if we are going to adopt a postmodernist vocabulary to interrogate our own past, we must begin from the assumption that we were not only the "first new nation" but were from the outset a postmodernist nation. American life is one long crisis of social representation. Our experience and identity as individuals, along with the contours of a knowable society, are forever going opaque. We live, in Raymond Williams' phrase, a "long revolution": a ceaseless, continuous transformation of the forms of economic, political, cultural, and community life. We experience this long revolution as a continuous epistemological crisis: the incipient breakdown and obsolescence of all we know about ourselves and our world. I go too far, of course, and I will retreat in a minute. But for the moment we need to recognize that we always seem to be behind in the race to catch up with a knowable society. Baudrillard (1988, pp. 79–80), our most recent European spectator, argues this way in his latest book, *America:*

> Not only can history (in America) not be caught up, but it seems that in this "capitalist" society capital can never actually be grasped in its present reality. It is not that our Marxist critics have not tried to run after it, but it always stays a length ahead of them. By the time one phase has been unmasked, capital has already passed on to another. . . . Capital cheats. It doesn't play by the rules of critique, the true game of history. It eludes the dialectic which only reconstitutes it after the event, a revolution behind.

If you strip away the suffocatingly narrow economic reference, Baudrillard has usefully described, without intending to, the attempts of progressives to catch up with a rapidly and endlessly changing society, one that defied representation in fixed terms. They were not the first, and obviously not the last, to be entrapped in this catch-up game. And they were not the first or the last to play it with the terms and technology of communication.

Why have we been forever living the postmodern? Presumably the inhabitants of North America, from the first settlements to the War of Independence, knew who they were, happily or not: colonials, planters, settlers, indentured servants, loyalists—in short, English subjects. Following independence, the question of who we were was no longer so easy to answer. We defined ourselves negatively through revolution—we were no longer English subjects—but what was an American? More to the point, how was the new country—its geography, culture, and political institutions— to be defined? The answers to these inescapable questions have always involved the homeopathic medicine of communication. However, communication has always referred to two separable and contradictory aspects of this social process.

COMMUNICATION AND THE SOCIAL PROCESS

The first part of the process was the actual creation of physical communities: town building and the creation of the institutions of local life—schools, courts, churches, assemblies, legislatures. This occupied a full century as the nation expanded west and south. It was carried out by groups of strangers who did not necessarily share a common background, experience, or tradition. What tradition is to the rest of the world, communication is to us: the process and resource through which we constitute ourselves and the little worlds we inhabit. By making a revolutionary break, we oriented to the future not the past, to posterity not tradition, and this made us unusually reliant on explicit processes and procedures of debate, discussion, negotiation: mutual sense-making in radically undefined situations. It is this sense of communication, the sense of community building, of communion, that gives the word one kind of weight in our culture. However, the felt experience of communion always has involved a contradiction. We ceaselessly create communities out of need, desire, and necessity but then continually try to escape from the authority of what we have created. We are forever building a city on the hill and then promptly planning to get out of town to avoid the authority and constraint of our creation. Both the creation and the escape, the organization and disorganization, involve intense episodes in sense-making, in the formation and reformation of human identity, in communication in its most fundamental sense.

The second task was that of nation building. We have always had a problem of scale. The country has always been too large for a democracy or republic. Today we forget the problem of scale, but it is well to remember that the most powerful of the European democracies, West Germany, can be safely tucked into Oregon. In the eighteenth century, the plan to create a democracy on a continental scale was taken to be folly. The question of scale was central to the debates of the Constitutional Convention and *The Federalist Papers*. In 1759, less than 30 years prior to the convention, Montesquieu had restated the conventional wisdom: democracies could only work in societies severely restricted in size and population. The question for the convention was the following: Could a representative democracy—a republic—effectively function if it were continental in size and virtually undefined in population? The debate on that question was fierce. Hamilton, it is reported, angrily inquired who had appointed Montesquieu a delegate to the convention. The delegates were aware that the last republic had dissolved when Caesar crossed the Rubicon in defiance of an edict of the Roman Senate. They were aware they were recreating an ancient and fragile form of nationhood, one that could easily be dissolved and rendered ineffective by the sheer problems of space and scale. In The Federalist No. 14, Madison gives us a shaky geography lesson when he describes the actual size of the new republic and projects it forward to a half continent from the Gulf of Mexico to the Canadian border, from the Atlantic to the Mississippi. He tried to demonstrate how it was possible to have a country on a scale virtually unimagined—1,000 x 1,000 miles with a population large enough, even if spread thinly, to defend and exploit it—and still maintain it as a republic. He summarized his position, the one that eventually carried, as follows:

> . . . the intercourse throughout the union will be daily facilitated by new improvements. Roads will every where be shortened, and kept in better order; accommodations for travelers will be multiplied and meliorated; and interior navigation on our eastern side will be opened throughout, or nearly throughout the whole extent of the Thirteen States. The communication between the western and Atlantic districts, and between different parts of each, will be rendered more and more easy by those numerous canals with which the beneficence of nature has intersected our country, and which art finds it so little difficult to connect and complete. (Cooke, 1961, p. 64)

The country could be cemented together in space by technology: turnpikes, roads, canals, navigable rivers, post offices, printing, and literacy. But this view of communication contained its own contradiction; for the very long lines of communication which cemented the nation together could leave it prey to the principal dangers facing democracies or republics: they might be overwhelmed by contagion or faction, swept up in antidemocratic enthusiasms, or captured by special interests who lacked regard for the commonwealth.

In summary, the crisis in *self*-representation turns on the nature of community life and the need both to construct and to escape authoritative institutions. The crisis in *social* representation turns on the need to give democratic coherence to a large nation with a diverse population without allowing it to decline into factionalism or combust into those enthusiasms that Mr. Dooley likened to a "bonfire on an icefloe." I once tried to catch these multiple contradictions as a contrast between a ritual and transmission view of communication. The progressive intellectuals of whom Professor Peters writes tried to describe these contradictions as they resurfaced in the 1890s in a language and sensibility appropriate to those times, a language and even more a sensibility that no longer can be ours. Moreover, and for the first time, they attempted to deal with the crisis of social and self-representation in a distinctively American vocabulary. Our social and intellectual thought for pretty much the first 100 years was a European import. Not until the 1890s did the sale of domestically written books exceed that of imported ones, and the rise was initially an artifact of new copyright laws. As Sidney Hook (1974, p. 3) has written:

> In the realm of thought and culture America has largely been a colonial dependency of Europe. Its own authentic history—the conquest of a virgin continent, the bloodiest of all civil wars, the technological revolution, the extension of social democracy—has not been reflected in a characteristic philosophy of life. As the pioneer settlements struggled across river and mountain, New England divines were still wrestling with age-old problems of freedom and predestination. When the nation was locked in arms over the issue of slavery, its leading teachers were still justifying the ways of God to man while the more daring were beginning to unwind the cobwebby speculations of German idealistic philosophy. Only towards the end of the nineteenth century did a distinctively American philosophy emerge. The names associated with it were Charles Peirce, William James, and John Dewey. This philosophy was labeled pragmatism or instrumentalism or experimentalism.

For our purposes, Hook makes the case too narrowly. Coincident with and central to the progressive movement was an attempt to shed or radically transform European categories of thought and to reevaluate and reconstruct American experience: pragmatism in philosophy, the frontier hypothesis in history (democracy did not arrive on the Mayflower but was created on the frontier), the creation of an authentic American canon in literature (Emerson, Whitman, Melville, Hawthorne), the beginnings of the American studies and American folklore movements. Most important, for our purposes, American social thought both rejected and transformed the basic dichotomies between gemeinschaft and gesellschaft, status and contract, organic and mechanical solidarity, feudalism and capitalism—the distinctions that framed European social theory. The product of revolutionary circumstances on a "virgin continent," we were never a gemeinschaft society, never one of status and organic solidarity, never one with a feudal tradition and, therefore, as Marx recognized in the *Grundrisse*, a strange type of capitalist democracy that demanded distinctive terms of description and explanation.

The problem of identity and the problem of scale, then, have been from the outset central terms of American experience, and the resolution of the conflict between them has continuously involved the vocabulary of communication. For most of the nineteenth century, these conflicts and contradictions were debated and resolved at the level of the community and the state, in town building and constitutional conventions. Most people lived in hamlets or modestly sized cities and took on identity from an often interchangeable village and church. There was little traffic between the federal union and the community, and what existed was regulated by political parties that had local organization.

The crisis of representation of the 1890s occurred as the national system of "end points" in communications was extended into the small towns and hamlets that had been by-passed in the earlier extension of the railroad and telegraph. The maturing of the wire services, the growth of national magazines, the development of national retail organizations and catalog sales, rural free delivery, national advertising and marketing, and national political parties all had the effect of eclipsing the local, of terminating the existence of self-contained, island communities. Urbanization, industrialization, the maturing of industrial capitalism (with increasingly international connections), the closing of the frontier, the eclipse of agriculture as a predominant way of life and with it the country town as a cultural force, these were the events that set the agenda for the progressive intellectuals. It was in this milieu of a national, urban society, a society which both invaded and transcended the local, that progressive intellectuals took up the task of representation. But these problems of scale and identity were the same, though larger, as had bedeviled the society from the outset: democracy versus scale, capitalism versus republican politics, Puritanism versus antinomianism, a continental political economy versus local life. These were the issues that had to be rethought with a new and transformed vocabulary. The crucial dimension and conflict, then as now, was between the local and national.

Surrounding those structural changes were a variety of cultural and social movements that were both "responses" and assertions: progressivism itself, populism, the creation of ethnic groups, nativism, the know-nothings, women's suffrage, temperance, the Grange. These movements expressed a restless search for new identities and for new forms of cultural and political life. Taken together, these movements offered new ways of being for a new type of society. The 1890s appears to be a moment when people actively shed their past, shed old ways of being and belonging, and created a society in motion that lacked a clear sense of where it was going or what it would be when it got there. Charles Beard (1914, p. 164) conveyed something of this complexity:

> Deep, underlying class feeling found its expression in the conventions [of 1896] of both parties, and particularly that of the Democrats, and forced upon the attention of the country, in a dramatic manner, a conflict between great wealth and the lower middle and working classes, which had hitherto been recognized only in obscure circles. The sectional or vertical cleavage in American politics was definitely cut by new lines running horizontally through society. . .

To capture what Raymond Williams has called the "structure of feeling" of that era, one might raise the questions about it that *we* raise about *our* time, about what is happening to *us* now that the fruits of the progressive era have yielded a more global or at least transnational structure of politics, commerce, and culture. What is the relation between the social disorganization of our time and the new forms of communication that have emerged since World War II? How does one represent the social totality and the period through which we are living? The Global Village? Spaceship Earth? The Post Industrial, Post Modern, Post Everything Society? Who are we in this new age? World Citizens? Feminists? Post Marxists? Neo-conservatives? Religious Fundamentalists? What are we going to do about the new plutocrats, Donald Trump, T. Boone Pickens, Ivan Boesky? Now that we are part of an international community, how do we understand the marriage of socialism and capitalism in Western Europe? The marriage of communism and capitalism in the Soviet Union and China? We struggle with these questions in the same way the progressives did with questions of the 1890s.

PROGRESSIVISM AND THE PUBLIC

The first generation of progressive intellectuals attempted to preserve the best of the American past—republican political institutions, democratic cultural forms—while controlling and transcending the most destructive features of American capitalism. That they failed to do so adequately is not particularly to their dishonor, for no one else has managed to provide a means to pull off this particular miracle. However, in the midst of that struggle they managed to produce in pragmatism a peculiarly American, antifoundational and anti-essential, philosophy, and in symbolic interactionism a vital tradition of sociology that focused on the details of the social process and a social psychology of the self and identity peculiarly well adapted to the fluid conditions of American life. At the same time, they maintained an unshakable commitment to democracy and undertook social action on its behalf. Above all, they cultivated a benign, generous, and optimistic outlook, an outlook of energy and hope. It is the latter structure of feeling that most decisively differentiates them from modern intellectuals and that the self-pitying modern mind finds most abhorrent about them. But pessimism or irony is as much a pose as optimism, and a far less useful one, at least for those of us who are still hostage to the future.

The first attempt of Dewey, Park, and Cooley to produce a response to the crisis of social representation was surely a disaster. The newspaper they envisioned and came close to producing, *Thought News*, was an attempt to represent society statistically, to produce order out of chaos by generating what we would call today a daily, continuously updated program of social indicators: a national bureau of standards charting every movement in the social body. As I wrote at length about this experiment some 15 years ago (Sims & Carey, 1976), I will not repeat myself. John Peters has given a reasonable account of this attempt to generate not a science of society but to set loose science in society: a way to know the world that was a product of scientific procedure and imagination.

John Dewey and Franklin Ford felt that changes in journalism and communication fostered by the telegraph and railroad brought with it a need for "scientific" reporting. Scientific reporting was a vision for a future organization of society based on the new dynamics centered around the telegraph. The news report of the future would supersede literature, and the literary consciousness, of the past. It was to be tied to an irreducible, statistical order of facts documenting the state of the social organism. The hopes and aspirations of the scientific attitude rested on the possibilities of a new form of social intelligence, achieved through the workings of the newspaper, which could establish an integrated republic and an ordered social life. Franklin Ford (1892, p. 18) suggested that:

> A tremendous movement is impending, when the intellectual forces which have been gathering since the Renaissance and Reformation, shall demand complete free movement and, by getting their physical leverage in the telegraph and printing press shall through free inquiry in a centralized way, demand the authority of all other authorities.

Dewey and Ford shared the conviction that the growth of the telegraph, overlaid upon earlier developments in printing, had created the material basis for a national society. However, this society was dormant as a spiritual or cultural reality. For a national community to emerge out of a national society, they looked to the union of modern communications technology (the material basis) with science (inquiry) as the agent of a shared intelligence. Ford's *Draft of Action* was an attempt to present a practical justification for the aspiration. Now that space was eclipsed, the opportunity was present:

> The great extent of the United States, the bigness of the country has compelled the elimination of distance. But this was only to prepare the way for the organization of its intelligence and the correlation therewith of the intelligence of the whole world. . . . Democracy in America is not organized till we have consciously brought its intelligence to a center and have related it to the past, that the light might be had for the morrow's guidance. The means of communication are in place but these could not be brought to the highest use until the realities flowing out from the locomotive and the telegraph, their spiritual meaning should be wrought out. . . . (Ford, 1892, p. 20)

Dewey (1920, 1949, p. 211), at his most mystical, similarly suggested that "when the emotional force, the mystical force one might say of communication, of the miracle of shared life and shared experience is spontaneously felt, the hardness and crudeness of contemporary life will be bathed in a light that never was on land and sea."

This entire notion seems to us a little silly—indeed it was silly—but it faithfully mirrors both a characteristic American motive and a general pattern in the development of modern communications: the desire for a nationally integrated system of communications, for a scientific journalism based on the sanctity of the fact, a naive faith that shared information would dissolve social disagreements, that opinion was medieval and knowledge modern, that commerce could provide an adequate model for human communication, and that science and technology would be twin solvents of all our difficulties. This is not much different from the rhetoric of modern computer enthusiasts, though they are both more opaque and enthusiastic.

The romance with thought news and the scientific newspaper was a brief interlude, relatively early in Dewey's career, rather than a lifetime preoccupation. To my knowledge, Dewey never returned to it, though he did maintain a lifelong interest in the relation of science, communication, and the media. However, his views on these central terms shifted markedly over the course of time.

A much more important statement of Dewey's general views is *The Public and Its Problems*, published in 1927. The book was an answer to Lippmann's *Public Opinion*. Dewey, without forswearing a commitment to science or the scientific method, criticized Lippmann's notion of elitist democracy and took Lippmann's book to be the "greatest indictment of democracy yet written."

The Public and Its Problems is an analysis of the eclipse of the public and a plea for its restoration. It is squarely in the tradition of Jefferson and *The Federalist Papers*. The public in eclipse was, of course, the face-to-face public of direct interaction. In trying to restore the public, Dewey gave the matter a somewhat different twist. He used the notion of the public to argue against individualism and to point out a domain of shared, cooperative experience and identity formation. Individualism assumes that transactions occur between discrete individual persons—bound usually by contract—and, properly speaking, concern only the parties directly involved. Dewey argued that a public interest arises whenever there are indirect consequences of individual, private transactions. These indirect consequences are what economists call externalties. Thus, an agreement to purchase a car is an individuated transaction between two private parties: a buyer and a seller. Yet the transaction depends upon and calls forth certain externalties such as the provision of roads, the regulation of traffic, the policing of highways, etc. Dewey argued that a public and a public interest came into existence whenever such externalties were created. In the modern world, few transactions have solely private consequences; externalties are pretty much coextensive with interaction. While externalties had steadily expanded, the domain and competence of the public had steadily shrunk. The interdependencies created by industry and commerce were nowhere matched by interdependencies of public life. It was Dewey's hope, forlorn as it turns out, that the new instruments of mass communication could transform the great society into the great community, bring externalties into conscious awareness, and create or restore public life on a scale matching that of industry and politics.

In *The Public and Its Problems*, Dewey produced an unusually abstract definition of the public, one defined by the function of dealing with externalties. This was his means of countering the elitist notions of democracy being put forth by Lippmann and others, notions that eventually, in the work of Paul Lazarsfeld and like minded social scientists, carried the day. Dewey, however, never quite detached the public or the community from the necessities of face-to-face interaction, from the oral tradition, from the belief that whatever the scale of society, democracy demands and rests upon the foundations of group life. Here, stitched together without ellipses, are his final conclusions:

> The generation of democratic communities and an articulate democratic public can be solved only in the degree in which local communal life becomes a reality. Signs and symbols, language, are the means by which a fraternally shared experience is ushered in and sustained. Conversation has a vital import lacking in the fixed and frozen words of written speech. Ideas which are not communicated, shared and reborn in expression are but broken and imperfect thought. Expansion of personal understanding and judgment can be fulfilled only in the relations of personal intercourse in the local community. We lie, as Emerson said, in the lap of an immense intelligence. But that intelligence is dormant and its communications are broken until it possesses the local community as its medium. (1927, pp. 217–219)

Those may be liberal pieties, but nothing in modern experience suggests they are anything other than liberal truths.

At a practical level, there is little that differentiates Dewey's views from those of Park, Cooley, or Josiah Royce. Royce (1969a, p. 31) introduces his autobiographical sketch by saying that his "earliest recollections include a very frequent wonder as to what my elders meant when they said that this [Grass Valley, California] was a new community." Although a person of wide cosmopolitan interests, Royce was profoundly influenced by his American experience. As John McDermott says, "Even John Dewey, a lifelong student of American democracy, did not conduct so extended a scrutiny of his own cultural roots as did Royce" (Royce, 1969a, p. 41). His history of California, his novel about California, along with the *Philosophy of Loyalty* and his essay, "Provincialism," were all attempts to recultivate and restore the local or provincial in the face of the national and cosmopolitan. Royce did not have the same political interests as Dewey, but he did recognize the critical part played by the local, face-to-face community in the cultivation of democratic life. He enlarged the local to the province and contrasted the province not with the city but with the nation:

> ... a country, a state, or even a large section of a country, such as New England, might constitute a province. For me, then, a province shall mean any one part of a national domain which is geographically and socially, sufficiently unified to have a true consciousness of its own unity, to feel a pride in its own ideals

and customs and to possess a sense of its own distinction from other parts of the country. (1969b, p. 1069)

This commitment to a province did not deny the importance of the national: "Our national unity, moreover, will always require of us a devotion that will transcend in some directions the limits of our provincial ideas" (1969b, p. 1070). In Royce's view, the idealization of the provincial experience would aid in the resolution of a serious "American problem," namely, "the problem of educating the self-estranged spirit of our nation to know itself better" (1969b, p. 952). Royce saw no contradiction in the deepening of provincial experience as a way of fostering an enhanced sense of national life. Actually, he held that "they cannot prosper apart" (1969b, p. 1071).

In one of his last writings, Royce (1969b, p. 1156) warns us that we must avoid the plight of the detached individual who belongs "to no community which he loves and to which he can devote himself. . . . For mere attachment, mere self-will, can never be satisfied with itself, can never win its goal. What saves us on any level of human social life is union."

I find no sharp break between Dewey and Royce, no difference that makes a difference, at least for the matters which concern us. Nor, for that matter, do I find Cooley and Park to be altogether outside this consensus. Park was more interested in social conflict and the ecology of racial and ethnic urban villages; Cooley was more attuned to the nature and role of primary groups. Both, however, were oriented to the same phenomena.

The key to understanding Cooley is to recognize that he spent his entire life in Ann Arbor, Michigan. The modern world came to him, and he took delight in the expanded contact and sympathy, connection and understanding, that the new media permitted. Events of his lifetime such as the Chicago fire of 1871 reinforced his view that the media could be a vehicle for an expanded civic and cultural awareness. As news of the fire spread out over the new international telegraph system, the residents of the city were overwhelmed by the response of people to their plight, a response of sympathy, mutual aid, and cooperation that spread back into the city over the same network. Cooley unfortunately was less attuned to the economic consequences of the new forms of communications, which in the words of the historian Lee Benson (1951, p. 62) produced in 1893 "an international agrarian market, an international agrarian depression and, as a climax, international agrarian discontent."

The strength of Cooley's work was not in his confused understanding of the new media but in his recognition that the transcendence of time and space by technology could not or at least ought not be allowed to produce a mass society of atomized individuals. His social psychology was a continuing argument against individualism and a recognition that even in the modern world the human personality would be formed within the context of local life, within a network of social interaction. However, a question needed to be answered: If the local community was eclipsed by the formation of a national society, what would replace the community as the agency of character formation, the site where a looking glass self developed, where the significant other and the generalized other came together to form an I and a me? Cooley invented the notion of the "primary group" to carry this indispensable burden. The primary group is, of course, a gross abstraction. Cooley was thinking of the nuclear family and the tiny circle of friends and relatives who surrounded it. Now that the primary group has been largely destroyed (destroyed, I might add, at the very moment it was being rediscovered by Elihu Katz and Paul Lazarsfeld), a victim to the advance of the postmodern, Cooley seems more than a little quaint. But the question he leaves behind is still very much with us: What kind of people are we to become in the postmodern world, where courts, counselors, schools, child care centers, and self-help groups assume the social role of the primary group?

The consistent strategy of the early progressive intellectuals was to tack back and forth between the great society brought about by industry and mass communication and the local as a site of community, politics, and character formation. Their emphasis was clearly on the latter, though they invested much misplaced hope in the great society. These were men, we must remember, who grew up in and were formed by the experience of the small town: Cooley in Ann Arbor, Michigan; Dewey in Burlington, Vermont; Park in Red Wing, Minnesota; Royce in Grass Valley, California. Each wrestled with the relationship between the idea of community as experienced in their youth, the world of European philosophy and education which, in different ways, formed their intellectual outlook, and the cosmopolitan world, national and international, in which they lived as adults. Their work is an attempt at reconciling the tensions between these three poles: between the identity-forming habitat of community, the national life of the modern period, and the European intellectual tradition. Their experience of actual communities was the pole magnetizing their beliefs, and it is what makes them so antique in their outlook, makes them available to our sophisticated condescension, to the easy dismissal of nostalgia or romance whenever the experience of community life creeps into their thought.

THE ATTACK ON THE SMALL TOWN

The closest thing to a tropism carried about by the modern intellectual is a heightened disdain for the community and the small town. But it is an unachieved tropism. Our entire life has been an attempt to escape the constraints of the proximate. We never seem to grasp the point that our view of the small town as either barren or romantic is one of the most ambiguous achievements of a later phase of the progressive movement itself. The image of the American small town, the country town, as a seat of unrelieved bigotry, Babbitry, and philistinism, a site of class conflict and exploitation, is an achieved image and an unquestioned one at that. The attack on the small town was a necessary part of a later phase of the progressive movement. The emergence of a national society depended in part on a burning over of the agricultural society and the small town credo that justified it. Just as the emergence of the postmodern depends on the destruction of the modern in all its forms, the emergence of "the progressive" relied upon the denigration of that phase of history which preceded it.

The appearance in 1914 of Edgar Lee Masters' *Spoon River Anthology* provided a damning indictment of the spiritual and cultural aridity of the small town. In scene after scene, Masters depicted the barren, mean, and vicious lives of villagers and created a picture of small town moral and intellectual depravity. Masters was a product of the Abraham Lincoln country in Illinois, and so his attack was directed at the very center of a faith embodied in the historical figure of Lincoln, namely, that small town America could produce figures of intelligence, culture, and learning, armed with the wit, probity, courage, and eloquence necessary for great stature. Six years after Masters' book, in 1920, Sinclair Lewis published *Main Street*, a novel destined for a much larger audience. Almost overnight Gopher Prairie and Carol Kennicott came to symbolize sterile towns and despondent heroines. Didactic and simply written, *Main Street* penetrated the minds of the more intellectually obtuse and joined with *Spoon River Anthology* in forming the indictment of small town America. Three years later Thorstein Veblen (1923a; 1923b), with his savage irony and wit, waded in with his economic critique of the small town and rounded out a picture that is today indelibly imprinted in the minds of everyone whether they grew up in such towns or have done no more than drive by them on the interstate.

The significance of such works and the many that have followed is this: for several generations Americans had at least pretended to believe that log cabins surpassed mansions in producing people most fit for democracy, that agriculture and country towns, close to nature and people, constituted the proper environment for creating leaders in the arts and professions, and that pastoral pursuits contributed to virtue, the good life, and happiness. Masters, Lewis, and Veblen, and a host of imitators, challenged all this, and in doing so they served a new age of industry, urbanization, and nationalization by weakening the credo which justified small town and agricultural America. Even now we confront the novels of Mark Twain, the paintings of Thomas Hart Benton, the poetry of Carl Sandburg, not as a residue of *our* past but as an exhibition of the primitive that might have descended from a South Sea island.

The truth of the attack and the distance are not what is in question. Our view of the small town is a discursive achievement, not a natural fact. It is the outlook of those who have never read the celebrations of small town life one finds in Edward Howe (1884) or William Allen White (1946) or Hamlin Garland (1924). It is the outlook of those who confront Lincoln as a legend, not as a person. It is the outlook of those who have disdained the rich secondary literature on small town life: Lewis Atherton's *Main Street on the Middle Border* (1954), Hugh Duncan's *Culture and Democracy* (1965), Stanley Elkins and Eric McKittrick's studies of democracy on Turner's frontier (1954), or even Richard

Sennett's application, in *The Uses of Disorder* (1973), of the lessons of this phase of our history to today's urban problems.

The lesson we should learn from the early progressives is not that of romantic and nostalgic attachment to a vanished way, to a world in many ways happily lost, but the image of democratic possibility still present in local life whether in academic departments, the villages of Iowa City or Urbana, or the urban villages of San Jose. We might also learn from the progressives something about how it is that social change depends upon a complex reconstruction of the past, a reconstruction that delegitimates an older order so as to pave the way for a new world of industry, the city, the professions, and modern styles of life.

ELEMENTS OF PROGRESSIVISM

The progressive movement contained three separable but closely connected moments. First, it was an attack upon the plutocracy, upon concentrated economic power, and upon the national social class that increasingly had a strangle hold over wealth and industry. The economic dimension of the movement, however, also included the struggle by middle class professionals— doctors, lawyers, journalists, social workers, etc.—to become a national class, to find a place in the national occupational structure and the national system of class influence and power: progressives sought to become, in Pierre Bourdieu's useful phrase, the dominated element of the dominant class. The national class of progressive professionals was, in many ways, merely a less powerful imitation of the national class of plutocrats. Progressivism was also a movement of political reform at the national level and, even more, an attempt to reclaim the cities from the political bosses and the urban machines. In many cases this was an attempt to uproot the political influence of ethnic working class groups who had earlier on seized city politics from local commercial and cultural elites. Progressivism was devoted to "good government" (read: honest, middle class government) and created the chain of Better Government Associations that one still finds in major American cities. Progressivism was for merit and against patronage, for science and against tradition, for middle class politics and against working class privilege.

Progressivism was also a cultural movement that sought to define new styles of life, patterns of child rearing, modes of family life, taste in art, architecture, urban planning, and personal conduct. Progressive education, progressive child rearing, progressive art, progressive science, and progressive taste were as important in this movement as progressive economics and politics.

The three wings of progressivism were joined to one common desire: a desire to escape the merely local, an enthusiasm for everything that was distant and remote, a love of the national over the provincial.

The national media of communication, particularly magazines and books, were the arena where the progressive program was set out and the place where the struggle for its legitimation occurred. Quite different judgments about the progressive movement are likely depending upon which aspect of it comes into question. For example, one can admire the economic attack on concentrated wealth without being enthusiastic for the movement of professionalism and elitist democracy that went along with it. The political reform movement, by contrast, has been a colossal failure, marked by a hypermoralism and middle class self-satisfaction. I would still prefer to elect judges rather than have them appointed by the American Bar Association; I find middle class civil service patronage no improvement over working class friendship patronage; and I would rather be governed by the first 100 names in the Boston phone directory than the faculty at Harvard. Similarly, I find much of the progressive cultural program—its attack on popular culture and the life of the working class, its espousal of Dr. Spock's methods of child rearing, its contempt for religion except as an appurtenance to politics and middle class life styles—to be in most instances what Saul Bellow called high IQ idiocy.

The economic wing of the progressive movement gave rise to the "muck-rakers," who directed their attack against the plutocracy. Later, they turned their attention to the press, for in the early decades of the century the press did not become the organ of neutral intelligence desired by Dewey and Cooley but an arena of struggle between the "special interests" that increasingly dominated American life. The progressive propaganda critics, of whom Professor Sproule writes, picked up the muckraking tradition of Lincoln Steffens and attempted to do systematically and, by their lights, scientifically what the muckrakers did journalistically. A paradigmatic figure in all of this is Upton Sinclair. In three significant volumes *(The Jungle* [1930] on meat packing, *The Goose Step* [1923] on higher education, and *The Brass Check* [1931] on the press), Sinclair attempted to unmask the power, privilege, and special interest that stood behind the presumed general beneficence of both private and public institutions. Muckraking and propaganda analysis were an American version of *Ideologiekritik* but with significant differences from the European counterpart. First, they were framed within an American language of democracy rather than a theory of mass society. Second, they were straightforward, descriptive, and aimed at provoking public action rather than theoretical reflection. Third, and most important, while they were overwhelmingly aimed at unmasking bourgeois ideology, they examined the propaganda efforts of all of the groups, both on the Left and Right, labor unions as well as manufacturers' associations, that were corrupting public discourse by control and manipulation of the press.

THE DECLINE OF PROPAGANDA ANALYSIS

The eventual decline and elimination of both the muckraking tradition and propaganda analysis has been ably analyzed by Professor Sproule. But we should add a couple of additional factors to his account. When the progressives were attacking concentrated wealth and power in the name of democracy, their arguments had support and resonance. Unfortunately, following the Russian Revolution, those attacks became intertwined with a long and decisive set of political struggles: among Bolsheviks, Mensheviks, Trotskyites, socialists, and liberals, and over issues such as social-fascism, the popular front, the Stalin trials, the Nazi-Soviet pact, isolationism, and the entrance of the United States into World War II. What discredited propaganda analysis, fairly or not, was that it became deeply involved in those struggles, was unable to maintain neutrality, and was often a pawn of the shifting position of the Communist party. The career of Upton Sinclair is instructive.

Sinclair was the universal champion of the underdog and lost cause. As Sidney Hook (1987, p. 250) says of him, "There was something endearing in the freshness of his spirit, its perennial youthfulness, and his never-failing sympathy for the down-and-out." At the same time, he was enormously gullible toward the propaganda of the Soviet Union. "He simply believed in the good intentions of those who used the same liberal and socialist vocabulary he did." Although a lifelong socialist and constitutionally wedded to peaceful persuasion, he became an impassioned defender of the Stalinist regime during the years when the purge and terror were at their height. He endorsed the Moscow trials, supported the Nazi-Soviet pact, and generally followed the predictable turns and reversals of Soviet foreign policy as it was transmitted through the American Communist party. Like so many others, late in his life he turned on the Soviet Union, and in the Lanny Budd novels "his hostile treatment of that country was as crude as his earlier support" (Hook, 1987, p. 252).

Sinclair's career was not an unusual one among the muckrakers; the same fate befell Lincoln Steffens. When propaganda analysis was devoted to unmasking the interest groups that were manipulating the channels of public communications with increased effectiveness, it performed a valuable service. Later, when it got caught in the squeeze, many of the same analysts simply used propaganda analysis to propagate another piece of propaganda. The deep divisions in the Left during the 1930s, divisions between social democrats like John Dewey and, principally, the Communist party, opened a space in American intellectual and political life through which those with an elitist conception of democracy and a statistical/experimental view of science could march to victory. The lessons of that period still have not been learned by progressive intellectuals.

We should remember that many Americans, John Dewey among them, had a romance with the Soviet Union in the years immediately following the Russian Revolution. Dewey visited the country in 1928 and issued glowing reports on its educational system. The Soviet Union became a concrete embodiment of the hopes of the progressive movement. The crunch came when these same intellectuals were forced to deal with the control of the American Communist party from Moscow, the evidence of the Stalin trials, and the Nazi-Soviet pact, in short, with the emergence of a totalitarian state. At that point, American discourse deteriorated into blast and counterblast with both the Left and the Right engaged in the most cynical, propagandistic attempts to manipulate American public opinion. In all of this, Max Eastman is another paradigmatic figure. Eastman, founder of *The Masses*, was a heroic opponent of the United States entering World War I and a powerful force in radicalizing American intellectuals. The translator of Trotsky's *History of the Russian Revolution*, he stood practically alone in 1924 when upon his return from the Soviet Union he presented the first evidence of the Stalinization of the Bolshevik regime. He then became a rebel and pariah in the radical movement and a continuous object of propagandistic attack by the Left. In the 1930s, he took on the heroic task of counteracting the shameless but effective propaganda of Walter Duranty, *The New York Times* Moscow correspondent, through whom the Kremlin concealed the truth about the great famines, liquidations, and purges that resulted from the collectivization campaigns. But by then American public discourse had degenerated into a propaganda war. What had started out as a form of analysis quickly became itself implicated, unwittingly or not, in a concrete political struggle.[1]

John Dewey and Lewis Mumford were two early champions of the Soviet Union who were also progressives, socialists, and advocates of propaganda analysis. They later broke from these positions in concrete circumstances: Dewey because of the Stalin trials, Mumford because of the propaganda campaign against American entrance into World War II. This latter campaign was conducted, one should remember, by forces on the Left and the Right, by isolationists, by the America First movement, and by the Communist party, which defined Britain as the enemy of Western democracy during the period of the Nazi-Soviet pact.

John Dewey and Lewis Mumford do not need my defense; their lives are testimony to the enabling power of democratic values, and they represent the best scholarship the American liberal tradition has to offer. Dewey's *Liberalism and Social Action* (1935) is an eloquent and I think decisive plea for pragmatism over partisanship in the conduct of intellectual work. He recognized that it was not enough to critique ideology as propaganda; one also had to have a program of political action that was something more than a defense of the American plutocracy or an apologia for the Soviet Union. Lewis Mumford's *Values for Survival* (1946), a book much opposed to Dewey's brand of liberalism, written before the war but published after it, a war which took his only son Geddes, is an attempt to find standards of intellectual conduct that transcend the ideological immediacies of the moment. His 1946 footnote to a 1940 essay (p. 39), a footnote to which Professor Sproule alludes, is still an apt critique of the failings of propaganda analysis at a moment of truth:

> A pathological resistance to rational persuasion characterized a great part of the civilized world during this period (the late 1930s). Even now that resistance remains: witness the people who still believe that the horrors of the German extermination factories are but the figments of propaganda. The responsibility for this state of mind must be widely distributed: it is the end-product of a general campaign of de-valuation and de-verification in which many supposedly decent people took part. Thus the well-attested record of German atrocities at

the beginning and at the end of the first World War was dismissed by an historian like Dr. Charles A. Beard as a "tale for babes." Analysts of propaganda, exposing the rhetorical devices of persuasion, themselves put over one of the biggest propaganda frauds of our time: namely, the conviction that the important part about a statement is not its truth or falsity, but the question whether someone wishes you to believe it. Such analysts held in effect that the mere desire to persuade is a sufficient ground for rejecting a statement: hence any unwelcome truth could be dismissed out of hand as "propaganda" if he who uttered it sought to move the hearer to action. On those terms only indifference and paralysis were guarantees of reputability. As a result, a large part of our fighting men went into the war thinking that there was no essential difference between their own cause and that of the enemy. In a world where no universal principles were valid and where no values were universal, skepticism and relativism, by undermining the reasons for fighting, also vitiated the will to fight. This will-to-disbelieve produced a grave moral debacle.

The progressive movement, and the propaganda analysis that grew out of it, remains among our most worthy traditions of scholarship and one from which there remains much to be learned. Will we learn from it? Judging from current evidence, it seems unlikely. There has been a resurgence of interest in propaganda analysis, but on the evidence of the first major work of the revival, Edward Hermann and Noam Chomsky's *Manufacturing Consent* (1988), we are still stuck back about 1936. We have learned very little in 50 some years, and I doubt there is much to be learned on these matters from postmodernism. We have little need for yet another unmasking of bourgeois ideology: an unmasking of an unmasking of an unmasking to the point of parody. We also have little need of a sludge that combines Lacan, Foucault, Derrida, Adorno, and Marx into a language of impotence and intellectual privilege. We might begin the task of reconstruction, taking a suggestion from the early progressives, in the place we live now, amidst generally undemocratic practice and anti-civil habits—the departments we currently call home, which are largely the site of our homelessness.

NOTE

1.   This account is largely taken from Hook (1987, pp 142).

REFERENCES

Atherton, L. (1954). *Main Street on the middle border*. Bloomington: Indiana University Press.

Baudrillard, J. (1988). *America*. New York: Verso.

Beard, C. A. (1914). *Contemporary American history*. New York: Macmillan.

Benson, L. (1951). The historical background of Turner's frontier essay. *Agricultural History*, *25*, 59–82.

Cooke, J. E. (Ed.). (1961). *The federalist*. Cleveland: Meridan Books.

Dewey, J. (1927). *The public and its problems*. New York: Henry Holt.

Dewey, J. (1935). *Liberalism and social action*. New York: G. P. Putnam's Sons.

Dewey, J. (1949). *Reconstruction in philosophy*. Boston: Beacon Press. (Original work published 1920)

Duncan, H. L. (1965). *Culture and democracy*. Totowa, NJ: The Bedminster Press.

Elkins, S., & McKittrick, E. (1954). A meaning for Turner's frontier. *Political Science Quarterly*, *69*, 321–355.

Ford, F. (1892). *Draft of action* (unpublished manuscript). University of Michigan, Ann Arbor.

Garland, H. (1924). *A son of the middle border*. New York: Macmillan.

Herman, E., & Chomsky, N. (1988). *Manufacturing consent*. New York: Pantheon Books.

Hook, S. (1974). *Pragmatism and the tragic sense of life*. New York: Basic Books.

Hook, S. (1987). *Out of step: An unquiet life in the 20th century*. New York: Harper & Row.

Howe, E. (1884). *The story of a county town*. Boston: J. R. Osgood & Company.

Lewis, S. (1920). *Main Street*. New York: Harcourt, Brace, & Company.

Masters, E. L. (1915). *Spoon River anthology*. New York: Macmillan.

Mumford, L. (1946). *Values for survival*. New York: Harcourt, Brace, & Company.

Peters, J. D. (1989). Satan and savior: Mass communication in progressive thought. *Critical Studies in Mass Communication*, *6*(3), 247–263.

Royce, J. (1969a). *The basic writings of Josiah Royce* (Vol. 1, J. J. McDermott, ed.). Chicago: University of Chicago Press.

Royce, J. (1969b). *The basic writings of Josiah Royce* (Vol. 2, J. J. McDermott, ed.). Chicago: University of Chicago Press.

Sims, N., & Carey, J. W. (1976, August). *The telegraph and the news report*. Paper presented at annual meeting of the Association for Education in Journalism and Mass Communication Convention, Madison, WI.

Sinclair, U. (1925). *The goose step*. Pasadena, CA: Author.

Sinclair, U. (1930). *The jungle*. New York: Vanguard Press.

Sinclair, U. (1931). *The brass check*. Pasadena, CA: Author.

Sproule, J. M. (1989). Progressive propaganda critics and the magic bullet myth. *Critical Studies in Mass Communication*, *6*(3), 225–246.

Veblen, T. (1923a, July 11). The country town. *Freeman*, pp. 417–420.

Veblen, T. (1923b, July 18). The country town. *Freeman*, pp. 440–443.

White, W. A. (1946). *The autobiography of William Allen White*. New York: Macmillan.

3 The New Validation of Popular Culture:
Sense and Sentimentality in Academia

MICHAEL SCHUDSON

In the past generation, popular culture has attained a new legitimacy in American universities. Popular culture is now studied more often, in more different courses, in more departments, and with more sympathy than before. In literature, serious scholars can write on science fiction or on detective fiction or on romance novels, in short, on what is still often labeled as "trash." In history, the attention to popular culture has moved even further; the attention to the beliefs and practices of ordinary people actually has displaced studies of political, diplomatic, and military elites as the leading edge of historical writing. In the interpretive social sciences, now rubbing up against and taking inspiration from the humanities, there is also a new freshness and new import-ance to the study of popular cultural forms.

The concept of popular culture has been revised entirely, and revitalized, by these developments. The result has been, in my opinion, a salutary new valuation of popular culture combined with an undiscriminatingly sentimental view of it. In the pages that follow, I describe the main intellectual lines that have produced this change, and I suggest that the new study of popular culture now offers a serious challenge to the identity of the modern university.

Popular culture can be understood broadly as beliefs and practices, and the objects through which they are organized, that are widely shared among a population.[1] These include both "folk" or "popular" beliefs, practices and objects rooted in local traditions, and also "mass" beliefs, practices, and objects generated from political and commercial centers. Until recently, scholars have tended to praise folk culture for its authenticity and decry mass culture for its commercial origin, its ideological aims, or its aesthetic blandness. Today the picture is more complex with scholars finding that authentic folk traditions often have metropolitan or elite roots and that mass culture often is authenti-cally incorporated into ordinary people's everyday lives. It is therefore more hazardous than it used to be to make a rigid distinction between folk and mass culture. I will lump both categories under the general term, popular culture.

49

Conventionally, objects taken to be part of popular culture are *readable* objects, written or visual materials for which there are available traditions of interpretation and criticism. In recent years, the range of what is considered readable has expanded vastly: now spatial arrangements, household objects, advertisements, food and drink, dress, and youth cultural styles are all parts of readable cultural systems. The special task of interpretation, for many years left to the humanities, has become a more general subject to which anthropology, sociolinguistics, and psychoanalysis have contributed, creating a new convergence of the social sciences and humanities.

The study of popular culture can be broken down as the study of (a) the production of cultural objects, (b) the content of the objects themselves, and (c) the reception of the objects and the meanings attributed to them by the general population or subpopulations. In all three dimensions—the study of the production of culture, the study of texts, and the study of audiences—intellectual developments of the past generation have provided a new validation for the study of popular culture. This development raises a fundamental question that I will take up later in the essay: what rationale remains for distinguishing "high" or "elite" culture from popular culture? If popular culture is valid for serious study, is there still a high culture that is *more* valid? That is, what justification remains for teaching—and thereby legitimating, even enshrining—some texts rather than others in university courses in the humanities? There is new thinking on this question, too, that has come out of historical and sociological accounts of the development of popular and high culture traditions and the evolution of a distinction between them. But let me begin with an examination of changes in the study of the producers, texts, and audiences of popular culture.

PRODUCING CULTURE: THE SOCIOLOGICAL EYE

In the 1960s, and 1970s, the study of the mass media in sociology changed in a way that has had influence well beyond the discipline. In sociology, there were two lines of discussion of popular culture dating to the 1940s and 1950s. One line of empirical studies, in both political science and sociology, looked for specific influences of mass media content on the attitudes or behavior or voting preferences of citizens. Growing out of a concern over propaganda in the 1930s and 1940s and, to some extent, out of a concern to make propaganda *effective* during World War II, these studies came to a surprising conclusion: the effect of the mass media on popular opinion was very small. People inherited voting inclinations from their parents or had their party preferences shaped by their occupational situations and their networks of friends and co-workers. Moreover, they attended to material in the mass media most likely to reinforce views they already held. Even when they came upon opinions contradicting their own, they tended to misperceive them, very often as supportive of their own views. In the face of this selective attention and perception, the power of the media to persuade seemed much less than researchers had imagined.[2]

A second line of thought came out of European social criticism, especially the Frankfurt School work, rather than out of the American tradition of empirical social research. This body of thought developed a concept of "mass society" within the context of Nazi Germany but with an urgent sense that all of modern industrial society was vulnerable to "massification." Theorists of mass society saw the modern individual as alienated, isolated, lonely, and privatized. They saw institutions of social solidarity, the family, the neighborhood, the church, and the party, to be weakening, while the state and its connection to individuals through the mass media was growing steadily more powerful. Without local social institutions to fall back on, the individual became more and more susceptible to the siren song of the mass media and any demagogue who could control mass communication. In one of the most radical statements of this position, Max Horkheimer and Theodor Adorno (1972) argued that popular entertainment, music, the movies, and the comics, spoke in a unified voice, drowning opposition to capitalism in the United States. The "culture industry," a term they coined for the whole array of entertainment industries, was an agent of mass deception, and they repeatedly drew parallels between the propaganda of Hitler and Goebbels and American commercial entertainment.

The one tradition, then, looked hard to find evidence of "media effects" and found little; the other tradition developed a coherent theoretical stance that imagined overpowering ideological influence. In the period from the mid-fifties until the late sixties, American sociologists and political scientists largely stopped studying the mass media (although studies continued in the relatively new departments of communication or mass communication in major universities in the Midwest). Only with the rise in public concern over the news media during the Civil Rights Movement and especially during the war in Vietnam, and with the involvement of a good many social scientists themselves in these movements, did research on the mass media revive. When it did, it returned with people whose personal experiences or personal convictions made them think the media were quite powerful. The difficulty, however, was to say *how* powerful or powerful *in what way.*

There have been both theoretical and empirical answers to these questions. A theoretical effort has been to replace the notion of an overwhelmingly powerful mass culture with the more subtle, and more slippery, notion of "hegemony." The term comes from the work of Italian communist Antonio Gramsci who held that the state achieves its power not only through force but through defining a reality that citizens freely accept, a reality whereby the natural or inevitable right of the ruling class to rule is popularly taken for granted.[3]

Empirical studies have taken another road to the media effects question; many scholars have abandoned efforts to answer it directly and ask, instead, how mass media content is created, not what influence it has. This work can be seen as a different kind of reaction against the mass culture theorists. As Paul DiMaggio (1977) has suggested, the left wing critics of mass culture implicitly assume that mass culture is produced in a monopoly situation: The public will absorb whatever the culture offers because only one product is available. The right wing critics of mass culture, on the other hand, implicitly assume a situation of perfect competition where the public gets whatever it desires (mass culture is of a miserable quality because the public is uncivilized). DiMaggio argues, instead, that the central features of mass culture are the "attributes of industries, not of societies" (p. 437). Some mass culture industries *are* in monopoly situations—the television industry (before cable) or public school textbook publishers. Other mass culture industries—trade books, records, movies, and magazines—create objects for specialized audiences, and their situation more closely resembles free competition. The diversity or innovativeness of the culture materials available to the public, DiMaggio concludes, has "more to do with the market structures and organizational environment of specific industries than with strongly felt demands of either the masses or their masters for certain kinds of homogeneous cultural materials (p. 448).

DiMaggio and the others in sociology and political science who have contributed to "production of culture" studies helped turn the social sciences toward the simple observation that cultural objects are *produced* by specific individuals and organizations under specific legal, economic, political, cultural, and organizational constraints. This obvious truth has had a number of far-reaching consequences for an understanding of culture.[4]

First, the insight has drawn attention to the role of *organizations* and *markets* in determining production. It has thus radically subsumed the sociological study of culture under the sociology of economic life and organizations. To the extent that paintings or novels or films are things made by people and organizations as part of their effort to earn a living, they are not unlike automobiles and hardware and widgets. Important recognitions follow from this. For instance, once a cultural object is seen as an *organizational* product, some of its formal features and thematic content can be traced not to individual minds but to organizational interactions and constraints. For instance, over time, a newspaper's front page devotes about an equal measure to metropolitan, national, and foreign news. This is done not because an editor determines that they are of equal weight in the greater scheme of things. It is done because the news organization is divided into metropolitan, national, and foreign desks, each with an editor who vies for front-page play and whose demands must be satisfied by a managing editor. One of the things a managing editor manages is not news but people in their organizational roles (Sigal, 1973).

Second, if cultural objects such as romance novels or comic books or B movies are organizational products, are not fine fiction published by Farrar, Straus or experimental films made by independent film makers also organizational products? The *balance* of commercial motive and respect for artistic integrity may be different, but commercial motive is rarely absent in the production of high culture, and respect for artistic integrity often has a place in the production of popular culture.

The sociologizing influence of production of culture studies, then, has succeeded in democratizing or relativizing an approach to the study of culture. If Norman Mailer is distinguishable from Sidney Sheldon or Pablo Picasso from LeRoy Neiman, it is not on the basis of craftsmanship versus crassmanship.

One factor that has boosted this sociological insight is that more of the arts have become *collective* than was once the case. For the most part, the novel is as much an individual enterprise today as in the 1800s; to some extent, it has even become more individual and less institutional since a writer can write at his or her own pace without the institutional constraints of having to come up with a serial installment for a daily newspaper as Charles Dickens did. But the rise of *film* as a central modern art, and then its off-shoots in television and video, has made the notion that art is the result of idiosyncratic individual effort difficult to maintain. We *do* maintain it, and the whole point of "auteur" theory in film criticism is to rescue the concept that film, like the novel and like painting or sculpture, can be seen as a traditional art expressive of individual genius. Surely there is *some* truth in this. But with film, it is apparent that other candidates for genius arise, not just the director, who has been lifted by critics to the central role, but also (to name just two) the cinematographer and the leading actors.

Further, some of the modern arts, and particularly those connected to film, require not only a collection of skilled people for production but require a great deal of money, much more than the funds required to support a single artist. It may be, then, that the producer or fund raiser for film or for modern theater deserves some of the credit for authorship. It is certainly true that there is a more coherent critical community for fiction, where most skillful aspiring authors can find a publisher, than there is for film, where the aspiring film maker may very well not find the funds to support the equipment to do technically good work or, finding the funds, may not find a way to exhibit the product.

Some voices in literary theory now question the whole idea of "authorship," and people speak of the death of the author. Changes in the character of artistic production along with the recognition that, even with individual authors, art making happens within a social and institutional context have contributed to a sociologizing of the idea of authorship and some radical questioning of taken-for-granted distinctions between high culture and popular culture.

CULTURAL TEXTS: THE ANTHROPOLOGICAL EYE

One of the most stunning intellectual developments of the past generation came in the advances made by linguists in studying the structure of language. The advances of Noam Chomsky's structuralist revolution are today hotly debated inside linguistics, but the lesson for people outside has remained clear and constant: All human languages are equally complex. No language is closer to nature than the next. All have complicated, rule-governed arrangements for sound, syntax, and meaning. Even pidgins and creoles and dialectical variations are not degradations of a pure form of language, sloppy in adherence to rules, but new ruled systems of their own.

This insight served in some cases as inspiration for and, in most cases, can serve as metaphor for the relativizing trend in the social sciences and humanities for what objects are deserving of study. It is not that the humanities *needed* Chomsky or Jakobson or Levi-Strauss; they had, after all, a tradition of rhetorical studies on which they might have drawn. Rhetoricians saw the entire range of human verbal productions as appropriate objects for study. Aristotle drew special attention to political, legal, and ceremonial speech, but a 20th century descendant, Kenneth Burke, was just as ready to examine aphorisms and advertisements. Yet the tradition of the humanities and especially literary study in the universities generally ignored Burke and others who sought to democratize the range of study-able texts and, instead, took it as their responsibility to define a canon of classic texts. This has been as true in art as in literature. Not simply students of art, university humanities departments have been promoters of their favorite artists and authors. More than most departments in a university, humanities departments are, perhaps necessarily, employers of scholars *engagé*, people deeply involved in *making* the very thing— elite culture—that they study. Barbara Herrnstein Smith describes the process with respect to Homer:

> . . . the value of a literary work is continuously produced and reproduced by the very acts of implicit and explicit evaluation that are frequently invoked as "reflecting" its value and therefore as being evidence of it. In other words, what are commonly taken to be the *signs* of literary value are, in effect, also its *springs*. The endurance of a classic canonical author such as Homer, then, owes not to the alleged transcultural or universal value of his works but, on the contrary, to the continuity of their circulation in a particular culture. Repeatedly cited and recited, translated, taught, and imitated, and thoroughly enmeshed in the network of intertextuality that continuously *constitutes* the high culture of the orthodoxly educated population of the West . . . that highly variable entity we refer to as "Homer" recurrently enters our experience in relation to a large number and variety of our interests and thus can perform a large number of various functions for us and obviously has performed them for many of us over a good bit of the history of our culture. (1984, pp. 34–35)

This is the kind of observation that literary scholars in recent years have begun to accept as they adopt a loosely sociological view of their own institution, understanding it as a hierarchical social structure with larger social functions. Frank Kermode (1983), for instance, writes of literary studies as an institution, that "professional community which interprets secular literature and teaches others to do so" (p. 168). It has authority (not undisputed, he observes) "to define (or indicate the limits of) a subject; to impose valuations and validate interpretations." It is, he says, "a self-perpetuating, semipaternal corporation" (p. 169).

This skeptical stance toward the academic institution as an imposer of valuations has enlarged the number and kinds of texts acceptable for study in the humanities. More kinds of literary texts have been added to the reading lists. Further, the whole concept of textuality has been applied to materials not previously regarded as textual at all, and here anthropology has made the most notable contribution.

The field of anthropology long has been concerned with texts in the collection of oral tales and myths of primitive peoples. Different anthropologists, studying the same group at different times and working with different informants, naturally picked up different variants of stories and folk tales. Piecing together from different variants the most authentic one, or concluding that *each* variant is authentic by its own light, anthropologists have worked with texts, the written-down versions of the orally transmitted tales, in understanding cultures. But anthropology has gone far beyond this still conventional understanding of the text to look upon rituals, games, and performances as interpretable texts that people *make*, and intend as meaningful objects that should be interpreted.

The most widely known instance of this kind of work is the essay by Clifford Geertz on the cockfight in Bali (1973). This essay shows the ways the Balinese cockfight represents and heightens the importance of social solidarities and social divisions in Balinese society. It also shows how the cockfight represents and heightens important psychological tendencies in Balinese personality, especially those surrounding the relationship between the Balinese man and his "cock." Geertz treads familiar ground here in connecting a cultural object to its social and psychological moorings, but he refuses to reduce the cultural object to its underpinnings. He insists that the cockfight is textual in that it is not only a reflection of a social setting or a psychological predisposition but an articulation and production of meaning. The cockfight does not express what Balinese society is but what, in a kind of collective thought-experiment, Balinese society might be if certain emotional tendencies were taken to their logical extreme. The cockfight is a safe way, culturally framed, to test out what happens when certain tendencies in the social order go unchecked, just as, Geertz argues, *King Lear* is a collective thought-experiment about what happens when fathers and daughters do not show appropriate love and respect for one another. Geertz holds that an observer can *read* the cockfight as a text just as a critic can read *King Lear* as a text.

Another anthropologist, Victor Turner, also emphasizes the readability of performances and the centrality of performances in social life. He looks especially at what he calls "social dramas," be they in a court of law or an assembly of elders or in some other ritual mode for dramatizing social conflict.

Like Geertz, Turner (1984) argues that the social drama does not re-state or mirror underlying social structure but acts as a performance in society's "subjunctive" mood. Ritual, carnival, festival, theater, and other cultural performances express "supposition, desire, hypothesis, possibility" rather than fact. All of these cultural forms can be seen as ways a culture thinks out loud about itself. Barbara Babcock (1984, p. 107), for instance, discusses Southwest Indian clown performances as a kind of acted-out philosophizing, a meta-language and commentary on social life that "disrupts and interrupts customary frames and expected logic and syntax and creates a reflexive and ironic dialogue, an open space of questioning."

The anthropology of performance is linked closely to conventional literary criticism since, of course, there long has been attention to the performative genres of theater and, to a limited extent, poetry. A performance, like a literary work, is an activity in which the author is oriented to and intends to have some effect on an audience. This attention to performance has not only added something to the conventional notion of text but acts back upon it as sociolinguists, anthropologists, and folklorists have urged the re-integration of the study of texts into their social and often "performed" contexts. Studies of oral poetry leapt ahead when scholars showed that the structure and form of works such as the *Iliad* and the *Odyssey* derive from their roots in an oral, memorized, improvised, and performed mode of composition (Finnegan, 1977).

In this regard, one might go so far as to say that the literary text, as conventionally understood, is a peculiar form of a cultural performance where the author does not relate to the audience face to face and where the relative permanency of the mode of recording separates the performance also from the immediacy of even the author. A literary text, one might say, is a performance that has a life of its own.

Anthropologists have gone further still. With respect to texts and performances, there is always the supposition that the cultural act or object is a somewhat self-conscious commentary on social life. With some aspects of culture, there may be a symbolic system operating at an identifiable level but one of which people are so little conscious that they may even deny its existence. Mary Douglas (1982) has "deciphered" the meaning of a meal, seeing food as a system of cultural communication and the meal as an organized, structured text that comments on social organization. She also has examined consumer goods as a medium through which culture is constituted. Commodities, in her view, are not so much good for consuming as they are "good for thinking; treat them as a nonverbal medium for the human creative faculty" (Douglas, 1979, p. 62). Vast areas of human activity then become expressions of human creativity, texts that can be deciphered, structures that have interpretable forms: not only staged performances or culturally framed rituals but the performances and rituals of everyday behavior that Erving Goffman studied so well—etiquette, public displays, the small interactions at a bus stop or in nearly any interactional setting where a person communicates messages about him or herself to others nearby.

Compared to this radical extension of the notion of textuality, the inclusion of new literary forms into the acceptable canon for literary studies seems a minor footnote in intellectual history. Of course, it has not been experienced that way. The universities are conservators of tradition, protectors of what they regard as the best and most valuable monuments to human invention and creative expression. It is therefore in some ways easier to accept the cockfight for study than the popular romance or the codes of fashion than television soap operas. The cockfight is sufficiently exotic to be beyond our own culture's status ranking of cultural forms. The romance and the soap opera, in contrast, hold a place—a very low place—in this society's established hierarchy of literary taste.

Now that sociologists and literary scholars alike hold up for examination the social processes whereby hierarchies of taste get established, should the hierarchies be granted any remaining authority? If the "lower" forms of culture deserve study, not just as data for social science but as literary texts meriting the same attention one might give Shakespeare, does this change what the university is supposed to be about? Does it call for a radical change or extension in what we take the mission of the university to be? This is a thorny and a fundamental issue. On the one hand, nothing that is human should be foreign to the "humanities" in a university, and African or Asian or American Indian literature should have as much place as Shakespeare or Dickens in a university education; on the other hand, American universities are, and intend to be, carriers of and promoters of Western traditions of art and thought, and their curricula cannot and should not be encyclopedic. They must be pedagogic. That is, the selection of materials presented, let alone the ways of presenting them, are a vital part of the university's educational endeavor. Selection is *the* vital part, in the view of Bartlett Giamatti (1980), who argues that the main task of the teacher is the task of *choosing* where to begin and what to begin with. On the one hand, it seems perfectly appropriate to study formulaic literatures, romances or detective stories, to see how they work, to think about *why* so many people respond so eagerly to them, and to contemplate the meaning of form and formula and genre in literature generally. On the other hand, there is justification for a critical tradition that pays greatest tribute to work that challenges form, breaks or becomes self-conscious about formula, blurs the boundaries of genres, or seems to surpass the limits of meaning possible within a genre. Watchers of baseball are more interested in learning lessons from Pete Rose than from Joe Schmo, and people who enjoy eating pay greater attention to the Sunday dinner that someone takes hours to prepare than the Wednesday leftovers dumped on the table. The making of distinctions and the making of judgments of better or worse, more or less complex, more or less memorable or enduring or pleasing were not invented by power-hungry elites or greedy institutions (though elites and institutions certainly have taken advantage of their power to make *their* judgments the reigning judgments).

It may be—it certainly remains the common-sense intuition—that different qualities of art reside in the thing itself: some paintings or performances or poems are better than others. But it is now argued with equal vigor that the quality of art lies in how it is received, or in how it is created within the context of reception, rather than in some quality intrinsic to the art object itself. Roland Barthes argues we have moved from an emphasis on the Work (the pristine object with intrinsic quality) to engagement with the Text, something that is produced by reader as much as by writer, by critic or interpreter as much as by author. The quality of *reading* rather than the quality of the object then takes center stage and the critic is more producer than evaluator or consumer. Indeed, for Barthes, as long as a person reads passively, it matters little if the reading matter is Shakespeare or subway graffiti. The task is to read *playfully*, playing the text "in the musical sense of the term" (Barthes, 1979, p. 79). And the task for the humanities in the university, I would infer from this, is not to create hierarchies of Works but to educate readers in reading. If this can be done with Shakespeare, fine; if it is better achieved with newspaper cartoons, that's fine, too. The task is to diminish the distance between writer and reader, writing and reading, and encourage students to be players.

The notion of the ideal reader as a "player" is not the only model of how a reader should read. Perhaps a more common understanding is that a good reader reads *critically*, reads "against the text" in the terms of one critic or reads "as a process of inaugurating disbelief" according to another (Altieri, 1984, pp. 60–61). Charles Altieri urges that good readers read through a text, submitting to "its provisional authority" as a work of art. Without abandoning a sense of critical reading, this position comes close to Barthes' notion of play and recommends to the reader an attitude that the anthropologists cited earlier would recognize as resembling the "subjunctive" mood.[5] It emphasizes gaining familiarity and facility more than distance and perspective but nonetheless a kind of facility that presumes perspective.

Suppose that the university sees its task as one of educating students to read against texts and to be players of texts. At some point, the question will still arise about who is a better player and who a worse player and who is to judge and what rules of play need to be observed. The radical democratization that appears when the Work is demoted to the Text does not do away with the desire for distinctions; the university must still determine, in a re-defined context, what values it should be promoting.

THE AUDIENCE: THE TEXT'S VULNERABILITY

The movement in literary studies that Barthes identifies as a shift from Work to Text has parallels in a different field of inquiry, the sociology of ideology and the sociology of culture. The audience, in social science studies of the mass media and popular culture, has been (like the weather) something that everybody talks about and nobody does anything about. And yet in recent years a number of scholars have finally paid attention to how audiences use the media and how they employ popular culture, while reshaping it, in their own lives.

One exemplary study is sociological without having come from sociology: Janice Radway's *Reading the Romance* (1984), a study of romance novels and their readers. Feminist literary critics have begun to pay some attention to "women's literature" meaning, by that, literature frequently read by women. Most critics, including Radway, find the romance novels to be politically reactionary, generally suggesting in very predictable and stylized plots that a woman's fulfillment in life comes from capturing a man, a man with repressed emotions and a somewhat brutal attitude toward women who, nonetheless, because of some prior suffering in his own life, can learn (through the guidance of the heroine) to express true love. Not infrequently, romance novels even rationalize or explain away the hero's rape of the heroine.

What more, then, needs to be said to condemn romance novels? Radway interviewed at length some 20 women who read large quantities of romance fiction. She learned a number of very interesting things about them. First, she learned that there is not one generalized mass public for romances but that different women respond to and seek out very different kinds of romantic fantasies. (The women she interviewed devour novel after novel but look down contemptuously upon women who watch television soap operas.) Second, she learned that the women interpret the novels very differently from feminist critics. They read *more literally*. When the narrator says that the heroine was a beautiful, bright, and independent woman, and then presents incident after incident that deny her independence (and shed some doubt on her intelligence), the romance readers see the story as one of a strong woman who makes the best of her life in the midst of great adversity. The feminist critic, in contrast, takes the initial description of the independent woman to be ironic in the context of the heroine's actual behavior. Third, whatever ideological message the women may take from the novel, they use the *act of reading* the novels as a bid for independence in their home lives. Most of the women Radway interviewed were high school or, in some cases, college-educated women with part-time or full-time work outside the home and a full set of wifely and motherly chores inside the home, too. In many instances, opening their novel and propping up their feet to read signaled to husband and children that these women were temporarily unavailable and should not be disturbed. It was an assertion of independence and of a right of their own time that apparently was effective in protecting them from demands of the domestic scene.

Of course, there is a lot more one would like to know about these women and their reading. But the point Radway makes most provocatively is that the presumptuousness of the critic to say what a work means has to be questioned and can be questioned, in part, on the basis of empirical studies of what readers get from books. This is an empirical or sociological enactment of the theoretical developments in criticism that suggest that readers and critics construct texts in the act of reading. This does not necessarily mean, however, that the readers construct the texts creatively or playfully or critically. Their responses, while not determined by the text of the romance novel as a prefabricated and autonomous entity, may be shaped by other prefabricated texts, the ideologies and fantasies of popular culture at large that serve as background for reading the romance.[6]

The view that readers construct their own texts (whether critically and creatively or not) is supported by a long line of psychological research on selective attention and selective perception. There is, for instance, a study by Neil Vidmar and Milton Rokeach (1974) that found that the message of *All in the Family* was read differently depending on people's preconceptions. Highly prejudiced viewers enjoyed the show because they could applaud Archie Bunker's sentiments and see him portrayed as a likeable hero. Tolerant viewers enjoyed the show because they could sympathize with the other characters and see Archie Bunker as the butt of jokes, his own prejudices coming back to haunt him or tie him in impossible contradictions.

There is also support for this view in sociological studies of working class culture and youth culture, which demonstrate that people outside the dominant power structures of society can turn commercial products, including music, movies, and television, to their own use, creating a mocking vernacular out of the culture that comes down to them from on high. Whether it is working-class "lads" creating a culture of resistance inside the British school system (Willis, 1977) or hot rodders turning mass-produced vehicles into individual signatures of machismo and power (Moorhouse, 1983), sociologists are finding significant instances where the conventional meaning of a standard product has been altered, reversed, or upended by small or local groups and subcultures with traditions and agenda of their own. (There are also important instances where an authentic subculture uses a mass culture industry as its own medium—Southern black blues musicians in the 1920s preserved and spread their art through the popular record industry [Levine, 1977].)

Are these audiences, then, playful? Able to read against or through texts? Or are they, alternatively, egocentric, making their own meanings from the texts not because they have read through them expertly but because they have not learned to truly read? Are Radway's romance readers *good* readers? Do they see the novels as displaying possible strategies for coping with women's subordinate role in patriarchal society? Is romance reading in their experience a "collectively elaborated female ritual through which women explore the consequences of their common social condition as the appendages of men and attempt to imagine a more perfect state where all the needs they so intensely feel and accept as given would be adequately addressed" (Radway, 1984, p. 221)? If so, then these readers are, as Radway sometimes suggests, very good readers indeed. But do the women experience reading this way? Why do they read the books' endings before buying them? Why do they insist that sad endings are unsatisfactory? Why are they uneasy with genres (like the television soap opera) that do not come to conclusions? Why do variations in the basic, prefabricated, predictable plot line and character line of romances make them uncomfortable? Have they really played with the novels or simply drifted under their spell? Have they submitted to the provisional authority of the work or given it, momentarily, absolute authority? And what would be the measure of their quality as readers?

Think of the readers of Eugene Sue's serialized melodramas in 19th century France: many of them were very active readers, even to the point of writing letters to Sue to implore him to change the plot or to protect a particularly lovable character from harm. Sue, in fact, altered his writing to accord with some of these requests. Other readers treated Sue's characters the way some television soap opera viewers treat the characters they follow so avidly—as real people, not engaging fictions. Sue was asked, for instance, to release one of his evil-fighting heroes to deal with actual crimes (Brooks, 1984, p. 164).

Here the space between writer and reader has narrowed, but is this the kind of reader Barthes or anyone else would want to encourage? These readers, we might say, are active but *not* playful; they do not understand that fiction is play, and, consequently, they do not learn to play with fiction. The first lesson about reading is probably that reading can be useful (you can read instructions) or that it can provide a measure of independence (you can entertain yourself in the absence of mother or father) or that it can be fun and exciting. Sue's readers knew all this. But the second lesson about reading is that a written text is not, or not only, a window on the world but is an imaginative construction. I agree with Peter Brooks that critics have spent too much energy on the second lesson—how is a text constructed to do its task—and not enough on the first: Why do people want to know what happens next? But is a person genuinely a reader if he or she remains unaware of the second lesson?

The study of specific audiences should be linked also to the study of the emergence of audiences historically. There has been important work recently on the development of the distinction between high culture and popular culture in the United States and the cultivation of an audience for high culture. Lawrence Levine's study of Shakespeare performance in 19th century America (1984) and Paul DiMaggio's study of the creation of a sphere of high culture in 19th century Boston (1982) both demonstrate that creating high culture was as much a task of shaping an audience as of consolidating a canon of legitimated works. In the early 19th century, Shakespeare was part of general popular culture in America. By 1900, this was no longer true. In part, the nature of Shakespeare's work matched other cultural currents and inclinations more closely in 1850 than in 1900; it better fit a population that delighted in and responded to oratory, melodrama, and heroes who could be seen as "architects of their own fortunes" (Levine, 1984, p. 53) than it did a population grown used to utilitarian uses of language and grown more interested in heroes and anti-heroes struggling in complex social and institutional webs. But also, in part, an upper class that felt threatened by a growing and ethnically diverse group of upwardly mobile seekers sought out certain features of culture, especially English language culture, that it could assign special moral and aesthetic value and keep safe and apart. After 1900, Shakespeare no longer belongs to the general public but to Culture, capital-ized. To attend Shakespeare not only costs money but requires an educated audience, educated to appreciate the plays and to behave properly in the theater. Shakespeare audiences in 1850 were players, not consumers, of theatrical presentations (Would Barthes have approved?) and would respond vocally and demonstratively to the action on stage. We have very little comparable to this today in film or theater except among the audiences for certain cult films such as *Rocky Horror Picture Show* and, perhaps, among audiences for professional wrestling. Audiences for sporting events today are probably closest to the Shakespeare audiences of 1850.

The audience itself, then, not just the products created for cultural consumption, is a social construction, a product of a sort in its own way. This is true for the audiences of elite culture as much as for audiences of popular culture, although the two audiences are cultivated and maintained by two very different organizational forms—mass culture industries for the popular audi-ence and private associations supported by private philanthropy and some governmental subvention, plus the institutions of higher education, for the elite audience. While social scientists have begun to study the audiences that differ from middle class expectations of audience behavior, they so far have paid only scant attention to the social processes that create the standard audience for high culture. The work of Pierre Bourdieu (1984) has begun to open up this area, but there is much to be done to understand how the rules of audience behavior and etiquette are arrived at, how the norms of polite conversation and comment following a play or concert are constructed, or even what the regulations of appropriate behavior in the school classroom mean.

Audiences, including the audiences for high culture, are not born but made. If anything, this is even more true in the age of modernism and its successors than it was before. Most justifications of the humanities tend to rest on the virtues of their study for moral education, for an enlargement of the individual's vision of what the human condition is and can be. But it is not clear to me, at any rate, that this rationale can be connected to many of the leading experiments in art, music, and literature in our time. Many of these developments seem to focus on the formal properties of art, music, and literature themselves; their subject turns out to be art making, music making, or writing as activities. They may comment on but do not intend to comment on the human condition except insofar as art making *is* the human condition (a contention they do not explore). Many of the leading movements in modern arts posit or hope for a degree of autonomy of the aesthetic sense unprecedented in human experience. The equivalent in popular culture is the emphasis on "special effects," in films, in theme parks, or in 4th of July celebrations. Audiences may enjoy the dazzle or they may engage in the intellectual detective work of trying to figure out how a special effect was achieved, but they are not likely to be looking to these effects for moral guidance or commentary on the human condition.

SENSE AND SENTIMENTALITY

So far, I have reviewed, generally approvingly, intellectual developments of the past two decades that have profound implications for our understanding of culture. First, I have reviewed the sociological insight that cultural products are created by groups as well as by individuals and that, even with individual artists, cultural products are oriented to a small or large degree to a marketplace and to a socially constructed "art world." This insight relativizes or democratizes works of art and raises questions about the distinction that universities have made between high culture and popular or mass culture. Second, I have reviewed developments in the study of texts that vastly enlarge the range of texts appropriate for serious study. This trend suggests an equivalence across texts whereby judgments of quality do not have pride of place and may not have much of a place at all. Third, I have looked at changing views of the audience that give credit to the audience, any audience, as a privileged critic or reader, even, *creator* of the texts it reads or watches. Once again, the tendency is to relativize the concept of culture, to whittle away at the props that maintain some elements of culture as higher than others.

There is a lot of justifiable excitement about these developments. Barriers to the halls of academe are breached by cultural objects that never before had seen the inside of a classroom; hallways between departments where professors did not know one another existed are now well worn. There has been a real liberation in all of this, based, in my view, on very good intellectual sense.

But with each of the intellectual movements I have reviewed here, there is a corresponding danger. With the sociological approach to artistic production, there is the threat of cynicism; with the democratization of the number and kinds of texts worthy of study, there is a danger of obscuring the special features of *written* texts; and, most of all, with the recognition of the active role of audiences in constructing the works they engage, there is a danger of romanticizing and sentimentalizing audiences as they exist in certain inhumane social conditions.

Production

While it is true that all art is produced by someone or some ones, not all production aims to manufacture or manufactures art. Some organizations produce toothpicks or ball bearings or toilet paper, not textbooks or soap operas. And producing the textbooks or soap operas *is* different. Certainly useful things (toothpicks) may have meanings and just as surely meaningful things (soap operas) may be useful, but for most things there is no difficulty in distinguishing whether utility or meaning is the primary feature. That there are university departments and international conferences and bibliographies overflowing on William Shakespeare, who produced plays, and not on Clarence Birdseye, who produced frozen foods, is not just an accident nor just a prejudice of people who disdain mass culture. The difference between meaning and utility remains important; the sociologizing trend in the understanding of artistic production does not erase it but asks that it be understood more carefully.

Texts

The fact that an anthropologist or literary critic can read an evening meal or a fast food advertisement or the names of athletic teams or the design of Disneyland as a commentary or metacommentary on culture does not mean that participant natives also read the texts that way. There is some danger that the recent trends in the study of popular culture may inadvertently romanticize the semiotic process itself; the academy's professional interest and pleasure in the act of interpreting can be self-indulgent, and the readings of meals or ads may be only academic *études* if these objects are not privileged as signs by the general community. Anthropologist Bruce Kapferer has recognized this problem:

> Most anthropologists argue that rituals make metacommentaries, and thus are reflexive upon the nonritualized, paramount reality of everyday life. But the anthropologist is in a position that would lead to such an observation: the anthropologist is never completely part of the culture being studied, but always apart from it. The subjects of research, the people, are also objects; and this is demanded by the nature of the anthropological discipline. The anthropologist, in a sense, assumes the role of a critic, for particular events are placed in the context of other events, are interrelated, contrasted, and evaluated. Therefore, while rituals might typically be regarded as reflexive events by anthropologists, it does not necessarily follow that they will be similarly regarded by participants. (1984, p. 203)

There is something democratic about opening up the range of things taken to be textual and accessible to interpretation, but it is as presumptuous to offer critical readings of popular artifacts as it is to interpret high culture artifacts without reference to what the actual audiences may be thinking. Sometimes, as Kapferer suggests, the artifact may be one in which the natives invest a great deal of interpretive energy themselves; sometimes, however, it will be an object that the people in question do not, in fact, think with. Vincent Crapanzano (1986) has made this point about Geertz's celebrated cockfight, that Geertz offers no evidence that the Balinese themselves see the cockfight as a text to be read, no evidence that the cockfight is marked in Balinese culture as a cultural object to be interpreted. Geertz's own interpretive virtuosity, without such support, may then be an instance of the academy's semiotic aggrandizement.

But do we not think with *all* the objects in our environment? Yes, at some level we do. But cultures do not invest all objects with equal amounts of meaning. For urban Americans, say, the power of the distinctions among street/road/avenue/court/place is much greater than that among elm/oak/maple/spruce, even though both sets of categories are part of the culture. These natives may find it worthwhile to interpret both the Sunday comics and the Sunday sermon, but they will most likely find disagreements over the sermon more troubling and the task of interpretation more significant and the value of skilled interpreters correspondingly greater.

Moreover, there is with some objects in the culture a tradition of interpretation that is cumulative and, for this reason, has acquired a sophistication or refinement that everyday interpretation does not attain. While such cumulative traditions exist with respect to a number of kinds of objects, they are especially noteworthy with respect to *written* materials, and, not incidentally, the interpretations themselves are carried on in writing. Written texts provide something that most other objects do not: the possibility of a tradition of criticism that makes an enormous difference in developing and elaborating reflective thought (Goody, 1977). It is not that analysis and reflection are impossible or even unlikely without writing, but a *sustained* tradition of reflection *is* unlikely. Certainly there can be a connoisseurship with respect to cockfights or culinary arts that exists primarily in oral culture. But with all its richness, oral culture also has its limits. The celebration of cockfights and culinary arts and clown dances in the university is all to the good so long as we do not forget that the medium of that celebration, the medium that makes thinking about these objects so interesting and enables an enlargement of our vision about what human cultures are about, is still the written word.

Audiences

It is right to observe that audiences do not absorb culture like sponges. The popular audience is selective, reflective, and constructive in its use of culture. But this is not to say that the popular audience is always critical or creative in its responses any more than elite audiences are. Even within an individual, a person responds differently to different cultural experiences. Very critical and searching readers of fiction may let music wash right over them at a concert; a discerning reader of poetry may not be able to stand before a painting in a gallery for more than a few seconds. Some people who are discriminating consumers of theater may rely on "name brands" for dance. Such people know very well, or should know, that they are more active, playful, critical, or creative in responding to some cultural objects than in responding to others.

If we can recognize such distinctions for individuals, then why not for groups? If we know, further, that in many of the areas where we *are* critical readers we have gone through a process of education, formal or informal, why can we not conclude that processes of education are central to critical and playful readings in general? And if we can say this, can we not also say, indeed, must we not affirm also that one of the tasks of education, not only in the schools and universities but in the structure of society as a whole, is, as Raymond Williams put it, "to deepen and refine the capacity for significant responses" (1983, p. 62)? The fact that popular audiences respond actively to the materials of mass culture is important to recognize and understand, but it is not a fact that should encourage us to accept mass culture as it stands or popular audiences as they now exist. The fact that different subgroups in the population respond in different ways to common cultural objects or have developed refined critical temperaments with regard to some local or provincial cultural form unrecognized by elites is important to understand and should lead us to recognize a wide variety of connoisseurships and a plurality of educational forms that lead to them. But this is not or should not be to admit all cultural forms equal, all interpretations valid, all interpretive communities self-contained and beyond criticism.

The celebration of popular culture and popular audiences in the universities has been a political act; it could not have been otherwise. The challenge popular culture now presents the university is not a call to erase all boundaries to what is to be treated in a classroom. Rather, it is to force a self-conscious and sociologically self-aware defense of the boundaries the university draws. The challenge is not to deny a place for judgment and valuation but to identify the institutional, national, class, race, and gender-bound biases set deep in past judgments and to make them available for critical reassessment. The new validation of popular culture should not lead higher education to abandon its job of helping students to be critical and playful readers, helping to deepen and refine in them a capacity for significant response. Instead, it should enhance these efforts with new respect for how, in some spheres and in some ways and despite some limits, students (and others) have been critical and playful readers all along.

The essay should end there. It would have, if I thought I had resolved the problems I presented.

I do not. I end up caught between a belief that the university should be a moral educator, holding up for emulation some values and some texts (and not others), and a reluctant admission that defining the basis of moral education is an unfinished, often unrecognized, task. I know, of course, that the university is a moral educator whether this is intended or not. Students learn from teachers what we value, by what values we "profess" to work, and what turns of mind or character we approve. But if we learn to be self-conscious about the implicit hierarchies of taste and value we live and teach by, will we locate adequate grounds for our moral claims? What ground can we stand on, especially when the trends that favor relativism are so much more powerful and cogent (to my own mind) than the rather arbitrary and ill-defended hierarchies of value they so pointedly confront?

If there is sentimentality on one side—would-be populists waving the banner of people's culture—there is piety on the other—ardent champions of a traditional curriculum wailing at the decline of literacy, values, morals, the university, or their students' ability to write (or even recognize) a good English sentence. Neither side seems to me very clear about the pass we have reached. We can all carry on, nevertheless: Departments and professional associations will sustain the structures for individual careers; institutional and personal investments in things as they are will keep us from looking too closely at the intellectual crisis we have come upon. But if we ever come to separating sense from romance and standards from nostalgia in all of this, it is not going to be easy.

Acknowledgments: This essay was originally commissioned by the University of Virginia's Colloquium on the Humanities and the American People. The author thanks Merrill Peterson, colloquium director, for supporting this work and Paul DiMaggio, Janice Radway, and Richard Terdiman for comments on earlier drafts of the essay.

NOTES

1. This definition and some of the framework for this essay are adapted from Mukerji and Schudson (1986).
2. A review and critique of much of this literature is Sears and Freedman (1971). Another critique that takes a broader look at the conclusion that the media have limited effects is Gitlin (1978).
3. Gramsci's views and the uses of his concept of hegemony are well reviewed in Lears (1985).
4. There is now a large literature on the production of culture within sociology. For a sampling, see Peterson (1976). An early and influential essay in this vein is Hirsch (1972). Some of the work is reviewed in Peterson (1979). A related approach coming out of fieldwork and symbolic interactionist traditions is well represented in Becker (1982).
5. On the subjunctive mood as a feature of literature generally, see Bruner (1986).
6. I am grateful to Richard Terdiman for this observation.

REFERENCES

Altieri, C. (1984). An idea and ideal of a literary canon. In R. von Hallberg (Ed.), *Canons* (pp. 41–84). Chicago: University of Chicago Press.

Babcock, B. A. (1984). Arrange me in disorder: Fragments and reflections on ritual clowning. In J. MacAloon (Ed.), *Rite, drama, festival, spectacle* (pp. 102–128). Philadelphia: Institute for the Study of Human Issues.

Barthes, R. (1979). From work to text. In J. Harari (Ed.), *Textual strategies: Perspectives in post structuralist criticism* (pp. 73–81). Ithaca, NY: Cornell University Press.

Becker, H. S. (1982). *Artworlds.* Berkeley: University of California Press.

Bourdieu, P. (1984) *Distinction: A social critique of the judgment of taste.* Cambridge, MA: Harvard University Press.

Brooks, P. (1984). *Reading for the plot.* New York: Vintage Books.

Bruner, J. (1986). *Actual minds, possible worlds.* Cambridge, MA: Harvard University Press.

Crapanzano, V. (1986). Hermes' dilemma: The masking of subversion in ethnographic description. In G. Marcus & J. Clifford (Eds.), *Writing culture.* Berkeley: University of California Press.

DiMaggio, P. (1977). Market structure, the creative process, and popular culture: Toward an organizational reinterpretation of mass-culture theory. *Journal of Popular Culture, 11*, 436–452.

DiMaggio, P. (1982). Cultural entrepreneurship in nineteenth-century Boston: The creation of an organizational base for high culture in America. *Media, Culture & Society, 4*, 33–50.

Douglas, M. (1979). *The world of goods*. New York: Basic Books.

Douglas, M. (1982). *In the active voice*. London: Routledge & Kegan Paul.

Finnegan, R. (1977). *Oral poetry*. Cambridge, MA: Cambridge University Press.

Geertz, C. (1973). Deep play: Notes on the Balinese cockfight. In C. Geertz (Ed.), *The interpretation of cultures* (pp. 412–453). New York: Basic Books.

Giamatti, A. B. (1980, July). The American teacher. *Harper's*, pp. 24–29.

Gitlin, T. (1978). Media sociology: The dominant paradigm. *Theory and Society, 6*, 205–253.

Goody, J. (1977). *The domestication of the savage mind*. Cambridge, MA: Cambridge University Press.

Herrnstein Smith, B. (1984). Contingencies of value. In R. von Hallberg (Ed.), *Canons* (pp. 5–40). Chicago: University of Chicago Press.

Hirsch, P. (1972). Processing fads and fashions: An organization-set analysis of cultural industry systems. *American Journal of Sociology, 77*, 639–659.

Horkheimer, M., & Adorno, T. (1972). The culture industry. In M. Horkheimer & T. Adorno, *Dialectic of Enlightenment* (pp. 120–167). New York: Seabury Press.

Kapferer, B. (1984). The ritual process and the problem of reflexivity. In J. MacAloon (Ed.), *Rite, drama, festival, spectacle* (pp. 179–207). Philadelphia: Institute for the Study of Human Issues.

Kermode, F. (1983). *The art of telling: Essays on fiction*. Cambridge, MA: Harvard University Press.

Lears, T. J. J. (1985). The concept of cultural hegemony: Problems and possibilities. *American Historical Review, 85*, 567–593.

Levine, L. W. (1977). *Black culture and black consciousness*. New York: Oxford University Press.

Levine, L. W. (1984). William Shakespeare and the American people: A study in cultural transformation. *American Historical Review, 89*, 34–66.

Moorhouse, H. F. (1983). American automobiles and workers' dreams. *Sociological Review, 31*, 403–436.

Mukerji, C., & Schudson, M. (1986). Popular Culture. *Annual Review of Sociology, 12*, 47–66.

Peterson, R. A. (Ed.). (1976). *The production of culture*. Beverly Hills: Sage.

Peterson, R. A. (1979). Revitalizing the culture concept. *Annual Review of Sociology, 5*, 137–166.

Radway, J. A. (1984). Reading the romance: Women, patriarchy, and popular literature. Chapel Hill: University of North Carolina Press.

Sears, D. O., & Freedman, J. L. (1971). Selective exposure to information: A critical review. In W. Schramm & D. F. Roberts (Eds.), *The process and effects of mass communication* (pp. 209–234). Urbana: University of Illinois Press.

Sigal, L. (1973). *Reporters and officials*. Lexington, MA: D. C. Heath.

Turner, V. (1984). Liminality and the performance of genres. In J. MacAloon (Ed.), *Rite, drama, festival, spectacle* (pp. 19–41). Philadelphia: Institute for the Study of Human Issues.

Vidmar, N., & Rokeach, M. (1974). Archie Bunker's bigotry: A study in selective perception. *Journal of Communication, 24*(1), 36–47.

Williams, R. (1983). *The year 2000*. New York: Pantheon Books.

Willis, P. (1977). *Learning to labor: How working class kids get working class jobs*. New York: Columbia University Press.

4 On the Dialogic Aspects of Mass Communication

HORACE M. NEWCOMB

TEXTS AND SOCIAL PRACTICE

A fundamental problem for the cultural studies approach to mass communication focuses on relations between mediated texts and social practices. Rooted in literary and rhetorical criticism, philosophical proofs, historical analysis, and persuasive argumentation, cultural studies continues, but is often critical of these traditions. A culturalist approach rejects, for example, formalist tendencies to exclude questions regarding the social basis and social influence of texts. And while more and more mass media critic-scholars have come to rely on techniques of close analysis associated with formalist studies, reading the political content of mediated texts in more and more sophisticated ways, it is still necessary to argue that politics cannot exist solely in signification. What happens in practice cannot be deduced solely from what happens in texts or structures.

At the same time, however, culturalists are unwilling to accept text/practice links claimed in traditional mass communications research. Connections established through positivist-empirical methodologies focusing on bits of mediated content are seen as insufficiently complex, often marred by the unexamined presuppositions of contemporary social science. Still, cultural studies has not created an adequate means of its own to relate texts, societies, and the individuals and groups that constitute those societies. Little wonder then, that some scholars call for the relegation of textual studies to a secondary position and a return to the analysis of social practices involved in production, distribution, and reception as the best means of understanding the social role of texts (Murdock & Golding, 1978).

On the one hand, then, we have the problem of establishing a link between texts and practices. On the other we have the problem of the gap between the *study* of texts and the *study* of society. In recent years, it is true, social scientists have intensified a search for notions of text that add needed complexity to their empirical studies. And humanists have increasingly sought for some means of dealing with "real," socially active users of the texts they study. Cultural studies can be seen as a middle position, mediating between and drawing from both the humanities and the social sciences. But the problem remains, and many scholars find themselves at an impass.

One way out is found in grand theory—theories of society, culture, and the individual that explain interactions between text and individual, text and group, text and institution. Thus we have analyses based in Freudian psychology (see, for example, Wood, 1976), in the various *"Screen* theory" appropriations of psychoanalytic models, (e.g. Heath & Skirrow, 1977), in various versions of semiotics (e.g. Barthes, 1967; Eco, 1977; Fiske & Hartley, 1978), in structural anthropology (e.g. Schatz, 1981), and symbolic anthropology (e.g. Newcomb & Hirsch, 1983; Newcomb & Alley, 1983).

Among the most important and successful studies are those based in Marxist theory. These analyses take various forms, for Marxist theory itself has, in recent decades, undergone continual analysis and interpretation. As Becker (1984) shows, a great deal of this work has taken place in England.

Further discussion of the ongoing process of interpretation and definition is presented by Gurevitch et al. (1982). These shifts are also richly amplified and concretely detailed within a specific context in one particular essay, "Cultural Studies at the Center," in Hall et al. (1980, pp. 15–47). This account traces the development of ideas leading to the use of Gramscian notions of hegemony as an account both rigorous and flexible enough to explain the interaction of text and society.

Hegemony is taken as an explanation that allows for individual variation in production and reception, but that also illuminates the ways in which larger social patterns are contained within dominant ideologies. Using hegemony as an overarching concept British scholars have produced re-readings of various popular art forms and social practices (Hall et al., 1980). In this country Kellner (1979) and Gitlin (1982) have applied the concept in analyses of television content and structure.

The advantages of the hegemonic model are manifold. It focuses on complex and subtle patterns of common-sense thought, suggesting that many forms of communication present as "natural" that which is socially motivated and politically implemented. It avoids arguments for homogeneity in production, the "culture industry" perspective. Instead it examines the range of variation in mass-mediated content, accepting the fluid boundaries found there. Yet it points to the alternatives that are left, or forced, out of media content, the ways in which basic questions are dominantly framed, and the terms which are permitted within debate (see Wander, 1981).

Hegemony also recognizes multiple perspectives in the reception of mass-mediated texts, calling into question readings that posit "single meanings" for texts *and* empirical analysis that searches for single effects or sets of effects following from media exposure. In his influential essay, "Encoding/Decoding Television Discourse," Hall (1980, pp. 128–138), suggests a range of possible responses to mediated forms, a range limited by hegemonically structured thought. Recipients may produce a "dominant reading" that accepts the content without question. They may produce a "negotiated reading" in which parts of the content are questioned, but the fundamental socio-political attitude is unquestioned. Or they may produce an "oppositional reading" in which the content is seen to be the product of a social system with which the recipient is fundamentally at odds. This overview, then, contains a model connecting the text to social practice. It also suggests the need for corroborative research, and, indeed, implies a design for that research. In *Everyday Television: Nationwide* (Brunsdon & Morley, 1978) and *The Nationwide Audience* (Morley, 1980a), we have a first key step building on the model of multiple, but hegemonically contained, interpretations of television.

Here, some problems begin to emerge, problems related once again to the thorny connection between texts and recipients. The Brunsdon and Morley analysis of *Nationwide* demonstrates some of the ways in which the program controls content in order to foster a hegemonic depiction. Their work shows how the discussion of certain subject matters is constrained by dominant ideology in contemporary Britain. This interpretive analysis of the *text* was followed by a study of various *audiences* viewing the program, in an attempt to test both the limits imposed by the text and the range of interpretations that might be associated with class-defined social position. But the study of the audience suggests a larger variety of interpretations, some expected, some unexpected, some more idiosyncratic, some more politically situated than others. As Morley puts it in an analysis building on the *Nationwide* work:

> In short, the relation classes/meaning systems has to be fundamentally reworked by taking into account the full effectivity of the discourse level. Discursive formations intervene between "classes" and "languages." They intervene in such a way as to prevent or forestall any attempt to read the level of the operation of language back in any simple or reductive way to economic classes. Thus we cannot deduce which discursive frameworks will be mobilized in particular reader/text encounters from the level of the socioeconomic position of the "readers." But position in the social structure may be seen to have a structuring and limiting effect on the *repertoire* of discursive or "decoding" strategies available to different sectors of an audience. They will have an effect on the pattern of the distribution of discursive repertoires. What is more, the key elements in the social structure which delimit the range of competences in particular audiences may not be referable in any exclusive way to "class" understood in the economic sense. The key sites for the distribution of discursive sets and competences are probably—following some of the leads of Bernstein and Bourdieu—the family and the school—or, as Althusser (following Gramsci) argued, the *family-school couplet*. (Hall et al., 1980, p. 173)

What Morley does not go on to say is that even the influence of *these* powerful forces of discursive patterning, of ideology formation, can be altered when subjects enter the active processes of making meaning, evaluating, and creating personal and group perspectives. As stated by Hall, "Ideological discourses can win to their ways of representing the world already-languaged subjects, i.e., subjects already positioned within a range of existing discourses, fully-social speakers" (Hall, 1982, p. 80). It is only in this way that we can account for "conversion" to different ideological perspectives, or for the "raising" or changing of "consciousness." These comments by Morley and Hall indicate that while the notion of hegemony is a distinct advance over more rigid models, it still fails to account completely for actual social practices involving communicated "texts" and their "readers."

Apparent weaknesses in the hegemonic model, failures to explain interpretation within the expected outline of dominance, however, are not seen as basic flaws. Because it is flexible the model is able to respond to challenge from criticism, theoretical or experimental, by simply enlarging the scope of containment, expanding the boundaries of the hegemonic corral, as it were. For example, after exploring the ways in which American television creates a hegemonic version of popular entertainment, but after also pointing out some of the "leaky" aspects of that same system, Gitlin suggests that "What is hegemonic in consumer capitalist ideology is precisely the notion that happiness, or liberty, or equality, or fraternity can be affirmed through the existing private commodity forms, under the benign, protective eye of the national security state. This ideological core is what remains essentially unchanged and unchallenged in television entertainment, at the same time the inner tensions persist and are even magnified" (Gitlin, 1982, p. 452).

Used in this sense, hegemony is merely a synonym for "ideology," or "culture," or for whatever term is used in whatever discipline to stand for the "natural," the "neutral," the "taken for granted," or that which is assumed to be "unmediated." Put another way, how could we conceive of a "consumer capitalist economy" in which the core would be different? Hegemony theory in most mass media analyses, then, gestures toward the complexities of textual and social processes, but expands at will to explain complexity in conventional terms of dominance. Challenge and change are already accounted for with pre-defined concepts of accommodation and co-optation.

But we can conceive of a "consumer capitalist economy" in which persistent and magnified tensions are themselves seen as challenges, in which the terms of the core are redefined or given varied application. We can conceive of an ideological system that changes into something else, just as we can conceive of individuals who change their minds about ideological systems, and conceive of the rise of groups from within which challenge the systems. I would argue that we can study the contributions of mass communication to these processes of change precisely because of the dialogic aspects of mass-mediated texts. A view of mass communication that begins with a recognition of the dynamic processes of production and reception calls for different forms of textual analysis and audience research. In exploring those aspects I turn to the works of V. N. Volosinov (1973) and M. M. Bakhtin (1981), who give us, respectively, a theory of language and a theory of text that offer a processual, dynamic, dialogic perspective on communication without sacrificing an understanding of the struggle for dominance central to that process.[1]

VOLOSINOV, BAKHTIN, AND THE STRUGGLE FOR TEXTUAL MEANING

In *Marxism and the Philosophy of Language* Volosinov emphasizes the fundamentally ideological nature of language. He rejects the notion that language is essentially the product of consciousness, referring to this view as "individual subjectivism." Within his perspective languages are always born in social practice. They exist in social structures *before* they take root in consciousness. Only in the understanding that cements social groups, on the "outside" and not within interior consciousness, can meaning be constituted. As a result, language is always becoming. Precisely because it is grounded in practice, this creation of meaning is the site of ideological struggle.

He is equally adamant, however, in rejecting grand theories of language. Linguistic theories—his term is "abstract objectivism"—are frozen descriptions of a living, active, on-going process. They, too, miss the ideological nature of the struggle for meaning within language, and have significance primarily for the linguists who create them rather than for the users of language or for those who would study communication as, or as totally determined by, ideology. The distinction, then, is between living languages, linguistic *practices*, and the static systems used to describe them. Volosinov's critique of Saussurian semiotics, for example, centers in the observation that Saussure's system overlooks the multi-vocality of signs and the *process* that accompanies the establishment, or choice, of a particular conventional usage.

The full effect of Volosinov's analysis of Saussure, however, is far more than a critique of that particular system. It stands as a general critique of theoretical systems that extract particular moments from an ongoing process and lock them into an explanatory model. This insight suggests further critiques applicable to all communication studies that deemphasize process and change. Thus, psychological models that "read" the "position" of the "subject" from theories of texts, styles, or practices can only result in static descriptions that cannot accommodate change. A related critique would hold for various forms of structuralism if they posit total explanations that purportedly can account for all patterns of meaning and their inflections. In a similar way, the notion of hegemony discussed above works only by constant expansion of the enclosing "net" in the face of clear textual multi-vocality and varied response on the part of actual "readers." The rhetoric is often processual, but the effect is finally a new formalism.

These difficulties result from the tendency on the part of such theoretical explanations to make social reality, practice, into a "text," and to follow with a "reading" of this text that explains it as if it were a closed system, a dead language, a world without struggle and change. Whenever research or analysis confronts actual experience, however, the struggle must be acknowledged. For this reason, perhaps, grand theories themselves are often internally conflicted, and explanations of enclosure must be repeatedly expanded.

None of this should be taken to ignore the *attempt* on the part of dominant groups to consciously or unconsciously impose meaning, to restrict usage and interpretation, to frame the terms of communication process and content, or to manipulate access to interpretive ability. That attempt is constant. But to assume from this acknowledgement that the attempt is always successful is to miss the point of Volosinov's critique. Language (communication) is both material and social. It is therefore mutable. Makers and users, writers and readers, senders and receivers can do things with communication that are unintended, unplanned for, indeed, unwished for.

To analyze these processes it is not enough merely to point out the essential multi-vocality of signs of various sorts. We also need a model grounded in a recognition of communicative change. Such a model is available in Bakhtin's (1981) study, "Discourse in the Novel," an analysis that can be used to study the dialogic aspects of other forms of communication, including mass communication.

Bakhtin's argument for the dialogic aspects of the novel is based on the recognition and study of the many languages embedded in any given social language. This, in simplified form, is what he means by his central concept, "heteroglossia."[2] On the one hand this variety reflects traditional notions of racial, regional, and ethnic dialects, class distinctions, gender distinctions, and so on. But Bakhtin also applies the term "language" to professional and occupational categories, age groups, religious groups, social circles, "movements," journals, and other patterns for grouping. Even the times of the day, the days of the week, and the seasons have their "languages." As he puts it:

> Thus at any given moment of its historical existence, language is heteroglot from top to bottom: it represents the co-existence of socio-ideological contradictions between the present and the past, between differing epochs of the past, between different socio-ideological groups in the present, between tendencies, schools, circles and so forth, all given a bodily form. These "languages" of heteroglossia intersect each other in a variety of ways, forming new socially typifying "languages." (Bakhtin, 1981, p. 291)

Within this communication polyglot we know as society, then, every utterance that goes out from speaker to listener, from writer to reader, from creators to audience, is bound into a system of multiple meanings. Every "word"—and Bakhtin uses the notion of "the word" to imply all utterance—is constructed upon, overlaid and inlaid with these meanings.

There is first the history of the word, the actual linguistic and etymological past that is borne in it and can never be completely erased. There is the context in which it goes forth; its generic base, its history, its "competing" words. Even in forms we might think of as uni-vocal, as purely rhetorical, or as persuasive—political speeches, journalistic prose, advertising—this multiplicity of voice is present. Within expressive forms such as the novel an added layer of complexity is present because we must consider utterances as part of the reality of the character who speaks, or of the narrator, or of an interpolated genre such as a letter or a speech. Every such representation is "an image of a language," and thus the image of an entire way of life, an ideological system required to interact with other systems in social dialogue. All these "voices" are woven into the dialogue that forms the work as a process.

The simple identification or extraction of these multiple voices, however, is not the primary task of the critic or analyst. The purpose is not merely to unravel the text. Rather it is to recognize the essential *dialogic* nature of all forms of communication. The "languages" and "words" interact with one another to form a new totality. There the author may strive to establish a *hegemony of intention*, the ascendancy of one "word" over another, but that attempt will never be fully successful. In recognizing the blend, the thrust, at times the combat, of these combinations we come to a fuller understanding of the work in question.

Still, there is another step in this dialogic process. For beyond utterance there is reception. Each listener, each reader, each viewer brings a similar sort of complexity to the reception of communication, brings a range of contexts in which the "word" is received and made part of the receiver's world. The receiver may "hear" the word as a member of a particular occupational group, a member of a political party, or a member of a religious community, each having its own "language," not always in total harmony with the others. As Bakhtin's editor-translator, Michael Holquist, explains it:

> ... Bakhtin's basic scenario for modeling variety is two actual people talking to each other in a specific dialogue at a particular time and in a particular place. But these persons would not confront each other as sovereign egos capable of sending messages to each other through the kind of uncluttered space envisioned by the artists who illustrate most receiver-sender models of communication.
>
> Rather, each of the two persons would be a consciousness at a specific point in the history of defining itself through the choice it has made—out of all the possible existing languages available to it at that moment—of a discourse to transcribe its intention *in this specific exchange*. (Bakhtin, 1981, p. xx)

One powerful result of this model is that the intentions of an originator of communication are constantly refracted by the contexts of reception. Bakhtin compares the message to a ray of light, a ray-word that enters "an atmosphere filled with alien words, value judgments and accents through which the ray passes on its way toward the object; the social atmosphere of the word, the atmosphere that surrounds the object, makes the facets of the image sparkle" (Bakhtin, 1981, p. 277). Clearly it is this "social atmosphere of the word" that is at work in the reception of mass-mediated content, the reception captured in studies such as Morley's and leading to the conclusion that we cannot predict responses merely from social class any more than we can predict from theories of textuality. Prediction is impossible because abstract notions cannot account systematically for variation. But Bakhtin refuses to accept abstractions. The forms he studies are, like the living languages examined by Volosinov, inevitably bound to practice. Meaning is made in *use*, not in theory.

Bakhtin's explanations bring to mind Benjamin's admonition regarding works of art in an age of mechanical reproduction. As put in Peter Uwe Hohendahl's translation: "The masses in their diversion submerge the work of art into themselves" (Hohendahl, 1982, p. 82). It is this submersion, I would suggest, that leads Benjamin to say that when the work of art loses its aura, when it is no longer based on ritual, "it begins to be based on another practice—politics" (Benjamin, 1968, p. 226). An adequate understanding of such politics must allow it to be practiced within texts and by the users of texts. Bakhtin makes the point this way: ". . . an intentional artistic hybrid is a *semantic* hybrid; not semantic and logical in the abstract (as in rhetoric), but rather a *semantics of the concrete and social*" (1981, p. 360. Emphasis in original.).

In order to better understand the complex, heteroglotic nature of any text, and more importantly, to understand the relations between texts and their recipient-users it is necessary to develop a sociological semiotics and an adequate sociology of interpretation. In this way we may more adequately explore the semantics of the concrete and the social, the collision of ideologies that inheres in complex forms such as the novel, and, I would argue, in the even more complex forms of contemporary mass communications. In order to illustrate the necessity for these sorts of analysis, I will focus on the texts of commercial television.

THE DIALOGUE IN TELEVISION

In our time the novel suffers little of the prejudice it faced when Bakhtin made it the topic of his studies. Indeed, it has been endowed with all the status, the aura, that attend socially privileged modes of expressive culture. It has been honored as the premier form of the age, and its previously debased state has all but disappeared from memory. The visual media have, for the most part, assumed the positions of dishonor previously reserved for some forms of literature, and even among them film has managed to move upward on the scale as it has been replaced by television as a central medium.

Television is, in many ways, more "novelistic" than the novel in this regard, for the serious novel in our day frequently assumes the status of poetry in Bakhtin's scheme—it becomes the form that restricts multiple voices, bends them all to the special "word" of the poet-author, fails to reproduce the mixture of "languages" that surrounds it, and chooses to remain thoroughly stylized, "aesthetic" in focus.[3] But almost every aspect of television draws from the heteroglot environment and contributes to the dialogic nature of the medium.

Quite clearly, any single episode of television drama is structured by conflicting points of view. Groups of central characters are designed to offer this sense of difference and the guest characters who appear in single episodes bring with them individualized perspectives. Often it is the entry of these guest characters that establishes conflict within the group or between some members of the group and the guest. Each character, then, represents a language, and each language an ideological inflection related to ongoing social negotiation. Put another way, each character responds to the central ideologies from a different perspective, making that centrality something other than a monolithic system. With this application we can begin to see some of the richness of Bakhtin's observations when applied to television.

In his discussion of the novel he reminds us repeatedly that represented characters are "images" of languages. How much more powerful is this sense of image when we actually see the representations. We *see* the choices made for costume, the make-up, the body itself—selected to represent a perspective within this small world of the series. Characters must be understood, then, as embodying what Bakhtin refers to as "character zones." They carry with them a range of meaning associated with their particular total language, and these meanings interact with other zones, other ranges. The result is the creation of dialogue even when characters do not speak. At this level the visual analysis of television is necessary. In camera patterns, in editing, in set design, dialogue is at work. It is true, of course, that description and narration in prose carry similar ideological weight. But the power of visual media is that in a single frame we may find layers of ideological content presented instantly with relations in place before action or sound begin to cue responses. The effect of sequential narration in prose may ultimately be similar, but the process of representation is quite different, leading, I argue to a different understanding of ideological conflict.

We must remember, of course, that these reproductions are not exact. The representations are not empirically "correct." On the one hand they are purposive distortions, a means of enclosing individual "languages" and bending them to the intentions of the creators. But there is more to it then that. As Bakhtin (1981) says:

> ... typical aspects of language are selected as characteristic of or symbolically crucial to the language. Departures from the empirical reality of the represented language may under these circumstances be highly significant, not only in the sense of their being biased choices or exaggerations of certain aspects peculiar to the given language, but even in the sense that they are a free creation of new elements-which, while true to the spirit of the given language, are utterly foreign to the actual language's empirical evidence. (pp. 336–337)

Using these observations as analytical directives we can watch an ordinary episode of television develop the system of world-views inherent in its visual representation. An "inconsequential" line of dialogue, a reference to a topic not crucial to the plot, becomes a statement, a marker of meaning, an inflection, a refraction. Characterization itself becomes the creation of a language, perhaps unclear until the episode is completed in the case of a new or guest character. The orchestrated appearance of two characters in a room, an exchange of glances, gestures, can all present us with dialogues, images of multiple languages engaged with one another. Changes in dress or other aspects of appearance take on new significance, especially if a character parodies, satirizes, or otherwise inflects someone *else's* language-world, as is often the case in comedy built around error, mistaken identity, or misunderstood *languages*.

All of this "discussion" is directed for the most part, of course, to a set of central issues forming the plot of the episode. Here problems are faced. Decisions must be made. Varying perspectives are outlined in explicit as well as implicit fashion. In "solving" or "resolving" the issues embedded at the plot level the languages that structure any television show expose themselves most directly. Arguments among characters outline and highlight points of view. Resolution is usually, though not always, structured in dominance, in an acceptance, often strained, of the perspective of dominant ideology. But individual differences within the discussion may be equally as important as outcomes. These specific, perhaps aberrant perspectives may form the basis for individual responses to the program rather than the "narrative' wholes" that attract the attention of critics.

Recognizing this internal dialogue can greatly assist our analysis of what goes on within a television show, just as it can assist us in understanding a given novel. But there is much more available than the study of such single, enclosed texts. For if we choose to study a television *series* every episode of a series is part of the larger dialogue involving every other episode. We see characters repeat their "statements" through a range of plot issues. While we may assume consistency for the most part, a careful study of a series over time will also reveal change, developments that demonstrate complexities embedded in character-languages, contradictions of various sorts. A series is an object in evolution, even when its episodes are self-contained and nonreflective. Characters are allowed to "reveal" their languages in confrontation with new issues as writers and producers explore previously undeveloped aspects of the series. In those series structured on the principles of serial narrative (the open-ended, "soap-opera-like" programs such as *Dallas* or *Hill Street Blues*), the opportunities for interaction, change, development, and modification are much greater. But this merely points to genre history and comparative genre studies, still other dialogic inflections within television narrative.

The evolution of television genres provides us with a kind of archaeology of television's dialogic universe. Thomas Schatz's (1980) argument for generic evolution in film can be applied almost directly to television. Fiske and Hartley (1978) point to this sort of generic change in the newer medium, and argue for the ideological significance of generic shifts. But they overlook one significant difference that is unique to television. In television we must add the complexity provided by the existence of re-runs. As David Thorburn (1976) explains, television provides its own "living museum." The development of genres occurs ever anew, before our eyes. Older versions of the genres remain in dialogue with their newer relatives. It is not merely that we can mark the "languages" of *Dragnet, Ironside,* and *Starsky and Hutch* as different inflections within the generic pattern we know as "police show. " It is much more important that we can see these shows or others surrounded by still other inflections from different periods, different ideological stages in the genre's history. We should be able to produce fruitful analyses of various generic interactions, particularly if we examine the use of re-runs in particular television "markets" which purchase and program a range and variety of older television content.

Dialogue within genres, however, pales in comparison to the dialogue *among* genres which is produced more powerfully by television than by any previous medium. Double-bill movies, mixed content magazines, newspapers, and radio have all, at one time or another, offered something that foreshadows the generic mix offered by television, but none of them has provided such range or bulk. Bakhtin noted, of course, that varying genres do exist alongside one another in time, and he focused even more specifically on the ways in which the novel interpolates other genres, gobbling up the letter, the speech, the essay, shaping with report, satire, and most importantly with parody. But television depends on the actual physical proximity of generic patterns, the immediate availability of generic switch. I refer here not only to the fictional genres—comedies, westerns, detectives, soap-operas—but to the news shows, to commercials and news spots, to conferences, public service announcements, sports programs, and to every other aspect of this medium that is instantly available to the viewer. Many of these types are embedded in the television text in ways that force generic shifts, force dialogue, upon us.

It is no wonder that some students of the medium choose to find this "flow" confusing and limiting (Williams, 1976) or analyze everything without reference to difference, positing an industrial sameness without prior analysis (Gerbner et al., 1976). But close analysis of TV texts does indicate forms of difference, of inflection. Indeed, it is quite possible to argue that the task of the successful television producer is to generate novelty, to refract in a slightly altered language, the given patterns of television's generic constructs. In this way he or she tries to capture the attention of a program buyer, who may then attempt to use that novelty to attract an audience. For the ordinary viewer the problem of flow hardly seems to be as confusing as it is for some scholars. Not only can differences be marked in basic generic patterns, but there is evidence that viewers can identify a particular producer or production company responsible for a particular style within a genre (Newcomb & Alley, 1983).

The role of the viewer becomes crucial in outlining yet another version of television's dialogue. For even the most channel-loyal viewer, the person who makes no conscious selection beyond the on-off decision, television programming provides strips of dialogically constructed content. Varied presentations of similar material mark a range of world views, "languages" within which that material is "discussed." But many viewers do change channels and make selections. Thus, the viewer has the option to "reprogram" the strips of television provided by networks and cable-casters. In effect, the viewer is creating his or her own text with such moves. I have argued elsewhere (Newcomb & Hirsch, 1983), that the concept of the "strip" offers a more powerful model of the television text, a model that most televiewers actually experience. We can even model strips, by switching channels in previously taped material, to alter television's dialogue into a variety of patterns. The analysis of strips, as experienced or modeled, allows us to consider the various dialogues that viewers enter. This analysis must, of course, account for series history and generic development as well as for the immediate context provided within the strip. Ultimately it would have to account for overall individual and social viewing patterns. But with the strip as the basic unit of analysis we maintain the concept of dialogue even in our primary examinations of the television text. We are able to see how the internal dialogue is altered by shifting a program, turning off of the set before another program begins, or blocking or otherwise avoiding all the commercials.

I do not have the space here to offer a full analysis of a television strip-text. I do want to illustrate the concept of television's dialogic nature, however, with a partial analysis of a single program, remarking on the ways in which the more complete analysis might develop. I purposely choose a densely dialogized program, *Hill Street Blues*, not (or not only) because it corroborates my argument, but also because it represents, in my view, a trend in television. That trend has to do with an increasing sense of, and manipulation of, television's dialogic aspects on the part of program makers. This tendency can be seen in generic self-reflexivity of all sorts, in various developments of "fringe" television's late-night parodies and generic hybrids (*Saturday Night Live, SCTV, The David Letterman Show*), and in increasing interest in popular and nostalgic television history.

The task of the critic who recognizes the dialogic form of mass communication is to attempt a reconstruction *and* a critical analysis of the dialogue that is the work. The task of the researcher, as we will see later, is equally magnified. Let me demonstrate with a few of the threads I would follow in what is surely not an exhaustive reading of *HSB*.

We must first recognize the generic base of this pattern of meanings. The prime-time serial, or soap, can obviously cross prior generic lines. The similarities of *HSB* to *Dallas* are significant, but no more so than the differences. We need only think of violence experienced in *Dallas* to recognize that the police procedural with all its generic history inflects that topic differently than the melodrama. Beyond this double-based formula we would also consider, in a complete analysis, something of the extra-television history of the police procedural and the melodramatic serial.

We might move from considerations of generic inflection to those of character. With our knowledge of the formula, we recognize a number of "types," commonly used "character zones." The strong central figure, the captain, is familiar to us. So, too, are various types of side-kicks and comic characters. Each of these bears with him or her the larger sense of a "language," so that specific words in the mouth of Furillo will mean something different from similar words in the mouth of Goldblume or Callentano. Each "type" is, in effect, a singular meaning system. This is especially true in *HSB* where race, ethnicity, class, education, background, gender and other "languages" are often the sources of conflict and topics for plot development. But each type is also presented anew in this "symphony" of meaning systems called *Hill Street Blues*, just as *HSB* is presented anew within the systems called "cop shows."

What is doubly important here, and central to this analysis is that the *form* of this new show significantly modifies the use of the character types. Because of the program's serial nature we can see them change and develop, act and react. As various aspects of their personalities are progressively revealed, we learn more quickly about the richness of their "languages" than we would in enclosed episodes. As a result, they become less and less "typical," and more "individualistic." As we come to know the individual "utterances" of these characters they become more like people with whom we are personally acquainted. Their "word," their meaning within the constellation of characters and actions, becomes more complex, more difficult to understand—yet for many of us, far more rewarding. This is the type of fiction that we, as intellectuals, often value and appreciate. Let me illustrate with my own favorite character from the series, Howard Hunter.

Initially I was intrigued by the use of Hunter as straight parody, dropped into the middle of an otherwise highly realistic narrative. He broke the frame, ruptured the sequence whenever he appeared. Later, however, I came to know something of his vulnerability, his fear of death and bodily injury. I saw more of his racism and militarism and related both to his experiences in Vietnam. I watched his difficulties in sexual relations and saw them as linked to the other aspects of his personality. And most recently I have seen him become involved with a Vietnamese massage parlor attendant in a move that now seems perfectly natural and, for all its humor, quite realistic. In short, as I have learned more of how Howard Hunter actually constitutes a language within the social system of this show, I have realized that he is, quite simply, an exceptionally complex individual and that the earlier representations of him as parody were merely selective, restricted exposures, much like the exposures we allow of ourselves on meeting new people. Much of his parodic style now seems self-planned, a defensive posture designed to protect a damaged personality. That it is so ineffective is, I think, part of the intention of his creators, for whom the parody is, in the traditional manner, subversive of his military posturing, his racist attitudes, his authoritarianism. If this is intentional it is highly successful— not only because it makes Howard silly. In fact, we are perhaps sympathetic toward him, but not because he is a failure at militarism and racism. Rather it is because he *and* his attitudes are so pathetic.

Significantly, the "language" I know as Howard Hunter is not made up merely of words. As suggested earlier, Bakhtin's insights should be extended to other forms of communication as well, and in television and other visual media we have presentations of those dialogic aspects of life and communication that can only be *re*presented in prose. Thus, the uniforms, the bearing, the hair, the cap, the pipe, the gestures—all these are part of the language of Howard Hunter. While these descriptive features would all be significant in a novel, Hunter's language is "heard," it enters the ideological dialogue, even when he crosses a room, out of focus in the background of a frame.

This focus on character and character development is but one aspect of the dialogue that is *HSB*. Similar analyses could be performed with plot elements, with visual elements, with movement, and so on. A thorough analysis must discover the ways in which these are organized, in which control is attempted and subverted. This sort of analysis might more accurately be termed an "inventory" of the show, a survey of the range of possible interpretations rather than an interpretation in itself.

From this level of close reading we can now leap to far more expansive level of dialogic interaction, to the "grand system" that is television. Surely much of our understanding of the power of *Hill Street Blues* comes from its contrasting style *within* that larger system and its inclusion in a generic grouping that contains, as yet, few shows. This is why I argue that the appropriate "text" of television is the strip of viewing experienced by a viewer in a given evening. It will make a difference in the dialogic interaction of television if a viewer comes to *HSB* from *Cheers* or from *Simon and Simon* or from *Amanda's*. Even this cursory analysis of the dialogic context of a single show should suggest to us that this medium is packed with the dense threading of multiple perspectives. That they are somehow only slight removes from one another makes their unravelling all the more important, and difficult.

So far I have concentrated on the "texts" of television, viewed largely from the perspective of the critic-analyst. But the concept of "dialogue" goes far in providing a new and more precise understanding of the production process as well. As described by Newcomb and Alley (1983), Gitlin (1983), and Cantor (1981), that process is one of constant negotiation. Simple notions of network containment and domination of the creative process are insufficient explanation. From the collaborative writing process common in film and television, to the negotiation between writer and producer, producer and network, network and internal censor—dialogue is the defining element in the creation of television content. The evolution of a character illustrated here with the brief description of Howard Hunter can even be described as the dialogic interaction between writers and their own creations. As they discern possibilities for a new "word" within a character, that variation can be "written into" the series, with the clear implication that it alters all other aspects of the total system. Ultimately, of course, there is the implied social dialogue between the potential audience and the creative and programming communities. As Schatz (1980) has indicated in his study of the evolution of film genres, audience participation and acceptance is crucial to the cultural dialogue surrounding formal development and refinement.

I have also focused on the ways in which *texts* are accepted and altered through program stripping, channel switching, commercial blocking, and other forms of viewer activity. But in looking so closely at textual forms of dialogue we run the risk of relegating the viewer to the position of respondent or the passive artifact "constituted" by the text. Indeed, that perspective is one often accepted explicitly or implicitly in traditional mass communication research. In a dialogic view of communication, however, the viewer is active, accepting, rejecting, and modifying what is offered. It is finally to the viewer's participation in this meaning-making process that we must turn in order to refine our notions of the role of mass communication in the social dialogue.

TEXTS, AUDIENCES, AND DISCOURSE ANALYSIS

All these dialogic features of television, of course, are but microcosmic reflections of the totality of mass communication. We must remember that television interacts with other forms in that totality and with forms of communication that cannot be considered "mass" in nature. As previously indicated we must move beyond the study of texts to fully understand these dialogic interactions. We must move to the responses of those who communicate. As put by Bakhtin:

> In the actual life of speech [we can substitute television content], every concrete act of understanding is active: it assimilates the word to be understood into its own conceptual system filled with specific objects and emotional expressions, and is indissolubly merged with the response, with a motivated agreement or disagreement. To some extent, primacy belongs to the response, as the activating principle: it creates the ground for understanding, it prepares the ground for an active and engaged understanding. Understanding comes to fruition only in the response. Understanding and response are dialectically merged and mutually condition one another, one is impossible without the other. (Bakhtin, 1981, p. 282)

In mass communication studies this sense of exchange is often denied. The "dialogue" has generally been marked as one-sided, with little opportunity or attempt to "talk back." But such an attitude is based on a narrow and simplistic notion of how meaning might be generated and exchanged. The few observational studies of television viewing available to us are beginning to suggest something else, that viewers absorb television into other forms of dialogue, respond with parallel stories and comments, that they block, mold, and shape the "words" of television in a range of ways (see, for example, Wolf, Meyer, & White, 1982).

An adequate response to the dialogic aspects of mass communication, then, calls for a fully developed, critical sociology of interpretation. That work will include more ethnographic work such as that by Anderson (1984) and his associates in discovering precisely how individuals and groups view and understand television, more studies such as those now being conducted by Elihu Katz (personal communication, 1983) and his groups in Jerusalem and Los Angeles examining the interpretation of *Dallas* in multi-cultural contexts.

Morley's work on the *Nationwide* audience is, in this regard, pioneering. Throughout this essay I have used Bakhtin's terms—the "word," the "utterance," "languages"—to identify the dialogic embodiment of ideologies in communication practices. Morley's term, the more familiar "discourse systems," is perhaps better, more precise, for this task. Put succinctly, then, the discourse system is the unit of analysis that relates texts and audiences, texts and society. Or, to be as accurate as possible, it is the interaction among *systems* of discourse systems that provides the central content for the cultural study of mass media. Morley's own views on the ideological manipulation of those systems can be tested with careful research cognizant of the dialogic model. I advocate no simplistic application of "technique" as an answer here. We may have to create completely new skills to deal with these questions. But the testing is necessary because in a dialogic view of mass communication, discourse is not "given." It is made.

We cannot predict how viewers will interpret television, for example, from our knowledge of their positions as student, church-goer, retiree, female, any more than from class. And this is so even, or especially, if we "read" our definitions of "student," "church-goer," "retiree," or "female" from dominant ideology. Instead we must continue to study the interactions of discourse systems employed in response to the systems used in mass communications. In so doing we may discover how those systems intersect one another, how the systems that any given individual might competently employ are perhaps in conflicted dialogue with one another. We need to know if certain systems are used to interpret certain generic patterns and not others, if certain types of content elicit particular responses in certain audiences. It is crucial that we understand how dialogue about mass communications—e.g., in the viewing or post-viewing context of television—contributes to the refinement and development of systems with which viewers interpret in the future. As Volosinov constantly reminds us, neither subjective individualism nor abstract objectivism is adequate here. It is discourse in the social arena that is our object. Both the texts that we study and the responses to them are forged there.

Ultimately we will need to investigate how all the dialogic aspects of mass communication relate to dominant ideologies. It is quite obvious that much mass communication appropriates the languages of actual social practice and bends them to its will, deploys them in dominant strategies, depletes them of their fundamental oppositional force. Current theories, even the more flexible notions based in the concept of hegemony, argue that all dialogue is thus ultimately contained. In this view, process either ceases or is deflected and employed primarily by oppressive interests. My references to characters and actions as "languages" would not be accepted as legitimate variation in such a view. They would be seen instead as *terms* within the *single language* of commodity systems, of advanced capitalism. Yet it is precisely on this point that the Volosinov-Bakhtin advancement is so powerful. Terms can no longer be conceived as "units" whose meaning is determined by the system in which they occur. Such a view is precisely what Volosinov argues so cogently against. Terms bear the history of social conflict and negotiation and whenever and wherever used they enter that conflict once again. There is no way to predict which aspect of the term will be seized upon by a viewer.

Even when the most powerful, controlled messages are dominant, they must still face the answering "word" of the viewer and the world of experience. Responses cannot be predicted from the text or from social theory but must be defined and described in the practice of research that acknowledges their varied possibilities. In this sense, Hall's "dominant," "negotiated," or "oppositional" readings should all be collapsed into versions of negotiation, for one respondent's acceptance may be another's opposition. Even in the study of international communications these dialogic aspects of mass communication can command our attention, for there the world itself is in discussion.

We can posit the enclosure, the total mastery and control of this heteroglot mixture known as mass communication in society, then, only at the broadest level. What does this gain us other than the most commonplace observation that cultures and societies seek to reproduce themselves and maintain social relations as they are? What we need to know is how that happens, and we need to ask questions without focusing solely on the forms of successful dominance. Some aspects of various societies should be maintained. And some aspects that should be changed have been.

In that process of maintenance and reproduction ideologies, world views, "languages," discourse systems will always struggle for ascendency. The only escape from the ongoing process might lie in the transcendental ideal of nondistorted discourse. It is a worthy goal indeed. But the only way to reach it is along the rugged path of *conflicted* discourse, the struggle for meaning that is truly ideological. There, the images of languages we find in mass mediated texts—embodiments of social realities that do at time posit true alternatives will be dealt with by individuals, groups, movements, societies, in ways that can initiate as well as retard social practices actually necessary for us to implement our ideals. New languages—that is to say, new worlds—may be built from the discussions, the dialogues, occurring among the old.

Acknowledgments: The author expresses appreciation to Thomas Schatz, James Hay, Jimmie Reeves, Richard Allen, Hilary Radner and Richard Simon for reading and suggesting changes in earlier drafts of this essay.

NOTES

1.   A great debate continues among scholars of Slavic Studies regarding the authorship of these works. Some, among them Bakhtin's editor, Michael Holquist, argue

that Bakhtin, the center of the "Bakhtin circle," is the author of both books, of Volosinov's work on Freud, and at least co-author (with Medvedev) of the work on Formalism. Others argue for clear, sole authorship by Volosinov of the works in his name. Suffice it to say that those of us not conversant with the original languages had best make no judgment. We must be content with the "dialogue" that continues within and among the works, no matter who the authors.

2. I do not dwell here on another of Bakhtin's powerful insights, the notion of "carnivalization" in the novel. That concept, however, is related to other work I have done on television as "liminal" or "liminoid" space, following the work on anthropologist Victor Turner. See Newcomb and Alley (1983) and Newcomb and Hirsch (1983).

3. This perspective does not hold, of course, for the popular novels in various genres. They are still considered "out of bounds" by many readers and scholars.

REFERENCES

Anderson, J. (1984). Cultural norming and the active audience. *Culture and ideas*. New Delhi: New Concepts Press.

Bakhtin, M. (1981). *The dialogic imagination* (C. Emerson and M. Holquist, Trans.). (M. Holquist Ed.), Austin: University of Texas Press.

Barthes, R. (1964). *Elements of semiology*. New York: Hill & Wang.

Becker, S. (1984). Marxist approaches to media studies: The British experience. *Critical Studies in Mass Communication*, 1(1), 66–80.

Benjamin, W. (1968). *Illuminations* (H. Zohn, Trans.). (H. Arendt, Ed.), New York: Harcourt, Brace World.

Brunsdon, C. & Morley, D. (1978). *Everyday television: "Nationwide."* London: BFI.

Cantor, M. (1981). *Prime-time television: content and control*. Beverly Hills: Sage.

Eco, U. (1977). *A theory of semiotics*. London: McMillan.

Fiske, J. & Hartley, J. (1978). *Reading television*. London: Methuen.

Gerber, G. & Gross, L. (1976). Living with television: The violence profile. *Journal of Communication*, 26(2), 173–199.

Gitlin, T. (1982). Prime-time ideology: The hegemonic process in television entertainment. In H. Newcomb (Ed.), *Television: The critical view* (pp. 426–454). New York: Oxford University Press.

Gitlin, T. (1983). *Inside prime-time*. New York: Pantheon.

Gurevitch, M., Bennett, T., Curran, J., & Wollacott, J. (Eds.). (1982). *Culture, society, and the media*. London: Methuen.

Hall, S., Willis, P., Hobson, D., & Lowe, A. (Eds.). (1980). *Culture, media, language*. London: Hutchinson.

Hall, S. (1982). The rediscovery of ideology: Return of the repressed in media studies. In Gurevitch, M., Bennett, T., Curran, J., & Wollacot, J. (Eds.), *Culture, society, and the media* (pp. 56–90). London: Methuen.

Heath, S. & Skirrow, G. (1977). Television: A world in action. *Screen*, 18(2).

Hohendahl, P. (1982). *The institution of criticism*. Ithaca: Cornell University Press.

Kellner, D. (1982). TV, ideology, and emancipatory popular culture. In H. Newcomb (Ed.), *Television: The critical view* (pp. 386–421). New York: Oxford University Press.

Morley, D. (1980a). *The "Nationwide" audience*. London: BFI.

Morley, D. (1980b). Texts, readers, subjects. In Hall, S., Willis, P., Hobson, D., & Lowe, A. (Eds.), *Culture, media, language* (pp. 163–173). London: Hutchinson.

Murdock, G. & Golding, P. (1978). Theories of communication and theories of society. *Communication Research*, 5(3), 339–356.

Newcomb, H. (1976, 1979, 1982). *Television: The critical view*. New York: Oxford University Press.

Newcomb, H. & Alley, R. (1983). *The producer's medium: Conversations with America's leading television producers*. New York: Oxford University Press.

Newcomb, H. & Hirsch, P. (1983). Television as a cultural forum: Implications for research. *Quarterly Review of Film Studies*, Winter.

Schatz, T. (1980). *Hollywood genres*. New York: Random House.

Thorburn, D. (1976). Television melodrama. In R. Adler & D. Cater (Eds.), *Television as a cultural force* (pp. 77–94). New York: Praeger.

Volosinov, V. N. (1973). *Marxism and the philosophy of languages*. New York: Seminar Press.

Wander, P. (1981). Cultural studies. In D. Nimmo & K. Sanders (Eds.), *Handbook of political communication* (pp. 497–528). Beverly Hills: Sage.

Williams, R. (1976). *Television: Technology and cultural form*. New York: Schocken Books.

Wolf, M., Meyer, T., & White, C. (1982). A rules-based study of television's role in the construction of social reality. *Journal of Broadcasting*, 26(4), 813–829.

Wood, P. (1976). Television as dream. In R. Adler & D. Cater (Eds.), *Television as a cultural force* (pp. 17–36). New York: Praeger.

Signification, Representation, Ideology: Althusser and the Post-Structuralist Debates

STUART HALL

Althusser persuaded me, and I remain persuaded, that Marx conceptualizes the ensemble of relations which make up a whole society—Marx's "totality"—as essentially a complex structure, not a simple one. Hence, the relationship within that totality between its different levels—say, the economic, the political, and the ideological (as Althusser would have it)—cannot be a simple or immediate one. Thus, the notion of simply reading off the different kinds of social contradiction at different levels of social practice in terms of one governing principle of social and economic organization (in classical Marxist terms, the "mode of production"), or of reading the different levels of a social formation in terms of a one-to-one correspondence between practices, are neither useful nor are they the ways in which Marx, in the end, conceptualized the social totality. Of course a social formation is not complexly structured simply because everything interacts with everything else—that is the traditional, sociological, multifactoral approach which has no determining priorities in it. A social formation is a "structure in dominance." It has certain distinct tendencies; it has a certain configuration; it has a definite structuration. This is why the term "structure" remains important. But, nevertheless, it is a complex structure in which it is impossible to reduce one level of practice to another in some easy way. The reaction against both these tendencies to reductionism in the classical versions of the marxist theory of ideology has been in progress for a very long time—in fact, it was Marx and Engels themselves who set this work of revisionism in motion. But Althusser was the key figure in modern theorizing on this question who clearly broke with some of the old protocols and provided a persuasive alternative which remains broadly within the terms of the marxist problematic. This was a major theoretical achievement, however much we may now, in turn, wish to criticize and modify the terms of Althusser's break-through. I think Althusser is also correct to argue that this is the way the social formation is in fact theorized in Marx's "1857 Introduction" to the *Grundrisse* (1953/1973), his most elaborated methodological text.

Another general advance which Althusser offers is that he enabled me to live in and with *difference*. Althusser's break with a monistic conception of marxism demanded the theorization of difference—the recognition that there are different social contradictions with different origins; that the contradictions which drive the historical process forward do not always appear in the same place, and will not always have the same historical effects. We have to think about the articulation between different contradictions; about the different specificities and temporal durations through which they operate, about the different modalities through which they function. I think Althusser is right to point to a stubbornly monistic habit in the practice of many very distinguished marxists who are willing, for the sake of complexity, to play with difference so long as there is the guarantee of unity further on up the road. But the significant advances over this delayed teleology are already to be found in the "1857 Introduction" to the *Grundrisse*. There, Marx says, for example, of course all languages have some elements in common. Otherwise we wouldn't be able to identify them as belonging to the same social phenomenon. But when we have said that we have only said something about language at a *very* general level of abstraction: the level of "language-in-general." We have only begun our investigation. The more important theoretical problem is to think the specificity and difference of different languages, to examine the many determinations, in concrete analysis, of particular linguistic or cultural formations and the particular aspects which differentiate them from one another. Marx's insight that critical thought moves away from abstraction to the concrete-in-thought which is the result of many determinations, is one of his most profound, most neglected epistemological propositions, which even Althusser himself somewhat misinterprets (cf. "Notes on the '1857 Introduction,'" Hall, 1974).

I have to add right away, however, that Althusser allows me to think "difference" in a particular way, which is rather different from the subsequent traditions which sometimes acknowledge him as their originator. If you look at discourse theory,[1] for example—at poststructuralism or at Foucault—you will see there, not only the shift from practice to discourse, but also how the emphasis on difference—on the plurality of discourses, on the perpetual slippage of meaning, on the endless sliding of the signifier—is now pushed *beyond* the point where it is capable of theorizing the necessary unevenness of a complex unity, or even the "unity in difference" of a complex structure. I think that is why, whenever Foucault seems to be in danger of bringing things together, (such as the many epistemic shifts he charts, which all fortuitously coincide with the shift from *ancien regime* to modern in France), he has to hasten to assure us that nothing ever fits with anything else. The emphasis always falls on the continuous slippage away from any conceivable conjuncture. I think there is no other way to understand Foucault's eloquent silence on the subject of the State. Of course, he will say, he knows that the State exists; what French intellectual does not? Yet, he can only posit it as an abstract, empty space—the State as Gulag—the absent/present other of an equally abstract notion of

Resistance. His protocol says: "not only the State but also the dispersed microphysics of power," his practice consistently privileges the latter and ignores the existence of state power.

Foucault (1972/1980) is quite correct, of course, to say that there are many marxists who conceive the State as a kind of single object; that is, as simply the unified will of the committee of the Ruling Class, wherever it is currently meeting today. From this conception flows the necessary "yoking together" of everything. I agree that one can no longer think of the State in that way. The State is a contradictory formation which means that it has different modes of action, is active in many different sites: it is pluricentered and multi-dimensional. It has very distinct and dominant tendencies but it does not have a singly inscribed class character. On the other hand, the State remains one of the crucial sites in a modern capitalist social formation where political practices of different kinds are *condensed*. The function of the State is, in part, precisely to bring together or articulate into a complexly structured instance, a range of political discourses and social practices which are concerned at different sites with the transmission and transformation of power—some of those practices having little to do with the political domain as such, being concerned with other domains which are nevertheless articulated to the State, for example, familial life, civil society, gender and economic relations. The State is the instance of the performance of a condensation which allows that site of intersection between different practices to be transformed into a systematic practice of regulation, of rule and norm, of normalization, within society. The State condenses very different social practices and transforms them into the operation of rule and domination over particular classes and other social groups. The way to reach such a conceptualization is not to substitute difference for its mirror opposite, unity, but to rethink both in terms of a new concept—articulation.2 This is exactly the step Foucault refuses.

Hence we have to characterize Althusser's advance, not in terms of his insistence on "difference" alone—the rallying cry of Derridean deconstruction—but instead in terms of the necessity of thinking unity *and* difference; difference *in* complex unity, without this becoming a hostage to the privileging of difference as such. If Derrida (1977) is correct in arguing that there is always a perpetual slippage of the signifier, a continuous "deference," it is also correct to argue that without some arbitrary "fixing" or what I am calling "articulation," there would be no signification or meaning at all. What is ideology but, precisely, this work of fixing meaning through establishing, by selection and combination, a chain of equivalences? That is why, despite all of its fault, I want to bring forward to you, not the proto-Lacanian, neo-Foucauldian, pre-Derridean, Althusserean text—"Ideological State Apparatuses" (Althusser, 1970/1971), but rather, the less theoretically elaborated but in my view more generative, more original, perhaps because more tentative text, *For Marx* (Althusser, 1965/1969): and especially the essay "On Contradiction and Over-determination" (pp. 87–128), which begins precisely to think about complex kinds of determinacy without reductionism to a simple unity. (I have consistently preferred *For Marx* to the more finished, more structuralist *Reading Capital* [Althusser & Balibar, 1968/1970]: a preference founded not only on my suspicion of the whole Spinozean, structuralist-causality machinery which grinds through the latter text but also on my prejudice against the modish intellectual assumption that the "latest" is necessarily "the best.") I am not concerned here with the absolute theoretical rigor of *For Marx*: at the risk of theoretical eclecticism, I am inclined to prefer being "right but not rigorous" to being "rigorous but wrong." By enabling us to think about different levels and different kinds of determination, *For Marx* gave us what *Reading Capital* did not: the ability to theorize about real historical events, or particular texts (*The German Ideology*, Marx & Engels, 1970), or particular ideological formations (humanism) as determined by more than one structure (i.e., to think the process of overdetermination). I think "contradiction" and "overdetermination" are very *rich* theoretical concepts—one of Althusser's happier "loans" from Freud and Marx; it is not the case, in my view, that their richness has been exhausted by the ways in which they were applied by Althusser himself.

The articulation of difference and unity involves a different way of trying to conceptualize the key marxist concept of determination. Some of the classical formulations of base/superstructure which have dominated marxist theories of ideology, represent ways of thinking about determination which are essentially based on the idea of a necessary correspondence between one level of a social formation and another. With or without immediate identity, sooner or later, political, legal, and ideological practices—they suppose—will conform to and therefore be brought into a necessary correspondence with what is—mistakenly—called "the economic." Now, as is by now *de rigueur* in advanced post-structuralist theorizing, in the retreat from "necessary correspondence" there has been the usual unstoppable philosophical slide all the way over to the opposite side; that is to say, the elision into what sounds almost the same but is in substance radically different—the declaration that there is "necessarily no correspondence." Paul Hirst, one of the most sophisticated of the post-marxist theorists, lent his considerable weight and authority to that damaging slippage. "Necessarily no correspondence" expresses exactly the notion essential to discourse theory—that nothing really connects with anything else. Even when the analysis of particular discursive formations constantly reveals the overlay or the sliding of one set of discourses over another, everything seems to hang on the polemical reiteration of the principle that there is, of necessity, no correspondence.

I do not accept that simple inversion. I think what we have discovered is that there is *no necessary correspondence*, which is different; and this formulation represents a third position. This means that there is no law which guarantees that the ideology of a class is already and unequivocally given in or corresponds to the position which that class holds in the economic relations of capitalist production. The claim of "no guarantee"—which breaks with teleology—also implies that there is no necessary *non*correspondence. That is, there is no guarantee that, under all circumstances, ideology and class can never be articulated together in any way or produce a social force capable for a time of self-conscious "unity in action," in a class struggle. A theoretical position founded on the open endedness of practice and struggle must have as one of its possible results, an articulation in terms of *effects* which does not necessarily correspond to its origins. To put that more concretely: an effective intervention by particular social forces in, say, events in Russia in 1917, does not require us to say either that the Russian revolution was the product of the whole Russian proletariat, united behind a single revolutionary ideology (it clearly was not), or that the decisive character of the alliance (articulation together) of workers, peasants, soldiers and intellectuals who did constitute the social basis of that intervention was guaranteed by their ascribed place and position in the Russian social structure and the necessary forms of revolutionary consciousness attached to them. Nevertheless 1917 did happen— and, as Lenin surprisingly observed, when "as a result of an extremely unique historical situation, *absolutely dissimilar* currents, *absolutely heterogeneous* class interests, *absolutely contrary* political and social strivings . . . merged . . . in a strikingly 'harmonious' manner." This points, as Althusser's comment on this passage in *For Marx* reminds us, to the fact that, if a contradiction is to become "active in the strongest sense, to become a ruptural principle, there must be an accumulation of circumstances and currents so that whatever their origin and sense . . they 'fuse' into a ruptural unity" (Althusser, 1965/1969, p. 99). The aim of a theoretically-informed political practice must surely be to bring about or construct the articulation between social or economic forces and those forms of politics and ideology which might lead them in practice to intervene in history in a progressive way—an articulation which has to be *constructed* through practice precisely because it is not guaranteed by how those forces are constituted in the first place.

That leaves the model much more indeterminate, open-ended and contingent than the classical position. It suggests that you cannot "read off" the ideology of a class (or even sectors of a class) from its original position in the structure of socio-economic relations. But it refuses to say that it is impossible to bring classes or fractions of classes, or indeed other kinds of social movements, through a developing practice of struggle, into articulation with those forms of politics and ideology which allow them to become historically effective as collective social agents. The principal theoretical reversal accomplished by "no necessary correspondence" is that determinacy is transferred from the genetic origins of class or other social forces in a structure to the effects or results of a practice. So I would want to stand with those parts of Althusser that I read as retaining the double articulation between "structure" and "practice," rather than the full structuralist causality of *Reading Capital* or of the opening sections of Poulantzas' *Political Power and Social Classes* (1968/1975). By "double articulation" I mean that the structure—the given conditions of existence, the structure of determinations in any situation—can also be understood, from another point of view, as simply the result of previous practices. We may say that a structure is what previously structured practices have produced as a result. These then constitute the "given conditions," the necessary starting point, for new generations of practice. In neither case should "practice" be treated as transparently intentional: we make history, but on the basis of anterior conditions which are not of our making. Practice is how a structure is actively reproduced. Nevertheless, we need both terms if we are to avoid the trap of treating history as nothing but the outcome of an internally self-propelling structuralist machine. The structuralist dichotomy between "structure" and "practice"—like the related one between "synchrony" and "diachrony"—serves a useful analytic purpose but should not be fetishized into a rigid, mutually exclusive distinction.

Let us try to think a little further the question, not of the necessity, but of the possibility of the articulations between social groups, political practices and ideological formations which *could* create, as a result, those historical breaks or shifts which we no longer find already inscribed and guaranteed in the very structures and laws of the capitalist mode of production. This must not be read as arguing that there are no tendencies which arise from our positioning within the structures of social relations. We must not allow ourselves to slip from an acknowledgment of the relative autonomy of practice (in terms of its effects), to fetishizing Practice—the slip which made many post-structuralists Maoists for a brief moment before they became subscribers to the "New Philosophy" of the fashionable French Right. Structures exhibit tendencies—lines of force, openings and closures which constrain, shape, channel and in that sense, "determine." But they cannot determine in the harder sense of fix absolutely, guarantee. People are not irrevocably and indelibly inscribed with the ideas that they *ought* to think; the politics that they *ought* to have are not, as it were, already imprinted in their sociological genes. The question is not the unfolding of some inevitable law but rather the *linkages* which, although they can be made, need not necessarily be. There is no guarantee that classes will appear in their appointed political places, as Poulantzas so vividly described it, with their number plates on their backs. By developing practices which articulate differences into a collective will, or by generating discourses which condense a range of different connotations, the dispersed conditions of practice of different social groups *can* be effectively drawn together in ways which make those social forces not simply a class "in itself," positioned by some other relations over which it has no control, *but also* capable of intervening as a historical force, a class "for itself," capable of establishing new collective projects.

These now appear to me to be the generative advances which Althusser's work set in motion. I regard this reversal of basic concepts as of much greater value than many of the other features of his work which, at the time of their appearance, so riveted Althusserian discipleship: for example, the question of whether the implicit traces of structuralist thought in Marx could be systematically transformed into a full blown structuralism by means of the skillful application to it of a structuralist combinatory of the Levi-Straussean[3] variety—the problematic of *Reading Capital*; or the clearly idealist attempt to isolate a so-called autonomous "theoretical practice;" or the disastrous conflation of historicism with "the historical" which licensed a deluge of anti-historical theoreticist speculation by his *epigoni*; or even the ill-fated enterprise of substituting Spinoza for the ghost of Hegel in the Marxist machine. The principal flaw in E. P. Thompson's (1978) anti-Althusserean diatribe, *The Poverty of Theory*, is not the cataloging of these and other fundamental errors of direction in Althusser's project—which Thompson was by no means the first to do—but rather the inability to recognize, *at the same time*, what real advances were, nevertheless, being generated by Althusser's work. This yielded an undialectical assessment of Althusser, and incidentally, of theoretical work in general. Hence the necessity, here, of stating simply again what, despite his many weaknesses, Althusser accomplished which establishes a threshold behind which we cannot allow ourselves to fall. After "Contradiction and Overdetermination," the debate about the social formation and determinacy in marxism will never again be the same. That in itself constitutes "an immense theoretical revolution."

IDEOLOGY

Let me turn now to the specific question of ideology. Althusser's critique of ideology follows many of the lines of his critique of general positions in the classical marxist problematic sketched above. That is to say, he is opposed to class reductionism in ideology—the notion that there is some guarantee that the ideological position of a social class will always correspond to its position in the social relations of production. Althusser here is criticizing a very important insight which people have taken from *The German Ideology* (Marx & Engels, 1970)—the founding text of the classical marxist theory of ideology: namely, that ruling ideas always correspond to ruling class positions; that the ruling class as a whole has a mind of its own which is located in a particular ideology. The difficulty is that this does not enable us to understand why all the ruling classes we actually know have actually advanced in real historical situations by a variety of different ideologies or by now playing one ideology and then another. Nor why there are internal struggles, within *all* the major political formations, over the appropriate "ideas" through which the interests of the dominant class are to be secured. Nor why, to a significant degree in many different historical social formations, the dominated classes have used "ruling ideas" to interpret and define their interests. To simply describe all of that as *the* dominant ideology, which unproblematically reproduces itself and which has gone on marching ahead ever since the free market first appeared, is an unwarrantable forcing of the notion of an empirical identity between class and ideology which concrete historical analysis denies.

The second target of Althusser's criticism is the notion of "false consciousness" which, he argues, assumes that there is one true ascribed ideology per class, and then explains its failure to manifest itself in terms of a screen which falls between subjects and the real relations in which subjects are placed, preventing them from recognizing the ideas which they ought to have. That notion of "false consciousness," Althusser says quite rightly, is founded on an empiricist relationship to knowledge. It assumes that social relations give their own, unambiguous knowledge to perceiving, thinking subjects; that there is a transparent relationship between the situations in which subjects are placed and how subjects come to recognize and know about them. Consequently, true knowledge must be subject to a sort of masking, the source of which is very difficult to identify, but which prevents people from "recognizing the real." In this conception, it is always other people, never ourselves, who are in false consciousness, who are bewitched by the dominant ideology, who are the dupes of history.

Althusser's third critique develops out of his notions about theory. He insists that knowledge has to be produced as the consequence of a particular practice. Knowledge, whether ideological or scientific, is the production of a practice. It is not the reflection of the real in discourse, in language. Social relations have to be "represented in speech and language" to acquire meaning. Meaning is produced as a result of ideological or theoretical work. It is not simply a result of an empiricist epistemology.

As a result, Althusser wants to think the specificity of ideological practices, to think their difference from other social practices. He also wants to think "the complex unity" which articulates the level of ideological practice to other instances of a social formation. And so using the critique of the traditional conceptions of ideology which he found in front of him, he set to work to offer some alternatives. Let me look briefly at what these alternatives are, for Althusser.

"IDEOLOGICAL STATE APPARATUSES"

The one with which everybody is familiar is presented in the "Ideological State Apparatuses" essay. Some of his propositions in that essay have had a very strong influence or resonance in the subsequent debate. First of all Althusser tries to think the relationship between ideology and other social practices in terms of the concept of reproduction. What is the function of ideology? It is to reproduce the social relations of production. The social relations of production are necessary to the material existence of any social formation or any mode of production. But the elements or the agents of a mode of production, especially with respect to the critical factor of their labor, has itself to be continually produced and reproduced. Althusser argues that, increasingly in capitalist social formations, labor is not reproduced inside the social relations of production themselves but outside of them. Of course, he does not mean biologically or technically reproduced only, he means socially and culturally as well. It is produced in the domain of the superstructures: in institutions like the family and church. It requires cultural institutions such as the media, trade unions, political parties, etc., which are not directly linked with production as such but which have the crucial function of "cultivating" labor of a certain moral and cultural kind—that which the modern capitalist mode of production requires. Schools, universities, training boards and research centers reproduce the technical competence of the labor required by advanced systems of capitalist production. But Althusser reminds us that a technically competent but politically insubordinate labor force is no labor force at all for capital. Therefore, the more important task is cultivating that kind of labor which is able and willing, morally and politically, to be subordinated to the discipline, the logic, the culture and compulsions of the economic mode of production of capitalist development, at whatever stage it has arrived; that is, labor which can be subjected to the dominant system ad infinitum. Consequently, what ideology does, through the various ideological apparatuses, is to reproduce the social relations of production in this larger sense. That is Althusser's first formulation.

Reproduction in that sense is, of course, a classic term to be found in Marx. Althusser doesn't have to go any further than *Capital* (Marx, 1970) to discover it; although it should be said that he gives it a very restrictive definition. He refers only to the reproduction of labor power, whereas reproduction in Marx is a much wider concept, including the reproduction of the social relations of possession and of exploitation, and indeed of the mode of production itself. This is quite typical of Althusser—when he dives into the marxist bag and comes out with a term or concept which has wide marxist resonances, he quite often gives it a particular limiting twist which is specifically his own. In this way, he continually "firms up" Marx's structuralist cast of thought.

There is a problem with this position. Ideology in this essay seems to be, substantially, that of the dominant class. If there is an ideology of the dominated classes, it seems to be one which is perfectly adapted to the functions and interests of the dominant class within the capitalist mode of production. At this point, Althusserean structuralism is open to the charge, which has been made against it, of a creeping marxist functionalism. Ideology seems to perform the function required of it (i.e., to reproduce the dominance of the dominant ideology), to perform it effectively, and to go on performing it, without encountering any counter-tendencies (a second concept always to be found in Marx wherever he discusses reproduction and precisely the concept which distinguishes the analysis in *Capital* from functionalism). When you ask about the contradictory field of ideology, about how the ideology of the dominated classes gets produced and reproduced, about the ideologies of resistance, of exclusion, of deviation, etc., there are no answers in this essay. Nor is there an account of why it is that ideology, which is so effectively stitched into the social formation in Althusser's account, would ever produce its opposite or its contradiction. But a notion of reproduction which is only functionally adjusted to capital and which has no countervailing tendencies, encounters no contradictions, is not the site of class struggle, and is utterly foreign to Marx's conception of reproduction.

The second influential proposition in the "Ideological State Apparatuses" essay is the insistence that ideology is a practice. That is, it appears in practices located within the rituals of specific apparatuses or social institutions and organizations. Althusser makes the distinction here between repressive state apparatuses, like the police and the army, and ideological state apparatuses, like churches, trade unions, and media which are not directly organized by the State. The emphasis on "practices and rituals" is wholly welcome, especially if not interpreted too narrowly or polemically. Ideologies are the frameworks of thinking and calculation about the world—the "ideas" which people use to figure out how the social world works, what their place is in it and what they *ought* to do. But the problem for a materialist or nonidealist theory is how to deal with ideas, which are mental events, and therefore, as Marx says, can only occur "in thought, in the head" (where else?), in a nonidealist, nonvulgar materialist manner. Althusser's emphasis is helpful, here—helping us out of the philosophical dilemma, as well as having the additional virtue, in my view, of being right. He places the emphasis on where ideas appear, where mental events register or are realized, as social phenomena. That is principally, of course, in language (understood in the sense of signifying practices involving the use of signs; in the semiotic domain, the domain of meaning and representation). Equally important, in the rituals and practices of social action or behavior, in which ideologies imprint or inscribe themselves. Language and behavior are the media, so to speak, of the material registration of ideology, the modality of its functioning. These rituals and practices always occur in social sites, linked with social apparatuses. That is why we have to analyze or deconstruct language and behavior in order to decipher the patterns of ideological thinking which are inscribed in them.

This important advance in our thinking about ideology has sometimes been obscured by theorists who claim that ideologies are not "ideas" at all but practices, and it is this which guarantees that the theory of ideology is materialist. I do not agree with this emphasis. I think it suffers from a "misplaced concreteness." The materialism of marxism cannot rest on the claim that it abolishes the mental character—let alone the real effects—of mental events (i.e., thought), for that is, precisely, the error of what Marx called a one-sided or mechanical materialism (in the *Theses on Feuerbach*, Marx, 1963). It must rest on the material forms in which thought appears and on the fact that it has real, material effects. That is, at any rate, the manner in which I have learned from Althusser's much-quoted assertion that the existence of ideology is material "because it is inscribed in practices." Some damage has been done by Althusser's overdramatic and too-condensed formulation, at the close of this part of his argument, that—as he quaintly puts its: "Disappear: the term ideas." Althusser has accomplished much but he has not to my way of thinking actually abolished the existence of ideas and thought, however convenient and reassuring that would be. What he has shown is that ideas have a material existence. As he says himself, "the 'ideas' of a human subject exists in his [or her] actions" and actions are "inserted into practices governed by the rituals in which those practices are inscribed within the material existence of an ideological apparatus," which is different (Althusser, 1970/1971, p. 158).

Nevertheless, serious problems remain with Althusser's nomenclature. The "Ideological State Apparatuses" essay, again, unproblematically assumes an identity between the many "autonomous" parts of civil society and the State. In contrast, this articulation is at the center of Gramsci's (1971) problem of hegemony. Gramsci has difficulties in formulating the state/civil society boundary precisely because where it falls is neither a simple nor uncontradictory matter. A critical question in developed liberal democracies is precisely how ideology is reproduced in the so-called *private* institutions of civil society—the theatre of consent—apparently outside of the direct sphere of play of the State itself. If everything is, more or less, under the supervision of the State, it is quite easy to see why the only ideology that gets reproduced is the dominant one. But the far more pertinent, but difficult, question is how a society *allows* the relative freedom of civil institutions to operate in the ideological field, day after day, without direction or compulsion by the State; and why the consequence of that "free play" of civil society, through a very complex reproductive process, nevertheless consistently reconstitutes ideology as a "structure in dominance." That is a much tougher problem to explain, and the notion of "ideological state apparatuses" precisely forecloses the issue. Again, it is a closure of a broadly "functionalist" type which presupposes a necessary functional correspondence between the requirements of the mode of production and the functions of ideology.

After all, in democratic societies, it is not an illusion of freedom to say that we cannot adequately explain the structured biases of the media in terms of their being instructed by the State precisely what to print or allow on television. But precisely how is it that such large numbers of journalists, consulting only their "freedom" to publish and be damned, do tend to reproduce, quite spontaneously, without compulsion, again and again, accounts of the world constructed within fundamentally the same ideological categories? How is it that they are driven, again and again, to such a limited repertoire within the ideological field? Even journalists who write within the muckraking tradition often seem to be inscribed by an ideology to which they do not consciously commit themselves, and which, instead, "writes them."

This is the aspect of ideology under liberal capitalism which most needs explaining. And that is why, when people say "Of course this is a free society; the media operate freely," there is no point in responding "No, they operate only through compulsion by the State." Would that they did! Then all that would be required would be to pull out the four or five of their key controllers and put in a few controllers of our own. In fact ideological reproduction can no more be explained by the inclinations of individuals or by overt coercion (social control) than economic reproduction can be explained by direct force. Both explanations—and they are analogous—have to begin where *Capital* begins: with analyzing how the "spontaneous freedom" of the circuits actually work. This is a problem which the "ideological state apparatus" nomenclature simply forecloses. Althusser refuses to distinguish between state and civil society (on the same grounds which Poulantzas (1968/1975) also later spuriously supported—i.e., that the distinction belonged only within "bourgeois ideology"). His nomenclature does not give sufficient weight to what Gramsci would call the immense complexities of society in modern social formations— "the trenches and fortifications of civil society." It does not begin to make sense of how complex are the processes by which capitalism must work to order and organize a civil society which is not, technically, under its immediate control. These are important problems in the field of ideology and culture which the formulation, "ideological state apparatuses," encourages us to evade.

The third of Althusser's propositions is his affirmation that ideology only exists by virtue of the constituting category of the "subject." There is a long and complicated story here, only part of which I have time to rehearse. I have said elsewhere[4] that *Reading Capital* is very similar in its mode of argumentation to Levi-Strauss and other non-marxist structuralists. Like Levi-Strauss (1958/1972), Althusser also talks about social relations as processes without a subject. Similarly, when Althusser insists that classes are simply "bearers and supports" of economic social relations, he, like Levi-Strauss, is using a Saussurean conception of language, applied to the domain of practice in general, to displace the traditional agent/subject of classical western epistemology. Althusser's position here is very much in line with the notion that language speaks us, as the myth "speaks" the myth-maker. This abolishes the problem of subjective identification and of how individuals or groups become the enunciators of ideology. But, as Althusser develops his theory of ideology, he moves away from the notion that ideology is simply a process without a subject. He seems to take on board the critique that this domain of the subject and subjectivity cannot be simply left as an empty space. The "decentering of the subject," which is one of structuralism's main projects, still leaves unsettled the problem of the subjectification and subjectivizing of ideology. There are still processes of subjective effect to be accounted for. How do concrete individuals fall into place within particular ideologies if we have no notion of the subject or of subjectivity? On the other hand, we have to rethink this question in a way different from the tradition of empiricist philosophy. This is the beginning of a very long development, which begins in the "Ideological State Apparatuses" essay, with Althusser's insistence that all ideology functions through the category of the subject, and it is only in and for ideology that subjects exist.

This "subject" is not to be confused with lived historical individuals. It is the category, the position where the subject—the I of ideological statements—is constituted. Ideological discourses themselves constitute us as subjects for discourse. Althusser explains how this works through the concept, borrowed from Lacan (1966/1977), of "interpellation." This suggests that we are hailed or summoned by the ideologies which recruit us as their "authors," their essential subject. We are constituted by the unconscious processes of ideology, in that position of recognition or fixture between ourselves and the signifying chain without which no signification of ideological meaning would be possible. It is precisely from this turn in the argument that the long trail into psychoanalysis and post-structuralism (and finally out of the marxist problematic) unwinds.

There is something both profoundly important and seriously regretable about the shape of this "Ideological State Apparatuses" essay. It has to do exactly with its two part structure: Part I is about ideology and the reproduction of the social relations of production. Part II is about the constitution of subjects and how ideologies interpellate us in the realm of the Imaginary. As a result of treating those two aspects in two separate compartments, a fatal dislocation occurred. What was originally conceived as one critical element in the general theory of ideology—the theory of the subject—came to be substituted, metonymically, for the whole of the theory itself. The enormously sophisticated theories which have subsequently developed have therefore all been theories about the second question: How are subjects constituted in relation to different discourses? What is the role of unconscious processes in creating these positionalities? That is the object of discourse theory and linguistically-influenced psychoanalysis. Or one can inquire into the conditions of enunciation in a particular discursive formation. That is the problematic of Foucault. Or one can inquire into the unconscious processes by which subjects and subjectivity as such are constituted. That is the problematic of Lacan. There has thus been considerable theorizing on the site of the second part of the "Ideological State Apparatuses" essay. But on the site of the first part—nothing. Finito! The inquiry simply halted with Althusser's inadequate formulations about the reproduction of the social relations of production. The two sides of the difficult problem of ideology were fractured in that essay and, ever since, have been assigned to different poles. The question of reproduction has been assigned to the marxist, (male) pole, and the question of subjectivity has been assigned to the psychoanalytic, (feminist) pole. Since then, never have the twain met. The latter is constituted as a question about the "insides" of people, about psychoanalysis, subjectivity and sexuality, and is understood to be "about" that. It is in this way and on this site that the link to feminism has been increasingly theorized. The former is "about" social relations, production and the "hard edge" of productive systems, and that is what marxism and the reductive discourses of class are "about." This bifurcation of the theoretical project has had the most disastrous consequences for the unevenness of the subsequent development of the problematic of ideology, not to speak of its damaging political effects.

IDEOLOGY IN *FOR MARX*

Instead of following either of these paths, I want to break from that impasse for a moment and look at some alternative starting points in Althusser, from which I think, useful advances can still be made. Long before he had arrived at the "advanced" position of the "Ideological State Apparatuses" essay, Althusser said, in a short section in *For Marx* (1965/1969, pp. 231–236), some simple things about ideology which bear repeating and thinking about. This is where he defined ideologies as, to paraphrase, systems of representation—composed of concepts, ideas, myths, or images—in which men and women (my addition) live their imaginary relations to the real conditions of existence. That statement is worth examining bit by bit.

The designation of ideologies as "systems of representation" acknowledges their essentially discursive and semiotic character. Systems of representation are the systems of meaning through which we represent the world to ourselves and one another. It acknowledges that ideological knowledge is the result of specific practices—the practices involved in the production of meaning. But since there are no social practices which take place outside the domain of meaning (semiotic), are *all* practices simply discourses?

Here we have to tread very carefully. We are in the presence of yet another suppressed term or excluded middle. Althusser reminds us that ideas don't just float around in empty space. We know they are there because they are materialized in, they inform, social practices. In that sense, the social is never outside of the semiotic. Every social practice is constituted within the interplay of meaning and representation and can itself be represented. In other words, there is no social practice outside of ideology. However, this does not mean that, because all social practices are within the discursive, there is nothing to social practice *but* discourse. I know what is vested in describing processes that we usually talk about in terms of ideas as practices; "practices" feel concrete. They occur in particular sites and apparatuses—like classrooms, churches, lecture theatres, factories, schools and families. And that concreteness allows us to claim that they are "material." Yet differences must be remarked between different kinds of practice. Let me suggest one. If you are engaged in a part of the modern capitalist labor process, you are using, in combination with certain means of production, labor power—purchased at a certain price—to transform raw materials into a product, a commodity. That is the definition of a practice—the practice of labor. Is it *outside* of meaning and discourse? Certainly not. How could large numbers of people either learn that practice or combine their labor power in the division of labor with others, day after day, unless labor was within the domain of representation and meaning? Is this practice of transformation, then, nothing but a discourse? Of course not. It does not follow that because all practices are *in* ideology, or inscribed by ideology, all practices are *nothing but* ideology. There is a specificity to those practices whose principal object is to produce ideological representations. They are different from those practices which—meaningfully, intelligibly—produce other commodities. Those people who work in the media are producing, reproducing and transforming the field of ideological representation itself. They stand in a different relationship to ideology in general from others who are producing and reproducing the world of material commodities—which are, nevertheless, also inscribed by ideology. Barthes observed long ago that all things are also significations. The latter forms of practice operate in ideology but they are not ideological in terms of the specificity of their object.

I want to retain the notion that ideologies are systems of representation materialized in practices, but I don't want to fetishize "practice." Too often, at this level of theorizing, the argument has tended to identify social practice with social discourse. While the emphasis on discourse is correct in pointing to the importance of meaning and representation, it has been taken right through to its absolute opposite and this allows us to talk about all practice as if there were nothing but ideology. This is simply an inversion.

Note that Althusser says "systems," not "system." The important thing about systems of representation is that they are not singular. There are numbers of them in any social formation. They are plural. Ideologies do not operate through single ideas; they operate, in discursive chains, in clusters, in semantic fields, in discursive formations. As you enter an ideological field and pick out any one nodal representation or idea, you immediately trigger off a whole chain of connotative associations. Ideological representations connote—summon— one another. So a variety of different ideological systems or logics are available in any social formation. The notion of *the* dominant ideology and *the* subordinated ideology is an inadequate way of representing the complex interplay of different ideological discourses and formations in any modern developed society. Nor is the terrain of ideology constituted as a field of mutually exclusive and internally self-sustaining discursive chains. They contest one another, often drawing on a common, shared repertoire of concepts, rearticulating and disarticulating them within different systems of difference or equivalence.

Let me turn to the next part of Althusser's definition of ideology—the systems of representation in which men and women *live*. Althusser puts inverted commas around "live," because he means not blind biological or genetic life, but the life of experiencing, within culture, meaning and representation. It is not possible to bring ideology to an end and simply live the real. We always need systems through which we represent what the real is to ourselves and to others. The second important point about "live" is that we ought to understand it broadly. By "live" he means that men and women use a variety of systems of representation to experience, interpret and "make sense of" the conditions of their existence. It follows that ideology can always define the same so-called object or objective condition in the real world differently. There is "no necessary correspondence" between the conditions of a social relation or practice and the number of different ways in which it can be represented. It does not follow that, as some neo-Kantians in discourse theory have assumed, because we cannot know or experience a social relation except "within ideology," therefore it has no existence independent of the machinery of representation: a point already well clarified by Marx in the "1857 Introduction" but woefully misinterpreted by Althusser himself.

Perhaps the most subversive implication of the term "live" is that it connotes the domain of experience. It is in and through the systems of representation of culture that we "experience" the world: experience is the product of our codes of intelligibility, our schemas of interpretation. Consequently, there is no experiencing *outside* of the categories of representation or ideology. The notion that our heads are full of false ideas which can, however, be totally dispersed when we throw ourselves open to "the real" as a moment of absolute authentication, is probably the most ideological conception of all. This is exactly that moment of "recognition" when the fact that meaning depends on the intervention of systems of representation disappears and we seem secure within the naturalistic attitude. It is a moment of extreme ideological closure. Here we are most under the sway of the highly ideological structures of all—common sense, the regime of the "taken for granted." The point at which we lose sight of the fact that sense is a production of our systems of representation is the point at which we fall, not into Nature but into the naturalistic illusion: the height (or depth) of ideology. Consequently, when we contrast ideology to experience, or illusion to authentic truth, we are failing to recognize that there is no way of experiencing the "real relations" of a particular society outside of its cultural and ideological categories. That is not to say that all knowledge is simply the product of our will-to-power; there may be some ideological categories which give us a more adequate or more profound knowledge of particular relations than others.

Because there is no one to one relationship between the conditions of social existence we are living and how we experience them, it is necessary for Althusser to call these relationships "imaginary." That is, they must on no account be confused with the real. It is only later in his work that this domain becomes the "Imaginary" in a proper Lacanian[5] sense. It may be that he already had Lacan in mind in this earlier essay, but he is not yet concerned to affirm that knowing and experiencing are only possible through the particular psychoanalytic process which Lacan has posited. Ideology is described as imaginary simply to distinguish it from the notion that "real relations" declare their own meanings unambiguously.

Finally, let us consider Althusser's use of this phrase, "the real conditions of existence"—scandalous (within contemporary cultural theory) because here Althusser commits himself to the notion that social relations actually exist apart from their ideological representations or experiences. Social relations do exist. We are born into them. They exist independent of our will. They are real in their structure and tendency. We cannot develop a social practice without representing those conditions to ourselves in one way or another; but the representations do not exhaust their effect. Social relations exist, independent of mind, independent of thought. And yet they can only be conceptualized in thought, in the head. That is how Marx (1953/1973) put it in the "1857 Introduction" to the *Grundrisse*. It is important that Althusser affirms the objective character of the real relations that constitute modes of production in social formations, though his later work provided the warrant for a quite different theorization. Althusser here is closer to a "realist" philosophical position than his later Kantian or Spinozean manifestations.

Now I want to go beyond the particular phrase I have been explicating to expand on two or three more general things associated with this formulation. Althusser says these systems of representation are essentially founded on unconscious structures. Again, in the earlier essay, he seems to be thinking the unconscious nature of ideology in ways similar to those in which Levi-Strauss used when he defined the codes of a myth as unconscious—in terms of its rules and categories. We are not ourselves aware of the rules and systems of classification of an ideology when we enunciate any ideological statement. Nevertheless, like the rules of language, they are open to rational inspection and analysis by modes of interruption and deconstruction, which can open up a discourse to its foundations and allow us to inspect the categories which generate it. We know the words to the song, "Rule Brittania" but we are "unconscious" of the deep structure—the notions of nation, the great slabs and slices of imperialist history, the assumptions about global domination and supremacy, the necessary Other of other peoples' subordination—which are richly impacted in its simple celebratory resonances. These connotational chains are not open nor easily amenable to change and reformulation at the conscious level. Does it therefore follow that they are the product of specific unconscious processes and mechanisms in the psychoanalytic sense?

This returns us to the question of how it is that subjects recognize themselves in ideology: How is the relationship between individual subjects and the positionalities of a particular ideological discourse constructed? It seems possible that some of the basic positionings of individuals in language, as well as certain primary positions in the ideological field, are constituted through unconscious processes in the psychoanalytic sense, at the early stages of formation. Those processes could then have a profound, orienting impact on the ways in which we situate ourselves in later life in subsequent ideological discourses. It is quite clear that such processes *do* operate in early infancy, making possible the formation of relations with others and the outside world. They are inextricably bound up—for one thing—with the nature and development of, above all, sexual identities. On the other hand, it is by no means adequately proven that these positionings *alone* constitute the mechanisms whereby all individuals locate themselves in ideology. We are not entirely stitched into place in our relation to the complex field of historically-situated ideological discourses exclusively at that moment alone, when we enter the "transition from biological existence to human existence" (Althusser, "Freud and Lacan," 1970/1971, p. 93). We remain open to be positioned and situated in different ways, at different moments throughout our existence.

Some argue that those later positionings simply recapitulate the primary positions which are established in the resolution of the Oedipus complex. It seems more accurate to say that subjects are not positioned in relation to the field of ideologies exclusively by the resolution of unconscious processes in infancy. They are also positioned by the discursive formations of specific social formations. They are situated differently in relation to a different range of social sites. It seems to me wrong to assume that the process which allows the individual to speak or enunciate *at all*—language as such—is the same as that which allows the individual to enunciate him- or herself as a particular gendered, raced, socially sexed, etc., individual in a variety of specific representational systems in definite societies. The universal mechanisms of interpellation may provide the necessary general conditions for language but it is mere speculation and assertion which so far suggests that they provide the sufficient concrete conditions for the enunciation of historically specific and differentiated ideologies. Discourse theory one-sidedly insists that an account of subjectivity in terms of Lacan's unconscious processes is itself *the* whole theory of ideology. Certainly, a theory of ideology has to develop, as earlier marxist theories did not, a theory of subjects and subjectivity. It must account for the recognition of the self within ideological discourse, what it is that allows subjects to recognize themselves in the discourse and to speak it spontaneously as its author. But that is not the same as taking the Freudian schema, reread in a linguistic way by Lacan, as an adequate theory of ideology in social formations.

Althusser himself appeared, earlier (in his "Freud and Lacan" essay, first written in 1964 and published in Althusser, 1970/1971), to recognize the necessarily provisional and speculative nature of Lacan's propositions. He repeated the succession of "identities" through which Lacan's argument is sustained—the transition from biological to human existence paralleling the Law of Order, which is the same as the Law of Culture, which "is confounded in its formal essence with the order of language" (p. 193). But he does then pick up the purely *formal* nature of these homologies in a footnote: "Formally: for the Law of Culture which is first introduced as language . . . is not exhausted by language; its content is the real kinship structures and the determinate ideological formations in which the persons inscribed in these structures live their function. It is not enough to know that the Western family is patriarchal and exogamic . . . we must also work out the ideological formations that govern paternity, maternity, conjugality and childhood. . . . A mass of research remains to be done on these ideological formations. This is a task for historical materialism" (p. 211). But in the later formulations, (and even more so in the Lacanian deluge which has subsequently followed) this kind of caution has been thrown to the wind in a veritable riot of affirmation. In the familiar slippage, "the unconscious is structured like a language" has become "the unconscious *is* the same as the entry into language, culture, sexual identity, ideology, and so on."

What I have tried to do is to go back to a much simpler and more productive way of beginning to think about ideology, which I also find in Althusser's work though not at the fashionable end of it. Recognizing that, in these matters—though our conceptual apparatus is extremely sophisticated and "advanced," in terms of real understanding, substantive research, and progress to knowledge in a genuinely "open" (i.e., scientific) way—we are very much at the beginning of a long and difficult road. In terms of this "long march," *For Marx* is earlier than the flights of fancy, and occasionally of fantasy, which overtake the "Ideological State Apparatuses" essay. It ought not, however, be left behind for that reason alone. "Contradiction and Overdetermination" contains a richer notion of determination than *Reading Capital*, though not so rigorously theorized. *For Marx* has a fuller notion of ideology than does "Ideological State Apparatuses," though it is not as comprehensive.

READING AN IDEOLOGICAL FIELD

Let me take a brief, personal example as an indication of how some of the things I have said about Althusser's general concept of ideology allow us to think about particular ideological formations. I want to think about that particular complex of discourses that implicates the ideologies of identity, place, ethnicity and social formation generated around the term "black." Such a term "functions like a language," indeed it does. Languages, in fact, since the formations in which I place it, based on my own experience, both in the Carribean and in Britain, do not correspond exactly to the American situation. It is only at the "chaotic" level of language in general that they are the same. In fact what we find are differences, specificities, within different, even if related, histories.

At different times in my thirty years in England, I have been "hailed" or interpellated as "coloured," "West-Indian," "Negro," "black," "immigrant." Sometimes in the street; sometimes at street corners; sometimes abusively; sometimes in a friendly manner; sometimes ambiguously. (A black friend of mine was disciplined by his political organization for "racism" because, in order to scandalize the white neighborhood in which we both lived as students, he would ride up to my window late at night and, from the middle of the street, shout "Negro!" very loudly to attract my attention!) All of them inscribe me "in place" in a signifying chain which constructs identity through the categories of color, ethnicity, race.

In Jamaica, where I spent my youth and adolescence, I was constantly hailed as "coloured." The way that term was articulated with other terms in the syntaxes of race and ethnicity was such as to produce the meaning, in effect: "not black." The "blacks" were the rest—the vast majority of the people, the ordinary folk. To be "coloured" was to belong to the "mixed" ranks of the brown middle class, a cut above the rest—in aspiration if not in reality. My family attached great weight to these finely-graded classificatory distinctions and, because of what it signified in terms of distinctions of class, status, race, color, insisted on the inscription. Indeed, they clung to it through thick and thin, like the ultimate ideological lifeline it was. You can imagine how mortified they were to discover that, when I came to England, I was hailed as "coloured" by the natives there precisely because, as far as they could see, I *was* "black," for all practical purposes! The same term, in short, carried quite different connotations because it operated within different "systems of differences and equivalences." It is the position within the different signifying chains which "means," not the literal, fixed correspondence between an isolated term and some denoted position in the color spectrum.

The Caribbean system was organized through the finely graded classification systems of the colonial discourses of race, arranged on an ascending scale up to the ultimate "white" term—the latter always out of reach, the impossible, "absent" term, whose absent-presence structured the whole chain. In the bitter struggle for place and position which characterizes dependent societies, every notch on the scale mattered profoundly. The English system, by contrast, was organized around a simpler binary dichotomy, more appropriate to the colonizing order: "white/not-white." Meaning is not a transparent reflection of the world in language but arises through the differences between the terms and categories, the systems of reference, which classify out the world and allow it to be in this way appropriated into social thought, common sense.

As a concrete lived individual, am I indeed any one of these interpellations? Does any one of them exhaust me? In fact, I "am" not one or another of these ways of representing me, though I have been all of them at different times and still am some of them to some degree. But, there is no essential, unitary "I"—only the fragmentary, contradictory subject I become. Long after, I encountered "coloured" again, now as it were from the other side, beyond it. I tried to teach my son he was "black" at the same time as he was learning the colors of the spectrum and he kept saying to me that he was "brown. " Of course, he was *both*.

Certainly I am from the West Indies—though I've lived my adult life in England. Actually, the relationship between "West-Indian" and "immigrant" is very complex for me. In the 1950s, the two terms were equivalents. Now, the term "West Indian" is very romantic. It connotes reggae, rum-and-coke, shades, mangoes, and all that canned tropical fruit-salad falling out of the coconut trees. This is an idealized "I." (I wish I felt more like that more of the time.) "Immigrant" I also know well. There is nothing remotely romantic about that. It places one so equivocally as *really* belonging *somewhere else*. "And when are you going back home?" Part of Mrs. Thatcher's "alien wedge." Actually I only understood the way this term positioned me relatively late in life—and the "hailing" on that occasion came from an unexpected direction. It was when my mother said to me, on a brief visit home: "I hope they don't mistake you over there for one of those immigrants!" The shock of recognition. I was also on many occasions "spoken" by that other, absent, unspoken term, the one that is never there, the "American" one, undignified even by a capital "N." The "silence" around this term was probably the most eloquent of them all. Positively marked terms "signify" because of their position in relation to what is absent, unmarked, the unspoken, the unsayable. Meaning is relational within an ideological system of presences and absences. "Fort, da."

Althusser, in a controversial passage in the "Ideological State Apparatuses" essay says that we are "always-already" subjects. Actually Hirst and others contest this. If we are "always-already" subjects, we would have to be born with the structure of recognitions and the means to positioning ourselves with language already formed. Whereas Lacan, from whom Althusser and others draw, uses Freud and Saussure to provide an account of how that structure of recognitions is formed (through the mirror phase and the resolutions of the Oedipus complex, etc.). However, let us leave that objection aside for a moment, since a larger truth about ideology is implied in what Althusser says. We experience ideology as if it emanates freely and spontaneously from within us, as if we were its free subjects, "working by ourselves." Actually, we are spoken by and spoken for, in the ideological discourses which await us even at our birth, into which we are born and find our place. The new born child who still, according to Althusser's reading of Lacan, has to acquire the means of being placed within the law of Culture, is already expected, named, positioned in advance "by the forms of ideology (paternal/maternal/conjugal/fraternal)."

The observation puts me in mind of a related early experience. It is a story frequently retold in my family—with great humor all round, though I never saw the joke; part of our family lore—that when my mother first brought me home from the hospital at my birth, my sister looked into my crib and said, "Where did you get this Coolie baby from?" "Coolies" in Jamaica are East Indians, deriving from the indentured laborers brought into the country after Abolition to replace the slaves in plantation labor. "Coolie" is, if possible, one rung lower in the discourse of race than "black." This was my sister's way of remarking that, as often happens in the best of mixed families, I had come out a good deal darker-skinned than was average in my family. I hardly know any more whether this really happened or was a manufactured story by my family or even perhaps whether I made it up and have now forgotten when and why. But I felt, then and now, summoned to my "place" by it. From that moment onwards, my place within this system of reference has been problematic. It may help to explain why and how I eventually become what I was first nominated: the "Coolie" of my family, the one who did not fit, the outsider, the one who hung around the street with all the wrong people, and grew up with all those funny ideas. The Other one.

What is *the contradiction* that generates an ideological field of this kind? Is it "the principal contradiction between capital and labor?" This signifying chain was clearly inaugurated at a specific historical moment—the moment of slavery. It is not eternal, or universal. It was the way in which sense was made of the insertion of the enslaved peoples of the coastal kingdoms of West Africa into the social relations of forced labor production in the New World. Leave aside for a moment the vexed question of whether the mode of production in slave societies was "capitalist" or "pre-capitalist" or an articulation of both within the global market. In the early stages of development, for all practical purposes, the racial and the class systems overlapped. They were "systems of equivalence." Racial and ethnic categories continue today to be the forms in which the structures of domination and exploitation are "lived." In that sense, these discourses do have the function of "reproducing the social relations of production." And yet, in contemporary Caribbean societies, the two systems do *not* perfectly correspond. There are "blacks" at the top of the ladder too, some of them exploiters of other black labor, and some firm friends of

Washington's. The world neither divides neatly into its social/natural categories, nor do ideological categories necessarily produce their own "appropriate"
modes of consciousness. We are therefore obliged to say that there is a
complicated set of articulations between the two systems of discourse. The
relationship of equivalences between them is not fixed but has changed
historically. Nor is it "determined" by a single cause but rather the result of
an "over-determination."

These discourses therefore clearly construct Jamaican society as a field of
social difference organized around the categories of race, color and ethnicity.
Ideology here has the function of assigning a population into particular
classifications organized around these categories. In the articulation between
the discourses of class and race-color-ethnicity, (and the displacement effected
between them which this makes possible), the latter is constituted as the
"dominant" discourse, the categories through which the prevailing forms of
consciousness are generated, the terrain within which men and women "move,
acquire consciousness of their position, struggle, etc." (Gramsci, 1971, p. 377),
the systems of representation through which the people "live the imaginary
relation to their real conditions of existence" (Althusser, 1965/1969, p. 233).
This analysis is not an academic one, valuable only for its theoretical and
analytic distinctions. The overdetermination of class and race has the most
profound consequences—some of them highly contradictory—for the *politics*
of Jamaica, and of Jamaican blacks everywhere.

It is possible, then, to examine the field of social relations, in Jamaica and
in Britain, in terms of an interdiscursive field generated by at least three
different contradictions (class, race, gender), each of which has a different
history, a different mode of operation; each divides and classifies the world in
different ways. Then it would be necessary, in any specific social formation, to
analyze the way in which class, race and gender are articulated with one another
to establish particular condensed social positions. Social positions, we may say,
are here subject to a "double articulation." They are by definition over-deter-
mined. To look at the overlap or "unity" (fusion) between them, that is to say,
the ways in which they connote or summon up one another in articulating
differences in the ideological field, does not obviate *the particular effects* which
each structure has. We can think of political situations in which alliances could
be drawn in very different ways, depending on which of the different articulations in play became at that time dominant ones.

Now let us think about this term, "black" within a particular semantic
field or ideological formation rather than as a single term: within its chain of
connotations. I give just two examples. The first is the chain—black-lazy,
spiteful, artful, etc., which flows from the identification of /black/ at a very
specific historical moment: the era of slavery. This reminds us that, though the
distinction "black/white" that is articulated by this particular chain, is not
given simply by the capital-labor contradiction, the social relations characteristic of that specific historical moment are its referent in this particular
discursive formation. In the West Indian case, "black," with this connotative

resonance, is a way of representing how the peoples of a distinctive ethnic character were first inserted into the social relations of production. But of course, that chain of connotations is not the only one. An entirely different one is generated within the powerful religious discourses which have so raked the Caribbean: the association of Light with God and the spirit, and of Dark or "blackness" with Hell, the Devil, sin and damnation. When I was a child and I was taken to church by one of my grandmothers, I thought the black minister's appeal to the Almighty, "Lord, lighten our darkness," was a quite specific request for a bit of personal divine assistance.

IDEOLOGICAL STRUGGLE

It is important to look at the semantic field within which any particular ideological chain signifies. Marx reminds us that the ideas of the past weigh like a nightmare on the brains of the living. The moment of historical formation is critical for any semantic field. These semantic zones take shape at particular historical periods: for example, the formation of bourgeois individualism in the 17th and 18th centuries in England. They leave the traces of their connections, long after the social relations to which they referred have disappeared. These traces can be re-activated at a later stage, even when the discourses have fragmented as coherent or organic ideologies. Common sense thinking contains what Gramsci called the traces of ideology "without an inventory." Consider, for example, the trace of religious thinking in a world which believes itself to be secular and which, therefore, invests "the sacred" in secular ideas. Although the logic of the religious interpretation of terms has been broken, the religious repertoire continues to trail through history, usable in a variety of new historical contexts, reinforcing and underpinning more apparently "modern" ideas.

In this context, we can locate the possibility for ideological struggle. A particular ideological chain becomes a site of struggle, not only when people try to displace, rupture or contest it by supplanting it with some wholly new alternative set of terms, but also when they interrupt the ideological field and try to transform its meaning by changing or re-articulating its associations, for example, from the negative to the positive. Often, ideological struggle actually consists of attempting to win some new set of meanings for an existing term or category, of dis-articulating it from its place in a signifying structure. For example, it is precisely because "black" is the term which connotes the most despised, the dispossessed, the unenlightened, the uncivilized, the uncultivated, the scheming, the incompetent, that it can be contested, transformed and invested with a positive ideological value. The concept "black" is not the exclusive property of any particular social group or any single discourse. To use the terminology of Laclau (1977) and Laclau and Mouffe (1984), the term, despite its powerful resonances, has no necessary "class belongingness." It has been deeply inserted in the past into the discourses of racial distinction and abuse. It was, for long, apparently chained into place in the discourses and practices of social and economic exploitation. In the period of Jamaican history when the national bourgeoisie wished to make common cause with the masses in the fight for formal political independence from the colonizing power—a fight in which the local bourgeoisie, not the masses, emerged as the leading social force—"black" was a sort of disguise. In the cultural revolution which swept Jamaica in the later 1960s and 1970s, when for the first time the people acknowledged and accepted their African-slave-black heritage, and the fulcrum or center of gravity of the society shifted to "the roots," to the life and common experience of the black urban and rural underclasses as representing the cultural essence of "Jamaican-ness" (this is the moment of political radicalization, of mass mobilization, of solidarity with black struggles for liberation elsewhere, of "soul brothers" and "Soul," as well as of reggae, Bob Marley and Rastafarianism), "black" became reconstituted as its opposite. It became the site for the construction of "unity," of the positive recognition of "the black experience": the moment of the constitution of a *new* collective subject—the "struggling black masses." This transformation in the meaning, position and reference of "black" did not follow and reflect the black cultural revolution in Jamaica in that period. It was one of the ways in which those new subjects were *constituted*. The people—the concrete individuals—had always been there. But as subjects-in-struggle for a new epoch in history, they appeared for the first time. Ideology, through an ancient category, was constitutive of their oppositional formation.

So the word itself has no specific class connotation, though it does have a long and not easily dismantled history. As social movements develop a struggle around a particular program, meanings which appear to have been fixed in place forever begin to loose their moorings. In short, the meaning of the concept has shifted as a result of the *struggle* around the chains of connotations and the social practices which made racism possible through the negative construction of "blacks." By invading the heartland of the negative definition, the black movement has attempted to snatch the fire of the term itself. Because "black" once signified everything that was least to be respected, it can now be affirmed as "beautiful," the basis of our positive social identity, which requires and engenders respect amongst us. "Black," then, exists ideologically only in relation to the contestation around those chains of meaning, and the social forces involved in that contestation.

I could have taken any key concept, category or image around which groups have organized and mobilized, around which emergent social practices have developed. But I wanted to take a term which has a profound resonance for a whole society, one around which the whole direction of social struggle and political movement has changed in the history of our own life times. I wanted thereby to suggest that thinking that term in a nonreductionist way within the theory of ideology opens the field to more than an idealistic exchange of "good" or "bad" meanings; or a struggle which takes place only in discourse; and one which is fixed permanently and forever by the way in which particular unconscious processes are resolved in infancy. The field of the ideological has its own mechanisms; it is a "relatively autonomous" field of constitution, regulation and social struggle. It is not free or independent of determinations. But it is not *reducible* to the simple determinacy of any of the other levels of the social formations in which the distinction between black and white has become politically pertinent and through which that whole "unconsciousness" of race has been articulated. This process has real consequences and effects on how the whole social formation reproduces itself, ideologically. The effect of the struggle over "black," if it becomes strong enough, is that it stops the society reproducing itself functionally, in *that* old way. Social reproduction itself becomes a contested process.

Contrary to the emphasis of Althusser's argument, ideology does not therefore only have the function of "reproducing the social relations of production." Ideology also *sets limits* to the degree to which a society-in-dominance can easily, smoothly and functionally reproduce itself. The notion that the ideologies are always-already inscribed does not allow us to think adequately about the shifts of accentuation in language and ideology, which is a constant, unending process—what Volosinov (1930/1973) called the "multiaccentuality of the ideological sign" or the "class struggle in language."

NOTES

1.   The general term, "discourse theory," refers to a number of related, recent, theoretical developments in linguistics and semiotics, and psychoanalytic theory, which followed the "break" made by structuralist theory in the 1970s, with the work of Barthes and Althusser. Some examples in Britain would be recent work on film and discourse in *Screen*, critical and theoretical writing influenced by Lacan and Foucault, and post-Derrida deconstructionism. In the U.S., many of these trends would now be referred to under the title of "post-modernism."

2.   By the term, "articulation," I mean a connection or link which is not necessarily given in all cases, as a law or a fact of life, but which requires particular conditions of existence to appear at all, which has to be positively sustained by specific processes, which is not "eternal" but has constantly to be renewed which can under some circumstances disappear or be overthrown, leading to the old linkages being dissolved and new connections—re-articulations—being forged. It is also important that an articulation between different practices does not mean that they become identical or that the one is dissolved into the other. Each retains its distinct determinations and conditions of existence. However, once an articulation is made, the two practices can function together, not as an "immediate identity" (in the language of Marx's "1857 Introduction") but as "distinctions within a unity."

3.   This idea is explicated in chapter 3 of *Cultural Studies* (Hall, forthcoming).

4.   This is the subject of chapter 5 of *Cultural Studies* (Hall, forthcoming).

5   In Lacan (1966/1977), the "Imaginary" signals a relationship of plenitude to the image. It is opposed to the "Real" and the "Symbolic."

REFERENCES

Althusser, L. (1969). *For Marx* (B. Brewster, Trans.). London: Penguin Press. (Original work published 1965)

Althusser, L. (1971). *Lenin and philosophy and other essays* (B. Brewster, Trans.). London: New Left. (Original work published 1970)

Althusser, L., & Balibar, E. (1970). *Reading Capital* (B. Brewster, Trans.). London: New Left. (Original work published 1968)

Derrida, J. (1977). *Of grammatology* (G. C. Spivak, Trans.). Baltimore: Johns Hopkins University Press.

Foucault, M. (1980). *Power/knowledge: Selected interviews and other writings 1972–1977.* (C. Gordon, Ed.), (C. Gordon, L. Marshall, J. Mepham, & K. Soper, Trans.). New York: Pantheon. (Original work published 1972)

Gramsci, A. (1971). *Selections from the prison notebooks* (Q. Hoare & G. Nowell-Smith, Trans.). New York: International Universities Press.

Hall, S. (forthcoming). With J. Slack, & L. Grossberg. *Cultural Studies.* London: Macmillan.

Hall, S. (1974). Marx's notes on method: A 'reading' of the '1857 Introduction.' *Working Papers in Cultural Studies, 6,* 132–170.

Lacan, J. (1977). *Ecrits: A selection.* (A. Sheridan, Trans.). New York: International Universities Press. (Original work published 1966)

Laclau, E. (1977). *Politics and ideology in Marxist theory.* London: New Left.

Laclau, E., & Mouffe, C. (1985). *Hegemony and Socialist strategy.* London: New Left.

Levi-Strauss, C. (1972). *Structural anthropology.* (C. Jacobson & B. G. Schoepf, Trans.). London: Penguin. (Original work published 1958)

Marx, K. (1963). *Early writings.* (T. B. Bottomore, Trans.). London: C. A. Watts.

Marx, K. (1970). *Capital* (Vol. 3). London: Lawrence and Wishart.

Marx, K. (1973). *Grundrisse.* (M. Nicholaus, Trans.). London: Penguin. (Original work published 1953)

Marx, K., & Engels, F. (1970). *The German ideology.* London: Lawrence and Wishart.

Poulantzas, N. (1975). *Political power and social classes* (T. O'Hagan, Trans.). London: New Left. (Original work published 1968)

Thompson, E. P. (1978). *The poverty of theory and other essays.* New York: Monthly Review Press.

Volosinov, V. N. (1973). *Marxism and the philosophy of language.* (L. Matejka & I. R. Tutunik Trans.). New York: Seminar. (Original work published 1930)

6

Feminism and Cultural Studies

ELIZABETH LONG

British cultural studies is now in the process of redefinition through appropriation. This process appears to be both especially difficult and consequential. Difficult because, as both Grossberg (1989) and O'Connor (1989) point out, it is not a sharply bounded or "single fathered" intellectual lineage. This is a radical heritage, and its political standpoint appears in danger of being compromised by absorption into the American scene as just another paradigm for sale on the marketplace of ideas.[1]

I am struck by the ways in which the summary or presentational statements about British cultural studies that have been made in this country have already practiced an exclusion that seems to have marginalized its feminist practitioners, ironically the strand of that tradition that has arguably the best chance of maintaining a critical stance in its appropriation by feminist scholars in America, both because of their connections with a broad social movement and because of the nature of their practices within the academy. This is particularly troubling given the tendency for feminist thought to have a truncated "circuit" (Escarpit, 1965) of distribution and readership beyond feminist circles, which are often on the margins of "general" theory and research. It is this lacuna that I address by discussing, first, what British cultural studies feminists have contributed to cultural studies in "general" and, second, some of the ways feminist British cultural studies have been—and might be—well used by Americans.

THE FEMINIST CHALLENGE

The small number of women at the Birmingham Centre for Contemporary Cultural Studies began their work mainly in reaction to the invisibility of women in the theoretical and empirical analyses of their male senior colleagues and peers, and their work bears some of what Leslie Roman and Linda Christian-Smith

114

(1988) call a "reactive" stamp. However, they were responding not only to the absence of women as subjects and as a category—an absence that fueled the early years of feminist critique in the United States—but from within a theoretical, methodological, and institutional position that allowed the simple question "What about women?" to have large consequences. One methodological and three conceptual arenas seem to have been especially significant both for engendering British feminist contributions to cultural studies and for those Americans who refer back to their work. I discuss each in turn.

First, Birmingham feminists took issue with the valorization of the public sphere that marked the Centre's work on subcultural forms and the media. As Angela McRobbie's articles on the study of subcultures pointed out, the focus on spectacular male group behaviors on the street or in other public places tended to address girls only by the terms of derogation common among participants. For the most part, this focus simply made females invisible, since the "public" bias of subcultural studies marginalized the family and other contexts in which girls might be participating in "equivalent rituals, response, and negotiations" (McRobbie, 1980; McRobbie & Garber, 1976).

Similarly, Dorothy Hobson and Charlotte Brunsdon challenged media studies that valorized news and public affairs programs over soap operas and other "female" genres (see also Ang, 1985). Their early identification of the family as an important site for the appropriation of television programming opened the way for innovative investigations of the interpellation of public and private life. In her book *Crossroads* (1982), about a soap opera of the same name, Hobson, for example, discusses how the family context influences both the concentration and perspective that people bring to their viewing, and the ways in which the women viewers "use" the program to reflect on their own family issues, linking women's sense of "ownership" of the program not only to its content but to its inclusion in their domestic routine.[2] Such early feminist formulations clearly demanded further theoretical and empirical work, for asserting the importance of women and the domestic sphere did not address the issue of how the structural and ideological boundaries between public and private are historically constituted and hierarchized so as to devalue women, their domestic and market-oriented labor, and the social settings and cultural forms in which they are "at home."

If the feminists' challenge to the Centre's valorization of public life was somewhat inhibited by their refusal to problematize "the private," they were much clearer about the need to challenge the regnant assumption that social class was the primary or singular mechanism of domination. Yet, all remained convinced of the importance of class as well as gender. So instead of posing these as exclusive claimants for analytic attention (class vs. gender vs. race), the writings of Mica Nava (1984a; 1984b), Erica Carter (1984), McRobbie (1978a; 1978b; 1980; 1982; McRobbie & Garber, 1976), Valerie Amos and Prathiba Parmar (1981; Parmar, 1982), Brunsdon (1981), and Hobson (1981; 1982) manifest a concern with how to integrate class and gender in cultural studies.

I think this work is particularly exciting for two reasons. First, informed by the Centre's commitment to keeping a close and dialectical connection between theory and empirical research, these feminist culturalists discuss the intersection of systems of subordination in the lived experience of active and sense-making human beings, rather than as static determinant variables or as purely abstract theoretical categories that must somehow be brought together. In general, work of this kind seems crucial for understanding the complexly contradictory ways in which subjectivity is constructed under late capitalism and for gaining the leverage (both scholarly and political) to understand the often conflicted ways our many-stranded identities are positioned within the existing social order, the first stage of working toward resistance of its imperatives.

Second, especially in their essays about the state and its role in enforcing gendered as well as class relations of domination, Birmingham feminists began to undermine still prevalent assumptions that gender can somehow be equated with a marginal "woman's sphere" of sexuality and the family. Rather, as essays by Nava (1984a; 1984b) and Barbara Hudson (1984) in *Gender and Generation*, as well as those by Anne Strong (1981), Trisha McCabe (1981; McCabe & Sharon, 1981), and Gill Frith (1981) in *Feminism for Girls*, detail, the work of educational and judicial authorities in enforcing what Robert Connell (1987) calls "hegemonic" masculinity and "emphasized" femininity in their class-related inflections has consequences that pervade the social order.

This kind of work seems particularly important today, when new wave conservatism is centrally concerned with enforcing a regressive-utopian vision (or visions, since all such policies are differentiated by class and race) of "traditional" womanhood, of homophobic masculinity, and of sexuality and the family in ways that legitimize other repressive political, military, and economic initiatives.

It is because of the deep connection between sexuality, desire, and the emotional roots of both domination and resistance that articles like McRobbie's "Dance and Social Fantasy" (1984) are so important not only for feminists but for all those concerned with modifying the rationalistic bias of Marxism and, indeed, most academic representations of human action. British feminists, like their American counterparts, have pushed their exploration further, theoretically working through their assignment as women to the realm of intuition and sexuality. Worth noting is McRobbie's insistence on mapping out the *social* nature of the construction of female subjectivity, pleasure, and desire—by a discussion of the history of popular dance, its representations in the media, several ethnographic experiences in modern discos, and the relationship of dance to working class family customs and women's life cycles.[3]

Perhaps because of their understanding of the cross-cutting complexities of power relations, the British feminists extended not only the Centre's substantive interests but also their methodological program in regard to producing and disseminating scholarly work. Another McRobbie article

(1982) is, again, exemplary of feminist cultural studies discussions about ethnography. In it, she criticizes "naturalistic" sociology by pointing out that researchers do not lose their social privilege while in the field, which undermines the "innocence" of the knowledge field encounters generate, as well as the "transparency" of the process by which data become text.

There is some indication in McRobbie's work, and that of other British feminists who interviewed mainly women, that the relations between women informants and women ethnographers—as well as the Women's Liberation Movement's preoccupation with domination by authoritative talk, disempowerment through silence, and with ways to democratize access to the spoken and written word—informed her insights about ethnographic knowledge. The connection with an oppositional social movement certainly influenced McRobbie and McCabe's attempt to make an innovative political intervention through publishing an "engaged" feminist collection of essays, *Feminism for Girls* (1981), written by academics, politically involved teachers, and students, and also directed to those students, teachers, and youth workers as well as to scholars. The book is an impressive but awkward attempt to speak beyond the academy, one that founders in the reality of the divergences in interest and vocabulary between these constituencies. In some ways, it stands for certain qualities of the British feminist presence in cultural studies that are both strengths and limits: its theoretical eclecticism, its often informal methodological stance, and its enthusiastic risk-taking in the name of nurturing resistance.

THE AMERICAN CONTEXT

If British cultural studies in general has had something of a blind spot about feminism because of what feminists from various perspectives have called class "essentialism" or economic or class "reductionism," mainstream American feminists have until recently manifested a similar blind spot toward British cultural studies (feminist or nonfeminist) because of a tendency toward "gender essentialism" and an accompanying sympathy toward models drawn from individual psychology that obscure questions of class and race.[4] Even now, it is mainly feminists influenced by Marxism or neo-Marxisms who find this tradition sympathetic. This is admittedly a gross generalization about a many faceted intellectual/political movement—and one I modify later—but, even insofar as it holds, feminists may be the scholars who can best maintain the critical stance of British cultural studies in the United States—for two major reasons.

First, feminist scholarship in America has remained in touch with an oppositional social movement—however embattled or embourgeoisified—and thus has had a genuine (self) interest in critical thinking; domination and subordination are, for the Birmingham thinkers, more than academic categories. Further, while this critical stance is often ambivalent—because of the possibility of some rewards from the status quo—it is always being reconstituted by "the environing society." Indeed, as mentioned earlier much of the thrust of the New Right has been in the arenas of family, sexuality, and the proper "sphere" for women, as well as in policies, such as the erosion of affirmative action, that make explicit the connection between women's oppression and that of other subordinate social groups. This environing society comprises, as well, the still male-dominated academy; so even intellectual workers find themselves, as women, at odds with the prevailing hierarchies of scholarly value and open to critical thought.[5]

Second, feminist scholarship displays many of the institutional features and work practices argued by both O'Connor and Grossberg to be not only characteristic of the Birmingham Centre but constitutive of their radical intellectual politics. For instance feminists work across disciplines and often in marginal positions in relation to mainstream academic departments or subspecialties. So, feminist reception of British cultural studies has occurred not only in communication but also in education, sociology, women's studies, popular culture, American studies, and rhetoric. The interdisciplinary nature of the feminist response to British cultural studies in America has militated against its simplistic encapsulation within a specific field as one of that field's "paradigms" (as has been true for feminist scholarship as a whole) and has supported the desire, enacted at Birmingham, to challenge the existing, depoliticizing, disciplinary fragmentation of cultural studies.

There is also a strong tradition of collective work among feminist scholars and an equally strong desire to undercut the hierarchical nature of academic life (although this stands in tension with the desire to amass individual "intellectual capital"). More often than men, women are apt to have nonstandard careers and thus are more likely to make contributions as graduate students, to need support within inhospitable university environments, and to work out innovative "spaces" to develop this support. Thus, the feminist scholarly community in America, being composed of "deviants" who have feminist traditions of anti-hierarchical and democratic processes, finds sympathy with the "processual" aspects of the British cultural studies tradition and, indeed, has had a history of similar work processes.

The already constituted nature of feminist scholarship in the United States (marginal, interdisciplinary, and collectivist in action or desire) may also explain why such a wide-ranging group of critically oriented feminist scholars has begun to take up British cultural studies as formative of their work. It appears that the political and intellectual scenes were similar enough to engender some parallel developments in critical scholarship in Britain and the United States, so that when American feminists of a critical orientation became aware of British cultural studies they incorporated it very quickly.

This appropriation, however, is relatively recent.[6] So, just as British cultural studies has appeared in the discipline of communication as part of the almost generational paradigmatic "ferment" of the past few years, its feminist "wing" has become most influential among a generation of scholars finishing graduate school or in the junior stages of their academic careers. These are women for whom the theoretical advances of a decade ago—such as object relations or Lacanian perspectives, post-structuralism, the Frankfurt School—are taken-for-granted and somewhat constraining aspects of their intellectual background. This is also a group who, in the conservative, jumpy eighties, is searching for ways to invest political/theoretical energy in analyses that have the critical power to intervene in both the academy and the world outside it, because they are informed by a theoretical tradition that understands them both as sites whose cultural or symbolic practices are also social struggles.

The point here is that American feminist appropriations of British cultural studies challenge both mainstream feminism and mainstream cultural studies less by transforming substantive areas (the study of subcultures, curricula, popular media, etc.), or by a focus on women's popular culture, sexuality, and the family, than by foregrounding a multidimensional understanding of power, domination, and possibilities for resistance.[7] Particularly important contributions are the feminist culturalists' appreciation that people's social identities and allegiances are multivalent and bring them into often contradictory positions in regard to hegemonic discursive practices, and their equally perspicacious understanding of the multiplicity of sites wherein repressive forms of social subordination can be reproduced or can provide opportunities for contestation. To make this point more concrete, I discuss the work of two American women scholars whose projects powerfully integrate these issues.

THE CRITICAL POTENTIAL OF CULTURAL STUDIES

Tricia Rose's studies of rap music (1989a; 1989b)—the central component of Hip Hop, predominantly black urban youth culture also known for break dancing and graffiti art—argue that it is not a natural outgrowth of oral Afro-American forms but a complex fusion of oral forms, modern notions of individual authorship, and postmodern technology. She also contextualizes rap as a cultural response to the brutal policies of urban renewal in the South Bronx that abandoned a gutted neighborhood to blacks and Hispanics. Moving from social history to "close readings" of rap songs and their live performances, she demonstrates that the music incorporates highly self-conscious references to a musical and cultural tradition that is recuperated through reconstitution, as well as artful critiques of dominant social values and their replication in the power relations of the commercialized music industry. Showing how women in Hip Hop are marginalized in mainstream and leftist journalism, Rose analyzes how the songs, videos, and style of women rappers, and fans challenge hegemonic notions of sexuality, courtship, and bodily aesthetics, articulating a community-based feminist perspective within the subculture. Her work urges consideration of the complex interrelationships among gender, race, and class as they are constructed at specific historical junctures in struggles between collectivities of sharply different power, as they are represented by the performances of cultural activists—whether on the streets, at concerts, or in the studio, ambivalently legitimated by the music industry—and as they are framed by diverse wings of the media and the academy.

Leslie Roman's ethnographic and semiotic analyses (1987; 1988; 1989) of how middle and working class Punk young women culturally produce their feminine sexualities in the slam dance examine a smaller social "scene," with equally challenging theoretical and empirical consequences. Addressing three problems within cultural studies—romanticization of "resistance," "class essentialism," and "productivism"—Roman shows how the young women's class-differentiated experiences within the family (often including sexual abuse and family violence), school, and their different opportunities and histories in the work world provided them with very different symbolic and material resources for self-articulation within the subculture. She explores the "asymmetries in subjectivity" that kept the young women's gender- or class-based alliances from transcending momentary insight and becoming socially transformative. Moreover, her activist and "dialogic" ethnography illuminates the epistemological ramifications of ethical and political research choices. Roman's work links the most private levels of subjectivity to its multiple sites of structuration, illuminating the complexities of motivation for action, whether defensive or challenging in relation to an equally complex understanding of the landscape of power relations.

This kind of political engagement, methodological innovation, and willingness to use gender as an entry into a more multiplex and less romantic understanding of the constituents of power, subordination, and resistance *in general* demonstrates—as does the work of other feminists using the British tradition to grasp the specificity of contemporary America—that feminism is central for developing the critical potential of cultural studies. Moreover, at a time when hegemonic interests are vested in remapping the relations between public and private, family and work, in redefining dependency and individual responsibility, and in tapping into the wellsprings of terror and desire for dubious purposes of pacification and mobilization, the feminist contribution to critical cultural studies will be critical indeed.

NOTES

1. My thanks to Michele Farrell, George Lipsitz, Ellen Wartella, and Joe Dumit.
2. Likewise, feminist and other criticisms of Morley's study (1980) of viewer response to the news program *Nationwide* (he constructed artificial audience "groups" on the basis of occupation, though also attending to gender and race)

led to his book *Family Television* (1986), which begins to address how that most domestic of media is incorporated within and constitutive of the relations of familial power and authority.

3. This is, as well, a project vital for feminist scholarship in the United States, and McRobbie often appears in citations as the authorization for a move to undercut the essentialist tendencies that psychoanalysis—as received in America—often seems to encourage vis a vis issues of fantasy, desire, and subjectivity.

4. Different aspects of this discussion have been taken up by scholars as varied as Michelle Barrett, Allison Jaggar, Sandra Harding, Heidi Hartmann, Toril Moi, and Leslie Roman.

5. The link of a (at least potentially) broad social movement with other oppressed social groups has tended to keep even liberal American feminist cultural studies work in touch with issues of power, and thus somewhat protected from falling into the two intellectual camps or tendencies that have marked American cultural studies "high" and often pessimistic theory vs celebration (often optimistic, pluralistic, and blind to issues of power) of the popular. See my 1986 work for a fuller discussion of this issue.

6. From an interview with Ellen Wartella (4/30/89). As examples of American work that may not have been directly influenced by British cultural studies but engaged with similar problematics, I would note my own writing on middle class women's reading groups (1986; 1987; 1988) and the work by Radway (1984), McCormack (1983), and Tuchman (1978), to name just a few examples from the realms of sociology and literary studies.

7. This quality characterizes scholarship in all three of the categories under which I have grouped some recent American "cultural studies" publications by feminists. For instance, a fair number of scholars deal primarily with texts. Their work is not only politically informed but also tends to be historically, contextually, or institutionally grounded rather than formalistic (Carter, 1988; Christian-Smith, 1988), to be concerned with the relation between constraints like gender and class, ethnicity, or race, rather than with gender alone (Bright, 1989a; Franco, 1986; Steeves & Smith, 1987), and to be oriented toward the intersection between "texts" and audiences' cultural practices even when not engaged in empirical studies of cultural usages by specific people (Byars, 1987; Ellsworth, 1988; Lewis, 1987a; 1987b; Silverman, 1986; Taylor, 1989). Another strand of research examines culturally mediated social relations, usually using some combination of ethnographic, historical, and institutional analysis (Banks & Zimmerman, 1987; Press, 1991). Of particular note are Bright's discussion (1986b) of the ethno-aesthetics of masculine identity among Mexican-American low riders, Henderson's work (1989) on the social construction of "individual" talent at a film school and the undermining effects of that ideology on women's attempts to organize against a male dominated establishment there, Lesko's work (1988) on style, authority, and class among girls at a Catholic high school, Amesly's work (in press) on *Star Trek* culture, and Rakow's work (1988b) on gender and technology in communication. More theoretical or programmatic works (Henderson, 1988; Press, 1987; Rakow, 1986; Schwichtenberg, 1986; 1989b; Steeves, 1987) have been particularly useful to me when they understand theory and methodology as cultural practices in themselves. Essays by McCarthy (1988), Smith (1988), Treichler (1986), Treichler and Wartella (1986), Henderson (1987), and Rakow (1989) are especially noteworthy in this regard.

REFERENCES

Amesly, C. (1989). How to watch *Star Trek*. *Cultural Studies*, *3*.

Amos, V., & Parmar, P. (1981). Resistances and responses: The experiences of black girls in Britain. In A. McRobbie & T. McCabe (Eds.), *Feminism for girls: An adventure story* (pp. 129–152). London: Routledge & Kegan Paul.

Ang, I. (1985). *Watching Dallas: Soap opera and the melodramatic imagination*. London: Methuen.

Banks, J., & Zimmerman, P. (1987). The Mary Kay way: The feminization of a corporate discourse. *Journal of Communication Inquiry*, *11*(1), 85–99.

Bright, B. (1989a). *Nade y Nade: Language, power and emotion in the poetry of Evangelina Vigil*. Unpublished manuscript.

Bright, B. (1989b). *Gendered voices in Chicana poetry*. Unpublished manuscript.

Brunsdon, C. (1981). "Crossroads" Notes on soap opera. *Screen*, *22*(4), 32–37.

Brundson, C. (1986). *Films for women*. London: British Film Institute.

Brunsdon, C., & Morley, D. (1978). *Everyday television: "Nationwide."* London: British Film Institute.

Byars, J. (1987). Reading feminine discourse: Prime-time television in the U.S. *Communication*, *9*, 289–304.

Carby, H. (1982). White woman listen! Black feminism and the boundaries of sisterhood. In Centre for Contemporary Cultural Studies (Ed.), *The empire strikes back* (pp. 212–235) London: Hutchinson.

Carter, E. (1984). Alice in consumer wonderland. In A. McRobbie & M. Nava (Eds.), *Gender and generation* (pp. 185–214). London: Macmillan.

Carter, E. (1988). Intimate outscapes: Problem-page letters and the remaking of the 1950s West German family. In L. Roman, L. Christian-Smith, & E. Ellsworth (Eds.), *Becoming feminine: The politics of popular culture* (pp. 60–75). London: Falmer Press.

Christian-Smith, L. (1988). Romancing the girl: Adolescent romance novels and the construction of femininity. In L. Roman, L. Christian-Smith, & E. Ellsworth (Eds.), *Becoming feminine: The politics of popular culture* (pp. 76–101). London: Falmer Press.

Clifford, J., & Marcus, G. (Eds.) (1986). *Writing culture: The poetics and politics of ethnography*. Berkeley: University of California Press.

Connell, R. (1987). *Gender and power: Society, the person and sexual politics*. Cambridge: Polity Press.

Ellsworth, E. (1988). Illicit pleasures: Feminist spectators and personal best. In L. Roman, L. Christian-Smith, & E. Ellsworth (Eds.), *Becoming feminine: The politics of popular culture* (pp. 102–119). London: Falmer Press.

Escarpit, R. (1965). *The sociology of literature*. Painesville, OH: Lake Erie College Press.

Franco, J. (1986). The incorporation of women: A comparison of North American and Mexican popular narrative. In T. Modleski (Ed.), *Studies in entertainment: Critical approaches to mass culture* (pp. 119–138). Bloomington: Indiana University Press.

Frith, G. (1981). Little women, good wives: Is English good for girls? In A. McRobbie & T. McCabe (Eds.), *Feminism for girls: An adventure story* (pp. 27–49). London: Routledge & Kegan Paul.

Glazer, N. (1980). Overworking the working woman: The double day in a mass magazine. *Women's Studies International Quarterly*, *3*, 79–95.

Grossberg, L. (1989). The circulation of cultural studies. *Critical Studies in Mass Communication*, *6*(4), 413–420.

Henderson, L. (1987, November). *Critical ethnography and the duality of structure.* Paper presented at a meeting of the American Studies Association, New York.

Henderson, L. (1988, April). *Picturing women: Feminism and popular culture.* Paper presented at a meeting of the Symposium on Women, Language and Power, Haverford College, Pennsylvania.

Henderson, L. (1989, May). *Interpreting "talent": Local meaning and ethnographic evidence.* Paper presented at a meeting of the International Communication Association, San Francisco.

Hobson, D. (1981). "Now that I'm married . . . ." In A. McRobbie & T. McCabe (Eds.), *Feminism for girls: An adventure story* (pp. 101–112). London: Routledge & Kegan Paul.

Hobson, D. (1982). *"Crossroads": The drama of a soap opera.* London: Methuen.

Hudson, B. (1984). Femininity and adolescence. In A. McRobbie & M. Nava (Eds.), *Gender and generation* (pp. 31–53). London: Macmillan.

Lesko, N. (1988). The curriculum of the body: Lessons from a Catholic high school. In L. Roman, L. Christian-Smith, & E. Ellsworth (Eds.), *Becoming feminine: The politics of popular culture* (pp. 123–142). London: Falmer Press.

Lewis, L. (1987a). Consumer girl culture: How music video appeals to women. *One Two Three Four: A Rock and Roll Quarterly, 5,* 5–15.

Lewis, L. (1987b). Female address in music video. *Journal of Communication Inquiry, 11*(1), 73–84.

Long, E. (1986). Women, reading and cultural authority: Some implications of the audience perspective in cultural studies. *American Quarterly, 38*(4), 591–612.

Long, E. (1987). Reading groups and the crisis of cultural authority. *Cultural Studies, 1*(2), 306–327.

Long, E. (1988). *The quest for the "serious": A study in contemporary reading practices.* Unpublished manuscript.

McCabe, T. (1981). Schools and careers: For girls who do want to wear the trousers. In A. McRobbie & T. McCabe (Eds.), *Feminism for girls: An adventure story* (pp. 57–79). London: Routledge & Kegan Paul.

McCabe, T., & Sharon, K. (1981). A note on lesbian sexuality. In A. McRobbie & T. McCabe (Eds.), *Feminism for girls: An adventure story* (pp. 178–186). London: Routledge & Kegan Paul.

McCarthy, C. (1988). Marxist theories of education and the challenge of cultural politics of non-synchrony. In L. Roman, L. Christian-Smith, & E. Ellsworth (Eds.), *Becoming feminine: The politics of popular culture* (pp. 185–203). London: Falmer Press.

McCormack, T. (1983). Male conceptions of female audiences: The case of soap operas. In E. Wartella, D. C. Whitney & S. Windahl (Eds.), *Mass communication review yearbook* (pp. 273–283). Beverly Hills: Sage.

McRobbie, A. (1978a). *Jackie: An ideology of adolescent femininity.* Birmingham: The Centre for Contemporary Cultural Studies.

McRobbie, A. (1978b). Working class girls and the culture of femininity. In Women's Studies Group (Eds.), *Women take issue: Aspects of women's subordination* (pp. 96–108). London: Hutchinson.

McRobbie, A. (1980). Settling accounts with subcultures: A feminist critique. *Screen Education, 34,* 37–49.

McRobbie, A. (1982). The politics of feminist research: Between talk, text and action. *Feminist Review, 12,* 46–57.

McRobbie, A. (1984). Dance and social fantasy. In A. McRobbie & M. Nava (Eds.), *Gender and generation* (pp. 130–161). London: Macmillan.

McRobbie, A., & Garber, J. (1976). Girls and subcultures. In S. Hall & T. Jefferson (Eds.), *Resistance through rituals* (pp. 209–223). London: Hutchinson.

McRobbie, A., & McCabe, T. (Eds.) (1981). *Feminism for girls: An adventure story.* London: Routledge & Kegan Paul.

Morley, D. (1980). *The "Nationwide" audience: Structure and decoding.* London: British Film Institute.

Morley, D. (1986). *Family television: Cultural power and domestic leisure.* London: Comedia.

Nava, M. (1984a). Drawing the line. In A. McRobbie & M. Nava (Eds.), *Gender and generation* (pp. 85–111). London: Macmillan.

Nava, M. (1984b). Youth service provision, social order and the question of girls. In A. McRobbie & M. Nava (Eds.), *Gender and generation* (pp. 1–30). London: Macmillan.

O'Connor, A. (1989). The problem of American cultural studies. *Critical Studies in Mass Communication, 6*(4), 405–413.

Parmar, P. (1982). Gender, race, and class: Asian women in resistance. In Centre for Contemporary Cultural Studies (Ed.), *The empire strikes back* (pp. 236–275). London: Hutchinson.

Press, A. (1989) The ongoing feminist revolution. *Critical Studies in Mass Communication, 6,* 196–202.

Press, A. (1991). *Women watching television.* Philadelphia: University of Pennsylvania Press.

Radway, J. (1984). *Reading the romance: Women, patriarchy, and popular literature.* Chapel Hill: University of North Carolina Press.

Radway, J. (1988). The Book-of-the-Month Club and the general reader: On the uses of "serious" fiction. *Critical Inquiry, 14,* 516–538.

Rakow, L. F. (1986). Rethinking gender research in communication. *Journal of Communication, 36*(4), 11–26.

Rakow, L. F. (1988). Gendered technology, gendered practice. *Critical Studies in Mass Communication, 5,* 57–70.

Rakow, L. F. (1989). Feminist studies: The next stage. *Critical Studies in Mass Communication, 6,* 209–215.

Roman, L. (1987). *Punk femininity: The formation of young women's gender identities and class relations in the extramural curriculum within a contemporary subculture.* Unpublished doctoral dissertation, University of Wisconsin, Madison.

Roman, L. (1988). Intimacy, labor, and class: Ideologies of feminine sexuality in the Punk slam dance. In L. Roman, L. Christian-Smith, & E. Ellsworth (Eds.), *Becoming feminine: The politics of popular culture* (pp. 143–184). London: Falmer Press.

Roman, L. (1989). *Double exposure: The politics of feminist materialist ethnography.* Unpublished manuscript.

Roman, L., & Christian-Smith, L. (1988). Introduction. In L. Roman, L. Christian-Smith, & E. Ellsworth (Eds.), *Becoming feminine: The politics of popular culture* (pp. 1–34). London: Falmer Press.

Rose, T. (1989a, November). *"Hit the road Sam": Black women rappers and sexual differences.* Paper presented at a meeting of the American Studies Association. Toronto, Canada.

Rose, T. (1989b). Orality and technology: Rap music and Afro-American cultural resistance. *Popular Music and Society, 13*(4), Winter, 1989.

Schwichtenberg, C. (1986, June). *Feminist politics and feminine style: Central issues in feminist film theory.* Paper presented at a meeting of the International Communication Association, Chicago.

Schwichtenberg, C. (1989b). The "mother lode" of feminist research: Congruent paradigms in the analysis of beauty culture. In B. Dervin, L. Grossberg, B. O'Keefe, & E. Wartella (Eds.), *Re-thinking communication: Paradigm exemplars* (Vol. 2, pp. 291–306). Newbury Park, CA: Sage.

Silverman, K. (1986). Fragments of a fashionable discourse. In T. Modleski (Ed.), *Studies in entertainment: Critical approaches to mass culture* (pp. 139–152). Bloomington: Indiana University Press.

Smith, D. (1988). Femininity as discourse. In L. Roman, L. Christian-Smith, & E. Ellsworth (Eds.), *Becoming feminine: The politics of popular culture* (pp. 37–59). London: Falmer Press.

Steeves, H. L. (1987). Feminist theories and media studies. *Critical Studies in Mass Communication, 4*, 95–135.

Steeves, H., & Smith, M. (1987). Class and gender in prime-time television entertainment: Observations from a socialist feminist perspective. *Journal of Communication Inquiry, 11*(1), 43–63.

Strong, A. (1981). Learning to be a girl: Girls, schools, and the work of the Sheffield education group. In A. McRobbie & T. McCabe (Eds.), *Feminism for girls: An adventure story* (pp. 186–198). London: Routledge & Kegan Paul.

Taylor, E. (1989). *Prime time families: Television culture and postwar America.* Berkeley: University of California Press.

Treichler, P. A. (1986). Teaching feminist theory. In C. Nelson (Ed.), *Theory in the classroom* (pp. 57–128). Urbana: University of Illinois Press.

Treichler, P. A., & Wartella, E. (1986). Interventions: Feminist theory and communication studies. *Communication, 9*, 1–18.

Tuchman, G. (1978). The symbolic annihilation of women. In G. Tuchman, A. Kaplan Daniels, & J. Benet (Eds.), *Hearth and home: Images of women in the mass media* (pp. 3–38). New York: Oxford University Press.

7 Strategies of Marxist Cultural Interpretation

LAWRENCE GROSSBERG

There is a growing recognition and acceptance of what is often euphemistically called "critical" or "materialist" theories of communication and culture. If we are to believe the cumulative description offered in *Ferment in the Field* (Gerbner, 1983), we have not advanced very far since Lazarsfeld first introduced the conflict between administrative and critical research into the canonical constitution of the discipline. First, each side is still attacked as if it held the same positions and faced the same theoretical quagmires as when Lazarsfeld attempted a liberal rapprochement between them. Second, each side continues to attack the other as if the "enemy" were a monolithic, theoretical, methodological and political monster. Third, and most importantly, each side often presents itself in similarly monolithic terms, ignoring not only their differences, but the contributions that such differences make to their alliance. The origins of such "reductionist" strategies are complex. To be sure, they are a risk of any interdisciplinary endeavor, and they seem, too often, to be the almost inevitable effects of the self-nominations, "science" and "marxism."

Given the increasingly confusing proliferation of models for marxist communications research, it should be useful to document some of the differences that exist. There are, however, a number of ways to divide the terrain; the framework constitutes as well as describes the differences. Positions are "necessarily" misrepresented because they respond to different issues. The framework I propose focuses on the practice of interpreting specific messages or cultural forms, rather than centering on any theory per se. On the other hand, I will "read" such practices as responses to two related theoretical questions: (1) the politics of textuality, and (2) the problematic of cultural studies.

The *politics of textuality* signals the changing meaning and function of the category "text" (or "message"), both within everyday life and in the specific work of intellectuals. The analysis of the functions[1] of a text depends in part on how one conceptualizes the nature of signifying practices and structures, and their relations to processes of creativity, determination and interpretation.

126

In more traditional marxist terms, the interpretation of texts also depends upon how and where they are inserted into the circuit of production and consumption. These terms are reproduced in a model of communication as the circuit of the exchange of meanings, information or signifiers. Consequently, the investigation of the text is divided into questions of encoding—the relation between production and text—and decoding—the relation between text and consumption or reception.

The second issue, the *problematic of cultural studies*, concerns the division between culture and society within the social formation. It questions the difference, as well as the relations, between signifying and nonsignifying practices. The "culture/society" couplet brings together the Chicago School pragmatists, marxist models of base and superstructure, and contemporary theories of ideology and power. In fact, there is a third term implicit in the question: not only cultural meaning (forms, practices, etc.) and social structures (processes, forces, etc.), but also experience or the domain of everyday life. This third term slides between culture and society. Williams (1958) identifies the ambiguity *in* the concept of culture, although he then projects it into the social. Culture refers to both the anthropologically constituted notion (with its liberal democratic politics) of a "whole way of life," and the critical humanistic notion (with its sharply demarcated class politics) of a special set of signifying activities. The latter can be "cleansed" of its inherent elitism by broadening the institutional sites of such practices beyond the narrow domain of art to include the entire range of "ideological state apparatuses" (Althusser, 1970/1971); in other words, the forms and practices of interpersonal and mediated communications.

Just as the question of textuality creates an analytical, if not theoretical, gap between encoding and decoding, the problematic of cultural studies produces a gap between culture and society in describing how particular structures of meaning determine or are determined by social processes. The task apparently requires both a hermeneutics of faith and a hermeneutics of suspicion (Ricoeur, 1965/1970). The latter sees the text determined by a context and functioning in part to hide that determination. The former treats the text as transcending that context, its message potentially universal. A "hermeneutics of faith" interprets the meaning or message of a text; it reaches into literary, symbolic and semiotic theory. A "hermeneutics of suspicion" connects that meaning to a determinate context; it must already have described the social realm, and the organization of power and domination within it. The intersection of these two hermeneutics defines the "ideological function" of the text and it is often in terms of "ideology" that the problematic of cultural studies is theorized.

The questions of the politics of textuality and the problematic of cultural studies, taken together, provide one way of defining the task of marxist interpretation: to describe (and intervene in) the way messages are produced by, inserted into, and function within the everyday lives of concrete human beings so as to reproduce or transform structures of power and domination. I will describe ten different positions (organized into three larger categories or approaches) to the study of cultural texts or communicative messages coexisting within the space of a marxist theory.[2] For each position I will briefly describe its methodological practice and the (often implicit) theoretical responses to the two questions described above. While I will provide at least one example of an interpretation for each position, the mix of abstract and concrete analysis will vary depending upon the availability and accessibility of the work. I will conclude with a schematic summary of this admittedly partial and oversimplified map of the marxist terrain.

THE CLASSICAL APPROACH

Under this heading, I describe three different positions sharing a number of assumptions: *false consciousness, critical theory* and *economism*. All three positions seek to find direct relations between cultural texts and social/economic realities. Not surprisingly, they often find intentional and malevolent voices speaking in the messages, voices seeking to protect their own positions of power and economic domination. Thus, we might describe all three as "reflection" or causal theories. Finally, such classical positions describe both the social and cultural practices of capitalism in terms largely derived from Marx's earlier, humanistic rhetoric: Capitalism creates false needs; modern experience is built upon standardization, the sensationalization of everyday life, dehumanization, escapism, and fragmented if not false understandings of the world. Both the economic interests behind particular texts and the processes of production are always hidden.

Classical approaches, then, never question textuality. The text is assumed to be a transparent medium, or it is erased, or it is simply a conduit which determines the necessary modes of its own consumption. A confrontation with the text is strategically avoided by bracketing decoding processes. Such analyses focus on the relationship between the producer and the text, implying that consumers are passive and unaware of the ways in which messages act upon them. Mass communication becomes a process of the self-colonization of the individual. Culture cannot be the site of a struggle for power unless there are radically alternative and competing economic and political systems of media production. The result is that change can only occur through action upon the economic and political systems which determine the media messages.

False Consciousness

This position assumes that texts are collections of images that can be extracted from the text and treated as isolated, ideological representations of reality; that is, they are motivated by and function to protect the class interests already structured into the economic relations of capital. How the critic reads this meaning/ideology in the text is mystified within the critical practice and there is no consideration of how the critic is able to escape the ideological machinations of the text. These meanings are then projected back into the processes of production (as intentions) and forward into the everyday lives of its audience. The unexamined practice of text-interpretation defines both the origin and effects of the text.

Perhaps the most compelling and important example of this approach is Dorfman and Mattelart's *How to Read Donald Duck* (1971/1975). They interpret the comics as a series of image-codes which organize and define the characters and the relations amongst them. Using techniques as diverse as semiotics and psychoanalysis, the authors describe the structures of social identity and social relationships that constitute the world of Donald Duck. They assume that these meanings are found in the text by its diverse Latin American audiences. The text becomes a simple link between the producer and the consumer. The meanings "transmitted" by the text are placed there by the producers and directly determine their own reception in ways which support the interests of the producers. The text, then, is determinately univocal. For example, they argue that the comic texts consistently re-present a particular familial politics predicated upon an absent father (and an absent mother), creating a relationship between international capitalism and imperialism on the one hand, and familial and gender politics on the other.

Their reading is based on two assumptions: (1) that people take the media to be a realistic representation of reality which then reflects back onto it to reproduce systems of distorted knowledge (ideology); and (2) that people consume such messages by a determined and direct identification with a single (set of) character(s). For example, their interpretation is predicated on the child's identification with his (the authors do not seem to acknowledge the importance of the gendered determination of consumption) counterpart in the comics. Their practice is manifested and exhibited in the conclusions they draw throughout the text:

> It is the manner in which the U.S. dreams and redeems itself, and then imposes that dream upon others for its own salvation. (p. 95)
>
> The bourgeois concept of entertainment, and the specific manner in which it is expounded in the world of Disney, is the superstructural manifestation of the dislocations and tensions of an advanced capitalist historical base. In its entertainment, it automatically generates certain myths functional to the system. It is altogether normal for readers experiencing the conflicts of their age from within the perspective of the imperialist system, to see their own daily life, and projected future, reflected in the Disney system. . . . Behind the Coca Cola stands a whole structure of expectations and models of behavior, and with it, a particular kind of present and future society, and an interpretation of the past. (Dorfman & Mattelart, 1979/1975, p. 97)

This ability to, as Blake might say, "see the world in a grain of sand," is based on a vision of the culture/society couplet as a system of reflexes, moving from the base to the superstructure, through the audience, and returning to the base. Thus, the complex and necessary ideological mechanisms of economic and political domination are "part of the metabolism of the system" (p. 56).[3]

It may be useful to provide a second, more widely accessible example of this approach—Gitlin's *The Whole World Is Watching* (1980). Gitlin examines how the "routine practices" of news organizations define the structures of, and possibilities for, the production of news messages. Although Gitlin's theoretical framework suggests a "hermeneutic" position built upon Williams (1973) and Gramsci (1971), his methodological practice contradicts this. Like other classical positions, he assumes that the media have the power to "orchestrate everyday consciousness" (p. 2) in rather unproblematic ways, and that the structures of meaning which the media impose upon the audience can be simply read off the surface of the texts themselves. Ideology is "distributed by the media," which "bring a manufactured public world into private life" (p. 1). Although he argues that critics must pay attention to the symbolic contents of the media before questions of concrete effects can be raised, Gitlin assumes that the texts are univocal. Consequently, he is not compelled to offer any theory of how one is to discover the "frames" within which the media place events. They are there, on the surface, available to anyone who looks for them, that is, that has the proper political awareness. But most importantly, Gitlin's analysis of the ideological encoding in news production, raises questions of its consumption. While he wants to allow for an active audience, that activity is limited to the ability to disagree with the ways in which media have framed a particular event, or to respond to the textual framing in future activities. The frames are the meaning of the text, and they apparently determine the terms within which the audience can respond to the message, either in sympathy or in opposition. That frames themselves may take on different functions, or that audiences may respond to the messages according to an alternative reading of the encoded frames, does not enter into his argument.

Critical Theory

The work of the Frankfurt School has, for a number of reasons, been one of the most influential interpretations of marxism in communication studies. Critical theory sees cultural texts as an imposition of the categories of mass production onto the domain of consciousness, imagination and thought. That is, the text becomes a conduit through which practices of production determine practices of consumption. The text is critically evaluated in terms of the ways in which it demands to be consumed. Thus, once again, the relations between encoding and decoding, and between society and culture, are assumed to be simple reflexes or reflections.

This can be seen most clearly in Adorno's (1941) discussions of popular music. This critique, typical of the Frankfurt School, is enacted in ways that are qualitatively different from the analysis of "art." Adorno condemns mass or popular music as a standardized industrial product (commodity) which determines an infantilized (fetishized) mode of consumption. He acknowledges that, while the manufacturing, distribution and marketing of the music are industrialized, the production itself must retain some artisanal character, but this merely functions as a rationalization of the music's commodification; it provides the illusion of individuality and masks its standardization. This contrasts sharply with Adorno's modernist vision of art as a transcendental, autonomous activity which, by projecting utopian possibilities, opens up a space for social critique.[4]

Critical theory assumes: first, that there is an abstract process of the "colonization of consciousness" by economic, industrialized forms which defines the power of the media; second, that there are direct relations between socio-economic and socio-psychological processes; and third, that these can be read off the surface of the text, not as a particular signifying form but as an exemplar of an abstract category of cultural practices. By assuming that the text is a mere exemplar of a superstructural commodity, Adorno collapses the distinction between production and consumption, making the consumer's alienation the same as the laborer's. Thus, while he recognizes that the consumer is an active coproducer of the cultural text, his view of the text as nothing more than a commodity-form leads him to see this work as the production of the (economic) success of the text. That is, the consumer's work is the production of pure exchange value. The superstructure has not only been industrialized; it has collapsed into the forces of production. For critical theory, the cultural object is pure exchange value, with no use value whatsoever, except perhaps as an ideological mystification in the service of the already existing structures of power:

> To be sure exchange value exerts its power in a special way in the realm of cultural goods. For in the world of commodities this realm appears to be exempted from the power of exchange, to be in an immediate relationship with the goods, and it is this appearance, in turn, which alone gives cultural goods their exchange value. . . . The appearance of immediacy is as strong as the compulsion of exchange-value is inevitable. The social compact harmonises the contradiction. The appearance of immediacy takes possession of the mediated exchange-value itself. If the commodity in general combines exchange-value and use-value, then the pure use-value, whose illusion the cultural goods must preserve in completely capitalist society must be replaced by pure exchange-value, which, precisely in its capacity as exchange-value deceptively takes over the function of use-value. The specific fetish-character of music lies in this quid pro quo. The feelings which go to the exchange-value create the appearance of immediacy at the same time as the absence of a relation belies it. It has its basis in the abstract character of exchange-value. Every "psychological" aspect, every ersatz satisfaction, depends upon such social substitution. (Adorno, cited in Bradley, n.d., p. 28)

This results in a rather odd view of consumption and the consumer, as well as of signifying practices and processes of encoding. In the *Grundrisse* (1953/1973), Marx struggled with the problem of consumption, though unsuccessfully. He finally concluded that consumption involves the "gratification of needs" which exist in a sphere of individual appropriation. Adorno psychologizes this need, and reduces the object of that appropriation to exchange value (in which both text and consumer are alienated and reified). This forces Adorno to confront the ultimately undecidable question of whether this need is real and unsatisfied, or illusory and produced by capitalism.

However, critical theory need not take that particular turn. John Berger (1972) has provided a reading of the "language" of publicity. Following Benjamin (1955/1968), Berger argues that, in the age of mechanical reproduction, the meaning of such visual language is no longer *in* the representations themselves. Thus, while publicity is "about" social relations, the message is embodied in its consumption—in how it is used, who uses it and for what purposes. Publicity is a language which, in its very consumption, produces its message: it is both the "life" of capitalism (as the necessary condition of consumption) and the "dream" of capitalism (as the celebration of future possibilities over present realities). Publicity is a "way of seeing" which proposes the possibility of transformation by consumption, a transformation which is measured by the "happiness of being envied" rather than by the actual possession of commodities. Berger makes the assumption, constitutive of critical theory, that there is a correspondence between social use and meaning. The text embodies a way of seeing only insofar as its appropriation is already defined by the moment of production or encoding. However, consumption is neither psychologized nor explained simply in terms of exchange value.

Economism

The third classical approach to the interpretation of cultural texts is perhaps the most difficult to fit into the framework of the present discussion since its "interpretive practice" negates the practice of interpretation. It responds to neither the question of the politics of textuality nor to the problematic of cultural studies. Instead, it erases any textuality by treating the cultural text as (just another) commodity; it not only refuses to consider the relation of encoding and decoding, but denies the specificity of cultural practices. And hence, the question of the relationship between culture and society is replaced by questions of determination within the economic sphere.[5] There is, in a sense, no necessity for cultural interpretation to ever look at cultural texts.

Economism looks behind the messages to see the mode of economic forces and relations, the systems of production and distribution. Consumption is monolithically determined by production, and hence both cultural texts and decodings are epiphenomenal products of the "economic base." At its most extreme, economism proposes that a concern with specific textual and consumption practices is itself a mystification of the actual relations of power in which cultural commodities are implicated. However, such reductionism is not inherent in the practice of economism. On the contrary, it is obvious that economic and technological practices, not only determine cultural texts in part, but also insert them into already existing social relations of power. And there may be features of such texts, or moments in the history of particular cultural forms, which depend crucially on such factors.

Economism assumes a series of correspondences or identities between the cultural text, its status within the circuit of production and consumption, the economic relations embodied within that circuit and the social relations of power. Most frequently, it analyzes the economic structures of media industries (e.g., modes of production, patterns of ownership, systems of distribution). But such "political economy" does not, by itself, constitute "economism" as an interpretive practice. Economism is based on implicit responses to the two questions discussed above, which allow it to read such analyses as making significant statements about the social functions of cultural texts, without any further interpretive mediations. For example, as Shore (1983) demonstrates, the six so-called "major" record companies control an enormous share of the records produced and sold in the world. But as he recognizes, the issue is what this tells us about the music being produced, the constraints that the system imposes upon the concrete production of particular records, how the record is consumed, and what the relations are between this "economic" power and forms of ideological and political domination. On the other hand, Smythe's (1977) article, "Communications: Blindspot of Western Marxism," is certainly correct to argue that the product of the media, which they then sell for a profit, is the audience itself. Advertisers buy time only to obtain the real commodity—an audience. The interpretation, however, slides from the commodity status of the audience to claims about the media's concrete functions in structures of social power. To do so, it must equate the accumulation of capital (surplus value at the expense of labor) with the particular organization of political, ideological and moral power (Murdock, 1978). And it must negate the ability of the text, as a cultural practice, to enter into the equation in specific (e.g., ideological) and even contradictory ways.

In summary, classical approaches can take a number of different forms. All of them refuse the problematic of cultural studies by making culture at best a reflection or mechanical reproduction of the social. They are thus able, not only to erase the specificity of cultural practices (even when talking about ideology), but also, to refuse to raise the question of production and consumption in terms of encoding and decoding. By identifying the determining moment of social life with economic forces and relations, they establish a correspondence between production and power. The text is nothing more than an impediment which must be shattered if its real functions are to be constituted within this equation. The differences amongst classical positions depends largely upon the assumed status of the epiphenomenal text: as a distorting but representational mirror; as alienated consumption; as another form of capital accumulation.

THE HERMENEUTIC APPROACH

Within this approach, I want to describe a number of positions which give cultural or signifying practices a more active (ideological) role in the construction of power relations. Such positions assume that the relationship between cultural texts and social reality is always mediated by processes and structures of signification. Thus, texts reveal their social significance, not on the surface of images and representations, but rather, in the complex ways that they produce, transform and shape meaning-structures. Texts orchestrate social reality, producing a symphonic experience which is not reducible to the cumulative contributions of each social determination. A text is not a simple reflection of a social reality, even a distorted one, nor is it a reflex response to the material conditions of its production. Thus, the interpretation of a text requires an appreciation of the specific rules of its formal existence as a signifying practice.

Furthermore, according to such positions, it is not primarily the factual, material social structure itself that is reworked and reshaped by the cultural text. Rather, society itself is already mediated through signifying practices. The question of the relationship between culture and society is answered by appealing to the third term—experience—which already locates the social within the cultural. Thus, social power is always to be viewed through the mediating structures of social experience, defined and determined, in the last instance, by class position. The "raw material" represented in cultural texts is social experience, and only indirectly then, social structures of power and domination. The critic, using the resources of literary theory, must look at the complex ways in which the text codes, reworks, and potentially transforms the very fabric of lived experience.

The result is a practice which seeks to find homologies or correspondences between the workings of the text and the social structures of experience; relationships embedded within the concrete mediations performed by the text. They exist only at a deeper level of textual meaning. At the level of this deep structure, points of correspondence can be identified and meanings which comment upon and enter into the experienced social reality of consumers and producers can be uncovered.

Structural Mediation

Perhaps the most significant figure in the emergence of marxist cultural studies has been Raymond Williams. For Williams, the crucial mediation by which cultural text and social reality are linked is defined by the notion of the "structure of feeling" (Grossberg, 1977; Williams, 1961). This concept identifies a series of homologies between cultural texts as organizations of meaning, social reality as lived experience, and the "objective" structures of social organization and power. One can see the force of this concept in Williams' (1974) interpretation of television as a text, in which he seeks to uncover the common structure underlying television's existence within multiple social and cultural dimensions. As an economic-technological system, television was marketed as a privately owned commodity for the home, receiving messages from centralized transmitters outside the home, in the public world. There are, obviously, political and economic interests "behind" these historical production/marketing decisions. More importantly, this insertion of the technology according to a particular structuring of the world connects it to, and corresponds with, other dimensions of television's existence:

> The technical possibilities that were commonly used corresponded to this structure of feeling: the enclosed internal atmosphere; the local interpersonal conflict; the close-up on private feeling. Indeed these emphases could be seen as internal properties of the medium itself, when in fact they were a selection of some of its properties according to the dominant structure of feeling. (Williams, 1974, p. 56)

This dominant structure of feeling, which apparently emerged in the nineteenth century to organize the experience of modernization, is described as "mobile privatisation." For Williams, it organizes particular television texts, as well as other cultural texts, and provides the central images defining the "feel" of contemporary life: waiting inside the home for the outside world to be "transmitted" into one's private life. Moreover, Williams (1974) uncovers it as well as in the very social experience of television broadcasting, which he describes as *planned flow*: "This phenomenon, of planned flow, is then perhaps the defining characteristic of broadcasting, simultaneously as a technology and as a cultural form" (p. 86). And even this flow of programming, comprised of diverse cultural forms as well as advertising, previews, etc., can be itself read as embodying the same structure of feeling:

> The apparently disjointed 'sequence' of items is in effect guided by a remarkably consistent set of cultural relationships: a flow of consumable reports and products, in which the elements of speed, variety and miscellaneity can be seen as organising: the real bearers of value. (p. 105)
>
> Yet the flow of hurried items establishes a sense of the world: of surprising and miscellaneous events coming in, tumbling over each other, from all sides. (p. 116)
>
> This, essentially, is how a directed but apparently casual and miscellaneous flow operates, culturally, following a given structure of feeling. (p. 111)

The structure of feeling is produced and responded to at the level of experience. Even when Williams finds, within a particular structure of feeling the intentional roots of its production (in structures of class power), such intentions are neither conscious nor individual. That is, the structure of feeling—mobile privatisation—organizes the television text, its form, its technology and even its socio-economic institutions, not by some conscious design nor as a simple reflection of those class relations, but only through the mediating interventions of the production, within signification, of homologies between society and culture.

This explains, in part, the apparent slippage of production and consumption, encoding and decoding, in Williams' work. One cannot draw direct links between the structure of feeling and the conscious interests of the agents of production, nor can one assume that the structure of feeling defines the terms within which the texts of television are immediately consumed. Yet neither relationship can be denied. Certainly, the dominant structure of feeling has become dominant precisely insofar as it supports the interests (both political and economic) of the ruling classes. Similarly, the structure of feeling sets limits and exerts pressures on how the audience is able to interpret the television text. Yet it functions below the surface, mediating these moments. The dominant structure of feeling defines the experiential context within which both the production and the consumption of particular meanings are to be grounded.

Thus, Williams has collapsed the difference between encoding and decoding by simultaneously collapsing the social into the cultural. The relation between society and culture (a hermeneutics of suspicion) is accomplished through an anlaysis of the common textuality of both (a hermeneutics of faith). Society, now understood as the structure of social experience (which can be read off of the surface of class position) is part of the same dialectical processes as culture; both are symbolic productions of meaning. The two are interrelated and homologous processes. Their relation is defined at the point of their intersection—the structure of feeling. Their correspondence is guaranteed by the necessary relation between class position and social experience through which class can be defined simultaneously as a structure of feeling and, in the last instance, as a set of economic and political interests.

Let us consider more carefully Williams' solution to the question of the politics of textuality; that is, the relation between encoding and decoding. As the discussion of Adorno demonstrates, merely accepting an "active" audience does not necessarily guarantee that the issue is acknowledged. One can take that active audience to be producing the text according to the interests of the dominant class, interests preprogrammed into the text itself. The issue is linked directly to the possibility of "political" struggles over and within cultural processes. In Williams' work, when we find the existence of different structures of feeling (embodying and producing different class experiences/positions), the clash between them is distant and global, having little to do with the concrete text. The reason for this is clear: the struggle is not in and over the text, as an attempt to impose a structure of meaning from one class position onto another (Volosinov, 1973). Rather, since there are two competing cultures, the question is deferred into the process of mediating between alternative structures of feeling.

While Williams maintains the possibility of struggle in his analysis of television, the question of the source of that struggle and its relation to the texts is submerged within his description of the dominant structure of feeling embedded within the texts. This is not simply a submission to the pessimism so often characterizing classical positions. It is, rather, the point at which the totalization implicit in the "dominant structure of feeling" and its necessary correspondence to social position breaks down. For, if this simple correspondence is ruptured, as it clearly is in his actual practice (which recognizes the complexity of interests within the media), then Williams can only locate the source of resistance and struggle in some place outside of the already consti-tuted class relations: hence, the importance of residual and emergent forma-tions, each with its own structure of feeling. But such notions bring the question of decoding back to origins, forcing consumption to reproduce the model of production. Origins replaces effects, and the question of decoding is indefinitely deferred.

Mediation through Appropriation

This dilemma sets the agenda for the next position to be discussed. This position attempts to understand the ways in which the struggles between different social groups are enacted within the domain of culture, as a contra-diction between different meaningfully organized formations. The major rep-resentative of this position is the work of the Centre for Contemporary Cultural Studies, under the leadership of Stuart Hall (Hall, 1980a; Grossberg, 1983).

As the Centre attempted to move beyond Williams' assumption of a single correspondence between class position, experience, and culture, much of their work focused on the phenomenon of subcultures and subcultural styles (Hall & Jefferson, 1976). Style, in fact, provided a new mediating term between the social and the cultural. Rather than beginning with two separable realms, each embodying a common structure, this position locates the homology within the subcultural formation itself. Style is a representation of, and an imaginary solution to, the experienced contradictions within the everyday lives of the members of the subculture. Such experience is "overdetermined," so that it can no longer simply be read off the class position of the members. In fact, the experienced contradictions are often the result of the contradictions between various social registers of determination and identity. Furthermore, the "fit" between the pieces that are appropriated by the subculture and constructed into its style defines the homology. It includes, as a part of its very structure, the experienced contradictions as that to which the style responds by present-ing itself as a "magical" solution. Thus, the relationship between culture and society is not a structural homology but rather, the homology of question and answer, of an "imaginary" solution to experienced contradictions. The corre-spondence cannot be read off the text itself, even as a deep structure. It can only be uncovered by placing the text within the social experience of its producers and consumers. Thus, the question of textuality is partially shifted (but only partially) from origins to effects, only partially because the text is still inserted into a pregiven structure of experience. (I will forego giving an example of such subcultural analysis until the discussion of Hebdige below.)

By changing the grounds on which the relation between culture and society was understood, the Centre found itself directly confronting the question of the relationship between encoding and decoding. For if subcultures could appropriate cultural practices into their own constructed style, then one has to begin by acknowledging that cultural texts can be read and used in different ways. Drawing upon semiotics, Hall (1980b) argued that texts are polyvocal and that there is no necessary correspondence between language (the surface of the text) and signification. The question then becomes that of identifying the relations between the origins of alternative readings and the possibilities for struggling against the interests of the existing structures of domination. On the one hand, Hall argued, processes of cultural production encode particular meanings into the structure of the texts. Such "preferred meanings" attempt to represent experience in ways which support the interests of those already in power, both economically and politically. Such encoding is, however, often the product of, and could be read alternatively through, "negotiated codes" which constitute particular social and professional identities (such as the "routine practices" of newsmaking). Thus, one cannot assume that the intentions behind the production of news are simply those of the ruling class; the question is rather, how journalists, operating with professional codes seeking to produce objectively neutral reports, nevertheless consistently produce texts which encode the preferred meanings of the existing structures of power. Finally, the fact that texts encode certain preferred readings does not guarantee that they are read accordingly; that is, we cannot assume effects simply from origins. Rather, there are alternative and even oppositional codes, derived from their own subcultural formations, which allow audiences to decode texts in ways that are not only significantly different from, but even opposed to, the preferred readings.

However, because it remains within a hermeneutic approach which seeks correspondences between experience and textual meanings produced through particular decoding practices, this position ends up with an abyss which threatens to sunder the relation between culture and social structures of power. In one of the clearest applications of this theory, Brunsdon and Morley (1978) undertook a semiotic reading of the *Nationwide* television program. Their analysis focuses neither on a simple explication of meanings or images, nor on the uncovering of an underlying structure of the text. Instead, they are concerned with the codes which the text seems to offer for its own interpretation, revealed in such semiotic features as modes of address (which determine the status of actors and the formality or informality of the presentation), and the ways in which the text defines it own "ideological problematic." For example, they conclude that:

the 'persona' of the programme, then is a professionally formulated reconstruction based in and on 'popular speech' and its sedimented wisdom. The
use of this linguistic register is one of the ways in which *Nationwide* constructs
'ordinary people' as the subject of its particular kind of speech. This 'populist
ventriloquism' is a crucial strand in the way the programme attempts to forge
an 'identification' with its audience. (pp. 8–9)

Here we can clearly see the shift in interpretive interest, no longer focused on
the text as an isolated and autonomous cultural object, but as part of a specific
cultural-social formation in which strategies encoded into the text attempt to
define the ways audiences bring these texts to bear on their own social
experiences—according to the encoded, preferred reading.

In a second part of the study, Morley (1980) attempted to describe how
different groups within the audience of the program actually decoded the text.
He argues that it is through the mechanism of identification that the audience
is brought into the circuit of meaning of the preferred reading, but if these
identifications are ineffective or challenged, alternative decodings become
possible. Thus, "we must assume that there will be no necessary 'fit' or
transparency between the encoding and decoding ends of the communication
chain" (p. 11). "We need to see how the different subcultural structures and
formations within the audience, and the sharing of different cultural codes and
competencies amongst different groups and classes, 'determine' the decoding
of the message for different sections of the audience" (p. 15). Using Bourdieu's
(1980) idea of "cultural capital," Morley argues that how a text is decoded
depends upon the codes available to the interpreter. Codes function within the
domain of culture much as capital functions within the domain of economic
production; they allow for the generation of surplus meaning. But while capital
is defined only by its circulation through the circuit, Morley fixes cultural
capital within the individual, defined as the intersection of social identities or
experiences. That is, a particular experiential position within the social formation predetermines the availability of particular resources for decoding. Once
again, the interpreter is seen as appropriating the text into the already
constituted space of his or her cultural formation, understood as a structure of
experience. And, once again, the question of effects is postponed into that of
the origins of such resources.

Morley found, not surprisingly, very little relationship between the
"preferred meaning" encoded into the text, and the diversity of alternative
decodings made by the audience. He also found it impossible to specify the
cultural resources of a particular group as a function of their social experience.
In the end, the two studies together foregrounded the very real gap between
encoding and decoding, origin and effects, production and consumption. He
could find relations between the social and cultural within both the production
and the consumption of the text, but he could not bring the two sets of relations
into relation. While he begins by arguing that the "key question" is "exactly
what is the nature of the 'fit' between, say, class, socio-economic or educational

position and cultural/interpretive code" (p. 20), he concludes that "social position in no way directly correlates with decodings" (p. 137). His conclusion questions the very assumption of a distinction between the social and cultural, and he argues that experience itself must be located within the field of discourse: "This is to insist on the social production of meaning and the social location of subjectivity/ies—indeed it is to locate the production of subjectivity within specific discursive formations" (p. 157). But such a move would make the assumption of an homology between social experience and cultural meanings fortuitous. This apparent contradiction between the two issues originally described grounds the shift into "discursive approaches" to cultural interpretation (Morley, 1981; Coward 1977).

Mediation through Signifying Practices

If hermeneutic positions seek correspondence, homologies or fits between structures of signification and experience, the Centre's work attempted to reproduce this structure on top of the split between encoding and decoding. But they sought to describe both signification and experience at the level of meaning, or signifieds. There is another tradition in marxist thought, rooted in the work of Brecht, Benjamin and perhaps Bakhtin, which locates meaning within its specific cultural mode of production. Consequently, the relation between culture and society, and that between encoding and decoding, are reconceptualized as competing forms of signifying practices.

One example of this strategy is Hebdige's *Subculture: The Meaning of Style* (1979), which combines the hermeneutic subcultural theory of the Centre with certain ideas taken from a discursive approach. For Hebdige, style is not merely an alternative construction of meaning, but an alternative mode of production. It does not merely offer different "cultural capital" but challenges the very way in which the signifier and the signified, language and meaning/experience, are connected. Subcultural styles deny and disrupt "the deceptive innocence of appearances" (p. 19) on which dominant structures of meaning are built and maintained. This "naturalness" of the meaning of reality, of the world of experience, of the circuit connecting object and sign, is not only problematized but ultimately rejected by the practice of style. The social processes of production, reproduction and consumption, depending as they do on the processes by which objects are given meaning and transformed into signs, are contradicted by the very production of style as a signifying practice.

Hebdige fails to see the implication that style is the de-construction of the possibility of any representation of reality as natural, (i.e., of both ideology and experience). This would move style outside of an hermeneutic approach for one would no longer be comparing structures of meaning. The relation between culture and society, and the struggle between encoding and decoding would be located within the contradictions between competing modes of (symbolic) production. Hebdige, however, continues to see style as a representation of, and an imaginary solution to, experienced contradictions. Thus, following the Centre's model, the first half of the book is an ethnographic description of the experience of particular social groups. But in the second half—a description and elucidation of subcultural styles—it becomes clear that we can not seek structural homologies or cultural resources. One is, if you like, still comparing these two planes, but the relationship between them is only describable in terms of the reproduction of the same constitutive signifying practice within each.

Hebdige continues the Centre's hermeneutic position: "The succession of white subcultural forms can be read as a series of deep-structural adaptations which symbolically accommodate or expunge the black presence from the host community. . . . We can watch, played out on the loaded surface of British working class youth cultures, a phantom history of race relations since the War" (pp. 44–45). Hebdige argues that subcultural styles construct "forbidden identities" which reflect the experience of the group. This representational identity provides the appearance of a magical resolution, within experience, of the contradictions. But because this identity is the product of signifying practices, it is always open to reappropriation and is, at best, temporary.

When the analysis turns to modes of symbolic practice, it opens up wider and even more disparate readings. For example, on the one hand, punk involved an "open identification with Black British and West Indian Culture" which antagonized, not only the dominant culture, but other youth subcultures as well. On the other hand, "despite the strong affinity, the integrity of the two forms—punk and reggae—was scrupulously maintained, and . . . punk music, like every other aspect of punk style, tended to develop in direct antithesis to its apparent source" (pp. 67–68). Here we have an origin which is negated by the signifying practice of punk; it is this transformation of origins into effects which characterizes, above all, the punk style:

> punk style had made a decisive break not only with the parent culture but with its own *location in experience*. This break was both inscribed and re-enacted in the signifying practices embodied in punk style. The punk ensembles, for instance, did not so much magically resolve experienced contradictions as represent the experience of contradiction itself in the form of visual puns. (Hebdige, 1979, p. 121)

Punk style does not so much "fit" within and answer to experience as reproduce within itself the practice of contradiction, a practice which constitutes the signification of that experience. Punk style is the deconstruction of all meaning in a world in which meaning is already deconstructed.

Punk has become an emblem for Hebdige's argument that all style is "a semiotic guerilla warfare." But when he seeks the representation of experience in style, the emblem forces him beyond his own descriptions: "The safety pins and bin liners signified a relative material poverty which was either directly experienced or sympathetically assumed, and which in turn was made to stand for the spiritual paucity of everyday life" (p. 115). Accounting for a particular style, Hebidge moves from a particular contradiction to a general one, from a phantom history of race relations to a general history of the deconstruction of experience, of the collapse of the future, and with these, the end of all spiritual meaning. The 'homology' between culture and social experience is reconstituted by making the signifying practice of style "represent different signifying practices" (p. 120).

The issue has slid from what style signifies to the homology between the way in which it signifies and the very structure of experience within the class formation: as reality has lost its meaning (i.e., as social signifying practices have been altered, whether or not this is experienced as such), so the subculture constructs a style which is defined by its practice of intentionally collapsing all meaning. The collapse itself—the production of the very reality it represents—is not the issue. Rather, the focus is on the relation between the practice of style and the practice by which experience is dismantled within a subculture's reality. The correspondence, so to speak, is located in a common signifying practice, represented in both style and experience.

Mediation through Narrative

Before leaving the hermeneutic approach, I want to briefly discuss positions which use narrative structures as the basis for cultural interpretation. Such positions read the narrative structure of a cultural text as an attempt to represent or work out the contradictions of social life. There are many sources for contemporary narrative theory (Rimmon-Kenan, 1984), including Propp (1928/1968), Levi-Strauss (1958/1963), Barthes (1970/1974), Bakhtin (1981), Greimas (1966), Frye (1957), and Burke (1945), as well as theories of historical narrative. Furthermore, the different positions describe the narrative structure and its relation to the social world differently (e.g., mythic narratives; narrative structures which reconcile contradictions, psychoanalytic processes of identification through which the reader is carried through the narrative, and semiotic circuits of transformation).

Perhaps the most significant contemporary use of narrative theory within Marxist cultural interpretation can be found in the work of Fredric Jameson (1981). Although this is only part of his larger theory of interpretation, its centrality is evident in his description of his project as the attempt to "restructure the problematics of ideology, of the unconscious and of desire, of representation, of history, and of cultural production, around the all-informing process of narrative" (p. 13). In fact, the subtitle of his book, *The Political Unconscious: Narrative as a Socially Symbolic Act*, is somewhat misleading, for narrative is *the* social-symbolic act, the very structure and production of history, the mediation of reality and fantasy, and the nature of the "political unconscious." Jameson wants to rescue the possibility of a hermeneutic reading of history as narrative which would also rescue the utopian projects of culture and marxism.

Jameson has a unique, indeed postmodern, view of the relationship between culture and society. While he argues that the social has collapsed into the cultural, this is the product and sign of the "consumer society" and its associated modes of production:

> I will say that culture, far from being an occasional matter of the reading of a monthly good book or a trip to the drive-in, seems to me the very element of consumer society itself; no society has ever been saturated with signs and messages like this one . . . until the omnipresence of culture in this society is even dimly sensed, realistic conceptions of the nature and function of political praxis today can scarcely be framed. (1979a, p. 139)

By both accepting (as an historical fact) and refusing (as a theoretical position) this collapse, Jameson reconstitutes the hermeneutic correspondence between particular narrative structures, narrative (and culture) as a mode of production, and social modes of production (with their associated class contradictions).

The assumption of this series of homologies grounds Jameson's attempt to understand the utopian possibilities of history and the ideological functions of culture. According to Jameson (1981), while history is a real materiality never reducible to the symbolic, it is available to us only as texts. The real is always mediated to us through interpretive paradigms ("ideologemes"). Culture, then, involves an ongoing transformation of these received texts and defines the intertextual existence of history by constructing and transforming the narrative paradigms within which we have received history. History is constantly displaced into and created within the semiotics of narrativization; that is, the practice of organizing particular narratives.

This narrativizing process, however, does not dissolve the distinction between society and culture, base and superstructure. Rather, it allows Jameson, following Levi-Strauss, to reconstitute the relationship. Culture transforms and provides resolutions in the realm of the symbolic or ideological to more basic political and economic contradictions:

> This is why a book like *The Nether World*, . . . is best read, not for its documentary information on the conditions of Victorian slum life, but as testimony about the narrative paradigms that organize middleclass fantasies about those slums and about "solutions" that might resolve, manage, or repress the evident class anxieties aroused by the existence of an industrial working class and an urban lumpenproletariat. (p. 186)

The function of the political unconscious is to seek "by logical permutations and combinations to find a way out of its intolerable closure and to produce a 'solution,' through the semiotic transformation of the narrative" (1981, p. 167). This "intolerable closure" is the particular and often contradictory desires, determined by social position and class struggles, that are unavailable to us except through such symbolic mediations. The function of the narrative apparatus, then, is to rechart these libidinal investments at the site of competing and multiple modes of production, in order to open up the multiplicity of generic narratives-both ideological and utopian—within the text.

The ideological function represses the contradictions, as well as the real possibility of their resolution, by the projection of an imaginary solution, for example, by the symbolic construction of a semiotic position within the logical possibilities of the "combinatoire" of characters (see Jameson's (1979c) reading of the fascism of Wyndham Lewis' narratives). On the other hand, the utopian function of such narratives is to offer the symbolic possibility of a real (i.e., utopian) transformation of history through compensatory structures.

Consequently, we must "grasp mass culture not as empty distraction or 'mere' false consciousness, but rather as a transformational work on social and political anxieties and fantasies which must then have some effective presence in the mass cultural text in order subsequently to be 'managed' or repressed" (1979a, p. 141). Unlike Adorno, Jameson argues that "the works of mass culture cannot be ideological without at one and the same time being implicitly or explicitly utopian" (1979a, p. 144). We can see this method at work, briefly, in Jameson's readings of contemporary popular films. For example, concerning *Jaws*, he writes:

> We are thus authorized to read the death of Quint in the film as the two fold symbolic destruction of an older America—the America of small business and individual private enterprise of a now outmoded kind, but also the America of the New Deal and the crusade against Nazism, the older America of the depression and the war and the heyday of classical liberalism.
>
> Now the content of the partnership between Hooper and Brody projected by the film may be specified socially and politically, as the allegory of an alliance between the forces of law-and-order and the new technocracy of the multinational corporations: an alliance which must be cemented, not merely by its fantasized triumph over the ill-defined menace of the shark itself, but above all by the indispensable precondition of the effacement of that more traditional image of an older America which must be eliminated from the historical consciousness and social memory before the new power system takes place. This operation may continue to be read in terms of mythic archetypes, if one likes, but then in that case it is a Utopian and ritual vision. (1981, pp. 143–144)

Similarly, concerning *The Godfather*, Jameson argues that its ideological function is to displace the problem of the "deterioration of daily life" from the economic to the ethical realm. On the other hand, its utopian impulse lies in its projection of the family as the fantasy of a resolution, a fantasy because it is located in the terms of an alien (non-American) other. That such solutions are the product of narrative acts is made even clearer in Jameson's reading of *Dog Day Afternoon*, in which it is the construction of a crucial narrative place—that of the FBI agent—which provides the resolution, within which "the whole allegorical structure of *Dog Day Afternoon* suddenly emerges in the light of the day" (1979b, p. 88).

We have now returned to the dilemma which Williams' hermeneutic reduction of the social to the cultural made obvious: the reading of a particular text assumes that the positions of producers and consumers vis à vis the text are identical within the common intertextual space of culture. This dilemma suggests that marxist interpretive theory must rethink the question of the relationship between culture, society and experience.

THE DISCURSIVE APPROACH

Within this category of interpretive practices, I want to describe a number of positions which refuse the hermeneutic binarism of text and experience while even more radically sliding the social into the cultural. Within such positions, textuality is a productive practice whose (imaginary) product is experience itself. Experience can no longer serve as a mediation between the cultural and the social since it is not merely within the cultural but is the product of cultural practices. As Hall (1980c) suggests, this move can be traced to Althusser's (1970/1971) interpretation of ideology as the unconscious system of representation of the imaginary relationship between people and their real conditions of existence. That is, the way in which we experience our relationship to the world is precisely that which ideological signifying practices manufacture. Ideology works as a practice, not merely by producing a system of meanings which purport to represent the world but rather, by producing its own system of meanings as the real, natural (i.e., experienced) one. Thus, the issue of ideology is not merely the conflict between competing systems of meaning but rather, the power of a particular system to represent its own representations as a direct reflection of the real, to produce its own meanings as experience. It is a question of signifying practice and representation rather than signification alone.

Experience can no longer be seen as something pregiven, outside of particular cultural or textual practices. It is already inherently implicated with structures of power. Power is no longer outside of culture (in the social) but within the very structures of signifying practices themselves. This radical negation of the binarism of culture and society implies as well a reconceptualization of the gap between encoding and decoding. For the subject, whether producer or consumer, cannot be defined by resources or experience existing outside of the network of cultural practices. Neither the production nor the consumption of particular texts can be approached as if the already socially constituted subject comes to the text, from somewhere outside of the intertextual cultural environment. The issue is reconceptualized in terms of competing forms of signifying practices, or the different ways in which the text locates the subject within its construction of experience. Thus, it is the cultural practices themselves which define identities for their producers and consumers by inserting them into the fabric of their discursive spaces. It is this power of the text to locate the subject by producing its intertextual domain of experience that becomes the object of critical interpretation. It cannot be read off the surface of the text as a system of meaning, nor is it to be found by a hermeneutic excavation of some deeper structure of signifieds. It is rather to be found in the ways in which the text produces meaning through its practices of structuring signifiers around the subject. The issue is not so much the particular knowledge of reality (true or false, mystified or utopian) which is made available, but the way in which the individual is given access to that knowledge and consequently, empowered or de-powered. Rather than seeking a series of mediations or correspondences, discursive positions seek the processes of encoding and decoding as a series of discontinuities and ruptures which are woven together, by signifying practices, around the sites of social identity and subjective power.

Positioning the Subject

Althusser, drawing upon the structural psychoanalysis of Lacan (1966/1977), argued that ideology works by producing or positioning the subject within its circuit. Lacan argued, more generally, that language (signification) is made possible only by a "splitting" of the subject. One accedes to language and enters into the cultural only by representing oneself in language (I) but this entails the repression of the speaking subject as the absent source (the unconscious). The subject within language is, then, already a position within a system of cultural power. Althusser identifies the specificity of ideological practices precisely by the specific point at which the subject is inserted into signification, a point from which the apparent givenness of experience cannot be problematized. Ideological practices locate the individual language user within language as its absent source who is therefore responsible for the meanings produced, the transcendental agent of experience. The individual as a subject becomes complicitous with his or her own insertion into the ideological production of an imaginary but lived reality. Ideology accomplishes its task, on such a view, by having already defined the phenomenological relationship of subject and object, and thus, the possibilities of power and knowledge.

This position is most clearly and influentially exhibited in the work of *Screen*, a British film journal, in the seventies (Heath, 1981). Their analyses of films focused on the ways in which the camera functions to produce a particular series of identifications for the viewer. For example, they argued that in the classic Hollywood cinema, one is positioned by the cameras as if one were seeing the scene of the film from an omniscient position outside of the scene of action itself. That identification with the camera slides into the particular characters within the film, through the way in which the camera relates to the positions of the characters themselves (as agents of knowledge). Consequently, the viewer is "stitched" or "sutured" into the text. Furthermore, the camera of the Hollywood film identifies with the male protagonists and renders the

female the object of the voyeuristic sight/site of the camera, the male characters, and the spectator. Alternatively, the avant-garde cinema often places the
camera within the mise-en-scene, imposing a reflexively limited point of view
on the spectator, and dispersing the viewing subject into a multiplicity of
positions, no longer claiming a privileged point of entry into or existence
within the text, and thus, declaring no single access to its truth.

The implications of this position, thus far, are apparently not that
different from those of the classical positions (Allor, 1984). If the subject is
totally the product of the encounter with the filmic texts, which create a
monolithic identification with the camera, then the audience is once again
merely the object of a (now textual) manipulative practice. The simplest
solution is, of course, to allow for a multiplicity of contradictory subject
positions and their different accessibilities to different audiences. A text may
in fact embody different textual practices and thus, produce fractured subjectivities. But more importantly, the consumer of the text is already a subject;
he or she has a history of textual or ideological existence. Thus, rather than
speaking of experiences, codes or resources that the individual brings to the
text, we can talk about the intertextuality of the practice of consumption itself,
a discursive history in which both the text and the subject have already been
determined and through which they are reinserted into that process of determination. As some feminist film critics (Kuhn, 1982) have argued, many
Hollywood films can not totally render the female into the passive object of
the camera's male gaze. Rather, there are points in the text itself in which the
female cannot be coded within the dominant signifying practices and consequently ruptures, or threatens to rupture, the text. There are then alternative
and resistant readings already coded into the text, insofar as the text always
exists only within the larger intertextual context of encoding and decoding.

While this position seems to ignore the question of encoding, it is actually
raised as the constitution of the terms of decoding. That is, such readings must
identify the particular relations of power that are coded by the production of
particular subject positions. The dominant practices of the Hollywood
"cinematic apparatus" produce subject positions which are identified with the
preexisting categories of domination: capitalist, male, white, etc. This assumed
correspondence allows those practices which differ to be comfortably identified
with the opposition or dominated other (e.g., socialist, female, etc.).

Of course, such identifications are not as serendipitous as they may appear.
Obviously, one might appeal to the marxist maxim that, at the very least, the
dominant culture will attempt to reproduce the dominant relations of power.
There are, however, other dimensions to the practice of such positions, which
ground its ideological readings, and which are already implicit in its semiotic
and psychoanalytic foundations. The former depends upon the film's production of signifiers in particular ways which leave "structured absences" within
its narrative or surface textuality. By locating particular characters and events
within a connotational chain, the film must attempt to hide the particular
moments which it is unable to code according to its own ideology.

A more powerful critical tool of such practices is based upon a psychoanalytic narrative theory which focuses on the ability of cultural practices to "stitch" the consumer into the structure of signifiers itself. For example, by using our identification with the position of the camera and its own narrative structure, the film can displace that identification, making it slide through a series of identifications within the narrative practices of the representation. We not only identify with the camera, but with the narrator and even further, as a result, we enter into the narrative itself by virtue of the narrator's own identifications within the text. Thus, we are not only positioned within the circuit of signifier and signified (whether as a unified or fragmented subject), but in the narrative movement of the signifiers themselves. This use of narrative theory constructs the film's power, not only in terms of its subject positions, but also in terms of how it uses such identificatory processes to code and render acceptable the contradictions and movements of resistance that threaten to disrupt the ideology of the particular textual system of power.

Articulating the Subject

The question of the positions which ideology creates for the individual as a subject does not, however, exhaust the concerns of marxist criticism, nor is it the only use which has been made of Althusser's critique of experience. Recent work has returned to the relationship between signifying practices and social reality, without appealing to the humanistic assumption of a pregiven social experience. It focuses on the construction of social positions or identities, and the "articulation" of particular practices and meanings as belonging to these identities.

This position has been defended in the more recent work of Stuart Hall (1983; forthcoming), as well as by a number of Marxist feminists such as Angela McRobbie (1982). Arguing that experience is the product of complex processes of overdetermination, Hall transposes the question of cultural criticism from the search for necessary correspondences (whether direct or mediated) between culture and society, to the analysis of the specific ways in which different practices, meanings and identities are "articulated" together. The critic can no longer assume that there is a necessary relationship between a text and a particular meaning, or between a practice and its representation in signification, or between a particular social position and a structure of experience. But there are always relations or correspondences *produced* between practices, texts and identities. The problematic of cultural studies is transformed, concerned with how a particular practice—signifying or social—is located in a network of other practices, at a particular point, in particular relations.

This reconceptualization of the relation between culture and society is accomplished by rejecting the gap between encoding and decoding. The question of power is transposed from origins to concrete effects. If the ideological significance of a cultural text cannot be read off of the text itself, the task of the analyst is to examine how the particular text or practice has been "inflected" or inserted into its context in such a way as to have identifiable ideological consequences.

While acknowledging the existence of the real (e.g., as the nonsignifying social practice), Hall argues that the effects of such practices are always articulated within the cultural regime of signification. The critic cannot escape ideology, and so must always talk about the politics of the representations of the social. Cultural criticism becomes the study of the connotational codes within which a particular term (such as nation or democracy) or a particular point of social identity (such as black, female, or adolescent) are located. We examine the specific ideological inflections or effects that, while not inherent in the texts, are produced for the text by its insertion within a set of connotational codes, its articulation to other signs.

Althusser argues, in essence, that the question of ideology is how particular significations appear as the natural representations of reality, so that individuals accede and consent to their explicit organizations of reality and their implicit structures of power and domination. Rejecting a psychoanalytic theory of subject-positioning, Hall (1980d) turns to Gramsci's (1971) theory of hegemony. Hegemony is the ongoing process by which a particular social block (made up of various class fractions) maintains its position of power by mobilizing public support for its social projects in a broad spectrum of social life. Hegemony is a question of leadership rather than explicit domination and control, containment rather than incorporation. It involves the colonization of popular consciousness or common sense through the articulation of specific social practices and positions within ideological codes or chains of connotational significance.

The fact that hegemony must operate on a broad terrain of social and cultural life means, for Hall, that the politics of its articulations cannot be assigned to preconsituated structures or categories of power. One cannot explain particular ideological moments by reducing them to a single contradiction within the real. Rather, such effects are determined by a multiplicity of power relations which can only be identified within the particular context of the articulation. Thus, Hall argues that the contradictions of race and gender are at least as fundamental as, and certainly irreducible to, the economic contradictions (whether in terms of class—capital versus labor, or of modes of production—forces versus relations of production) that have preoccupied marxists. These three planes on which power is organized may have different relations to each other at different points within the struggle for hegemony.

Angela McRobbie's (1982) study of the ideology of adolescent feminity within a mass circulation magazine, *Jackie, is* one of the best examples of this approach:

> It will be argued here that the way *Jackie* addresses 'girls' as a monolithic grouping, as do all other women's magazines, serves to obscure differences, of class for example between women. Instead it asserts a sameness, a kind of

> *false* sisterhood, which assumes a common definition of womanhood or
> girlhood. Moreover by isolating out a particular 'phrase' or age as the focus
> of interest, one which coincides roughly with that of its readers, the magazine
> is in fact creating this 'age-ness' as an ideological construction. 'Adolescence'
> and here, female adolescence, is itself an ideological 'moment' whose conno-
> tations are immediately identifiable with those 'topics' included in *Jackie*.
> And so, by at once defining its readership vis à vis age, and by describing
> what is of relevance to this age group, *Jackie* and women's magazines in
> general create a 'false totality.' (p. 265)

The appearance of this totality allows the significations of *Jackie* to function
ideologically, to appear as representations of the real. It allows no space for
alternative constructions of identity around adolescence and feminity. The
ideological significance of any text within the magazine can only be understood
in terms of its inflection by its existence within the larger cultural and social
context of the magazine and adolescent feminine culture, that is, in terms of
the project of constructing a "false totality" around the particular identity.

A second example is provided by Hall, Critcher, Jefferson, Clarke &
Roberts (1978) *Policing the Crisis: Mugging, the State, and Law and Order*, which
examines the ideological articulation of the crime of mugging within a larger
crisis of the social formation, defined by issues of both race relations and "law
and order." By looking at the complex intertextuality within which mugging
was given an ideological significance, the authors attempt to describe the ways
in which this particular construction participated in the production of a
hegemonic formation.

Perhaps most radically, and unlike the other positions I have discussed,
this position locates, within its own analysis of the relationship between
culture and social power, the possibility of, and the sites for resistance. For,
corresponding to the struggle for hegemony, the struggle against it must
involve the struggle to disarticulate the ideological inflections which are
produced on a broad number of issues and social identities.

Thus, rather than being concerned with the production of subjectivities
within texts, a discursive theory of articulation examines the ways in which
particular sites of social identity are articulated (and hence, the experiences to
be associated with them produced) in an intertextual context of ideology. In
the end, the question of encoding and decoding becomes, if not irrelevant, a
misleading way of framing relations of cultural power. Rather, the question is
the existence of particular inflections of social identities and practices within
the articulating cultural environment, and the gaps within this network which
allow for struggle and resistance. While previously discussed positions must,
at best, find it difficult to find an optimistic place for the broad range of
actively struggling social groups, within this position it is precisely the actions
of such groups that articulate particular messages with particular meanings or
inflections, into particular connotative networks. But this decoding process,
if we are to continue referring to it in this way (since it includes resistance to,

and the reproduction of, existing structures of domination) is not the product of already available cultural capital, preconstituted social identities or domains of experience which necessarily correspond to positions of power or powerlessness. Both encoding and decoding are only artificial moments within the struggle for and resistance to hegemony, defined by the particular context of the text itself. Nevertheless, because it locates social reality or power within culture, this position continues to see power in terms that escape signification and the differences it constitutes (e.g., in various social and economic positions of domination).

Power and the Materiality of Culture

This final position is best represented in the work of Michel Foucault, and reverses the premise of a discursive approach, by collapsing culture into the social (Grossberg, 1982). Nevertheless, given the primarily methodological interest of this inquiry, Foucault's position bears important similarities to the two discursive positions previously described. Like these, Foucault refuses to begin with either experience as an innocent measure of social reality, or with an appeal to a transcendental, autonous subject (i.e., the determiner of its own determinations, unified and transparent to its own self-reflection). But unlike other discourse positions, Foucault refuses to assume any absolute distinction between culture (the signifying) and society (the nonsignifying locus of a power which is represented in and maintained through signification). Finally, Foucault refuses to define questions of culture and power around the central issue of subjectivity or identity as the primary sites or vehicles for the production of power-effects.[6]

This position attempts to describe the contextual articulations of discursive and nondiscursive events together. Like the previous one, it is concerned with the particular network of effects and rejects the assumption that any event has inherent within it its own meanings or effects or even, political implications. But Foucault is not willing to limit the category of effects to the production of connotational webs or codes of meaning (i.e., ideology). Rather, the very fact of a text's existence at a particular social site—its materiality—is the occasion for multiple planes of effects beyond the ideological. Hence, power can neither be located entirely within this plane, nor entirely outside of it (as if merely the reproduction of external relations of power upon the organization of meaning).

Rejecting the separation of culture and society, Foucault (1979) locates any event in a multiplicity of interacting planes or regimes of power within the social formation. We can see this demand for specificity in Foucault's own use of "event":

> It is not a question of putting everything on a certain plane, that of the event, but of seeing clearly that there exists a whole series of levels of different types of events, which do not have the same range, nor the same chronological

breadth, nor the same capacity to produce effects. The problem is to both distinguish the events, differentiate the networks and levels to which they belong, and to reconstitute the threads which connect them and make them give rise to one another. (p. 33)

The materiality of events points to the ways in which we live and act, ways over which we have no control and about which we are unaware. This is not simply the ideologically constructed plane of experience, for experience itself (phenomenologically understood) is merely another set of events or facts, to be included within the analysis of the network of effects.

The identity of an event is only given in its contextual specification; it is fractured and dispersed into the multiplicity of its effects. These effects define the "conditions of possibility," operating in either direction, of the particular practice. In a sense, Foucault (1978a) carries the theory of overdetermination to its logical conclusion, and this has important methodological consequences for cultural criticism. If any event is articulated at a particular point in a network of effects, whether its existence is primarily determined by its production of meaning-effects is an empirical question. That is, a text may be more than, or other than its meaningfulness, depending on whether its most powerful effects are mediated by processes of signification:

I do not question the discourses for their silent meanings but on the fact and the conditions of their manifest appearance: not on the contents which they may conceal, but on the transformations which they may have effectuated; not on the meaning which is maintained in them like a perpetual origin, but on the field where they co-exist, remain and disappear. It is a question of the analysis of the discourses in their exterior dimensions. From whence arise three consequences:

1. Treat past discourses not as a theme for a commentary which would revive it, but as a monument to be described in its character-disposition.

2. Seek in the discourse not its laws of construction . . . but its conditions of existence,

3. Refer the discourse . . . not to the subject which might have given rise to it, but to the practical field in which it is deployed. (p. 15)

Of course, once we have allowed that our concern is with the multiplicity of effects which may both exceed and absent the meaningful, then the issue of encoding and decoding is itself called into question. For Foucault, this dilemma embodies marxism's inability to confront the reality of power as the very microstructure of effects or relations. The dilemma, by recreating the duality of culture and society, always locates power as something outside of an event, something brought into it (intentions or interests) or something taken away from it (hegemonic consent). Power is, instead, the intricacies of the particular network in which events make possible other events; it is a "capillary action," organizing and extending the possibilities of its own existence. Thus, power is always located in "apparatuses" which are built upon "technologies," programmings of behavior (Foucault, 1981). An apparatus not only emerges at a particular site, it is also located within or excluded from "regimes of jurisdiction and veridication" (p. 8). The former prescribes what can be done: procedures and strategies; the latter justifies these ways by producing particular discourses as "true."

If Foucault refuses to locate power outside of the apparatus itself, he also refuses to center or hierarchize it. He rejects notions of ideology, hegemony, the State, or capitalism, as if these could explain the materiality of power. For example, in his consideration of the Gulag (1979, p. 51), he refuses any category which reduces its specific structuring of power: For example, treating it as a structure of meaning to be read off texts; or as a single effect, perhaps with multiple causes; or as a specific instance of a repeated historical phenomenon; or as the negation in practice of its explicit ideology. Foucault, in fact, refuses any reductionism; human life itself is not merely labor, nor the production of meaning: "The life and time of man are not by nature labour, but pleasure, restlessness, merry-making, rest, needs, accidents, desires, violent acts, robberies, etc." (1979, p. 62). Life is both chance and determinations, both power and pleasure. It is the complex interweaving of power, knowledge and desire that defines the politics of an event.

The analytic task (Foucault, 1972/1980) is to provide a "genealogy" of specific practices and apparatuses, mapping out the conditions of possibility into which they emerged, and out of which they elaborated new (and even unintended) effects. And the political task is similarly transformed; no longer seeking to identify the conspiracy or structure of power behind the surfaces of everyday life, Foucault seeks instead to locate those voices and practices which have been excluded by the contemporary technologies of power, and to struggle to open a space within which their resistance can be heard. It is then the already existing history and context of struggle which needs to be organized, not as the attempt to develop alternative or counter-hegemonic strategies but as the ongoing struggle against all moments of power and domination.

My own work on rock and roll (Grossberg, 1983/84; 1984) attempts to use this position to analyze rock and roll as a set of apparatuses within which a variety of events are empowered as sites of pleasure for youth cultures. These are, simultaneously, both the condition of possibility of rock and roll and yet, deconstructed by the very technologies it organizes. We can see another example of this position in the recent work of Hebdige who has, in a series of articles (1981a, 1981b; 1983a, 1983b), sought to describe the complex "effectivities" of particular cultural texts: the motorscooter, pop art, and the products and discourses through which "America" was constructed as in "imaginary" category within the British social formation. To consider one example in more detail, Hebdige has begun a "genealogy" of youth in England, pointing to the complex and productive relations between a range of discourses, social institutions and technologies of surveillance: "The vectors of power I want to trace cut across a number of heterogeneous sites—discursive categories, institutions and the spaces between institutions. Those sites are youth, sexuality, fashion, subculture, display, and its corollary, surveillance" (1983a, p. 71). He draws three conclusions. First, youth only exists when it is posed as a problem and consequently, the power of youth is precisely, through a variety of practices, to pose a threat. Second, the resistance or "insubordination" of youth can only be understood as a "micropolitics of pleasure" which exceeds the current boundaries of "legitimate" political practice. And third, the politics of youth is enacted on the material surface, at the interface between surveillance and the evasion or transformation of surveillance into pleasure (i.e., as style). Although Hebdige attempts to return this politics of style to the space of the sign, it is clear that it exceeds the question of signification and representation. It is the production of youth as difference, in the gaps between the signs, in the leaks within hegemony, in the contradictions within institutions, and in the heart of the capillary existence of power. Further, if we accept Foucault's (1976/1978b) argument that the contemporary technologies of power articulate a "biopolitics" in which the body of the population—the very materiality of human existence—becomes the object for new strategies of control, then Hebdige seems to be suggesting that the construction, emergence and elaboration of "youth" is both a product of and a resistance to this apparatus.

CONCLUSION

In conclusion, I will attempt to provide a useful schematic summary of the ten positions described above, emphasizing their methodologies of cultural interpretation. I have tried to point to the necessity for a more reflective consideration of the theoretical, methodological and political assumptions which organize the ways in which we interpret cultural texts:

Classical approaches: culture reflects society; decoding is unproblematic.

1. False consciousness: the text is a distorting mirror which acts directly upon its audience.

2. Critical theory: the text imposes forms of consumption which reflect their industrialized modes of production.

3. Economism: the text is erased in favor of the forces and relations of its production.

Hermeneutic approaches: culture represents society; decoding is problematic.

4. Mediation through structure: the relation between the text and social experience is defined by a common "structure" or organization of meaning which links the encoded interests and the decoded interpretations.

5. Mediation through appropriation: the relation between the text and social experience is defined by the former's ability to be "fit" into the codes which structure interests (encoding) and experience (decoding); the absence of any necessary relation between the two sets of codes results in a gap between encoding and decoding such that the homology between text and social experience must be examined at each end of the circuit of the communication.

6. Mediation through signifying practices: the relation between the text and social experience is defined by the cultural mode of production of the former which is a response to the structures of the latter. Encoding and decoding are differentiable as embodying different forms of response.

7. Mediation through narrative: the relation between text and social experience is defined by the narrative structure of the former which provides, in its own narrative trajectory, possibilities for the resolution of experienced and unconscious social conflicts. Both encoding and decoding, albeit not necessarily equivalent, are constructed within the narrative through processes of identification.

Discursive approaches: culture produces not only the structures of experience but experience itself, which functions within social structures of domination; the question of encoding is one of the dominant forms of decoding.

8. Positioning the subject: the text creates a space within the experience it produces into which it inserts the reader as the subject or source of that experience, and thus, of its claim to be true knowledge of reality. The possibility of different decodings points to the existence of different positions which may be taken up within the text.

9. Articulating the subject: the text is inserted into a network of other texts which define the particular ways in which it produces the meaningfulness or experience of particular social identities. Decoding is precisely this intertextual articulation understood as a struggle over the power to constitute experience.

10. Materializing power: the effects of the text are defined by its existence at a particular place within a network of other practices which it both enables and is enabled by. Neither the subject nor the terms in which power is organized exist outside of this fabric of material effects.

My own biases are, I am sure, painfully obvious in the summary, if only by the trajectory of the presentation. Nevertheless, I want to emphasize that I think that all of these positions have made, and will continue to make, important contributions to our understanding of communications in the contemporary world. The point is not so much to choose between them, although one inevitably must do so, but to define new forms of alliance and cooperation amongst them.[7]

Acknowledgments: The author expresses appreciation to Martin Allor, James W. Carey, Stuart Hall, Jennifer Daryl Slack and Ellen Wartella for their comments on earlier drafts of this essay.

NOTES

1. I use the term "function" broadly to encompass any theory of the relationship between discourse and practice. Thus, it includes theories of meaning, effects and functions (understood in a narrower, 'functionalist' sense).

2. These positions have developed in response to historical conditions and events, as well as through theoretical arguments. The positions or strategies presented here could be described in different frameworks, although the results would be, to differing degrees, not entirely equivalent. For example, Ellen Wartella has suggested that the distinction between classical, hermeneutic and discursive approaches can be seen in terms of the problem of the audience. Classical approaches tend to ignore the audience or assume that it is passive; hermeneutic approaches assume an active audience; and discursive approaches attempt to insert the audience into the very structures of cultural textuality. Similarly, Martin Allor has suggested that the three approaches can be distinguished on the basis of their differing views of determination: as a simple causal process, as a process of defining constraints and exerting pressures, or as "overdetermination" (see Slack, 1984). I could have also chosen to make the distinctions on the basis of competing theories of ideology.

3. Of course, in the last analysis, a text must be evaluated in the different contexts within which it functions. Thus, one must acknowledge that Dorfman and Mattelart's work has an important place, not only in the development of a Marxist interpretation of popular culture, but also within the concrete political struggles of the Latin American left against the power of the United States. And despite what I take to be its methodological weaknesses, the analysis is still an insightful critique of Disney's texts.

4. The problems with Adorno's critique are obvious. Adorno, like other modernists, sees art as a transcendental, autonomous activity capable of utopian criticism. His definition of art, however, is derived from a particular historical moment which is then generalized into a universal measure. Thus, the "standardization" of popular music is defined by comparison to the harmonic and structural complexity of the "canon." He ignores other normative measures—such as rhythmic complexity, timbre, texture, etc.—which may give different aesthetic conclusions. Further, he ignores the conventionality of all cultural forms—based in the specificity of signifying practices—which would make the question of individuality and creativity a problematic matter of degree and local judgment.

5. I am not concerned here with the historical and theoretical adequacy of the economic theory that such positions use to describe specific media contexts. Obviously, such considerations should form an important part of the ongoing development and elaboration of the various "economisms."

6. One other comparison may be useful. While post-structuralist theories such as *Screen*'s tend to deny the very possibility of correspondences ("necessarily no correspondence") and Hall's denies both the classical assumption of a "necessary correspondence" and the post-structuralist position (arguing for "no necessary correspondence or non-correspondence"—a "Marxism without guarantees"), Foucault makes the question an empirical one in each instance. Thus, there may be events which are, for all practical purposes, inserted into necessary correspondences. For example, a practice already embedded within an apparatus may be articulated in already defined ways. Note that there are significant methodolog-

ical similarities between Foucault and the work of "Annales" school of history (Braudel, 1978/1981).

7. Such alliances, motivated and shaped by the political contexts of both the discipline of communications research and the present State-formation, would require a critique of the various political practices that have become associated with the interpretive strategies presented here. For such alliances must avoid reproducing, at either the structural or practical level, the very forms of power they seek to challenge.

REFERENCES

Adorno, T. (1941). On popular music. *Studies in Philosophy and Social Science, 9*, 17–48.

Allor, M. (1984). *Cinema, culture and the social formation: Ideology and critical practice.* Unpublished doctoral dissertation, University of Illinois, Urbana.

Althusser, L. (1971). Ideology and ideological state apparatuses. In (B. Brewster, Trans.), *Lenin and philosophy and other essays* (pp. 127–186). New York: Monthly Review Press. (Original work published 1970)

Bakhtin, M. (1981). *The dialogic imagination.* (C. Emerson and M. Holquist, Trans.). Austin: University of Texas Press.

Barthes, R. (1974). S/Z: *An essay.* (R. Miller, Trans.). New York: Hill and Wang. (Original work published 1970)

Benjamin, W. (1968). *Illuminations* (H. Zohn, Trans.) (H. Arendt, Ed.). New York: Schocken Books. (Original work published 1955)

Berger, J. (1972). *Ways of seeing.* London: BBC and Penguin.

Bourdieu, P. (1980). The aristocracy of culture. *Media, Culture and Society, 2*, 225–254.

Bradley, D. (n.d.). *The cultural study of music.* Stencilled occasional paper. Birmingham, England, Centre for Contemporary Cultural Studies.

Braudel, F. (1981). *The structures of everyday life: Vol 1. The limits of the possible* (S. Reynolds, Trans.). New York: Harper & Row. (Original work published 1978)

Brunsdon, C., & Morley, D. (1978). *Everyday television: 'Nationwide.'* London: British Film Institute.

Burke, K. (1945). *A grammar of motives.* Englewood Cliffs, NJ: Prentice-Hall.

Coward, R. (1977). Class, 'culture' and the social formation. *Screen, 18*, 75–105.

Dorfman, A., & Mattelart, A. (1975). *How to read Donald Duck: Imperialist ideology in the Disney comic* (D. Kunzle, Trans.). New York: International General. (Original work published 1971)

Gerbner, G. (Ed.). (1983). Ferment in the field. *Journal of Communication, 33*(3).

Foucault, M. (1978a). Politics and the study of discourse. *Ideology and Consciousness, 4*, 7–26.

Foucault, M. (1978b). *The history of sexuality: An introduction* (R. Hurley, Trans.). New York: Pantheon Books. (Original work published 1976)

Foucault, M. (1979). *Power, truth, strategy* (M. Morris and P. Patton, Eds.). Syndey, Australia: Feral Publications.

Foucault, M. (1980). "Two Lectures." In C. Gordon (Ed.). *Power/knowledge: Selected interviews and other writings 1972/1977* (pp. 78–108). New York: Pantheon Books. (Original work published 1972)

Foucault, M. (1981). Questions of method: An interview. *Ideology and Consciousness, 8*, 3–14.

Frye, N. (1957). *Anatomy of criticism*. New York: Atheneum.

Gitlin, T. (1980). *The whole world is watching: Mass media in the making and unmaking of the New Left*. Berkeley: University of California Press.

Gramsci, A. (1971). *Selections from the prison notebooks*. London: Lawrence and Wishart.

Greimas, A. J. (1966). *Semantique structurale*. Paris: Larousse.

Grossberg, L. (1977). Cultural interpretation and mass communication. *Communication Research, 4*, 339–354.

Grossberg, L. (1982). Experience, signification and reality: The boundaries of cultural semiotics. *Semiotica, 41*, 73–106.

Grossberg, L. (1983). Cultural studies revisited and revised. In M. Mander (Ed.), *Communications in Transition* (pp. 39–70). New York: Praeger.

Grossberg, L. (1983/84). The politics of youth culture: Some observation on rock and roll in American culture. *Social Text, 8*, 104–126.

Grossberg, L. (1984). Another boring day in paradise: Rock and roll and the empowerment of everyday life. *Popular Music, 4*, 225–257.

Hall, S. (1980a). Cultural studies and the Centre: Some problematics and problems. In S. Hall, D. Hobson, A. Lowe, & P. Willis (Eds.), *Culture, Media, Language* (pp. 15–47). London: Hutchinson.

Hall, S. (1980b). Encoding/decoding. In S. Hall, D. Hobson, A. Lowe, & P. Willis (Eds.), *Culture, Media, Language* (pp. 128–138). London: Hutchinson.

Hall, S. (1980c). Cultural studies: Two paradigms. *Media, Culture and Society, 2*, 57–72.

Hall, S. (1980d). Popular-democratic vs. authoritarian populism: Two ways of 'taking democracy seriously.' In A. Hunt (Ed.), *Marxism and democracy* (pp. 157–185). London: Lawrence and Wishart.

Hall, S. (1983). The problem of ideology-Marxism without guarantees. In B. Matthews (Ed.), *Marx 100 years on* (pp. 57–86). London: Lawrence and Wishart.

Hall, S. (forthcoming). With J. Slack., & L. Grossberg. *Cultural Studies.*

Hall, S., & Jefferson, T. (Eds.). (1976). *Resistance through rituals*. London: Hutchinson.

Hall, S., Critcher, C., Jefferson, T., Clarke, J., & Roberts, B. (1978). *Policing the crisis: Mugging, the state, and law and order*. London: Macmillan.

Heath, S. (1981). *Questions of cinema*. Bloomington: Indiana University Press.

Hebdige, D. (1979). *Subculture: The meaning of style*. London: Methuen.

Hebdige, D. (1981a). Towards a cartography of taste 1935–1962. *Block, (4)*, 39–56.

Hebdige, D. (1981b). Object as image: The Italian scooter cycle. *Block, (5)*, 44–64.

Hebdige, D. (1983a). Posing . . . threats, striking . . . poses: Youth, surveillance, and display. *Substance, 37/38*, 68–88.

Hebdige, D. (1983b). In poor taste. *Block, (8)*, 54–68.

Jameson, F. (1979a). Reification and utopia in mass culture. *Social Text, 1*, 130–148.

Jameson, F. (1979b). Class and allegory in contemporary mass culture: "Dog day afternoon" as a political film. *Screen Education, 30*, 75–92.

Jameson, F. (1979c). *Fables of aggression: Wyndham Lewis, the modernist as fascist*. Berkeley: University of California Press.

Jameson, F. (1981). *The political unconscious: Narrative as a socially symbolic act*. Ithaca, NY: Cornell University Press.

Kuhn, A. (1982). *Women's pictures: Feminism and cinema*. Boston: Routledge and Kegan Paul.

Lacan, J. (1977). *Ecrits: A selection* (A. Sheridan, Trans.). New York: W.W. Norton. (Original work published 1966)

Levi-Strauss, C. (1963). *Structural anthropology* (C. Jacobson and B. G. Schoepf, Trans.). New York: Basic Books. (Original work published 1958)

Marx, K. (1973). *Grundrisse* (M. Nicholaus, Trans.). New York: Vintage Books. (Original work published 1953)

McRobbie, A. (1982). Jackie: An ideology of adolescent femininity. In B. Waites, T. Bennett, & G. Martin (Eds.), *Popular culture: Past and present* (pp. 263–283). London: Croom Helm.

Morley, D. (1980). *The 'Nationwide' audience: Structure and decoding.* London: British Film Institute.

Morley, D. (1981). The 'Nationwide' audience—a critical postscript. *Screen Education, 39,* 3–14.

Murdock, G. (1978). Blindspots about western Marxism: A reply to Dallas Smythe. *Canadian Journal of Political and Social Theory, 2,* 109–119.

Propp, V. (1968). *The morphology of the folk tale* (L. Scott, Trans.). Austin: University of Texas Press. (Original work published 1928)

Ricoeur, P. (1970). *Freud and philosophy: An essay on interpretation* (D. Savage, Trans.). New Haven, CT: Yale University Press. (Original work published 1965)

Rimmon-Kenan, S. (1984). *Narrative fiction: Contemporary Poetics.* London: Methuen.

Shore, L. (1983). *The crossroads of business and music: The music industry in the United States and internationally.* Unpublished manuscript.

Slack, J. D. (1984). *Communication technologies & society: Conceptions of causality for the politics of technological intervention.* Norwood, NJ: Ablex.

Smythe, D. (1977). Communications: Blindspot of western Marxism. *Canadian Journal of Political and Social Theory, 1,* 1–27.

Volosinov, V. N. (1973). *Marxism and the philosophy of language.* New York: Seminar Press.

Williams, R. (1958). *Culture and society 1780/1950.* London: Chatto and Windus.

Williams, R. (1961). *The long revolution.* London: Chatto and Windus.

Williams, R. (1973). Base and superstructure in Marxist cultural theory. *New Left Review, 82,* 3–16.

Williams, R. (1974). *Television: Technology and cultural form.* London: Fontana.

II | THE APPLICATION OF CRITICAL APPROACHES

8

For Whom the Bell Tolls: Causes and Consequences of the AT&T Divestiture

ROBERT BRITT HORWITZ

The third major attempt this century to break up the American Telephone and Telegraph Company succeeded in 1982. In a settlement directed by Federal District Court Judge Harold Greene, AT&T and the Justice Department came to an agreement which spins off the local telephone operating companies from AT&T and allows a slimmer AT&T to enter competitive telecommunications and information markets (*United States v. American Telephone and Telegraph Company*, 1982). The 22 former Bell Operating Companies have become seven separate and independent regional regulated telephone monopolies. AT&T remains a vertically integrated company consisting of Long Lines, Western Electric, and Bell Labs (some of which have been given new names), but is no longer in the business of providing basic local switched telephone service. Instead, the company continues to provide long distance telephone and special common carriage service, and to manufacture and sell telecommunications equipment.[1] And, significantly, AT&T now may enter into both US domestic and international competitive markets. With the important exception of services for the national defense, AT&T had been confined to the provision of domestic regulated telecommunications services since 1956.

The principal aim of this essay is to examine the causes of the AT&T divestiture. A settlement of such dramatic and potentially longlasting significance does not come out of the blue. As it is argued, even trumpeted, constantly, the American telephone system is the finest in the world—and this distinction has been achieved in an environment of regulated monopoly. Why, then, change telephony's basic structure? The essay will demonstrate that the traditional structure of American telephony constituted a precarious balance between the benefits and drawbacks of regulated monopoly. So long as the technology and uses of telephony were relatively simple, regulators and policy makers ("assisted" by AT&T's massive lobbying power) found the benefit side of monopoly to outweigh its problems. The advent of digital technology and the rise in large corporate telecommunications use forced the disintegration of the older framework of monopoly common carriage in the public interest. But divestiture is a complex historical event, a mosaic of intertwined technological, economic, legal, and political determinations. This essay reconstructs this mosaic in a history of the regulation of AT&T and the transformation of telecommunications into information technology.[2] It also begins to explore some of the consequences of the breakup, looking at divestiture's ramifications on the US domestic telecommunications industry. The divestiture of AT&T, though it resolves many regulatory and economic contradictions, serves to undermine many of the traditional principles of American telecommunications policy. Though divestiture and deregulation are not necessarily the same political phenomenon, divestiture is being used to expand the program of the deregulation of telecommunications.

INTRODUCTION: THE MULTIPLE, INTERRELATED CAUSES OF DIVESTITURE

Many reasons have been advanced in the effort to explain the breakup of the American Telephone and Telegraph Company—the largest divestiture in the American industrial history. Indeed, there may be several versions of "conventional wisdom." Among economists, a standard explanation is that divestiture was motivated by the economic need to free AT&T to respond to challenges from unregulated domestic competitors. Freedom for AT&T would have the added advantage of spurring innovation in telecommunications. Many in the legal community attributed divestiture to clear and convincing evidence that AT&T had violated the antitrust laws. As the Justice Department's (1982) case against AT&T made plain, the corporation had illegally cross-subsidized its unregulated services by the guaranteed profits of its regulated services, and used this illegal cross-subsidy to practice predatory pricing in competitive markets. Students of international political economy attributed divestiture to the shared desire of the U.S. government and AT&T to free the corporation to compete in international markets in the increasingly important area of information technology. Because telecommunications is a key—perhaps *the* key growth area for industrial capitalist economies for the near future—policymakers considered the freeing of AT&T for international markets to be of paramount importance.[3] The general public was treated to technologically based explanations, that the advent of the "information age" had destroyed the line between the telephone and the computer.

Each of these reasons has its merits. That is to say, each of these reasons correctly captures a genuine dynamic which constituted a factor in divestiture. The problem is that alone, each argument is oddly decontextualized, and is insufficient to explain divestiture. In fact, each argument requires reference to all the others to make sense of the divestiture. It is the premise of this essay that there is one major contradiction which organizes or canalizes the above-listed issues and contradictions into an interrelated set of causes. The roots of the AT&T divestiture lie in the antitrust and regulatory contradictions generated by the regulated monopoly structure in telecommunications, and the business and associated technological developments which bring the rationality of that structure into question. It is the particular *regulatory* history of AT&T which can be said to "overdetermine" the breakup.

Telecommunications policy-making has been centered largely in the Federal Communications Commission since 1934. For reasons to be examined shortly, the regulatory arrangement had been one in which the perception of the public interest in telecommunications was tied to the health of the Bell System. AT&T provided end-to-end telephone service (and other carriage services) as a regulated monopoly. The FCC oversaw a system which obliged that AT&T provide service to all, and which presumably enforced internal subsidies for certain types of service. Regulation guaranteed the corporation a fair rate of return on its investment. Until the mid 1960s, policymaking in common carrier telecommunications was a stable, largely "private" matter of the FCC accommodating the complex needs of AT&T. Inasmuch as telephone rates declined and service expanded and improved over that 30-year period, the FCC's mode of regulatory oversight was commonly thought to be in the public interest.

But certain antitrust matters, concerning the nature of the Bell System as a vertically integrated regulated monopoly, continually called into question the rationality of the regulatory arrangement. Whereas the provision of telephone service was thought to constitute a "natural" monopoly, the monopoly manufacture of telephone equipment was questioned. Accusations surfaced as early as the mid 1930s that AT&T used its Western Electric manufacturing arm to inflate its overall rate base. In a separate development of great consequence, the FCC initiated a series of regulatory decisions beginning in the mid and late 1950s which served to open special parts of the Bell monopoly's operating environment to competition. These regulatory decisions were in response to the specific demands of the community of large users of telecommunications services and the vendors which served those users (Schiller, 1982). These small entry "liberalizations" encouraged the emergence of new technologies and new players into telecommunications common carriage, notably in "private lines" and "terminal equipment." Over the years, these new players would push continuously at the borders of the Bell System with new technologies and new services.

Such regulatory developments had two inadvertent and serious ramifications. First, they raised serious issues of public policy regarding the appropriate boundary between regulated and unregulated activities. And second, they placed AT&T's rate structure in potential jeopardy. Because both antitrust and competition issues derive from the structure of the Bell System and its legally constructed operating boundaries, the 1956 Consent Decree (which permitted AT&T to remain a vertically integrated monopoly but restricted its business to the provision of telecommunications common carriage only) is centrally important.

These antitrust and liberalized entry matters became inexorably intertwined in the late 1970s. Faced with new competitive players and unclear regulatory boundaries, AT&T found its external operating environment and its policy arena, both for decades remarkably stable and certain, becoming increasingly unstable and uncertain. By 1976, partly at AT&T's urging, the policy-making arena opened to include Congress in an attempt to rewrite the 1934 Communications Act. Soon, however, all branches of government were engaged in efforts to formulate new national telecommunications policy—a process likened by AT&T's Chairman Charles L. Brown to "nothing less than a three-ring circus" (Brown, 1983, p. 6).

An antitrust suit was filed in 1974 on the basis of AT&T's alleged anti-competitive and predatory pricing actions. What began as a complex antitrust case inadvertently became by 1981 a *closed* policy forum within which various economic and political concerns could be *joined*. In the context of Reagan Administration Justice Department negotiations, the need to solve pressing contradictions in domestic telecommunications common carriage could be reconciled with AT&T's desire to be freed of regulatory barriers, with national security considerations, and finally, with the growing concern to protect American global interest in information technology.

The nature of the bargain struck between AT&T and the Justice Department reflects these considerations. The settlement resolves many technological and business contradictions, yet essentially leaves the vertically integrated nature of the corporation alone. It is the least expensive option for AT&T and for a Reagan Administration at once hostile to antitrust and solicitous of US expanded investment in information technology. AT&T's corporate initiatives following divestiture confirm its rapid movement into the international arena and in information technology generally.[4] The settlement also changes the nature of telecommunications in the United States.

The telephone was a communications device which Congress thought necessary to extend to all citizens. The social good (or "public interest") embodied in national communication was embodied in the Communications Act of 1934, and regulated monopoly secured universal and relatively cheap telephone service. In contrast, the divestiture sets up a dynamic of competition in expanded or "enhanced" telephony; its goal is economic efficiency. Competition seems to advance rapid expansion and innovative service, whereas monopoly secured relatively cheap (if unsophisticated) service to all. Large telecommunications users will be served by competition-generated new technologies and services. (This has the added consequence of lowering domestic business costs generally—a result looked upon with favor by the government.) On the other hand, the traditional recipient of "universal service" likely will suffer from poorer telephone service and higher rates.

Thus, a major consequence of divestiture is to structurally reorient telecommunications policy away from equity in favor of "theoretical" economic efficiency. "Theoretical," because the efficiencies which competition will undoubtedly bring to telecommunications will not necessarily assure the kind of *system-wide* improvement guaranteed by the old monopoly arrangement. Further, divestiture serves to undermine the traditional regulatory rationale of separation of "content from conduit," or, put differently, the message from its transmission. The common ownership of information and the means of transmitting it raises First Amendment concerns. Finally, the added thrust that the AT&T divestiture gives to the deregulation movement augurs the collapse of the common carrier principle in telecommunications.

To make sense of the divestiture of AT&T, then, it is necessary to follow the two interrelated, but separate histories of antitrust and regulation. These histories underscore the changes in technology and the changing pattern of telecommunications use. The antitrust and regulatory problems induce a transformation of policy-making from a closed FCC arena, to the open arena of Congress, finally to the closed arena of the Justice Department.

EARLY HISTORY AND BASIC POLICY PRINCIPLES

The early history of American telephony was characterized by alternating periods of monopoly and competition. Its patent position permitted the Bell Telephone Company to integrate vertically and monopolize telephony from 1876 to 1894. With the expiration of Bell's two basic patents a spate of independent telephone companies sprouted, and the second phase of telephone history was characterized by direct intra-industry competition. Expansion of service during this period (1894–1913) was prodigious. Bell reacted to competition with various strategies, including the refusal to interconnect other telephone companies into Bell local or long distance lines. The strategy which proved successful for Bell was an aggressive campaign to buy out many independent systems (FCC, 1938; Gabel, 1969).

Bell's actions against independents prompted the Wilson Administration to propose antitrust action against the company. This threat led to the "Kingsbury Commitment" of 1913, wherein AT&T agreed to dispose of its holdings in Western Union (which it had acquired in 1910) and refrain from acquiring any directly competing independent telephone companies. Bell was permitted to purchase only noncompeting independents. Most important, AT&T agreed to allow independents to interconnect into the Bell system (Brooks, 1975; Loeb, 1978). With the blessings of AT&T and state regulators, a period of consolidation ensued and direct competition was discouraged. The 1921 Willis-Graham Act expanded the scope of the Kingsbury Commitment, and established the presumption that telephony constituted a natural monopoly. That Act permitted AT&T to purchase competing independent telephone companies, under approval of the Interstate Commerce Commission. In exchange, the Justice Department exempted AT&T from antitrust prosecution. This had the effect of stabilizing the telephone industry by permitting AT&T to consolidate control over it.

Those early regulatory parameters recapitulated the philosophy of AT&T President Theodore Vail; that telephony constituted a natural monopoly. "One policy, one system, and universal service," was Vail's slogan (Vail cited in Pool,

1983, p. 22). Two general arguments were advanced to support the natural monopoly contention. The economic argument claimed that competing telephone systems squandered resources and duplicated services, and that the value of telephone service increased with the number of subscribers. The technical argument asserted that a single entity could best provide technically integrated, end-to-end service. Vail envisioned government regulation, if enlightened and uncorrupt, as a beneficial and stabilizing force for telephony. Vail's vision was certainly different from most of the corporate leaders of his day. But AT&T changed its attitude toward government regulation only after the elimination of competition from independent telephone companies was nearly a *fait accompli*. Moreover, Bell support for regulation had the effect of politically disarming whatever calls for nationalization existed at the time.

Though it seems on its face that non-interconnected, competing telephone service imposes burdens (duplication of plant, subscribers requiring more than one telephone) which support the contention that telephony is a natural monopoly, the period of 1894 to 1913 indicates that competition brought certain benefits. The competitive era was chaotic and many of the independents provided poor and unreliable service. Nonetheless, it was the competition from the independents which forced Bell to vastly expand its services and which extended service to more people in general. Competition also functioned to bring down the price of telephone service and to spur technical innovation (Bornholz & Evans, 1983; Trebing, 1969). The question whether or not telephony is a natural monopoly resurfaces in contemporary debates. The issue—competition vs (regulated) monopoly—is not simply an economic one, but also a political policy issue. Again, competition seems to advance rapid expansion and innovative service, whereas regulated monopoly seems to advance relatively cheap service to all.

The Communications Act of 1934 provided for centralized regulation of a telephone industry which by then was more or less monopolized by AT&T. The FCC was empowered to control entry into and exit from the industry, to require and to set just and reasonable rates, to ensure nondiscriminatory access, and to mandate interconnection between carriers. The FCC (formally restricted to the regulation of radio and *interstate* wire communications only) and state regulatory agencies (whose jurisdiction extended to *intrastate* wire communications) fashioned a cooperative system of telephone oversight. In general, regulation granted local monopoly franchises and secured the stabilization of business risk. This was accomplished through a guaranteed fair rate of return and a policy of long-term capitalization. To determine the rate of return, the FCC must assess the net value of used and useful property and plant—known as the rate base. The fair rate of return was calculated to permit the carrier to accrue revenues sufficient to cover all reasonable operating expenses, the cost of acquiring capital, depreciation expenses, *and* give a "fair" profit on its investments (e.g., in the 1970s, the ostensible rate of return fluctuated between 8 and 11%). In return, regulation was able to "extract" from AT&T the public service obligation of service to all, or, "universal service."

Universal service means that telephone service should be available to, and affordable by, everyone. The policy was stated in general terms in section one of the Communications Act (1934).

> . . . to make available, so far as possible, to all the people of the United States a rapid, efficient, Nation-wide, and world-wide wire and radio communications service with adequate facilities at reasonable charges . . .

Long amortization of plant and equipment was inherent in the principle of universal service. Because telephony was characterized by large capital investment in a comparatively simple technology, a long amortization schedule would have the effect of spreading service as broadly as possible and of keeping operating costs down. Universal service also served the sociopolitical goal of increasing the utility of the network, since the utility of the network increased exponentially as more subscribers were hooked in.

This regulatory scheme seemed to presuppose monopoly, for universal service could be accomplished only through a complex amalgam of value-of-service pricing and general rate averaging. Value-of-service pricing takes advantage of different demand curves in order to expand the telephone network. Users willing to pay more for a given service are charged more, even though it may actually cost more to provide service to those least willing to pay. This has meant that urban residents pay more than rural subscribers for telephone services, and businesses pay more than residential subscribers. Rate averaging is the policy of charging equally for interstate calls of the same distance, regardless as to whether there were different actual costs due to different routing (Oettinger & Berman, 1977).

In addition, utilizing procedures known as "separations," the FCC and the state public utilities commissions divided assets and costs between the interstate and intrastate jurisdictions. "Settlements" was the term for similar averaging procedures worked out between AT&T and independent telephone systems. This regulatory action could enforce an internal cross-subsidy which shifted costs indirectly to business users and directly to long distance in order to support local (and especially rural) telephone service. Simply put, separations and settlements constituted procedures by which AT&T paid local telephone operating companies for handling the local-exchange ends of long distance traffic. This was a clear social policy since the decision in *Smith v. Illinois Bell Telephone Co.* (1930). These policies had the effect of bringing unified control to the national network, even though that network was owned by many different entities.

The *Smith* decision established the legality of separations procedures, though the subsidy of local telephone rates by long distance did not amount to much until the 1950s and 1960s, when developments in microwave transmission and direct distance dialing resulted in cheaper long distance costs. Administratively, cost-averaging was infinitely simpler than determining the fairest way to allocate the *joint costs* between urban local, rural local, intra- and interstate long distance services. These services share much of the same equipment and plant, but in proportions which are exceedingly difficult to determine. Some costs are calculable on the basis of the type and amount of telephone traffic. However, with respect to large portions of shared equipment, costs simply are not calculable. This portion of the equipment is referred to as "nontraffic-sensitive" costs, that is, those costs which do not vary with the extent to which the facilities are used. The basic cost of installing and maintaining a local loop remains the same whether it is used for one call or hundreds, or whether those calls are local or long distance.

The amalgamation of services, costs, and charges was and is so complex that any attempt to set rates is fundamentally *arbitrary* (Oettinger & Berman, 1977; Sichter, 1977). Thus the rate-setting process historically has been a process half acknowledged as one of *political* accommodation between telephone providers, various regulatory bodies, and (more recently) consumers. The process is only partially acknowledged as political because all the players must rely on the statistics and analyses provided by AT&T before they deal.

Notwithstanding the intent of the cost-averaging and separations policies, universal service cannot be attributed wholly to these procedures. The post-World War II economic boom and the explicit government subsidies provided through the Rural Telephone Bank and Rural Electrification Administration were of equal importance (Cornell, Kelley, & Greenhalgh, 1980). But given this general regulatory arrangement, the protection, indeed, the definition of the public interest in telephony became equated with the successful operation of the Bell System (Trebing, 1969; Breyer, 1982, chap. 15).

The Question of "Subsidy"

It is generally accepted that local telephone rates have been subsidized by long distance. But there has never been a comprehensive study which establishes the amount of the cross-subsidy. According to one AT&T source, local service (intrastate) accounts for 92% of usage of the common facilities. Long distance (interstate) accounts for 8%. Under 1982 FCC rules the share of joint costs allocated to interstate long distance was over 26% (*National Association of Regulatory Utility Commissioners [NARUC] v. Federal Communications Commission*, 1983). This amounted to a subsidy of approximately $7 billion to local telephone companies. But for the very reasons that the joint uses and costs were difficult to calculate at the time of the *Smith* decision, some AT&T critics have questioned the figures provided on the cross-subsidy.

Several arguments have been raised which undermine the subsidy claim. One involves the pricing of "private line" services. A private line consists basically of an open line between two fixed points, and is used primarily by corporations to interconnect distant offices, by news wire services to newspapers, or by television networks to transmit signals to distant affiliate stations.

The FCC historically did not require users of private line services to contribute, as ordinary long distance callers do, to local plant costs allocated to the interstate jurisdiction (*NARUC v. FCC*, 1983). Now, it is only efficient to purchase AT&T private line facilities if one uses the facilities a great deal. Consequently, the purchasers of private lines historically have been large corporations. Thus the largest users of the telephone system were exempted from contributing toward the support of the local telephone plant. To the extent that private line users utilize local exchanges, these users and these services have benefited from a subsidy.

Another argument which calls into question the existence and amount of the traditionally alleged subsidy harkens back to the first antitrust investigation of AT&T. The Bell Operating Companies (BOCs) bought equipment and services from AT&T, at prices which may have been inflated. At the very least, it seems likely that the BOCs purchased more equipment and services than was cost effective. This follows the Averch-Johnson-Welliscz hypothesis that the firm under rate of return regulatory constraint will tend to invest more capital than necessary as a means of increasing its rate base (Averch & Johnson, 1962; Cornell, Pelcovits, & Brenner, 1983). The overbuilding or "goldplating" of local plant would constitute a capital flow back to AT&T (through equipment purchases) as well as increase the overall rate base.

These claims, of course, are not settled issues. But even if the BOCs' capital investments cannot be characterized as overbuilding, such investments usually were legitimized as being necessary to meet "peak demand." Yet peak demand generally meant the upgrading of local plant to accommodate the local exchange needs of long distance and business users during the business day. The added costs of such investment would be charged to the local operating company, though the principal beneficiaries were long distance and business users. Lastly, it is claimed that other subsidies flow to AT&T from the local companies. The "license contract fee" was a percentage of local telephone operating company revenues paid to the AT&T central organization in exchange for services provided to the BOCs. The amount of this percentage basically was arbitrarily determined by AT&T, and long had been the subject of regulatory disputes (FCC, 1938).

"Subsidy," then, must be seen as part of the politics of representation. Another way of looking at the subsidy is that without the local connections, there could be no long distance. The above arguments highlight the fact that it is not the numbers and statistics *per se* which are subject to dispute in matters of telephone costs and prices, but rather the fundamental assumptions upon which the numbers are based. Again, the purpose of this excursus is not to claim that the traditionally construed subsidy does not exist. Rather, the point is that given the absence of any definitive studies on the subject, the entire area is highly problematic. In light of the above arguments, the subsidy claim (and matters of telephone costs generally) might be seen as a sort of shell game that AT&T has played with regulators.

ANTITRUST PROBLEMS AND THE 1956 CONSENT DECREE

Some of the basic issues that underlie the previous discussion of the "subsidy" first surfaced in a 1935 FCC investigation of AT&T. Known as the Walker Report, the investigation found that Western Electric prices for telephone equipment to AT&T and the Bell operating companies were unreasonably high. The report claimed that Western Electric overcharges cost telephone subscribers approximately $51 million per year. The result of these pricing practices was to create an internal subsidy which functioned to inflate the rate base from which telephone rates were derived. Part of the explanation of Western Electric's pricing had to do with an inadequate cost accounting system, but most of the problem rested in the fact that telephone equipment simply was not a natural monopoly. Without competition or *direct* regulation (the FCC could regulate Western Electric only indirectly and inadequately, by the reduction of AT&T's rate base), Western's prices could be entirely arbitrary. But because of the complex interrelation between the maintenance of the telephone system and the *integrated* nature of the Bell System, the Report's suggestion to enact competitive bidding on purchases of telephone equipment was dropped in the FCC final report (Brooks, 1975; Danielian, 1939).

This issue, however, would not go away. It was resurrected in January, 1949, when the Justice Department filed suit against Western Electric and AT&T for violations of the Sherman Act in the manufacture and sale of telephone equipment and supplies. State public utilities commissions had complained to the Justice Department that they were unable to determine the reasonableness of Western Electric's charges. AT&T's control of the market for telephone equipment, together with Western Electric's position as exclusive supplier for the system, in the words of Attorney General Tom Clark, "permits these two concerns to control both plant investments and operating expenses, factors upon which the federal and state regulatory authorities must fix rates to be charged subscribers for local and long distance telephone calls" (Zerner, 1949, p. 1). The suit also alleged that AT&T's monopoly of basic patents in the area of wire telephony had led to the suppression of improvements. The Justice Department recommended that Western Electric be split into three companies, require that AT&T and the Bell Operating Companies buy telephone equipment only under competitive bidding, and require that Western Electric and AT&T license their patents to all applicants on a nondiscriminatory and reasonable royalty basis (Goulden, 1968).[5]

The 1956 Consent Decree

The 1956 Consent Decree settled the antitrust suit, but it did not truly address the monopoly issue. The settlement placed most of its emphasis on patents, owing largely to AT&T's hold on the patent of the newly discovered transistor. The settlement formalized an already existing policy to allow any applicant the use of some 8,600 existing AT&T patents, without having to pay royalties to AT&T. The rationale for this was based in part on the recognition that AT&T research and development were publicly subsidized. In a bow to AT&T, however, companies which applied to use AT&T patents had to share their own patents with AT&T (Lewis, 1956). The Consent Decree constituted a combination of minimal AT&T concessions and the construction of new regulatory barriers. It called for Western Electric to institute uniform cost accounting procedures and enjoined Western Electric from paying any patent royalties to AT&T (which could inflate the rate base). Most significant for the future, AT&T agreed not to engage in any activities external to those of a regulated communications common carrier (except, importantly, for military work). In exchange, the Consent Decree legally sanctified AT&T as a vertically integrated monopoly (*United States v. Western Electric Co.*, 1956; George, 1969).

The Consent Decree later was discovered to be marred by improprieties. According to a 1958 report of the House Judiciary Committee, Eisenhower's Attorney General, Herbert Brownell, improperly suggested to AT&T's general counsel that the company examine its operations and tell the Justice Department what practices might be enjoined without subjecting the corporation to any real injury (Shanahan, 1974; Solomon, 1978). The House Report stated, "Upon all the evidence adduced in the committee's investigation, the consent decree entered in the AT&T case stands revealed devoid of merit and ineffective as an instrument to accomplish the purpose of the antitrust laws" (cited in U.S. Senate, 1982a, p. 1). In addition, there is ample evidence that the Defense Department and Atomic Energy Commission exercised influence to maintain the integrated nature of AT&T. The following quotation from a July 10, 1953 letter from the Secretary of Defense, C. E. Wilson, to the Attorney General reveals the intense pressure to dismiss the suit:

> The Department of Defense wishes to express its serious concern regarding the further prosecution of the antitrust case now pending against Western Electric Co. and AT&T Co. in which it is asked that Western Electric be completely severed from the Bell System. . . . The pending antitrust case seriously threatens the continuation of the important work which the Bell System is now carrying forward in the interests of national defense. This is for the reason that the severance of Western Electric from the system would effectively disintegrate the coordinated organization which is fundamental to the successful carrying forward of these critical defense projects, and it appears could virtually destroy its usefulness for the future. This result would, in the judgment of this Department, be contrary to the vital interests of the Nation. . . . That work [electronics and atomic energy] is still underway on an expanded scale and new responsibilities in these and other critical areas have been assumed by the Bell System organization. It is now clear that no terminal date can be placed upon the special usefulness of that organization. Its importance to the national defense will increase as the race for supremacy in the application of advancing technology to military uses continues, as we

must assume that it will for the indefinite future. For these reasons, it is now evident that a mere postponement of the prosecution of this case does not adequately protect the vital interests involved. It is therefore respectfully urged that the Department of Justice review this situation with a view of making suggestions as to how this potential hazard to national security can be removed or alleviated. (U.S. House, 1958b, pp. 2026–2027)

Many letters attesting to the crucial integrated nature of the Bell System are extant in the Celler Committee files. These reflected the role of the Bell System as virtually a "quasi-state apparatus" with regard to its relations with the Defense Department. After all, in 1949 Bell was asked to manage and operate the Defense Department's high-tech weapons installation known as Sandia Laboratory. Western Electric's original five-year contract was renewed in 1954, in 1959, and throughout the 1960s. In 1950 the US Army chose Western Electric as prime contractor for the Nike Ajax guided aircraft missile; in 1954 AT&T became a key player in the vast project to extend the Distant Early Warning air defense radar system (Brooks, 1975; Fagen, 1978).

Not all the testimony rested on the importance of AT&T as a prime defense contractor. AT&T consistently claimed that the integrated nature of the Bell System served to keep costs *down*. Certain evidence convinced some Justice Department attorneys that divestiture might increase the cost of telephone communications equipment. It is likely this evidence was part of the general web of improprieties surrounding the case (Goulden, 1968; B. Strassburg, personal communication, March 24, 1985). Nonetheless, according to the account of one commentator, some of the attorneys believed that the government would lose if the case went to trial. Once Justice dropped its insistence on divestiture, a settlement could ensue (Madsen, 1959).

AT&T Agrees to Stay Out of Computers

At the time, the Consent Decree clearly was a victory for AT&T. What is interesting, though, is that AT&T was able to remain "whole" at the expense of forgoing entry into computers and data processing at the dawn of the computer age. The Consent Decree sought to fashion an operating boundary for AT&T, but did so in a manner which relied on a technological distinction which was to become obsolete. The murkiness of the technological distinction partly would be the cause of monopoly-competitive economic boundary problems later. Because the regulatory boundary between common carrier and non-common carrier activities becomes so crucial in later years as the technological distinction blurs, it is necessary to spend some time on the Consent Decree.

The company's desire for an out of court settlement is understandable. After all, by settling with the government AT&T avoided the uncertainty posed by a negative Court judgment. And along with that possibility came the spectre of numerous private antitrust suits, which would use a Court judgment as *prima facie* evidence of antitrust violations. A judgment entered by consent cannot be used as *prima facie* evidence of violation of the antitrust laws in subsequent civil action.

That the maintenance of AT&T's monopoly was a victory for the corporation is unquestionable. And it is consistent with AT&T's long tradition of advocacy of end-to-end service and monopoly in telephony. What is perplexing about the Consent Decree is the concession to limit the corporation's legal operating arena to communications common carriage. Given the rise in computers and data processing—beginning contemporaneously with the period of the Consent Decree—why would AT&T forgo the possibility of getting into the computer field at the dawn of the computer age? After all, the most critical technological component of the second generation of computers, the transistor, was invented by research scientists at Bell Labs in 1947. The 1954 and 1955 Annual Reports to its shareholders indicate that AT&T had a fairly good idea of the possibilities of the transistor's applications. In the 1954 Annual Report, the corporation claimed that the computer was fast becoming an important business technology, and that AT&T would begin to move in ways to "service" these developments.

In fact, the corporation was involved in more than just service to the emerging computer industry. AT&T had been experimenting with computers since the late 1930s (Hanscom, 1961). AT&T built the first all-transistor computer, named TRADIC, for the Defense Department in 1954. (In contrast, IBM did not market an all-transistor computer until 1959, when it introduced its 7090 series.) AT&T even flirted with the idea of designing a machine to handle all of its own data processing, but dropped the idea in 1958 when IBM came out with a better model (Brock, 1975; Fishman, 1981). Nonetheless, AT&T did subsequently build computers for telephone switching. The renowned UNIX computer operating system came out of AT&T's computer research. Lastly, military contracts for continuing transistor-based military hardware were forthcoming throughout the 1950s (Fagen, 1978; AT&T Annual Report, 1955).

Thus the constriction of AT&T business operations posed by the 1956 Consent Decree is puzzling. In an address before the Spring Joint Computer Conference in Atlantic City on April 30, 1968, AT&T Chairman, H. I. Romnes, offered this explanation of AT&T's actions:

> We did in fact—using relays—build the very first electrically operated digital computer (in 1939) and up to 1950 had produced more than half of all the large ones made. With that kind of head start, and considering also our position in transistors and solid-state technology generally, what might have been a surprise was that we took ourselves completely out of the business of providing computer services. The reason was simply that we wanted to concentrate on communications. (Romnes cited in Mathison & Walker, 1970, p. 6)

This explanation is insufficient. After all, it took RCA's threat to construct a competing long distance telephone system via radiotelephone to finally push AT&T to negotiate the corporate division of industry in 1926 and get out of radio broadcasting. And it took the threat of antitrust action to get AT&T out of motion picture projection equipment in 1935. It is unlike the corporation to withdraw from a market within which it promises to be a major player. The claim that a company under regulatory constraints becomes risk-averse, especially in this case where AT&T would have to face IBM in head-to-head competition, does seem compelling. But this must be taken in a highly specific context. The context indicates that AT&T's decision to agree to stay out of computers and data processing was very intelligent, indeed.

The 1956 Consent Decree specifically suspended the boundary between regulated common carriage and unregulated markets if the customer of such AT&T provided services was any agency of the federal government or other communications carriers. In the 1950s the market for computers was growing, but the scope and extent of growth was very uncertain. In a 1980 advertisement IBM claimed, perhaps disingenuously, that in the early 1950s it had estimated its market for computers to be about 50 machines ("One of the great miscalculations," 1980). One aspect which was very clear, however, was that the federal government (particularly the Department of Defense) would be a major, if not the major customer of computers and data processing for the forseeable future. Computer industry historians generally agree that the first electronic computers were built for the federal government, and ever since then, the federal government has been the largest purchaser and lessor of computers (Brock, 1975; Sharpe, 1969). AT&T's experience with computers and its obvious expertise with interconnection presumably would keep the company in excellent bidding position for federal contracts. Given the fact that the federal government was the effective market for such services, the terms of the Consent Decree allowed AT&T access to the best customer without running the considerable risks of entering the public marketplace. This arrangement also underscored the tendency of the government to integrate AT&T as a quasi-state apparatus.

The risk management factor joins another important economic factor. The intense post-war boom in telephone demand taxed AT&T's capacity. Despite staggering increases in investment and manpower, for several years through the middle 1950s AT&T could not meet telephone demand (AT&T, 1948–1957; FCC, 1949–1956). The new business of television interconnection revealed other AT&T service shortfalls. In the early 1950s, AT&T could not provide the four fledgling television networks with as much carriage as they requested. Notwithstanding its experience with computers, AT&T could not have easily entered another equipment market, especially an intensely competitive one. Lastly, AT&T could have expected to gain peripherally from a strong computer market, because the company would expect to carry computer generated data via its telephone lines. This would affect certain equipment as well. In fact, until 1969, only AT&T-manufactured modems could be used to interface computers to the telephone network. Modem devices manufactured by others, including IBM, were considered illegal "foreign attachments."

NEW DEMANDS AND TECHNOLOGIES:
REGULATORY LIBERALIZATION

Antitrust notwithstanding, traditional regulatory policy was to minister to the needs of AT&T. According to Bernard Strassburg, chief of the FCC Common Carrier Bureau from 1964–1973, normal FCC practice was to deal with AT&T in negotiation rather than through formal procedures. The FCC would watch AT&T reported earnings and then ask for a rate adjustment (B. Strassburg, personal communication, March 25, 1985). By the early 1950s, however, a new feature of regulatory policy surfaced. New telecommunications users were generating demands for new or increased services. These demands taxed AT&T's ability to provide service. The lobbying of large users and the insufficient capacity of AT&T pushed the FCC to allow the entry of new providers of "specialized" telecommunications services. The policy of liberalized entry for special service providers began completely *within* the dominant protectionist regulatory paradigm. Specialized providers were thought by the FCC to have no adverse impact on AT&T. But the policy of partially liberalized entry, with time, did have an impact on AT&T, inasmuch as it created small competitive markets at the borders of the AT&T monopoly.

The long process of liberalized entry began with seemingly innocuous rulings on television signal carriage. At the beginning of commercial television, private line relay facilities were not sufficient to meet all network demands to transmit television signals to their affiliates. Though broadcasters floated the idea of a privately owned and operated relay system, the FCC supported the common carrier approach. Thus, the FCC disallowed competitive entry in the developing market for the transmission of television signals. But because of AT&T's insufficient capacity, the Commission declined to address AT&T's argument that video interconnection should be supplied on a monopoly basis. Though it felt the insufficient availability of facilities in 1948 was only a temporary problem, the FCC authorized the operation by broadcasters of private microwave relaying facilities on an interim basis, pending the availability of common carrier facilities. A 1958 rule-making granted permanent authorization of private interconnection facilities based upon the petition of a small market television station which claimed it could not afford AT&T facilities at prevailing rates and could build and operate private system links at substantially less cost. The open entry policy was limited to the lower quality technique of picking off-the-air signals of other television stations and relaying them for rebroadcast. It did not hold for direct private interconnection systems (FCC, 1980; U.S. House, 1958a).

Television interconnection set the stage for another controversy over private line carriage. The advent of computers and the rise of digital data transfer highlighted both the shortage of AT&T (and Western Union) carriage facilities and, more crucially, the inappropriateness of terminal devices and carriage networks geared for analog voice communications for the transmission of digital data. High-speed, error-free business data transmission was a "broadband" service, that is, it required much larger carriage capacity than the telephone network normally provided for "narrowband" telephone service. Most important at the time, data processing required unfailingly high transmission quality, because uncompensated interruptions can mean the loss of network synchronization and the garbling of signals. "Noise" creates errors.

Strictly technological matters were hardly the only issues in the private line controversy. In many respects the technological concerns were secondary, a smokescreen for issues of control over telecommunications prerogatives. New technologies and new economic players emerged together. Independent electronics and computer manufacturers wanted access to the lucrative new field of computer communications. New suppliers could emerge because, in contrast to the earlier years, AT&T no longer was the exclusive source of research and development in telecommunications. The massive amounts of research underwritten by the Defense Department during World War II had significant spillover effects in the post-war electronics industry. The development of microwave technology (from wartime radar research) permitted radio equipment firms to enter the telecommunications market. Later, the development of satellite technology permitted large Department of Defense and NASA aerospace contractors to enter the telecommunications market.

Perhaps more important, potential *users* of private line systems sought to break the external hold AT&T held on management telecommunications prerogatives, especially given new forms of capitalist expansion with multi-unit outposts and overseas factories (Schiller, 1982). Here, new telecommunications needs must be seen as arising within a larger context of the pattern of post-World War II capitalist expansion. Large multi-unit and nascent transnational corporations, needing to communicate quickly with their geographically dispersed operations, experienced the slow, analog, narrowband Bell System as a hindrance. With the 1959 *Above 890* case, the technological and economic power issues came to a head.

Opening of Private Line Entry

In *Above 890* the FCC established a presumption in favor of the authorization of new communications services, permitting the establishment of private transmission facilities for all private line services, including video delivery, irrespective of the availability of common carrier services. In this case, an alliance of prospective private users and manufacturers (including the Automobile Manufacturers Association, the National Retail and Dry Goods Association, the American Newspaper Publishers Association, the National Association of Manufacturers, and the Central Committee on Radio Facilities of the American Petroleum Institute) asked the FCC for permission to use the frequencies above 890 megacycles in the spectrum for non-common carrier microwave service. *Above 890* was more an instance of victory for AT&T's opponents than a theoretical ruling on the virtues of competition. The FCC noted that the common carriers which opposed the liberalization of entry had failed to substantiate their claim that the indiscriminate authorization of private facilities would cause them substantial financial injury. The Commission also noted that AT&T had not met the need for private point-to-point systems. And, significantly, the FCC implicitly addressed an aspect of the Western Electric antitrust problem as well. Asserting that "the expanded eligibility will afford a competitive spur in the manufacturing of equipment and in the development of the communications art," the Commission implicitly acknowledged the problem that, as a regulated monopoly, AT&T was in the position to slow down the pace of technical innovation *(Allocation of Microwave Frequencies Above 890mc,* 1959, p. 414; Wiley, 1981).

Above 890 revealed the two power blocs behind the liberalization of common carrier entry regulations. These were the heaviest corporate users of telecommunications and the potential competitors to AT&T in servicing those users. The efforts of these two blocs have continued unabated for 30 years. And it is they who, in the latest battle, most wanted divestiture.

Above 890 itself had little direct effect on the industry, but it had three important indirect effects. First, AT&T's response to the threat of its major corporate customers building their own private systems was to institute a bulk discount service called "TELPAK." TELPAK and other associated moves later would be seen as part of the company's efforts to illegally thwart competition, and would constitute evidence in the government's 1974 antitrust suit. Second, the delimited liberalization of entry established in *Above 890* set the stage for later regulatory decisions which opened entry much more widely for other carriers of specialized telecommunications services. Third, spurred by charges that AT&T priced TELPAK rates artificially low, the FCC initiated a series of proceedings on AT&T's tariffs. In the mid 1960s, to the tremendous pique of AT&T, the FCC instituted the first formal inquiry into AT&T rates and rate base calculation procedures. These ongoing investigations were consolidated into a proceeding known as "Docket 18128" (FCC, 1976b).

The 1969 *MCI* decision permitted the MCI Corporation to offer specialized private line service for hire *(In re Applications of Microwave Communications Inc.,* 1969). In the aftermath of this decision, the FCC was innundated with requests to construct private line systems for hire. In *Specialized Common Carrier,* the FCC sought to formulate general policy (FCC, 1970). These rulings favored new entry into the specialized communications (primarily data carriage) field. The FCC's logic was that entrants would provide new services to customers with needs that had not been met by the established carriers. AT&T would have to make its local telephone exchanges accessible to the new firms under reasonable terms. This position was strengthened in 1974 when the FCC (with appellate court backing) held that AT&T had to provide its private line service competitors with the same types of facilities that it provided to its own private line operations *(Bell System Offerings,* 1974). Finally, in a series of decisions in the mid 1970s, the Commission permitted the entry of what are known as "value-added" carriers. These were companies which proposed to lease channels from existing common carriers and attach computers and software in order to transmit data with more efficiency and less error *(Graphnet Systems Inc.,* 1974; *Packet Communications Inc.,* 1973; FCC, 1976c; *Telenet Communications Corp.,* 1974).

Though the corporate proponents of these liberalizations legitimated their policy positions on the basis of the *general* beneficence of "competition," in reality this meant freedom of choice for the very largest corporate telecommunications users. And though the FCC did not authorize such liberalizations of entry on the basis of direct competition with traditional carriers, clearly this general policy was in response to heavy corporate demands for efficient computer-communications. Without impugning the motives of the FCC, the Commission did not (perhaps could not) foresee the consequences of the liberalization of private line services (British Telecommunications Union Committee, 1983). After all, at the time of *Specialized Common Carrier* in 1970, private line services accounted for only about 4% of Bell's total revenues (FCC, 1970).

The liberal private line rationale likewise partially underlay the "Open Skies" policy for domestic satellite communications networks in 1972. The Nixon Administration-sponsored domestic satellite policy was a clear victory for large telecommunications users. The creation of a privately owned and operated satellite system amounted to a stupendous give-away to capital of the benefits of over $20 billion in publicly subsidized research and development in the space program. Further, it permitted the creation of a new telecommunications infrastructure largely outside the control of AT&T. AT&T was permitted to lease satellite circuits, but not to own a satellite for many years. Nor was AT&T allowed to lease satellite facilities for its commercial private line services until 1979. The FCC believed that precluding AT&T from engaging in satellite-delivered private line service was necessary to assure that AT&T did not foreclose entry by other firms. The FCC also worried that if AT&T were permitted full access to the satellite business, the company's great strength might permit it to engage in cross-subsidization and to forestall innovation *(Domestic Communications-Satellite Facilities [DOMSAT],* 1970).

Thus, by the early 1970s, the tenor of FCC policy must be recognized as having changed to some extent. The Commission seemed to have bought the logic of the large telecommunications users that satellite services be *competitive* and that AT&T be kept out of the satellite business. Clearly, the FCC no longer thought of specialized services as "peripheral" to common carrier telecommunications. Yet, the general tone of the *DOMSAT* decision is one which sees AT&T as potential predator, not a company in danger of being hurt by a potential challenge to its monopoly. *DOMSAT* reveals a FCC promoting competition in specialized services on the one hand, and expecting to protect AT&T's traditional monopoly turf on the other.

The "Hush-a-Phone" Precedent

What *Above 890* was to private lines, *Hush-a-Phone* was to foreign attachments. *Hush-a-Phone* concerned a mechanical device which could be attached to a telephone receiver. The device enabled more private conversations in crowded office conditions. AT&T had a complete prohibition against non-Bell attachments and the Hush-a-Phone Corporation appealed to the FCC. After a six-year delay, the FCC upheld Bell's invocation of tariff restrictions against the device. The Court of Appeals reversed the FCC, finding that there was no evidence to show that the Hush-a-Phone device harmed the telephone system. In remanding the case to the FCC, the Court of Appeals also raised the antitrust spectre, seeing an inherent danger in tariff restrictions which placed control over a potential competitor's business in the hands of the regulated manufacturer. *Hush-a-Phone* did little to alter the terminal equipment market, largely because AT&T's response was to allow mechanical attachments but to restrict electrical attachments, again on the basis of preserving the technical integrity of the telephone system *(Hush-a-Phone Corp. v. United States*, 1956).

The *Hush-a-Phone* precedent was used by the FCC to rule against such AT&T restrictive tariffs in the 1968 *Carterfone* decision. The Carterfone device connected the national telephone land line system with two-way mobile radios to provide radio telephony to oil drillers too far away from local networks. Though the *Carterfone* decision was decided on the narrow grounds that there was no showing of harm to the telephone system, the FCC also found that the device satisfied an unmet demand. Again, large users argued for the liberalization of entry, including the American Petroleum Institute and the National Retail Merchants Association. And in this case, the Justice Department indicated to the Commission that the tariff provisions against foreign attachments were contrary to the antitrust laws. *Carterfone* served to open the telephone attachment market generally. As part of the *Carterfone* decision, the FCC ordered the common carriers to submit recommendations which would protect the telephone system against technically harmful devices, but which otherwise would allow the customer to provide his/her own terminal equipment *(In the Matter of Use of the Carterfone Device in Message Toll Telephone Service*, 1968).

In private lines, the FCC's rationale for liberalizing entry was tied to the idea of responding to new service demands from large corporate users. In foreign attachments, it was judicial constraints which pushed the Commission in a parallel liberalizing direction. With *Hush-a-Phone*, the FCC was bound by judicial thinking which took seriously the *public utility* rationale embedded within common carrier regulation. *Hush-a-Phone* asserts "the telephone subscriber's right to reasonably use his telephone in ways which are privately beneficial without being publicly detrimental" *(Hush-a-Phone Corp. v. United States,* 1956, p. 269). This logic seemed to resurrect a strict common law conception of common carriage, by which the carrier could have no control over how the lines would be used by patrons.[6]

It is essential to see that the liberalizations of private line and terminal equipment regulations were undertaken *not* on the basis of a theoretical rationale which advocated head-to-head competition with AT&T. Rather, given AT&T's inability or slowness to meet specific demands, and faced with heavy lobbying from major corporate entities, the FCC reasoned that new entry would mean new services and that these new services were unlikely to have any significant adverse effects on AT&T. Specialized common carriers were thought to provide *new* services and markets (primarily for large corporate users), and would tap latent but undeveloped markets for existing services. The FCC thought this would thus expand the size of the total communications market rather than take business away from AT&T. With regard to the liberalization of the terminal equipment market, the FCC was bound by judicial constraints deriving from strict interpretation of common carrier and antitrust law.

On the other hand, the FCC did promote competition *indirectly* in ways which harken back to the antitrust complaints against Western Electric. As the new ancillary products and services came into being, the FCC hoped that these could create an environment where the established carriers would be pressured to provide their specialized services at rates wholly related to costs. The Commission stated this explicitly in *Specialized Common Carrier*:

> In an industry of the size and growing complexity of the communications common carrier industry, the entry of new carriers could provide a useful regulatory tool which would assist in achieving the statutory objective of adequate and efficient services at reasonable charges. Competition could afford some standard for comparing the performance of one carrier with another. Moreover, competitive pressure may encourage beneficial changes in AT&T's services and charges in the specialized field and stimulate counter innovation or the more rapid introduction of new technology. (FCC, 1970, p. 333)

In other words, faced with the herculean problems of rate tariff determination in common carriage generally (problems owing to the fact that service tariff requests were largely unrelated to actual costs), the FCC saw in resale carriers a possible tool for comparison.

CONSEQUENCES OF ENTRY LIBERALIZATION

The consequences of these developments are extremely complex. The regulatory decisions which favored open entry in private lines and terminal equipment could not effectively *contain* those services, especially as technological innovation blurred service lines and inasmuch as the courts often *widened* the scope of FCC decisions. For instance, genuine competition in long distance telephony was created when the Court of Appeals reversed the FCC in the 1977 *Execunet* case. Again, this pivoted around MCI. MCI offered a service ("Execunet") which effectively duplicated AT&T's regular message toll service, and the FCC ordered MCI to terminate it (FCC, 1975). Reversing the FCC decision, the court ruled that once the FCC licensed a firm to provide *any* service, that firm could provide *every* service (with the same equipment) unless the FCC specifically focused upon, and denied it, the right to do so. The FCC had not so stipulated, and thus MCI was allowed to offer the service. The Court's reasoning is significant. The Court conceded that the FCC

> . . . did not perhaps intend to open the field of common carrier communications generally, but its constant stress on the fact that specialized carriers would provide new, innovative, and hitherto unheard-of communications services clearly indicates that it had no very clear idea of precisely how far or to what services the field should be opened. *(MCI Telecommunications Corp. v. FCC*, 1977, p. 379)

Moreover, the Court explicitly raised the question of the legitimacy of AT&T's monopoly. The decision concluded:

> The question whether AT&T should be granted a *de jure* monopoly was not among those proposed to be decided in *Specialized Common Carriers*, and nowhere in that decision can justification be found for continuing or propagating a monopoly that, according to the staff, had theretofore just grown like Topsy. Of course, there may be very good reasons for according AT&T *de jure* freedom from competition in certain fields; however, one such reason is not simply that AT&T got there first. *(MCI Telecommunications Corp. v. FCC*, 1977, p. 380)

In other words, microwave private lines, computer-based terminal equipment, and domestic satellite delivery created not only new services, but also new possibilities for delivering older services which had been the sole province of the traditional common carriers. Though for years the FCC had allowed entry into *specialized* markets, the Commission had sought to contain entry to those markets *only*.[7] It was the courts which permitted head-to-head competition in what thereto had been regulated monopoly services. This could serve only to make even more ambiguous the boundary between regulated and competitive markets in common carrier services.

This had two serious consequences. As the line between computer and communications technologies became less and less clear (and these technologies became increasingly compatible, interchangeable, and mutually supplementary), alternative delivery systems became available for myriad uses. Large users could opt out of the Bell System partially or completely. This became known as the "bypass" problem. Although estimates differed as to its immediate economic impact, bypass potentially could place AT&T's internal-subsidy, average-pricing rate structure in danger. Moreover, because carriage competitors (as in long distance or data) did not have to include any of the local plant costs that AT&T had to allocate to its interstate rate base, the competitors could always undercut AT&T rates. AT&T vigorously opposed this iniquity, labeling the practice "cream-skimming." Second and conversely, because AT&T now was just one (albeit the largest by far) of several players in a few competitive markets, it could use the guaranteed fair rate of return profits of its monopoly switched telephone service to practice "predatory pricing" (or, more accurately, pricing without regard to cost, because no one knew AT&T costs) in those competitive markets.

These developments raised significant issues of public policy regarding the appropriate *boundary* between *regulated* monopoly communications activities and *unregulated* competitive data processing services. The boundary between these created by the 1956 Consent Decree was undermined by the interaction of new technologies and regulatory liberalizations. The FCC attempted to deal with this situation in the first of two "Computer Inquiries" (FCC, 1966). In this policy (under heavy pressure from large users) the Commission sought to segregate data processing, which was presumed to lie outside FCC jurisdiction, from regulated telecommunications. But the intrinsic versatility of computerization defied regulatory compartmentalization. After all, time-sharing use of a central computer via scattered locations creates a communication system. By the time of the Second Computer Inquiry, the Commission essentially abandoned the notion of a well-defined, fixed domain of regulated monopoly service (FCC, 1976a; Frieden, 1981).

The FCC, in the meanwhile, was faced with the problem of determining AT&T rate charges in a situation where historically, charges were not cost-based (for the reasons raised earlier in the discussion of universal service), but now AT&T no longer had monopoly control over common carriage. Remember, it was the monopoly provision of services which permitted the relatively easy non-cost-related determination of tariffs and political accommodations between carriers, regulators, and customers.

These developments served to make the cost, price, and shared equipment problem of AT&T even more complicated and difficult to resolve. The presence of competitors forced the FCC to face the issue of cost allocation, which it did in the 1976–78 proceeding known as "Docket 18128." By this point in time, the FCC and all parties agreed that the actual costs of providing service should be the dominant criterion in rate-setting, and thus moved toward a fully distributed cost approach to the pricing of both AT&T's monopoly and competitive services. The problem was which methodology to employ in such rate determination. The methodology would determine whether, for instance, AT&T could offer private line services equivalent to, or even below, competitors. And the issue this raised was whether AT&T would then use its regulated monopoly profits in basic telephone to cross-subsidize its operations in competitive markets. The Commission found that the returns from AT&T's private line services were in fact being cross-subsidized by its monopoly services. AT&T was ordered to file tariff rate revisions for all services in order to yield rate levels in accordance with the costing guidelines and methodologies established in its decision (FCC, 1976b).

The problem, of course, went again to the difficulty of figuring what was what within the Bell System. As economist Leland Johnson has written, evaluating Bell's underlying costs to determine whether it is competing "fairly" is a monumental task (Johnson, 1978, p. 140). Echoing this conclusion was the Justice Department itself. Justice pointed to AT&T's control over cost information and its demonstrated ability to frustrate any attempt to penetrate the relationship between its costs, by whatever definition, and its prices (United States Department of Justice, 1981).

Such anti-competitive practices constituted part of the suit against AT&T, filed late in 1974. The suit charged the company with illegal methods of keeping out competitors mainly in the area of services provided to business, but also in long distance and customer equipment. The Justice Department also charged that AT&T tried to thwart competition in intercity communication by refusing interconnection with the local exchanges and by engaging in predatory pricing. In fact, Justice charged that AT&T had used the regulatory process to impose costs on entrants, and give itself time to develop competitive offerings. The 1974 suit again addressed the longstanding issue of Western Electric being the sole equipment provider to the local telephone operating companies.

A SUMMARY OF REGULATORY AND ANTITRUST PROBLEMS

The boundary issue primarily and rate structure issue secondarily begged for a dramatic solution, especially as they increasingly called into question the relevance of the regulatory formulae which defined the life of AT&T. The major corporate users also were quite concerned with the boundary issue, inasmuch as they feared that the regulatory quagmire could bring specialized services and data processing under more regulatory supervision. At the same time, the major corporate users were concerned over the possible degradation of the basic switched network system (FCC, 1976a; Schiller, 1982). Thus, the roots of the divestiture lay in the contradictions between regulatory formulae, which sought to structure the telecommunications industry, and the business and technological developments which over time challenged both the rationality of those formulae and the balance of political forces that supported the formulae.

Original government policy sanctioned the monopoly of telephony by the American Telephone and Telegraph Company, for clear economic and political reasons. Monopoly status took advantage of economies of scale and provided for universal and affordable service. But in a modern capitalist society, monopoly, even when government-sanctioned for the larger public good, seems to engender economic contradictions, ideological opposition, and businesses seeking a piece of the action. This is especially true given the inadequate oversight by the FCC. On the one hand, evidence of possible abuses and economic inefficiencies practiced by the Bell System induced large-scale investigations to determine whether AT&T had violated the antitrust laws. On the other hand, the same monopoly structure which permitted systematic control of telecommunications eventuated in various limitations on the service and technical prerogatives of large telecommunications users.

The early antitrust dilemma was how to safeguard the economic and political benefits which monopoly secured from the economic (and political) abuses that monopoly status posed. The 1956 Consent Decree reflected this dilemma; by "solving" the problem conservatively, it created new problems. The Consent Decree left intact the integrated nature of the Bell System, but at the expense of constructing judicial barriers which, even then, were becoming obsolete. Moreover, the Consent Decree chose to ignore the problem side of monopoly. The peculiar inefficiencies of the monopoly firm under regulatory constraint (to wit, slow innovation and limited service options) left the Bell System open to challenge. *Above 890* can be interpreted as little more than large corporate users prevailing in the regulatory arena over AT&T in the face of new technological needs and the demonstrated incapacity of AT&T to provide for them. It was a clear example of interest group liberalism—abetted by technological change—at work in the regulatory arena. An ongoing dynamic of liberalized entry in specialized markets was set in motion by the large user community's demand for increased and enhanced telecommunications services. Liberalized entry created competitive markets which, in turn, confused boundaries between regulated and nonregulated realms, and jeopardized AT&T's averaged rate structure.

Hush-a-Phone and court ordered decisions like *Execunet* constitute a separate level of constraint and determination, beyond interest politics *per se*. The law does not stand "outside" socioeconomic life, and it would be foolish to assert its complete "autonomy." And of course it is the conflict between economic players which allows the courts to play a role at all. Nonetheless, socioeconomic factors influence law only indirectly most of the time. Law is affected as much by its own independent history, language and logic. The essential characteristic of modern rational law, as a body of rules and procedures, is to apply logical criteria with reference to standards of universality and equity. Thus, legal rationality and precedent, as in *Hush-a-Phone* and *Execunet*, constitute another dimension of determination. The FCC's belief that partial entry liberalizations were containable was exploded by subsequent judicial decisions. The ramifications of FCC and court-ordered entry liberalizations, then, engendered a further spiral of legal constraint. AT&T's actions to circumvent the effects of entry liberalization put the corporation in direct conflict with the antitrust laws.

Together, these liberalizations and boundaries had the significant consequences touched upon above. But if these regulatory and judicial decisions "forced" a restructuring of common carrier telecommunications, they did not determine the *actual* restructuring. That determination is found in the policy arena. In a sense, the long process of regulatory change set up an alteration of the forum for policy-making.

ACCUMULATED CONTRADICTIONS
CREATE NEW POLICY-MAKING ARENAS

Finding itself in losing battles with the FCC and the Court of Appeals in the matter of safeguarding its monopoly, in the mid 1970s AT&T turned to Congress to preserve as much of its dominance in telecommunications common carriage as was possible. This was embodied in a 1976 bill called "The Consumer Communications Reform Act," which was so pro-AT&T it came to be known colloquially as the "Bell Bill." This bill was the last hurrah of the traditionally constituted Bell *System*, and fittingly was directed by traditionalist AT&T Chairman John deButts.[8] The bill failed, and in many respects the move toward Congress backfired. The issues first posed in the "Consumer Communications Reform Act" were taken up in subsequent Congressional attempts to rewrite the Communications Act—in ways not always to AT&T's liking. The first rewrite would have forced AT&T to divest itself of Western Electric in exchange for permission to enter the computer and data processing fields. By the late 1970s, many other players possessing conflicting agendas, and large numbers of experts armed with competing testimony, were part of the relatively open Congressional policymaking arena. Notwithstanding its enormous lobbying power, the legislative arena could not be stage-managed by AT&T (Rowland, 1982).

The 1974 antitrust suit, passed on to the Reagan Administration Department of Justice, became the one policy arena where AT&T could exercise its voice and be heard. The Reagan Administration did not want divestiture. It had convened a working group on telecommunications composed of the Departments of Agriculture, Defense, Commerce, and Energy, and the Federal Energy Management Agency to deal with the AT&T antitrust suit. This working group cared less about the merits of the case than the national interest in telecommunications (see Commerce Secretary Baldridge's comments at note 3 *supra*). But Commerce's interest in international competition had to be balanced against the longstanding Defense interest in safeguarding the integrated nature of the telecommunications network. As Department of Defense General Counsel, William H. Taft, IV, testified at Senate Judiciary Committee hearings in 1981:

> Court-ordered divestiture could cause substantial harm to our national
> defense and security, and emergency preparedness telecommunication capac-

> ities. . . . From a national defense and security and emergency preparedness standpoint, the telecommunications network cannot properly be artificially divided between the inter-city and local exchange functions. . . . Artificial division of the Bell System between local exchange and intercity functions ignores the physical and functional operation of the telecommunications network, will reduce or eliminate the incentives for the Bell Operating Companies to participate in joint network planning and management, and will eventually result in fragmentation of the nationwide telecommunications network. (U.S. Senate, 1982a, pp. 51–52)

After all, all national defense circuitry, Strategic Air Command (SAC) circuitry, Presidential support circuitry, warning circuitry and North American Radar Air Defense (NORAD) circuitry is provided by the common carrier system. The Defense establishment worried that the divestiture of AT&T would jeopardize this system and would destroy standards in telecommunications as well (U.S. Senate, 1982b).

The Reagan Administration appeared to have tied the fate of the lawsuit with that of pending telecommunications legislation, the Telecommunications Competition and Deregulation Act of 1981 (U.S. Senate, 1981, S.898). Whereas the antitrust suit sought *again* to divest AT&T of Western Electric (and some BOCs), S.898 advocated the much less radical solution (already approved by the FCC in its Second Computer Inquiry) of creating fully separate subsidiaries to be overseen by the FCC. (This action, of course, would create new responsibilities for the FCC to allocate costs—which it already could not do.) Thus in July, 1981, the Justice Department, joined by AT&T, requested that the Federal District Court grant an approximate one-year continuance in the antitrust case. The Administration's argument was that the AT&T case was just part of the larger issue of reformulating telecommunications policy. Congress, it was argued, was the proper arena for this rather than the "much narrower" judicial forum.

But the Congressional arena was stalemated. More important, Federal District Court Judge Harold Greene, the judge presiding over the case, denied the request for a continuance. In contrast to the usual course of large antitrust matters, Judge Greene intended to bring the suit to trial in relatively quick fashion and he denied all requests for postponements. Greene's power lay in his being positioned as the key mediating player between adversaries whose options had narrowed. Judge Greene's *Opinions* on AT&T's motion for dismissal and on the settlement proposal gave clear indication that he would have found that AT&T had violated the Sherman Act *(United States v. AT&T*, 1982). But if it was clear that Judge Greene would have found AT&T guilty, it is not so clear, his statements notwithstanding, that he would have had the chutzpah to order so consequential a move as divestiture. Speculation regarding Greene's opinion is largely irrelevant. Regardless of the court's decision, it is extremely likely the case would have been appealed by some party (if not AT&T), and drag on for another decade.

In contrast, the negotiating forum between AT&T and the Justice Department could keep out all other players. Though they were "adversaries" of a sort, AT&T and Justice nonetheless had many interests in common. A settlement offered many potential advantages to the principal players. A settlement would benefit the various state interests in telecommunications and information technology. Unlike a judicial ruling, a settlement forum would allow the deeply conflicting interests of defense and commerce to be ironed out in negotiation. Not surprisingly, the actual settlement is one which protects the commerce interest, for it preserves, even enhances, the international business capabilities of AT&T. The settlement also represents a near-total realization of the historic agenda of the large telecommunications users. The large users are able to utilize the competition-generated spate of new technologies and services. At the same time, the settlement does minimally safeguard the financial and technical viability of the basic switched telephone network, upon which the new technologies depend.[9] For the Department of Defense, the settlement is a good "second best" solution. A provision of the Consent Decree allows AT&T to provide the very end-to-end telecommunications services the settlement was designed to disallow, so long as those services meet certain national security needs. The settlement thus safeguards the interests of the Defense Department through the back door.

For AT&T, a settlement would preclude the use of the government's antitrust case as *prima facie* evidence in private antitrust actions against the company. Most important, unlike a judicial ruling (whose appeal, and hence further delays, was likely), a settlement presumably would end the uncertainty of action for AT&T. The company needed to move quickly into the "information age." The settlement reflects that need. It resolves most of the technological and business contradictions discussed above, *and* leaves intact the vertically integrated nature of AT&T. Though this is not what AT&T wanted—up to the end, AT&T publicly sought to preserve the System—it is a very good second best for AT&T.

And it may be that AT&T was somewhat disingenuous in its public pronouncements. The transition in chairmanship of the company from deButts to Brown in 1979 reflected a change in corporate philosophy from the traditional "universal service in the public interest" to a plea to be rid of the barriers to diversification.[10] The form divestiture took (i.e., the spinning off of the BOCs from the remaining vertically integrated AT&T) met the new needs of AT&T in two crucial ways. *Without* divestiture, AT&T would have faced intolerable regulatory and antitrust pressures—due to the continuing problem between regulated and unregulated spheres. Even had the company created a wholly independent subsidiary to enter competitive markets, it is likely that AT&T's competitors would continue to have hounded AT&T in regulatory and legal arenas. Second, there is the matter of the company's size. It is at least an open question how quickly the company would have been able to introduce new services or new products with a hugely capitalized, regulated monopoly dragging it down.[11]

CONCLUSION: SOME RAMIFICATIONS OF DIVESTITURE

Whether the settlement is in the public interest is another question. The settlement's many defenders highlight the vast profusion of service options, the potential rush of technological innovation, and the promise of rich diversity in sources and modes of communication. Undoubtedly, much of this will come to pass. But as others point out, these options and innovations will come to specialized information users, while basic telephone users can look forward to higher rates and perhaps a decline in the quality of service. The 22 severed BOCs (regrouped as seven independent "Regional Holding Companies," or RHCs), barred from the provision of interexchange, long distance, or unregulated services, are looking to raise local rates considerably. The bypass problem can only get worse as technical innovation gets better. Indeed, the new AT&T itself has begun to bypass its former local phone companies (Berg, 1985a).

All long distance and private line carriers which interconnect into the local telephone lines will have to pay an access fee for this interconnection service. It is here where a new version of the traditional subsidy could be resurrected. However, if that access fee is too large, corporate users would have an incentive to build their own internal networks, bypassing the local telephone companies partly or totally (Pollack, 1983). The bypass threat has a technological as well as an economic component. The crucial issue here is that broadband data and video carriage are hindered enormously by the small bit capacity of the so-called "local loop," now owned and operated by the regional holding companies. Companies with big data needs may find interconnection into the local loop a burden—slow and error-prone. Bypass could reduce the revenues of the regional holding companies considerably, because the very corporations which would engage in bypass are those which generate the most revenue for the local telephone companies.

At this time, there are no definitive studies of the bypass threat, and it probably is true that local telephone monopolies exaggerate the threat as an added ploy in rate increase requests (FCC, 1982). But the anecdotal evidence is noteworthy. Many large users have installed bypass systems, including Westinghouse in Pittsburgh, Boeing in Seattle, and ARCO in California. Martin Marietta, for example, connects its Data Systems Center to its Orlando, Florida plant via fibre optic cable. It currently is installing an earth station to bypass the local exchange, enabling it to make interstate calls directly via satellite. Bell South estimates current losses at $500,000 per year, projected to $3 million when Martin Marietta completes its system (*NARUC v. FCC*, 1983). In response to divestiture, local telephone companies (telcos) have asked for significant rate increases. But increased phone rates attack the heart of the traditional social policy of universal service. It is as if the traditional social policy has been reversed—local service subsidizing specialized business services. This may be the real meaning behind the telecommunications "revolution."[12]

Because basic telephone service is thought to be a flat market, and the local telephone companies will lose the long distance cross subsidy, the telcos face a financing dilemma. There are three identifiable strategies. The first is to find a way to increase local telephone rates, whether by requesting rate hikes through the various Public Utilities Commissions (PUCs) or instituting FCC mandated "end-user access," charges to the local loop. Actual rate hikes have been below requests, but approved increases have been hefty nonetheless. Though Congress slowed the implementation of access charges, residents began paying a $1 per month fee as of June, 1985. A corollary to this is for the telcos to institute "zone usage measurement," that is, charging callers for local calls on the basis of distance and duration. Telcos have been pushing PUCs hard on this. But there is evidence that the cost of installing equipment to measure all local calls throughout the nation would itself cost between $1 billion and $2 billion annually over the next several years. This would create further upward pressure on phone rates (Dawson, 1984; Schmuckler, 1984; Trice, 1984). Nonetheless, the telcos are successfully imposing zone usage measurement.

Another strategy finds the telcos moving quickly into competitive businesses, so as to diversify their holdings. These include ventures in real estate, international telecommunications consulting, and equipment leasing. There even have been efforts to move into long distance service. In December, 1984, Judge Greene approved some of the telco new business plans. These unregulated businesses must be offered through separate subsidiaries, and must be closely monitored by the Justice Department. The telcos must limit their investments in the new companies to 10% of their estimated revenues, ostensibly to make sure that they do not neglect their primary business of providing regulated, monopoly phone service. But, this development has its dangers. After all, one of the problems of the old regulatory arrangement in telephony was the danger of AT&T using guaranteed profits from its regulated service to subsidize nonregulated ventures. The FCC's inability to monitor AT&T does not augur well for the Justice Department's ability to monitor the divested telcos ("Regional phone firms win ok for ventures," 1984).

The third strategy is most interesting, in part because it has great bearing on the coming battle over the so-called "last mile" of wire into homes and businesses. So as to recapture or prevent the loss of the business telecommunications market, the telcos have been contemplating the construction of broadband networks. The Consent Decree, while barring telcos from developing and offering enhanced services (including video and videotex), does appear to allow them to build whatever types of plant they deem essential to their roles as providers of local telecommunications facilities. The FCC's rules bar telcos from owning and operating cable television systems in their service areas. However, the companies believe Judge Greene's order gives them latitude to build broadband networks capable of providing the full range of CATV-style video, so long as they themselves are not the operators of such services. On the state level, PUC's appear friendly to the idea, because cross-use of the facilities could lower the cost of phone service.

The telcos are going about testing the feasibility of building broadband networks in several cities across the country, including Baltimore, Detroit, Philadelphia, Chicago, Milwaukee, Washington DC, and Palo Alto, California. In many cases, this strategy puts telcos in direct conflict with aggressive multi-system cable TV operators, which have constructed institutional loops to link businesses and government in major cities. The broadband network would replace the old telephone truck lines with optical fiber, and the telco would lease back a large share of the channel capacity to the city (Baer, 1984; Holsendolph, 1983). Arrangements such as this hold the possibility that telephone rates could be kept from exorbitant increases. But, whereas such broadband strategies may keep large data users inside the telephone system, they entail enormous investments in plant, the costs of which will be passed on largely to the residential customer.

This latter scenario illustrates one more ramification of divestiture. On the one hand, divestiture seems to reconstruct a 1956 Consent Decree-type operating barrier for telcos—with all of the problems associated with such a boundary. Judge Greene likely will spend the rest of his judicial life overseeing various aspects of divestiture. On the other hand, new burdens and responsibilities have fallen onto state public utility commissions. PUCs, which previously ruled on local telephone depreciation plans and rates, must act on many more public policy issues in the wake of divestiture. They must decide whether or not to allow competition in long distance markets within a state; how to regulate the intrastate services of AT&T and its long distance competitors; how to minimize bypass; and how to police the marketplace in a period of rapidly improving technology. It appears that, to the extent PUCs have jurisdiction, they are attempting to slow the pace of telephone deregulation (Barnes, 1984b).

The jurisdiction question is crucial, however, for jurisdiction partly determines how future substantive issues are fought out. In a major blow to state regulatory commissioners, a federal appeals court recently affirmed the right of the FCC—rather than state regulators—to fix telephone company depreciation schedules ("FCC's regulatory role," 1984). Such depreciation schedules are a key factor in determining local telephone rates. This jurisdictional dispute thus highlights the divergence in policy goals between state and federal regulatory bodies. The states continue to regulate in the interests of equity, whereas the FCC clearly has moved toward regulation whose goal is economic competition (Noam, 1983).[13] Yet, the overall move toward cost-based pricing may not mean the end of regulation at all—it may signal the emergence of an *ad hoc* form of "regulated competition." The recent FCC moves on customer choice of primary long distance carrier underscore this. But unlike the old regulatory arrangement, which dealt (however inadequately) with a *system*, the forthcoming regime of regulated competition will have no system on which to get a handle (Phillips, 1983). The most common complaint of all parties involved in post-divestiture telecommunications is that there is no consistent, stable set of federal and state rules (Pagano, 1985).

As for the telecommunications system itself, it now may be more difficult to coordinate and manage the basic switched network. This fact is alluded to in the behind-the-back provision of the Consent Decree regarding AT&T's relations with the Defense Department and the Strategic Air Command. This allows AT&T to provide integrated, end-to-end telecommunications services (precluded by the settlement) so long as those services meet certain national security needs. And AT&T has asked the FCC for permission to offer complete end-to-end services for *all* agencies of the U.S. government (Ricci, 1984a). But for the non-government sectors, research and development in telecommunications no longer will be undertaken with *systemwide* improvement in mind. As Bell Labs reorients its activities toward the market, its unique role in the overall construction and maintenance of the telephone system will disappear. Given the many players and service resellers and equipment suppliers, each with different technical standards and tariffs, the AT&T breakup and the onset of competition may mean innovation in specific parts of the system, but neglect of other parts, and a fair degree of anarchy for the system as a whole. As if to underscore this, business and residential complaints about telephone service and equipment have been rampant since the divestiture (Ricci, 1984b; Sahagun, 1984). Many analysts forsee large problems ahead due to generally poorer standards and a deterioration in the physical plant of local telephone companies (Pollack, 1984).

This essay has shown that the traditional regulated monopoly structure in telecommunications was inherently precarious. The incontrovertible public good of expanding the system of telephony throughout the nation has to be seen against a backdrop of Bell System inefficiencies and antitrust violations. These inefficiencies and antitrust problems did not generate major economic or political contradictions so long as the usage of the telephone system remained relatively simple. However, in a period of rapid business growth and associated technological advance, the particular monopoly structure of AT&T could not forever withstand the weight of powerful corporate demands. In many ways, the breakup of the Bell System, if not inevitable, certainly was likely in some form. The point of this conclusion, though, is to underscore that the specific terms of the breakup are not in the public interest. The benefits and drawbacks of divestiture are by no means evenly distributed. The breakup serves the interests of the large telecommunications users, AT&T, and government interests in commerce and defense. As AT&T moves into unregulated information technology markets and large corporate users opt out of the regulated telephone network, the regulated telephone system likely will suffer and traditional customers will pay far more. It remains to be seen whether the system as a whole is threatened. The breakup thus augurs the possible collapse of the public utility principle in telecommunications.

Acknowledgments: The author wishes to thank Dennis Costa and A. Margot Gordon for their help with parts of the research, and Lew Friedland, Dan Schiller, Nicholas Garnham, and Herbert Schiller for their comments on earlier drafts of this essay.

NOTES

1. In the United States, "common carriage" designates the legal framework which applies to the means, or conduits, of transportation and mass communication. As it emerges in transportation law, the main principle of common carriage is that a carrier must allow nondiscriminatory access to its service. Often, common carriers are characterized by economies of scale and thus are granted monopoly franchises. Such carriers are considered to be imbued with a public function, and often are labeled "public utilities." In communications, common carriers are barred from exercising any control or from having an interest in the content transmitted over their lines.

2. "Information technology" or "telematics" are neologisms given to describe the melding of two previously separate technologies, telecommunications and computers, into one industrial complex. The computerization of telephone switching and the ability to digitalize information have served to transform the traditionally capital-intensive, but relatively simple technology of the telephone. Telecommunication links allow the creation of computer networks—which then can function as telephone-like information circuits. In other words, recent developments have rendered telephone and computer technologies virtually indistinguishable. This is the basis of the so-called "information revolution" about which we have heard so much (see Forester, 1985; Nora & Minc, 1980).

3. Indeed, testimony from Assistant Attorney General, William F. Baxter, the official most directly involved in the prosecution and settlement of the government's antitrust suit against AT&T, illuminates this perspective quite baldly. He testified to the Senate Judiciary Committee, in its oversight hearings on the *US v ATT* case: "A great deal more than the enforcement of the antitrust laws is involved in this situation. The telecommunications industry arguably is our most important industry even at the present time. The boundary lines between telecommunication and data processing and word processing are rapidly becoming blurred beyond recognition. I think there is almost no doubt that it will be our most important industry by a wide margin over the next quarter of a century" (Baxter cited in US Senate, 1982a, p. 28). Later in those hearings, Baxter linked the AT&T and IBM cases explicitly. He testified, "In some respects, I thought the most effective relief I could find in the IBM case was freeing AT&T from the 1956 Consent Decree, and in some respects the most appropriate relief in the AT&T case was freeing IBM from further harassment in that litigation" (Baxter cited in US Senate, 1982a, p. 73). Or, as Secretary of Commerce, Malcolm Baldridge, testified at an earlier session of those Senate Judiciary hearings, "We found in this task force that the state of the art in the [telecommunications] industry had leapfrogged itself so many times that it was imperative to deregulate and make this competitive if we were not going to relinquish leadership to other countries in the future" (Baldridge cited in US Senate, 1982a, p. 11). Baldridge tied together the commerce and defense interest in settling the AT&T antitrust case. "This is vitally important to this country, for our national defense effort

among other things, that we get legislation on this. Otherwise we are going to be buying telecommunication equipment and electronics from the Japanese in 10 years" (Baldridge cited in US Senate, 1982a, p. 11). Also of interest in this regard is a report of the National Telecommunications and Information Administration (NTIA) on US long-range international telecommunications and information goals (US Senate, 1983).

4. AT&T has acted quickly to move into domestic and international competitive markets. Since the divestiture, the company has introduced its "3B" line of minicomputers, a new computerized office switchboard, and its version of a personal computer. The corporation has announced plans to construct a fibre optic digital transmission network for the United States (to be expanded internationally). Domestically, AT&T is engaged in cooperative ventures with Wang Laboratories and Digital Research. Together, these represent the first component package for a so-called "local area network" to link telephones, data processors, workstations and other office equipment. AT&T's aim here is to move quickly into the "office of the future" market ("AT&T plans to blend computers," 1984; "AT&T set to expand," 1984). The corporation has gone after big computer contracts, as well. In June, 1985, the U.S. National Security Agency awarded AT&T with a $946 million contract to supply it with minicomputers and services (Sanger, 1985). Internationally, AT&T has entered into an agreement with Philips of Holland for the manufacture of telephone exchanges. It has offered to purchase Inmos, the largest British silicon chip maker (in which the British government holds a 75% share) for $70 million. The company has purchased a 25% chunk of Olivetti, the Italian business machine company (with the option to increase its share to 40%), for the production of terminal equipment. AT&T has entered into joint ventures for specific equipment with Taiwan, Korea, and Spain ("Did it make sense," 1984). Through these international intercorporate links AT&T is positioning itself to gain access to the otherwise "protectionist" Post, Telegraph, and Telephone national monopolies for the sale of equipment and services.

5. One reason why the Western Electric antitrust problem did not "go away" was that Holmes Baldridge, who had served as the principal attorney for the Walker investigation, subsequently became chief of the general litigation section of the Justice Department's antitrust division. It must be understood that, of the three major antitrust moves against AT&T, both the Walker investigation and the 1949 antitrust suit came out of the milieu of New Deal antagonism to corporate power. A New Deal Congress specially allocated $750,000 in 1935 to fund the Walker investigation. In contrast, as we shall see, the impetus for the 1974 antitrust suit came from the coalition of newly competing companies and large telecommunications users to break open the AT&T monopoly.

6. Under the law that had evolved for railroads, carriers may not ask their customers to waive their rights, for these rights arise from common or statute law and not from the contract for service (*Hannibal and Saint Joseph Railroad Co. v. Swift*, 1870; *Philadelphia and Reading Railroad Co. v. Derby*, 1852). Moreover, this separation between medium and use seems a reasonable extension of the principle of the separation between medium and message—a principle which embodies the traditional concern with the protection of freedom of speech. In this case, however, the separation between medium and use effectively created a market for emerging microelectronics manufacturers and equipment suppliers. The other legal foun-

dation underlying *Hush-a-Phone* was a 1936 antitrust decision which declared illegal IBM's compulsory tie-in between its tabulating cards and tabulating machines *(IBM v. US, 1936)*.

7. This point was emphasized in interviews by Henry Geller (FCC General Counsel, appointed 1964; Assistant Secretary for Communications and Information, and Administrator of NTIA, appointed 1977) and Bernard Strassburg (H. Geller, personal communication, March 24, 1985; B. Strassburg, personal communication, March 25,1985).

8. See John D. de Butts' address to NARUC's 1973 annual convention, entitled, "An Unusual Obligation." In this address, deButts vigorously defended the traditional AT&T monopoly and the common carrier principle (de Butts cited in Von Auw, 1983, pp. 422–432).

9. The original, or "unmodified" settlement underscores how well AT&T's and Justice's interests meshed—to the detriment of the local telephone companies. The financial viability of the divested BOCs was not a major concern in the original settlement. It was only Judge Greene's post-Decree intervention which took away Yellow Pages (producing $3 billion in revenues annually) from AT&T and gave the service to the BOCs. This intervention also limited the share of debt each BOC would have to bear post-divestiture. Judge Greene permitted the BOCs to market telephone equipment so long as it was manufactured by some other entity.

10. In his speech before the shareholders in 1981, Charles L. Brown said that AT&T's "long distance services must be relieved of the burden of contributing to the support of local service." Brown outlined AT&T's "Statement of Policy," which claimed that increasing local rates is the key to enabling AT&T expansion into data processing and related fields ("AT&T lifts earning," 1981, p. D5). In another context, Brown as much as admitted that divestiture was necessary. In an address at AT&T's annual meeting in 1982, he stated, "Slowly, indeed painfully, it had become clear over the last few years that the Bell System would have to be significantly restructured. And it had become clear that the choice was not between preserving the Bell System as it is today or restructuring it in some new way. . . . The real issue was how and when to undertake a radical transformation" ("Ma Bell speaking," 1982, sec. 3, p. 2).

11. For all of the analysis which claims that divestiture was a good move for AT&T, several caveats need to be acknowledged. At least for the short term in the domestic arena, divestiture will not be easy for the company. It is not accustomed to having to compete in an open marketplace. And deregulation is by no means complete. AT&T must continue to abide by the requirement (imposed by the FCC's Second Computer Inquiry) that it maintain a separate subsidiary to market telephone equipment and enhanced telephone services. Hence the company's actions likely will be cautious and conservative. The introduction of AT&T's personal computer in June, 1984 appears to confirm this. Rather than come out with a major new product, the AT&T model 6300 is another IBM-compatible computer. For all the hoopla, AT&T barely figured in the computer market in 1984 (Sanger, 1984). On other fronts, AT&T continues to suffer from a large servicing backlog for business customers. In California, the company claims large losses on its long distance service since divestiture (Keppel, 1984). The telephone equipment market, according to economist Thomas C. Spavins, Deputy Chief of the FCC Office of Plans and Policy, will stabilize with AT&T having only one

quarter of that market (T. C. Spavins, personal communication, June 20, 1984). Already, AT&T's share of phones leased and sold to customers has fallen to 67% from a high of 85% in 1982, according to the Electronic Industries Association (Rempel, 1985). A similar slide has occurred in the domestic Private Branch Exchange (PBX) market. AT&T's share of PBX sales dropped from 51% in 1976 to 22% in 1983 (Barnes, 1984c). Lastly, AT&T is expected to lose a large share of the long distance market. In 1982 before divestiture, AT&T controlled nearly 93% of the nation's toll revenue. Now, according to estimates, the company has 80% of total long distance revenues (Barnes, 1984a). Notwithstanding AT&T rate decreases, the competitors' share has risen. And the announcement in June, 1985 that IBM has purchased a major share of MCI bodes ill for AT&T's continued dominance in long distance. By its own count, AT&T is losing 5000 long distance business and residential customers a day to competitors (Barnes, 1984c).

12. AT&T's own figures show that just 10% of residential users make over $25 worth of long distance calls per month; just 14% of business users make over $50 worth of long distance calls per month (AT&T, 1984). It is *these* users who will benefit from divestiture. Thus, the assessment of the divestiture which claims that any increase in local telephone rates will be balanced by a corresponding decrease in long distance rates fails to recognize the vast difference in *user classes*. Moreover, the "balancing" claim, thus far, is untrue. Although long distance rates have fallen 5–6% since divestiture, these have failed to offset actual and foreseeable increases in local phone service. For example, in November, 1984, New York Telephone sought to raise its average residential bill by 16.3%, to $29.67 from the current $25.52. Pacific Bell has asked the PUC for a rate increase of $1.36 billion in 1984. Consumer groups figure that the increase proposals would raise overall local rates 55% by 1986—even Pacific Bell concedes the raise would come to 36% (Guyon & Saddler, 1984). According to a study by the Consumer Federation of America, a Washington-based consumer group, residential phone rates rose by an average of 20%, or $2.5 billion, in 1984, the first year following the breakup (Berg, 1985b). Finally, in order to keep major data customers inside the local telephone companies, the companies have offered such customers special low rates (Keppel, 1985).

13. The FCC's moves toward competition threaten the viability of the telcos in one more respect. Recent decisions to approve cellular radio and Digital Termination Systems encourages the entry of technologies which can bypass the telco "last mile."

REFERENCES

Allocation of Microwave Frequencies Above 890mc, 27 FCC 359 (1959).

American Telephone and Telegraph Company. (1948–1957). *Annual report*. New York: Author.

AT&T lifts earnings 11.1%, calls for higher local rates. (1981, April 16). *The New York Times*, p. D5.

AT&T set to expand fiber optic network. (1984, November 9). *The New York Times*, p. D1.

AT&T plans to blend computers and phones. (1984, November 10). *The New York Times*, p. D1.

Averch, H., & Johnson, L. L. (1962). Behavior of the firm under regulatory constraint. *The American Economic Review, 52* (5), 1052–1069.

Baer, W. S. (1984). Telephone and cable companies: Rivals or partners in video distribution? *Telecommunications Policy, 8* (4), 271–289.

Barnes, P. W. (1984a, June 25). Long-distance phone battle. *The New York Times,* pp. D1, D5.

Barnes, P. W. (1984b, July 10). States slowing telephone deregulation. *The New York Times,* pp. D1, D6.

Barnes, P. W. (1984c, August 5). AT&T: Hot products, high costs. *The New York Times,* sec. 3, p. 4.

Bell System Offerings, 46 FCC 2d 413 (1974), aff'd sub nom. Bell Tel. Co. v. FCC, 503 F.2d 1250 (3rd Cir. 1974), cert. denied, 422 U.S. 1026 (1975).

Berg, E. N. (1985a, March 11). New phone company twist. *The New York Times,* pp. D1, D3.

Berg, E. N. (1985b, May 31). $1-a-month phone fee takes effect tomorrow. *The New York Times,* pp. D1, D5.

Bornholz, R., & Evans, D. S. (1983). The early history of competition in the telephone industry. In D. S. Evans (Ed.), *Breaking up Bell: Essays on industrial organization and regulation* (pp. 7–40). New York: Elsevier.

Breyer, S. (1982). *Regulation and its reform.* Cambridge, MA: Harvard University Press.

British Telecommunications Union Committee. (1983). *The American experience . . . a report on the dilemma of telecommunications in the USA.* London: Author.

Brock, G. W. (1975). *The U.S. computer industry: A study of market power.* Cambridge, MA: Ballinger.

Brooks, J. (1975). *Telephone: The first hundred years.* New York: Harper & Row.

Brown, C. L. (1983). Recasting the Bell System. *The Columbia Journal of World Business, 18*(1), 5–7.

Communications Act of 1934, Pub. L. No. 416, 73rd Congress, 48 Stat. 1064 (1934).

Cornell, N. W., Kelley, D., & Greenhalgh, P. R. (1980). *Social objectives and competition in common carrier communications: Incompatible or inseparable?* (Working paper No. 80–01, Office of Plans and Policy). Washington, DC: Federal Communications Commission.

Cornell, N. W., Pelcovits, M. D., & Brenner, S. R. (1983). A legacy of regulatory failure. *Regulation, 7* (4), 37–42.

Danielian, N. R. (1939). *AT&T: The story of industrial conquest.* New York: Vanguard Press.

Dawson, F. (1984). Born Bell. *Cable Television Business, 21*(1), 42–52.

Did it make sense to break up AT&T? (1984, December 3). *Business Week,* pp. 86–124.

Domestic Communications-Satellite Facilities ("DOMSAT"), First Report and Order, 22 FCC 2d 86 (1970); Second Report and Order, 35 FCC 2d 844 (1972), aff'd sub nom. Network Project v. FCC, 511 F.2d 786 (DC Cir. 1975).

Fagen, M. D. (Ed.). (1978). *A history of engineering and science in the Bell System: National service in war and peace, 1925–1975.* New York: Bell Telephone Laboratories, Inc.

FCC's regulatory role over phones affirmed. (1984, June 20). *The Washington Post,* p. F1.

Federal Communications Commission. (1938). *Telephone investigation: Proposed report.* Washington, DC: Government Printing Office.

Federal Communications Commission. (1949–1956). *Annual report*. Washington, DC: Government Printing Office.

Federal Communications Commission. (1966). In the matter of regulatory and policy problems presented by the interdependence of computer and communication services and facilities (first computer inquiry). FCC Docket No. 16979 (Notice of inquiry November 10, 1969), final decision, 28 FCC 2d 267 (1971), aff'd in part sub nom. GTE service corp. v. FCC, 474 F.2d 724 (2nd Cir. 1973).

Federal Communications Commission. (1970). In the matter of establishment of policies and procedures for consideration of application to provide specialized common carrier services in the domestic public point-to-point microwave radio service, and proposed amendments to parts 21, 43 and 61 of the Commission's rules. FCC Docket No. 18920 (Notice of inquiry, notice of proposed rulemaking released July 17, 1970), 24 FCC 2d 318.

Federal Communications Commission. (1975). In the matter of MCI Telecommunications Corp., 34 R. R. 2d 539 (1975), 37 R. R. 2d 1339 (1976), rev'd sub nom. MCI Telecommunications Corp. v. FCC, 561 F.2d 356 (DC Cir. 1977), cert. denied sub nom. FCC v. MCI Telecommunications Corp., 434 U.S. 1040 (1978).

Federal Communications Commission. (1976a). In the matter of amendment of section 64.702 of the Commission's Rules and Regulations (second computer inquiry). FCC Docket No. 20828 (Notice of inquiry and proposed rulemaking 1976), final decision, 77 FCC 2d 384 (1980), aff'd sub nom. CCIA v. FCC, 693 F.2d 198 (DC Cir. 1982).

Federal Communications Commission. (1976b). In the matter of Amer. Tel. & Tel. Co. Long Line Dept. revisions of Tariff FCC No. 260 Private Line Service Series 5000 (TELPAK). FCC Docket No. 18128. 61 FCC 2d 587 (1976), recon., 64 FCC 2d 971 (1977), further recon., 67 FCC 2d 1414 (1978).

Federal Communications Commission. (1976c). In the matter of regulatory policies concerning resale and shared use of common carrier services and facilities. 60 FCC 2d 261 (1976), recon. 62 FCC 2d 588 (1977), aff'd sub nom. AT&T v. FCC, 572 F.2d 17 (2nd Cir. 1978), cert. denied, 439 US 875 (1978).

Federal Communications Commission. (1980). Video interconnection: Technology, costs and regulatory policies. In Network Inquiry Special Staff, *Preliminary report on prospects for additional networks*.

Federal Communications Commission. (1982). In the matter of MTS and WATS market structure. FCC Docket No. 78–72.

Fishman, K. D. (1981). *The computer establishment*. New York: Harper & Row.

Forester, T. (Ed.). (1985). *The information technology revolution*. Cambridge, MA: MIT Press.

Freiden, R. M. (1981). The computer inquiries: Mapping the communications/data processing terrain. *Federal Communications Law Journal, 33*(1), 55–115.

Gabel, R. (1969). The early competitive era in telephone communication, 1893–1920. *Law and Contemporary Problems, 34*(2), 340–359.

George, G. F. (1969). The Federal Communications Commission and the Bell System: Abdication of regulatory responsibility. *Indiana Law Journal, 44*(3), 459–477.

Goulden, J. C. (1968). *Monopoly*. New York: G. P. Putnam's Sons.

Graphnet Systems Inc., 44 FCC 2d 800 (1974).

Guyon, J., & Saddler, J. (1984, December 17). A year after breakup of AT&T, the benefits mostly remain elusive. *The Wall Street Journal*, pp. 1, 26.

Hannibal and Saint Joseph Railroad Co. v. Swift, 12 Wall 262 (1870).

Hanscom, C. D. (1961). *Dates in American telephone technology*. New York: Bell Telephone Labs, Inc.

Holsendolph, E. (1983, March 7). Bell units weighing cable TV role. *The New York Times*, pp. Dl, D8.

Hush-a-Phone Corp. v. United States, 238 F.2d 266 (D.C. Cir. 1956).

In the Matter of Use of the Carterfone Device in Message Toll Telephone Service, 13 FCC 2d 420 (1968), recon. denied, 14 FCC 2d 571 (1968).

In Re Applications of Microwave Communications, Inc., 18 FCC 2d 953 (1969), recon. denied, 21 FCC 2d 825 (1970).

International Business Machines Corp. v. United States, 298 U.S. 131 (1936).

Johnson, L. L. (1978). Monopoly and regulation in telecommunications. In G.O. Robinson (Ed.), *Communications for tomorrow: Policy perspectives for the 1980s* (pp. 127–155). New York: Praeger.

Keppel, B. (1984. June 24). Citing early losses, AT&T Communications asks PUC to give it a break. *The Los Angeles Times*, part 5, pp. 3, 8.

Keppel, B. (1985, June 3). PUC trying to adapt to new environment. *The Los Angeles Times*, part 4, pp. I, 5–6.

Lewis, A. (1956, January 25). AT&T settles antitrust case; shares patents. *The New York Times*, pp. 1, 16.

Loeb, G. H. (1978). The Communications Act policy toward competition: A failure to communicate. *Duke Law Journal*, 1978 (1), 1–56.

Ma Bell speaking. (1982, April 25). *The New York Times*, sec. 3, p. 2.

Madsen, K. E. (1959). Antitrust: Consent Decree: The history and effect of Western Electric Co. v. United States, 1956 Trade Cas. 71,134 (D.C. N.J. 1956). *Cornell Law Quarterly*, 45(1), 88–96.

Mathison, S. L., & Walker, P. M. (1970). *Computers and telecommunications: Issues in public policy*. Englewood Cliffs, NJ: Prentice-Hall.

MCI Telecommunications Corp. v. FCC, 561 F.2d 365 (D.C. Cir. 1977).

National Association of Regulatory Utility Commissioners v. FCC, No. 83–1225, U.S. Court of Appeals (D.C. Cir. 1983).

Noam, E. M. (1983). Federal and state roles in telecommunications: The effects of deregulation. *Vanderbilt Law Review*, 36(4), 949–983.

Nora, S., & Minc, A. (1980). *The computerization of society: A report to the President of France*. Cambridge, MA: MIT Press.

Oettinger, A. G., & Berman, P. J. (1977). The medium and the telephone: The politics of information resources. In A. G. Oettinger, P. J. Berman, & W. H. Read (Eds.), *High and low politics: Information resources for the 80s* (pp. 1–145). Cambridge, MA: Ballinger.

One of the great miscalculations in IBM history [advertisement]. (1980, May 4). *The New York Times Magazine*, p. 127.

Packet Communications Inc., 43 FCC 2d 922 (1973).

Pagano, P. (1985, June 24). Phone industry wants U.S. to clarify goals. *The Los Angeles Times*, part 4, pp. 1–2.

Philadelphia and Reading Railroad Co. v. Derby, 14 How. 468 (1852).

Phillips, A. (1983). Regulatory and interfirm organizational burdens in the U.S. telecommunications structure. *The Columbia Journal of World Business*, 18(1), 46–52.

Pollack, A. (1983, December 1). Sidestepping the telephone company. *The New York Times*, pp. 29, 31.

Pollack, A. (1984, February 18). Omens for phone technology. *The New York Times*, pp. 29, 31.

Pool I. de Sola. (1983). *Forecasting the telephone: A retrospective technology assessment of the telephone.* Norwood, NJ: Ablex.

Regional phone firms win ok for ventures. (1984, December 15). *The Los Angeles Times*, part 4, p. 1.

Rempel, W. C. (1985, January 21). Not all phone users buy freedom. *The Los Angeles Times*, part 4, pp. I, 5.

Ricci, C. (1984a, April 2). AT&T will seek waiver to offer services to U.S. *The Wall Street Journal*, p. 3.

Ricci, C. (1984b, April 30). Heavily reliant on phones, brokers are hit hard by AT&T breakup. *The Wall Street Journal*, sec. 2, p. I.

Rowland, W. D. (1982). The process of reification: Recent trends in communications legislation and policy-making. *Journal of Communication*, 32(4), 114–136.

Sahagun, L. (1984, May 27). AT&T split takes toll on customers. *The Los Angeles Times*, pp. 1, 25.

Sanger, D. E. (1984, June 22). Challenge to AT&T computer. *The New York Times*, pp. D1, D2.

Sanger, D. E. (1985, June 28). Big U.S. computer deal for AT&T. *The New York Times*, pp. 27, 29.

Schiller, D. (1982). *Telematics and government.* Norwood, NJ: Ablex.

Schmukler, E. (1984). The war of the wires. *Channels*, 4(2), 36–39.

Shanahan, E. (1974, November 21). U.S. sues to divest AT&T of Western Electric Co., charges wide conspiracy. *The New York Times*, pp. 1, 68.

Sharpe, W. F. (1969). *The economics of computers.* New York: Columbia University Press.

Sichter, J. W. (1977). *Separations procedures in the telephone industry: The historical origins of a public policy.* Cambridge, MA: Program on Information Resources Policy.

Smith v. Illinois Bell Telephone Co., 282 U.S. 133 (1930).

Solomon, R. J. (1978). What happened after Bell spilled the acid?—Telecommunications history: A view through the literature. *Telecommunications Policy*, 2(2), 146–157.

Telenet Communications Corp., 46 FCC 2d 680 (1974).

Trebing, H. M. (1969). Common carrier regulation—The silent crisis. *Law and Contemporary Problems*, 34(2), 299–329.

Trice, J. A. (1984). Cable wars. *California Lawyer*, 4(7), 54–56.

United States Department of Justice. (1981). Plaintiff's Memorandum in Opposition to Defendents' Motion for Involuntary Dismissal Under Rule 41 (b) in United States v. American Telephone and Telegraph Company (August 16, 1981).

United States House of Representatives. (1958a). 85th Congress, 2nd Session. Interstate and Foreign Commerce. *Network Broadcasting* (Report No. 1297). Washington, DC: Government Printing Office.

United States House of Representatives. (1958b). 85th Congress, 2nd Session. Committee on the Judiciary. Antitrust Subcommittee (Subcommittee No. 5). *Consent Decree Program of the Department of Justice* Hearings, 25 March–22 May 1958 (Serial No. 9). Washington, DC: Government Printing Office.

United States Senate. (1981). 97th Congress. The Telecommunications Competition and Deregulation Act of 1981 (S. 898).

United States Senate. (1982a). 97th Congress, 1st and 2nd Sessions. Committee on the Judiciary. *The Department of Justice Oversight of the United States v. American Telephone and Telegraph Lawsuit* Hearings, 6 August 1981 and 25 January 1982 (Serial No. J–97–53), part 1. Washington, DC: Government Printing Office.

United States Senate. (1982b). 97th Congress, 2nd Session. Committee on Commerce, Science, and Transportation. *AT&T Proposed Settlement* Hearings, 25 January and 4 February 1982 (Serial No. 97–92). Washington, DC: Government Printing Office.

United States Senate. (1983). 98th Congress, 1st Session. Committee on Commerce, Science, and Transportation. *Long-Range Goals in International Telecommunications and Information: An Outline for United States Policy.* Committee Print (11 March 1983). Washington, DC: Government Printing Office.

United States v. American Telephone and Telegraph Company, Western Electric Company, Inc., and Bell Telephone Laboratories, Inc., U.S. District Court (D.C. Cir. 1974), Civil Action 74–1698, Civil Action No. 82–0192 ("Modified Final Judgment," 1982).

United States v. Western Electric Co., Inc., Civil Action No. 17–49 (D. N.J. 1956).

Von Auw, A. (1983). *Heritage and destiny: Reflections on the Bell System in transition.* New York: Praeger.

Wiley, R. E. (1981). Competition and deregulation in telecommunications: The American experience. In L. Lewin (Ed.), *Telecommunications in the United States: Trends and policies* (pp. 37–59). Dedham, MA: Artech House.

Zerner, C. (1949, January 15). U.S. sues to force AT&T to drop Western Electric Co. *The New York Times*, pp. 1, 30.

9 Investigative Journalism and the Moral Order

THEODORE L. GLASSER, JAMES S. ETTEMA

$\mathbf{I}$f investigative reporting is American journalism at its most vigorous and often its most influential, it is also American journalism at its most paradoxical. The essential energy of investigative journalism is still best characterized as "righteous indignation," a term coined by Ida Tarbell nearly a century ago as the anthem of the muckrakers. The contemporary version is *IRE!*, the acronym for Investigative Reporters and Editors, a national organization founded in 1975. This unmistakable tone of moral judgment stands in apparent opposition to the presumed objectivity of the press. How can the press function as the "custodian of conscience," as Bethell (1977) puts it, and at the same time claim to be only a detached observer? That is, how can investigative reporters expose wrongdoing without making moral judgments?

In *Deciding What's News*, Gans (1980, pp. 185–186) offers an insightful, if underdeveloped, answer to these questions: "Like social scientists and others, journalists can also feel objective when they assume, rightly or wrongly, that their values are universal or dominant. When values arouse no dissent or when dissent can be explained away as moral disorder, those who hold values can easily forget that they are values."[1] Indeed, it is a commitment to enduring and consensual social values that makes journalistic objectivity possible. "Being part of news judgment, the enduring values are those of journalism rather than of journalists," Gans (p. 197) concludes. "Consequently, journalists can feel detached and need not bring in their personal values." Investigative reporters thus can set aside explicit consideration of the normative "ought" and concentrate instead on documentation of the empirical "is" by limiting their investigative stories to violations of widely shared values.

In their dealings with presumably incontrovertible instances of wrongdoing, reporters typically describe two aspects of the empirical "is." One aspect is the wrong itself: the actions of the violators and, perhaps, the reactions of their victims (cf. Ettema & Glasser, 1988). The second aspect is some empirically determined standard that has been violated by those actions. As Gans

(p. 183) points out, the quintessential investigative story, the expose, "typically judges the exposed against their own expressed values, and these can be determined empirically by the reporter." If nothing else, then, the exposed are found to have violated the widely shared proscription against hypocrisy, but often they are also found to have violated such "objective" standards as laws, codes of professional conduct, and the like. By appealing to standards external to journalism, investigative reporters are able to treat questions of right and wrong as questions of fact. And because this objectification of moral claims, as it might be called, necessarily upholds, not challenges, the prevailing moral order, Gans (p. 293) posits a fundamentally conservative role for an adversarial press: it conserves the moral status quo insofar as it "reinforces and relegitimates dominant national and societal values by publicizing and helping to punish those who deviate from the values."

Gans' central insight is that investigative journalists can claim to be objective to the extent that they operate within what Hallin (1984) calls a "sphere of consensus" and can therefore locate "objective" standards of conduct. We argue, however, that Gans underestimates the amount of moral work that must be accomplished by journalists because the consensus upon which they rely is neither stable nor complete. While there may be "enduring values" upon which the claim to objectivity depends (e.g., antipathy to hypocrisy), such values are not consistent, and their application to the situation at hand is seldom clear. Appropriate objective standards are rarely self-evident, and the task of "empirically determining" them is rarely simple. Investigative journalists do not, indeed cannot, simply reiterate, and thereby reinforce, a clearly articulated moral order by exposing incontrovertible transgressions against that order. Journalists themselves must articulate the moral order by showing that transgressions are, in fact, transgressions. While they stop short of making moral judgments, if such judgments are understood to be unequivocal and carefully justified pronouncements of right and wrong (in order to help maintain the necessary fiction of disengagement), they do locate, select, and interpret the standards that can be used by the public to make such judgments. This objectification of moral standards, we conclude, is the special contribution of investigative journalists to the ongoing cultural process by which morality is not only reinforced but also defined and refined through application to new and ever-changing conditions.

Investigative reporters are thus participants in what Condit (1987) describes as the "crafting of public morality," though the terms of their participation are problematic. They are called upon not so much to maintain as to produce standards of moral judgment, but they are denied by the canons of objectivity the opportunity to explicitly make and, more important, analyze and defend such judgments. Despite the focus on apparently incontrovertible instances of wrongdoing, escape from the paradox is not, then, as easy as it may first have seemed. This paradoxical, but necessary, connection between moral custodianship and moral disengagement is our point of embarcation for the intellectual territory that Hallin (1985) identifies as most in need of exploration by communication scholars: the realm of social and cultural life wherein media power is brought to bear in the ongoing struggle to legitimize the existing order. Specifically, our objective is threefold: (1) to review briefly the enduring relationship between adversarialism and objectivity, (2) to examine the diverse styles that contemporary investigative reporters have adopted to live within that difficult relationship, and (3) to assess the special moral craftwork of these reporters (i.e., their objectification of standards for moral judgment). We conclude with an argument concerning journalism's role in the process of legitimation and, in turn, the consequences of that process for continuity and change in the moral order.

THE PARADOX OF THE DISENGAGED CONSCIENCE

No doubt fueled by *The Washington Post*'s now legendary efforts in the early 1970s to uncover corruption in the Nixon White House, the rise of investigative journalism represents a renewed interest in a watchdog or adversary press. To be sure, the adventures of Carl Bernstein and Bob Woodward, and especially the adventures of their celluloid counterparts, Dustin Hoffman and Robert Redford, mark the beginning of what has become an extended celebration of those hard-hitting reporters whose bravado spirit affirms the importance of a free and unintimidated press. Above all else, it is a celebration of the notion that the public interest is best served by a continuing rivalry between the press and the powerful.

The pitting of the press against power, particularly the power of the state, reflects a fundamentally populist conception of the press in contemporary society. Though not unmindful of the drudgery of long hours of routine and often mundane work, a burgeoning literature with titles like *The Typewriter Guerillas* (Behrens, 1977) and *Raising Hell* (Weir & Noyes, 1983) presents an unabashedly heroic profile of investigative reporters whose stories "attack, charge, inflame, accuse, harass, intimidate, incriminate, and sometimes damage or destroy organizations, agencies, and government on your behalf and mine" (Behrens, 1977, p. xxiv).[2] These "news room irregulars" appear as our last hope for a challenger to the authority of government, a role which is important, we are told, because "realistically, the public cannot count upon any administration to do a strict job of policing itself" (Mollenhoff, 1981, p. 354).

Whether the ideal of an adversary press manifests itself as exaggerated cynicism or healthy skepticism, whether it reflects journalists' "psychic baggage" (cf. Lichter, Rothman, & Lichter, 1986) or their commitment to their constitutionally sanctioned duty (cf. Blasi, 1977), it is an ideal which has long endured as the ethos of American journalism. It may be true that the genre of investigative journalism, despite occasional flashes of high visibility, appears relatively infrequently on America's front pages. It may also be true that only a minority of journalists expressly endorse an adversarial role (Weaver &

Wilhoit, 1986), but it is probably just as true that an adversarial attitude "has always lurked in the psyche of American journalists" (O'Neill, 1983, p. 8). The notion that the press should be a relentless adversary of the powerful, a "lifeline of democracy in reporting upon the use, misuse, and abuse of power" (Mollenhoff, 1981, p. 355), does, in fact, have deep roots in American journalism. But the notion that the press is an unbiased recorder of fact is also sustained by deep roots. Indeed, any full account of the intimate relationship between adversarialism and objectivity would begin where the history of modern journalism begins: the penny press.

As James Gordon Bennett himself explained, the penny press sought both to reach "the great masses of the community" (Lee, 1923, p. 95) and to gain independence from the mercantile and political elites whose interests dominated the press of the 1830s (cf. Schudson, 1978). This self-proclaimed independence enabled this new journalism to pursue what was then an entirely novel approach to reporting: "surveillance of the public good" (Schiller, 1979, p. 47). With no narrow cause to advocate and no special interest to promote, the penny press could offer, it claimed, a more dependable and authentic journalism: news untainted by the political, social, and economic values that for so long had defined the content of the daily papers. Championing the values of its predominantly working class public served not to diminish but to strengthen faith in the authenticity of its news; for the values of its readers, especially when those values were cast in terms of political or economic opportunity, were not treated as mere values but as natural rights. Drawing upon these enduring values, the penny press could, without apparent contradiction, claim to be at once the recorder of what Bennett stated would be "facts of every public and proper subject, stripped of verbiage and coloring" (Lee, 1923, p. 195) and the "private defender of the public good" (Schiller, 1981, pp. 45–47). This new journalism thus spoke for, and thereby helped to realize, a vision of public interest by telling stories which exemplified and defended that interest.

Any account of the relationship between adversarialism and objectivity also needs to highlight the alliance between journalism and the Progressive Movement. Journalism's sense of independence, its disdain for special interests, and its commitment to news of "public interest," all a legacy of the penny press, coincided well with the Progressive call for reform. Much in the tradition of the penny press, the muckraking magazines of the pre-World War I years, according to Leonard (1986, p. 185), had "triple the circulation of the older monthlies and sold at a third of the price"; and with "bolder editing and greater use of photographs, the new monthlies brought vivid stories of corruption to hundreds of thousands of Americans who were used to nothing more than disjointed newspaper accounts." This "new, moral, radical type of writing," as Filler (1968, pp. 9–10) termed it, may have bewildered and shocked conservative readers who probably felt that "it was no business of theirs if someone's factory was a firetrap," but to the ordinary reader "the new writing was as gripping as it was educational: they had never known that business and politics could be so interesting." Once again, a new journalism helped to consolidate the very value system upon which it based its claim to speak on behalf of the public interest.

The muckrakers' exposé, and even the sensational journalism of Hearst and Pulitzer, benefited enormously from what was becoming the hallmark of the new century: reverence for the logic of science and faith in the power of detached observation. The Progressive Era marked the beginning of what Hallin (1985, p. 129) describes as the "scientization of journalism," when the "changing conventions of journalism paralleled the rise of science as a cultural paradigm against which all forms of discourse came to be measured." With straightforward fact-filled reports, journalists, like scientists, could position themselves and their work as value free. The ideal of objectively reported fact was soon rationalized into journalism's dominant paradigm:[3] "a canon of professional competence and an ideology of professional responsibility" which conveyed a "reassuring sense of disinterest and rigor" (Carey, 1969, pp. 33, 36). Consequently, the independence of the press came to mean an allegiance to unadorned—if sometimes outrageous—facts, and news judgment came to appear as an impartial and disinterested response to the day's events, issues, and personalities rather than as a value-laden determination. Similarly, bias came to be understood as manifest partisanship that could be easily neutralized rather than as latent presuppositions about "the world outside" that end up, to complete the title of Walter Lippmann's famous essay, as "pictures in our heads."

By this account, the paradoxical connection between moral custodianship and moral disengagement is less a logical contradiction than a necessary tension in the historical development of American journalism. Tarbell's journalism of righteous indignation has been made credible (indeed, it has been made intellectually possible in the age of science) by its "appearance of disinterest and rigor." For no one can "unearth a scandal," according to Weisberger (1961, p. 160), "as effectively as a man with no vested interest in any part of the scandal-making mechanism." But if the triumph of objectivity as the professional ethic of journalism has worked to make muckraking credible, it has worked also to further obscure the very values upon which it depends. Allegiance to objectivity has made it difficult for journalism to ask explicitly what constitutes the public interest or even what constitutes a scandal, because that allegiance has made it difficult explicitly to make, analyze, or defend moral judgments. Values are now submerged into what Hall (1982), borrowing from Noam Chomsky, terms the "deep structure" of journalism.

And yet this "hidden consensus," to use another of Hall's phrases, has never been entirely secure. In turn, the journalistic deep structure is never completely submerged. In our own time, journalism has come under fire for its values even though, as Gans finds, it has retained the value system of the Progressive reformers (cf. Sorauf, 1987). Like the Progressives, it supports individualism and resists "collective solutions other than at the grassroots level." The resemblance, Gans (p. 69) argues, "is often uncanny, as in the common advocacy of honest, meritocratic, and anti-bureaucratic government, and in the shared antipathy to political machines and demagogues, particularly of populist bent." Nevertheless, contemporary journalism is often seen to be dangerously adversarial in its stance toward "traditional values." For example, Daniel Moynihan's celebrated *Commentary* essay on "The Presidency and the Press" (1971), published three years before Richard Nixon's resignation, lamented a feckless hostility to power among members of the press. Due in large measure to the rising social status of its practitioners, Moynihan (p. 43) argued, "the press grows more and more influenced by attitudes genuinely hostile to American society and American government." Journalism had become yet another manifestation of what Lionel Trilling (1965) terms the "adversary culture" or Moynihan the "culture of disparagement" (cf. Callahan, Green, Jennings, & Linsky, 1985; Lichter et al., 1986).

Even journalists themselves sometimes argue that the values they detect within journalism are not proper values. In his presidential address to the American Society of Newspaper Editors, Michael J. O'Neill (1983, p. 8) complained bitterly about the press' "adversarial posture toward government and its infatuation with investigative reporting." A more appropriate editorial philosophy, O'Neill (p. 15) proposed, would involve a "clear but uncrabbed view of the world"; it would be "more positive, more tolerant of the frailties of human institutions and their leaders" (p. 12). Similarly, journalists' own commentary on the "Janet Cooke scandal" often suggested that in the 1960s and 70s journalism had gone too far in its attempt to overcome the limitations of traditional objectivity (Eason, 1986). Indeed, some observers argued that the excesses of investigative journalism along with the experiments in New Journalism had created a disorder in the professional arena that undermined not only the authority of government but the authority of truth itself.

And so, it seems, the boundaries of the moral order that journalists are to defend are not clearly demarcated even among journalists themselves. Their response, unsurprisingly but nonetheless ironically, may be to demand a renewed commitment to a "clear . . . view of the world," which is to say, of course, "objectivity." A simplistic call for resolution of the paradox in favor of more objectivity and less adversarialism, however, is not the only response of contemporary journalists.

NEWS JUDGMENT AND MORAL CONSENSUS

Our ongoing, on-the-record series of interviews with distinguished investigative journalists shows these reporters to have a sophisticated, though not necessarily consistent, sense of the necessary tension between adversarialism and objectivity in their work.[4] These indepth interviews reveal diverse approaches to that paradoxical relationship, but they also reveal commonalities that unite these reporters in a shared intellectual enterprise. Here, we reconstruct at least a little of that unity within diversity.

Some of these reporters celebrate active adversarialism. An example is Jonathan Kaufman, who, with a number of colleagues at the *Boston Globe*, won the Pulitzer Prize for a series of articles on the persistence of racism in some of Massachusetts' most esteemed institutions, including the *Globe* itself. "I love getting people's attention," he said of his reporting. Kaufman wants his readers to think: "This is an outrage!" He understands very well that routine reporting cannot be the venue for presentation of the issues he wants his readers to confront:

> Typical reporting gets the charge and gets the response and stops there. But what we tried to do with the racism series, what investigative reporting tries to do, is to go back and say, "Well, that response doesn't make sense," or "That response is a lie. . . ."

> Traditional objectivity here would not advance the argument at all. Traditional objectivity would basically have white people saying what white people have always said and black people saying what black people have always said. What these pieces tried to do was to move the argument ahead.

Kaufman's goal is to make Boston the best city that it can be. "I do the kind of reporting I do, in part, because I think newspapers should write for people who have no voices," he said. "If we're not going to write about homeless people and poor people and people discriminated against, who will?" Here, then, is a reporter who takes pride in his ability to influence his community but who also recognizes that any claim to moral leadership within the community is problematic for journalism. He expressed discomfort with the idea that the series on racism was driven by either the *Globe*'s or his own sense of morality:

> I think it was driven by a sense that it was important to the city. The *Globe* has been accused of being above the city and pointing down and saying, "You people should act better. You people should act like good, well-to-do liberals." My feeling here, and the way we wrote about institutions, was that this was crucial for the city to face. It wasn't something we wanted to impose on people, but the city was being torn apart.

> Newspapers are not just repositories of what happened yesterday. This was a very activist piece. It tried to say, "There's something important going on here that we must think about and think about hard."

Thus, when pressed by a persistent questioner, even this unabashed advocate was more comfortable characterizing his work in terms of what is "important" to the community rather than what is right.

In contrast to Kaufman, William Marimow of the *Philadelphia Inquirer* ringingly reaffirmed objectivity, particularly the distinction between fact and value. Marimow was adamant in his insistence that moral values are not problematic for the investigative reporter. "Right and wrong may be a threshold question but not a fundamental question," he argued. The fundamental questions are whether the transgression really did occur, whether it can be documented in a reasonable period of time, and whether that documentation will yield "information that would be important to *Inquirer* readers." The expertise of the reporter, according to Marimow, is brought to bear not in judgments of morality but in judgments of practicality and newsworthiness. He elaborated with reference to his Pulitzer Prize-winning investigation of the Philadelphia police department's K-9 unit whose dogs and officers were "out of control":

> Let's go to the K-9 cases. Are these attacks warranted? Yes or no? No, they look questionable. Is there a standard by which I can gauge whether they're justifiable, questionable, or really unwarranted? Not a clear one, but you can get a sense of it. . . .
>
> Is it newsworthy? Well, in my opinion, if people sworn to uphold the law are alleged to be violating people's civil rights over and over again, that's important. Why is it important? It's important because these people are entrusted with great power and authority and these dogs are capable of inflicting great physical and psychological harm. And the city must know about [it] because there are dozens of civil suits being filed and nothing's happening. The officers go back to the street time and time again. So I think, for me, the ultimate question becomes a question of importance and not right or wrong.

Just as Kaufman implicitly recognized a limit to adversarialism in his defense of it, Marimow implicitly recognized a limit to objectivity. Even as Marimow argued that morality is an unproblematic, "threshold" question, while newsworthiness is the ultimate question, he acknowledged that moral issues are both present and problematic. His commentary provides a brief glimpse of the enduring values (e.g., individualism manifested here in terms of individual civil rights) which are submerged in the journalistic judgments of "importance." It also provides a glimpse of the moral work to be done: Marimow suggested that there were standards to judge the situation, but he acknowledged that they were not unequivocal. While his goal is to report on obvious violations of the moral order, he knows the exact boundaries of the order are not well defined. Wrongdoing is not entirely self-evident, and he must demonstrate, after all, that the transgression is indeed a transgression.

If the interviews with Kaufman and Marimow were studies of intellectual life at the polar extremes, interviews with most other reporters examined life in the domains between. Loretta Tofani of *The Washington Post*, for example, acknowledged that her Pulitzer Prize-winning investigation of sexual assaults against inmates in a Maryland county jail evoked a strong "gut reaction" within her and that it began as a "conscious choice" to show "the wrong" in a situation that is often seen as an inevitable consequence of incarceration. Elsewhere in our interview with her, however, she rejected the role of moral leadership for her paper or for herself. She said that she was sure her readers, when confronted with the facts, would agree with her response to the situation. "I think my judgment reflects people outside of journalism," she said. "I really felt that people outside would see it as wrong as well." Thus any morally inflected judgments she may have made were not, as she views it, her judgments but those of her community.

At the same time, she backed away from the notion that she had helped define for her readers an ambiguous situation as wrong. "I don't know if I'm helping them see what's right and wrong as I am showing them a problem that they otherwise would not be able to learn about in any sort of detail," she argued. "You don't end up saying, 'And this is wrong.' You stop at the point of describing the problem." With many of her colleagues, she sought refuge in the notion that she had not made explicit moral judgments but had merely described a situation that was important to her community. It is the community, Tofani argued, that must ultimately say, "This is wrong."

The argument that any moral judgments made by the journalist reflect the moral values of the community was fundamental to the reporters of the middle domain. Jon Sawyer who, with longtime partner in the *St. Louis Post Dispatch*'s Washington bureau William Frievogel, has distinguished himself as an investigator of waste and fraud in defense procurements. He acknowledged that investigative reporters are constantly making judgments concerning "immorality, the potential [for] immorality, the appearance of immorality." But he argued that journalists cannot dictate values to their audiences. If the investigation does not uncover something that is "really wrong," he maintained, "the story will sink without a trace." To have an impact, the story must reflect "the community consensus on those values and how they apply in particular instances."

Stephen Kurkjian of the *Boston Globe*'s much-decorated Spotlight Team also recognized a value-based relationship between journalist and community. "With more experiences in various systems, when you pay your bills, when your kids go to school, you become more of a judge as to what shouldn't be and what should be," he argued. "The more part of a community you get, the more cautious you become, but the more accurate becomes your sense of personal outrage." Kurkjian conceptualized the values of his community as a "common-man set of standards," personified in the standards of his aunt whom he described as an average citizen who graduated from high school. "I think, 'Gee, I gotta see it the way she would see it.'" Her sense of outrage, he argued, has become his.

Journalists' value judgments can therefore reflect the community consensus on values until in the final analysis these judgments, as Sawyer said, are so "ingrained" that they become news judgments. "I make a judgment whether something's worth going after, whether it meets my own standard of what's significant," Sawyer acknowledged. When asked to articulate these standards, however, he revealed just how ingrained or, in our terms, submerged such standards are. "I don't know that I can [articulate them]," he said. "It would depend entirely on the situation, the circumstances that you're talking about." But whatever these unarticulated standards may be, they seemed to Sawyer to concern "what's newsy, what's jazzy, what's interesting, what's out of the ordinary, more than what's immoral."

In the simultaneous embrace of adversarialism and objectivity, these investigative reporters have found a variety of ways to live with, though not resolve, the paradox of their craft. While these examples do not exhaust the diversity of reporter thinking, they do capture the key features of the modus vivendi that continues to make investigative journalism credible, indeed possible. Although these reporters do not always articulate it clearly or consistently, they do acknowledge that their connection to a community and its moral order allows them to identify outrages against that order. While their conceptions of "the community" and its values may not encompass everyone in their city or everyone in their audience, these conceptions reference an "interpretive community" (Fish, 1980) within which values seem to be "pretty black and white," as one reporter said; "the facts," as another reporter said, "speak for themselves." Thus journalists make judgments of news value (i.e., "importance" to the community), not of moral value. With Gans, these reporters do realize that their claim to moral detachment depends upon a moral relationship of long standing to the community, or at least those segments of the community with which they identify. Once in that relationship, values come to be "ingrained" or, in Gans' terms, "included unconsciously . . . because they are built into importance judgments" (p. 196). Investigative journalists are not, then, moral arbiters who can recreate the moral order anew with each story, but neither do they simply and uncritically reinforce that order. Rather, they contribute something to the ongoing moral relationship with their communities. Indeed, these reporters do seem to understand at some level that, even if values are "pretty black and white," there is particular moral work which they must do. It is to this work, a role in the crafting of morality not fully appreciated by either Gans or the reporters themselves, that we now turn.

FROM MORAL CLAIMS TO EMPIRICAL CLAIMS

Documenting the existence of a transgression is largely a matter of gathering evidence and assessing its quality (Ettema & Glasser, 1987). But establishing that the transgression *is* a transgression requires a process which we have termed the "objectification" of moral standards. In this process, reporters attempt to make good on their claim that they make news judgments rather than moral judgments, that is, that they attempt to transform moral claims into empirical claims so that, ultimately, the moral standards used to appraise the transgression appear as empirically unambiguous as the evidence used to document its existence. By the logic of this process, the moral order is made a fact, and facts, of course, can be observed and reported with detachment.

In general terms, the task of objectifying a moral claim is accomplished through an appeal to some self-evidently credible moral authority. Among the reports and reporters we have studied, these appeals to authority include (1) appeal to the law, (2) appeal to formalized codes or guidelines, (3) appeal to recognized expertise, (4) appeal to normality as evidenced in statistical or other comparisons, and (5) appeal to common decency. By locating and selecting moral authorities and by interpreting and applying their judgments, investigative reporters can recognize and expose wrongdoing and at the same time maintain their allegiance to the ethic of objectivity. These appeals, like the strategies identified by Tuchman (1972) in her analysis of the conventions of objective reporting, serve to insulate reporters from responsibility for their own judgments.

Even if the law is the product more of politics than morality, reporters know it as the most concrete and objective standard for the evaluation of questionable actions. "I can hang my hat on the law," said one reporter. "I'm always trying to find the legal edge to the story," said another. An excellent example of putting a "legal edge" on the story is the *Boston Globe*'s series on racial discrimination. For Jonathan Kaufman and his colleagues, federal law was "the rock to cling to" throughout any storm of criticism directed at their analysis of racism:

> One of the key things that we decided was that whatever definitions we used would have to be federal law, things like affirmative action and discrimination. . . . That was our fall back, saying, "Look, these are definitions that the courts have decided. Its not something we decided would make a good city. This is what the law is."

Kaufman and his colleagues thus located and used a source of moral authority outside their own personal or organizational values. It is important to note, however, that the term "fall back" is well chosen, for it captures well the process by which a moral claim is objectified. Kaufman and the *Globe* attacked discrimination not merely because it was illegal. They *had* decided that discrimination made a bad city and, as Kaufman said, they wanted Boston to be "the best city it could be." The law provided a ready objectification of moral judgment that served not merely as a shield against criticism but as an instrument of moral craft.

The legal edge may be the sharpest edge among the journalist's tools, but the law is not the only or even the most important tool of moral craftwork. Reporters recognize that much evil is not illegal. Stephen Kurkjian, for example, succinctly summarized the range of wrongdoing encountered by the investigative reporter as "illegal, improper, irregular." Bill Marimow offered a strikingly parallel summary:

> I'll go through the categories that I have in my mind. First, there's the issue of legality and then there's the issue of ethicality, then there's the issue of propriety and then there's the issue of appearance of impropriety, four levels.

Marimow presented these "categories" (or more accurately, typifications) as a hierarchy of news value, but they can also be seen as a hierarchy of transgressions.[5] Marimow strives, in his own words, "to find some objective standard" that can transform impropriety into unethical behavior, or at least transform apparent impropriety into impropriety.[6] These "objective standards," the tools to objectify wrongdoing that is not illegal, often include codes of ethics and formalized guidelines for behavior. At best, codes and guidelines are those of the individual or organization under investigation. If those do not exist, Marimow may borrow relevant codes or guidelines from others. He may also call upon the testimony of experts to establish usable standards. Once again, he used his investigation of Philadelphia's K-9 unit to illustrate this process:

> If you look at the K-9 story, you'll see I like to have something to measure conduct by. . . . After the questions were raised about the necessity for these attacks, I said, "Well, what specifically do the guidelines say?" I found a deposition given by Morton B. Solomon, former police commissioner of Philadelphia, in which he equated the use of dogs to the use of deadly force. You can use them when the police officer's life is in mortal danger, when another citizen's life is in mortal danger . . . or to apprehend a fleeing felon. That was what the police commissioner said was the appropriate use of dogs. I wasn't satisfied with that. I went out and found the head of the New York Transit Authority's K-9 unit and he said, "No Solomon's wrong. Dogs are like night sticks, another law enforcement tool." So through those two people I was able to establish parameters.

In the series that appeared in the *Inquirer*, however, Marimow (1984, p. 1) used the stricter standard set by the former police commissioner. He also made news of the fact that police did not have their own guidelines in this regard:

> A three-month *Inquirer* investigation has found that a hard core of errant K-9 police officers and their dogs is out of control. Furthermore, the police department has made no attempt to hold these men or their colleagues to any sort of written guidelines or standard procedures spelling out when to attack and when to hold back. . . .

> Former police commissioner Morton B. Solomon, in a deposition taken in February 1982, stated that there were only three circumstances in which he believed a dog should be commanded to attack: protect an officer's life, to protect another person's life, or to apprehend a fleeing felon. But these are only Solomon's beliefs, not the rules that actually govern the officer and dog on the street.

Marimow defended this borrowing of standards, and implicitly acknowledged his role as moral craftsman, with the notion that it is not the violation of particular codes or guidelines per se which makes the story important. "Ethicality isn't determined by whether or not there's a strict set of definitions," Marimow argued, "rather, it really deals with one's values and what's right and wrong." Just as Kaufman fell back upon the law, so Marimow fell back upon other modes of objectification for a story in which values were not so unproblematic after all.

The practice of confirming an intuitive sense of wrong by "falling back" upon codes, guidelines, or experts is illustrated by Jack Reed and Lucy Morgan's investigation of a county sheriff's department for the *St. Petersburg Times*. Reed was responsible for examining the financial relationship between the sheriff and an independently wealthy deputy:

> I felt almost immediately, because of the things I looked into, that there was something wrong . . . . One of the first things I did was look into [the sheriff's] dealings with Mr. Moorman, the deputy, and I realized something was wrong. I went to a professional property appraiser in that county and ran it by him and said, "What's going on here in this transaction where [the deputy] apparently sells a piece of property for a fraction of its value and buys a business from the sheriff for a lot more than it was worth, apparently it is worth nothing. What do you say about this?"

> He agreed that this was an unusual transaction, so immediately I know that there was something unusual going on.

Just as wrong extends beyond the illegal to the unethical, so it may extend beyond the unethical to the abnormal, the "unusual" in Reed's terms or the "irregular" in Kurkjian's. The reporter, however, tries to move the wrong up the hierarchy by pursuing the possibility that the irregular is, in fact, unethical. And in Florida, the unethical behavior of an official may also be illegal, which is a judgment made by the Commission on Ethics once a complaint has been lodged.

> When it came to land dealings and bank dealings, I would try to talk to professionals in the field . . . . They backed up my feelings that we were on to something that was unusual. You know, at the time I didn't even think, "Is it illegal?"

> The next thing I got into was [whether] it was illegal for a public official to be doing this. I would call Larry Gonzales who is the director of the Commission on Ethics for the state in Tallahassee. He wouldn't answer specific questions but he would answer hypotheticals: You know, what if a public official does this . . . ? He'd say, "Yes, potentially there's conflict with this certain code of ethics."

Reed was adamant in his conviction that it is not appropriate for the newspaper or an individual reporter to lodge the complaint with the Commission on Ethics, and so a conclusive judgment could not be reported in the story. Nevertheless, with Gonzales' help, Reed found precedent for strongly implying in the story that the sheriff's behavior was unethical. At the same time, the reporter allowed the sheriff to make his own appeal to normality:

> When Pasco County Sheriff John M. Short wants to buy or sell a piece of property or find a business partner, he often turns to his employees . . . . The sheriff says it's all proper, sheriff's business comes first. . . . Short also says that "many sheriffs" and other elected officials do business with subordinates because they are "people they know and trust."

> Yet Florida law prohibits a public official from having a work relationship that "will create a continuing or frequently recurring conflict between his private interests and the performance of his public duties."

> In interpreting that law in 1982, the State Ethics Commission said that "an ongoing business relationship with a subordinate" can cause conflicts for a public official, since it could impede that official's "duty of impartially evaluating the subordinate's job performance." (Reed & Morgan, 1983, pp. B1, B8)

While the abnormal is low on reportorial hierarchies of wrongs, the documentation of abnormalities may play a useful role in the moral craft of the investigative journalist. An investigation by Pam Zekman of WBBM-TV in Chicago concerning the suppression or "killing" of crime reports by the Chicago Police Department provides an example: "In the case of 'killing crime' there were no laws being broken," said Zekman, "but there are FBI guidelines for crime reporting and we hung a lot on that." It was not, however, merely the violation of arcane federal guidelines that objectively demonstrated something was wrong in the police department. It was that Chicago's unfounding rate was abnormally high for crime reports when compared with other major cities. (A crime report is classified as "unfounded" if the initial investigation yields little or no evidence of a prosecutable offense.) In her report, which aired in a 1982 newscast, Zekman combined these two elements into her explanation of Chicago's "secret weapon" against crime:

> Here's how it works: the police say the victim's complaint is unfounded, in effect, that the crime never happened. The police rubber-stamped that conclusion on more than 9,000 robbery cases last year, 1 out of every 3. By comparison, New York, Los Angeles, and St. Louis unfounded fewer than 1 out of 100. We wondered why Chicago is so out of line when it's supposed to follow the same FBI guidelines as all other cities.

According to the report, Chicago's unfounding rate for rape was 6 times higher and for burglary was 50 times higher than other major (i.e., normal) cities. Such statistics were central to the conclusion that the Chicago Police Department "lies about the number of crimes."

For Kaufman and his colleagues, statistical comparisons provided another of the "rocks" to which they could cling in their assessment of racism in Boston:

> With the rock of statistics you were able to go to the Bank of Boston and say, "Only 1% of your managers are black."
>
> They'd say, "Well, you know, there are very few black bankers."
>
> And then you could say, "Well, the national average is 5% and Chicago has 6% and Washington has 2%. . . ."
>
> That was probably the thing that gave the story the most credibility because otherwise you would have been hooked into competing anecdotes. You never would have had any evidence.

Altogether, these sorts of data helped the reporters to objectify the claim that, among a number of large cities, Boston was "the least liveable" for blacks.

If statistics are not available, a comparative case study may suffice. For the *Globe*'s Kurkjian, who does many stories on the machinations of governmental bureaucracies, a basic principle is "the system should work." He regularly finds norms for system performance through comparison to other systems. "In each of our series, we try to show a system which has worked out there," said Kurkjian, "and why it works there and doesn't work here." Statistics and comparisons thus objectify the normal, and through the implicit equation of morality with normality they turn moral claims into empirical claims.

While objective standard-bearers (federal antidiscrimination laws, state ethics codes, opinions of experienced police officers, federal employment statistics) may speak with substantial authority, they may not speak eloquently enough to summon the community's righteous indignation. Laws, guidelines, and the rest are really only echoes of the enduring values that are at stake in these stories. But, of course, the ability of journalists to speak explicitly and forcefully of values is severely constrained. Thus, even with careful objectification of standards, journalists may not elude the dilemma of moral craftwork within the culture of objectivity.

The solution to this dilemma is often an appeal to common decency, an appeal that provides essential moral energy to even the most elaborately objectified story. This appeal differs from the others because it is not an explicit enumeration of objective standards but rather an implicit invocation of commonsensical standards. The authority of this appeal lies not merely in its invocation of widely shared interpretations of right and wrong but in its embedding of the interpretations within the facts of the situation. The appeal is powerful precisely because it is implicit. It is made within and through an "objective" description of the situation, a story in which the facts seem to speak for themselves.

A masterful example of the appeal to common decency is Loretta Tofani's series on sexual assaults in a county jail. While the rape of one inmate by another was obviously illegal, Tofani knew that "there would be some really highly insensitive people in the world who would not view that as wrong, who would say, 'Look, the guy was in jail. What do you expect in jail?'" Tofani's personal response to such a point of view is a classic statement of moral common sense:

> The first thing I would say is, "How would you feel if that happened to you?" Then I would say, "Human beings are entitled to a certain amount of dignity. That [experience] really robbed this man of that. The jail is entrusted with keeping these people secure and that was violated. People ought to have a certain peace of mind and not have to spend their lives thinking of this really traumatic thing that happened to them."

Tofani's appeal—"How would you feel if it happened to you?"—is a variation on that cornerstone of moral common sense, the Golden Rule.

Tofani attempted to objectify her "gut sense" of this terrible wrong by searching for experts who could testify as to what, in fact, could be expected in other jails and to the psychological consequences of jail rape. All she could find, however, were "self-styled experts" who seemed to be "on Mars." Most of these were academics to whom "theories were more important than people." Few had any clinical knowledge of jail rape. "Some of the worst experiences I had were talking to those so-called experts," she recalled. "I just wanted to puke every time I got them on the phone." The importance of this failure to objectify the evil of jail rape with expert opinion or statistical comparison was clearly demonstrated by the reporter's need to explain the absence of such information from her series:

> It is not known whether the rape problems in the Prince George's County jail are more or less serious than in other jails throughout the country. Few people have studied the problem of jail rapes; those who have studied it tend to produce more theories than facts. Perhaps as a result, the problem of jail rape is not a public issue; only rarely is it even a topic of discussion at conventions for jail officials, according to penologists.

> Yet it is a problem with serious consequences. Men who were raped in the county jail say the experiences left them shocked, disoriented, and unable to concentrate on their upcoming trials. Of 15 victims who were interviewed, three were later treated in mental institutions. (Tofani, 1982a, pp. A1, A18)

While this passage from one of the stories acknowledged the absence of objectified standards, it also laid the foundation for an appeal to common decency. Narratives of victimage and villainy, as we have argued elsewhere (Ettema & Glasser, 1988), are central to the moral force brought to bear in and through investigative journalism. In this series, the narrativized appeal to common decency began with terrifying case studies of young men who were typically charged with minor offenses but who were punished with brutal rapes; and it continued with a grotesquely callous appeal to normality by the head jailer who dismissed any rapes that may have occurred with the notion that "the same thing happens in schools." Thus, through narrative, the reporter showed her readers what it would be like if it *did* happen to them: terror, pain, humiliation, and abandonment. She showed them that what was wrong here was not a failure of officials to obey a law or follow a guideline but rather a failure to meet the most basic expectations of common decency. The appeal concluded with an explicit condemnation of the situation voiced in the story by a source: "'We're not rehabilitating people,' says District Court Judge Joseph Casula, referring to the rapes. 'We're not even punishing them. We're subjecting them to torture and degradation'" (Tofani, 1982b, p. A1). While explicit, this summary judgment was brief and hardly necessary. It was through storytelling itself that the reporter made her appeal to common decency and thereby evoked righteous indignation at a situation that was, until she began the series, morally ambiguous. These stories not only documented events in a county jail, they proposed standards which revealed those events to be a moral outrage. These stories, in short, defined evil.

THE LIMITS OF LEGITIMATION

In this essay, we have tried to understand how the tensions between detached observation and active moral agency are mediated within the institution of investigative journalism. We have taken seriously the arguments of distinguished investigative journalists who maintain that they make news judgments rather than moral judgments. But we have argued as well that news judgments draw upon a historically given moral order and have implications for the future of that order. Obviously, these judgments concern the selection of breaches in the moral order for public attention. Less obviously, perhaps, they concern the objectification of evaluative standards (the location, selection, and interpretation of standards appropriate to the situation at hand). These news judgments thus represent the transformation of moral claims into empirical claims.

In deciding where, as one reporter phrased it, "the curative powers" of journalistic scrutiny are to be brought to bear and in deciding which evaluative standards are to be used, investigative journalism contributes to the process by which the moral order may be defined and developed as well as simply reinforced. Journalism is not the only agent active in this process, however, for as the journalists themselves vigorously argue, the community (the public or at least public officials) must also participate. Moral guardianship and moral neutrality are not contradictions for these reporters so long as journalists only tell the story and let the public decide what, if anything, is to be done. "It really wasn't my job to make that final decision: Is this illegal or not, is this immoral or not?" argued Jack Reed of his investigation of the county sheriff. "I raise the question. I can tell you what he did and I can tell you what the law is and you can take it from there."

These reporters maintain that their power as well as their responsibility are limited to presenting their community with a story. Sometimes the public may turn a county sheriff from office at the next election or their representatives may commission the construction of new jail facilities, but sometimes the public and government officials do nothing. These reporters all have examples of stories that evoked no indignation or even interest. To this, Bill Marimow said, "So be it. My job, I think, is to present important information to the public." He argued that his work has not been proven less valuable if there is no reaction to the story. "The value to me is getting important information to readers . . . so that they, based on their judgment, can either bring public pressure to bear or ignore it."

Whether the story summons outrage or "sinks without a trace," as Jon Sawyer said, the story is nonetheless always a test of "the community consensus on . . . values and how they apply in particular instances." The story is always a call for the community to affirm by word or deed that an action is, indeed, a transgression of the moral order or else to affirm by indifference that once, perhaps, the act might have been a transgression, but it is no longer. Those stories that provoke public outrage reward both the journalists' selection of the transgressions for public scrutiny and their application of the "objective" moral standards to the case at hand. Such stories may simply reinforce the authority of the standards and, in turn, the boundaries of the consensus, but they may also define and develop standards through their application to new and different situations. Those stories met with indifference, on the other hand, may not be told again, the standards revised and the boundaries redrawn. Thus investigative reporting may be a party not only to the definition and development of values but also to their debasement and dissolution.

This process, this call and response, cannot be understood fully at the psychological level of analysis (although individuals may experience "media effects") or at the organizational level (although organizational imperatives within journalism and government do influence both story and response) or even at the sociological level (although social institutions such as the law are involved). This process is authentically cultural: a candidate for characterization as that often discussed but rarely documented phenomenon, the mass mediated ritual. These stories and the response to them are, as Victor Turner (1968, p. 6) writes of ritual, "a periodic restatement of the terms in which men [sic] of a particular culture must interact if there is to be any kind of a coherent social life." They serve, in Geertz's terms (1973), both as a model *of* social structure and moral value and as a model *for* their reproduction. But, as both anthropologists suggest, these maintenance functions do not exhaust the meaning of ritual in and for the life of a culture. Ritual is not only reflective but also reflexive, an occasion for deconstruction and, perhaps, reconstruction of structure and value. It is an agent not only of cultural maintenance but also of cultural change.

As ritual, investigative journalism embraces this eternal tension between continuity and change. On the one hand, it hardly constitutes the "culture of disparagement" envisioned by Moynihan. Rather, the press generally, and investigative reporting particularly, serves as a fundamentally conservative influence insofar as it typically reifies but also vivifies enduring values and evokes among the public indignation at their violation. On the other hand, investigative journalism is not the simple apology for traditional values that Gans depicts; it does not simply reinforce and relegitimate the status quo. Rather, it is a process in which new outrages are identified and standards to evaluate them are proposed, and it is a process in which old outrages are shown to no longer capture the moral imagination. Values, therefore, are not only reinforced but renewed or realigned in the attempt to apply them to new and ever-changing conditions. The complexity of this ongoing process is, perhaps, best captured in Hall's phrase (1982), "the production of consensus," which suggests that the press actively helps fashion and simultaneously helps legitimize the very consensus it ostensibly only conveys.

In emphasizing the open-ended, ongoing character of this process, we diverge from legitimation theorists—among them, Horkheimer and Adorno (1972), Marcuse (1964), and Milliband (1969)—whose work casts the media in an unproblematic role as producers of a "one-dimensional" consciousness, an ideological consensus that uncritically reflects and thus functions to legitimize the existing order. With Gouldner (1976), Hallin (1985), and others, whose understanding of the process of legitimation derives from Habermas' reformulation of it (1975), we are not inclined to ascribe to the press the power to achieve any complete or lasting ideological closure. We recognize instead that what may be functional for the press may not always serve the interests of society's "hegemonic elites"; at times, in fact, it is a matter of self-interest for the press to publish news "*dis*creditable to powerful and reputable elements" in society (Gouldner, 1976, p. 109).[7] And even when the press can be counted on to act as a legitimizing force in society, legitimacy so gained tends to be ideologically weak, incoherent, and, most certainly, tentative.

In the case of investigative journalism, there is little doubt that the press can serve as an agent of legitimation for dominant or enduring values, but there is also reason to believe that, on occasion, it can serve as an agent of change for those values. To Gouldner's appreciation of the complexity of this situation, we would add a final, ironic complication. Any effect of investigative journalism on the moral order, whether in the direction of continuity or change, is made weaker, less coherent, and more tentative by the very tactic that presumably makes journalism more credible: a mode of discourse that distances reporters from the knowledge claims they report and also denies them what Rorty (1983) calls "a morally sensitive vocabulary." Callahan and his colleagues (1985, p. 19) make largely the same point in their assessment of the relationship between the press and congressional ethics:

> Journalists are reluctant to raise ethical issues or to analyze them on their own. For the most part they approach ethical issues only indirectly, through quotes elicited from others. As a result, legislative ethics is molded by journalistic practice into the form of charges and countercharges, accusations and denials. This distorts the process of moral dialogue and reflection in the legislative setting and leads to a preoccupation with . . . "scandal ethics."

Thus, while investigative journalism may function to conserve or to change the moral order, journalistic traditions and practices also function to undermine the rationality of that order by subverting critical discussion of it.[8] The impoverishment of journalism's moral resources may well equip it to preside most comfortably over the debasement and dissolution of values, more comfortably, certainly, than over their definition and development. When stories of transgressions do summon moral outrage, the vocabulary necessary for rich and rigorous discussion of underlying values gives way to a vocabulary of guilt and innocence, praise and condemnation. And when stories do not summon outrage, journalism needs only to fall silent.[9] Thus, in finding Gouldner (1976, p. 111) to be quite correct when he observes that news "devalues, censors, and represses" the very values in which journalists ground their judgments, we once again are forced to confront the paradoxical nature of news. Throughout this essay, we have argued that the ideological consequence of a press seeking to be the "custodian of conscience" is an intimate, if always tentative, connection between the press and the moral order. We also recognize, however, that the consequence of a press seeking, at the same time, to be a detached observer is a devalued, censored, and repressed connection between the press and the public conscience.

Acknowledgments: The research was supported by a grant from the Gannett Foundation with supplementary funding from the authors' universities.

NOTES

1. Moral disorder news, as Gans (1980, p. 56) defines it, reveals "instances of legal or moral transgressions, particularly by public officials and other prestigious individuals who, by reason or virtue of their power and prestige, are not expected to misbehave." In contrast to social disorder news, which "monitors the respect of citizens for authority," moral disorder news evaluates "whether authority figures respect the rules of the citizenry" (p. 60). Both investigative reporting and

day-to-day crime reporting are genres of moral disorder news. Unlike crime news, however, investigative journalism is not as a rule limited to instances of illegal conduct. Rather, it deals more broadly with instances of illegitimate conduct.

2. See, for example, Dygert (1976), whose book *The New Muckrakers* is subtitled "Folk Heroes of a New Era," and Bolch and Miller (1978), whose introductory chapter is called "The New American Hero."

3. For an excellent discussion of objectivity as the dominant paradigm of journalism, see Hackett (1984).

4. The interviews with the investigative journalists were conducted from June 1985 to February 1987.

5. Unlike the term "category," which implies a "classification of objects according to one or more relevant characteristics ruled salient by the classifiers," the term "typification" denotes a phenomenological orientation, a "classification in which relevant characteristics are central to the solution of practical tasks or problems at hand and are constituted and grounded in everyday activity" (Tuchman, 1973, pp. 116–117).

6. Of all the improprieties that public officials might conceivably commit, it is probably hypocrisy that most outrages Kurkjian's "common man." Thus, the peccadilloes of the powerful may become stories if they suggest hypocrisy. Use of marijuana by a public official, for example, may or may not be a story according to Bill Marimow. "I don't think anybody knows, on the hierarchical scale of values, where the usage of marijuana is in contemporary society," he says, "but I would say that it is definitely a story if the guy is an outspoken critic of marijuana usage." If mere impropriety seems too ineffectual a basis for a powerful investigative story, consider the fall of Gary Hart.

7. The press may want to publish news discreditable of the powerful in society in part because such news enhances journalism's "fourth estate" or "watchdog" role; or as Hallin (1985, p. 124) puts it, "the ability of the mass media to support the structure [of social power] ideologically is limited by their need to maintain the integrity of the process of communication on which their own legitimacy depends." Also, there may be economic incentives to publish news critical of the status quo in that attacks on the powerful tend to sell newspapers: "This would seem to be an inescapable implication of the competiveness characteristic of capitalist production, in which each economic unit is quite ready to profit from disaster to another" (Gouldner, 1976, p. 109).

8. Habermas speaks to this point in his distinction between instrumental and communicative rationality. What underpins the discourse of journalism is a kind of instrumental rationality, a *monologic* use of language that strives for technical control over objectified process. In contrast, communicative rationality rests on a *dialogic* use of language that honors the intersubjectivity between subjects and objects (cf. Habermas, 1971, p. 137). The importance of this distinction, Held (1980, p. 303) explains, "arises from the fundamental difference . . . between the interaction of a subject with an object, which can be regarded as another subject, and that of a subject with an object which cannot be so construed."

9. That the press does not always fall silent in this situation may be evidence of a moral courage that should command our respect, or at least our attention. The *Globe*'s series on racism, for example, was undertaken even though its earlier reporting on school busing had been, as Kaufman described it, a "whole trauma . . . where people had shot at the building and all." Kaufman and his colleagues

undertook the project despite the fact—or perhaps because of the fact—that they would be "writing against the grain with this piece, that, in fact, the overwhelming sense in Boston was, 'Don't bring this up; things are okay.'"

REFERENCES

Behrens, J. C. (1971). *The typewriter guerillas*. Chicago: Nelson-Hall.

Bethell, T. (1977, January). The myth of an adversary press. *Harper's*, pp. 33–40.

Blasi, V. (1977). The checking value in First Amendment theory. *American Bar Foundation Research Journal*, 520–642.

Bolch, J., & Miller, K. (1978). *Investigative and in-depth reporting*. New York: Hastings House.

Callahan, D., Green, W., Jennings, B., & Linsky, M. (1985). *Congress and the media*. Hastings-on-the-Hudson, NY: Hastings Center.

Carey, J.W. (1969). The communications revolution and the professional communicator. *The Sociological Review, 13*, 23–38.

Condit, C. M. (1987). Crafting virtue: The rhetorical construction of public morality. *Quarterly Journal of Speech, 73*, 79–97.

Dygert, J. H. (1976). *The investigative journalist*. Englewood Cliffs, NJ: Prentice-Hall.

Eason, D. L. (1986). On journalistic authority: The Janet Cooke scandal. *Critical Studies in Mass Communication, 3*, 429–447.

Ettema, J. S., & Glasser, T. L. (1987). On the epistemology of investigative journalism. In M. Gurevitch & M. R. Levy (Eds.), *Mass communication review yearbook 6* (pp. 338–361). Newbury Park, CA: Sage (Originally appeared in *Communication, 8*, 183–206).

Ettema, J. S., & Glasser, T. L. (1988). Narrative form and moral force: The realization of innocence and guilt through investigative journalism. *Journal of Communication, 38*(3), 8–26.

Filler, L. (1968). *The muckraker*. Chicago: Henry Regnery.

Fish, S. (1980). *Is there a text in this class? The authority of interpretive communities*. Cambridge: Harvard University Press.

Gans, H. (1980). *Deciding what's news*. New York: Vintage Books.

Geertz, C. (1973). *The interpretation of cultures*. New York: Basic Books.

Gouldner, A. W. (1976). *The dialectic of ideology and technology*. New York: Seabury Press.

Habermas, J. (1971). *Knowledge and human interests*. Boston: Beacon Press.

Habermas, J. (1975). *Legitimation crisis*. Boston: Beacon Press.

Hackett, R. A. (1984). Decline of a paradigm? Bias and objectivity in news media studies. *Critical Studies in Mass Communication, 1*, 229–259.

Hall, S. (1982). The rediscovery of "ideology": Return of the repressed in media studies. In M. Gurevitch, T. Bennett, J. Curran, & J. Woollacott (Eds.), *Culture, society and the media* (pp. 56–90). London: Methuen.

Hallin, D. C. (1984). The media, the war in Vietnam, and political support: A critique of the thesis of an oppositional media. *Journal of Politics, 46*, 2–24.

Hallin, D. C. (1985). The American news media: A critical theory perspective. In J. Forester (Ed.), *Critical theory and public life* (pp. 121–146). Cambridge: Massachusetts Institute of Technology Press.

Held, D. (1980). *Introduction to critical theory*. Berkeley: University of California Press.

Horkheimer, M., & Adorno, T. W. (1972). *Dialectic of enlightenment*. New York: Seabury Press.

Lee, J. M. (1923). *History of American journalism* (rev. ed.). Cambridge MA: Riverside Press.

Leonard, T. C. (1986). *The power of the press*. New York: Oxford University Press.

Lichter, S. R., Rothman, S., & Lichter, L. S. (1986). *The media elite*. Bethesda, MD: Adler and Adler.

Marcuse, H. (1964). *One-dimensional man*. Boston: Beacon Press.

Marimow, W. K. (1984, April 15). A city ruffed up: The K-9 cases. *Philadelphia Inquirer*, p. 1.

Milliband, R. (1969). *The state in capitalist society*. London: Weidenfeld and Nicolson.

Mollenhoff, C. R. (1981). *Investigative reporting*. New York: Macmillan.

Moynihan, D. P. (1971, March). The presidency and the press. *Commentary*, pp. 41–52.

O'Neill, M. J. (1983). A problem for the republic—And a challenge for editors. In *The adversary press* (pp. 2–15). St. Petersburg: Modern Media Institute.

Reed, J., & Morgan, L. (1983, December 11). Doing business with the boss in Pasco. *St. Petersburg Times*, pp. B1, B8.

Rorty, R. (1983). Method and morality. In N. Haan, R. N. Bellah, P. Rabinow, & W. M. Sullivan (Eds.), *Social science as moral inquiry* (pp. 155–176). New York: Columbia University Press.

Schiller, D. (1979). An historical approach to objectivity and professionalism in American news reporting. *Journal of Communication*, 29(4), 46–57.

Schiller, D. (1981). *Objectivity and the news*. Philadelphia: University of Pennsylvania Press.

Schudson, M. (1978). *Discovering the news*. New York: Basic Books.

Sorauf, F. J. (1987). Campaign money and the press: Three soundings. *Political Science Quarterly*, 102, 25–42.

Tofani, L. (1982a, September 26). Terror behind bars. *The Washington Post*, pp. Al, A18.

Tofani, L. (1982b, September 27). Justice may not be served. *The Washington Post*, p. Al.

Trilling, L. (1965). *Beyond culture*. New York: Harcourt, Brace, Jovanovich.

Tuchman, G. (1972). Objectivity as strategic ritual: An examination of newsmen's notions of objectivity. *American Journal of Sociology*, 77, 660–679.

Tuchman, G. (1973). Making news by doing work: Routinizing the unexpected. *American Journal of Sociology*, 79, 110–131.

Turner, V. (1968). *The drums of affliction*. Oxford: Clarendon.

Weaver, D. H., & Wilhoit, G. C. (1986). *The American journalist*. Bloomington: Indiana University Press.

Weir, D., & Noyes, D. (1983). *Raising hell*. Reading, MA: Addison-Wesley.

Weisberger, B. A. (1961). *The American newspaperman*. Chicago: University of Chicago Press.

10 An Ethics of Vision for Journalism

DOUGLAS BIRKHEAD

Most of our literature on media ethics centers on the conduct of the journalist in a professional world of news-handling decisions and reporting practices. In this orientation, ethics is associated primarily with right actions. Ethical questions are seen to arise when the need for action arises or when the need for justifying action is pressing. Journalists are taught that ethical deliberation, like news judgment, calls for special expertise. Ethical behavior depends upon skilled reasoning and a knowledge of theorems, principles, or a code of right action, or at least a familiarity with a range of case studies from which general guidance can be abstracted.

I argue in this essay that this pervasive view of ethics is not in harmony with the essential interpretive task of the craft of journalism. Being ethical does not hinge on "moving things about in the public world," in Iris Murdoch's apt phrase (1970, p. 5). Ethical journalism begins with a capacity for socially constructing a moral realism. When the need for specific decision and action in journalism is at hand, the search for ethical insight already is essentially over. Believing that the crucial opportunity for ethics resides in the deliberation of public acts may actually impede a journalist's moral development.

My argument covers three points of discussion. First, I consider why journalism has the ethical stance that it does and why it presents a moral and social difficulty. Second, I acknowledge some previous scholarship that relates to the issues of this essay, drawing ideas for further elaboration. Third, I present and explore an alternative view of ethics for framing the work of the journalist. These aims are not neatly sequential. Rather, they invite "circles of speculation" to uncoil from a central problem: how we are to understand journalism as an ethical activity.[1] No claim is made about a final solution to the problem here, or even about a very orderly advance toward one.

I use the terms "ethics" and "morality" as largely interchangeable. As Jaksa and Pritchard (1988, p. xiii) observe, neither textbooks nor common language exhibits a clear or consistent distinction between these concepts.

Many researchers, and most ordinary writers and speakers, depend upon a natural sense of context for their application.

THE ETHICAL JOURNALIST

When there is talk of ethics or morality in journalism, we are prepared to hear about matters of conduct. Such discussions typically assume and depend upon a common behavioral focus. The issues deal predominately with professional behavior or performance in terms of the roles, goals, and norms of the journalist in the institutional setting of the press (Goldman, 1980, p. 1). The thrust of my essay is to treat this commonplace discourse as problematic. Such talk about ethics is not only bureaucratic in its topical concerns but also in the direction it sets for moral deliberation. I want to discuss briefly why this is so and why it raises ethical and social questions.

Journalism's bureaucratic nature is itself a commonplace observation. Its study has generated such familiar subjects of research as the routines and rituals of news room operations and the organizational construction of news. One cogent theme of analysis that attempts to draw out the ethical ramifications of the craft's performance setting involves the social function of ideology as embedded in the news production system. Glasser and Ettema (1989), for example, characterize the press as performing a reproachful morality play under the guise of journalism's investigative zeal. They argue that journalists, despite a historical "righteous indignation," subvert critical discussion in society by constructing a self-protective "news as discourse."

I believe that a more deeply human failing is at issue than the ideological analysts suggest. In approaching essentially the same drama of ideological intrigue, Kenneth Burke (1959) identifies a dilemma that is also phenomenological and literary. He describes a historical decline in the character of journalism as a cultural performance of perception and mediation of meaning. The conduct he critiques is not just the occupational maneuvering of an ideological discourse but the praxis of a "haphazard philosophy" of interpreting reality (p. 250).

For analysis, Burke offers us a parable on journalism's passage as literature into the modern age. At one time, Burke relates, subtle standards such as meter and alliteration were used to shape an imaginative story genre of news. The inventive effort, however, constrained the productive rhythm of story output. The progress in skill from composing alliterative reports to assembling "All the news that's fit to print" represents the craft's journey to full capacity: the bureaucratization of the ancient bard. The distortion of accomplishment in equating performance with efficiency is readily apparent, Burke (p. 250) concludes, "but we can only speculate gropingly, on paper, as to the ways *all* journalistic efficiency becomes distortion methodized."

The bureaucratic nature of journalism reflects and promotes a power structure. But, as Burke suggests, a bureaucratized press also embodies the more mundane perspectives of a broadly defined urban and industrial order. The habits of the craft are thoroughly mannered by "headline thinking," the concern for a mass audience, a preoccupation with output and speed (pp. 250–252). The result is less a tactical subversion of society's critical self-reflection than a bureaucratized imagination, an organized method of dealing with topics, events, and people from without. Intimacy and complexity are sacrificed for ease of handling. For the journalist, "His problems of craft 'transcend' his problems as layman" (p. 201). The journalist is alienated, not so much from his or her own labor as from what the news product is purported to transform into reality: the "original imaginative stimulus" of the ongoing world. The underlying issue for Burke in the performance of the press is what the contemporary practitioner is able to "see" at all.

Burke's concern about the sentient alienation of journalists is not drawn up explicitly in ethical terms. But the estrangement from imaginative stimulation that he describes, which denies "art for art's sake," has a moral equivalent. The practitioner of an ethically formalized and coded journalism is separated from what constitutes moral ordering as an intricately linked, personal and communal, undertaking. Ethics framed largely in terms of profession and organization setting, even if the purpose is to curb the exploitation of news by applying standardized norms of conduct, seems to misdirect moral attention. What the practice appears to control just as much are ethical *experiences*, what there is to be conscious of, and expressive about, even before the fashioning of an ideological discourse. As complex events are reduced to formula stories to maximize efficiency in reporting, a moral complexity is managed through an expedient ethics of action. We may speculate about the kind of world the journalist imagines as possible, a reality where moral comprehension is not only shaped by but inherently limited to bureaucratically credible stories.

Burke's account of the fate of imagination in journalism points to a possible "methodical distortion" in the way most journalists, and many of their academic mentors, approach an ethics of press performance. Ethics is treated primarily as a style of behavior tied to a productive task. Moral righteousness functions as an "insignia of privilege," reinforcing vocational authority (p. 201). Moral deliberation is a method for determining or justifying acts rather than a human capacity for comprehending value in the world. The ethical journalist is a moral agent rather than a moral being. These are the matters this essay explores.

COSMOPOLITANS AND PROVINCIALS

One researcher who has dealt with concerns similar to Burke's is Howard Ziff in "Practicing Responsible Journalism: Cosmopolitan Versus Provincial Models" (1986), an analysis of ethical relativism in contrasting settings of practice. His study begins with a critique of professionalism and its limits in setting ethical standards. But the argument ultimately turns to the elaboration of an inherently different approach to understanding the nature of ethics in relation to journalism, an outlook associated more closely with perception and expression as focal activities rather than decision making.

Ziff contends that in journalism "uniform professional standards of ethics and responsibility do not exist in fact and ought not exist in principle" (p. 154). That they do not exist is evident in the practice of journalism in diverse settings world-wide. But there is actually no uniform ethical perspective in the American press as well, Ziff maintains, and he draws a significant distinction between urban and provincial media. "Great journalistic organizations and moral journalists are not necessarily engaged in the same endeavor, traveling toward the same goal" (p. 166). The diversity of performance, Ziff concludes, enriches a democratic society and its culture. He offers a number of ethical values—such as being accurate in statements about others, making amends for inaccuracies, avoiding duplicity in dealings, honoring promises, and abstaining from indecencies—which could be argued as universally binding. But they are not values that need to be identified as particular to journalism and its practice. Their appeal for conformity, if any, would oblige all members of a society. What Ziff holds as rightfully relative are values that guide the specialization of journalism in engaging the communal setting of its practice, at times through participation, on occasion through the experience of moral alienation.

In Ziff's view, professionalism is a doxology of disengagement. A primary occupational end of professionalism is autonomy from local setting, with codified ethics and responsibility serving as obligations of independence. The obligations are discharged through principles of practice such as objectivity and disinterestedness. Ziff argues that other vocational ends of journalism are possible. He identifies professionalism with a particular scale and style of social interaction and experience, broadly characterized as metropolitan life or cosmopolitanism. He introduces provincialism as an abstraction of an alternative life style with different goals, other sensibilities, and modified imperatives. Under provincialism, subjectivity and compassion might emerge as appropriate moral obligations in a number of journalistic situations. Community service takes on ethical weight. Perhaps in greatest contrast, individualism as a focus of craft (real or imagined) is devalued. Although Ziff sketches his cosmopolitan and provincial models primarily in geographical terms, or big-city versus small-town journalism, he claims that either ethos can prevail in any setting, depending upon the cultivation of an identity with a mass or communal audience for news. Even national media can be unabashedly community minded (p. 165). Media also may reflect orientations toward both models to some degree.

The dualism, of course, is hardly new. Ziff's argument echoes a classic sentiment for community to scale down modern society to more human proportions (see Dewey, 1927). Media researchers continue to probe the communal value tradition for ethical insight. Clifford Christians, for instance, declares "persons-in-community" as the irreducible category of human exis-tence and focuses on society as a mosaic of subcultures (1986, pp. 123–124). Ziff sees in provincial journalism and its ethical relativism of engagement an affinity for this multiform social design.

Still, as I have summarized them to this point, Ziff's contentions do not seem to raise any serious questions concerning ethics as a process of moral deliberation aimed toward action, even if his critique of professionalism and ethical universalism is taken as well founded. It is one thing to warn against thinking about ethics as detached rules of performance that neatly fit all situations. It is quite another matter to suggest that the moral reasoning involved in applying such rules may itself be problematic. It is this possibility I explore next, using Ziff's analysis as a base of discussion.

MORAL DELIBERATION

In the study of journalism ethics, a model of moral reasoning, the Potter Box, has been adapted by Christians and others to frame typical ethical appraisals in journalism as case studies (Christians, Rotzol & Fackler, 1983, pp. 2–8). It formalizes what is perhaps the everyday approach that many journalists take in ethical deliberation, or approximates in the abstract what is an actual, real-world procedure of handling ethical dilemmas. Four basic categories of potential disagreement are identified by the model: how the situation of the dilemma is defined, the values involved, the principles at stake, and the loyalties that come into play. It is assumed that when journalists differ in their ethical judgment, either among themselves or with others involved in the news, the disagreement may be characterized in terms of these dimensions of an ethical decision-making act. The box is used to locate misunderstandings and to "construct action guides" (p. 2).

In terms of the model, the differences in judgment that might arise from the cosmopolitan and provincial orientations, and the antipathy between the orientations, might reasonably be reduced to essentially an issue of conflicting loyalties. Ziff himself writes of provincialism as fundamentally an attitude of loyalty. The principal source of his positive concept of provincialism is the American philosopher Josiah Royce, who called his turn-of-the-century ethical system based on community the "philosophy of loyalty" (1969). Dealing with a situation in which conflicting loyalties arise may be a trying task, but facing such a condition is unexceptional in everyday decision making. A uniform resolution of differences in every case is hardly to be expected. In this light, what Ziff observes as a basic difference in ethical orientation among journalists is unsurprising. The difference may be accounted for and assessed to some degree by rationally examining the moral weight of allegiances derived from the different perspectives. The issue is thus "contained" by the likes of a Potter Box. It might be argued that Ziff gives us another ethical orientation to think about, but not to think with.

While the Potter Box provides a frame for some aspects of the distinction Ziff develops, I do not believe such a device accommodates the kind of moral activity he advocates. There are features of Ziff's analysis which lie outside the formal reasoning encouraged by the box, and a deeper, implied disposition that what the box represents, ethical decision making, particularly as a procedure of determining or justifying specific acts, is not the most appropriate focus of moral concern in journalism.

Ziff (pp. 151–152) introduces his study with a seemingly far-afield anecdote, an episode in the life of Samuel Johnson and his friend, James Boswell. In Boswell's account of a journey together to Scotland (1961), a reference is made to their staying together in an "indifferent inn," where Johnson is inconvenienced by the windows and is "constantly eager for fresh air." In Johnson's writing on the trip (1775), a digression is made from his formal account of Scotland to include a description of Scottish windows, including their supposed hindrance to fresh air. Johnson concludes with an apology for detracting from the "dignity of writing" with such a detail but then asserts the demand of truth for such seemingly insignificant observations in the appropriate style of depiction: "The true state of every nation is the state of common life."

The anecdote is a rough epistemology or a prescribed method for acquiring and reporting an understanding of social reality that is clearly sympathetic to a provincial model of journalism. But Ziff's use of it as an analogue in his discussion of ethics goes beyond this affinity in perspective. He asserts that his relativistic principle of diverse media ethics is a condition of observing the world properly. It is essential to the journalist's task of *contracting and explicating experience*. As Johnson adapted his prose to give an accounting of the mundane because it was necessary to capture the essence of everyday life in a specific setting, Ziff suggests that a similar flexibility is required in ethics that apply to journalism's task of faithfully exploring and reporting reality, for determining "what stories it is necessary to tell ourselves to realize the ideal significance of our communal life" (p. 166). Ettema and Glasser (1985, p. 200) also write of such an integration of ethics and epistemology in the work of investigative reporters but only as a method of justifying behavior in making observations with "moral certainty." Ziff argues that an ethical sensitivity is necessary to make meaningful observations.

In this view, media ethics is a form of participant observation in particular and deeply felt communal beliefs. A diversity of ethical considerations fosters and preserves "differing ways of imagining and accounting for community experiences" (Ziff, p. 154). The ultimate ethical crisis is not indecision but exile—to stand against community and risk the extreme of alienation on an issue of individual conscience. Cosmopolitanism stands as a separate "world of journalism" detached from community involvement (p. 164). It is a moral haven for standing above local values when the needs of individual conscience are seen to demand it. But it is less involved with the *lived* social world, Ziff implies, and the detachment can limit comprehension of that world. Burke's argument, although made without reference to the concept of community, nevertheless reaches a similar conclusion. The moral imagination as a source of comprehensive insight and expression is constrained if dominated by a craft consciousness embedded in a material order of production. The conscientious journalist, Ziff concludes, alternates between provincial and cosmopolitan frames of vision to guide in the making of authentic assessments of everyday experience.

As a more general theme of philosophy, this perspective predates modern urban and industrial culture. It shares an affinity with a more fundamental and durable cultural debate concerning the rise of rationalism. Johann Gottfried Herder, for example, also grappled with the dualism of provincial and cosmopolitan perspectives as ethical orientations for constructing a meaningful social reality. Sharing the communitarianism of a political romanticism emerging in the late eighteenth century, he nevertheless recognized that an observer solely dependent upon a role of participation in common forms of life could not avoid distorting perception. Despite the "blurred heart of the indolent cosmopolitan," he wrote, the reflexiveness of the cosmopolitan viewpoint, its detachment and critical opportunity, could not be excluded from the process of understanding the world (Larmore, 1987, p. 95). Although "belonging" was the ideal psychological state for meaningful comprehension, it did not satisfy the requirement of observation to leave understanding open to other possibilities of vision, to the complexities of pluralism in meaning, value, and even fact (Larmore, pp. 96, 166–167; see also Berlin, 1976). Herder thus advocated a mixed perspective, provincial and cosmopolitan, much as Ziff suggests for journalists.

How well does a moral reasoning device such as the Potter Box frame the kind of assessment that Ziff advocates? Perhaps such a device is not being fully applied if we consider only the category of loyalties and thus is not being fairly assessed in this discussion. Ziff's call for ethical diversity as a means or condition of explicating experience could also be taken as a principle of truth seeking on which journalists might differ. This is a judgment covered by another category of the box. Since the practical result of much of his discussion is to argue for the removal of certain professional ethical pressures on small-town journalists by defining their situation differently or by appealing to the importance of local values, virtually any category of the Potter Box—loyalties, principles, definition of the situation, values—could be used to "manage" our thinking about Ziff's two orientations or about choices that may arise in relation to them. Trying to "contain" Ziff's argument within the box is, of course, a probing of the radical reach of his position. The exercise is not entirely suitable to the heuristic design of the box, but it does perhaps open Ziff's analysis to the inference that a different *kind* of moral deliberation is involved in his approach, even different human faculties. Although the Potter Box may be only a formalized approximation of how journalists engage ethics in their craft, there is a disposition in Ziff's discussion which hints at a misplaced focus. That focus is the familiar *manner* in which the box approaches ethics, that is by breaking up ethical decisions into deliberative parts. Applying ethics to make decisions in news handling is typical of the craft, and is the topic I explore next.

ACTION VS. VISION

Ziff's provincial model touches upon a more traditional view of ethics as a state of being through authentic comprehension of an essential moral realism, specific in its complexity with regard to time and setting though not without its universal aspects as well. What differs between cosmopolitan and provincial journalists, Ziff (p. 163) describes, is a "context and fabric of sensibility" for making decisions, which results in divergent ethical styles. Morality is concerned not just with the quality of a decision when the need arises but with states of attention, perception, and consciousness. There is a crucial notion of antecedence involved. Moral reasoning as deliberative action to be consummated in behavior is preceded by a contemplation, the cultivation of a way of seeing the world, that is not concerned with specific acts.

Morality is thus more than a mode of behavior. It is a form of reality construction, a technique for observing and expressing interpretations about aspects of the world which are humanly unobservable and ineffable without an ethical sensitivity. Ethical action depends upon an ethics of vision, a "seeing" before doing. The journalist is a moral observer before he or she is a moral agent. Ziff's exploration of provincialism, as quaint as it may strike some readers, is a search for what Iris Murdoch (1970, p. 83) calls the "genetic background" of moral acts. Access to this precondition to willed and controlled performance of duty is limited by any organized method of dealing with the world without intimacy, Burke's bureaucratized imagination. But the imagination in ethics is crucial. As Charles Larmore (1987, p. 12) observes, it reflects "intrinsic interest" in ethical matters and expresses "a far more active and thoughtful interest in the moral life than does the observance of fully determined moral rules." The nature of moral judgment itself may be closer to the play of the imagination in nurturing a sensitized engagement with the world than it is to reason as a process of applying abstract principles. Larmore (p. 21) writes of its complexity:

> We should not hesitate to say that we know that moral judgment exists and know how to recognize it when it occurs just because it appears not to be a phenomenon constituted by reconstructible rules. We should realize not only that there are limits to *theoretical* understanding, but also that there are other kinds of understanding that are more appropriate for grasping the nature of moral judgment.

Our capacity for moral insight, he concludes, thrives on examples as derived through literary expression.

Historical observers as diverse as Friedrich Nietzsche and Henry James have tended to give greater authority to the imagination than to human will, holding that the imagination is "the only human faculty capable to challenging the will with a revelation of what lies beyond its mental frames" (Gunn, 1987, p. 40). Murdoch has written extensively on what she considers the unwise forgetting of the concepts of inner experience and consciousness in formulating moral philosophy. In her book, *The Sovereignty of Good* (1970), she draws a distinction in basic metaphors for conceptualizing an ethical condition. On the one hand is a metaphorical system of motion, the regulation of the human will as it functions in action. A moral reasoning device such as the Potter Box may be seen as a manifestation of this metaphorical system. It attempts to schematize a logic for taking ethical action. In contrast is a system of images and concepts based on vision, the surmising of what "goodness" might be as an end in itself, the treating of virtue as if it were an observable dimension of a fully meaningful world (pp. 3–5). In what she describes as doing "justice to both Socrates and the virtuous peasant," Murdoch identifies virtue with a just vision fostered by humility and suppression of the "fat relentless ego" (pp. 2, 52). This precondition of behavior defines a moral being by quality of consciousness, or sensibility in the broadest perceptive sense.

French philosopher Simone Weil argues in a similar vein. Moral virtue involves a "detachment from the fruits of action," or agency, she writes, in order that a person be prepared to act from a general predisposition of perception (Dunaway, 1984, p. 60). She calls for an attitude of objectivity toward the world in the classic meaning of the concept, or selflessness. This moral sensibility requires a social mediation to be realized. In her book, *The Need for Roots* (1952), Weil calls for its nurturing in the "real, active and natural participation in the life of community" (Dunaway, 1984, p. 52). Royce's moral philosophy based on loyalty advocates a similar social commitment (1969). Murdoch (1970, p. 92) writes that we "act rightly 'when the time comes' not out of strength of will but out of the quality of our usual attachments and with the kind of energy and discernment we have available."

This perspective on ethics suggests that behind the veil of formal moral deliberation may be a different kind of groping altogether. Believing may be seeing, inextricably meshed in an acquaintance with the world through human association. When the need for decision and action arises, the quest for morality may already be essentially over. There is no "formula which can be illuminatingly introduced into any and every moral act," Murdoch (1970, p. 43) observes. "The task of attention goes on all the time and at apparently empty and everyday moments we are 'looking', making those little peering efforts of imagination which have such important cumulative results." The moral life is continuous; the hope of the would-be virtuous person is for "just attention" beyond the duration of the moment of explicit moral choices: "What happens in between such choices is indeed what is crucial" (pp. 37–38).

All ethical thought addresses how people should relate to one another. The apprehension of a real "otherness" in persons appears to be crucial to morality and is what Murdoch perceives to be the essence of having moral vision (Weldhen, 1986, p. 124). Murdoch calls the faculty, simply if also boldly, love. Love is the ideal "imaginative recognition" of the uniqueness of persons and, if connected to a consideration of aesthetics, to the particularity of things as well (Weldhen, p. 123). The activities of ethics and aesthetics merge in a phenomenological poetic of perception and expression. The poetic is articulated in metaphorical language, emerging in images and ultimately as stories in the process of making sense of everyday life.

In this view, moral stories naturally *precede* what journalists construct in their craft as reports. They make authentic observation possible. They preface action. Ideally, they condition the decisions and actions of journalists as laypeople, before craftspeople, in Burke's terms, if not for the alienation of the bureaucratized imagination. For Ziff, the alienation is manifest in the unwise break with community through professionalism, limiting the sense-making perspective by undermining its collective source. Although exile from community can occur on occasions of conscience, the world is not "made right" by the choice. The meaning of the act remains, for the conscientious journalist, embedded in the culture being opposed. In this cosmopolitan deferring, there is no detachment of sensibility. There is instead the heroic price of authentic tragedy: suffering for the sake of virtue.[2]

An ethics of vision does not discount action or the need for deliberating choices of behavior. As Murdoch emphasizes, its realm of concern is the appropriate background for ethical behavior. The approach attempts to reintroduce the importance of inner states of being, a morality of consciousness, socially negotiated, and to stress the importance of a moral imagination as an aspect of moral reasoning (Weldhen, 1986, p. 125). The approach seems to address the function of the journalist as a vital observer in society and would appear to offer a framework for devising an occupational stance toward ethics in harmony with the essential interpretive task of the craft.

This view of ethics, however, has its own problematic tension. If morality is a quality of vision, there is seemingly less of an imperative for action. It appears to invite passivity, a dilemma pondered by Hannah Arendt in *The Life of the Mind* (1978). This issue of passivity is the topic of the final section of this essay.

ACTION AND ABSTENTION

Freeing the moral imagination has been described as a precondition of ethical behavior. But it entails an orientation toward ethics that could be described as preoccupied with perception through a socially mediated consciousness. If the essence of ethics precedes action, what is left for the will to achieve *in* action? It could be argued that "just vision" makes just action possible, and what is necessary for action cannot also be held accountable for inaction. This is not a totally adequate response, but it is enhanced by a compelling corollary: the widening of moral vision makes the unconscionable act less likely. With imagination, we might comprehend the extremes of *no* imagination. That was the speculation claimed by Hannah Arendt, sitting in a courtroom in Jerusalem at the trial of Adolf Eichmann, when she came to her famous conclusion on the "banality of evil" (1978). She describes it as the realization of a "manifest shallowness in the doer that made it impossible to trace the uncontestable evil of his deeds to any deeper level of roots or motives" (p. 4). Faced with comprehending the monstrous and the demonic, she was struck by absences: of firm ideological conviction, of realized purpose, of rhetorical flair, of imposing manner. The only notable characteristic beyond the brute reality of deed was another negative—the sheer *thoughtlessness* displayed by the man in the glass booth:

> Cliches, stock phrases, adherence to conventional, standardized codes of expression and conduct have the socially recognized function of protecting us against reality, that is, against the claim of our thinking attention that all events make by virtue of their existence. If we were responsive to this claim all the time, we would soon be exhausted; Eichmann differed from the rest of us only in that he clearly knew of no claim at all. (p. 4)

Perhaps it is arguable that a bureaucratized imagination has no such extreme of absence, the complete annihilation of sensibility. It is certainly not an appropriate caution to raise with regard to journalism. But it grounds the moral imperative of Burke's view in the need for continuous possibilities of the imagination to arise in all realms of public life. A bureaucratic imagination is "functional" and that is precisely the problem. It is the kind of solution to problems of action and decision making that ends in circularity: the only course of the imagination is to make something more so. This is the course toward efficiency becoming "distortion methodized" that Burke invites speculation about.

Arendt posed a question in response to her experience in Jerusalem which appeals to an ethics of vision, although her treatment of the query is almost entirely intellectual, as a problem *of* reason rather than its limitation. Her question redirects the priority of Murdoch's contemplation of a moral realism as a precondition for action, but the insight is the same: "Could the activity of thinking as such, the habit of examining whatever happens to come to pass or to attract attention, regardless of results and specific content, could this activity be among the conditions that make men abstain from evil-doing or even actually 'condition' them against it?" (p. 5). She perceives the pertinent danger in this possible solution, that is its identity with passivity. She describes this danger as the potential revalidation in the modern world of an ancient Greek desire: to watch and contemplate the world as godlike spectators, largely invisible and withdrawn (pp. 69–91). But her intellectualization of the question ("What are we 'doing' when we do nothing but think?" [p. 8]) nevertheless retains its powerful ethical attraction. And she might well have asked a slightly less motionless question with the same force of argument: What are we doing when we *pause* to think?

Murdoch (1960, p. 255) writes of the proper ethical attitude as the consideration of another being as more than just "a clear-cut piece of drama." This appeal to moral evaluation as involving total being, as quality of consciousness and behavior, finds a parallel in modern literature. Henry James (1934), for example, explored an "action" of inner experience in his characters of fiction, particularly women, identifying contemplation as a worthy accomplishment in itself. Martha Banta (1987) argues that historically this inner activity has been useful cultural work, contributing to the refinement of human sentience. For James, depicting this fact was a fundamental problem of literature: how to capture the essence of moral drama as involving consciousness as well as literature's "living wage" of melodramatic action (James, 1934, p. 54). Failure to adequately address the problem had led to a historical underevaluation of the moral contribution of women as represented in fiction and drama. As James describes the difficulty, a woman offered a "frail vessel" for portraying significance in literature because she could be depicted as "doing" little in a patriarchal culture where action was the domain of men. The success of James' *The Portrait of a Lady*, Banta (1987) argues, was in making the story's principal performance a meditative vigil, the "representation simply of her motionlessly *seeing*. . ." (James, p. 57).

In balance, however, action properly may be seen as continuous from inner to outer states of being, consummated at every point, compelled by the impulse to be responsible if freedom of thought and behavior allows. The dilemma of being self-satisfied with ethical vision is perhaps resolved. As David Eason (1984, p. 57) writes, "To become an observer is to see social reality as composed of active participants, who must take responsibility for their acts, and passive spectators, who bear no responsibility for what they watch." It is difficult to imagine an observer with moral vision, and the freedom to choose, having only the inertia to become the latter.

And what of Burke and journalists? Do we meet them again to close these circles of speculation? This essay began with Burke's "simpler" lament about a distortion in journalism rather than just an ideological rigging of the news discourse. The argument that has been presented here has been an exploration of the possibility that Burke's notion of a bureaucratized imagination, introduced to account for the literary shallowness of modern journalism, may also apply to the realm of journalism ethics as well. If *"all* journalistic efficiency becomes distortion methodized," then perhaps some of the complexity of a moral existence is lost, too, in a production-minded and decision-oriented professionalism looking to "design" an expedient ethics of action. The stories of such a craft may be failing as moral interpretations for want of imagination, from an *abdication* of the imagination, in a world whose activity and structure may well be poetic, or at least one in which the historical "conversation" of human intercourse has been vitally poetic at its most lucid moments (Oakeshott, 1962, pp. 197–247).

If the achievement of morality is the full apprehension of "otherness," the kind of ethical intimacy that "mass" media can strive for would at least suggest the suitability of more humility and less righteousness over the prospect of comprehending the lives of so many others. The sensibility of a provincialist may help a little. A character molded of communal insight, tempered by a cosmopolitan self-determination and courage to see things reflexively, may give us the exceptional journalist. But journalism by its nature is probably not great moral work. It is a craft of the faintly damned and the inveterate outcast who take up the calling in the first place. May their souls be saved elsewhere. That is perhaps the first, and most important, moral lesson of the craft.

NOTES

1. I owe this description of the argument to a reviewer of the manuscript.
2. One reviewer suggests that the argument of this essay contains religious dimensions that ought to be made explicit. Murdoch claims her philosophy is totally secular in its assumptions. Weil is recognized as a religious mystic. My own views fall somewhere in between.

REFERENCES

Arendt, H. (1978). *The life of the mind*. New York: Harcourt, Brace, Jovanovich.

Banta, M. (1987). *Imaging American women: Idea and ideals in cultural history*. New York: Columbia University Press.

Berlin, I. (1976). *Vico and Herder*. New York: Viking.

Boswell, J. (1961). *Boswell's journal of a tour to the Hebrides with Samuel Johnson, L.L.D. 1773*. (F.A. Pottle & C.H. Bennett, Eds.). New York: McGraw-Hill.

Burke, K. (1959). *Attitudes toward history*. Berkeley: University of California Press.

Christians, C. G. (1986). Reporting and the oppressed. In D. Elliott (Ed.), *Responsible journalism* (pp. 109–130). Beverly Hills: Sage.

Christians, C. G., Rotzoll, K. B., & Fackler, M. (1983). *Media ethics: Cases and moral reasoning*. New York: Longman.

Dewey, J. (1927). *The public and its problems*. Chicago: Swallow Press.

Dunaway, J. M. (1984). *Simone Weil*. Boston: Twayne Publishers.

Eason, D. (1984). The new journalism and the image-world: Two modes of organizing experience. *Critical Studies in Mass Communication, 1*, 51–65.

Ettema, J. S., & Glasser, T. (1985). On the epistemology of investigative journalism. *Communication, 8*, 183–206.

Glasser, T. L., & Ettema, J. S. (1989). Investigative journalism and the moral order. *Critical Studies in Mass Communication, 6*, 1–20.

Goldman, A. (1980). *The moral foundations of professional ethics*. Totowa, NJ: Rowman and Littlefield.

Gunn, G. (1987). *The culture of criticism and the criticism of culture*. Oxford: Oxford University Press.

James, H. (1934). *The art of the novel: Critical prefaces*. New York: Charles Scribner's Sons.

Jaksa, J., & Pritchard, M. (1988). *Communication ethics: Methods of analysis*. Belmont, CA: Wadsworth.

Johnson, S. (1775). *A journey to the western islands of Scotland*. London: W. Strahan.

Larmore, C. E. (1987). *Patterns of moral complexity*. Cambridge: Cambridge University Press.

Murdoch, I. (1960). The sublime and the beautiful revisited. *Yale Review, 49,* 247–271.

Murdoch, I. (1970). *The sovereignty of good*. London: Ark Paperbacks.

Oakeshott, M. (1962). *Rationalism in politics and other essays*. London: Methuen.

Royce, J. (1969). Provincialism. In J. J. McDermott (Ed.), *Basic writings of Josiah Royce* (Vol. 2, pp. 1067–1088). Chicago: University of Chicago Press.

Weil, S. (1952). *The need for roots*. London: Ark Paperbacks.

Weldhen, M. (1986). Ethics, identity and culture: Some implications of the moral philosophy of Iris Murdoch. *Journal of Moral Education, 15,* 119–126.

Ziff, H. (1986). Practicing responsible journalism: Cosmopolitan versus provincial models. In D. Elliott (Ed.), *Responsible journalism* (pp. 151–166). Beverly Hills: Sage.

11 *Hill Street Blues* as Narrative

CAREN J. DEMING

How *Hill Street Blues* began is a story for the Hollywood book of apocrypha. The series was the personal project of Fred Silverman, who at the time was head of programming at NBC. He wanted Steven Bochco and Michael Kozoll to produce a seriocomic cop show, a combination of *Barney Miller* and *Fort Apache, the Bronx*. Silverman took the reluctant Bochco and Kozoll to an expensive lunch at La Scala. In the restaurant they agreed to make the pilot, but only after dealing for carte blanche to break all of the rules of television police drama (and any others they might think of as the project progressed).[1]

The series went on the air January 15, 1981. Few people watched it, in part because it was shown in five different time periods on four different nights of the week during its first months on the air. The ratings were abysmal, but the critics were euphoric. Moreover, the series received an unprecedented twenty-one Emmy nominations; it won eight.[2] It also won the Humanitas Prize. Despite its failure to find a large audience, *Hill Street Blues* stayed in the NBC schedule for the fall of 1981. Official network rhetoric holds that the show was retained because of its quality (audiences needed time to get familiar with anything so innovative) and because letters from the show's loyal fans were uncommonly persuasive. Cynics say that NBC had nothing aborning with which to replace a failing series. However motivated, the decision proved to be a good one.

Through the reductive lens of history, *Hill Street Blues* will be seen as a milestone in American series programming, a marker of a place where (program) quality won out over (viewer) quantity. The purpose of this essay is to explore the claims to quality and innovation by examining *Hill Street Blues* as a narrative. More specifically, what follows is an analysis of the series as a modernist text cast primarily as melodrama. *Hill Street Blues* revels in complexity, ambiguity, and discontinuity. At the same time, it maintains its intelligibility by remaining anchored in a narrative mode that is characteristically straightforward and ideally suited to the television medium. The result is a

240

mixture of forms and their conventions (televisual, filmic, and literary) that skates on the edges of our assumptions about such structures.

Utilizing a structuralist definition of narrative, this paper begins with a reconstruction of the stories told in the episode entitled "Film at Eleven," first broadcast on February 7, 1981. The analysis proceeds with explication of the program's melodramatic form and style, its rendering of time, space, characters, and events as discourse, and the audience implied by the text. The essay concludes with a brief summary of research on the real audience and the significance of *Hill Street Blues* as a television narrative.

NARRATIVE AS STORY

Contemporary narratology (acknowledging a debt to Aristotle) defines narrative as a bifurcated entity in which the story is separable from its rendering. The story is the chain of events, together with characters and setting, abstracted from their disposition in the text and reconstructed in chronological order.[3] The story is rendered as discourse manifested in a medium. The story and its discursive manifestation together constitute the narrative text (Chatman, 1978, p. 27). This approach to the definition of narrative allows for the transposability of stories among media. It, thereby, also allows for the analysis of dramatic presentations as narratives.[4]

More importantly, the concept of narrative is fundamentally communicative. Notions of a "teller" and a "told to" are immanent to narrative. As this analysis of *Hill Street Blues* attempts to demonstrate, the narrative approach to television criticism provides convenient means to talk about aspects of message creation and reception in a more comprehensive context than other frameworks have allowed.[5] Put this way, the aim of this article is to account for elements of content as organized into a narrative system under the exigencies of the television medium for the purpose of engaging the viewer.

The model employed in this analysis is a slightly simplified version of Chatman's (1978, p. 267) diagram of narrative structure.[6] The model contains five essential elements: a real author, an implied author, the discourse, an implied audience, and a real audience. The real author constructs the narrative by arranging symbolic elements appropriate to the medium of manifestation. In television, the real "author" is a group made up of the producer, the writer, the director, and their support personnel. *Hill Street Blues* also makes use of a supervising producer, creative consultants, and (because it is shot on film) a cinematographer.

The implied author is a controlling principle (re)constructed by the viewer from elements of discourse manifested in the medium. The implied author is more or less covert, depending on the transparency or opacity of the medium in the discourse. In *Hill Street Blues*, the implied author is apparent in the many devices used to call attention to the medium. Abrupt editing and temporal discontinuity, for example, give the viewer a sense of being led through the narrative by an omnipresent (though not omniscient) camera eye. Frequent use of handheld camera shots and occasional use of rolled focus call attention to the medium, reminding viewers that they are experiencing art and, thereby, establishing aesthetic distance. In retrospect, viewers' awareness that vital information has been withheld also contributes to the sense that events are being manipulated.

The discourse is the form of the narrative expression, a series of statements organized to tell a story. Statements (the constituents of discourse) include events, characters, and setting. The term *statements* is used literally in references to verbal narratives; for television, the term is broadened to include visual information as well as dialogue and other sound. Statements are made by the real author and interpreted by the real viewer.

The implied audience is a construct implicit in the demands made by the narrative in order for comprehension to occur. The real audience reconstructs and interprets the narrative from cues in the manifestation by comparing them to cultural codes and life experience. The real audience may bear little resemblance to the implied audience, as real viewers operate independently of any role cut out for them by authors or critics.

Story Characters and Events

The complexity of the *Hill Street Blues* narrative is apparent from the onset in that it tells several stories at once. "Film at Eleven," a representative episode from the first season, advances five stories. The cast consists of twenty-nine identified characters: twelve regular main characters, eleven more main characters, and six minor characters. The stories involving these characters are:

1. Television reporter Cynthia Chase and camera operator Bernard are assigned to do a news feature on the police. They choose Hill Street Station as their subject and begin to interview the officers and shoot videotape. Chase meets Public Defender Joyce Davenport, and they become friends.

2. Kevin Herman Dracula has been harassing women on the streets. He bites Wilma (a prostitute) on the neck. Detective Mick Belker arrests Dracula and books him. Dracula is put in a cell, and someone gives him a television set. No one takes his fantasy seriously. Davenport is assigned to his case, and she persuades Captain Frank Furillo to release him. Meanwhile, Dracula hangs himself in his cell. Sergeant Philip Esterhaus and Davenport discover the body. Davenport and Furillo discuss the suicide and their feelings of guilt.

3. A Haitian woman steals a Peruvian llama named Cookie from the zoo; she also steals several chickens and a goat from her neighbors for use in voodoo sacrifices. Officers Bobby Hill and Charlie Renko, accompanied by Chase and Bernard, go to a tenement to arrest the woman. Renko breaks in the door to her apartment, and they take her to the station. Cookie is returned to the zoo.

4. Billie Riles steals a purse and a gun from Rita Perez. Detectives Neal Washington and Johnny LaRue arrest Riles after they see her throw the purse in a trash can. Attempting to escape, Riles throws her bag of loot at Washing-

ton, spilling the contents, including the gun. They take her to the station for interrogation, where she confesses to the robbery. She is released.

5. Officers Hill and Renko inadvertently interrupt a dope deal. They are shot by an assailant who hides the gun in the back of a liquor store owned by Louie Decarlo. Decarlo's handy man George finds the gun and trades it to Chico Perez (Rita's husband). Billie Riles steals the gun from Rita. LaRue and Washington discover the gun while arresting Riles. Ballistics tests identify the gun as the one that was used to shoot Hill and Renko. Chico Perez and Rita Perez are arrested and charged with the shooting. Furillo and Lieutenant Ray Calletano trick Perez into telling them that he got the gun from George. Perez is released. Washington and LaRue talk to Decarlo, who identifies Eddie Hoban. They arrest Hoban. Renko identifies Hoban as the man who shot him. Hoban professes his innocence, and Detective Henry Goldblume expresses his doubt that Hoban is guilty.[7]

With the exception of the Hill-Renko shooting, the stories are relatively simple. By standards of complexity and amount of discourse devoted to it, the Hill-Renko story is the main story of this episode. Only one of the subsidiary stories (Billie Riles) is intimately related to the main story. The other three are related by their occurrence in roughly the same time, by occasional spatial intersection, and by the involvement of certain main characters in more than one story.

Story Time

The five stories occur virtually simultaneously in a contemporary urban setting. Only the main story has a specified duration, approximately six months. The other stories appear to take place in less time, though the discourse does not reveal their duration specifically.

Vagueness with regard to story time is characteristic of *Hill Street Blues*. That fact raises an analytical issue that is important to address. As Chatman (1978, p. 137) points out, story structure, discourse structure, and manifestation structure are "independently systematic." The temporal dimensions of *Hill Street Blues* illustrate this point. The duration of the manifestation structure is one hour. It takes one hour to view the program, including the nonstory elements that reside in segments within the broadcast time (station identifications, commercials, promotional announcements, credits). At this level of analysis, events occur in strictly linear sequence (the episode contains no superimposures or splitscreen effects).[8]

The discourse structure occupies a duration of roughly one day. The episode opens with the usual roll call that begins the day shift at seven o'clock and closes with a late-night conversation between Furillo and Davenport. The hours of discourse time are contracted to fill the manifestation time through the use of ellipsis. The sequence of events portrayed is essentially chronological (progressing from morning through evening), but events in the story often are revealed anachronically. For example, the discourse unravels the events in the Hill-Renko shooting story largely in reverse order, following the more or less logical process by which the officers work their way back in time from the discovery of the gun to its use in the shooting. Specifically, the technique is analepsis, which Rimmon-Kenan (1983, p. 46), following Genette, defines as "a narration of a story-event at a point in the text after later events have been told."[9]

The stories, each of which occurs in its own strict chronology, must be reconstructed from the discourse. Being metonymic to the discourse, which, in turn, is metonymic to the manifest text, the story is accessible to the viewer only through elaborate decoding. As a complete structure, it is available only in retrospect, and only if sufficient information is provided in the discourse. Therein lies the analytical problem.

NARRATIVE AS STRUCTURE

Considering narratives as structures, Chatman (1978, pp. 21–22) attributes to them the characteristics of structure identified by Piaget: wholeness, transformation, and self-regulation. Of these, transformation is the least problematical, as the discussion of time above demonstrates. The very process of manifesting the story structure in narrative structure is transformational. Wholeness and self-regulation are more troublesome because they require a structure to be distinct from the elements that compose it and to maintain and close itself. If closure is immanent to narrative, how can *Hill Street Blues* (or any serial drama) be analyzed as narrative? More particularly, how can narrative be said to exist at the episode level of analysis in such a text?

In response to the first question, let us look at the five stories in "Film at Eleven." The story of Chase and the news feature hardly can be called a story. The problem it addresses, the relationship of the police to the news media, is not presented as clearly-defined conflict. There is no clear climax, but rather a sustained level of tension that seems to dissipate rather than to reach closure. As a plot, its shape is almost flat.

The stories of Dracula and the Haitian woman are somewhat more traditional. The Dracula story has a kind of closure, but his suicide appears to be a shockingly inappropriate climax to the problem of what to do with a young man who believes he is Dracula and acts upon the fantasy. The Haitian woman's story is almost complete, although her ultimate fate is omitted.

The story of Billie Riles builds fairly fully but has a throw-away ending, as if to get her out of the way as inconspicuously as possible. The mystery of the Hill-Renko shooting is the fullest narrative; and yet its resolution is bathed in doubt. Clearly, none of these stories contains the kind of closure that Aristotle preferred. The stories are, in fact, the result of reconstruction from what Chatman (1978, p. 22) would describe as "ill-formed narratives" in the Piagetian sense. Traditional narrative closure is a convention of the story artifact[10] that *Hill Street Blues* acknowledges the importance of, even draws attention to, by repeatedly avoiding it.

This practice puts *Hill Street Blues* squarely in fiction's modernist camp. An "open" text by virtue of its ambiguity and complexity, it self-consciously lays the problem of closure at the feet of the viewer much as a modernist novel leaves the problem to the reader. Resistance to resolution, as Ellis (1982) indicates, is also characteristic of series television. In contrast to film:

> The TV series repeats a problematic. It therefore provides no resolution of the problematic at the end of each episode, nor, often, even at the end of the run of the series. . . . Fundamentally, the series implies the form of the dilemma rather than that of resolution and closure. This perhaps is the central contribution that broadcast TV has made to the long history of narrative forms and narrativised perception of the world. (p. 154)

Ellis goes on to say that television does resolve narrative problems at the level of particular incidents, whether within an episode or across several episodes.

Hill Street Blues exploits television's tendency to answer the little questions (who committed the crime?), at least provisionally, and to leave the big question (how can order be restored to the society?) defiantly unanswered.[11] The program also exploits television's habit of asking questions over and over again; but it complicates everything by asking several at the same time, intermixing the narrative pieces necessary for the formulation of answers, and leaving out a fair share of those pieces. In the hermeneutic game it plays with the audience, *Hill Street Blues* invokes the idea of closure in the refusal to manifest it.

NARRATIVE AS DISCOURSE

Form as Discourse

By repeatedly invoking closure without manifesting it, *Hill Street Blues* embodies a central theme of melodrama, the attempt to restore order to a chaotic world. As Brooks (1976, p. 12) describes it, melodrama is a theatrical substratum found in works of low art (those which attempt little, risk little, and are, therefore, conventional and unself-conscious) as well as high (ambitious works whose conception and mode of representation constitute "the very process of reaching a fundamental drama of the moral life and finding terms to express it"). Melodrama polarizes good and evil and demonstrates their operation as real forces in the world. It uses "heightened dramatic utterance and gesture" to demonstrate the moral drama in ordinary, private life. It assumes that "the quotidian life, properly viewed, will live up to the expectations of the moral imagination." Finally, it posits good and evil as moral *feelings*, thus asserting that emotion is the realm of morality (p. 54).

In *Hill Street Blues*, the classically melodramatic battle between order and chaos takes place on three interactive levels: on the societal level (where the evil is violent crime or political corruption), on the interpersonal level (where evil is behavior that undermines the goals of the group), and on the personal level (where evil is insanity or less total personal disintegration, failure to cope).

For the *Hill Street* characters, the public battle against crime is engaged from the perspective of the private struggle to do good. The grimy realities of life on The Hill are, thus, the stuff of which the moral drama is concocted: drug busts and torn shirts, sexual baiting and broken vending machines, racial hatred and babysitting. The action is intense physically and emotionally. As portrayed in the narrative, life on The Hill contains no dull moments. Every act and every utterance (including the humorous) is loaded with social or personal meaning, and frequently with both. Violence and insanity always lurk somewhere in the *Hill Street* picture, and frequently they are ascendant.

Melodrama is essentially a modernist form, an artistic response to the shattering of myth and the loss of tragic vision which Brooks (1976) traces to the French Revolution. It is a response to "a world in which the traditional imperatives of truth and ethics have been violently thrown into question, yet where the promulgation of truth and ethics, their instauration as a way of life, is of immediate, daily, political concern" (p. 15). Having abandoned the likelihood of the absolute triumph of virtue, melodrama rehearses the confrontation with its enemies (labeled as villains), expunging them over and over again. The drama "represents both the urge toward resacralization and the impossibility of conceiving sacralization other than in personal terms" (Brooks, 1976, p. 16).

Lacking vital moral absolutes, finding the government and police bureaucracies corrupt and family life in disarray, the inhabitants of The Hill take life one day at a time, expunging villains and sticking together as best they can. Unable to eradicate evil, they try at least to keep it at bay. They find the strength to keep fighting the losing battle in interpersonal relationships. The *Hill Street* "family" thus provides the web of personal relations "that must be carefully nurtured, judged, handled as if they mattered" (Brooks, 1976, p. 22) basic to melodrama.

As a narrative structure, *Hill Street Blues* for the most part skips melodrama's first stage, the presentation of virtue-as-innocence. There are few innocents in *Hill Street Blues*. In "Film at Eleven," Kevin Dracula is a provisional innocent, though hardly entirely virtuous. Anonymous children are shown as innocent victims or employed in comic diversion (the case in "Film at Eleven"), though they are not central to the drama. Pollution in the world of The Hill is a given. The obstacles to innocence are everywhere, and virtue is in peril at every turn.

Virtue in *Hill Street Blues* is an impulse within the main characters put in peril by the very conditions of their daily lives. The triumph of evil is more typically melodramatic, however, in that its success often depends on the blindness or bad judgment of politicians, judges, or police officials (the uncles, guardians, and sovereigns Brooks identifies) who thwart *Hill Street*'s heroes. In "Film at Eleven," Kevin Dracula is lost in "a bureaucratic black hole" (scene

58), his death blamed on the failure of "Maintenance" to comply with Furillo's earlier orders to plaster over the exposed pipes from which he hangs himself (scene 61). Virtue, unable to articulate the cause of the right (try though it does again and again in *Hill Street Blues)* must undergo an unbearable experience, one which draws upon basic emotions in their primal, unrepressed condition (Brooks, 1976, p. 35). Then comes the race against the clock, the race to get there in time—to court, to the hospital, to the scene of the crime—to catch the criminal before more harm is done. Melodrama's overt judgment, offered in order to clarify the meaning of enigmatic or misleading signs, most often comes from the lips of Furillo. The *Hill Street Blues* narrative also includes large doses of discussion exploring the moral and ethical implications of actions by heroes and villains, however.

Violent action constitutes the physical acting out of virtue's liberation (Furillo and company are good at violence when they need to be); and the drama ends with the public recognition of virtue and evil, the eradication of one being the reward of the other. As in the case of innocence, *Hill Street Blues* never fully manifests this final stage. Although individual criminals may be caught, they are always subject to release; or else the suspicion that the right ones have not been caught lingers on. In addition to the ambiguity of story endings, the multilinear plot structure prevents the achievement of full resolution; for if one case is "solved," others remain to be continued in later episodes.

Thus, although *Hill Street Blues* is melodramatic in form, its refusals to fit the form precisely are numerous. Most importantly, the heroes lack the requisite certainty of virtue, though their ultimate goodness asserts itself. By contrast, the villains more often are unambiguously evil. However, as in the case of Kevin Dracula, antagonists sometimes turn out to be victims, if not total innocents. Sometimes, as in the case of Eddie Hoban, the identity of the villain is not certain. Other times, as with Billie Riles, misdeeds go unpunished. Unlike melodrama in its purest form, more villains are of the less privileged classes than of the privileged. Ultimately, then, *Hill Street Blues* raises more questions than it answers.

If *Hill Street Blues'* polarization of good and evil is less certain than usual in television melodrama, the program's failure to present a clear, uncritical vision of the new society is characteristically melodramatic. By providing its own self-critique (in the debates over ethics that occur between Furillo and Davenport or Goldblume, for example, in flaws such as LaRue's alcoholism, or in Hunter's caricature of militaristic extremism), *Hill Street Blues* declares itself to be high melodrama in Brooks' (1976) terms—the search for a fundamental drama of the moral life and the terms to express it. The manifestation of the debate is in keeping with Newcomb and Hirsch's (1983) notion of television as a cultural forum, in which televisual communication is the process of ritualized negotiation of cultural reality. In turn, Newcomb's thesis is consistent with Ellis' (1982) proposition that television narratives imply unresolvable dilemmas, as opposed to problematics subject to resolution and closure. In short, *Hill Street Blues* does more of what other television does best.

Hill Street Blues is unique in the extent to which it emphasizes contradictions and self-consciously resists closure. To borrow phrases from Kermode (1980, p. 89), the *Hill Street* discourse overtly "invites interpretation" more than it "appeals to consensus." Kermode's discussion of Joseph Conrad's *Under Western Eyes* distinguishes between the discursive "secrets" embedded in that text and its "relatively clean, well-lighted plot." By contrast, *Hill Street Blues* blatantly advertises its invitation to interpretation by keeping secrets in the plots themselves, declaring the *search* for answers and for the form to express them as its paramount concern and joining form and theme in exigent intimacy.

Style as Discourse

The moral complexity of *Hill Street Blues* is matched by stylistic complexity. On its surface, the narrative itself seems chaotic.[12] This effect is in large part a function of the movement among the various stories extant in any episode, as well as extensive elision. It is also a function of the emphasis on the middle stages of melodrama. As one critic put it, *Hill Street Blues* is a "collection of brilliant middles" (Gabree, 1981, p. 31).

The density of the action is matched by dense visual and aural texture and overall naturalism of style. That naturalism is achieved through harsh lighting, tightly-shot, crowded sets, handheld camera work, and thick ambient sound. The dialogue is blunt and often vulgar, though confused by the intentional garbling of lines.[13] Sex is lusty and open more than suggestive or titillating. Violence is random and shocking, not the pulse of the show, but heart-stopping.

Such naturalism perhaps is too intense for a medium normally thought of as realistic. What the style achieves, within the world represented in the narrative, is the subjective feel of life on The Hill. Because the intensity of affect is consistent with the melodramatic form and with the density of its treatment, the narrative achieves verisimilitude.[14] In other words, the excesses of style and content are acceptable under the artistic terms set up by the narrative.

The rhetorical excess characteristic of melodrama finds expression in the tendency to discuss the moral import of events explicitly. Villains frequently announce their own villainy publicly in the squad room or privately to Davenport. Like Furillo, she rarely misses the opportunity to give her moral analysis along with her legal analysis. The intense emotionalism of the dialogue in which such judgments are articulated is in keeping with what Brooks (1976)—returning to the idea that in melodrama good and evil are moral *feelings*—calls melodrama's "expressionism of the moral imagination" (p. 55).

The moralistic tone of the melodrama is relieved with humor, which is extensive enough to lend a seriocomic tone to much of the action. In keeping with the melodramatic tendency toward extremes, however, the humor can be hyperbolic. Such is the case with "Film at Eleven's" portrayal of Hunter's seminar on new prisoner restraining devices (scene 17). When Hunter puts his locking collar on Officer Santini, Hunter's "prisoner" yelps in painful surprise. Predictably, the collar refuses to release, and Santini returns to his chair with the ridiculous collar still attached. Such silliness turns humor to caricature and extracts the occasional cheap laugh from the situation.

Commonly, the humor is ironic because of its racial or sexual overtones. "Film at Eleven's" leering after Cynthia Chase, suggestive remarks to Furillo about Davenport, and race-flavored banter between Hill and Renko fall in this category. The absurdity of both verbal and visual humor is made palatable by its streetwise topicality. The repartee and wisecracking are quick, sharp, and hip. They emphasize the preoccupation of the narrative with current social reality. The humor's presence intensifies the impact of the dramatic action, and its topicality is a reminder that this drama is of the here and now. Though not common to the melodramatic form, such self-conscious humor appropriately blends conventions of situation comedy with the melodrama to intensely ironic effect.

Time as Discourse

Despite the use of analepsis, *Hill Street Blues* conveys the sense that events are portrayed in chronological order by revealing story events as they are discovered by the characters. This common storytelling convention provides chronology derived from a psychological focus. The effect is to diminish the importance of events as they occur in technical clock and calendar time and to enhance the importance of time and events as experienced by the characters. That the day covered by narrative time is specified more clearly than is the duration of any particular story, therefore, is appropriate.

Furthermore, the *Hill Street Blues* narrative capitalizes on television's illusion of liveness to emphasize the present tense and the irreversible flow of time. In contrast to film's historic mode of narration, television operates in the mode of the continuous update (Ellis, 1982, p. 59). Each episode of *Hill Street Blues* begins *in medias res*. The roll call is under way when the viewer is brought on the scene, and the time of day is superimposed briefly, a practice reminiscent of the way morning news programs keep viewers aware of the passage of time.[15] The emphasis on the present tense is enhanced by the commercials and promotional announcements that interrupt the narrative. These announcements remind the audience that the fiction is part of television's segmented flow, the flow that continues whether the set is on or not and whether the viewer watches or not. This effect is particularly acute near the end of the broadcast, when local news headlines are interleaved with the closing credits for *Hill Street Blues*. In effect, the news begins before the program ends. This practice, combined with the inadequate closure of the fiction, reinforces the notion that the episode is (like the news) a report on the day's events rather than a completed fiction.[16]

If in conveying a sense of liveness *Hill Street Blues* is decidedly televisual, it is more filmic in the way it compresses time. The alternation among the various stories advanced in the episode is a convention that film and television viewers recognize as signifying the simultaneity of events. In *Hill Street Blues* the practice, combined with the heavy use of ellipsis, results in time compression more typical of film than of television, however. One episode of *Hill Street Blues* conveys more events than one can imagine happening on even the most harried of days on The Hill. By contrast, the multiple stories told in one episode of *The Love Boat* or *Fantasy Island* seem to unfold in a most leisurely fashion, though even these programs compress time more than soap operas or dramas such as *Family* do (see Gronbeck, 1984).

The rapid pace of *Hill Street Blues* comes more from eliding events (and the time it would take to tell them) than from rapid cutting between short shots. Long takes containing references to multiple events and *mis-en-scene* shooting (involving camera movement or rolled focus in addition to character movement) are much more common in *Hill Street Blues* than they are in most television. The occasional use of the freeze frame at the end of an episode (which has become formulaic for some soap operas) or slow motion mirrors the way that psychological time slows down intensely emotional events.

Unlike more action-oriented police drama, in which the pace quickens as the heroes close in on the villains, the pace of the *Hill Street Blues* episode tends to slow down as it progresses. In "Film at Eleven," the pace is fastest at the beginning. By Act Four, only two stories are being told (Dracula and Hill-Renko), and most of the attention is focused on the shooting mystery as it is being unraveled through discussions in the precinct house. The final scene is a quiet conversation between Davenport and Furillo. Such a scene has become a conventional episode closing, though some episodes end much more abruptly. Variation in pacing is but one means by which *Hill Street Blues* achieves dramatic intensity more common to film than to series television.

Space as Discourse

The way that space is manipulated also contributes to a sense of intensity and compression. Although the action takes place in a limited geographical area (the Hill Street station house and its environs), a relatively large number of sets is utilized. "Film at Eleven" requires fourteen sets (ten interiors and four exteriors) in addition to the stock exteriors used in the title sequences. The interiors are dominated by precinct sets: the roll call room, Furillo's office, the squad room, the interrogation room, the corridor, a basement stairwell, a basement cell, and the viewing room. Other interiors are the tenement corridor and the Dee Boy Liquor Store.

The sets are tightly shot and crowded with detail. Establishing shots are almost always lacking. The lighting is harsh, the high contrast causing some of the detail to be lost in darkness. The result is crowded confusion, an effect intensified by the small size and low image resolution of the television screen. Even though regular viewers find the sets familiar, sudden shifts among them are common. The deliberately low-definition rendering of space[17] places a heavier than normal burden of interpretation on the viewer and increases the opaqueness of the medium.

The interior spaces of the precinct house are the "home" base of the main characters. In contrast to soap opera's portrayal of work through the perspective of home life, *Hill Street Blues* portrays the personal lives of the characters from the perspective of their work. The significance of domestic issues and problems in the narrative is enhanced by the extent to which characters use the workplace as a setting for working them out. At times the squad room is reminiscent of an old-fashioned kitchen, where family and friends exchange news and gossip, argue, and offer advice. Furillo's office is father's den, where people go for private conversations, advice, or discipline. The bathroom is a retreat, where characters indulge in private grief, anger, or consolation. Though their sanctity is violable, these spaces are safer than the more public areas of the precinct house (where confusion reigns and violence often erupts) and decidedly safer than the city outside the station.

In keeping with melodrama's preference for "those ordinary and enclosed spaces wherein most of us act out our deepest needs and feelings" (Thorburn, 1982, p. 542), exterior space is less important than interior space in *Hill Street Blues*. "Film at Eleven's" four exterior sets are 124th street, a tenement on 124th street, the outside of the liquor store, and a phone booth. The precise location of these places in relation to the station is vague. Although it is shot in Los Angeles and (less often) in Chicago, the *Hill Street Blues* narrative takes place in an unidentified northeastern city, effectively Hill Street, Anywhere (but Los Angeles) Urban, U.S.A. The most important thing about the exteriors is precisely that they are outside the station house. These are the mean streets from whose danger the station provides a modicum of shelter. Moreover, the shooting style makes the exteriors feel almost as claustrophobic as the interiors. In contrast to soap operas—whose occasional sequences shot on location are jarring because of changes in lighting, amount of detail, and perspective interiors and exteriors have a consistent look in *Hill Street Blues*.

Events as Discourse

Density in the treatment of space, reinforced by thick sound, coheres with the density of events created mainly by multilinear story development. In addition to relating five stories, "Film at Eleven" contains considerable nonstory material, however. The primary function of this material is to provide serious or humorous insight into the main characters. Its subject matter often concerns their personal problems, interpersonal relationships, or the ongoing problem of integrating professional life with private life.

Nonstory material interrupts the progress of story development in varying degrees. Least disruptive is dialogue unrelated to the story being developed in a scene. Such *digressions* distract attention from the story line but do not halt its progress altogether. Rather, they run parallel to it.[18] *Interludes*, on the other hand, are complete scenes. They portray events virtually unrelated to the stories told in the episode.[19] Digressions and interludes add texture to the narrative and increase the demand on the viewer in constructing the story structure from the discourse. What readers of simpler texts do with "'unconscious felicity'" (Chatman, 1978, p. 55, quoting Kermode) the viewer of *Hill Street Blues* must do more consciously and perhaps not always felicitously.

"Film at Eleven" demonstrates the complex interweaving of story and nonstory elements characteristic of the *Hill Street Blues* narrative. Act One opens with the familiar roll call in the squad room (scene 1).[20] Against a background of wisecracking officers, Sergeant Philip Esterhaus (Michael Conrad) introduces the stories of Dracula (Tony Plana) and the Haitian woman. Esterhaus refers to Kevin's antics as "previously described," an allusion to earlier episodes which suggests that his neck-biting behavior is iterative. The presence of a mobile video unit (scene 2) makes Esterhaus uncomfortable, but he concludes the briefing with a brave speech about a savage attack on the precinct's Busy Baker pastry machine. The setting quickly changes to an exterior location, where Detectives Johnny LaRue (Kiel Martin) and Neal Washington (Taurean Blacque) are on a drug stakeout (scenes 3–6). Their small talk concerns LaRue's "negative cash flow." The digression reveals a source of tension in their partnership, though they remain conscious of the assignment throughout the scene. The integration of this counterpoint to the plot demonstrates the characters' capacity for thinking about two subjects at once and, of course, asks the viewer to do the same. LaRue watches a tenement window through a telescope disguised as a liquor bottle in a paper bag, an indirect visual allusion to LaRue's alcoholism.

Two story inconsistencies emerge in the action involving the discovery of the gun used in the shooting portrayed in the series pilot. First, the closing of the pilot clearly implies that the officers died, and yet both Hill (Michael Warren) and Renko (Charles Haid) are alive in "Film at Eleven." Second, later on in the February broadcast, the shooting is referred to as having occurred in March. Such discrepancies call attention to the drama as fiction. The vagueness and confusion about the timing of past events is intensified when episodes are rerun because the episodes are not always rerun in sequence.[21]

The rest of Act One (scenes 13–31) is devoted mainly to the Chase and Dracula stories. In sum, the most important story of the episode begins late (relative to the other stories); it has a misleading beginning because its events are joined[22] to those of a subsidiary story (Billie Riles); and it is developed only slightly. Act One includes eight scenes interrupted by digressions. It also contains an interlude during which Lieutenant Hunter (James B. Sikking) demonstrates a new locking collar and a taser gun. All of this in less than a quarter-hour of narrative: five plot introductions, an interlude that at first appears to be an additional plot (the vending machine)[23] but that does not develop into a plot in this episode, and a substantial interlude (Hunter). Though most of the action takes place within the precinct house, the first act involves 31 scene changes. Not only the stations need a break.

The double plot significance of the shooting is an example of narrative enchainment adapted for episodic television. The shooting climaxes the pilot program. In retrospect, that is, from the point of view of "Film at Eleven," the incident launches the mystery that drives the episode's main story. The pilot and the episode were not written as a "two-parter." The finality of the shooting in the pilot made possible the full exploitation of its shock value. Picking the story up again (and changing its outcome in the process), the creators alert the audience that things will not always be what they seem in *Hill Street Blues*. The challenge reaches beyond the normal boundaries of misleading clues conventional to mysteries.

In *Hill Street Blues*, which is created week by week and season by season, needed information sometimes is missing, and the creators reserve for themselves the right to revise information after the fact. The audience is thereby reminded of the handicap under which it engages in the hermeneutic challenge posed by the *Hill Street* narrative. Causality, even inevitability, do not rule the episode or the series. The past always threatens to become the present again. As such, it is subject to revision. This is the kind of narrative to which we are accustomed in the novels of William Faulkner or Virginia Woolf, for example; but it is far less predictable than the customary narratives of series television.[24]

As Act Two begins, Billie is being questioned about the gun (scenes 37–38). A brief interlude occurs when Furillo leaves the interrogation room (scene 39). He notices a man clad only in a blanket. A terse exchange ensues:

FURILLO (*to Esterhaus, regarding man*): What's his story?
ESTERHAUS (*shrugs*): Claims that a group of rather large gentlemen jumped out of
    a black van on Hertel and stole all his clothes.
FURILLO (*thoughtful*): Black van, huh? 'Thought that was a harbor problem.
ESTERHAUS: We're a transient society, Francis.

No illumination of this allusive dialogue occurs until Act Three.

During the exposition of the Hill-Renko shooting story, we also learn a little more about Kevin Herman Dracula from Public Defender Joyce Davenport (Veronica Hamel). She interrupts Furillo to ask him where the "alleged vampire" has been taken (scene 45). Their staccato dialogue interweaves details about Kevin, about the gun, about Davenport's sexy reputation, and about Furillo's habit of stretching the edges of the law in his treatment of suspects. In less than two minutes, this remarkable scene advances three stories and incorporates two recurrent (but only tangentially related) *Hill Street Blues* themes. The scene is the equivalent of the summary scene in a narrative containing an overt narrator. According to Chatman (1978), such a scene in an unnarrated narrative indicates the implied author, the controlling presence accountable for the skillful selection and arrangement of the dialogue. By calling attention to the dialogue as artifice, the scene creates aesthetic distance.

Meanwhile, two other stories also advance in parallel fashion. In scene 40, we leave Billie and the shooting story to accompany Hill and Renko to the tenement in which we meet the Haitian woman. The landlord's complaint that she is keeping animals in her apartment has brought the officers, accompanied by the television crew, to investigate. The friction between the officers and the television people reaches its absurd climax when Bernard asks Renko to delay breaking in the woman's door while he (Bernard) reloads his camera. The Haitian woman's story, including denouement, takes less than four minutes to tell, and none of the key action occurs on the screen.

The story development in Act Two is interrupted six times in addition to the "nude-man" interlude. The conversation digresses to Detective Mick Belker's (Bruce Weitz) successful entertainment of Rita Perez' baby while his mother is being questioned (scene 43); to sexual baiting—twice in English, once in Spanish (scenes 45, 46); to an officer's concern over Freddie the Wino's poor health (scene 47); and to playful racial wise-cracks passed between Hill and Renko (scene 50).

In contrast to the first two acts, the last two are much briefer and simpler. Act Three opens with an exchange between Cynthia Chase (Andrea Marcovicci) and a man brought in to repair the demolished vending machine. Then Officer Harris (Mark Metcalf) tries to impress Chase by telling her that he is involved in an "investigation that would melt your film." The unimpressed Chase replies drily, "We shoot on tape" (scene 52). His big case turns out to be the nude man, whose story finally is explained by Officer Fuentes:

FUENTES (CONT'D): It's what you call the black van. Three four prostitutes 'll cruise an area turnin' tricks inside. If they think a john is really carryin' or gettin' outta line, they'll rip 'im off and toss 'im out the back.

In scene 56 comes the first substantial clue as to where the Chase story may be headed. While Chase interviews Davenport, they discover that they both are hampered professionally by their sex and their good looks. The dramatic purpose of the leering and sexual humor (directed at each of the women) that recurs throughout the episode at last is revealed. By itself, the Chase story goes nowhere; what it provides is a vehicle for exploring thematically the purpose of news and the relationship between the police and the news media. Furthermore, it lays groundwork rich in story potential. The Chase-Davenport friendship, the sexual harassment, and the reflexive media commentary themes all remain available for later development.

The subdued emotional tone of the Chase-Davenport conversation is sustained through scene 57, in which Davenport persuades Furillo to release Kevin. Then Esterhaus and Davenport (accompanied by Chase and Bernard) discover Kevin's body hanging in his cell, to the shock of characters and audience alike. Although the elision of a significant dramatic moment can effectually emphasize the event (as it does in Kevin's suicide), it can also detract from an event's importance (as in the case of the Haitian woman's arrest). The habit of eliding some of the events upon which action-adventure narratives thrive takes the accent off of the event *qua* event and puts it on the significance of the event for (primarily) the main characters, as is reflected in their extensive discussion of it.

Characters as Discourse

The certainties of the *Hill Street Blues* narrative are easier to locate in characters than they are in plot. The fourteen main characters are essentially good people—albeit consistently flawed and morally vulnerable—seeking to be better in the face of vital challenges. In contrast to heroes of romantic crime dramas, whose moral and physical superiority are beyond question, the main characters of *Hill Street Blues* are more ironic. They face ambiguous moral problems; and they sometimes weaken in the face of adversity. The struggle for order and sanity occurs, therefore, within and among them as well as between them and the chaotic world of the streets. Yet, despite apparently overwhelming odds, they never lose their essential goodness. They keep trying, and that makes them heroic.

In Frye's (1968) terminology, it might be said that the heroes of *Hill Street Blues* are cut mainly from the low mimetic template. Yet, in naive, silly, or morally frail moments, they can be ironic in the extreme. Because the narrative alternates between drama and comedy, its characters manifest elements of both.

Captain Furillo articulates the values of a moral order that transcends the police bureaucracy, thus exposing the inadequacy of the political system for coping with the social disintegration that threatens to engulf The Hill, as well as the system's inability to respond adequately to individual human need. Furillo bends the rules and stretches the law in order to do right as he defines it. Always pragmatic, he even violates his own moral code when necessary, acting forcefully and working through his guilt later.[25]

As narrative agent, Furillo functions as primary focalizer, whom Rimmon-Kenan (1983, pp. 71–76), following Genette, defines as the character in the represented world that provides perceptual, cognitive, emotive, and ideological orientation for understanding the narrative. On the perceptual level, Furillo is a limited observer, though he achieves a certain panoramic aspect through his centrality in the action and dialogue. The limits on his powers of observation lend plausibility to the withholding of information that creates suspense.

On the psychological level, Furillo's cognitive field is similarly limited, providing a subjective view of events open to discussion among characters and subject to misreading (as in the case of Kevin Dracula). Furillo's primary focalization is ideological, though events frequently are seen from the literal perspective of his space (through the door of his office) or through his eyes in subjective camera movement.

Furillo's perspective, although it dominates the narrative, is not the only one presented. The cast contains other leaders, who demonstrate an array of leadership styles. Male characters, such as Sergeant Esterhaus and Lieutenant

Ray Calletano (Rene Enriquez), tend to be sincerely and competently paternal when functioning as leaders.

In contrast, the women of *Hill Street Blues*—with the questionable exception of Fay Furillo (Barbara Bosson)—are hardly motherly by traditional television definition. They tend to be sexually and otherwise aggressive, independent, and tough. They wear the patina of experience more prominently than the dew of youth. Lucy Bates (Betty Thomas) is the stronger character in the team of Bates and Coffey (Ed Marinaro); and yet she will work all afternoon to find a blind date taller than she is. After months of study in the 1983–1984 season, she passes the examination that allows her promotion to sergeant. Then she is selected to replace Esterhaus after his death in February, 1984 (narrative time).[26] Placing Bates in this role sets the stage for exploration of her personal and professional growth more centrally in the drama than has been the case to this time.

The predominance of male focalization in the narrative has meant that female characters are seen through male eyes. From that perspective, Bates and the other female officers are struggling to make their way in the decidedly male world of law enforcement. They are frequent objects of sexual innuendo (Bates is the butt of jokes about the llama in "Film at Eleven"); and their struggle to keep their personal lives separate from their professional ones is often played out as opposition between their desire for acceptance in the brotherhood of The Hill (with the intense intimacy that implies) and their desirability as sexual partners.

The two main characters who are not police officers, Fay Furillo and Davenport, are more pointedly focalized by Furillo. The two women in his life are effective touchstones for his vulnerability. Fay's visits to The Hill are literal intrusions of domestic life on the job. Also, her ineptitude at managing her own life and her refusals to subordinate her needs and those of Frank Junior to the exigencies of Frank's police work cast her in the role of perpetual innocent. As such, it is easy to be impatient with her. Furillo passes judgment on her feisty incompetence by stoically standing by her and wishing she were stronger.

If Fay represents the innocence of Frank's earlier life, Joyce represents the experience of the current one. The competent public defender (as well as lover), she often articulates the point of view of Furillo's antagonists. Her criticism of his behavior comes closer to the target and cuts deeper into his vulnerability than does Fay's. When Joyce accuses him of "having a corner on the morality market" or "playing by his own rules," he offers a serious defense. Although both women provide opportunities for Furillo to articulate his moral code, Davenport (unlike the former wife) is his match.

Therefore, though both are enigmatic, Davenport's mystery is more intriguing. Exotically beautiful (as opposed to Fay's homegrown cuteness), tough-minded and successful—yet fragile-appearing—Davenport embodies apparent contradictions. Her ambiguity is an updated equivalent of the "problem" of female sexuality that has been the focus of so many Hollywood films. In Fiedler's (1969) typology of female characters, then, Joyce, is the Dark Lady to Fay's (used) Fair Maiden.

Because of her professional savvy and strength of character, Davenport is a force to be reckoned with in a way that Fay Furillo is not. In the light of this situation, Bates' promotion is an interesting rhetorical move. Having demonstrated competence on the street, Bates is now moved into the parental role defined by the late Esterhaus. As a character, she has the potential to bring together the two aspects of femaleness represented by Fay and Davenport in one person. Though it takes two women to balance the magnitude of Furillo's character, Bates is in a position to develop the capacity to manage all of the others singlehandedly. Whether the character will be allowed that development is a question that must be left for the future.

The main characters are highly individualized, as evidenced by their association with the actors who play them. (Replacing Michael Conrad with a new actor to play Esterhaus is unthinkable.) Though mainly focalized by Furillo, each of these characters provides a personalized version of how to cope with the evils they face alone and together.[27] The individuality and fullness of most regular main characters notwithstanding, *Hill Street Blues* draws heavily on stereotypes, particularly for portrayal of characters other than the police officers. Winos, pimps, prostitutes, dope pushers—not to mention sexy white dames (Cynthia Chase), fat black matrons (Haitian woman), young black shoplifters (Billie Riles), swaggering Puerto Rican thieves (Chico Perez)—all rely upon swift, efficient communication via stereotype for characterization. A humorous character easily becomes a caricature, a device effective only in small doses. In describing the projected humanizing of Howard Hunter in the 1982–1983 season, writer Anthony Yerkovich (Yerkovich & Anspaugh, 1982) observed that the writers must resist the temptation to write for their own amusement in order to prevent a character's "drowning in silliness." Thus, although *Hill Street Blues* is, in some ways, anything but formulaic, it draws deeply from the well of formula.

The Implied Audience

The *Hill Street Blues* narrative projects an implied audience unusual in television. While all television viewing requires more of the viewer than critics are in the habit of admitting, *Hill Street*'s open text insists that the audience engage in more conscious efforts to fill in and to comprehend the narrative. The text positions the viewer more as a gazer (akin to a film spectator) than as a "looker and glancer" (see Ellis, 1982, p. 128). As the characters have memories, so the viewer is responsible for keeping track of events from week to week. Even though there is more talk than one would expect in film, more strictly visual information occurs in *Hill Street* than in other television. Because there are few prompts (as opposed to soap opera, in which recapitulations within the narrative are common), *Hill Street* implies a viewer who watches every week and who pays attention.

The conscious neglect of the unities of time, place, and action described in earlier sections of this essay are an invitation to the viewer to participate in the drama. The roundness of the main characters and the intriguing faces of the actors (upon which the camera dwells) invite the viewer to identify with them. Yet, exploiting what Ellis (1982) refers to as television's conspiratorial nature, the narrative invites the viewer to participate in the discourse rather than to identify too strongly with individual characters.

Characters even go so far as to address viewers directly (direct address being the primary means by which television establishes its "we against they" relationship with the viewer) in series promotional announcements ("NBC— Be there!") or in transitions to station breaks (*"Hill Street Blues* will be right back"). Occasionally, a character looks directly into the camera lens during the narrative proper without the preparatory shot that establishes another character's point of view. The effect is penetration of the illusionary fourth wall conventional in film and television drama. The violated convention allows the character's gaze to enter the viewer's space. Thus, viewers are invited to share the implied author's view of reality—to view the agents of violence and chaos as "others" who must be expunged—and to imagine *themselves* as participants more than to imagine themselves as *these participants.*

The principal means by which the narrative accomplishes this rather delicate positioning of the viewer is by making artifice opaque. The thick texture of the interwoven story structures, extreme use of ellipsis, self-conscious shooting style (handheld camera, rolled focus, even the occasional swish pan)—all remind viewers to keep their aesthetic distance. Moreover, the creators intentionally seek opportunities to catch viewers off balance. Comedy suddenly turns to violence, a coffee break to disaster. Yerkovich calls the technique creating drama by "choreographing moods" (Yerkovich & Anspaugh, 1982). Such violent mood shifts increase the sense of aesthetic manipulation and call attention to the presence of the implied author.

Finally, the viewer is removed further from the drama by the segmentation of the narrative into acts separated by commercial breaks. The spell is broken three times by commercial breaks and numerous other times by reminders that the viewer has an interpretative job to do.[28] From this vantage point, audience satisfaction derives more from the reconstructive act itself than from witnessing closure in the traditional filmic or televisual senses. Indeed, the cliffhanging episode endings that *Hill Street Blues* sometimes borrows from other serial melodramas cause between-episode speculation so widespread as to find its way into the press.[29]

The narrative's assumption that the viewer will discern the large artistic whole at work in the segmented and discontinuous presentation allows it to indulge in content that in all likelihood would be offensive in a less ambitious undertaking. Furthermore, rampant racism, sexism, as well as class bias, occur in an overall context of social realism or critique (in the case of humor). That context casts them as the society's ailments even when they taint the heroes' behavior. Although negative stereotypes abound, they also are shared among a wide variety of groups. By being democratic in the distribution of villainy, *Hill Street* diffuses the offensive impact of objectionable material.

So, too, with the program's politics. Pollan (1983, p. 31) labels the political attitude of *Hill Street Blues* "post-liberal, shading to neoconservative." Rather than justice, the heroes strive for stability through the reassertion of authority. In the face of widespread anomie, liberal politicians get in the way and patience with civil liberties wears thin. Pollan concludes that although some (liberal) viewers find the program's politics dubious, they are drawn "into the logic of its values and conclusions, creating a fictional world so believable that its politics seem natural and appropriate."

In structuralist terminology, naturalization is the process by which the viewer "forgets" the conventional character of narrative conventions, "fills in" gaps in the text, and otherwise adjusts the elements of narrative to fit a coherent whole, "even when ordinary life expectations are called into question" (Chatman, 1978, p. 49). The openness of the *Hill Street* text seems to invite variant readings by viewers; and yet its overall unity—what Brooks (1976, p. 53) refers to as the "coherent interreferentiality" of any highly structured text—guarantees its accessibility as a narrative.

The Real Audience

The *Hill Street Blues* narrative is designed to attract an assemblage of real viewers with certain characteristics. Specifically, the target audience is "upscale," urban viewers 18 to 49 years old. These are the people the industry regards as trendsetters. They are the hope of an industry realigning itself in order to ride out the current decline in viewer loyalty to network television. Audience research, as summarized by Pollan (1983, p. 34), indicates that *Hill Street Blues* attracts and holds such viewers. Despite the fact that its overall audience share is relatively low, *Hill Street* is first in drawing men aged 18–49 and third in drawing women in that age group in its time period. The program is extremely popular in urban centers and particularly in homes with pay cable.

Moreover, the series' Q score (a measure of viewer loyalty) indicates that the viewers are avid fans. An advertisement in the February 20, 1984, issue of *Broadcasting* claimed that, based on performer Q rankings, "no other current series has so many stars who rank so high as favorites of their viewers." It is no accident that *Hill Street Blues* runs on Thursday, the night NBC runs advertisements for theatrical films the advertisers hope the viewers will attend on the weekend.

As well as filmgoers, *Hill Street*'s viewers presumably are frequent air travelers, buyers of business computers and foreign cars, and consumers of aspirin-free pain killers—if the advertisements shown with the program are any indication. By extension, these are viewers who also are likely to buy video recorders and to become what the industry calls "time shifters" (viewers who rearrange the broadcast day by taping shows and viewing or re-viewing them at their convenience). They also might edit out the commercials or otherwise reconstruct the narrative. With such behaviors, viewing becomes more like reading in terms of audience control over the process. With its demand for a high level of viewer participation in the construction of the narrative, the text of *Hill Street Blues* is well situated to capitalize on the emerging media age.

CONCLUSION

Despite the network's class-biased and materialistic approach to viewers, the *Hill Street Blues* narrative appeals to a wider audience. Although affluent urban viewers are most interesting to the network, the text speaks primarily in terms of melodrama, that innately modern and democratic form, opened up and expanded in the *Hill Street* narrative. In its openness—manifested as resistance to narrative closure, ambiguity, discontinuity, and ironic characters—the text advertises itself as modernist and invites interpretation in the demand for the viewer's participation. The narrative exploits televisual conventions—aesthetic distancing, extreme emphasis on interior space, close shooting, and emphasis on the present moment—to make the medium and form opaque. This process-oriented, constructivist attitude of the text signals the presence of high melodrama.

The form's concern with the urgency of restoring moral order out of chaos and its recognition of the impossibility of doing so except in personal terms permeate the *Hill Street Blues* narrative formally and thematically. Thus, viewers are free to interpret variously the meanings characters assign to specific events. More importantly, viewers can accept the ultimate meanings of the form, and the seriousness of the issues it addresses, even when presented with content that otherwise might be offensive on aesthetic, moral, or political grounds. In its refusal to answer melodrama's big question and its deliberate obfuscation of answers to even the little questions, *Hill Street Blues* declares its preoccupation with the search. The extent to which the narrative fulfills the promise of that emphatic declaration allows its creators and its viewers—not to mention critics—to explore the emancipatory possibilities of television narrative art.

NOTES

1. This is the account given by David Anspaugh (Yerkovich & Anspaugh, 1982). Anspaugh is a director, and Yerkovich is the author of the script for the episode analyzed in this article. "Film at Eleven" was produced by Gregory Hoblit and directed by Georg Stanford Brown. For a slightly different version of *Hill Street Blues'* beginning, along with a description of how the series' creators won autonomy from the network, see Gitlin (1983).

2. In the drama series category, *Hill Street Blues* won Emmys for best series, lead actor, lead actress, supporting actor, writer, director, cinematography, and film sound editing.

3. The controversy over the separability of story from discourse need not detract from the heuristic value of the exercise of separation. The attempt to separate

story from discourse in the present analysis helps to illuminate the narrative's fluid form and the intricate relationship between content and form in *Hill Street Blues*.

4. Some literary theorists, Rimmon-Kenan (1983), for example, limit the definition of narrative to verbal renderings. Others apply the concept fruitfully to visual media as well. See Chatman's (1978) comparison of narrative conventions in fiction and film and Ellis' (1982) study of narrative elements in film and television.

5. Although narrative theory may be capable of subsuming knowledge gained in other theoretical frameworks, I do not wish to imply that this or any other particular critical approach is capable of fully explaining any televisual event. However, narrative theory does provide a synoptic view, something television research in the main has been lacking.

6. In graphic presentation, Chatman's model is misleadingly unidirectional. Because the process of narrative communication he discusses is transactional, I have not reproduced his diagram here.

7. The Hill-Renko story continues in later episodes. Hoban is released when his alibi proves to be solid. The matter of who shot the officers is not resolved. The story instead becomes the new story of Hill and Renko's readjustment to duty after the trauma of the shooting, their estrangement from one another, and their eventual rapprochement as partners. This material is not included in the story outline because the information was not available to viewers of "Film at Eleven" when first broadcast. Were we examining the text as rerun, this material would have to be included.

8. Chatman (1980) appears to discount the significance of manifestation time. However, when the viewer does not control the time it takes to experience a narrative (as in film or television, as opposed to novels or paintings), manifestation time takes on greater significance. It becomes a third independent time system, through which the viewer accesses the other two. Taking into account broadcast time's inclusion of unrelated narratives (commercials) and nonnarrative content (station identifications, promotional announcements), as well as television's pre-occupation with the present tense, manifestation time becomes a force to be reckoned with if we are to understand television narrative adequately.

9. The discontinuity described here should not be confused with the cinematic or psychological flashback. The discourse progresses in the continuous present typical of television time. It is analeptic only in relation to the story chronology. The relationship is common in the mystery genre, where events that occurred in the past often are revealed in the present time of the narrative, which Chatman (1978, p. 63) refers to as the "narrative NOW."

10. Aristotelian notions of beginning, middle, and end apply to story elements *as imitated* by narrative. Such notions are meaningless in life. "No end, in reality, is ever final in the way 'The End' of a novel or film is. . . . Such a term marks out plot, the story-as-discoursed. It is strictly an artifact of composition, not a function of raw story-material (whatever its source, real or invented)" (Chatman, 1978, p. 47).

11. Television news, paradoxically narrative despite its claims to being life rather than art, demonstrates these tendencies. News stories repeatedly contain attempts at endings, but they reveal the paradox with conventional statements such as "The investigation is continuing." Ellis (1982, pp. 154–155) compares the rhetorical strategies of the current events series and the soap opera, pointing out that both forms pose as dilemmas the problems of repeated disturbances to domestic

equilibrium caused by outside forces. He contrasts this practice with film's articulation of a specific problematic, its resolution, and closure.

12. Despite the chaotic surface, *Hill Street Blues* is the product of the tight control that has become a trademark of MTM productions. Chaos is to be represented— not manifested—in the text. The technical merits of the production have been recognized in its many Emmy awards and nominations. Yet Anspaugh acknowledges that some confusion arises out of the pressurized shooting schedule. In 1981, the director of an episode had seven days of preparation (with one co-producer) and seven shooting days (Yerkovich & Anspaugh, 1982). The shooting schedule since has been extended to nine days.

13. See Gitlin (1983, pp. 291–295) for further discussion of shooting and sound recording techniques.

14. Thorburn (1976, p. 537), noting the implausibility of television melodrama's emotional intensity, suggests that the emotions dramatized are not in themselves unreal and that "television melodrama often becomes more truthful as it becomes more implausible."

15. The current practice of opening an episode with a brief recapitulation of events from the previous episode was not used initially. The recapitulation was added as a concession to network fear that viewers could not (or would not) keep track of series events from week to week. The heady dive into the middle of things was the original intent.

16. Weaving news headlines into breaks is common network practice. It occurs with heightened effect in *Hill Street Blues* because the *Hill Street* narrative treats time and its passage so consciously and because the *cinema verite* shooting brings news footage to mind.

17. I am indebted to Herbert L. Zettl for this phrase.

18. Chatman (1978, pp. 53–55) states that narrative events imply the logic of connection and hierarchy. The principle of connection (which may be causal or not) allows for the sorting of nonstory elements from story elements and elements of different stories one from another. The logic of hierarchy allows events to be sorted into what Chatman (after Barthes) calls *kernals* (major events that entail choices among one or more possible paths of development) and *satellites* (minor events that portray the workings-out of choices made at the kernals). Satellites imply the existence of kernals but not the reverse. The elements of narrative discourse I am calling digressions and interludes are neither satellites nor kernals. What is unusual about *Hill Street Blues* among television narratives is the relatively large amount of nonstory material present.

19. If one defines the narrative as the entire "strip" of segments, including program, commercials, etc., the commercial break becomes a more disruptive interlude, though this analysis concerns only those interludes contained within the program. In the strip view, the ultimate interlude would have to be all of the material broadcast between the close of one episode and the open of the next episode the following week. Although cumbersome for analytical purposes, such a view is particularly legitimate for *Hill Street Blues* and other serials because their stories continue across the weeks.

20. A scene is defined as a sequence of related shots. A change of scene may or may not involve a change in setting. For example, scenes 1 and 2 of "Film at Eleven" take place in the squad room. The scene numbers used here are those indicated in the script.

21. Episodes are selected and scheduled for repeat broadcast on the basis of their ability (as episodes) to draw audiences more than out of concern for story consistency. Ironically, the story outlines supplied to foreign purchasers contain a plea that the episodes be run in strict sequence.
22. The plot device of joining (presenting events with double narrative relevance) requires that events be shown redundantly on a plot diagram because they literally belong to both stories (Rimmon-Kenan, 1983, p. 23).
23. The problem of the vending machine recurs in many episodes. Eventually the attacks on the machine are treated more seriously. The problem does not receive enough development in "Film at Eleven" to allow it to be distinguished as a story. In the longer view, the problem might be interpreted as a sixth story disguised as an interlude.
24. Many of the series' narrative "innovations" quickly became conventions through recurrent use. Thus, the series appears to be more predictable in 1984 than it was in 1981. See Ellis (1982, pp. 6–10) for a discussion of realism as a function of taste. He observes the irony in the fact that new works appear realistic precisely because they break old canons of realism. Once the new becomes conventional—a development that may happen quickly—it is subject to being labeled as cliche. The paradox in a serial work is to maintain the conventions that define the series' appeal while at the same time keeping the narrative fresh by not overworking them.
25. Commenting on television's frequent use of melodrama, Brooks (1976, p. 204) observes that television's increasing tendency to "psychologize" cops and villains "in no sense violates the melodramatic context. It is not that melodramatic conflict has been interiorized and refined to the vanishing point, but on the contrary that psychology has been externalized, made accessible and immediate through a full realization of its melodramatic possibilities."
26. Michael Conrad died in November, 1983.
27. With the possible exceptions of Fay Furillo and Davenport, the characters do not represent alternate readings. Stories are told consciously from the cops' point of view, and no scene without a cop or Davenport occurs.
28. By contrast, see Gronbeck's (1984, p. 19) comment that the ideology of *Family is* pernicious in part because of its artistic seamlessness.
29. Hunter's suicide attempt in the 1983–1984 season is an example. Except for those who read about it in the newspaper, fans had to wait a week to find out for sure whether Hunter had died.

REFERENCES

Brooks, P. (1976). *The melodramatic imagination: Balzac, Henry James, melodrama, and the mode of excess*. New Haven: Yale University Press.

Chatman, S. (1978). *Story and discourse: Narrative structure in fiction and film*. Ithaca: Cornell University Press.

Chatman, S. (1980). What novels can do that films can't (and vice versa). In W. J. T. Mitchell (Ed.), *On narrative* (pp. 117–136). Chicago: University of Chicago Press.

Ellis, J. (1982). *Visible fictions: Cinema, television, video*. London: Routledge & Kegan Paul.

Fiedler, L. A. (1969). *Love and death in the American novel* (Laurel ed.). New York: Dell.

Frye, N. (1968). *Anatomy of criticism: Four essays*. New York: Atheneum.

Gabree, J. (1981, October 31). Can 'Hill Street Blues' keep dodging the Neilsen bullet? *TV Guide*, pp. 27–32.

Gitlin, T. (1983). *Inside prime time*. New York: Pantheon.

Gronbeck, B. E. (1984). Audience engagement in "Family." In M. J. Medhurst & T. W. Benson (Eds.), *Rhetorical dimensions in media: A critical casebook* (pp. 4–32). Dubuque, IA: Kendall/Hunt.

Kermode, F. (1980). Secrets and narrative sequence. In W. J. T. Mitchell (Ed.), *On narrative* (pp. 79–97). Chicago: University of Chicago Press.

Newcomb, H. M., & Hirsch, P. M. (1983). Television as a cultural forum: Implications for research. *Quarterly Review of Film Studies*, 8(2), 45–55.

Pollan, M. (1983, March/April). Can 'Hill Street Blues' rescue NBC? *Channels*, pp. 30–34.

Rimmon-Kenan, S. (1983). *Narrative fiction: Contemporary poetics*. London: Methuen.

Thorburn, D. (1982). Television melodrama. In H. Newcomb (Ed.), *Television: The critical view* (3rd ed., pp. 529–546). New York: Oxford University Press.

Yerkovich, A., & Anspaugh, D. (1982, April). *Television producing and directing*. Workshop presented at the San Francisco State University Broadcast Industry Conference, San Francisco, CA.

12 Securing the Middle Ground: Reporter Formulas in *60 Minutes*

RICHARD CAMPBELL

Since *60 Minutes* became a Nielsen ratings success during the mid-1970s, critics and journalists have tried to account for the phenomenon of a popular news program (see Arlen, 1977; Black, 1981; Funt, 1980; Kahn, 1982; Madsen, 1984; Moore, 1978; Stein, 1979; Weisman, 1983). One explanation points to the CBS decision to air the program on Sunday evenings in the fall following pro football and against children's programming on other networks. Another explanation suggests the importance of the arrival on the program of star reporter Dan Rather, fresh from the Watergate beat. Mike Wallace (1984, pp. 352–353) argues that viewers discovered the program when they were forced "to stay home on Sundays instead of visiting relatives or going for a late afternoon drive" during the 1973–1974 Arab oil embargo and subsequent fuel shortage. Don Hewitt, creator and executive producer of the program, credits *60 Minutes'* strong connection to narrative tradition as a major factor for the program's popularity:

> Documentaries were getting the same rating whether they were on ABC, CBS, or NBC . . . the same 15 to 20 percent share of the audience. I said to myself, "I'll bet if we made it multisubject and we made it personal journalism—instead of dealing with issues we told stories; if we packaged reality as well as Hollywood packages fiction, I'll bet we could double the rating." ("Father of '60 Minutes,'" 1981, p. 15)

In this study, I argue that not only are the meanings of *60 Minutes* embedded in the general narrative tradition Hewitt discusses but that the narratives of the show extend that tradition to carry a mythology for Middle America.

I define myths not as apocryphal stories associated with earlier cultures but as vital contemporary creators of meaning and value. Myths allow "a society to use factual or fictional characters and events to make sense of its environment, both physical and social. . . . They endow the world with conceptual values which originate in their language" (Hartley, 1982, p. 30). *60 Minutes* is a myth maker, constructing and reconstructing modern myths that signify "conceptual, intellectual or 'objective' values" (p. 26).

Myths help us make sense of experience. Within the human condition, as Edmund Leach (1968, p. 547) argues, "there are certain fundamental contradictions . . . with which all human beings must come to terms," and "myth provides a way of dealing with these universal puzzles." Similarly, Claude Levi-Strauss (1967, p. 226) argues that myth provides a logical model in the form of a narrative structure that resolves abstract conflicts such as life and death, good and evil, tradition and change, and nature and culture. Mythic narratives mediate their own constructed tensions and allow a culture to come to terms with contradiction and ambiguity.

The mythic narrative pattern provides the shape for many news reports, including those of *60 Minutes*. The pattern picks up people, issues, events, and other experiences and transforms them into narratives of two-dimensional conflicts. The reporters of *60 Minutes* perform as mediators who resolve tensions between nature and culture, good and evil, hero and villain, individual and institution, the abstract and concrete, presence and absence, and ultimately between their own reports and the reality those reports represent.

Here I offer an interpretive reading of *60 Minutes* as narrative and metaphor. With an emphasis on formula, myth, and text, my approach is linked closely to literary formalism (see Strine, 1985). I am, however, indebted to recent developments in cultural studies focusing on the interrelationships between text and audience (see Allen, 1987; Fiske, 1986; Hall, 1980; Jensen, 1987; Katz & Liebes, 1984; Morley, 1980; Newcomb, 1984; Radway, 1984). Although my analysis is textual, I do not mean to foreclose variant audience positions toward *60 Minutes* (e.g., note the "Letters" segment at the end of each program for selected oppositional readings). I do believe, however, that analysis of text and analysis of audience response still may be treated as separate questions. Whereas John Fiske (1986, p. 404) argues that "meanings occur only in the encounter between texts and subjects," I argue that producers of texts, the producers of *60 Minutes*, construct formulaic ways to read the text, maps for meaning, and I am concerned here with interpreting those maps. Although viewers may read *60 Minutes* in a variety of ways, they do so in relation to the program's formulas which offer a mediated middle ground (rather than a "dominant position") to engage. While variant negotiated and oppositional readings pose an intriguing research problem, I concentrate on interpreting the mythic narrative maps or formulas that feature *60 Minutes* reporters in their metaphorical performances as detectives, analysts, and tourists. I take this path because I believe with Horace Newcomb and Paul Hirsch (1983, p. 53) that "research and critical analysis . . . must somehow define and describe the inventory that makes possible the multiple meanings extracted by audiences, creators, and network decision makers."

Individuals and cultures construct identities and reality through the narrative process. As Joan Didion (1979, p. 11) suggests, we live "by the imposition of a narrative line upon disparate images, by 'ideas' with which we have learned to freeze the shifting phantasmagoria which is our actual experience." Narrative enables us to make sense of our own phantasmagoria because, in contrast to that experience, narrative is a familiar, concrete, and objectified structure. Narratives then *are* metaphors, shaping and containing the bodiless flow of experience within the familiar boundaries of plot, character, setting, problem, resolution, and synthesis.

Since its inception in 1968, *60 Minutes* has built its narratives around conceptual formulas that feature reporters chiefly in three roles: as detective, as analyst, and as tourist.[1] These metaphorical stances allow reporters to convert the abstract into the concrete, the unfamiliar into the familiar, and the contradictory into the clear, thereby resolving the narrative conflict each episode creates. These metaphors of the reporter present us with figures of modernity who offer mediated interpretations of experience, maps for negotiating our world.

REPORTER AS DETECTIVE

It is not mere coincidence that the fictional detective and the commercial reporter first appeared in the mid-nineteenth century. Both were products of a gradual cultural paradigm shift from romanticism to realism, from religion to science. Both were products of a utilitarian culture that took shape around the notion of conforming to "what is" rather than imagining "what ought to be" (Schudson, 1978). Many nineteenth century reporters associated their practices with the ideal of science, and the classical detective story, as personified by cerebral, rational detectives such as Arthur Conan Doyle's Sherlock Holmes and Edgar Allan Poe's Auguste Dupin, can be read similarly as an expression of faith in the "scientific mind" to gather facts and solve problems (see Cawelti, 1976; Nevins, 1970). By the end of the nineteenth century the identities and methods of both reporters and detectives were bound to a view of a world teeming with data waiting to be discovered, rationalized, organized, and transformed into frames of reference for the public to use in the explanation of immediate experience. Both news reports and detective stories in the nineteenth century then can be interpreted as vehicles for the new rationality of a utilitarian culture "in which the normative order moved from a set of commandments to do what is right to a set of prudential warnings to adapt realistically to what is" (Schudson, 1978, p. 121).

60 Minutes not only extends this tradition of faith in rationality, it has merged reporting practices with the literary traditions of the fictional detective. The detective formula describes a central narrative pattern in *60 Minutes*, featuring a variety of narrative characteristics that on the surface, at least, closely resemble those of the classical detective story (see Cawelti, 1976). As in classical detective stories, the *60 Minutes* detective episodes include the identification of a criminal situation followed by a series of actions to make sense of it: identifying victims, villains, and bystanders (who provide evidence and obstacles), reconstructing the factors contributing to the transgressions, revealing the perpetrators, and explaining the crime. The *60 Minutes* reporter, posed in front of the traditional *60 Minutes* storybook, introduces himself or herself and the "crime," which may range from political intrigue to deviation from Middle American values to murder. Next the reporter identifies major characters and settings, reconstructs the crime, and confronts a villain. Generally, there are characters who refuse to talk to the reporter and characters who try to hinder the search for evidence. But in the end the reporter fits together the puzzle and solves the crime. Instead of Sherlock Holmes revealing the crime's patterns for a befuddled Dr. Watson, however, the *60 Minutes* reporter ends the narrative posed again in front of the storybook frame, explaining in a direct address to the viewer the missing evidence, the fate of the villains, and any apparent contradictions.

The *60 Minutes* reporters carry no weapon but rely on rational analysis and their ability to outwit the other characters. They wear trench coats frequently when reconstructing crimes, a detail Don Hewitt notes with pride: "Those scenes of Mike Wallace on a stakeout in a trench coat are great if they produce anything . . ." (Henry, 1986, p. 29). And like their fictional counterpart, the *60 Minutes* detectives often succeed where traditional investigative agencies, victims of mediocrity or inferior intelligence, fail. Finally, following the tradition of the classical detective, the audience is privy to very little personal information about the reporters; we learn little about their private lives, their relationship to the stories they tell, or their own moral judgments of the stories. While unlike classical detectives, the *60 Minutes* reporters are real, they create and enact personae guided by audience expectations that detectives reveal the truth.

The Detective Formula

60 Minutes detective episodes reveal the following characteristics: (1) introduction of the detective and the crime, (2) reconstruction of the crime scene and the search for clues, (3) confrontation of villains and witnesses, and (4) explanation of the solution and/or the denouement. Three general conflicts serve to organize these narratives: individual versus institution, honesty versus deception, and safety versus danger.

Introducing the Crime

Detective episodes often explicitly frame the narrative *as* a detective story. For example, in "Land Fraud and a Murder" (3/2/75), a story about organized crime activity in Arizona, Morley Safer introduces "a new and frightening development," a tale of "dubious land sales involving shady characters," and "a story almost too hot to handle."[2] In "Warning: May Be Fatal" (12/14/75), a story about "potential lethal pollution" of chemical plant workers, Dan Rather suggests, "What we have here in no small way is a whodunit." Occasionally, too, reporters make direct allusions to the similarities between their narratives and the classical detective fiction of Doyle or Poe. Rather, for instance, begins "Equal Justice?" (8/24/80), a story about a black New Jersey political candidate who is allegedly framed for kidnapping, this way: "Tonight the strange case of Mims Hackett." And Mike Wallace introduces "The Stolen Cezannes" (10/14/79) similarly: "The case of the stolen Cezannes is not just the tangled tale of . . . three purloined paintings." In all of these episodes, the story begins with the reporter's introduction and the revelation of some crime that sets him off to unravel the mystery.

Searching for Clues

The reporter in these episodes sets off to unravel the mystery, stopping first at the place of the crime, where the crime's details and intrigue are recalled, then leading us to areas where clues reside and where the crime is resolved. In these scenes, *60 Minutes* visually mediates the conflict between safety and danger by displaying the reporter at the scene of the crime, a place once full of peril but now rendered safe by the passing of time and the reporter's presence. For example, Morley Safer in "Land Fraud and a Murder" takes us to a dark stairwell in a public parking garage to reconstruct a murder that has been connected to organized crime in Arizona. He points to blood-stained clues and shows us a newspaper photo with the victim lying in the very place that Safer now safely occupies. The episode also features safe, intimate interviews where characters recount details and clues. In "The Death of Edward Nevin" (2/17/80), Dan Rather poses on a rooftop in San Francisco to reconstruct the crime: how the government carried out a secret germ warfare experiment in 1950 that led to the death of an innocent man. In a trench coat, Rather demonstrates how villainous government agents collected dangerous bacteria samples. Again this public, once dangerous, place is now secure, filled by the reporter's presence. As in most *60 Minutes* episodes, the reporter, featured in an intimate mid-chest shot on the safe sets of a CBS studio, presents the final mediation and denouement.

Confronting Villains

The third detective element includes a confrontation segment where the reporter waylays a villain, an unwitting representative of an evil institution, or a befuddled witness or bystander. Because the reporter assumes certain risks in order to resolve a problem, the reporter's actions again embody and mediate the tension between safety and danger. For example, in "The Mystery in Building 213" (7/20/75), a story about spy satellites, the CIA, and national security, Mike Wallace approaches a building that is guarded by armed police and surrounded by a tall, barbed wire fence. This ominous setting reveals a public place full of potential intrigue and risk. Wallace, undaunted, confronts a security guard in the parking lot outside the building and suggests, "Everybody around here says it's a CIA building." The guard, appearing confused and guilty, refuses to link the building to the CIA, leaving this connection for Wallace to make later. Another example, "From Burgers to Bankruptcy" (12/3/78), tells a story about deception in the food franchising business. Wallace, in a trench coat, confronts an executive from a burger franchising company and tries to elicit a response. When the executive no longer will talk, Wallace stakes out his restaurant and in the parking lot confronts an employee (who nervously tells Wallace, "I'll watch what I'm saying") with information about his employer's past. These dramatic confrontations serve to display the reporter in some *danger* so that the tension later can be balanced against the *safety* provided by the reporter's revelation of and apparent solution to the crime.

Another aspect of confrontation scenes is the "probing, tough interview." In the detective episode, confrontation works to establish the oppositional structure and the values implicit in that structure. For instance, "Handcuffing the Cops?" (6/22/80) presents a prison confession scene between alleged murderer Barry Braeseke, whose constitutional rights were technically violated by police during an arrest, and Wallace:

BRAESEKE: I was in my room and I had my rifle with me, and I came downstairs, and I walked into the family room and the family was watching the TV set with their back to me.
WALLACE: Hm-hmm.
BRAESEKE: And then I started firing the rifle. I was standing behind my—my Dad and I shot him.
WALLACE: Through the head?
BRAESEKE: Yes.
WALLACE: And then right away—?
BRAESEKE: Almost instantly my mother. (CBS News, 1980, p. 629)

Here Wallace confronts the villain in his own dangerous space but elicits truth that renders the setting safe.

Solving the Crime

The explanation scene is one of the chief patterns of action in the detective formula, representing "the goal toward which the story has been moving" (Cawelti, 1976, p. 88). That goal is the resolution of narrative tension, "the pleasure of seeing a clear and meaningful order emerge out of what seemed to be random and chaotic events" (p. 89). As detective writer P. D. James (1984) notes regarding the formula, "No matter how difficult the problem, there is a solution. All of this is rather comforting in an age of pessimism and anxiety." In *60 Minutes*, interpreting events and identifying criminals serves to resolve major narrative conflicts. So, for example, in "Your Money or Your Life" (3/19/78), a world of normalcy is represented by Americans pitted against a world of deviance—foreign "terrorists" who threaten U.S. businessmen abroad and citizens at home. Dan Rather mediates this opposition by explaining how we can minimize threats from terrorists. In this narrative, Rather is located squarely between the worlds of normalcy and deviance. He is clearly neither a part of the deviant world of terrorism nor a member of an unsuspecting, victimized public. The reporter is the hero of this story, mediating the tensions between a normal world of middle class values and a deviant world of terrorism set upon destroying those values. As detached hero, Rather, however, does empathize with the normal, vulnerable world portrayed in the story. At one point he responds to a statement about terrorism in the United States: "Do you believe that? That scares the hell out of me." Such dramatic vulnerability actually heightens the reporter's credibility as a heroic figure who can live with contradictions and manage to interpret and resolve them.[3]

In a less dramatic example, "The Grapes of Wealth" (10/14/79), Morley Safer confronts wealthy southern California farmers who, through a bureaucratic loophole, qualify for special low interest loans designed to "save the family farm." *60 Minutes* juxtaposes expensive cars, homes, tennis courts, and horse stables owned by these farmers with narration about their acceptance of "low interest disaster loans" intended for poorer, struggling farmers. While the opposition between safety and danger is not displayed prominently in this episode, the reporter still must clarify tension between honesty and deception by portraying the practices of wealthy farmers set against honest, unsuspecting middle class farmers whom Safer represents in the narrative. In the final scene, the reporter, posed in front of the storybook frame, enumerates the deceptive practices. This ending or solution scene where the reporter wraps up the case is typical of most detective episodes, just as it is typical in much classical detective fiction where there is often a denouement featuring the "actual apprehension and confession of the criminal." But that denouement need not be an ingredient in the formula since "the classical story is more concerned with the isolation and specification of guilt than with the punishment of the criminal" (Cawelti, 1976, p. 90).

In some episodes, however, there is a clear denouement. "Another Elvis?" (8/12/79), for instance, presents a story about characters who pay money to shady record companies in return for recording careers. The disreputable president of a Nashville company (who, we learn, had a previous criminal record), is apprehended and subsequently confesses to the reporter, who has caught the villain in a lie. Mike Wallace reports at the end of the episode that this character has "quit the business" and now "thanks" *60 Minutes* for turning his life in an honest direction. In this episode, the reporter dissolves tension by placing himself between innocent victims and insensitive villains. Ultimately, he wraps up the case, reinstitutes safety, and reaffirms honesty in the denouement when the villain promises to reform.

Detective as Mediator

A major function of the detective formula in the mythic framework of *60 Minutes* is to display the reporter amid conflicts between safety and danger. Reporters, of course, always emerge from these dramatic situations safely by either resolving the crime or at least presenting an interpretation. They thus straddle and mediate the conflict. Implicit in their mediation are moral values such as security, democracy, honesty, loyalty, and justice. Safety affirms these middle class values that gain definition only in relation to the danger of insecurity, communism, dishonesty, disloyalty, and injustice.

A second narrative conflict frequently used in the detective formula is between individual and institution. In "Titan" (11/8/81), where the crimes are government ineptitude and insensitivity, the narrative creates the tension through a victimized character, a former Air Force sergeant reprimanded by his superiors after he tried to investigate a toxic leak and fatal explosion in a U.S. missile silo. According to the ex-sergeant, "I went down there for God, my country, the flag, my job—everything—I didn't go down there for any other reason. I gave them my all. And what did I get from them [the Air Force]? A letter of reprimand. . . . What about the little guy ?" 60 Minutes affirms the ex-sergeant's status as little guy by juxtaposing him with the absent Air Force who, as Safer tells us, "absolutely refuses to answer any questions." The reporter mediates the tension between the individual and institution by supporting the side of the innocent, unsuspecting victim and by affirming values of honesty and loyalty against the Air Force, the institutional villain.

A third major tension, between honesty and deception, organizes detective narratives. In "Taking on the Teamsters" (12/3/78), Safer's narration creates a Robin Hood metaphor by opposing individuals, the "dissident leader" of "the people" and "his small band," who are running for labor union offices against the long-entrenched institutional union heads who are under surveillance for possible payoff schemes and organized crime connections. Here again the presence of the small band of dissidents at various meetings contrasts sharply with the absence of the current union leaders, who, Safer tells us, "refused absolutely" to be interviewed. In their place are aerial shots of their expensive homes and swimming pools and accompanying narration tells of the alleged criminal activity. The reporter mediates the conflict by implicitly supporting and affirming the honest, hard-work ethic of the dissident band of union individuals against corrupt, indulgent, institutional leaders. This ability to mediate derives from the reporter's values. The allegiance to honesty provides a basis for moral superiority over deceptive institutions.

An important subconflict in these detective episodes features the *presence* of victims, heroes, and the 60 Minutes reporter and the *absence* of the villainous persons or institutions. Presence versus absence generally takes two forms on 60 Minutes: (1) certain parties refuse to be filmed or interviewed, and (2) certain parties simply are not interviewed by 60 Minutes even though their absence is used as a major opposition in the narrative (see Shaw, 1987). The absent, or faceless, villain generally represents some form of business, government, or labor institution. For example, in "Distressed" (5/3/81), a story about a flourishing Florida county listed by HUD (Department of Housing and Urban Development) as an economically distressed area, no top bureaucrat from HUD would grant Safer an interview. He tells us that one institutional representative said, "No way will I sit down for an interview." *60 Minutes* then introduces a General Accounting Office report that criticizes HUD for using 20-year-old statistics to determine economically distressed areas. Safer's narration, filmed outside the HUD building, displays the agency as a big, insensitive, inefficient bureaucracy under no individual's control. In contrast, the reporter's presence affirms values of efficiency, justice, and common sense against the inept, unjust, and illogical countervalues of the absent bureaucracy.

60 Minutes reinforces the narrative function of reporters as mediators by a style that gives them more visual or frame space in which to operate. With few exceptions, *60 Minutes* reporters are shot at a greater distance than the characters they interview. Frequently, in reaction or question shots, characters appear in extreme close-ups (usually with the top of the head cut from the frame), while the reporter appears in medium close-up shots (normally shown from the middle of the chest up). The greater space afforded the reporters in *60 Minutes* supports their function as mediators since it endows them with a medium position, with the appearance of more control over their place in the narrative. The greater distance granted the reporter also reinforces the posture of detachment. Often the reporter's hands, shoulders, and head are free in the frame, whereas other characters—unsuspecting victims or devious villains who are shot in tighter close-up shots—have less room to maneuver within the frame. As Meyrowitz (1985, p. 102) notes, interviewees are shot so tightly "that any move of the head makes it appear" that the subjects are "trying to escape scrutiny." With heads and sometimes chins cut off, these characters are reduced to eyes, noses, lips, foreheads, sweat, facial twitches, and tears. The greater space granted to the reporters of *60 Minutes* places them in a position to see the larger picture, control their environment, secure a middle ground, and thereby mediate narrative tension.

What empowers the classical detective to find clues and resolve problems is superior intelligence and detachment, a "lack of moral or personal involvement in the crime he is called upon to investigate" (Cawelti, 1976, p. 83). The *60 Minutes* reporters display these traits whenever they assume a more positive position than villains or inefficient institutions, the counterparts to the bungling and inefficient police of detective fiction. The greater visual space afforded the reporters' portrayal as *individuals* (rather than as institutional representatives of CBS News) grants them superior narrative positions.

James Fernandez (1974, p. 124) argues that a cultural "mission of metaphor" is to move the subject of the metaphor, in this case the reporter, "into optimum position in quality space," the space of the classical detective who is characterized by both superiority and detachment. In *60 Minutes*, the reporter occupies optimum position for mediating contradiction. The reporter receives metaphoric status as a heroic detective who champions Middle American individualism and integrity in the face of heartless bureaucracy. As Robert Bellah and his colleagues (1985, p. 149) note in *Habits of the Heart*, historically the detective first appeared as a popular cultural hero "when business corporations emerged as the focal institutions of American life. The fantasy of a lonely, but morally impeccable, hero corresponds to doubts about the integrity of self in the context of modern bureaucratic organization." Depicting *60 Minutes* reporters as individual loners, apart from a team of producers, researchers, and editors who construct the story, apart from the powerful CBS media corporation, allows the reporters' institutional identities to remain hidden. This portrayal enhances their preferred narrative position as mediators of tension, clarifiers of doubt, and affirmers of individualism.

REPORTER AS ANALYST

Like the detective, the analyst too has assumed a position in the quality space of our culture. The development of the analyst's social influence also can be traced to the late nineteenth century during a cultural shift from religion to science, a geographical shift from rural to urban living, and an economic shift from a producer to a consumer society. The analyst emerged from the changes as a prominent promoter of a "therapeutic ethos" that offered renewal of "a sense of selfhood that had grown fragmented, diffuse, and somehow 'unreal'" (Lears, 1983, p. 4). The analyst gained legitimacy by riding the coattails of prestige bestowed upon medical science and the ability of science in general to solve problems. Jackson Lears (pp. 6–11) identifies several crises and problems around the turn of the century including urbanization, which introduced the "anonymity of the city"; technological advance, which brought "prepackaged artificiality" along with "unprecedented comfort and convenience"; institutionalization, which created "an interdependent national market economy" and cut people off from ties to the land and "primary experience"; and secularization, which displaced religion and isolated people from traditions. The analyst stepped into these crises to try and restore a sense of individuality offering "harmony, vitality, and the hope of self-realization." The analyst offered, and continues to offer, cures for and mediations of cultural tension. As Bellah and his colleagues (1985, p. 47) point out, "the very term *therapeutic* suggests a life focused on the need for cure."

A second *60 Minutes* formula features the reporter as analyst who offers cures for contemporary tensions. In general, the reporter assumes two roles in these *60 Minutes* analyst episodes: that of the social or cultural commentator, and that of the psychoanalyst or therapist. And in any given analyst episode, the reporter may perform both roles. In each case, however, the reporter is, first of all, an interpreter who recasts, rearranges, and retells the stories of others. Such narrative interpretation, psychologist Roy Schafer (1981) suggests, is the essence of analysis:

> [People] tell the analyst about themselves and others in the past and present.
> In making interpretations, the analyst retells these stories. In the retelling,
> certain features are accentuated while others are placed in parentheses. . . .

The analyst's retellings progressively influence the what and how of the stories told. . . . The analyst establishes new, though often contested or resisted, questions that amount to regulated narrative possibilities. (pp. 31– 32)

In many episodes of *60 Minutes*, reporters function precisely as such analysts when they construct narratives about the lives of others.

One result of the reporter's analytical interpretations is to endow narratives with closure. The desire for closure in narrative, as Hayden White (1981) argues, is a desire for moral meaning:

The demand for closure in the historical story is a demand . . . for moral meaning, a demand that sequences of real events be assessed as to their significance as elements of a *moral* drama. Has any historical narrative ever been written that was not informed not only by moral awareness but specifically by the moral authority of the narrator? (p. 20)

The affirmation of values or morality, both explicitly and implicitly, is a chief function of *60 Minutes* where, as in other forms of factual storytelling, "narrativity . . . is intimately related to, if not a function of, the impulse to moralize reality" (White, 1981, p. 14).

The *60 Minutes* analyst episodes reflect the impulse to moralize reality in mediating three key dramatic tensions: success versus failure, tradition versus change, and the personal versus the social. While the tension between the personal and social realms is a variant of individualism versus institution, the different terms call attention to the more general nature of this opposition as it is worked out in the analyst formula. In the detective episodes, the institution typically is a government or business organization. In the analyst episodes, bureaucracies give way to a broader notion of "society" as a set of demands and rules that "individuals" must confront. In the detective episodes, characters serve mainly as a function of plot and their individual behavior and attitudes are rarely explored in depth. In the analyst episodes, a single character generally is the focus of the 14- to 15-minute story. Whereas detective episodes include on the average 8 to 10 characters who are named and interviewed, in the analyst episodes only 2 main characters are usually featured, the subject of the story and the reporter.

The Analyst Formula

Four characteristics of the analyst formula are: (1) the role of the reporter as social or psychological analyst, endowing the narrative with closure and moral meaning, (2) the personalized role of the analyst, (3) the treatment of characters as heroic or villainous, and (4) the style of the reporter as inquisitor, asking tough questions.

Social and Psychological Analysts

The role of the analyst on *60 Minutes* is that of the social commentator who analyzes and interprets political, economic, and cultural trends in relationship to the interview subjects, the major characters in these narratives. For example, in "Martin Luther King's Family at Christmas" (12/24/68), Mike Wallace tells a story about King's family and analyzes the effect of King's death on the civil rights movement which, in Wallace's words, was "leaderless" and "rudderless" without King. Wallace's role in this episode, the reporter's function in the social analyst episodes, is not so much to analyze historical events as it is to offer a narrative that explains the present and predicts future directions of social phenomena (in this case, the civil rights movement). In another example, "New York Yankee" (5/3/81), Harry Reasoner offers social commentary on Yankee owner George Steinbrenner, who is characterized by Reasoner as "almost impossible to work for." He "can't hit, run, or throw, but boy can he talk," Reasoner tells us. The reporter offers insights and forecasts trends regarding labor-management relations in baseball. Reasoner predicts ominously that Steinbrenner "should be heading toward another successful season—but don't bet on it." Reasoner's analysis implicitly rejects negative aspects of Steinbrenner's character (egocentrism, physical mediocrity, and self-indulgence), aspects that counter Middle American values.

A second analytic role features the reporter as psychoanalyst or therapist. Moving away from *public* events and issues, the reporter as psychoanalyst probes the *private*, emotional world of the characters in order to reaffirm values. Again in "Martin Luther King's Family at Christmas," Wallace probes the emotions of the King children by asking how they are adjusting to their father's assassination. The narrative then affirms the ability of the private family to overcome the chaos and conflict inherent in a public assassination. In another example, "The Shah of Iran" (10/14/76) episode allows Wallace to practice some confrontational psychology by reading to the Shah from his CIA psychological profile: "A brilliant but dangerous megalomaniac who is likely to pursue his own aims in disregard of U.S. interests." Wallace asks the Shah, "Should I go on?" and then concludes the scene with narration that analyzes the Shah's mental characteristics by juxtaposing them implicitly with positive values such as humility and democracy. As a final illustration, in "Anderson of Illinois" (2/17/80), Morley Safer overtly displays the therapist persona when he conducts a kind of verbal Rorschach test on 1980 presidential candidate John Anderson: "For an underdog, Anderson is a gentle soul who does not speak harshly of his rivals, even when you play the candidate game with him. I'll give you a name, and you give me an answer. Ronald Reagan?" Safer offers three more names to complete the test. In so doing, Safer as therapist constructs a story that implicitly supports Anderson's kindness and modesty as values for living. In each of these episodes, the reporter probes the emotional states of interviewees in order to offer a cure for the larger sociopolitical problem that these narratives are constructing as reality.

The Intimate Reporter

A second characteristic of the analyst formula features the reporter as a character with subjective likes and dislikes. One visual instance stands out, a scene from "Lena Horne" (12/27/81) where reporter Ed Bradley and interviewee Horne walk hand in hand across a busy New York street. Although not always as vividly, reporter intimacy also surfaces in other analyst episodes. In "Madame Minister" (9/19/82), actress and Greek cultural minister Melina Mercouri takes Harry Reasoner "on a date" to a Greek nightclub. In "Mister Right" (12/14/75), Mike Wallace, in a sweater and jacket, interviews presidential candidate Ronald Reagan during a jeep ride on Reagan's California ranch. In these examples, the analyst persona displays a more involved personal stance in the narrative.

A visual device that personalizes the reporter also comes into play in the analyst episodes. In contrast to the detective formula where the reporter is typically shot no closer than medium range, in the analyst formula the camera zooms in considerably closer in reaction or question shots with the interview subject. For example, in "More Than a Touch of Class" (4/7/74), an interview with actress Glenda Jackson in a London pub, Wallace appears three times in close-up shots and in one extreme closeup where part of his forehead is cut off; in none of the detective episodes featuring Wallace is he shot this tightly.

Interviewee as Hero or Villain

A third characteristic of the analyst episodes, the treatment of characters as heroes and villains, also involves the use of visual space. Interview subjects in these episodes are treated as either representatives of middle class values (heroic) or countervalues (villainous). In certain analyst episodes, the interview subject receives equal visual space with the reporter. These episodes generally portray the interviewee heroically, that is, the subject appears also as a mediator resolving oppositions, as an enforcer of or model for basic values. For example, in "Extremism in the Defense of Liberty" (7/20/75), Karl Hess, who has "progressed" from his job as Barry Goldwater's "arch-conservative" speech writer to inner-city social reformer, receives visual space similar to Morley Safer, who appears mostly in waist-up medium and long shots. Again in "What Became of Eldridge Cleaver?" (5/18/75), the camera helps us follow Cleaver's career from black revolutionary to reformed activist. In early shots in this episode, Mike Wallace asks Cleaver about his 1960s threat to "take off the heads" of established political figures; here Cleaver appears in extreme close-ups. Once Wallace establishes that "Cleaver is no longer a black symbol of resistance," no longer a villain, the camera pulls back and Cleaver too appears in waist-up medium shots. He now appears in similar visual space as Wallace. He is a mainstream, American figure who can resolve central contradictions in his own life and serve as a model for others.

When an interview subject appears as a deviant from basic values and a polarizer of tensions, the camera denies visual space (this is also true for victims, those who are caught in gray areas between conflicts they cannot resolve). For example, in "The Shah of Iran," Wallace battles the Shah in an interview that features tensions between American democracy and a foreign dictatorship. The villainous Shah appears almost totally in extreme close-ups that, at times, cut both his forehead and chin from the frame. Wallace, who is featured in nearly 40 shots in this episode, receives more visual space. In most shots, we can see the reporter's hands at work in the frame, demonstrating that Wallace is in more control of the space around him. And it is Wallace who affirms American ideals in the face of the Shah who stands for foreign, tyrannical countervalues.

Another visual technique that separates heroic from villainous or victimized subjects involves the camera's depiction of private artifacts, a visual technique that personalizes interview subjects. In "The Empress" (5/18/75), for instance, a profile story of the Empress of Iran, shots create a contrast between public ceremonies and private, more intimate moments featuring the empress with her children at a birthday party. Other shots in this episode also help resolve a conflict between public and private through intimate glimpses of a living room featuring family artifacts that portray the empress as a model of simplicity, modesty, and motherhood in spite of her regal position and wealth. In contrast, the camera mostly ignores the private, personal lives of villains. For instance, in "The Shah of Iran," we do not see him with his children, at birthday parties, in an intimate living room, nor are we told stories from his youth. The questions and the visuals focus not on the private but on the sociopolitical nature of his public, anti-American, anti-democratic postures.

Reporter as Inquisitor

A final characteristic of the analyst formula features the tough confrontational questions that generally probe deviations from basic values. The reporters display this characteristic by confronting and questioning characters who are portrayed, at least during a part of the interview, as representing countervalues. In "General Ky and Big Minh" (10/21/71), for instance, Mike Wallace asks General Ky if he plans to overthrow the South Vietnamese government. "No coups on your mind?" Wallace asks as he confronts Ky on questions of disloyalty, antidemocracy, and deception. In "Anderson of Illinois," Morley Safer challenges the presidential candidate on his plan to cut federal spending: "Well, so what are you saying? Abandon the cities?" At the end of this episode, Safer couches the tough question in negative comments made by other reporters:

> It's kind of interesting . . . the perception of John Anderson. For example, this *Washington Post* headline is "Dream Candidate Going Nowhere." Tom Wicker, a liberal columnist in *The New York Times*, says the man running on

either side can't win. Conventional wisdom? Leo Durocher says nice guys finish last. What do you say to all that? (CBS News, 1980, p. 339)

A major function of the tough question scenes in the mythic framework of *60 Minutes* is to locate the reporter in the middle, between us and them, between private and public tensions. Indeed, as Ian Connell (1978) has noted,

> The "hard," "tough" style of interviewing . . . was legitimized as an attempt "to get at the facts" on behalf of the public. This adoption of a "watchdog" role on behalf of the ordinary voters also led to the attempted identifications with "us," and the attempts to articulate the kinds of questions that "we" would ask of "our" powerful representatives if "we" only could. (p. 83)

In the analyst formula, posing tough questions includes the viewer in the reporter's point of view, clarifies narrative tension, and sets the stage for mediation.

Analyst as Mediator

Within the mythic framework, the analyst episodes call for resolution of central narrative tensions. As in the detective episodes, a chief mission of the reporter here is to mediate fundamental, emotional, and conceptual oppositions. In "Martin Luther King's Family at Christmas," Mike Wallace mediates tension between life and death in the closing scene: "Martin Luther King left a legacy for all of us that we cannot fail to understand especially at this Christmas season. But he left us, too, Coretta King." Mrs. King then discusses "creative suffering" and argues that the tragedy "doesn't mean we will sit around and bathe in our grief." Wallace, as mediator, celebrates the presence of Coretta King and her family as a solution to contradiction and ambiguity. Other episodes also offer the family as a solution for social as well as personal conflicts and suffering. Resolution and moral meaning for the audience in these episodes are enabled through the probing, guiding questions of the reporter.

Conflicts between person and society, tradition and change, which also shape many analyst episodes, are often resolved through the presence of a character whose moral code once deviated from Middle American values. In "What Became of Eldridge Cleaver?" Cleaver emerges as a man who formerly wanted to decapitate U.S. leaders but who, five years later, wants to return from exile in Paris to attend his father's funeral and the U.S. bicentennial celebration. In this episode, Wallace switches discussion from Cleaver's personal loss to the social change and "success" of the entire Black Panther organization. He offers a symmetrical closure, the Panthers following Cleaver's repentant course. Instead of violent revolutionaries, analyst Wallace describes a "changed outfit," now "working," "laboring," "muted." They too have become "nonviolent" reformers hard at work "inside the system." The Panthers' adjustment from deviance to normalcy obscures Cleaver's personal loss and closes the narrative with a positive image, parallel to Cleaver's own repentance and return to normalcy. Within the structure of this analyst formula, narrative mediation occurs as Wallace sorts positive values from their negative counterparts, thereby endowing the narrative with moral meaning: Cleaver and the Panthers must pay a price when they overstep the bounds of a society's rules, but once that price is paid, society accepts them back into the mainstream.

The Cleaver episode offers a metaphorical framework for transforming the abstract and less familiar categories of deviance and normalcy, tradition and change, into the more concrete and familiar terms of a mythic narrative structure. Wallace introduces the concept and value of repentance in order to resolve opposition between the concrete entities of the story, a radical Cleaver and the Black Panthers versus established government leaders, and the abstract concepts both sets of characters represent: revolution and status quo, deviance and normalcy, change and tradition. The transformation of Cleaver's idiosyncratic experience into the myth of the prodigal son resuming his place in normal society requires that Wallace become a mediating term in the mythic narrative between opposed sets of moral values. It is not merely the introduction of the concept of repentance that resolves this particular mythic narrative but the performance of Wallace domesticating deviant attitudes and comforting the audience.

In the analyst episodes, as in the detective episodes, metaphor locates the reporter in preferred narrative space. That quality space is provided by the legitimacy that comes through associating the reporter with those who know about social processes and psychological states, social commentators and therapists. Within the structure of the analyst formula, mediation occurs as reporters rescue reality from apparent contradiction, thereby endowing and enriching the narrative referent with moral meaning and sense.

THE REPORTER AS TOURIST

The same sets of nineteenth century historical conditions that prepared the way for the analyst also contributed to the importance of the tourist to twentieth century culture. Urbanization and secularization, technology and "prepackaged artificiality" severed connections to "primary experience" and older traditions (Lears, 1983). These changes initiated a twentieth century search for the past, for lost identity, for authentic experience. Dean MacCannell (1976, p. 3) describes this quest and defines modern tourists as "sightseers, mainly middle-class, who are at this moment deployed throughout the entire world in search of experience." What tourists implicitly seek, according to MacCannell (p. 3), is to resolve the contradictions between nature and civilization, tradition and modernization: "For moderns, reality and authenticity are thought to be elsewhere: in other historical periods and other cultures, in purer, simpler lifestyles." Dean O'Brien (1983, p. 9) finds MacCannell's quest for authentic experience at the center of reporting: "journalists, also in search of authenticity, travel from one source, event and sight to another," trying "to penetrate the markers and the 'staged authenticity' of front regions (news releases, government hand-outs, pseudo-events) to reach genuine back regions. . . ." Audiences, of course, vicariously accompany reporters in this contradictory quest to get beyond the artificial. Certain episodes of *60 Minutes* embody the quest for authentic experience, whether it be in a foreign land or in America's heartland.

The Tourist Formula

The tourist stories portray the reporter (1) acting as surrogate in exploring and describing the new or unfamiliar, (2) searching for authenticity: trying to recover the past, the natural, and smashing through the facade that is modern civilization, and (3) confronting villains, usually portrayed as either bureaucracies or modernity itself (often in the guise of Americanization). The reporter in these episodes mediates three major narrative conflicts: tradition and modernization, nature and civilization (or rural and urban), and individual and institution.

The episodes that portray the tourist in Middle America often begin with explicit acknowledgment of their mythic narrative structure. For example, Dan Rather as our tourist surrogate, in jeans, travels the country in "Wild Cat Trucker" (2/22/76). He begins the episode: "There's a new brand of folk hero around these days—the wildcat trucker. Like the cowboy and the gold miner and the aerial barnstormer of an earlier era, he's taking his place in Americana." Again in "Charity Begins at Home" (2/4/79), a story about a town that "takes on the state of New Jersey over the issue of welfare," Morley Safer, in the manner of Thornton Wilder, leads us on a tour of small-town America. "This is one of those *Our Town* kind of stories, and if you were writing it as fiction, there are certain things you'd have to include" such as an ice cream parlor and a hardware store. "The tale we have to tell is one of those late twentieth century American dramas."

Acting as Surrogate

In describing a guiding myth of modernity, MacCannell (1976, p. 159) notes that "the position of the person who stays at home in the modern world is morally inferior to that of a person who 'gets out' often," because "authentic experiences are believed to be available only to those moderns who try to break the bonds of their everyday existence and begin to 'live.'" To a certain extent, television and television news mediate the bind experienced by those of us caught in the routine of everyday life who also seek authenticity outside our homes. The *60 Minutes* reporters function in part as surrogates, as tour guides, who take us to unfamiliar, foreign places and remind us of "reality and authenticity elsewhere" (MacCannell, 1976, p. 16). Thus in "Paris Was Yesterday" (4/22/73), when Mike Wallace dines at a Parisian cafe and narrates a sightseeing tour about old and new Paris, he becomes our surrogate, rendering this unfamiliar place accessible and familiar. The reporter, as our representative in this foreign land, helps us "break the bonds of everyday existence and begin to 'live.'" In "Oman" (8/24/80), a story about a U.S. military base in the Middle East, Wallace dons shorts and relaxes with a newspaper at poolside. In voice-over narration, he comments about his tourist role in the narrative: "Even Americans aren't especially welcome as tourists," a comment that implicitly includes the viewers in partnership with Wallace as he dares to tour exotic lands.

Searching for Authenticity

The episode "How To Live To Be 100" (7/5/81) illustrates a second feature of the tourist formula. Here Morley Safer comments that a particular community of Russians live long because of their *authentic* lifestyle. The reporter lists the community's rules and values: "food from earth, not from a can; hard physical labor, not the so-called leisure years, and above all an unbreakable belief in family life that makes age more important than youth or wealth." A visual counterpart to this narration features a 107-year-old man bathing in the natural, authentic setting of a cold mountain stream. Similarly, in "Yanks in Iran" (1/2/77), Mike Wallace talks to disgruntled American citizens who came to Iran in search of identity and authenticity, but failed to find them. One character, who is leaving Iran after eight years, tells Wallace about other Americans who "think they're coming to the promised land." He then discusses the expenses, drugs, "smog, noise, cars," and other symbols of modernization that have disrupted the Americans' quest. These explicit symbols of *artificiality* pose a set of countervalues to moderation, good health, and small-town pastoralism, which are affirmed in this narrative.

In the heartland episodes, part of what is accomplished is not only the authentication of the reporter's presence, but the verification that these places display genuine small-town markers and symbols: the ice cream parlor, the hardware store, the meeting hall, the church, the diner, and main street. The established authenticity and individuality of the small town then is contrasted with the artificiality and impersonality of the big city. For example, the opening of "Away From It All?" (8/1/76) establishes a quest for an authentic experience that can be found only in a small-town setting. The reporter here asks if we ever had the feeling that we "wanted to get away from it all—pollution, taxes, pressure." Shots of neon signs and congested urban streets, the symbols for the artificial, impersonal big city, are then contrasted visually with shots of a lake, a church, an inn, barns, horses, and a waterfall in Derry, New Hampshire.

Whereas in the foreign-place episodes, the villain is typically modernization or foreign values, in these heartland episodes the villain is more often an institution (located in the artificial city rather than the natural country). Rarely represented visually, the invisible institution becomes more menacing. For example, in "Rural Justice" (2/22/76), the absent values of the legal profession are opposed to the law and order code of small-town South Carolina magistrates. Contrasted with the urban legal system that demands rural magistrates hold law degrees are these small-town judges, one of whom moonlights as a night watchman. In emphasizing the importance of humility and individualism, this rural judge tells Morley Safer that he refuses to wear a judicial robe "because it would scare people," and he wants to "make them feel at home. . . . I take this little magistrate's job to heart." While five rural judges visually are portrayed, no one from big city legal institutions appears in this story. The concrete presence of individual magistrates, who connote familiarity and friendliness, contrast here with the law profession which, reinforced by its menacing *absence*, connotes unfamiliarity and unfriendliness.

Confronting Modernity and Bureaucracy

Aligned with the search for authenticity is a third aspect of the tourist formula, modernization or bureaucracy as the villain that conceals or destroys authentic experience. In "Rolls-Royce" (6/22/80), which offers us a tour of a British Rolls factory, Safer describes the effects of modernization on authentic experience: "The trouble really is that nothing these days is built to last. . . . We live most of our lives in a junk society. Our durables aren't very durable. But when something is built by hand out of materials given by nature, old-fashioned pride is maintained." Later in the episode, Safer, who describes the Rolls auto factory as a "cottage industry" in contrast to the sprawling technology of an American auto plant, queries a British automobile "craftsman": "Well, what's the difference between this and a stamped-out car?" The worker responds, "Well, a stamped-out car is just a stamped-out car, isn't it? I mean, anybody can build them." In continuing the indictment of the U.S. car industry, Safer asks, "How would you like to work in one of the big auto plants and run a machine that simply punched out one of those doors every ten seconds?" The man responds, "Well, I think it would bore me within two or three hours. . . . I'd sooner use my hands and make it myself." The American auto industry symbolizes bureaucracy and the negative dimension of modernization. A modern villain, it holds values counter to tradition, to craftsmanship, and to quality that Safer finds in another modern corporation but one that represents premodern values.

The tension between individual and institution also plays a significant role in the heartland episodes, helping structure our readings of these stories. In "Charity Begins at Home," Safer's opening narration sets up a conflict between a small New Jersey town attempting to transform welfare into "workfare" and ready to confront the state. In the episode, a character explicitly sets up the conflict between individual and institution for Safer: "I think the bureaucracy worships paper gods as opposed to seeing the needs of people." A recurrent variation of individual versus institution (or small town versus big city) pits *place* against *space* rather than person against the larger social system.

O'Brien (1983) argues that *space* is more abstract, more hostile, less familiar and tranquil, more open and dangerous than *place*, which connotes security, stability, familiarity, serenity, closeness, and friendliness. And these connotations accompany the verbal and visual significations of small-town versus big-city conflict that underpin this set of 60 *Minutes* stories. For example, in "Away From It All ?" which looks at a small New Hampshire town facing the encroachment of urbanization, the episode's final narration explicitly acknowledges the opposition: "The scent of apple blossoms and the hum of honeybees are being replaced by the smell of asphalt and the noise of traffic. . . . Pastures are being turned into shopping centers." The visual accompaniment to the reporter's voice-over reveals the clutter of neon signs and fast food restaurants. In this episode, the pastoral serenity of an apple blossom setting represents the stability and authenticity of *place*, while the clutter of the "neon, asphalt" urban environment stands for the instability and artificiality of *space*.

Tourist as Mediator

The tourist formula establishes central contradictions that organize many 60 *Minutes* narratives. The conflict between tradition and modernization is displayed in "Paris Was Yesterday," where Mike Wallace and Janet Flanner, who wrote from Paris for *The New Yorker* for 50 years, recall the authentic Paris of the 1930s. Flanner comments, "Paris was more gracious in its pleasure—more customary. You knew who you were." This authentic, personal vision opposes shots of modern Paris overrun by litter, junkyards, crowds, and quick meal signs; modern buildings are "bogus new towers . . . hatched by vipers" that lack the majesty of the authentic Eiffel Tower. In "Yanks in Iran," shots of traditionally dressed Iranians and plain white homes oppose shots of modern billboards and a sound track of radio ads for Pepsi, 7-Up, Caterpillar tractors, and baseball. Tradition versus modernization also frames "Rolls-Royce," where Safer refers to the car as "a British institution with an almost mythical tradition." After he tours the Rolls plant, he visits a woman in Ireland who has been driving the same Rolls since 1927. Her complaints about the modernization of newer Rolls models ("not half as dignified," "too complicated") gain support from the reporter: "They said it [the new Rolls] looked like nothing more than something out of Detroit in the fifties. . . . [The] Rolls had finally fallen victim to the fickle hands of modernity." Safer here identifies modernity and the U.S. auto industry as villains whose presence has undermined traditional values represented by the older Rolls.

Through opposition between tradition and modernization, 60 *Minutes* constructs a map for meaning and sense. The reporter, in a metaphorical role as tourist, stalks authenticity, chastises modernity, and transforms the unfamiliarity of foreign space into a now familiar place. The reporter resolves the conflict between tradition and modernization by affirming places that suggest authenticity, simplicity, family, honesty, security, common sense, and other virtues of tradition.

While this tension between tradition and modernization generally features events, issues, and ideas in opposition, nature versus civilization is a tension of locale where natural settings oppose artificial cities. In "The Oil Kingdom" (6/9/74), which presents a tour of Saudi Arabia, shots of nomadic tribes herding sheep in the desert compete with crowded city street scenes and giant modern oil rigs springing from that same desert. Nature, visually portrayed by the desert, animals, and nomadic tribes, opposes civilization, visually portrayed by a modern city and oil rig technology. Similarly, in "Seward's Folly" (9/1/74), an Alaskan travelogue, an artificial enclosure houses and shields oil company workers from the stark, cold Alaskan tundra. American workers inside who are protected by that modern, artificial environment appear in contrast to the natural, native Eskimos who endure the tundra outside. This episode also juxtaposes spectacular mountains and waterfalls with scenes of prostitutes soliciting on the streets of Anchorage; the scenes display modern, urban values as undesirable, indeed villainous. The reporter, as mediator, once again resolves the meaning of the opposing images by framing elements associated with nature as real experience and elements associated with civilization as artificial. Symbols for nature emerge as affirmations of simplicity, purity, pastoralism, and unadorned beauty.

This romanticized vision of pure nature and false civilization occasionally gives way to a conflict where brutal natural elements become the villain in a test of the ingenuity and endurance of courageous individuals. Nature assumes this role, however, only in relation to individuals, not institutions. Again in "Seward's Folly," workers from oil companies tell their stories about surviving as a family in the brutal Alaskan frontier. Tour guide Morley Safer tells us that the growth of the oil industry, which these workers represent, could eventually "bring a dentist to town." Here civilization and modernization receive a personal face in the presence of an individual, a dentist. In this section of the narrative, nature opposes individuals who by courage, ingenuity, endurance, hard work, true grit, and a sense of family rise up to defeat this brutal villain. It is only by replacing institutions with workers and civilization with the individual dentist, however, that nature's villainous aspects emerge to create narrative tension.

In the heartland episodes, the mediation of individualism versus bureaucracy occurs when the reporter makes a connection between the story's characters and the promise of a better social system created by individuals. In "Wild Cat Trucker," Dan Rather mediates the conflict by placing himself at its center, traveling with the trucker, facing confrontations with the law, and surviving to summarize the spirit of individualism manifested by independent truckers. The visual frame that accompanies this concluding narration features a shot of a trucker, who Rather calls a cowboy, riding into the sunset with the popular mid-1970s song "Convoy" fading out in the audio background. Less dramatic mediation takes place in "Charity Begins At Home," where Morley Safer mediates between the state and a small town. Here he interviews individuals in town and a representative from the state over the issue of welfare. Even though the courts have ordered the town to comply with the state law in this particular case, Safer presents enough evidence (more than 10 local characters and lots of filmed small-town footage) supporting individualism to offset the position of the state (represented by one character in an impersonal office). Safer mediates the tension by siding with small-town values and by offering *hope* in his concluding narration: "The battle is not over." In most concluding scenes, the reporter mediates narrative tension by suggesting that individuals hold answers to institutional and social problems.

Finally, a minor opposition that is significant in these tourist episodes features conflicts between near and far or us (the United States) and them. When these tensions structure a story, generally the villain is some "backward," foreign, or alien set of values. In "Yugoslavia" (2/17/80), for example, Dan Rather interviews a foreign couple who affirm and mirror middle class American values in contrast to the apparently more repressive, centralized values of communism. This narrative portrays a view of communist Yugoslavia as a U.S. ally modeled on our own culture. Rather tells the Yugoslav couple, "It strikes me, as you talk, that your life here is very much like middle class life in the United States or England." *60 Minutes* then reveals a scene in a Yugoslav nightclub with the couple out for an evening of dinner and dancing. With "When the Saints Go Marching In" playing in the background, Rather offers this voice-over narration: "The scene is Korcula. It could be Saturday night in Kalamazoo. Dancing to American jazz music mixed with Yugoslav rock. In many other important ways, this is happening in Yugoslav society." With this episode, *60 Minutes* merges the themes of its foreign land and American heartland formulas. Rather mediates tensions between capitalism and communism, us and them, as he presents this communist country as small-town, middle class America. Its people support consumerism and speak proudly of newly purchased middle class conveniences. These individuals from a foreign country are heroic through association with values of democracy, individualism, and capitalism. This portrayal ultimately helps Rather resolve narrative opposition. The Soviet Union, as the agent for villainous communism, emerges here as a distant institutional force (visually unrepresented in this story) that has lost the support of individuals or at least the support of this couple who, in spite of their life in a communist society, seem to prefer Middle American values.

As in the detective and analyst episodes, the dichotomies posed in the tourist formula require resolution, not merely termination, of the narrative. One function of journalism is that it "stimulates by bringing opposites together in a single context, thus suggesting the possibility of synthesis" (O'Brien, 1983, p. 18). Reporters perform that synthesis in *60 Minutes*, acting as mediators of tension by affirming a set of basic values and thereby bring closure to the story. "Rolls-Royce" offers the best example. Here contradictions between humanity and technology, nature and civilization, are resolved as the Rolls acquires human and animal characteristics. In the narration, the Rolls receives a personality and pedigree. A lab technician dressed like a veterinarian or doctor probes a Rolls with a stethoscope. The plant's director refers to the car's "gestation period," and Morley Safer compares the plant's testing facilities to an "incubation ward." As the Rolls—a product of civilization and technology—takes on personal and natural traits of humans and animals, technology becomes natural. Machine becomes person.

The central conflict in the tourist episodes is between place and space. The mythic narrative structure transforms abstract, unknown space into concrete, known place, resolving conflict between the two and mediating contradiction. The reporter, as our surrogate, locates the self in the new or unknown and through the narrative transforms that space into a familiar place. *60 Minutes* draws a map that helps its audience to distinguish local from alien, authenticity from artifice, villain from heroes, and basic values from ideologies.

CONCLUSION

The mythic narratives of *60 Minutes* offer weekly mediation between the personal and social spheres. In its handling of changing social attitudes toward race, men and women, war, the economy, and foreign powers, among other issues, *60 Minutes* mediates the conflict between tradition and change by applying familiar formulas to a wide variety of experiences. The detective formula, for example, can accommodate raw experience as diverse as waterfront crime, a Vietnam colonel, spy satellites, racial protests, child pornography, valium, diamond scams, the Teamsters, horse doping, art theft, cocaine, and the Nazis, all within repetitive and familiar structures. Other *60 Minutes* formulas provide similar flexibility to assimilate a variety of unfamiliar realities into a handful of familiar representations. At the center of these formulas is the device of metaphor, transforming complex, abstract experience into more manageable, concrete formulas.

These metaphors also serve *60 Minutes* by rescuing the reporters from a tide of criticism leveled at the profession since Watergate. The power of *60 Minutes* resides in replacing reporters who work for bureaucratic news organizations with lone detectives, analysts, and tourists. It is important that the institutional identities of the *60 Minutes* reporters remain concealed; they appear to be operating as individuals, independent of their bureaucratic organizations. This narrative strategy is crucial in order to transform the reporters into heroes and elevate them to a position once-removed from the routine realm of institutional reporting. While the profession more and more draws public criticism as an invader of privacy and a threat to other individual rights, the metaphorical roles performed by the *60 Minutes* reporters, located somewhere outside Middle America, situate them more comfortably on a symbolic map located *within* the space of a middle class mythology.

The mythology is not without contradictions. Celebrated and admired for the performance of independent roles, the reporters also dramatize an institutional function as an arm of social justice that acts on behalf of individuals to right wrongs committed by villains and bureaucracies. Mike Wallace (1984) argues that viewers regard the program as a dramatic "unofficial ombudsman":

> [B]y the late 1970s . . . I kept bumping into people who jumped at the chance to alert me to some scandal or outrage that was ripe for exposure on *60 Minutes*. They would give me vivid accounts of foul deeds and the culprits perpetrating them, and urge me to take appropriate action: "You really should look into this, Mike. . . . " (p. 450)

Certainly a large number of episodes conclude with *60 Minutes* serving explicitly as ombudsman. In "The Selling of Col. Herbert" (2/4/73), for example, Wallace calls for a public hearing concerning an alleged Army coverup during the Vietnam War. In "Savak" (3/6/77), Wallace asks for a Senate investigation into the activities of Iranian secret police operating in the United States. And in "Equal Justice?" *60 Minutes* tracks down a witness (who police could not find) and, as a result, a federal judge reconsiders an earlier conviction. Leah Ekdom (1981, p. 149) classifies these kinds of stories as "heroic press narratives," that portray the press as an ideal, "the fourth estate, which monitors and checks government and other abuses of power, and calls our attention to instances in which the country fails to live up to its values." This heroic role of *60 Minutes* unites individual concerns and perceptions with a sense of social mission and order.

Like much of the news media, *60 Minutes* narrowly conceives its role as responsible ombudsman, as heroic press. The techniques of *60 Minutes* do reveal injustices, but they conceal as well. Some of what they conceal are the elements involved in constructing stories: the values of reporters and the economic self-interests of news organizations. While these elements mediate embedded conflicts between product and process, journalists and their audiences routinely assume that there is little distance between the narrative *product* and the raw experience that the product represents and accept one for the other without questioning the *process* of transformation. The taken for grantedness of formulaic narrative referents is so embedded in our consciousness that Hall (1980, p. 129) argues that "the event [reality] must become a 'story' before it can become a *communicative event.*"

I nonetheless disagree with research that fails to recognize the social value of news formulas and accuses news institutions, particularly television news, of ideological control. In a society as pluralistic as our own, institutions create centers and provide frameworks for making sense of experience. As Newcomb and Hirsch (1983, p. 49) note, "one of the primary functions of the popular culture forum, the television forum, is to monitor the limits and effectiveness of this pluralism. . . ." Peter Dalgren (1981, p. 111) is correct when he says that television journalism is often caught in a double bind "between its attempt to appear as an independent, critical agent, and its commitment to the prevailing social arrangements," but he is wrong when he argues that "TV news mystifies rather than clarifies." Dalgren and others disregard the formulaic and metaphoric power of news to provide a *center*, a cultural forum for discussion, that transforms complexity and contradiction through the narrative process. Television news helps to create a common reality and to clarify issues and events within that reality.

In *Habits of the Heart*, Bellah and his colleagues (1985, pp. 279–281) also miss the mark when they categorize television as part of the "culture of separation" because of its "disconnectedness" to reality, its "extraordinary discontinuity," and its failure to support "any clear set of beliefs or values." The mythic narrative impulse in television's "fictional" and "factual" programs seeks to resolve fundamental, archetypal conflicts between good and evil, tradition and change, individual and institution, and nature and culture. Not only does television offer a coherent vision that generally affirms individualism in the face of bureaucratic oppression, but it does so through the *coherence, continuity* and *assurance* of its formulas, through its romances, its mysteries, its melodramas, and its news.

Other studies also overlook or discredit diversity among audiences, arguing that news is merely a hegemonic device, a way for existing power structures to dominate. Fiske (1986, p. 392) points to the "failure of ideological criticism" to address both "the polysemy of the television text" and "the diverse subcultures in a society." While *60 Minutes* structures centered readings through its formulas, it cannot control the multiplicity of audience responses to that centering. And the program itself, in part, celebrates viewer diversity through the weekly "Letters" segment that offers viewpoints and values that oppose the program (*60 Minutes*, however, does frequently try to recenter this opposition by providing a roughly equal smattering of letters that support the program from week to week). I conceive of viewer response on a horizontal model (or as a map metaphor) rather than the vertical model of dominant, negotiated, and oppositional readings proposed by Hall (1980).[4] While *60 Minutes* attempts to position us at the center of its map, viewers still may find their own location on or off that map. As Newcomb (1986, p. 223) notes: "Whatever the messages and meanings of television, we, the viewers may read them in our own ways, receive them only as raw material for our own uses, bend them to our purposes, subvert, parody, distort, and otherwise appropriate them at will."

The mythic narrative formulas of *60 Minutes* provide a map or mythology for the middle class and affirm that individuals through adherence to Middle American values can triumph over institutions that deviate from central social norms. The term "middle" in middle class signifies a mediation between a variety of ambiguous oppositions: up and down, high and low, here and there, liberal and conservative, tradition and change, nature and culture, individual and institution. The electronic media, by taking us to once inaccessible places, "strip away layers of social behavior" to create a new *middle region* reality that merges the ordinary and extraordinary, the usual and unusual, the public and private (Meyrowitz, 1985, p. 311). (*60 Minutes'* preferred shot is the *middle* or *medium* shot that symbolically locates reporters advantageously in a region between close-ups and long shots where narrative conflict is mediated.)

In *60 Minutes*, stories affirm a set of central values: allegiances to family, education, religion, capitalism, health, democracy, competition, work, honesty, loyalty, duty, fidelity, moderation, fairness, team play, efficiency, simplicity, authenticity, discipline, common sense, modesty, humility, security, cooperation, and ingenuity. These stories celebrate the integrity of the individual and middle class norms. Don Hewitt, creator of *60 Minutes*, has argued that part of the reason for the program's success is his own ties to Middle America:

> My strength is that I have the common touch. I don't know why this is, because most of the people I hang around with are pretty elite. But Kiwanians, Rotarians, I understand them. . . . Maybe it's because I grew up in New Rochelle, the small town that George M. Cohan wrote "45 Minutes From Broadway" about. It was very Middle American. My father was in the advertising business and worked for Hearst. My mother was a housewife. We were middle class. (Henry 1986, p. 28)

Hewitt's small-town, middle class history taps into a fundamental mythic impulse in American culture, a nostalgic yearning to retreat from the "large scale organizational and institutional structures" that rob our lives of "meaning and coherence" (Bellah et al., 1985, p. 204).

The formulas and metaphors of *60 Minutes* penetrate deeply into American consciousness. The detective, for instance, taps into our desires for truth, honesty, and intrigue. The analyst helps us come to terms with our inner self, with order, and with knowledge about experience. The tourist cherishes tradition, nature, and authenticity. These metaphorical transformations of the reporter offer us figures of and for modernity, carriers of ways of knowing and interpreting complexity. In this way they offer the possibility of enriching rather than merely simplifying experience. Walker Percy (1975, p. 70) argues that while one function of metaphor is to mediate, "to diminish tension," more importantly metaphor is "a discoverer of being." Through metaphor we discover who we are. What *60 Minutes* ultimately offers its large audience through the detective, analyst, and tourist metaphors is the comfort, concreteness, and familiarity of a middle ground, a center to go back to (or start out from) each week. The power of its formula and metaphor is to reveal and conceal, transform and deform, enrich and simplify *experience* and secure a sense of place, a *middle ground*, where we map out meanings and discover once again *who we are*.

Acknowledgment: The author thanks Leah Ekdom for her suggestions.

NOTES

1. This analysis is based on a study of 154 *60 Minutes* episodes from 55 programs broadcast between 1968 and 1983, held by the Library of Congress (Motion Picture, Broadcasting, and Recorded Sound Division) in Washington. In addition to the three major formulas, I also identified a minor referee formula and four combination

episodes in which the reporter assumes a dual role (e.g., detective/analyst or tourist/analyst). Of the 154 episodes analyzed, 5 (mostly from the earlier years) did not fit into these formulas; I labeled these nonformulaic narratives as experimental.

At the time of my research, the *60 Minutes* collection at the Library of Congress was complete to 1983, except for 12 shows from 1968 and 1969 that were not copyrighted at the Library by CBS. It should be noted that *60 Minutes* was scheduled erratically by CBS at this time; the program was shown every other Tuesday evening and ran from late September to early or mid-June. The library's collection includes more than 500 *60 Minutes* programs available for viewing on 16mm film (1968–1975) or 3/4-inch videotape (since 1975). The library is about one to two years behind in cataloging more recent episodes. CBS News, which has a complete collection, said it did not have the facilities to accommodate my viewing and research requests. Viewing of more recent episodes suggests that the formulas remain intact, although more combination formulas featuring the reporters in dual metaphoric roles (rather than in the pure formulas described here) now dominate the program's structure.

In viewing each episode from the 55 sample programs, I utilized a viewing sheet on which I described the narrative sequence and the role of reporters as mediators of conflict. I identified each episode by (1) number in sample, (2) air date, (3) episode title, (4) episode position in program, (5) producer, and (6) reporter. I also summarized the chronological structure of each episode and identified the major characters in each narrative. I made notes on the reporter's location in the story both in terms of what he said, when he said it, and his relationships to the camera, other characters, and the setting. In addition, I broke down each episode into the following narrative elements: subject matter, plot, setting/locations, resolution/summary, conflicts, and values.

2. The numbers in parentheses refer to the broadcast dates of the *60 Minutes* programs I studied. CBS News published the transcripts of *60 Minutes* programs from the 1979–1980 television season as a book, *60 Minutes Verbatim*, and quotations from those programs refer the reader to that text (see CBS News under references). All other quotations from the programs come from my own viewing notes.

3. In this episode, Rather briefly resembles the hard-boiled American private detective typified by the works of Dashiell Hammett and Raymond Chandler in the 1920s and 1930s (see Cawelti, 1976). In this model, the detectives are vulnerable, reflective, and far less detached; they are morally and emotionally involved in their investigations, and they are as interested in "what ought to be" as "what is." In hard-boiled fiction, detectives emerge as characters defined and determined by an explicit value system rather than as mere functions of plot and dramatic tension. The world of clues becomes a means for revealing aspects of a more personal, more complex world. *60 Minutes*, however, rarely looks to this model which would violate journalistic codes of moral neutrality.

4. I am grateful to Robert Allen for suggesting this conceptualization.

REFERENCES

Allen, R. (1987). Reader-oriented criticism and television. In R. Allen (Ed.), *Channels of discourse: Television and contemporary criticism* (pp. 74–112). Chapel Hill: University of North Carolina Press.

Arlen, M. (1977, November 23). The prosecutor. *The New Yorker*, pp. 166–173.

Bellah, R. N., Madsen, R., Sullivan, W. M., Swindler, A., & Tipton, S. T. (1985). *Habits of the heart: Individualism and commitment in American life.* Berkeley: University of California Press.

Black, J. (1981, April/May). The stung. *Channels*, pp. 43–46.

Cawelti, J. (1976). *Adventure, mystery, and romance: Formula stories as art and popular culture.* Chicago: University of Chicago Press.

CBS News. (1980). *60 Minutes verbatim.* New York: Arno Press.

Connell, I. (1978). Monopoly capitalism and the media. In S. Hibbin (Ed.), *Politics, ideology and the state* (pp. 69–98). London: Lawrence & Wishart.

Dalgren, P. (1981). TV news and the suppression of reflexivity. In E. Katz & T. Szecsko (Eds.), *Mass media and social change* (pp. 101–114). Beverly Hills: Sage.

Didion, J. (1979). *The white album.* New York: Simon and Schuster.

Ekdom, L. (1981). *An interpretive study of the news: An analysis of news forms.* Unpublished doctoral dissertation, University of Iowa.

Father of "60 Minutes": Taking the heat as no. 1. (1981, April 3). *Chicago Tribune*, sec. 2, p. 15.

Fernandez, J. (1974). The mission of metaphor in expressive culture. *Current Anthropology*, *15*, 119–145.

Fiske, J. (1986). Television: Polysemy and popularity. *Critical Studies in Mass Communication*, *3*, 391–408.

Funt, P. (1980, November). Television news: Seeing isn't believing. *Saturday Review*, pp. 30–32.

Hall, S. (1980). Encoding/decoding. In S. Hall, P. Willis, D. Hobson, & A. Lowe (Eds.), *Culture, media, language* (pp. 128–138). London: Hutchinson.

Hartley, J. (1982). *Understanding news.* London: Methuen.

Henry, W. A. III. (1986, May). Don Hewitt: Man of the hour. *Washington Journalism Review*, pp. 25–29.

Himmelstein, H. (1984). *Television myth and the American mind.* New York: Praeger.

James, P. D. (1984). Interview on PBS' *Mystery* series, *Cover her face*, episode four [Television interview]. WGBH, Boston.

Jensen, K. B. (1987). Qualitative audience research: Toward an integrative approach to reception. *Critical Studies in Mass Communication*, *4*, 21–36.

Kahn, E. J. Jr. (1982a, July 19). Profiles: The candy factory—Part I. *The New Yorker*, pp. 40–41, 47–49, 54–61.

Kahn, E. J. Jr. (1982b, July 26). Profiles: The candy factory—Part II. *The New Yorker*, pp. 38–42, 45–46, 50–55.

Katz, E., & Liebes, T. (1984). Once upon a time, in Dallas. *Intermedia*, *12*, 28–32.

Leach, E. (1968). Claude Levi-Strauss: Anthropologist and philosopher. In R. Manners & D. Kaplan (Eds.), *Theory in anthropology: A source book* (pp. 541–551). Chicago: Aldine.

Lears, T. J. J. (1983). From salvation to self-realization: Advertising and the therapeutic roots of consumer culture, 1880–1930. In R. W. Wightman & T. J. J. Lears (Eds.), *The culture of consumption: Critical essays in American history, 1880–1980* (pp. 1–38). New York: Pantheon.

Levi-Strauss, C. (1967). The structural study of myth (C. Jacobson & B. Grundfest Schoef, Trans.). In *Structural anthropology* (pp. 202–228). Garden City, NY: Anchor-Doubleday.

MacCannell, D. (1976). *The tourist: A new theory of the leisure class*. New York: Schocken Books.

Madsen, A. (1984). *60 Minutes: The power and the politics of America's most popular tv news show*. New York: Dodd, Mead, & Company.

Meyrowitz, J. (1985). *No sense of place: The impact of electronic media on social behavior*. New York: Oxford University Press.

Moore, D. (1978, January 12). 60 Minutes. *Rolling Stone*, pp. 43–46.

Morley, D. (1980). *The "nationwide" audience*. London: British Film Institute.

Nevins, F. M. Jr. (Ed). (1970). *The mystery writer's art*. Bowling Green, OH: Bowling Green University Popular Press.

Newcomb, H. (1984). On the dialogic aspects of mass communication. *Critical Studies in Mass Communication, 1*, 34–50.

Newcomb, H. (1986). American television criticism, 1970–1985. *Critical Studies in Mass Communication, 3*, 217–228.

Newcomb, H., & Hirsch, P. (1983). Television as a cultural forum: Implications for research. *Quarterly Review of Film Studies, 8* (3), 45–56.

O'Brien, D. (1983, September). The news as environment. *Journalism Monographs, 85*.

Percy, W. (1975). Metaphor as mistake. In *The message in the bottle* (pp. 64–82). New York: Farrar, Straus and Giroux.

Radway, J. A. (1984). *Reading the romance: Women, patriarchy, and popular literature*. Chapel Hill: University of North Carolina Press.

Schafer, R. (1981). Narration in the psychoanalytic dialogue. In W. J. T. Mitchell (Ed.), *On narrative* (pp. 25–49). Chicago: University of Chicago Press.

Schudson, M. (1978). *Discovering the news*. New York: Basic Books.

Shaw, D. (1987, March 28). Grading "60 Minutes": It's still going strong—But needs help in one key area. *TV Guide*, pp. 4–10.

Stein, H. (1979, May 6). How "60 Minutes" makes news. *The New York Times Magazine*, pp. 28–30, 74–90.

Strine, M. S. (1985). The impact of literary criticism. *Critical Studies in Mass Communication, 2*, 167–175.

Wallace, M., & Gates, G. P. (1984). *Close encounters: Mike Wallace's own story*. New York: Berkeley Books.

Weisman, J. (1983, April 16). "60 Minutes"—How good is it now? *TV Guide*, pp. 5–14.

White, H. (1981). The value of narrativity in the representation of reality. In W. J. T. Mitchell (Ed.), *On narrative* (pp. 1–23). Chicago: University of Chicago Press.

13 Television, Black Americans, and the American Dream

HERMAN GRAY

William F. Buckley Jr. has observed, "it is simply not correct . . . that race prejudice is increasing in America. How does one know this? Simple, by the ratings of Bill Cosby's television show and the sales of his books. A nation simply does not idolize members of a race which that nation despises" (Demeter, 1986, p. 67). Buckley seems to suggest that if racial prejudice exists at all in the United States it does not figure significantly in the nature of American society, nor does it explain very much about social inequality based on race and characterized by racial discrimination, racial violence, economic dislocation, and social isolation. Still, what is perhaps most interesting about Buckley's observation is his reliance on Bill Cosby's successful media presence as a barometer of American racial equality.

An open class structure, racial tolerance, economic mobility, the sanctity of individualism, and the availability of the American dream for black Americans are represented in a wide range of media. Representations of such success are available in *The Cosby Show*, the box office power of Eddie Murphy, the international popularity of Michael Jackson, and the visibility of Oprah Winfry. Equally important to the contemporary ideology of American racial openness, however, are representations of deprivation and poverty such as those shown on network newscasts and documentaries. In media reports of urban crime, prisons overcrowded with black men, increased violence associated with drugs, and the growing ranks of the homeless are drawn the lines of success and failure.

As Buckley's observations demonstrate, the meanings of these representations are not given; rather, viewers define and use the representations differently and for different reasons. One message of these representations of success and failure is that middle class blacks (and whites) succeed because they take advantage of available opportunities while poor blacks and other marginal members of our society fail because they do not (Glasgow, 1981; Lewis, 1984). These representations operate not just in terms of their relationship to the

294

empirical realities of black life in America but also in relationship to other popular media constructions about black life. My interest here is in the relationship between representations of black life in fictional and nonfictional television and the ideological meanings of these representations when television is viewed as a complete ideological field (Fiske, 1987a). In the following section, I theoretically situate the problem. I then turn to a discussion of black failure as represented in the CBS News documentary *The Crisis of Black America*: The *Vanishing Family* and the representation of upper middle class black affluence in *The Cosby Show*.

THEORETICAL CONTEXT

In order to describe how television representations about race communicate and to examine their ideological meanings, I draw on Gramsci's notion of ideological hegemony (Gramsci, 1971; Hall, 1982). Media representations of black life (especially middle class success and under class failure) are routinely fractured, selectively assembled, and subsequently become a part of the storehouse of American racial memory. The social and racial meanings that result from these processes appear in the media as natural and given rather than as social and constructed. In *Ideology and the Image* (1981, p. 1) Bill Nichols states that "ideology uses the fabrication of images and processes of representation to persuade us that how things are is how they ought to be and that the place provided for us is the place we ought to have." I use "hegemony" to specify the material and symbolic processes by which these racial representations and understandings are produced and naturalized (Fiske, 1987a; Hall, 1982).

Media representations of black success and failure and the processes that produce them are ideological to the extent that the assumptions that organize the media discourses shift our understanding of racial inequality away from structured social processes to matters of individual choice. Such ideological representations appear natural and universal rather than as the result of social and political struggles over power.

The process of media selection and appropriation, however, is only one part of the play of hegemony. Mass media and popular culture are, according to Stuart Hall (1980), sites where struggles over meaning and the power to represent it are waged. Thus, even as the media and popular cultural forms present representations of race and racial (in)equality, the power of these meanings to register with the experiences (common sense) of different segments of the population remains problematic. Meanings constantly shift and are available for negotiation. It is in this process of negotiation that different, alternative, even oppositional readings are possible (Fiske, 1987a; Hall, 1980). Because of this constantly shifting terrain of meaning and struggle, the representations of race and racial interaction in fictional and nonfictional television reveal both the elements of the dominant racial ideology as well as the limits to that ideology.

Within this broad struggle over meaning, Fredric Jameson (1979) shows how popular cultural forms such as film and television work symbolically to establish preferred, even dominant ideological meanings. In popular culture, ideology is secured through the psychological appeal to utopian values and aspirations and a simultaneous repression and displacement of critical sensibilities that identify the social and economic organization of American society as the source of inequality. In television representations of blacks, the historical realities of slavery, discrimination, and racism or the persistent struggles against domination are displaced and translated into celebrations of black middle class visibility and achievement. In this context, successful and highly visible stars like Bill Cosby and Michael Jackson confirm the openness and pluralism of American society .

The commercial culture industry presents idealized representations of racial justice, social equality, and economic success. Idealized middle class black Americans increasingly populate fictional television. They confirm a middle class utopian imagination of racial pluralism (Gray, 1986). These idealized representations remain before us, driven, in the case of television, by the constant search for stable audiences and the centrality of advertising revenue as the basis for profits (Cantor, 1980; Gitlin, 1983).

As Jameson further notes, however, utopian possibilities are secured against the backdrop of reified nonfictional (and fictional) representations. In the case of racial representations, the black under class appears as menace and a source of social disorganization in news accounts of black urban crime, gang violence, drug use, teenage pregnancy, riots, homelessness, and general aimlessness. In news accounts (and in Hollywood films such as *Colors*), poor blacks (and Hispanics) signify a social menace that must be contained. Poor urban blacks help to mark the boundaries of appropriate middle class behavior as well as the acceptable routes to success. As a unity, these representations of black middle class success and under class failure are ideological because they are mutually reinforcing and their fractured and selective status allows them to be continuously renewed and secured. Furthermore, the meanings operate within a frame that privileges representations of middle class racial pluralism while marginalizing those of racial inequality. This constant quest for legitimacy and the need to quell and displace fears at the same time as it calls them forth are part of the complex ideological work that takes place in television representations of race.

The representations of black American success and failure in both fictional and nonfictional television, and the assumptions that organize them, are socially constructed according to commercial, professional, and aesthetic conventions that guide producers and consumers of television (Gray, 1986). These conventions guide personnel in the selection and presentation of images to ensure that they are aesthetically appealing, culturally meaningful, politically legitimate, and economically profitable.

Although fictional and nonfictional representations of blacks emanate from separate generic quarters of television, they activate meanings for viewers across these boundaries. That is, the representations make sense in terms of their intertextuality between and within programs (Fiske, 1987a; Fiske & Hartley, 1978; Williams, 1974). Television representations of black life in the late 1980s cannot be read in isolation but rather should be read in terms of their relationship to other television texts.

The meanings that these representations express and activate are also significant in terms of the broad social and historical context in which they operate. Fictional and nonfictional representations of black life appear at a time when political and intellectual debate continues over the role of the state in helping the black urban poor and whether or not affirmative action ought to remain an active component of public policy. Within the black political and activist community, sharp differences remain over the role of the black middle class and the efficacy of black generated self-help programs to battle problems facing black communities. Increased racial violence and antagonisms (including those on college campuses), economic dislocation, a changing industrial base, ethnic and racial shifts in the demographic composition of the population, and the reelection of a conservative national administration help set the social context within which television representations of black life take on meaning.

A myriad of community, institutional, social, political, and economic forces shape the broad public discourse on the conditions of blacks in contemporary American society. In the absence of effective social movements such as those for civil rights, students, women, and against the war, which, at the very least, helped ground and mediate media representations, these representations take on greater authority and find easier access to our common sense (Winston, 1983, p. 178). Under these conditions, the ideological potency of media representations remains quite strong.

Media representations of black success and failure occur within a kind of gerrymandered framework. Through production conventions, political sensibilities, commercial pressures, and requirements for social organization and efficiency, television news and entertainment selectively construct the boundaries within which representations about black life occur. The primacy of individual effort over collective possibilities, the centrality of individual values, morality, and initiative, and a benign (if not invisible) social structure are the key social terms that define television discourses about black success and failure.

REIFICATION AND THE UNDER CLASS

To explore the reification side of the Jameson formulation, I begin with a discussion of the CBS News report about the black urban under class. The special report which aired in January 1985 is titled *The Vanishing Family: Crisis In Black America*. CBS senior correspondent Bill Moyers hosted the 90-minute documentary which was filmed in Newark, New Jersey. Through interviews and narration by Moyers, the report examines the lives of unwed mothers and fathers, detailing their education, employment, welfare history (especially across generations), hopes, frustrations, and disappointments.

The appearance of the terms "vanishing family" and "crisis" in the title of the program implicitly suggests the normalcy of everyday life when defined by stable nuclear families (Fearer, 1986; Fishe, 1987a). Missing is recognition that families and communities throughout the country are in the midst of significant transformation. Instead, the program title suggests an abnormal condition that must be recognized and addressed.

In the report's opening segment, visual representations also help frame the ideological terms of the report. Medium and long camera shots are used to establish perspective on the daily life in the community. Mothers are shown shopping for food and caring for children; groups of boys and young men appear standing on street corners, playing basketball, listening to music, and working out at the gym. Welfare lines, couples arguing, the police, housing projects, and the streets are also common images.

These shots tie the specific issues addressed in the story into a broader discourse about race in America. Shots of black men and youth standing on corners or blacks arrested for crime are conventionally used in newscasts to signify abnormalities and social problems. These images operate at multiple levels, so even though they explicitly work to frame the documentary, they also draw on and evoke images of crime, drugs, riots, menace, and social problems. People and communities who appear in these representations are labeled as problematic and undesirable.

The documentary's four segments are organized around three major themes, with each segment profiling unmarried couples. By the end of the four segments, the dominant message of the report is evident: self-help, individual responsibility, and community accountability are required to survive the crisis. This conclusion is anticipated early in the report with a promotional tease from a black social worker. In a 30-second sound bite, the social worker notes that the problem in the black community is not racism or unemployment but the corruption of values, the absence of moral authority, and the lack of individual motivation. This dominant message is also reinforced in the introduction to the report by correspondent Moyers:

> A lot of white families are in trouble too. Single parent families are twice as common in America today as they were 20 years ago. But for the majority of white children, family still means a mother and a father. This is not true for most black children. For them things are getting worse. Today black teenagers have the highest pregnancy rate in the industrialized world and in the black inner city, practically no teenage mother gets married. That's no racist comment. What's happening goes far beyond race.

Since blacks dominate the visual representations that evoke images of crime, drugs, and social problems, little in the internal logic and organization of the documentary supports this contention. Even when voice-over data is used to address these issues among whites, it competes with rather than complements the dominance of the visual representations. Moyers' comment is also muted because the issues are examined primarily at the dramatic and personal level.

For example, the first segment considers the experiences of urban single parent families from the viewpoint of women. The opening piece profiles Clarinda and Darren, both young and poorly prepared emotionally or financially to care for an infant. Clarinda supports the baby with welfare and is also the baby's primary source of emotional nurturance. Darren occasionally sees his baby but takes little economic or emotional responsibility for her. On camera he appears distant and frustrated.

The second segment focuses on Alice, 23, and Timothy, 26. They are older but financially no more prepared to raise a family than Clarinda and Darren. Unlike Darren, Timothy is emotionally available to Alice. (On camera they confess their love for each other, and Timothy is present at a birthday party for one child and the delivery of another.) In the interview Alice freely shows her frustration with Timothy, especially his lack of work and unwillingness to take responsibility for his family.

Timothy on the other hand lives in a world of male sexual myths and a code that celebrates male sexual conquest and virility (Glasgow, 1981). Although he confesses love for Alice and his kids, he avoids economic and parental responsibility for them, especially when his own pleasures and sexual conquests are concerned.

The mothers in these segments are caring, responsible, and conscientious; they raise the children and provide for them. They are the social, economic, and emotional centers of their children's lives. As suggested in the interviews and visual footage, the fathers are absent, immature, selfish, irresponsible, and exploitive. Where women are shown at home with the children, the men are shown on street corners with other men. Where women talk of their children's futures, men speak in individual terms about their present frustrations and unrealistic aspirations.

The dramatic and personal tone of these representations makes them compelling and helps draw in the viewer. These strategies of organization and presentation also help personalize the story and, to a limited extent, give the people texture and dimension. Nevertheless, these representations are also mediated by a broader set of racial and class codes that continue to construct the people in the documentary as deviant and criminal, hence marginal. The members of the community are contained by these broader codes. They remain curious but distant "others."

The third segment features Bernard, a 15-year-old single male who still lives at home with Brenda, his 30-year-old single mother of three. This segment tells the story of life in this community from the young male point of view. The male voice takes on resonance and, in contrast to Darren and Timothy, we learn that the men in this community have feelings and hopes too. The segment shows Bernard's struggle to avoid the obstacles (drugs, educational failure, unemployment, homicide, jail) to his future. From Brenda's boyfriend (and role model for Bernard) we learn about the generational persistence of these obstacles to young male futures.

In each of these segments the dramatic dominates the analytic, the personal dominates the public, and the individual dominates the social. Individual mobility, character, and responsibility provide powerful explanations for the failures presented in the story. Indeed, by the final segment of the report the theme of moral irresponsibility and individual behavior as explanations for the crisis of the under class is fully developed. Moyers introduces the segment this way:

> There are successful strong black families in America. Families that affirm parental authority and the values of discipline, work, and achievement. But you won't find many who live around here. Still, not every girl in the inner city ends up a teenage mother, not every young man goes into crime. There are people who have stayed here. They're outnumbered by the con artists and pushers. It's not an even match, but they stand for morality and authority and give some of these kids a dose of unsentimental love.

As a major "actor" in the structure of this report, Moyers is central to the way that the preferred meanings of the report are conveyed. As an economically and professionally successful white male, Moyers' political and moral authority establishes the framework for identifying the conditions as trouble, for articulating the interests of the dominant society, and for demonstrating that in the continued openness of the social order there is hope. Through Moyers' position as a journalist, this report confirms the American dream even as it identifies casualties of the dream.

Moyers' authority in this story stems also from his position as an adult. During his interviews and stand-ups Moyers represents adult common sense, disbelief, and concern. This adult authority remains throughout the report and is reinforced (and activated) later in the story when we hear from caring (and successful) black adults of the community who claim that the problems facing the community stem from poor motivation, unclear and unsound values, and the lack of personal discipline. Like Moyers, these adults—two social workers, a psychologist, and a police officer—do not identify complex social forces like racism, social organization, economic dislocation, unemployment, the changing economy, or the welfare state as the causes of the crisis in their community. They blame members of the black community for the erosion of values, morality, and authority. This is how Mrs. Wallace, the social worker, puts it:

> We are destroying ourselves. Now it [the crisis] might have been motivated and plotted and seeded with racism, but we are content to be in this well now. We're just content to be in this mud and we need to get out of it. There are not any great white people running around this block tearing up stuff. It's us. We've got to stop doing that.

When combined with the personal tone of the documentary and Moyers' professional (and adult) authority, this comment, coming as it does from an adult member of the community, legitimates the emphasis on personal attributes and a benign social structure.

At the ideological level of what Stuart Hall (1980) calls preferred readings, each segment of the documentary emphasizes individual personalities, aspirations, and struggles for improvement. These assumptions and analytic strategies are consistently privileged over social explanations, and they provide a compelling vantage point from which to read the documentary. This displacement of the social by the personal and the complex by the dramatic both draws viewers into the report and takes them away from explanations that criticize the social system. Viewers question individual coping mechanisms rather than the structural and political circumstances that create and sustain racial inequalities.

MIDDLE CLASS UTOPIA

I consider the utopian side of the Jameson formulation by exploring the theme that media representations of black success and failure are ideological, precisely to the extent that they provide a way of seeing under class failure through representations of middle class success. Implicitly operating in this way of viewing the under class (and the middle class) is the assumption that since America is an open racial and class order, then people who succeed (and fail) do so because of their individual abilities rather than their position in the social structure (Lewis, 1984).

In contrast to the blacks in the CBS documentary, successful blacks who populate prime time television are charming, unique, and attractive individuals who, we assume, reached their stations in life through hard work, skill, talent, discipline, and determination. Their very presence in formats from talk shows (Bryant Gumbel, Arsenio Hall, Oprah Winfrey) to situation comedy (Bill Cosby) confirms the American value of individual success and mobility.

In the genre of situation comedy, programs like *The Cosby Show, 227, Frank's Place,* and *Amen* all show successful middle class black Americans who have effectively negotiated their way through benign social institutions and environments (Gray, 1986). Their family-centered lives take place in attractive homes and offices. Rarely if ever do these characters venture into settings or interact with people like those in the CBS documentary. As doctors, lawyers, restaurateurs, ministers, contractors, and housewives, these are representations of black Americans who have surely realized the American dream. They are pleasant and competent social actors whose racial and cultural experiences are, for the most part, insignificant. Although black, their class position (signified by their occupations, tastes, language, and setting) distances them from the codes of crime, drugs, and social problems activated by the urban under class. With the exception of the short-lived *Frank's Place,* the characters are never presented in situations where their racial identity matters. This representation of racial encounters further appeals to the utopian desire in blacks and whites for racial oneness and equality while displacing the persistent reality of racism and racial inequality or the kinds of social struggles and cooperation required to eliminate them. At the level of the show's dominant meanings, this strategy accounts in part for the success of *The Cosby Show* among blacks and whites.

In virtually any episode of *The Cosby Show*, the Huxtable children—Sandra, Denise, Vanessa, Theo, and Rudi—are given appropriate lessons in what appear to be universal values such as individual responsibility, parental trust, honesty, the value of money, the importance of family and tradition, peer group pressure, the value of education, the need for independence, and other important guides to successful living in America.

In contrast to the experience of the young men in the CBS documentary, *Cosby's* Theo learns and accepts lessons of responsibility, maintaining a household, the dangers of drugs, the value of money, and respect for women through the guidance of supportive parents. In Theo's relationship to his family, especially his father Cliff, the lessons of fatherhood and manhood are made explicit. Theo and his male peers talk about their aspirations and fears. They even exchange exaggerated tales of adolescent male conquest. Because similar discussions among the young men in the documentary are embedded within a larger set of codes about the urban black male menace, this kind of talk from Timothy, Darren, and Bernard signals their incompetence and irresponsibility at male roles. In the middle class setting of *The Cosby Show*, for Theo and his peers this same talk represents the ritual of adolescent male maturation. Together, these very opposite representations suggest a contemporary version of the culture of poverty thesis which attributes black male incompetence and irresponsibility to the absence of male role models, weak personal values, and a deficient cultural environment.

The strategy of imparting explicit lessons of responsibility to Theo (and to young black male viewers) is deliberate on the part of *Cosby*. This is not surprising since the show has enjoyed its greatest commercial success in the midst of increasing gang violence and epidemic teen pregnancy in urban black communities. The show's strategy illustrates its attempt to speak to a number of different audiences at a number of different levels (Fiske, 1987a; Hall, 1980).

Shows about middle class black Americans revolve around specific characters, settings, and situations (Gitlin, 1983; Gray, 1986). The personal dimension of social life is privileged over, and in many cases displaces, broader social and structural factors. In singling out *The Cosby Show*, my aim is not to diminish the unique qualities, hard work, and sacrifices that these personal representations stress. Nevertheless, I do want to insist that the assumptions and framework that structure these representations often displace representations that would enable viewers to see that many individuals trapped in the under class have the very same qualities but lack the options and opportunities to realize them. And in the world of television news and entertainment, where production conventions, ratings wars, and cautious political sensibilities guide the aesthetic and journalistic decisions of networks, the hegemony of the personal and personable rules. Whether it is Bill Cosby, Alicia Rashad, Darren, Alice, or Bill Moyers, the representation is of either deficient or gifted individuals.

Against fictional television representations of gifted and successful individuals, members of the urban under class are deficient. They are unemployed, unskilled, menacing, unmotivated, ruthless, and irresponsible. They live differently and operate with different attitudes and moral codes from everyone else; they are set apart. Again, at television's preferred level of meaning, these assumptions—like the images they organize and legitimate—occupy our common sense understandings of American racial inequality.

CONCLUSIONS

The assumptions that organize our understandings of black middle class success and under class failure are expressed and reinforced in the formal organization of television programming. Formally, where representations of the under class are presented in the routine structure of network news programming, it is usually in relationship to extraordinary offenses such as drugs, homicide, and crime. In contrast, middle class blacks are very much integrated into the programming mainstream of television. Successful shows about black life inhabit a format and genre that has a long tradition in television entertainment—the situation comedy. The rhythm, texture, and form of this type of show are comfortable and familiar to most viewers. Moreover, these programs are coupled with others that are similar. Thus, for instance, the Thursday evening schedule is built around *The Cosby Show* and *A Different World. 227* fits snugly into the Saturday evening programming flow with *Golden Girls* and *Amen*. Still, even though representations of under class and middle class life are presented in the "bracketed" space of the news documentary and the situation comedy, at the level of decoding, the meanings of these shows circulate in the programming flow across programs and genres.

Surely, then, the failure of blacks in the urban under class, as Mrs. Wallace suggested in the CBS documentary, is their own since they live in an isolated world where contemporary racism is no longer a significant factor in their lives. The success of blacks in the television middle class suggests as much. In the world of the urban under class, unemployment, industrial relocation, ineffective social policies, power inequalities, and racism do not explain failure, just as affirmative action policies, political organization, collective social and cultural challenges to specific forms of racial domination, and the civil rights movement do not help explain the growth of the black middle class.

The nonfictional representations of the under class and the fictionalized treatment of the middle class are significant in other ways. Contemporary television shows in general and shows about black life in particular have reclaimed the family; they are either set in the nuclear family of *The Cosby Show* and *227* or the work place family of *Frank's Place* and *Amen* (Feurer, 1987; Taylor, 1988). The idealized representations of family presented in these shows maintain the hope and possibility of a stable and rewarding family life. At the same time, this idealization displaces (but does not eliminate) possibilities for critical examination of the social roots of crisis in the American family (Jameson, 1979).

Family stresses such as alienation, estrangement, violence, divorce, and latch key kids are typically ignored. When addressed in the television representations of black middle class families, they are presented as the subject of periodic and temporary disagreements rather than as expressions of the social stresses and disruptive impulses that originate in the social organization of society and the conflicting ideologies that shape our understanding of the family as a social institution.

At the negotiated level of meaning (Hall, 1980), *The Cosby Show* effectively incorporates many progressive moments and impulses from recent social movements. The show presents Claire's independence, autonomy, and authority in the family without resorting to exaggeration and trivialization (Downing, 1988). Again, this utopian impulse is one of the reasons for the show's popular appeal. And yet it is also one of the ways the explicit critical possibilities of the show are contained and subverted. Claire's independence and autonomy are expressions of her own individual character; they are confined to the family and put in the service of running a smoother household. This claim on the family and the affirmation of female independence are especially appealing when seen against the crisis of the family dissolution, female-headed households, and teenage pregnancy presented in the CBS documentary. Ironically, this celebration of Claire's independence and agency within the family has its counterpart in the CBS documentary. In each case, black women are assertive and responsible within the contexts of their various households. Thus, even within the constraints of under class poverty this moment can be read as an appeal to the utopian ideal of strong and liberated black women.

Ideologically, representations of under class failure still appeal and contribute to the notion of the black poor as menacing and threatening, especially to members of the white middle class. Such a menace must, of course, be contained, and through weekly visits to black middle class homes and experiences, whites (and middle class blacks) are reasonably assured that the middle class blacks with whom they interact are safe (Miller, 1986). Whites can take comfort in the fact that they have more in common with the Huxtables than with those representations of the family in crisis—Timothy, Clorinda, Darren, and Alice.

The twin representations of fictional and nonfictional television have become part of the public discourse about American race relations. While, no doubt, both the fictional and nonfictional representations of blacks are real, like all ideology, the realities are selected, partial, and incomplete. Where the television lens is trained, how wide, which angle, how long, and with whose voice shapes much of what we see and how we understand it. As these fictional and nonfictional television representations indicate, television helps shape our understandings about racial (in)equality in America.

REFERENCES

Cantor, M. (1980). *Prime-time television: Content and control.* Beverly Hills: Sage.

Demeter, J. (1986). Notes on the media and race. *Radical America, 20*(5), 63–71.

Downing, J. (1988). "The Cosby Show" and American racial discourse. In G. Smitherman-Donaldson & T. A. van Dijk (Eds.), *Discourse and discrimination* (pp. 46–74). Detroit, MI: Wayne State University Press.

Feuer, J. (1986). Narrative form in American television. In C. MacCabe (Ed.), *High theory/low culture: Analyzing popular television and film* (pp. 101–115). New York: St. Martin's Press.

Feuer, J. (1987). Genre study and television. In R. Allen (Ed.), *Channels of discourse.* (pp. 113–134). Chapel Hill: University of North Carolina Press.

Fiske, J. (1987a). *Television culture.* London: Methuen.

Fiske, J. (1987b). British cultural studies and television. In R. Allen (Ed.), *Channels of discourse.* (pp. 254–291). Chapel Hill: University of North Carolina Press.

Fiske, J., & Hartley, J. (1978). *Reading television.* London: Methuen.

Gitlin, T. (1983). *Inside prime time.* New York: Pantheon.

Glasgow, D. (1981). *The black underclass.* New York: Vintage.

Gramsci, A. (1971). *Selections from the prison notebooks.* New York: International Publishers.

Gray, H. (1986). Television and the new black man: Black male images in prime-time situation comedy. *Media, Culture, and Society, 8,* 223–242.

Hall, S. (1980). Encoding/decoding. In S. Hall, A. Lowe, & P. Willis (Eds.), *Culture, media, language* (pp. 128–139). London: Hutchinson.

Hall, S. (1982). The rediscovery of ideology: Return of the repressed in media studies. In M. Gurevitch, T. Bennett, J. Curran, & J. Woollocott (Eds.), Culture, society, and the media. (pp. 56–91). London: Methuen.

Jameson, F. (1979). Reification and utopia in mass culture. *Social Text, 1,* 130–148.

Lewis, M. (1984). *The culture of inequality.* New York: American Library.

Miller, M. C. (1986). Deride and conquer. In T. Gitlin (Ed.), *Watching television* (pp. 183–229). New York: Pantheon.

Nichols, B. (1981). *Ideology and the image.* Bloomington: University of Indiana Press.

Taylor, E. (1987, October 5). TV families: Three generations of packaged dreams. *Boston Review of Books,* p. 5.

Williams, R. (1974). *Television: Technology and cultural form.* New York: Oxford.

Winston, M. (1983). Racial consciousness and the evolution of mass communication in the United States. *Deadalus, 111,* 171–183.

14

Out of Work and On the Air: Television News of Unemployment

STEVE M. BARKIN, MICHAEL GUREVITCH

The argument that television news ought to be regarded not only, or not even primarily, as a conveyor of information, but also, and perhaps more importantly, as a constructor of meanings is no longer radical or even novel (Adoni & Mane, 1984; Bennett, 1982). It is part and parcel of the paradigmatic shift in mass communication research from a transmission or conveyor belt model of the mass communication process to a view of the media (indeed, of all human communication) as a dialectical process in which meanings are produced and reproduced (Carey, 1975; Hall, 1982; see Davis & Robinson, 1986, for a more recent review). This shift has placed the notions of ideology and the ideological role of the media as central issues in mass communication research. But there is less than unanimity among scholars working in this vein about how to examine the role of the media as an ideological agency.

Disagreements abound both with regard to the general role of ideology in society and, more specifically, with regard to the ideological functions of the media. Abercrombie, Hill, and Turner (1980) provide a critique of the usefulness and applicability of the notion of "dominant ideology" for the analysis of the integration and coherence of modern capitalist societies. Their general critique also applies to the specific argument that the media act as central agencies for the promotion and dissemination of a dominant ideology. The debate on that issue, however, has produced different views and conclusions. Thus, for example, examinations of media content have led some scholars to note that the media "have certain inbuilt tendencies to present a limited and recurring range of images and ideas which form rather special versions of reality" (McQuail, 1977, p. 81) or, when focusing more specifically on television news, that "the content of the news is organized in such a way that coherence is given to only one set of explanations and policies" (Glasgow University Media Group, 1982, p. 59; see also 1976, 1980). Such statements appear to give credence to a view of the media as agencies of ideological manipulation and domination. An alternative view can be found in Newcomb and Hirsch (1984), who offer an approach that "begins with the observation, based on careful textual analysis, that television is dense, rich, and complex rather than impoverished" (p. 71). Coupled with sensitivity to the range and variation of audience interpretations of, and responses to, media contents, this approach yields a view of television as a "cultural forum"—an essentially pluralistic medium, rather than a dispenser of near-monolithic views of society. The debate, then, is between a hard-nosed Marxist interpretation of television as an instrument of the dominant ideology and a literary or aesthetically based approach that treats television as a "central cultural medium presenting a multiplicity of meanings rather than a monolithic dominant point of view." In Newcomb and Hirsch's words, the emphasis in this view is "on discussion rather than indoctrination, on contradiction and confusion rather than coherence."

Ideology, of course, can wear a thousand masks. It is plausible to assume that an ideology is more effective the more it is internally coherent. But it can also be argued that an apparent inconsistency among different beliefs and interpretations of social reality represents a more subtle form of ideological work that, precisely because of its apparent pluralism and diversity, renders the ideology more invisible and thus contributes to its power. We shall return to that issue at the conclusion of this paper.

BACKGROUND TO THE STUDY

The study reported in this paper reflects some of these concerns. It was conducted as part of a larger study that focused on the relationship between television's representations of different social issues and audience perceptions of these issues. That study was triggered in part by an awareness of the paucity of empirical research into the links between media representations and audience perceptions, links that are clearly essential if we are to establish the ideological role of the media in relation to their audiences. Recognition of the need to examine these links is not new, even among proponents of the dominant ideology thesis. Thus, Golding and Murdock (1978) have argued that:

> To say that the mass media are saturated with bourgeois ideology is simply to pose a series of questions for investigation. To begin to answer them, however, it is necessary to go on to show how this hegemony is actually reproduced through the concrete activities of media personnel and the *interpretive procedures of consumers*. This requires detailed and directed analysis of the social contexts of production *and reception* [italics added]. (p. 350)

Although some work in this vein has been done in the past few years (Morley, 1980, 1983), our methodology in the larger study differed from this work. Instead of focusing on "the relation between the dominant ideological forms of the media and the subcultures and codes inhabited by different classes and class fractions. . ." (Morley, 1983, pp. 104–105), we attempted to relate audience members' understandings of a given social issue, unemployment, to media explanations of that issue. We began by presenting a set of questions on unemployment to respondents in a national telephone survey conducted in May-June 1983, at the height of that period of unemployment. Respondents were first told: "There are many different explanations given for why we still have high unemployment," and then asked "What do you think are the main reasons for high unemployment?" The results are reported in Gurevitch and Levy (1986).

One of the main findings of that exercise was that the respondents offered diverse explanations. In all, 32 different types of causes of unemployment were cited by respondents. Almost one-fifth (19%) of the national sample offered no explanation ("don't know") for the continuing high levels of unemployment. About half gave one explanation, one-quarter gave two explanations, and one in ten respondents replied with three or more reasons. No single cause was mentioned by more than 11% of all respondents.

Explanations centering on economic forces (e.g., high interest rates, inflation, and vulnerable industries) accounted for one-third of all answers excluding "don't know." About one-fifth of all causes focused on unions or workers, with a slightly smaller proportion finding fault with politicians, government, or public policies. One-seventh of all responses dealt with foreign competition or imports, while only 6% of all answers (excluding "don't knows") specifically blamed the business community or management.

Where do these audience understandings come from? It could be assumed that all those who are either touched by unemployment directly or are exposed to the trauma of unemployment through their relationships with the unemployed seek to understand and explain to themselves what has gone wrong and why. One source of understanding is people's own direct experience with unemployment. When one in ten people in the work force is unemployed, such direct experience is quite prevalent. Even those who are not themselves unemployed might have a relative, friend, or neighbor who is the victim of unemployment (see Behr & Iyengar, 1985). As in many other perplexing and unsettling social problems, however, other important sources of explanatory frameworks for most people are the mass media. If the media are, indeed, the sources of such understandings for most people, we need to turn to the contents of the media to uncover the ways the problem of unemployment is framed, explained, and understood.

Ideology in Stories of Unemployment

While ideology may be said to pervade the entire contents of the media, it is probably more manifest in some forms of media contents than in others and is likely to be closer to the surface in discussions of some areas of social life rather than others. One such area is the economy. This is so not only because images of society and views of the social order are embedded in all representations of economic life but also because it is a domain of social life where conflict is integral and highly visible. Stories of economic conflict and displacement such as industrial strikes typically attract considerable media attention. (Hence the choice of industrial strife as the subject matter of the *Bad News* series of studies.) Unemployment is another economic issue that is especially apt for an examination of ideological representations in the media. Besides the threat that unemployment poses to the economic well-being of society and of its members—primarily, of course, its victims—it also touches a basic chord in the identity of all members of work-oriented societies. High unemployment therefore attracts the attention of the media not only because it reveals conflict but also because media organizations and professionals clearly assume (probably correctly) that it is a topic of high interest to the audience.

Since unemployment touches, directly or indirectly, every member of society, most people would seek to make some sense of the problem and to search for explanations and understandings of that issue. Television stories of unemployment constitute a prime source of such explanations. Although such stories come at a variety of levels, ranging from the strictly informative (as in "tell stories" read by the newscaster) to longer "field reports," most such stories, with the possible exception of brief headline items, contain a theme open to decoding, that is, a statement about the nature of a society where such threatening dislocation can occur. It is through the analysis of these themes that we sought to shed some light on the ideological uniformity or diversity of television news.

The Narrative Structure of Unemployment

In January 1983, the U.S. Department of Labor reported the December rate of civilian unemployment in the country at 10.7%. The jump to double-digit unemployment meant that the number of Americans out of work had reached a post-Depression record of more than 10 million. The unemployment rate stayed above 10% for the next six months, and by June 1983, 11,162,000 Americans were classified by the Department of Labor as unemployed (U.S. Department of Labor, 1984, pp. 74–80).

Television news presents such events as stories, relying on a narrative framework that adheres to the requisites of dramatic unity and plot development.[1] In unemployment stories, statistics are usually read by the anchor in a brief tell story. When unemployment statistics, or, for that matter, any official economic statistics, reach a symbolic threshold (in this case the 10% level), the statistics are likely to become the "news peg" for an expanded report. Correspondents in the field may personalize the issue by looking at unemployment through the perspective of the individual confronted with idle factories, lines at unemployment offices, lines created when 200 jobs are offered and 5,000 people arrive to claim them; or reporters may focus on the individual who has found work after a prolonged search, benefited from an innovative retraining program, or was sustained by the generosity of neighbors.

Field reports, bracketed by reporter introductions and "stand-up" conclusions, are self-contained narrative essays. Generally, though, the stories evoke more than just the plight or prospects of the individuals involved. "Despite the explicit concern with people and their activities," Gans writes, "the recurring subjects of the news are nation and society—their persistence, cohesion, and the conflicts and divisions threatening their cohesion" (1979, p. 19). The narrative structure of the television report places the elements of the story in dramatic relationship to one another: Characters act or are acted upon. The aspirations of individuals conform or conflict with the social and national contexts. Bennett and Edelman (1985) note that narrative becomes, in effect, a means of understanding the social world:

> The intriguing characteristic of a social world created by a narrative is the integral link among its components: the who, what, where, why, how, and when that gives acts and events a narrative frame. A choice among alternative settings or among origins of a political development also determines who are virtuous, who are threats to the good life, and which courses of action are effective solutions. (p. 159)

For casting light on the processes of nation and society, record unemployment is an especially resonant subject. For example, the single image of the line, in the 1930s the breadline, is easily connected to the visual literature of the Depression and to a more general view of a society in disrepair. In addition, images of boarded-up shops, idle factories, deserted Main Streets, empty landscapes, and job seekers clustered in front of campfires establish the linkage between present-day suffering and its historical and cultural contexts. High unemployment remains a disjunction in the American experience; perhaps more important, it runs counter to American expectations.

Television finds in unemployment a story rich with thematic possibilities. Unemployment has a direct bearing on individuals, while also conveying the sense that there is something seriously wrong at the societal level, that something is out of kilter in American life. The difficulties faced by individuals almost inevitably become a gauge of the problems of society at large. Because large-scale unemployment cuts across socioeconomic lines, the story may be told from a number of vantage points. Executives and factory workers alike face layoffs. Even the graduates of elite universities find their choices narrowed and their futures suddenly uncertain. The unresponsive economy may point to failings within the social structure, the failure of American business to modernize, for example, or to external challenges from Japan or from Third World labor. Unemployment may be viewed as the product of failed policies or as inherent in an existing economic system.

In the course of this study, we identified two levels of narrative framework within the coverage of unemployment that we have labeled *explanations* and *themes*. Explanations were defined as explicit, causal statements made either by anchors and reporters presenting the news of unemployment or by the subjects of the coverage, the sources cited or appearing on camera. To the extent that news relates dislocations in the economy, and consequently in the lives of people, to underlying causes, it provides explanations. Those explanations in turn provide some sense of how the society is structured, how it functions or falters, and where power resides.

Even if news broadcasts do not offer concrete or specific reasons for unemployment, the narrative treatment of the issue may be expected to frame the problem in particular ways and promote particular audience understandings. The narrative frame, specifically, the image of society conveyed in the news report, was treated as the theme of the story.

THE CONTENT ANALYSIS

Content analytic techniques applied to television news range from traditional item counts of words, sentences, and other linguistic elements to more holistic and semiotic approaches that treat the text as a structured and interdependent whole rather than as simply the sum of its parts. Traditional content analysis has been subjected to criticism for its narrow preoccupation with the frequency of appearance of different textual elements without an accompanying concern for the potential diversity of meanings carried in these elements and more generally for "counting the wrong things" (Winston, 1983). More recently, holistic, meaning-centered methods have been preferred. Hackett (1984, p. 242) is among those who have voiced the objection that conventional forms of content analysis "merely [count] repeated denotative signifiers, rather than searching for the underlying code which places the signifiers." Thematic analysis of media texts, on the other hand, is specifically concerned with narrative patterns, the broad outlines that establish a context for determining the significance of the elements.

Thematic examinations of television news have identified, for example, clusters of enduring values (Gans, 1979), categories of broad substantive interest (Larson, 1984), and dominant characteristics of news presentation (Frank, 1973). Our project began with a preliminary viewing of unemployment stories, conducted over a four-week period in a graduate seminar. In the course of viewing, the seven participants sought to distill the themes of the stories into sets of declarative statements. Coders then attempted to identify the principal theme, if one could be discerned, and as many as two subsidiary themes for each story. The method shares characteristics with literary analysis: the readings were the product of a shared culture developed over time and based upon extensive discussion.

Videotapes of stories dealing with unemployment on the ABC, CBS, and NBC evening newscasts between January 1, 1983, and June 30, 1983, were obtained from the Television News Archive of Vanderbilt University. The stories were selected initially through a search of the Television News Index and Abstracts. Index entries on unemployment, employment, jobs, the economy, and similar themes were consulted. All stories under these headings with any reference to unemployment were selected. In addition to straightforward stories on unemployment, this procedure resulted, for example, in the selection of stories on farm foreclosures that were described in the index as related to unemployment. A review of the videotapes was conducted with the purpose of eliminating those stories that were irrelevant to unemployment but were included due to the vagaries of the index.

A coding scheme was constructed that consisted of four sections. The first section dealt with such details as network, date, length of story, subject of story, and type of story (either anchor tell story, correspondent field report, anchor voice-over, or editorial/commentary). A second set of questions was aimed at uncovering the demography of unemployment as conveyed on television news. Our intention here was to address the familiar question of whether news reports accurately reflect "objective" or statistical reality. We are not arguing, of course, that statistical data necessarily constitute a more accurate or objective reflection of reality. They do offer, however, a version of reality that can be used as a yardstick for measuring the version offered by television news. In the case of unemployment, the federal government provides monthly indices of the unemployed population by age, race, sex, occupation, and geographical location. In applying classifications to news stories, we coded each story for the demographic characteristics of the unemployed people who were the principal focus of the report. Age, race, occupational, and geographical categories were chosen to correspond to the groupings used by the Department of Labor in compiling its official statistics.

In the third section, we coded explanations, as defined above, and sources, and made an effort to classify stories on a "good news"-"bad news" dimension. A cited source was defined as any individual, agency, or institution credited with providing information. Sources coded as appearing on camera included all interview subjects, identified or otherwise.

Whereas a bad news story might deal with a factory's closing, with no clear suggestion that things might be expected to improve, a good news story might deal with the reopening of a factory after a prolonged shutdown. A number of stories were labeled "good news-silver lining." In a silver lining story, the message of the report is that, although conditions are undeniably bad, a change for the better is clearly in sight.

The fourth section of the coding instrument dealt with themes, as defined earlier. Finally, each story was coded for the presence of key visual images. To examine the complex patterns of visual imagery in the stories would require a separate discussion. Nonetheless, the visual component of the stories is clearly one of the building blocks in the construction of the meaning of the stories and is thus reflected in the coding of the themes.

DATA BASE AND SELECTED FINDINGS

In the following section we present a summary of our findings on selected aspects of the contents. Since our main interest was the thematic content of the stories, that discussion is presented in extended form, following a brief overview of our other findings.

During the six-month period, the total number of stories was 253. Of those, 102 appeared on CBS, 80 on NBC, and 71 on ABC. Although the unemployment rate declined less than half a percentage point during the period (from 10.4% in January to 10% in June), the networks' attention to the subject faded rapidly; there were 92 stories on the three networks in January, followed by 45 in February, 42 in March, 38 in April, 21 in May, and 13 in June. On each of two days, January 7 and February 4, the networks broadcast a total of 8 unemployment-related stories, the most on a single day. During a period of 181 days, there was at least one unemployment-related story on 102 days. The length of the stories varied from about 10 seconds apiece (there were 22 such stories) to five minutes 40 seconds, the length of a special report on CBS. The significance given the stories by the networks is suggested by the presence within the 253 stories of 167 correspondent field reports, stories of generally more than two minutes apiece that require a fair investment of resources on the part of the networks; 67 were tell stories.

Coding the stories by subject yielded an extensive list, ranging from general unemployment or re-employment to subjects such as aid to the unemployed, youth employment, and general economic policy. The two subjects receiving attention most frequently were general unemployment stories and stories concerning a jobs bill under consideration by Congress, each subject representing about 14% of the total number of stories. More generally, government policy—stories on the jobs bill, administration policy, and efforts to reduce the deficit—was the subject of almost 30% of the stories. About 14% of the stories treated unemployment in the context of an economic recovery that was expected to dispel the problem.

On the face of it, unemployment could be assumed to be a bad story. Yet our initial viewing of the tapes revealed that the coverage of that issue was laced with a considerable dose of good stories. Hence the inclusion of that question in our coding scheme. And indeed, over 22% of the stories were eventually coded as good news or good news-silver lining stories. About 40% of the stories were straightforward bad news and 34% contained elements of both. The significant proportion of good news stories may well be the result of the interaction of the news practices guided by the search for "hard news" (for example, reporting the re-opening of a factory in a town with high unemployment is regarded as hard news), the reliance on principles of balanced coverage, and, perhaps, a basic optimistic streak in American culture. Inasmuch as news is a cultural product that both reflects and reinforces basic cultural themes, the possible tendency toward optimism in the culture may have significant consequences for the shaping of the news. We shall return to that issue in our discussion of the narrative themes in the stories.

The Demography of Unemployment

About 41% of the stories had a clear occupational focus and, of those, 78% concerned industrial occupations and 22% non-industrial occupations. Steel and automobiles were the most frequently covered industries, each representing about 5% of the total number of stories. According to Labor Department data for 1983, however, the industrial sector of the economy accounted for only 34% of the nation's total unemployment, while unemployment in the service sector represented 45% of the total. In that sense, television gives a skewed portrait of unemployment: comparatively few stories were devoted to the areas of economic activity where unemployment was most pervasive in the period.

Given an apparent concentration on "smokestack" unemployment, on failing factories and out-of-work factory workers, it is not surprising that, geographically, stories of unemployment were centered east of the Mississippi River in the country's traditional industrial belt. One-third of the stories either were set in or concentrated upon developments in the midwestern states (Illinois, Indiana, Michigan, Ohio, and Wisconsin); 20% of the stories focused on the mid-Atlantic states (New York, New Jersey, and Pennsylvania). During 1983, according to the Department of Labor, the two areas represented 37.5% of all U.S. unemployment. Taken as a percentage of all stories where location was specified, the figure for television news was 53%.

In focusing on industrial unemployment and locating it largely in the industrial East and Midwest, television news producers and reporters may reveal the influence of the stock of readily available cultural images that have long been associated with economic hard times, primarily images of the Depression. It is as if they searched for images to familiarize the trauma of unemployment to the viewers and found those images in the grim factory towns of Pennsylvania and Ohio, in steel, rubber, and automobile plants, usually bursting with productive energy, now quiet and forlorn, and in hard times mirrored in hard winters. But in 1983 those images were not fully descriptive of the changing face of unemployment. They ignored the numbers of unemployed service workers, secretaries, information processors, and bureaucrats, whose ranks had been swelling. With no idle smokestacks and rusting assembly lines to give pictorial quality to their unemployment, non-industrial occupational groups appeared less often in the coverage.[2]

In 1983, the unemployment rate for blacks was almost 20%, more than double the rate for whites. Females constituted 43% of all U.S. unemployed. Most television stories did not specify the race or sex of the unemployed, but

12 stories (4.7%) addressed the issue of black unemployment specifically. Only two stories (0.8%) dealt with female unemployment.

Sources

The sources appearing most frequently on camera were unemployed persons, a category that included farmers facing foreclosure of their holdings. The source cited most frequently was President Reagan. Government officials represented 35% of all sources appearing on camera and almost half of all sources cited (Table 1).

The figures clearly reveal the familiar preoccupation of journalists with authoritative sources or what Hall calls "primary definers" (see Hall, Critcher,

TABLE 1. Sources Appearing and Sources Cited

Source	Appearances on Camera	% of Appearances	Cited in Story	% of Citations
President Reagan	27	7	53	26
Cabinet Member/s	16	4	5	2
Elected Official, Republican	23	6	13	6
Elected Official, Democrat	28	7	12	6
Other Government Official	43	11	17	8
Government Agency	—	—	31	15
Congress/Courts	—	—	5	2
Unemployed Person (Includes Farmers Facing Foreclosure)	65	16	5	2
Family of Unemployed	12	3	—	—
Advocate for Unemployed	18	4	4	2
Employed Person	40	10	3	1
Family of Employed	2	*	—	—
Employer/Manager/ Employer Representative	41	10	16	8
Small Businessman/ Businesswoman	3	1	—	—
Union Member/Official	22	5	8	4
Banker/Business Representative	17	4	10	5
Employment Specialist	7	2	—	—
Expert	30	7	16	8
Health Care Professional	3	1	—	—
Media Representative/ Media Outlet	4	1	5	2
Man/Woman in Street	1	*	—	—
Total	402	99**	203	97**

*Less than 1%.
**Error due to rounding.

Jefferson, Clark, & Roberts, 1978, pp. 57–60). Authoritativeness, according to Gans (1979, pp. 130–131), is a principal consideration of journalists when selecting sources. Officials are considered knowledgeable and persuasive largely because of their formal designation as officials. In addition, should the subject of the story be controversial, authoritative sources provide journalists with a measure of protection from criticism by news executives. The President, members of his administration, and other government officials are regarded as obvious sources for newsworthy statements on all social issues. Their pronouncements also carry greater weight than, say, the views of an unemployed individual whose grasp of the issue is considered to be less authoritative, whose power to affect the problem is clearly very small, and whose value to the reporter is primarily in contributing a human interest angle to the story. Consequently, although the appearance of unemployed persons on camera may add a personal quality that authenticates and humanizes the story, those persons are not regularly cited. As Table 1 shows, unemployed persons appeared on camera 65 times in the network coverage, but were cited only 5 times. By contrast, President Reagan appeared as a source 27 times, while he was cited 53 times, considerably more often than was any other source.

EXPLANATIONS AND THEMES

The significance of examining news sources lies in the well-documented power that sources have to offer explanations and thus construct the framework for presenting different social issues in the media and for the audience's understanding. But when we examined the news stories for the explanations they contained, we discovered that only a relatively small proportion of all stories offered such explanations. (Explanations, as we suggested above, were defined as explicit, causal statements about the problem of unemployment.)

Only about 30% of the stories contained any explanation. In the 78 stories that had at least one explanation, 21 explanations were presented by reporters; 10 by employers, managers, and employer representatives; and 7 by anchors. The remainder of explanations were offered by a variety of sources. Only about 14% of stories contained more than one explanation; the total number of explanations was 113.

Twenty-two separate reasons for unemployment were offered in the television news stories. (In the audience survey, 24 causes were mentioned by at least 1% of the respondents.) In the television stories, no single explanation represented more than 9% of all explanations. This pattern was similar to that of the audience survey, where no single cause represented more than 8% of all causes mentioned. In general, television news stories mentioned economic forces more frequently as an explanation for unemployment than did audience members; television cited causes related to unions and workers, and to foreign competition, less frequently (Table 2).

TABLE 2. Television Explanations vs. Survey Respondents' Explanations of Unemployment

	% Explanations TV Content Analysis (N = 113)	% Responses Audience Survey (N = 544)
Economic Forces		
1. High Interest Rates	—	8
2. Inflation	—	4
3. Certain Industries Vulnerable	9	4
4. Recession	5	3
5. Technology, Automation	7	3
6 Low Consumer Demand	9	3
7. Public Lack of Confidence	7	1
8. Worldwide Economic Conditions	3.5	1
9. Industry Relocating	2	1
10. High Cost of Oil, Materials	—	—
11. Unemployment Inevitable, Structural	3.5	—
12. General Economic Forces	7	—
	53.0	28
Unions/Workers		
13. Unions/Union Demands/Labor Costs	3.5	7
14. Lack of Desire to Work	—	5
15. Poorly Trained Workers	5	3
16. Too Many Workers	—	2
	8.5	17
Government/Politicians/Policies		
17. Reagan/Republican Policies	8	6
18. Federal Debt, Budget Deficit	—	2
19. Cuts in Federal Programs	—	2
20. Monetary Policy	—	2
21. Taxes	2	1
22. Excessive Military/Space Spending	—	1
23. Carter/Democratic Policies	3.5	1
24. Anti-Inflationary Policies	—	—
25. Government Regulations	2	—
26. Not Enough Military Spending	—	—
27. General Government Policy	2	—
	17.5	15
28. *Foreign Competition/Imports*	3.5	11
Business Sector		
29. Unproductive U S. Industries	2.5	3
30. Poor Management/Business Practices	2.5	1
31. Failure to Plan	—	1
32. Management Decisions	3.5	—
	8.5	5

Continued

TABLE 2. *Continued*

	% Explanations TV Content Analysis (N = 113)	% Responses Audience Survey (N = 544)
Miscellaneous		
33. Not Enough Jobs	2	9
34. Racial Prejudice	—	—
35. God, Fate	—	—
36. Adverse Natural Conditions	1	—
37. Don't Know	—	12
38. Multiple Causes	6	—
	9.0	21
	100.0	100

What accounts for this paucity of direct explanations? In one sense, it should not be too surprising. Television news predictably is drawn more to consequences than causes. When questioned about the possibilities of enhancing the explanatory role of their medium, television executives typically cite time constraints as an inherent limitation on their ability to provide context and historical background. Beyond that consideration, however, and beyond the view of economic issues as somehow too narrow or technical for public comprehension and appreciation, are what might be called political constraints. A direct explanation for a social problem may require statements that depart from strict objectivity and carry dangers of perceived bias. The suggestion, for example, that misguided policies have caused unemployment certainly would be regarded in official circles as partisan. Straightforward explanations contain another significant hazard for journalists; there is always the possibility that later events may prove them and their explanations wrong.

Whereas direct explanations are laden with risk for journalists and their news organizations, themes represent a narrative framework that may not entail explicit journalistic commitment to a particular point of view or set of beliefs. A theme may be sufficiently diffuse or subtle to obscure accountability.

As we described earlier, our method in identifying themes was to immerse ourselves in stories about unemployment for a period of several weeks, much as Gans engaged in "continual scrutiny of the news" in producing a list of "enduring values" (1979, p. 19). The impressionistic nature of such an analysis should be emphasized: the array of themes we identified certainly do not exhaust the possibilities even within the rubric of unemployment stories. Yet, working with a team of five graduate students who acted as coders, we found that although the stories offered a relatively thin scatter of overt explanations, the stories nonetheless were rich in thematic lines of exposition. All but 32 stories—virtually all of them brief items read by the anchor—were coded as having a principal theme. Fifty-three percent of the stories were coded as having one subsidiary theme and about one-quarter of the stories as having two subsidiary themes. Twenty separate themes were identified. Some themes were, in effect, implicit explanations allowing causal inferences about the problem of unemployment, for example, the themes that technological advances continually result in the displacement of workers or that government policies have failed. Other themes took a more broadly based, societal frame of reference, among them the themes that Society Is Fragmented and Conflict Ridden or divided into Haves and Have Nots. Briefly defined, the 20 themes were as follows:

1. *Economic Darwinism: Failure*
   Ours is a society where the marketplace decides and everyone has the opportunity to fail. The unemployed are those who, for whatever reason, have not been equal to the task.

2. *Economic Darwinism: Success*
   In an economy built on the survival of the fittest, the marketplace determines the winners as well as the losers. Everyone has the chance to succeed.

3. *An Unfair Society*
   Ours is a society that is innately, structurally unfair. No particular interest may be held accountable for this situation, but the society, or system or economy, victimizes at least some of its members. Unemployment, like poverty, is a built-in cost.

4. *A Fair Society*
   Structurally, the society is fair to its various constituents. The social structure is arranged in such a way that opportunities are provided and equally distributed. In cases where this is not so, the system is self-correcting.

5. *Haves and Have Nots*
   Our society is one of haves and have nots. Acting in their own interests, powerful elements in society are responsible for the displacement that excludes and victimizes those who are less powerful.

6. *Times Are Tough*
   Our society and, hence, the economy are driven by elemental forces that no one can control. Ultimately, there may be some readjustment that eases individual misfortune, but there is not much to do but wait it out.

7. *Technology Displaces People*
   The engine of social progress is technological change. Just as the industrial revolution wrought personal upheaval, the changeover to a new economic order (the information society or the new industrial revolution) inevitably means that some will be left behind.

8. *Technology Creates New Opportunities*
Technological change will eventually make things better for all of us. It is not as if the pieces of the pie are being redistributed; the pie is getting larger.

9. *Policies Have Costs in Unemployment*
The decisions our leaders make always have consequences. In order to pursue particular ends, a defense buildup, for example, we have to realize that there are costs involved. Unemployment is one of them.

10. *Policies Are Wrong/Unfair*
Ours is a society that should be fair and *would* be fair, if it were not for those who govern. Unemployment is not ingrained or inherent in the system. It is caused by wrong or unfair policies.

11. *Policies Are Bungled/Incompetent*
Our leaders would like to improve the situation, but they aren't capable enough.

12. *Policies Work*
Our leaders have responsibility for the way the society functions, and they seem to be doing the job well.

13. *A Caring Society*
Ours is a society that cares for and nurtures its own. Being unemployed is a fate not unlike living in a house that burned down. It is a personal disaster. The neighbors rally round, provide shelter, offer a warm meal. The victims don't curse the gods; they are thankful that someone was there to help.

14. *An Uncaring Society*
If you're unemployed in this society, your troubles have just begun. Those who are unfortunate get taken advantage of. People care only for themselves.

15. *An Economy in Decline*
Ours is an economy in decline. The inroads made by overseas competitors are a symptom, not a cause, of whatever economic failings we experience. Steel mills and smokestacks almost suggest a civilization that is passing.

16. *Fighting Back*
Life may not be fair, but in the face of adversity we persist, and more. Expressions of anger, resolve, and determination and the willingness to fight for what should be ours are tales of courage.

17. *Society Is Fragmented, Conflict Ridden*
The society is fragmented by self-interested groups and constituencies. Unions, management, and other groups seek short-term benefits at the expense of the national good. The notion of common welfare has been lost.

18. *Society Can Pull Together*
    When competing elements work together, any problem can be overcome. We may need crisis or tragedy to stir our best American impulses, but in the midst of suffering, these petty divisions are being overcome.

19. *Times Are/Will Get Better*
    The economy has its cycles, and bad is followed by good. The good (or at least better) cycle either has already begun or is coming soon.

20. *Unemployment Is a Political Football*
    Government is mired in partisan squabbling. When serious issues such as unemployment present themselves, finding solutions to real problems seems to be secondary to the game of political advantage. Little changes for those who need or seek help.

A review of the entire list of themes makes it clear that television stories offered a variety of points of view and thematic implications. One story may suggest that something was fundamentally wrong in the basic structure of society, while another story may emphasize that the society was capable of self-correction. Some themes were thus expressed as pairs of directly contrasting statements. Whereas some stories, for example, portrayed the unemployed as the beneficiaries of the humanitarian assistance offered by others (A Caring Society), other stories portrayed them as the victims of those who could take advantage of their weakness and susceptibility (An Uncaring Society). While there were stories that presented the theme that society could overcome its problems when its members worked together, other stories implied that such cooperation was impossible given the fractious nature of society. Thus there are several obvious dimensions, among them conflict-consensus, social control-lack of control, that cut across a number of themes. In an effort to identify the most useful of these, we turned to the characteristics of the most prevalent theme (Table 3).

The dominant theme was Times Are Tough.[3] The characteristic Times are Tough story portrayed an individual or group of individuals under duress, usually unable to find work. No explicit causes for this situation were mentioned or intimated in the report. One aspect of this theme is the avoidance of placing responsibility on any human actors. The stories were pessimistic in tone to the degree that they portrayed individuals as victims of the innate cyclical fluctuations of the economy. Yet they carried undertones of optimism in the suggestion that this crisis, too, would pass.

Interestingly, the Times Are Tough rationale, the acceptance of hard times as a trial to be endured, is evident in the nation's first responses to the Great Depression. In a study of post-World War I America, William E. Leuchtenburg notes that at the outset of the Great Depression the country's first impulses were fatalistic:

> Business cycles were inevitable, the fatalistic argued, and there was nothing to do but wait out this latest disaster. Any attempt to interrupt the process

TABLE 3. Distribution of Themes

Theme	% of Primary Theme	% of All Themes
1. Economic Darwinism: Failure	1.8	3.1
2. Economic Darwinism: Success	0.5	1.2
3. An Unfair Society	3.2	6.7
4. A Fair Society	0.9	1.2
5. Haves and Have Nots	1.4	2.6
6. Times Are Tough	35.7	23.1
7. Technology Displaces People	2.7	4.0
8. Technology Creates Opportunities	1.4	1.2
9. Policies Have Costs in Unemployment	3.2	4.3
10. Policies Are Wrong/Unfair	5.4	6.9
11. Policies Are Bungled/Incompetent	1.4	1.9
12. Policies Work	2.7	3.1
13. A Caring Society	2.7	2.6
14. An Uncaring Society	1.2	1.9
15. An Economy in Decline	4.5	5.2
16. Fighting Back	2.7	5.2
17. Society Is Fragmented, Conflict Ridden	2.7	4.8
18. Society Can Pull Together	3.2	3.1
19. Times Are/Will Get Better	14.9	11.7
20. Unemployment Is a Political Football	7.8	7.1
Total	100.0	99.9*
	N = 221	N = 420
None, N/A	32	
Total	N = 253	

*Error due to rounding.

would only make matters worse. *The New York Times* contended that the "fundamental prescriptions for recovery [were] such homely things as savings, retrenchment, prudence, and hopeful waiting for the turn." (1966, pp. 249–250)

Similarly, Times Are Tough stories do not attempt to locate the causes of unemployment and do not offer explanations; unemployment, and the economic cycles that produce it, are depicted as natural forces residing outside the realm of social control (indeed, a few stories established a direct link between the arrival of harsh winter weather and the growth of unemployment lines, suggesting an elemental form of causality).

The Times Are Tough story combines strains of optimism and pessimism. It also combines the perspectives of the individual and the larger society in the sense that, while individuals are the focus of the story, they are not held accountable for their predicament and can do little to change it. This theme thus straddles the dimensions of optimism-pessimism and individual-society.

Examining the ways these two dimensions structure the entire list of themes, we produced a table with the following elements: optimistic themes focusing on the individual; optimistic themes with a societal perspective; pessimistic themes with an individual perspective; and pessimistic themes with a societal frame of reference (Table 4).[4]

At least two conclusions emerge from an examination of themes along these dimensions. First, unemployment stories contain a considerable number of stories with optimistic themes (29% of primary themes and 28.3% of all themes were labeled "optimistic") balanced against those stories with pessimistic themes (35.3% of primary themes, 48.5% of all themes). "Optimism" in the stories frequently takes the form of reassurance that, however grim the statistics, unemployment is transient, and the basic structure of society is sound. The two most frequent themes, Times Are Tough and Times Are/Will Get Better, both offer such direct reassurance. Second, the distribution of themes indicates that although stories often deal with the problems faced by individuals, the themes of the stories generally address broader issues of social structure and purpose. Themes with a societal perspective (57.9% of primary themes, 64.7% of all themes) are far more prevalent than themes with an individual perspective (6.4% of primary themes, 12.1% of all themes).

CONCLUSION

Two central conclusions concerning the explanatory function of television news emerge from our findings. First, television news stories offered few *direct explanations* of unemployment. By avoiding such direct explanations and shunning any didactic role, television news organizations remain true to the professional creed of dispensing objective information to their audiences. At the same time our analysis suggests that the narrative structures of these stories contain an abundance of *explanatory frameworks* or themes. Many themes provided implicit reasons for unemployment, embedded in broader statements about the nature of society. Even those themes that were more open-ended and could not be construed

TABLE 4. Two-Dimensional Structuring of Narrative Themes

	% of Primary Theme	% of All Themes
Individuals/Optimism	3.2	6.4
Individuals/Pessimism	3.2	5.7
Society/Optimism	25.8	21.9
Society/Pessimism	32.1	42.8
Times Are Tough	35.7	23.1
	100.0	99.9

as explanations—Times Are Tough is probably the prime example—nonetheless provided a way of thinking about the problem, a framework for understanding it and relating it to the nature of society and to its history.

In constructing a portrait of unemployment, television news personnel were clearly guided by a set of professional values and practices that explains much of what we found: the preference for authoritative sources, usually government officials; the reliance on traditional images of unemployment drawn from the nation's industrial belt; and the concentration on Washington-based partisan debate instead of examinations of America's place in a changing world economy or of the dynamics of supply and demand (not surprising, given television news producers' continuing view of economics as arcane, abstract, and difficult to visualize). The marked attention given to good news stories may also reflect a professional judgment that news, by definition, is deviational, so that with a record number of people out of work, re-employment, not unemployment, becomes noteworthy.

Beyond the professional values of television journalists, however, the coverage of unemployment seems rooted in a collective cultural memory of hard economic times. The demography of unemployment on television news evokes an era of assembly lines and boarded-up factories that may reflect the 1930s more accurately than the 1980s. Correspondingly, Times Are Tough and Times Will Get Better are archetypal themes of resignation and persistence, reminiscent of responses to the Great Depression.

Thematic Diversity and the Question of Ideology

We return then to the question with which we opened: what implications for the debate about the ideological role of the media can we draw from our analysis? What insights can be gleaned from our findings concerning the different positions in the debate about the dominant ideology?

The multiplicity of themes in the stories analyzed suggests that the story of unemployment is told in diverse, often contradictory, ways. The mixed thematic character of the stories seems to reinforce Newcomb and Hirsch's view of television as a cultural forum. In their words:

> In its role as a central cultural medium [television] presents a multiplicity of meanings rather than a monolithic dominant point of view. It often focuses on our most prevalent concerns, our deepest dilemmas. Our most traditional views, those that are repressive and reactionary, as well as those that are subversive and emancipatory, are upheld, examined, maintained, and transformed. (p. 61)

Clearly, the view of society as both caring and uncaring, fair and unfair, technologically advanced and perilously in decline offers little support to the idea that television is monolithic. We should also not be surprised, therefore, to discover that audience members' explanations of the causes of unemployment are wide ranging and diffuse.

Does that conclusion stand in opposition to the dominant ideology argument about television? If that argument requires that the universe of views of society offered by television should be internally coherent and near monolithic, the answer is clearly yes. If, on the other hand, the notion of dominant ideology only requires that the ideas and beliefs about society should be contained within the boundaries of a *dominant paradigm*, then the notions that television is both an instrument of the dominant ideology and also a cultural forum can be accommodated to each other. Indeed, Newcomb and Hirsch argue that the cultural forum, the variety of perspectives on American television, "works for the most part within the limits of American monopoly capitalism and within the range of American pluralism" (p. 61). Pluralism and monopoly capitalism thus may be seen as the key elements of the dominant ideology of American society and television then can be regarded as its servant.

Diversity and the fragmentation of audience understandings thus become the mechanisms for disseminating that dominant ideology. As Abercrombie et al. (1980, pp. 156–158) have argued, "In late capitalism the limited ideological unity of previous periods has collapsed. . . . This creates the paradox that, at the same time as the apparatus [of ideological transmission] becomes more forceful, the coherence of the dominant ideology becomes weaker." Diversity, as we have argued earlier, might be seen as a subtle form of ideology, and the fragmentation of the audience might indeed have social consequences beneficial to the economic order. Such fragmentation inhibits the opportunities for the emergence of a unified opposition to the basic premises of the existing economic order. It might sow confusion as to the causes of economic difficulties such as unemployment and reduce the potential emergence among individual members of society of a sense of political efficacy, of a feeling that there *are* answers to the problem and that these answers can be acted upon.

An Empty Vessel?

One final point. The notion of television as a cultural forum, much like the old metaphor of the media as a "marketplace of ideas," suggests that the media offer their audiences a variety of perspectives and meanings from which audience members can pick and choose. In the tradition of effects research, the idea of audience selectivity was applied primarily to differential exposure to diverse media contents. But selectivity can also operate at the level of decoding, where audience members attribute different meanings to the same contents. With regard to unemployment stories, our analysis suggests that viewers could choose between different themes and explanations and could also exercise selectivity by decoding the stories in different ways. Clearly, meanings cannot be "read off" straight from the text. They emerge and are reproduced in the interaction between texts and viewers. As Morley puts it, "The meaning of the text will be constructed differently according to the discourses (knowledges, prejudices, resistances, etc.) brought to bear by the reader, and the crucial factor in the encounter of audience/subject and the text will be the range of discourses at the disposal of the audience" (1983, p. 106).

The diversity of possible decodings however, is to some extent constrained by the degree of openness of story themes. While some of the themes we have identified, such as An Economy in Decline, Policies Work, and An Unfair Society, present a relatively well-defined view of society and its attendant problems, others, most notably Times Are Tough, skirt the issue of causation and are open-ended enough to enable viewers to inject into the stories the variety of their own readings.

Given the potential for selectivity both at the level of exposure, and of decoding and the construction of meaning, television might then be best described not merely as a cultural forum but indeed as an "empty vessel" that can be all things to all people. It is, perhaps, in terms of the combination of its textual richness and diversity on the one hand, and its open-endedness on the other, that the analysis of the ideological functions of television, as well as of its attractiveness to the audience, usefully can be pursued.

Acknowledgments: This research was supported by a grant from the University of Maryland. The authors thank Professor Mark R. Levy for his advice and Alan Lipke for assistance in data collection and processing.

NOTES

1. The central role of stories and storytelling in mass communication increasingly provides a basis for textual analysis as well as examinations of the social functions of journalists. See "Media and Society: Social Reality and Media Representations" in Gurevitch and Levy (1985, pp. 185–370). For discussion of narrative form in mass communication, see the "Homo Narrans" section of *Journal of Communication*, 35 (4).

2. Some might argue that the disparity between media representations and the picture of unemployment conveyed by government reports is tantamount to media distortion of reality. We suggest instead that the media portrayals and official accounts represent two separate versions of reality. For another example of the discrepancy between television representations and the reality of the "working world," see Foltin, 1983.

3. We noted only minor differences between networks in the thematic content of stories, with perhaps this exception: the Times Are Tough theme represented more than 40% of all ABC primary themes; about 34% of all NBC primary themes and 22.5% of all CBS themes.

4. The placement of themes along the dimensions of optimism-pessimism and individual-society was problematic in only one instance, the theme of Haves and Have Nots. The theme is clearly pessimistic but has elements of both individual and societal perspectives. We decided that, although the theme emerges from a general view of society, it rests on the notion that individuals are different; we therefore classified it as individual.

REFERENCES

Abercrombie, N., Hill, S., & Turner, B. (1980). *The dominant ideology thesis*. London: Allen & Unwin.

Adoni, H., & Mane, S. (1984). Media and the social construction of reality: Toward an integration of theory and research. *Communication Research, 11*, 323–340.

Behr, R., & Iyengar, S. (1985). Television news, real-world cues, and changes in the public agenda. *Public Opinion Quarterly, 49*, 38–57.

Bennett, T. (1982). Media, 'reality,' signification. In M. Gurevitch, T. Bennett, J. Curran, & J. Woollacott (Eds.), *Culture, society and the media* (pp. 287–308). London: Methuen.

Bennett, W., & Edelman, M. (1985). Toward a new political narrative. *Journal of Communication, 35*(4), 156–171.

Carey, J. (1975). A cultural approach to communication. *Communication, 2*, 1–22.

Davis, D., & Robinson, J. (1986). The social role of television news: Theoretical perspectives. In J. Robinson & M. Levy (Eds.), *The main source* (pp. 29–54). Beverly Hills: Sage.

Foltin, H. (1983). The working world as represented by the mass media in the Federal Republic of Germany. In V. Mosco & J. Wasko (Eds.), *The critical communications review: Labor, the working class, and the media* (pp. 153–166). Norwood, NJ: Ablex.

Frank, R. (1973). *Message dimensions of television news*. Lexington, MA: D. C. Heath.

Gans, H. (1979). *Deciding what's news*. New York: Random House.

Glasgow University Media Group. (1976). *Bad news*. London: Routledge & Kegan Paul.

Glasgow University Media Group. (1980). *More bad news*. London: Routledge & Kegan Paul.

Glasgow University Media Group. (1982). *Really bad news*. London: Writers and Readers.

Golding, P., & Murdock, G. (1978). Theories of communication and theories of society. *Communication Research, 5*, 339–356.

Gurevitch, M., & Levy, M. R. (Eds.). (1985). *Mass communication review yearbook*. Beverly Hills: Sage.

Gurevitch, M., & Levy, M. (1986). Information and meaning: Audience explanations of social issues. In J. Robinson & M. Levy (Eds.), *The main source* (pp. 159–175). Beverly Hills: Sage.

Hackett, R. (1984). Decline of a paradigm? Bias and objectivity in news media studies. *Critical Studies in Mass Communication, 1*, 229–259.

Hall, S. (1982). The rediscovery of 'ideology': Return of the repressed in media studies. In M. Gurevitch, T. Bennett, J. Curran, & J. Woollacott (Eds.), *Culture, society and the media* (pp. 56–90). London: Methuen.

Hall, S., Critcher, C., Jefferson, T., Clarke, J., & Roberts, B. (1978). *Policing the crisis: Mugging, the state and law and order*. London: Macmillan.

Journal of Communication. (1985). Homo narrans: Story-telling in mass culture and everyday life. 35(4), 73–171.

Larson, J. (1984). *Television's window on the world: International affairs coverage on the U.S. networks*. Norwood, NJ: Ablex.

Leuchtenberg, W. E. (1966). *The perils of prosperity: 1914–32*. Chicago: University of Chicago Press.

McQuail, D. (1977). The influence and effects of mass media. In J. Curran, M. Gurevitch, & J. Woollacott (Eds.), *Mass communication and society* (pp. 70–94). London: Edward Arnold.

Morley, D. (1980). *The 'nationwide' audience: Structure and decoding.* London: British Film Institute.

Morley, D. (1983). Cultural transformations: The politics of resistance. In H. Davis & P. Walton (Eds.), *Language, image, media* (pp. 104–117). New York: St. Martin's Press.

Newcomb, H., & Hirsch, P. (1984). Television as a cultural forum. In W. Rowland & B. Watkins (Eds.), *Interpreting television: Current research perspectives* (pp. 58–73). Beverly Hills: Sage.

U.S. Department of Labor. (1984, February). *Monthly labor review.* Washington, DC: U.S. Government Printing Office.

Winston, B. (1983). On counting the wrong things. In V. Mosco & J. Wasko (Eds.), *The critical communications review: Labor, the working class, and the media* (pp. 167–186). Norwood, NJ: Ablex.

15 Oppositional Decoding as an Act of Resistance

LINDA STEINER

A social group can use mass media in a couple of ways to express and dramatize its cultural life, its own definitions, visions, ideals, and frustrations. First, through its own media (newspapers, magazines, etc.), the group can articulate and sustain its cultural identity and styles by addressing its own concerns in its own language. Second, a social group can actively play with the texts of the larger culture, responding to and reworking both positive and negative images of the group in the dominant media. The group here deconstructs in order to reconstruct its own story.

Cultural studies acknowledges both forms of social usage in its concern with the varied ways events and objects can be encoded and decoded. With rare exceptions, however (see Morley, 1980a), media practices of real audience groups are largely ignored. Efforts of social groups to construct emotionally and intellectually satisfying discourses that give meaning and significance to alternative ways of seeing, feeling, and judging are not analyzed nearly so well as the contents and structure of more hegemonic mass media. Moreover, despite theoretic prohibitions against reducing texts to producers' conscious intentions, most communication research concentrates on relationships of texts and authors, not texts and readers.

In this essay, I focus on the interaction of encoding and decoding by describing a social group's creative reworking of already constructed but still polysemic texts distributed by the dominant culture. The object of analysis is *Ms.* magazine's "No Comment" section, which reprints items about women that readers submit from "outside" media. *Ms.* readers present these items as messages that are neither merely what they seem to be nor politically innocent. Instead, they judge these items to debase or devalue women, to rhetorically construct "women" as not only different from but also less than "men." *Ms.* readers articulate their own cultural style and identity, in part, by pointing to these examples of styles and identities they repudiate.

Specifically, I regard the "No Comment" department as reflecting what Stuart Hall (1980b) calls "oppositional" reading. *Ms.* readers call attention to "No Comment" items in ways not encoded by their producers, precisely to make the point that *Ms.* readers are not the women inscribed in dominant media. But bracketing these items does not simply recast what readers take to be their intended meanings. It repudiates them. My view is that the very act of capturing these texts and setting them in an oppositional frame is an act of resistance. After describing the kinds of subjects typically held up for scrutiny in "No Comment," I speculate on why this symbolic resistance is important to *Ms.* readers as a social group. Finally, I discuss what this implies for our understanding of the communication process.

OPPOSITIONAL DECODING

I understand communication to be a ritual process for articulating, transforming, and maintaining a social group's culture (Carey, 1975). Yet I take very seriously Hall's view (1980b, p. 128) of communication as a "complex structure in dominance." While Hall's references to "coding" and to the linked moments of the production, circulation, and consumption circuit seem more mechanistic than necessary and harken back to the very transmission definitions I want to avoid, Hall is correct to focus on language as the primary mediator between cultural texts and their social contexts, and on signs as a principal arena of struggle.

Hall begins, and ends, with the polysemic nature of signs. Producing meaning, he argues, is not a politically neutral practice; dominant power structures invariably try to influence signification, but success is not guaranteed. Dominant media provide sets of "preferred" readings that audiences tend to use in making meanings. Focusing on television messages, Hall and his colleagues (1977, p. 53) state that several meanings are delivered, but one is preferred and is offered to the viewers over the others as the most appropriate. These privileged readings do not wholly determine response, however. Oppositional readings continually contest the dominant ideology.

In "Encoding/Decoding," Hall (1980b) focuses mostly on how encoders seek to win assent to readings within the dominant ideology and devotes only the last paragraph (pp. 137–138) to oppositional decoding. While Hall implies that oppositional practices are insignificant and atypical, he concedes that a viewer might well understand the literal and the connotative inflection given by a discourse but decode the message in a globally contrary way: "He/she detotalizes the message in the preferred code in order to retotalize the message within some alternative framework of reference" (p. 138).

Robinson (1983, p. 322) takes more seriously the potential for interpreting media texts oppositionally: "My own assumption is that the range of possible reactions is a great deal wider than our mechanical metaphors would imply." She suggests that audiences may transform messages to provide social alternatives or to solve problems in ways that are very different from those suggested by the media. People also may resist the media, either by withdrawing from their assigned role as consumers or by actively struggling against the ideas and images projected.

We need not merely assume that resistance occurs; we can locate it in practices, such as in "No Comment." Moreover, television texts are not uniquely polysemic or uniquely resisted and repudiated. To understand how audiences accept or resist media, we should look neither to the individual viewer (which leads to the deterministic psychologizing of the uses and gratifications approach) nor to the masses (which, in the effects approach, simplistically empowers the text). Rather, we should look to the social group. We all recode messages we contest, dislike, or do not want to hear as we think they are intended. But it is the group, in its own communication, that publicly challenges preferred readings, uncovering hidden structures, implicit mythologies, and naturalized ideological operations, albeit within the framework of its own structures, mythologies, and ideology.

Reading is technically a private, solitary act, but subscribing to a magazine such as *Ms.*, self-consciously addressed to a specific community, is communal. Recent literary critics such as Fish (1980) emphasize that readers construct meaning according to assumptions and strategies they adopt by virtue of their participation in a specific interpretive community. Such reading is one of the ways that geographically separated people sustain "communities of sentiment" (Steiner, 1983).[1] What appears in "No Comment," then, is not the result of individual self-serving, idiosyncratic renderings of texts but a collective appropriation of texts from the dominant culture to suit group interests.

I anticipate two potential objections to my analysis. One is my usage of "oppositional." Hall, following Parkin's lead (1971), posits a third, "negotiated" code, which combines adaptive and oppositional elements.[2] According to Hall (1980b, p. 137), the negotiated code privileges dominant definitions but allows for some deviant applications, particularly in relation to the decoder's specific position. Hall states that negotiated decoding generally acknowledges the legitimacy of hegemonic definitions, but at a more situational level "it makes its own ground rules—it operates with exceptions to the rule." Given the spectrum of political philosophies represented among American feminists, I expect criticism for not according *Ms.* readers the more negotiated (co-optable) status. *Ms.* readers, after all, have been belittled as "insufficiently radical" and condemned as "mainstream." The bracketing by *Ms.* readers of every example of exploitation of women's bodies as "sexism" is, however, as oppositional as, to use Hall's example (1980b, p. 138), the British shop steward who interprets every mention on the evening news of "national interest" to mean "class interest." The gender politics of *Ms.* may be middle of the road and its articulation of problems and solutions naive and short-sighted.

As an organ of and for liberal feminists, *Ms.* typically does not challenge hegemonic modes of representation. The political philosophy of *Ms.* reflects both commercial and political considerations and is more broadly and loosely conceived than that expressed in other feminist publications. These factors, however, do not mean that *Ms.* is not feminist. *Ms.* translations and restructurings are consistent repudiations of the ever-gendered meanings, practices, and beliefs of the larger social world. As the expressive organ of a group dedicated to social change that is predicated on the basis of oppositional readings of dominant practices, *Ms.* is oppositional.

A second objection may be my failure to query *Ms.* readers on their thoughts while reading, submitting, or rereading these "No Comment" items. The reprinting of items without explicit comment suggests readers' certainty that none of them will mistake that the items devalue women. (On occasion, particularly insulting passages are underlined or circled.) From their vantage point, providing "explanations" would only compound the injury. Their silence about the items is therefore significant. *Ms.* readers take for granted that the contents are transparent, not hollow, already very much filled in by the dominant ideology.[3] Ironically, they probably seriously overestimate the effects of these messages. The fact that the items generate unintended decodings is a clue that they are not as powerful as the readers suppose. In any case, a shared response is more likely because what is taken to be problematic about these items has already been denaturalized by and for this particular interpretive community. The meanings of discrete items become more obvious when wrenched from their original contexts and combined over time. Liberal feminists typically prefer to isolate individual instances of discrimination and inequality, taking them to be symbolic of and complicit with general social valuations of women, rather than to critique an entire structure of relations. Not surprisingly then, *Ms.* readers ignore what might be salient about the relationship of these elements to the structure of their original context. But, while readers' responses may differ in kind and intensity, the page can be taken as a fairly straightforward representation of the concerns of a specific community. Magazines that dramatize a highly specific, defined world view are analytically interesting and sociologically powerful for precisely this reason. Finally, if indeed *Ms.* represents its audience and if "No Comment" carries obvious import for its readership, then I need not claim superior insight in order to understand readers' responses.

"NO COMMENT"

Ms. magazine, published monthly since it first appeared in 1972, was cofounded as a feminist magazine by Gloria Steinem and Patricia Carbine. Its circulation is 490,000 (small relative to a mainstream magazine like *U.S. News and World Report*, whose circulation is over 2 million). Recently, *Ms.* seems to be trying to attract a larger (and perhaps less ideologically committed) audience. From its beginning, however, *Ms.* has employed dominant coding strategies. It never looked out of place displayed at the corner drugstore. More articles now emphasize achieving personal growth, managing finances, and dressing for success, and fewer articles promote political activism. A *Washington Monthly* cover story (Milligan, 1986) claimed *Ms.* was nearly indistinguishable from *Cosmopolitan* or *Working Women*. The *Washington Monthly* cover shows photographs of two magazine covers, each featuring actor Richard Gere, and then asks, "Quick! Can you guess which one's *Ms.* and which one's *Playgirl?*" *Ms.* is fairly slick. It is published on glossy paper with sophisticated graphics and expensive-looking advertisements. Still, it can be distinguished from "general" women's magazines, and the staff, though not interested in losing money, does seem sincere in its claim that it is at one with its middle class liberal feminist audience and that the magazine's primary ambition is to serve that community.

The "No Comment" section first appeared in September 1972 (the magazine's third issue) and was a monthly feature until 1982. For 10 years, 6 to 12 items were displayed on one or two pages toward the back of each issue. Since then, it has appeared infrequently and in a different format, although a staff researcher says that entries sent to the New York office could fill up the entire magazine each month (Linda Bennett, *Ms.* staff member, personal communication, March 12, 1986). "No Comment" credits both the readers who provide the materials and the original sources.[4] To the extent it provides access to readers, the "No Comment" section may be seen as part of an attempt to operate the magazine oppositionally. At the least, it is consistent with the magazine's resistance to highly sophisticated (patriarchal) bureaucratic hierarchies. Often many readers submit the same item. For example, over 40 people (March 1977, p. 112) submitted a quote by General William Westmoreland, originally published in *Parade* and *The Family Weekly*, criticizing women for attending West Point and thus depriving men of positions there.

Items originate in a wide range of sources though the department focuses primarily on print ads. Other sources include medical journals, large and small newspapers, textbooks from several fields, office manuals from several industries, business letters and memos, mail-order catalogs, books, and dictionaries, as well as photographs of billboards, signs, and posters. For example, an August 1980 page (p. 96) includes an excerpt from a computer textbook, an article from the *Oregonian* of Portland, an ad from *The Citizen* of Ottawa, and an ad from *The Salt Lake Tribune* reading "DAD, KIDS—COME BOWL A LINE! (while mom prepares dinner)." The very diversity of sources gives evidence that *Ms.* women read everything from computer texts to *The Salt Lake Tribune*. This is a point of pride to *Ms.*, which claims to attract and speak for large numbers of feminists who manage to live various (other) roles.

"Men's" magazines and hard-core pornography are virtually ignored, although "No Comment" has reprinted vulgar photographs and references from advertising, billboards, and, especially, record album covers. Presumably, *Ms.* readers do object to *Genesis* and *Hustler*, since feminists are very concerned with the brutal nastiness of pornographic magazines. They direct their critical energies, however, toward transforming the practices of more visible or widely accepted mainstream media aimed at either large heterogeneous or more specialized, but not oppositional, audiences. They recognize that if changes in national status are marked by representations in dominant mass media, the more crucial challenge is monitoring *Family Weekly* where reigning understandings of hierarchies of power and status are embedded. Notably, in light of liberal feminists' belief that the power structure dares not mock or insult blacks the way it does women, "No Comment" presents nothing demeaning black women.[5]

"No Comment" items are juxtaposed ahistorically and without regard for the differing degrees to which they articulate oppressive systems. Many items rely on double entendres, puns, and sexually loaded variations of classic aphorisms. Other items suggest a more straightforward interpretation, perhaps challenging readers to understand the items' ideological implications. For example, the February 1980 issue (p. 104) includes an advertisement for a furniture refinishing company which purrs, "It happened in the boss' office, overnight, without removing a thing!" But next to it is an ad boasting that a $30 handkerchief is "Made of linen in China by young girls whose eyesight was permanently impaired by the fineness of the work."

Perhaps readers "get" the jokes in some messages but still view these messages as evidence of men's continuing insensitivity. And readers may decode these messages even more radically, discovering in them the oppressive structures of capitalistic patriarchy. Readers may recognize that producers' intentions are themselves slippery, that the complex texts cannot be reduced to a single meaning. *Ms.* readers do not care to critique the whys and hows of these items. They simply regard *what* they consistently find as insulting and insidious. If anything strikes them as remarkable, it is the extent of oppression and its location as revealed in the geography, class, and social interests reflected in the items. That is, despite this admixture of images and the ambiguity about the specific interpretations of individual readers, "No Comment" pages provide evidence of a shared map of meaning that enables relatively coherent and stable, if unspoken, responses for the group. To put the case more strongly: given the audience's commitment to a feminist discourse and the magazine's status as a relatively specialized magazine (compared to *Newsweek*), *Ms.*, as Hall uses the term, "prefers" new decodings that are not those authorized by their original producers but that most *Ms.* readers probably accept.

Ms. readers sense that most mass media consumers seeing the messages in their original context will not be offended, will not particularly attend to them, and may even be amused by or applaud their sentiment. As obviously wrong as the items seem to feminist readers, these meanings either will not be obvious or will appear natural and commonsensical to audiences using the intended coding. The dominant encoding actually prefers that the meanings it gives to "woman" not be analyzed or critiqued but only be taken as natural. This is what *Ms.* readers refuse to do. For *Ms.* readers, the very act of capturing and exposing images from the "outside" contests and resists what "they" say about "us."

Submitters and readers need not analyze, describe, or even categorize the items because *Ms.*' women and men (to be sure, the *Ms.* community includes men) are expected to comprehend them instantly. For example, a Department of the Army Field Manual (April 1976, p. 104) advises soldiers to treat natives as human beings and to "respect personal property, especially their women." Perhaps, if asked to voice their own interpretation, *Ms.* readers would decode this as "the United States government treats women as property." Within their own community, however, there would be no need to speak what is immediately known. More significantly, the absence of explicit markings on the problematic aspects of these messages lets readers feel superior because they have understood what outsiders missed. Lastly, the absence of categories and analysis forces neither readers nor staff to issue (or argue about) pretentious, heavy-handed ideological statements. *Ms.* readers who want to claim a sense of humor can still respond occasionally with a laugh, albeit a laugh tinged with horror or bitterness.

The double decoding by the *Ms.* audience has itself been normalized, routinized, ritualized. If the audience needs not be self-conscious about its specific code, it knows its shared ideological maps fundamentally contest the maps of the dominant social order and that its decoding system flaunts licensed readings.

PATTERNS IN "NO COMMENT"

Examination of a decade of monthly entries suggests that most items feature one of a limited number of general themes. A frequent theme is that women are defined as men's property. For example, 26 readers objected strongly enough to an advertisement in *The Washingtonian Magazine* to submit it to "No Comment" (March 1982, p. 74). A banner across the top of the ad proclaims, "BURGLARS DON'T ALWAYS TAKE WHAT YOU WANT THEM TO." A photograph shows a middle-aged matron, in curlers and dowdy chenille bathrobe, gagged and tied to a chair. Nearby is a desk, with one drawer open, having apparently been emptied. The text at the bottom of the ad reiterates: "Unfortunately, when a burglar strikes he always winds up taking your most valuable items and leaves behind the items you wouldn't mind doing without. Protect your home and belongings with the best security system available. . . ." The ad is ambiguous on whether or not the woman literally belongs to the man, but presumably she is something he "wouldn't mind doing without." Whether because she is female or because she is matronly, she is less "valuable" than whatever was stolen. The ad implies that men decide what to protect and how, although it is unclear whether this is because they are men or because they are smarter. (The ad also suggests that burglars are male.) Thus, while this text is perhaps unusually polysemic, a primary thrust has been preferred.

Some items value women more highly than does the security system advertisement. One such ad (September 1976, p. 115), for Knights of Columbus Insurance, is headlined, "Priceless Possessions . . . Your Wife and Children." Presumably, this ad cues men to make responsible decisions about insurance and other important issues, but feminists decode the ad as cuing men to objectify women. The text adds, "No one can place a price tag on your wife's time as she works as homemaker, nurse, cook, hostess, purchasing agent and business secretary." Perhaps Brother Knights are touched by the sentimental text and photograph of mother and children, but the language inflating mothers' responsibilities is, at best, a patronizing sop. Items in other ways define women in terms of their husbands. A news article (March 1980, p. 89) about a state representative who (along with her female flight instructor) survived a plane crash is introduced by the headline, "Drew Lewis' Wife Survives Crash." Items ostensibly advertising restaurants, bars, and dry cleaners invite men to regard their wives as things they can exchange, sell, use, and abuse.

Mocking or condemning feminism is another offensive theme. Readers collected a dozen headlines that either assert that "Women's Lib is Dead" (from *Educational Digest*), or rhetorically ask "Is feminism finished?" (*Mademoiselle*). *Ms.* readers reject the claim that the women's movement is dead and reject *Time* and *Newsweek* as legitimate coroners. More extreme language proclaimed the message on a sign outside a Denver church (February 1976, p. 102): "ADAMS RIB, PLUS SATANS FIB EQUALS WOMANS LIB [*sic*]."

While *Ms.* does not challenge advertising in principle, it does challenge the use of women's bodies in ways that are irrelevant to the product or service, that trivialize women, or that suggest social acceptance of sexual exploitation *Ms.* readers find objectionable. For example, a vacuum cleaner ad (January 1982, p. 103) features two buxom women, one wearing a t-shirt that says "FAST" and the other a t-shirt saying "BEST." The women serve only to attract attention; they are textually silent. More often, narrative materials further exploit women's bodies, often with sexual suggestions. A large percentage of such items use double entendres and sexually loaded puns (especially, but not always, to sell goods and services) or make jokes about women's bodies. These references objectify women in terms of sexuality, identifying women's gender with sex, and then invite men to enjoy or consume women's bodies. A sign (March 1977, p. 112) in a Long Island butcher's window reads, "IF YOUR HUSBAND IS A BREAST OR LEG MAN, ASK FOR MY CHICKEN PARTS." A hardware company flyer (December 1978, p. 103) features a woman in a bikini provocatively posed on top of a large tool chest. She murmurs, "THE BOX I'M SITTING ON IS BIG ENOUGH TO HOLD YOUR LARGEST

TOOL." And a notice (August 1979, p. 100) tacked to a hotel room bar announces: "This Servi Bar is sealed and virginal. But you don't have to marry it—just break seal and enjoy."

Some items present wild ideas about women and sexuality as scientific theory. What is problematic in these items is how so-called experts, always male, use the authority of science against women. An author in *Review of Medical Physiology* (November 1977, p. 102) calls menstruation "the uterus crying for lack of a baby." An article (July 1979, p. 100) from *Child Abuse and Neglect* explicitly blames wives for incest: wives actively encourage incest to compensate for their own promiscuity, or they precipitate incest by frustrating men sexually. An article (January 1977, p. 97) published in *Rehabilitation Literature* defends scientists' failure to study the sexual difficulties of women with spinal injuries on the grounds that because women are sexually passive these victims may lack feeling but can still "function." Although some items inscribe a lusty woman enormously interested in sex, *Rehabilitation Literature* is not unique in implying that for women not to enjoy sex is no great loss. Some items are bracketed because *Ms.* readers find them all too true. For example, an ad (February 1976, p. 102) for contraceptive foam warns, "It's up to the woman to keep love beautiful."

Other items particularly ugly, and frequent, suggest either that women enjoy sexual abuse or violence or that beating women is fun and unproblematic. Readers discover a lot of stylized but virulent brutality against women celebrated on album jackets. A billboard (May 1977, p. 99) promoting a Rolling Stones album features a woman, chained with legs spread, announcing, "I'm 'Black and Blue' from The Rolling Stones—and I love it!" The sign, however, testifies to someone's anger at its sexual politics. A handwritten inscription, "This is a crime against women," runs across its face. The common notion in the dominant code that joking about domestic violence is acceptable is aggressively demonstrated in a bowling alley ad (July 1973, p. 100) that recommends, in huge block letters, "HAVE SOME FUN. BEAT YOUR WIFE TONIGHT." And newspaper clippings, both American and foreign, detail how men were acquitted of murdering their wives because they had good reasons (an improperly cooked dinner, a late breakfast) or were acquitted of rape or other violent acts because they had explanations that a male judge accepted. Other items make light of rape in still other ways.

Some items highlight men's domination of various social institutions, especially those liberal feminists regard as high status and those aimed at women. For example, an *Advertising Age* photograph (April 1982, p. 80) of representatives of seven major women's magazines shows 11 men in business suits. It surprises no feminist that magazines like *Woman's Day* and *Ladies Home Journal* are managed by men, that men presume to speak for women and control their communication channels.

Another issue is gender stereotyping of adults and children. For example, a *New York Times* article (May 1982, p. 100), unusual only because it was submitted by a *Ms.* staff member, reports on a museum tour where girls see dollhouses while boys visit a fort. Trivializing notions of femininity are clearly enforced at a very early age, as indicated by a clipping about a 4-year-old girl chosen to be "Little Miss America" based on her looks. Other items further insinuate that girls are lesser humans than boys. A military chapel newsletter (March 1974, p. 108) boasts of its new altar servers, who elevate the chapel over "some less fortunate parishes and military posts [that] have had to resort to girls." A brochure (November 1979, p. 117) for the Ace Telephone Association argues the benefits of speaker phones: the lady of the house might use it when holding the baby or stirring a pot and men when taking extensive notes on an important call.

Some items explicitly call women stupid or silly. One ad (June 1975, p. 110) reads, "We taught our data entry system to speak a new language: Dumb Blond [*sic*]." The picture above the text shows lips, heavy with lipstick and puckered. This text not only blatantly defines women as dumb, but also, in addressing itself to male customers, excludes women.

Items often trivialize or undermine women's work and accomplishments (especially the responsibilities or careers typically seen as "women's work") or conversely, assign credit for meaningful or hard work entirely to men. Nothing is wrong with a report (October 1978, p. 104) about female officers working at New York toll crossings, but the headline is "Tollhouse Cookies on [the] Way." Help wanted items often deny that women can perform as well as men. A newspaper ad (April 1981, p. 102) for an office manager, described a "very good job for a retired man or energetic woman." One "No Comment" page (April 1976, p. 105) has six items implying that fathers are more important than mothers in the birth process. For example, the San Francisco *Examiner* announces the new births by the father's name only; a mock theatrical birth announcement, advertised in a crafts catalog, lists the father as "producer" and the mother as "associate." *Ms.* translates such "cuteness" as denigrating the mother's role in childbirth.

Ms. readers do not take strong stands against corporate hierarchy or status distinctions, but they do oppositionally bracket items that legitimate differential privileges along gender lines. For example, a business memo (August 1976, p. 102) announces that male employees have an hour for lunch, women a half-hour. Likewise, a Tucson paper reports (June 1975, p. 110) why a (male) Welsh darts league banned women's teams: "If the wives get into the league, who is to stop [*sic*] at home to look after the children?" the league president whines. *Ms.* reads this as demonstrating a pattern of husbands enjoying privileges denied wives.

Finally, "No Comment" implicitly ridicules the generic use of male pronouns, a practice that is seen as particularly ironic when the referent is logically female. For example, an Ohio General Assembly house bill (February 1975, p. 93) states, "NO PERSON MAY REQUIRE ANOTHER PERSON TO . . . UNDERGO AN ABORTION OF PREGNANCY, AGAINST HIS WILL."

In sum, the key concepts reflected in the items are asymmetry, bias, inequity, discrimination, and difference. Liberal feminists provide no overall critique of advertising agencies, businesses, schools, governmental units, or churches, much less of industrial capitalism, democracy, or secular religion. What *Ms.* readers do is catalog ways that major institutions, even in the twentieth century, unabashedly treat women as less intelligent, less creative, and less worthy than men—a pattern of essentializing women in terms of sex.

OTHER FEMINIST RESPONSES

Ms. is not the first feminist periodical to reprint comments about women from dominant media. Nineteenth century suffrage periodicals such as Elizabeth Cady Stanton and Susan B. Anthony's *Revolution* regularly included "Straws in the Wind" and "What They Say About Us" in order to mark shifts, or the lack thereof, in the status of the nascent breed of strong-minded women (Steiner, 1983).

A major thrust of the post-1960s women's liberation movement has been to indict mass media representations of women as false and demeaning. Feminists have published media criticisms and have picketed magazine offices, burned pornographic materials, and boycotted advertisers. Gloria Steinem (1981, p. 111), who wrote for television and for several national publications before co-founding *Ms.*, says she still spends hours composing mental letters to the editor and "talking back to the TV."

Robinson (1983, p. 308) claims early feminists' concern with media images influenced an entire spectrum of social movements. Whether or not feminists pioneered in this, various political, social, and cultural movements have been consistently and intensely concerned with mass mediated images of their goals and memberships, and analogous characterizations are often contested by other groups: For example, blacks and the elderly also resent being seen as irrational, weak, and stupid.

More recently, *New Woman* (September–October 1976, p. 9), a bimonthly magazine, has invited readers to submit quotations for its "Swap the Old Lady for a New Woman" page. Quotes, nearly always from well-known people, are divided into three sections: "Sounds Like an Old Lady" (Prince Rainier: "I must be the boss, or else I'm not a man"); "Sounds Like a New Woman" (Karen Black: "Strong men prefer strong women. It's only the sloshy ones who are afraid of being dominated by a woman"); and "Thump on the Head to" (Oregon Governor Bob Straub: "There's only two things wrong with women: Everything they do and everything they say"). If readers have submitted these, however, they are not so credited, and *New Woman* privileges the expressions of celebrities. More importantly, because items are not reprinted from originals, they lack compelling graphics.

In 1980, *Ms.* also established "One Step Forward" for reader-submitted items that "prove change possible—and keep optimism alive." The inaugural page spotlighted "positive images of grown-ups and children," according to a brief introduction by editor Letty Cottin Pogrebin (December 1980, p. 108). The feature, however, seldom appears. Perhaps readers locate little proof of progress. More likely, readers are not inspired to submit these items because they experience greater ambiguity about what constitutes improvement.

DECODING AND GROUP IDENTITY

Hall does not bother with why a particular community might commit itself to an oppositional code, nor does he speculate on how a group might experience itself having done so. Still, it is a topic that invites speculation. Why do readers choose to attend to markers of their low social status and of their status as sexual objects and to the hegemonic structures responsible for maintaining that status?

In celebrating the fifth anniversary of *Ms.*, the staff itself acknowledged the immense popularity of "No Comment" when it introduced a kind of "No Comment" olympics. Here the editors awarded prizes to personal favorites. For example, their Ayn Rand Free Enterprise Award went to designer Bill Blass, who justified his line of genital deodorants: "Honey, if there's a part of the human body to exploit, you might as well get into it." The editors (July 1977, p. 48) suggested, "Perhaps the sight of this nutty or enraging stuff in a feminist context is a relief in itself. Perhaps a reader's act of mailing it off to a sympathetic place is a minor catharsis."

Reclaiming and sharing insulting texts may have other purposes besides therapy. Most centrally, the activity gives shape and meaning to group experiences, symbolically marking the group's normative boundaries and reconfirming its convictions and commitments. The group must demarcate its world view from that of the dominant culture. The newly produced texts both violate the dominant code and, by extension, the value system it sustains. They also produce and nourish alternative codes and values. If *Ms.* magazine as a whole forms the group's prayer, then "No Comment" is its cursing. *Ms.* shows that constructions of reality have an actively reactive element, dramatizing worlds in which we refuse to dwell. "No Comment" itself may even remind readers that at some point they might have identified with "them" and so decoded according to "their" rules. "No Comment" constitutes a fairly comprehensive definition of who readers are not and what *Ms.* will not say in its own ads. The framing of these examples asserts that the *Ms.* woman is not stupid; she is not her husband's property; she does not measure herself by breast size; and she does not sell her body. Engaging in oppositional practice articulates and dramatizes an oppositional identity.

"No Comment" also serves the readers' community by encouraging converts to continue to believe in and work actively for their oppositional vision. Although collecting such materials might seem discouraging, this is crucial now that certain goals have been accomplished but so integrated into the fabric of the dominant culture that feminists' work is either forgotten or rendered invisible. The items provide visible evidence for the readers' sense of continuing oppression. As visible data, they provide a focus for resistance. Engaging in symbolic repudiation is both a part of the feminist identity and an inspiration for further commitment. Nevertheless, I do not regard this practice of decoding and recoding as pleasurable. To call attending to nasty insults "enjoyable" trivializes both political commitment and the notion of pleasure.

"No Comment" reconfirms the point that messages which violate women's sense of dignity and integrity are not limited to overtly pornographic magazines. Rather, "political pornography" is readily available, in rural newspapers, family magazines, and mail-order catalogs. The more salient political battles actually must be waged against and within these arenas. These items corroborate feminists' belief that dominant mass media do ideological work and that, regardless of media effects in the behavioral sense, mainstream content must be contested.

Oppositional decoding does not directly change the encoding or decoding performed under dominant rules. Coding systems are still very unequal in their abilities to privilege meanings for society. "No Comment" decoding hardly constitutes a "dialogue." Nor do resistant readers claim that their community-shared deconstructions materially affect dominant practices. Still, they can argue that such oppositional strategies work to shape and sustain their social identity and that a thereby strengthened social group can take up more effective interventions. Challenging and transforming ideological systems cannot occur without such access and commitment to an alternative, oppositional definition of reality.

The oppositional decoding of "No Comment," it must be added, differs somewhat from the decoding described by Radway (1984). Radway persuasively argues that the patriarchal surface of romance novels conceals a womanly subtext that women readers can interpret against the grain. More importantly, she sees time spent reading romances as potentially oppositional because it allows women to refuse momentarily the other-directed, self-abnegating role prescribed for them by the dominant patriarchal culture; the practice of reading romances is both combative and compensatory. Although the plots also may have some oppositional elements, Radway (p. 190) concedes that romance readers "rely on standard cultural codes correlating signifiers and signified that they accept as definitive." "No Comment," on the other hand, is oppositional neither because it allows subversive readings against the grain nor because it allows readers time for their private purposes. It involves both socialized, not privatized, acts of reading and the texts themselves, which, as texts usually addressed to men, are captured and communally repudiated.

CONCLUSION

Various transmission definitions of mass communication still in vogue assume a generally effective linear movement of discrete content from professional sources to receivers separated by time and space and only vaguely connected in the reverse by a feedback loop. Such definitions cannot account for the case of "No Comment," where a community understands messages delivered by various sources but reconstitutes those messages in its own terms, in the process of constructing and maintaining a uniquely, if only partially, satisfying and meaningful world. Although I have focused on a set of texts whose precise meanings from and to readers cannot be elaborated, it reminds us that an audience's symbolic activity should not be ignored.

I also have emphasized that cultural expression is not simply positive but also reactive, that communication involves struggle and power. It occurs within a larger social order which, while not wholly determining, works very hard to achieve hegemony. Cultural expression is not only a process by which we symbolically construct meaningful identities and worlds but also a rejection of who we are not and a repudiation of worlds in which we do not want to live.

More centrally for my purposes, the decoding and recoding in "No Comment" further illustrates the fruitfulness of Hall's notion (1980b) of oppositional code. Granted, besides the mechanistic language already noted, certain problems remain. Streeter (1984) criticizes Hall for not distinguishing his two uses of the term "oppositional code." In one sense, oppositional decoding represents an alternative interpretation from an opposing framework that individually supplants every dominant meaning with an alternative. In another sense, Hall denies the validity of a one-for-one substitution in order to bring to the foreground what the oppositional decoding otherwise leaves in the background.

Wren-Lewis (1983) mounts a more serious attack on Morley's application (1980a) of the Parkin-Hall model for audience decoding. (Morley himself raised some of these issues in his 1981 "Critical Postscript."[6]) Wren-Lewis suggests that Morley imposed his own decoding categories on both the content of the codes and the audience's socioeconomic structure and argues for the interviewing of decoders individually in order to understand intersubject differences. He correctly emphasizes that television is a signifying practice that produces meaning, rather than a secondary sign-fixing practice that only reproduces meaning.

Since I have not undertaken a reader ethnography, I can say nothing about variations in the basic oppositional recodings of an interpretive community. Media, however, are all primary practices that require "context" before "content" becomes meaningful, even though they may vary in the ways they open and close off audience interpretation. Precisely what makes "No Comment" interesting is the difficulty of distinguishing encoding and decoding in this practice. Readers are not only decoding, they are also recoding and decoding again. We should take seriously the notion that the meanings of texts are not set into place in some final, finite way just because they have been set into print. "No Comment" is not simply silent commentary about other people's meanings. It is a new text.

The temporally situated nature of readers' ongoing engagement with *Ms.* and "No Comment" is important. As readers teach themselves strategies for reading mass mediated messages (i.e., here, from the vantage of feminism), they grow more sophisticated in discovering and denaturalizing coded references to their own symbolic status. They may rethink old responses.

One issue not yet resolved is the distinction and connection of oppositional and negotiated codes. Hall (1980b, p. 138) suggests, "One of the most significant political moments . . . is the point when events which are normally signified and decoded in a negotiated way begin to be given an oppositional reading." Knowing what precipitates code changes might enable members of social groups to anticipate the possibility of co-optation. An in-depth examination and comparison of the texts of various groups across time and space may help indicate when or why a social group might change strategy. Such comparison also may reveal whether formulations of oppositional codes are consistent across groups, whether such formulations reconstitute parallel images or serve parallel values. And to understand readings preferred by alternative media, the example of "No Comment" implies attending to the relation of oppositional encoding and oppositional decoding.

Finally, I return to the importance of social group communication. Not every narrowcast cable television show or specialized magazine can be seen as sincerely emerging from and for a coherent cultural group, but studies of texts and contexts, of audience engagement with its own cultural materials, may bear witness to cultural communities that practice communication in different ways. Specifically, these may reveal surprising degrees of resistance to and active repudiation of apparently hegemonic ideology. Radway (1986, p. 97) states:

> . . . If mass culture does indeed allow for differential interpretation and use, if particular groups can adapt messages designed by others for their own purposes, it is conceivable that the ideological control achieved by any particular mass culture form may not be complete. . . . They might also successfully use those forms to analyze their material situation and to express their discontent with it.

We need not so pessimistically concede unitary effects of mass media on mass audiences. Indeed, even if the educational apparatus, reinforced by mainstream mass media, generally favors hegemonic meaning systems, looking at alternative publications may suggest how to teach oppositional and critical thinking.

NOTES

1. This contradicts the reasoning of an otherwise persuasive article contrasting romance novels and soap operas as resistive practices. Brown (1987) argues that soaps are more shared and communal than romances, which are consumed silently and individually.
2. Within the hegemonic code there is also a professional subcode, characterized by an ongoing attempt at neutrality and objectivity but ultimately supporting the dominant code.
3. In McLuhan's terms, the messages in their original contexts are "hot," thus enabling their "cool" reframing.
4. Staff researcher Linda Bennett explained (personal communication, March 12, 1986) that the sheer volume of entries requires editors to make a selection. But, according to Bennett, the staff has no criteria and no policy dictating the selection process. Nor do they keep records on what was submitted and published. And since "No Comment" is no longer a regular feature, no on-site observation of the selection process can now be done.
5. These patterns may perhaps be explained in other ways, that is, that women read pornography but do not want to admit it (although I doubt that *Ms.* readers would be ashamed of this). On the other hand, the absence of items featuring blacks, in part, may reflect the infrequency with which *Ms.* readers attend to black newspapers and magazines. I also doubt that it is a matter of the editorial process in New York. Given their willingness to use sexually explicit materials from other sources (like record covers), I doubt *Ms.* editors are averse to reprinting materials from pornographic magazines. Nor is there reason to believe that they want to protect against demeaning references to black women.
6. The encoding/decoding model is not perfect, but I believe some other critics (see Stevens, 1978) misunderstand the model and its conception of reading.

REFERENCES

Brown, M. (1987, May). *Questioning the politics of pleasure: Soaps and romance novels.* Paper presented at the International Communication Association, Montreal.

Carey, J. (1975). A cultural approach to communication. *Communication, 2,* 1–22.

Fish, S. (1980). *Is there a text in this class? The authority of interpretive communities.* Cambridge, MA: Harvard University Press.

Hall, S. (1980a). Cultural studies and the centre. In S. Hall, D. Hobson, A. Lowe, & P. Willis (Eds.), *Culture, media, language* (pp. 5–39). London: Hutchinson.

Hall, S. (1980b). Encoding/decoding. In S. Hall, D. Hobson, A. Lowe, & P. Willis (Eds.), *Culture, media, language* (pp. 128–138). London: Hutchinson.

Hall, S., Connell, I., & Curti, L. (1977). The "unity" of current affairs television. *Working Papers in Cultural Studies, 9,* 51–93.

Milligan, S. (1986, October). Has *Ms.* undergone a sex change? *The Washington Monthly,* pp. 17–21.

Morley, D. (1980a). *The "Nationwide" audience: Structure and decoding.* London: British Film Institute.

Morley, D. (1980b). Texts, readers, subjects. In S. Hall, D. Hobson, A. Lowe, & P. Willis (Eds.), *Culture, media, language* (pp. 163–173). London: Hutchinson.

Morley, D. (1981). The "Nationwide" audience: A critical postscript. *Screen Education*, *39*, 3–14.

Parkin, F. (1971). *Class inequality and political order*. London: Macgibbon and Kee.

Radway, J. (1984). *Reading the romance: Woman, patriarchy, and popular literature*. Chapel Hill: University of North Carolina Press.

Radway, J. (1986). Identifying ideological seams: Mass culture, analytic method, and political practice. *Communication*, *9*, 93–123.

Robinson, L. (1983). Women, media, and the dialectics of resistance. In A. Swerdlow & H. Lessinger (Eds.), *Class, race, sex: Dynamics of control* (pp. 308–324). Boston: G. K. Hall.

Steinem, G. (1981, November). Feminist notes: "Night thoughts of a media watcher". *Ms.*, p. 111.

Steiner, L. (1983). Finding community in nineteenth-century suffrage periodicals. *American Journalism*, *1*(1), 1–16.

Stevens, T. (1978). Reading the realist film. *Screen Education*, *26*, 13–34.

Streeter, T. (1984). An alternative approach to television research: Developments in British cultural studies at Birmingham. In W. Rowland & B. Watkins (Eds.), *Interpreting television: Current research perspectives* (pp. 74–97). Beverly Hills: Sage.

Wren-Lewis, J. (1983). The encoding/decoding model: Criticism and redevelopments for research on decoding. *Media, Culture and Society*, *5*, 179–197.

16 Television: Polysemy and Popularity

JOHN FISKE

Critical analysis of television texts has been with us for a number of years now. Early examples of this work, such as those by Hall, Connell, and Curti (1976), Heath and Skirrow (1977), and Brunsdon and Morley (1978) all tended to demonstrate that television was an ideologically closed medium. The thrust of their analyses was to reveal the subtle ways in which the dominant ideology was encoded into the text where it worked upon the viewer to constitute him or her as an Althusserian subject-in-ideology. These analyses and their theoretical origins matched perfectly Althusser's and Gramsci's explanations of the power of late capitalism to reproduce itself in the thought processes and subjectivities of those whose material social position (usually, in these studies, defined in terms of class, gender or race) would be expected to place them in opposition to the dominant ideology.[1]

These theories of ideology-in-the-text and ideology-in-capitalism led to a very subjected view of the subject, whether we conceive of one as a reading subject or a subject-in-ideology. The power of the dominant ideology, whether working textually or socially, to inform the sensemaking processes of its subjects seemed irresistible. As these sense-making processes extended beyond the sense made of texts to include the senses made of self, of social relations and of the social structure at large, television was seen as a homogenizing force whose preferred (and singular) meaning was an example of the way that the dominant ideology worked hegemonically to naturalize itself into the "common sense" of society in general (Brunsdon & Morley, 1978).

The preferred meaning theory elaborated by Hall (1980) challenged this position, but unfortunately remained a theory at the time, untested critically or empirically.[2] Morley (1980), in his watershed study, used empirical means to demonstrate a wide range of audience responses to a single TV program and to show that the audiences' powers to make meanings that suited their social position was far greater than that permitted by Hall's preferred meaning theory. But his work was an audience study. His earlier analysis of the text

346

(Brunsdon & Morley, 1978) was part of the school of Althusserian and Gramscian criticism and thus was not concerned to identify the fissures and excesses in the text that made such polysemic readings possible.

THE POLYSEMIC NECESSITY

The failure of ideological criticism to account for the polysemy of the television text is paralleled by its failure to account for the diversity of Western capitalist societies. Despite generations of life under the hegemony of capitalism there is still a wide range of social groups and subcultures with different senses of their own identity, of their relations to each other and to the centers of power. This diversity shows no signs of being homogenized into the unthinking mass so feared by members of the Frankfurt School, and, in a different way, by the ideological critics of the late 1970s. Rather, divergent and resistant subcultures are alive, well and kicking, and exerting various forms of pressure and criticism upon the dominant ideology of Western capitalist societies.

The main argument of this essay is this: In order to be popular, television must reach a wide diversity of audiences, and, to be chosen by them, must be an open text (Eco, 1979) that allows the various subcultures to generate meanings from it that meet the needs of their own subcultural identities. It must therefore be polysemic. But the television text is not anarchically open so that any meaning can be derived from it. The diverse subcultures in a society are defined only by their relations (possibly oppositional) to the centers of domination, so, too, the multiple meanings of a text that is popular in that society can be defined only by their relationships (possibly oppositional) to the dominant ideology as it is structured into that text. The structure of meanings in a text is a miniaturization of the structure of subcultures in society—both exist in a network of power relations, and the textual struggle for meaning is the precise equivalent of the social struggle for power.

Central to this theory is the notion that all television texts must, in order to be popular, contain within them unresolved contradictions that the viewer can exploit in order to find within them structural similarities to his or her own social relations and identity. The emphasis thus differs from Kellner's (1982), who also argues that television is necessarily contradictory, but who finds these contradictions largely in television's total output, that is, between programs that are in themselves essentially monosemic. Where he does find contradictions within a program, such as *Starsky and Hutch*, he claims that they are resolved within the program and not left comparatively open for the viewer's own subcultural sense-making:

> Television mythologies often attempt to resolve social contradictions. For instance, the cop show *Starsky and Hutch* deals with the fundamental American contradiction between the need for conformity and individual initiative, between working in a corporate hierarchy and being an individual. Starsky

and Hutch are at once conventional and hip; they do police work and wear flashy clothes *and* have lots of good times. They show that it is possible to fit into society and not lose one's individuality. The series mythically resolves contradictions between the work ethic and the pleasure ethic, between duty and enjoyment. Television mythology speciously resolves conflicts to enable individuals to adjust. (p. 400)

More recent work by Newcomb (1984) draws fruitfully upon the work of Volosinov (1973) and Bakhtin (1981) to argue persuasively for the multivocal nature of television: "almost every aspect of television draws from the heteroglot environment and contributes to the dialogic nature of the medium" (p. 41). This theory rests on the twin piers of all language (or communication) systems being understood as *heterglot* and *dialogic*. Bakhtin (1981) explains the heteroglossia of language:

> Thus at any given moment of its historical existence, language is heteroglot from top to bottom: it represents the co-existence of socio-ideological contradictions between the present and the past, between differing epochs of the past, between different socioideological groups in the present, between tendencies, schools, circles and so forth, all given a bodily form. These "languages" of heteroglossia intersect each other in a variety of ways, forming new socially typifying "languages." (p. 201)

Newcomb also quotes from Bakhtin's translator-editor, Holquist, to explain the dialogic nature of communication:

> . . . Bakhtin's basic scenario for modeling variety is two actual people talking to each other in a specific dialogue at a particular time and in a particular place. But these persons would not confront each other as sovereign egos capable of sending messages to each other through the kind of uncluttered space envisioned by the artists who illustrate most receiver-sender models of communication.

> Rather, each of the two persons would be a consciousness at a specific point in the history of defining itself through the choice it has made—out of all the possible existing languages available to it at that moment—of a discourse to transcribe its intention *in this specific exchange*. (Bakhtin, 1981, p. xx)

Newcomb (1984) concludes that:

> Language (communication) is both material and social. It is therefore mutable. Makers and users, writers and readers, senders and receivers can do things with communication that are unintended, unplanned for, indeed, unwished for. (p. 38)

He goes on to assert, after Volosinov, that terms (in language) bear the history of social conflict and negotiation and whenever and wherever used they enter that conflict once again.[3] There is no way to predict which aspect of a term will be seized upon by a viewer.

In this essay I agree broadly with Newcomb's theoretical position, but wish to challenge the thrust of his analysis. Newcomb finds most evidence of heteroglossia in the various "languages" (or discourses), often embodied in characters, that go to make up a television program. The dialogue that he traces is primarily one between "languages" in a text, and not between the languages of a text and the viewer. He allows for this, but offers no detailed account of how it might work. I argue that the polysemy of television lies not just in the heteroglossia from which it is necessarily constructed, but in the ways that different socially located viewers will activate its meaning potential differently. Thus, any one utterance can be a member of a number of different "languages": so when a character says, in an assumed southern accent, "Oh, that's the cutest thing you've ever said to me, sugar" (see p. 396) this can be read as part of a traditional chauvinist discourse of gender, or as a more modern, liberated one. We may not be able to predict the actual reading that any one empirical viewer may make, but we can identify the textual characteristics that make polysemic readings possible, and we can theorize the relation between textual structure and social structure that make such polysemic readings necessary. One illustrative aspect of this structural relationship can be understood in terms of authority, and here I wish to exploit the semantic link between author and authority. By using the term I do not intend to extend the fallacy that the notion of an individual, creative author can help us to understand television, but rather to use the notion of the author-in-the-text which works through the form to prefer certain readings and to attempt to impose these upon the reader.[4] This implies a power relationship between text and reader that parallels the relationship between the dominant and subordinate classes in society. In both instances authority attempts to impose itself, but is met with a variety of variously successful strategies of resistance or modification that change, subvert or reject the authoritatively proposed meanings.[5] Grossberg (1984) has identified the strategy of *excorporation* (the opposite of the Frankfurt School's *incorporation*), by which members of subordinate classes can take the cultural products of dominance, turn them against the cultural producers and excorporate them into resisting discourses. My theoretical position differs slightly from Newcomb's (and is, I believe, closer to Volosinov's) in that it stresses that heteroglossia and dialogue can only be understood in terms of power relationships and not just in terms of the social diversity of liberal pluralism.

In the words of Hartley (1984):

> The signifying practice of mainstream, broadcast television is not so much to exploit as to control television's semiotic potential. (p. 134)

or:

> television is a prolific producer of meaningfulness, which it seeks to discipline, by prodigious feats of ideological labor . . . but I have also tried to suggest that television's meaningfulness is, literally, out of control. (p. 137)

Meaning is as much a site of struggle as is economics or party politics, and television attempts (but fails) to control its meaning in the same way that social authority attempts (but fails) to stifle voices and strategies of opposition. It is the polysemy of television that makes the struggle for meaning possible, and its popularity in class structured societies that makes it necessary.

DEMONSTRATION OF IDEOLOGICAL CRITICISM

I propose to take a typical piece of prime time television as my example for analysis. It is a segment of *Hart to Hart* consisting of two short scenes in the first of which the husband and wife detective team, the Harts, discuss ways in which a jewel robbery may have been committed on a cruise liner, and plan to set a trap for the thieves. In the second the villain and villainess plan their next "hit." See Transcript (Figures 1–8).

An ideological analysis would have no difficulty in showing how the various codes of television are working to construct the Harts as embodiments of the dominant ideology, and to swing our affective allegiance towards them, so that hegemonically we are led to accept the point of view that they stand for as the common sense one even if we are not members of the same class, race, age group as they. Technical codes such as lighting, setting, music and camera work all function to make the Harts more attractive than the villain and villainess. Their cabin is lit in a softer, warmer light and is softened and humanized by flowers and drapes. The background music is in a major key when the Harts are on screen, but shifts to a minor for the jewel thieves. The camera treats them with the normal, respectful close-up, rather than the extreme close-up used for the villain and villainess. I have shown elsewhere (Fiske, 1985) that extreme close-ups (ECUs) are conventionally used to construct either villainy or intimacy, depending on the other codes working in their context. Here they are used to connote villainy by bringing us close to the villain so that we can see through his words and expression to the "truth" that lies behind them, not in them. Similarly the dialogue allows the Harts an "attractive" joke and metaphor (of which more later) and their actions and words show them as a couple cooperating together. The villain and villainess, on the other hand, have their dialogue restricted to their criminal plans and are shown disagreeing and physically pulling apart from each other. All these codes are working hegemonically to attract the viewer to adopt the social position whose ideology is embodied by the Harts as the one from which to make sense of the events, and to reward the adoption of this position with the

TRANSCRIPT

SCENE ONE

HERO: He knew what he was doing to get into this safe.

HEROINE: Did you try the numbers that Granville gave you?

HERO: Yeh. I tried those earlier. They worked perfectly.

FIGURE 1

HEROINE: Well you said it was an inside job, maybe they had the combination all the time.

HERO: Just trying to eliminate all the possibilities. Can you check this out for me. (He gestures to his bow tie)

HEROINE: Mm. Yes I can. (He hugs her) Mm. Light fingers. Oh, Jonathon.

FIGURE 2

HERO: Just trying to keep my touch in shape.

HEROINE: What about the keys to the door.

HERO: Those keys can't be duplicated because of the code numbers. You have to have the right machines.

HEROINE: Well, that leaves the window.

HERO: The porthole.

FIGURE 3

HEROINE: Oh yes. The porthole. I know they are supposed to be charming, but they always remind me of a laundromat.

HERO: I took a peek out of there a while ago. It's about all you can do. It's thirty feet up to the deck even if you could make it down to the window, porthole. You'd have to be the thin man to squeeze through.

FIGURE 4

HEROINE: What do you think? (She shows her jewelry) Enough honey to attract the bees?

HERO: Who knows? They may not be able to see the honey for the flowers.

HEROINE: Oh, that's the cutest thing you've ever said to me, Sugar. Well, shall we? (Gestures towards the door).

FIGURE 5

SCENE TWO

VILLAIN: I suppose you noticed some of the icing on Chamberlain's cupcake. I didn't have my jeweler's glass, but that bracelet's got to be worth at least fifty thousand. Wholesale.

VILLAINESS: Patrick, if you're thinking what I know you're thinking, forget it. We've made our quota one hit on each ship. We said we weren't going to get greedy, remember.

FIGURE 6

VILLAIN: But darling, it's you I'm thinking of. And I don't like you taking all those chances. But if we could get enough maybe we wouldn't have to go back to the Riviera circuit for years.

VILLAINESS: That's what you said when we were there.

FIGURE 7

VILLAIN: Well maybe a few good investments and we can pitch the whole bloody business. But we are going to need a bit more for our retirement fund.

FIGURE 8

twin pleasures of recognition and of familiarity with the dominant ideological practice.

The dominant ideology, so this argument runs, informs this text largely through the differences and similarities between hero/ine and villain/ess. As Gerbner (1970) demonstrates, heroes are distinguished from villains largely through their greater attractiveness and greater efficiency: in other characteristics they are remarkably similar.[6] Here the attractiveness of the hero and heroine's mode of representation is supported by the casting. The language and accent of the villain identify him as non-American, probably British (though some viewers have read his swarthy appearance to place him as Hispanic). The villainess, however, is blonde, white American and thus is less "villainous" than he (indeed, she finally repents and helps the Harts to catch the villain). The Harts are, of course, embodiments of American bourgeois appearance, morality and behavior.

The similarities between the hero/ine and the villain/ess are equally, if not more, significant, for they provide not the conflict that is to be resolved in the narrative, but the ideological common ground upon which that narrative is played out, and which is therefore not called into question, but remains at the level of common sense. Thus both sides take for granted that the getting and keeping of wealth is an unquestionable motive for action. Similarly, it is not called into question that in both cabins the men are planning, while the women are prettying themselves.

I cannot leave this type of ideological criticism without demonstrating it working in greater detail on two particularly significant textual devices in this segment.

The first is the porthole/window/laundromat joke, which is used to marshal the viewer's affective sympathy on the side of the hero/ine. But it does more than that. Freud tells us that jokes are used to relieve the anxiety caused by repressed, unwelcome or taboo meanings. This joke revolves around the "feminine" (as defined by our dominant culture) inability to understand or use technical language, and the equally "feminine" tendency to make sense of everything through domestic discourse. "Porthole" is technical discourse—masculine. "Window-laundromat" is domestic-nurturing discourse—feminine. The anxiety that the joke relieves is that caused by the fact that the heroine is a detective, is involved in the catching of criminals—activities that are part of the technical world of men in patriarchy. The joke is used to recuperate contradictory signs back into the dominant system, and to smooth over any contradictions that might disrupt the ideological homogeneity of the narrative. The fact that the joke is so feeble implies, as I shall argue later, that this ideological work is always less than fully effective, and that it necessarily leaves gaps for resisting readers to exploit.

The second device is that of jewelry. The getting and keeping of jewelry is the motor of the narrative. Jewelry operates within at least three interlocking discourses—those of economics, taste and gender and the cumulative meanings of these three merge unproblematically into the discourse that dominates the next level up in realism's "hierarchy of discourses" (MacCabe, 1981), that of class.

In the discourse of economics, the villain/ess stress the investment/exchange function of jewelry—"it's worth fifty thousand wholesale," it forms "a retirement fund." For the hero/ine, and in particular for the wealthy cruise passengers for whom they are metonyms, this function is left exnominated: for them, as for their class, jewelry is typically an investment to hold, not to exchange or cash in. It provides security rather than a coin of exchange—a class difference in the meanings within the economic discourse. The discourse of taste demonstrates class differences even more clearly. The heroine deliberately overdoes the jewelry, producing a vulgar, ostentatious effect in order for it to be meaningful within the lower class discourse of the villain/ess and thus be an effective bait for them. They, in their turn, liken it to the icing on a cupcake, foregrounding their inability to appreciate its aesthetic qualities. And as Bourdieu (1968) and others have shown us, the function of good taste in our society is to naturalize class differences, by displacing class-based differences of meaning onto the physical natural of the body (notice the metaphor of "taste" with its vehicle of the natural senses). Thus the different class tastes of the "cultured" classes are presented as functions of their "naturally" finer sensitivities and discriminatory abilities.

The meaning of jewelry in the discourse of gender is clear. Jewels are the coins by which the female commodity is bought, and wearing them constructs her as a sign that she is a male's possession.

Interestingly, in the discourse of gender there is no real class difference between hero/ine and villain/ess—the economics of patriarchy are the same, even to the extent of disguising their ideological naturalizing of the "fact" that man provides for "his" woman. We must also note here, that the narrative distinction between hero/ine and villain/ess is not made in class terms, but in terms of morality—the distinction between good and bad. This displacement of social differences into moral differences is typical ideological practice in popular television, and is repeated in the discourse of race/nation: the non-American villain is morally worse than the American villainess. The events of the narrative—the victory of the heroes, the death of the non-American, the survival of the Aryan—prove the morality and justify the way it displaces class and race/nation as markers of the narrative frame that surrounds, but is outside, the conflict-to-be-resolved.

A critical practice that goes no further than this is one hide-bound by the limits of the Frankfurt School or of the 1970s ideological criticism, both of which model the viewer as powerless, in the one case in the face of the manipulations of the producers in the culture industry, and in the other in the face of the authority of the text to construct a reading position for its subjects. The implication of this position is that texts such as this propagate American patriarchal capitalism internally and internationally and exert the irresistible hegemonic force of the dominant culture.

An inherent weakness of this model is its inability to accommodate either the possibility of social change or a theory of popularity that is capable of conceptualizing "the people" as anything other than "cultural dupes" (Hall,

1981) who are helpless before the power of the industry or of the text. The aim of this sort of ideological criticism then, is limited to the not insignificant, but finally negative, one of increasing the viewer's ability to resist the imposition of cultural meanings that may not fit one's own social identity, and in so doing to resist the homogenization of culture. But we need to develop a more positive critical practice than this, and the strategy for achieving this posture is the topic of the next section.

POLYSEMY, POPULARITY AND THE POLITICS OF READING

A more reader-centered critical theory leads us to investigate the extent to which the textual discourses may, or may not, correspond to the discursive practices of the wide variety of audiences that will have viewed this program over a large part of the Western and Third World. As these audiences have different material sociocultural positions, so their discursive practices and ideological frames must also differ. As Mattelart and Siegelaub (1979, p. 27) wonder:

> In how many countries, do the Aryan heroes of the television series, "Mission Impossible," fighting against the rebels, undergo a process of identification which is the exact opposite of that intended by the imperialist code, and how often are they viewed as the "bad guys" in the story?

Hodge and Tripp (1986) found instances of Australian Aboriginal children supporting blacks in television fights against whites and Indians against cowboys. They also found, less surprisingly, that they identified with Arnold and Willis (the two American blacks in *Diff'rent Strokes*). Using character as a category to think with, they constructed one that included Aboriginals, American blacks and Indians, which used as its prime semiotic marker racial subordination in opposition to white dominance.

But the different audiences worldwide are only a larger and more dramatic sign of the different audiences within a nation, and if any program is to be popular it must allow for the different discursive practices and ideological frames of different subcultures to be used in the reception and decoding of the text.

A theoretical strategy that might account for both social change and a notion of popularity that allows "the people" some say in the matter is one derived from deconstruction theory. The differences between this and the "preferred reading" school are not great, in fact, they are often ones of emphasis and methodology. One such difference is that deconstruction asserts the instability of all meaning, and thus denies the possibility of preferred meanings being structured into the text with any degree of clarity at all. If there is any stability of meaning, it can only derive from the ideology of the reader, never from the structure of the text. Another is that the preferred reading school derives the variety of textual readings from the varied social experiences of the readers; whereas deconstruction derives it from the inherent instability of language itself. It is this that finally invalidates deconstruction, for social struggle is always inscribed in language (Volosinov, 1973), and a preferred meaning is always structured into the mass media message. As Hall (1981) says:

> The cultural industries do have the power constantly to rework and reshape what they represent; and, by repetition and selection, to impose and implant such definitions of ourselves as fit more easily into the descriptions of the dominant or preferred culture. That is what the concentration of cultural power—the means of culture-making in the hands of the few—actually means. These definitions don't have the power to occupy our minds; they don't function on us as if we are blank screens. But they do occupy and rework the interior contradictions of feeling and perception in the dominated classes. (p. 233)

The dominated classes then, *do* have the power to make their own culture out of the products of the culture industry, which means that such excorporated culture cannot be defined in terms of its own essence, but only in terms of its (resisting) relationship to the dominant. The main enterprise of deconstruction is to deconstruct texts to reveal their instability, their gaps, their internal contradictions and their arbitrary textuality, and thus their potential for readings that are produced by the audiences, not by the culture industry or by the author-in-the-text. Thus when the villain says, "Well maybe a few good investments and we can pitch the whole bloody business. But we are going to need a bit more for our retirement fund," his words are treated by the text in a specific way. The ECU of his face, the heavy irony in his English accent, and the fact that the pretty American villainess has just characterized his attitude as greed combine to lead the viewer into a negative orientation towards him. Or do they? Is it not rather our own ideology or our capitulation to the dominant ideology-in-the-text that produces the reading? Can a subordinate non-white or non-American, whether in the U.S. or the rest of the world, read this to be a subversive use of the discourse and ethics of capitalism which turns the system back on itself? Could not this conjuncture of the discourses of race and capitalist economics also mean that the only way in which members of the subordinate race/class can participate in the validated activities of capitalism (looking after one's female and preparing for old age) is by what the dominant class calls crime? If so, the definition and motivation of crime would be shifted from the realm of the (evil) individual and placed firmly in the domain of the social system, and the semiotic needs of an oppositional subculture would be catered for. Excorporation will have worked. Irony, as a rhetorical device, is fertile ground for deconstructive criticism because it necessarily works by simultaneously opposing meanings against each other. Screen theory, like the preferred reading one, would place these meanings in a hierarchical relationship with each other. That is, we "know" that the moral one (this man is evil) takes precedence over, and is used to explain, the manifest "meaning" of the words (he is behaving responsibly). In this case irony prefers one meaning over the other, and is seen to work in the same way as the perfect camera viewpoint does. It gives the reader/spectator privileged knowledge; we understand the villain's words better than he does, we have a privileged insight into him, and our understanding is complete and adequate. Irony is, in this reading, also part of MacCabe's (1981) "hierarchy of discourses" that construct for the reader this position of "dominant specularity." But how do we *know*, the deconstructionist would ask, which meaning takes precedence? If "this-man-is-behaving-respon-sibly" does, then the moral condemnation is shifted away from the individual towards the social system, and the politics of the meaning is reversed. Recovering such meanings from the margins of the text is the strategy of deconstruction. Using such meanings to make the text make self-interested sense may be the reading strategy of one, or more, of the audiences.

Similarly, upon receiving a compliment the heroine says, "Oh, that's the cutest thing you've ever said to me, sugar," and she adopts a pseudo southern accent to say it. The patriarchal meaning of this emerges from the traditional, if not old-fashioned, myth of the southern belle as the most contentedly and severely subordinate of all female stereotypes. The irony lies in the tension between our liberated, northern heroine adopting this role and the self-aware, parodic way in which she does it. This might be seen to foreground the mythic nature of the stereotype and so comment critically on the myth as she triggers it. The opposing discourses involved in this irony, then, are those of the liberated northern woman and the traditional southern belle, and the hierarchical precedence is given by the text and context to the former—which is not to say that a traditional chauvinist of either gender, might not reverse this order of precedence. However, given that the "northern liberated" reading is the dominant, are there still gender differentiated readings of this? Both the preferred reading school, and the deconstructionists would claim that there must be. A reader who is resistant to patriarchy might find here a deliberate deconstruction of the sexism that is present even in the discourse of the liberated woman. For the meanings depend on the associations that are made between the various codes used in this exchange (see figure 5 and dialogue). First there is the irony of the dialogue, and irony, as we have seen, requires the presence of opposing discourses, but does not necessarily prescribe the nature of the relationship that these discourses bear to each other. Then there is the association between the dialogue and the self-consciously excessive jewelry, and the relationship between this and the heroine's make-up, which in the dominant code appears normal, though an opponent of patriarchy might see it as being at least as excessively sexist as the jewelry. Added to this is the metaphor of the bees, the honey and the flowers, which is also spoken in the tone of voice that draws attention to its metaphoric nature. It is worth noting here that metaphor works like irony in that two discourses are present but the relationship between them is open to negotiation. This metaphor, then, can be used either to "naturalize" sexism—the woman as the flower attracting the man as bee—or its ironic tone of voice can be used to demystify its sexism, thus foregrounding the ideological nature of the code of which it is a part.

There are here a number of codes that can be brought together in a number of different associative relations, and that can therefore produce a number of different meanings for different audiences. Thus a male chauvinist could associate the make-up, the jewelry (not seen as excessive) and the bees-honey-flowers metaphor in a mutually supportive relationship that would then deny the irony of the compliment and its response, and would read the exaggerated southern accent as sexual playfulness. An antipatriarch, on the other hand, would use the contradictions between the codes (e.g., that between the excess of the jewelry, and the normalcy of the makeup, and the way that both of these are in association with an assumed southern accent) to foreground their ideological origin, and the amount of ideological labor that is required to make them fit, to iron out the contradictions. This reading would also foreground the sexist pleasure that is the reward of this ideological labor.

In the same way, the window/porthole/laundromat joke does not have its meaning stabilized by either the text or the dominant codes structured into it, but only by the dominant reading of the sexist who finds it funny. The heroine's words, "I know they are supposed to be charming, but they always remind me of a laundromat," could be read to distance her from one traditional connotation of portholes—their romance—and there may be enough uncontrolled distanciation here to distance her also from the preferred masculine-technical meaning as well. Jokes, like metaphors, like irony, rely on the collision between discourses, and neither the text, nor the dominant ideology, can ever control all the potential meanings that this collision produces.

The fissures in the text which allow for meanings that escape the control of the dominant are at their most apparent and most exploitable when the text is composed of discourses or other elements which are related by association rather than by the laws of logic or cause and effect. The laws of association are looser, more resistant to closure and admit of greater reader participation in the negotiation of meaning.

This analysis has concentrated at the micro-level on identifying and investigating the fissures opened up by the relative freedom that associative structures offer the reader, but it can be argued that this is typical of television on a macro-level as well. In contrasting television with film, Ellis (1982) argues that a defining characteristic of television is the segmentation of its text. By this he means that its generic mode of presentation is by short, self-contained segments linked by association rather than by logic. This essay is concerned with two such segments in a narrative, but Ellis suggests that the televisual typicality of segmentation carries it beyond narrative to include news, commercials, game shows, sport and the whole of the television flow of output.

Segmentation, with its associative structure, is more likely to produce an open text (Eco, 1979) that offers more readily a range of semiotic potential than a text like a film that relies more on narrative sequence and cause and effect for its structuring principles, for these are agents of semiotic closure.

In order to explore how the relative openness of the television text might allow for ideologically contradictory readings we need to investigate the notion of semiotic excess. This has some affinities with both the "preferred reading" and the deconstructionist schools. It shares with the former the belief that dominant ideological values are structured into the text by the use of dominant codes and thus of dominant encodings of social experience. It shares with the latter the belief that the dominant reading does not exhaust the semiotic potential of the text. In a popular work of art these codes and their formal relationship must conform to the conventions of encoding and decoding that the dominant ideology has established as its natural signifying practice, because without them reader expectations would be defeated and popularity would be at risk. And here I am referring to that dimension of popularity that refers to a text's ability to give pleasure to as wide a range of audiences as possible. The text can appeal to this variety of audiences only if there is a common ideological frame that all recognize and can use, even if many are opposed to it. The preferred reading of a popular text in mass culture must necessarily, then, attempt a hegemonic function in favor of the culturally dominant. The reader, who statistically is almost certain to be one of the culturally subordinate, is invited to cooperate with the text, to decode it according to codes that fit easily with those of the dominant ideology, and if one accepts the invitation, is rewarded with pleasure. The pleasure is the pleasure of recognition, of privileged knowledge and of dominant specularity, and it produces a subject position that fits into the dominant cultural system with a minimum of strain.

Identifying and revealing this ideological work of the text is a vital part of critical practice, but when we have achieved this we are far from having exhausted the text's potential. The theory of semiotic excess proposes that once the ideological, hegemonic work has been performed, there is still excess meaning that escapes the control of the dominant and is thus available for the culturally subordinate to use for their own cultural-political interests. The motivation to use the semiotic excess for particular, possibly oppositional subcultural purposes, derives from the differences between the sociocultural experiences of the producers and readers. Hodge and Tripp (1986) are in no doubt about what happens when the meanings that TV seems to prefer are in conflict with those used to organize the reader's perception of the world: "non-television meanings are powerful enough to swamp television meanings." This brings us to the fuller definition of "popularity," its sense of being "of the people, serving the grass roots interests of the subordinate"—a meaning that is closer to folk art than mass art (O'Sullivan, Hartley, Saunders, & Fiske, 1983, pp. 174–176).

Bennett and Woollacott's (1986) work on James Bond has demonstrated the instability of the meanings of popular texts, and has shown that varying readings need not work by rejecting the dominant ideology, but rather by articulating their oppositionality in relation to it. The dominant and the oppositional are simultaneously present in both the text and its readings. The dominant is found in the preferred reading, the oppositional in the semiotic excess that the preferred reading attempts to marginalize, but that can never be finally or totally controlled by the dominant. It is this semiotic excess that a socially motivated deconstructionist reading recovers and attempts to mobilize in the interests of the subordinate; what is crucial here is the variety of readings that the variety of social experiences of subordination can produce. Hodge and Tripp (1986) argue that their work constitutes:

> a compelling argument for the primacy of general social relations in developing a reading of television, rather than the other way about, for it seems likely that the ideological meanings inscribed in general social relationships will have a powerful effect upon the total meanings of the television experience.

The subordinate reading may displace the dominant, or they may occur after and over the preferred ones; in this case they are necessarily mutually contradictory. Greenfield (1984) sees these contradictions as potentially dysfunctional:

> Television in the United States usually portrays members of racial minorities as less powerful and poorer than the majority. . . . In accord with the general principle that children identify with powerful figures rather than powerless ones, black children often model themselves after white rather than black characters in a show. This process, occurring in a racist society, can cause an identity conflict: how to have the status of a white person without ceasing to identify psychologically with one's own group? (p. 38)

Hodge and Tripp's work, however, lead them to the conclusion that children are not only able to handle these contradictions, but are able positively to turn them to their own advantage:

> By nine years old children seem to be remarkably adept at reading television programs designed for them. They effortlessly pick up ideological content. They also see lines of fissure in that content, contradictions which find analogous structures within their developing psyche. They try to balance these contradictions, between different aspects of the total semiotic potential of the given program, contradictions so diverse that a single coherent meaning for the program becomes unlikely if not impossible.

A black fighting with a white on television will presumably lose, and the Aboriginal child who identifies with that black will not allow this defeat to deny the characteristics that led him or her to make the identification in the first place, rather it will be seen as another example of white power within which black values must struggle for expression. The ideological progress of the narrative will not be effective in swinging this child's moral and affective affiliation onto the official hero. Identifying with the loser in a television narrative may be an important way of making meanings that are useful in the social experience of the subordinate. One of the aims of criticism must be to demonstrate that the narrative defeat of the subordinate is part of the same system that produces the social subordination; the characteristics and actions of heroes and villains must be read as social and not personal.

CONCLUSION

If the text is able to contain simultaneously contradictory readings, then my argument is that the reading subject must be able to cope with them, and use them, for meanings occur only in the encounter between texts and subjects. These contradictions in subjectivities are accounted for in the theory of the divided subject. According to Lacan (1968), our subjectivity is formed as we enter the symbolic, the language or meaning system that is always already awaiting us, and that has always already mapped out the subject position for us to occupy. But our material social experience may well contradict our given subjectivity, may demand meanings of experience that this given subjectivity cannot provide. So we develop a split subjectivity in which more recently acquired and less deeply rooted subject positions can and do conflict with the original, given one. This conflict frequently occurs within consciousness, whereas an uncontested subject position remains largely in the unconscious, its labor in the sense-making process that we call culture unrecognized and uninspected.

So a given bourgeois subjectivity can acquire a contradictory radical one, a patriarchal subjectivity can acquire a feminist one, and a white subjectivity can acquire a black one. Contradictions in society reproduce themselves in subjectivities. As texts can never be totally controlled by the dominant, so subjectivities can never be produced by the dominant ideology alone—otherwise social change would be impossible. The correspondence between text and subjectivity as theoretical constructs is close. Both are makers of sense and consciousness, both bear similar relations to the dominant ideology and both are capable of working contradictarily, and it is this potential to activate contradictions that provides for their ability to be oppositional and subversive. Hodge and Tripp's (1986) work accounts for the co-existence of the subversive meaning with the dominant—they suggest that not only is the subversive meaning necessary, but that, for the child viewer, it becomes the preferred one: "Of the two kinds of meaning, ideological (Parent) and subversive (Child) meanings, the emotional charge and attraction of the programme is invested in the subversive (Child) meanings." In this they are developing Eco's (1980) argument that aberrent decodings are the norm for mass media messages.

Ideological control of both the text and the reading subject attempts to work through the denial of any contradictions which might disrupt the seamless homogeneity of bourgeois ideology. A socially responsible critical practice must recover these contradictions, and must concern itself with that central one between the hegemony of the text and the social needs of the subordinate.

Stuart Hall (1981) uses different rhetoric to make a similar point when he writes:

> The people versus the power-bloc: this, rather than "class-against-class," is the central line of contradiction around which the terrain of culture is polarized. Popular culture, especially, is organized around the contradiction: the popular forces versus the power-bloc. (p. 238)

Critics need to develop strategies of textual analysis that are equally sensitive to the needs of the subordinate as to those of the controlling authority. We must first identify the semiotic excesses of the text, those potential meanings that escape the control of the producers of the dominant culture. This will enable us to identify where and how members of subordinate subcultures can use these semiotic opportunities to generate meanings for *them*, meanings that relate to their own cultural experience and position, meanings that serve their interests, and not those of cultural domination.

As a semiotician, I believe that meanings are the most important part of our social structure, and are potentially the main origin of any impetus to change it, for, as Hall (1984) has said, "a set of social relations obviously requires meanings and frameworks which underpin them and hold them in place" (p. 10). If we are to resist the centralization of meaning, if we are to preserve the subcultures and alternative cultures that serve the interests of the people and whose differences form the only possible source of social change, then a socially motivated deconstructive critical and teaching practice is essential. It is this practice that can explain and legitimate the ability of the subordinate to take the signifying practices and products of the dominant, to use them for different social purposes, and to return them from where they came, stripped of their hegemonic powers. A critical theory and practice of this type offers us a way of understanding how television can be *dialogically popular*, that is, how it can serve the interests of the dominant and of the subordinate at one and the same time.

NOTES

1.   Gitlin (1982) gives a thorough account of hegemony and its usefulness in the study of the mass media and popular culture. In particular, he stresses that the concept implies a constant struggle between the forces of domination and resisting subordinate classes. But despite this emphasis and his insistence that hegemony is not always effective, the main thrust of his essay is towards the conclusion that hegemony in late capitalism is difficult, if not impossible, to resist. Similarly

Newcomb and Hirsch (1984) theorize the possibility of divergent audience readings, but give no convincing examples.

2. See Fiske (1982) and Newcomb (1984) for an account of this theory and its relationship to Morley's (1980) work.

3. Hartley (1982) provides a useful analysis and theory of news on television (and in print) that takes account of Volosinov's theory.

4. See Newcomb and Alley (1983) and Marc (1984) for accounts of the role of the creative individual in the production process that challenge my assertion.

5. See Fiske (1986) for a fuller account of empirical work by Hobson (1982) and Hodge and Tripp (1986) that demonstrates how effectively subordinate classes of viewers (in Hobson's case, women and in Hodge and Tripp's, children) can construct *their* meanings, *their* culture, out of the products of the television industry. Radway (1984) gives a similar insight into the power of women readers of romance to produce a feminine culture from it.

6. Fiske and Hartley (1978) and Fiske (1982) discuss the implications of Gerbner's work for a cultural theory of heroes and villains in a society structured along axes of class, race, gender, nationality and age-group.

REFERENCES

Bakhtin, M. (1981). *The dialogic imagination*. Austin: University of Texas Press.

Bennett, T., Boyd-Bowman, S., Mercer, C., & Woollacott, J. (Eds.). (1981). *Popular television and film*. London: BFI/OU.

Bennett,T., & Woollacott, J. (1986). *Bond and beyond: The political career of a popular hero*. New York: Routledge, Chapman & Hall.

Bourdieu, P. (1968). Outline of a sociological theory of art perception. *International Social Sciences Journal, 2*, 225–254.

Brunsdon, C., & Morley, D. (1978). *Everyday television: Nationwide*. London: BFI/OU.

Davis, H., & Walton, P. (Eds.). (1983). *Language, image, media*. London: Blackwell.

Eco, U. (1979). *The role of the reader: Explorations in the semiotics of texts*. Bloomington: University of Indiana Press.

Eco, U. (1980). Towards a semiotic inquiry into TV messages. In J. Corner & J. Hawthorn (Eds.), *Communication studies: An introductory reader* (pp. 131–149). London: Arnold.

Ellis, J. (1982). *Visible fictions*. London: Routledge & Kegan Paul.

Fiske, J. (1982). *Introduction to communication studies*. London: Methuen.

Fiske, J. (1985). Television: A multilevel classroom resource. *Australian Journal of Screen Theory, 17/18*, 106–124.

Fiske, J. (1986). Television and popular culture: Reflections for British and Australian critical practice. *Critical Studies in Mass Communication, 2*, 200–216.

Fiske, J., & Hartley, J. (1978). *Reading television*. London: Methuen.

Gerbner, G. (1970). Cultural indicators: The case of violence in television drama. *Annals of the American Association of Political and Social Science, 338*, 69–71.

Gitlin, T. (1982). Prime time ideology: The hegemonic process in television entertainment. In H. Newcomb (Ed.), *Television: The critical review* (3rd ed., pp. 426–454). New York: Oxford University Press.

Greenfield, P. (1984). Mind and media. London: Fontana.

Grossberg, L. (1984). Another boring day in paradise: Rock and roll and the empowerment of everyday life. *Popular Music, 4*, 225–257.

Hall, S. (1980). Encoding/decoding. In S. Hall, D. Hobson, A. Lowe, & P. Willis (Eds.), *Culture, media, language* (pp. 128–138). London: Hutchinson.

Hall, S. (1981). Notes on deconstructing the popular. In R. Samuel (Ed.), *People's history and socialist theory* (pp. 227–239). London: Routledge & Kegan Paul.

Hall, S. (1984). The narrative construction of reality. *Southern Review, 17*(1), 3–17.

Hall, S., Connell, I., & Curti, L. (1976). The unity of current affairs television. *Working Papers in Cultural Studies, 9*, 51–94.

Hall, S., Hobson, D., Lowe, A., & Willis, P. (Eds.). (1980). *Culture, media, language.* London: Hutchinson.

Hartley, J. (1982). *Understanding news.* London: Methuen.

Hartley, J. (1984). Encouraging signs: Television and the power of dirt, speech and scandalous categories. In W. Rowland & B. Watkins (Eds.), *Interpreting television: Current research perspectives* (pp. 119–141). Beverly Hills: Sage.

Heath, S., & Skirrow, G. (1977). Television: A world in action. *Screen, 18*(2), 7–59.

Hobson, D. (1982). *Crossroads: The drama of a soap opera.* London: Methuen.

Hodge, R., & Tripp, D. (1986). *Children and television.* London: Polity Press.

Kellner, D. (1982). TV ideology, and emancipatory popular culture. In H. Newcomb (Ed.), *Television: The critical view* (3rd ed., pp. 386–421). New York: Oxford University Press.

Lacan, J. (1968). *The language of the self* (A. Wilden, Trans.). New York: Delta.

MacCabe, C. (1981). Realism and the cinema: Notes on some Brechtian theses. In T. Bennett, S. Boyd-Bowman, C. Mercer, & J. Woollacott (Eds.), *Popular television and film* (pp. 216–235). London: BFI/OU.

Marc, D. (1984). *Demographic vistas: Television in American culture.* Philadelphia: University of Pennsylvania Press.

Mattelart, A., & Siegelaub, S. (Eds.). (1979). *Communication and class struggle* (Vol. 1). New York: International General.

Morley, D. (1980). *The nationwide audience: Structure and decoding.* London: BFI/OU.

Morley, D. (1983). Cultural transformations: The politics of resistance. In H. Davis & P. Walton (Eds.), *Language, image, media* (pp. 104–117). London: Blackwell.

Newcomb, H. (Ed.). (1982) *Television: The critical view.* New York: Oxford University Press.

Newcomb, H. (1984). On the dialogic aspects of mass communication. *Critical Studies in Mass Communication, 1*, 34–50.

Newcomb, H., & Alley, R. (1983). *The producer's medium: Conversations with America's leading television producers.* New York: Oxford University Press.

Newcomb, H., & Hirsch, P. (1984). Television as a cultural forum: Implications for research. In W. Rowland & B. Watkins (Eds.), *Interpreting television: Current research perspectives* (pp. 165–198). Beverly Hills: Sage.

O'Sullivan, T., Hartley, J., Saunders, D., & Fiske, J. (1983). *Key concepts in communication.* London: Methuen.

Radway, J. (1984). *Reading the romance: Feminism and the representation of women in popular culture.* Chapel Hill: University of North Carolina Press.

Rowland, W., & Watkins, B. (Eds.). (1984). *Interpreting television: Current research perspectives.* Beverly Hills: Sage.

Samuel, R. (Ed.). (1981). *People's history and socialist theory.* London: Routledge & Kegan Paul.

Volosinov, V. (1973). *Marxism and the philosophy of language.* New York: Seminar Press.

17 The Rhetorical Limits of Polysemy

CELESTE MICHELLE CONDIT

The recent, energetic critical program focused on the receivers of mass communication emphasizes the autonomy and power of audiences to exert substantial control of the mass communication process and hence to exercise significant social influence. The polysemic character of texts, these studies argue, allows receivers to construct a wide variety of decodings and thereby prevents simple domination of people by the messages they receive (Fiske, 1986; Hall, 1980; Morley, 1980; Radway, 1986).

These theoretical claims are supported by substantial evidence demonstrating the active character of audience viewing. The theoretical conclusions, however, overstate the evidence because they oversimplify the pleasures experienced by audience members. As many of the preeminent scholars in critical audience studies themselves admit, audiences are not free to make meanings at will from mass mediated texts (Fiske, 1987c, pp. 16, 20, 44). Consequently, the pleasures audiences experience in receiving texts are necessarily complicated. In this essay, I employ a multidimensional rhetorical critique of a single television text to suggest that the ability of audiences to shape their own readings, and hence their social life, is constrained by a variety of factors in any given rhetorical situation. These factors include audience members' access to oppositional codes, the ratio between the work required and pleasure produced in decoding a text, the repertoire of available texts, and the historical occasion, especially with regard to the text's positioning of the pleasures of dominant and marginal audiences. I conclude that mass media research should replace totalized theories of polysemy and audience power with interactive theories that assess audience reactions as part of the full communication process occurring in particular rhetorical configurations.

CRITICAL STUDIES OF THE AUDIENCE

Audience-centered critical research argues that viewers and readers construct their own meanings from texts. Audiences do not simply receive messages;

they decode texts. Members of mass audiences are therefore not mere "cultural dupes" of message producers. As John Fiske (1987c) describes the process, viewers have the "ability to make their own socially pertinent meanings out of the semiotic resources provided by television" (p. 65). As a consequence, "viewers have considerable control, not only over its meanings, but over the role that it plays in their lives" (p. 74). Janice Radway (1984, p. 17) makes a similar argument about mass-produced fiction: "Because reading is an active process that is at least partially controlled by the readers themselves, opportunities exist within the mass-communication process for individuals to resist, alter, and reappropriate the materials designed elsewhere for their purchase."

Critical audience analysts position their work as a radical break with the history of critical media studies, which they depict as having emphasized the power of the media to impose a dominant ideology or to control beliefs and behaviors (Fiske, 1986; Morley, 1980; Radway, 1986). The new studies indicate that disparate audiences do not decode messages in uniform ways (Katz & Liebes, 1984; Morley, 1980; Palmer, 1986), in the precise directions critics have suggested they might (Radway, 1984), or even as the messages authors seemed to have intended (Hobson, 1982; Steiner, 1988).[1] These studies conclude that the texts which link producers' intended messages with actual audiences are not univocal. Reworking structuralist insights, they emphasize that all texts are polysemic (Fiske, 1986; Newcomb, 1984), that is, capable of bearing multiple meanings because of the varying intertextual relationships they carry (especially Bennett & Woollacott, 1987) and because of the varying constructions (or interests) of receivers.

The study of the polysemic character of texts has thus included two research schools, often not clearly distinguished. Works in the American school (Kellner, 1982; Newcomb, 1984) emphasize the variety of ideological positions contained within the mass media. In contrast, the British approach highlights the variety of decodings possible from a single text or message (e.g., Burke, Wilson, & Agardy, 1983; Morley, 1980).

Whether based in the variety of available texts or in the flexibility of decoding processes, polysemy has been taken to be a widespread or even dominant phenomenon, bearing significance for theories of social change. Rather than portraying the mass media as the channel of oppression generated through the top-down imposition of meanings, such a perspective allows for the suggestion that the pleasures of the popular media might in fact be liberating. Radway (1984, p. 184), for instance, claims that because of the pleasure women derive from romance reading, "they at least partially reclaim the patriarchal form of the romance for their own use." Fiske (1987c, p. 239) finds similar pleasures and effects operative in television: "The pleasure and the power of making meanings, of participating in the mode of representation, of playing with the semiotic process—these are some of the most significant and empowering pleasures that television has to offer." Fiske argues that, even without the additional step of circulating one's own representations, these pleasures may offer a real resistance to the dominant ideology. Escape, he indicates (p. 318), may itself be liberating, because to escape from dominant meanings is to construct one's own subjectivity, and that is an important step in more collective moves toward social change. Fiske (p. 230) concludes:

> While there is clearly a pleasure in exerting social power, the popular pleasures of the subordinate are necessarily found in resisting, evading, or offending this power. Popular pleasures are those that empower the subordinate, and they thus offer political resistance, even if only momentarily and even if only in a limited terrain.

Recent critical audience studies thus repudiate prior portrayals of television as a sinister social force in favor of a celebration of the ability of audiences, enabled by the broad referential potentiality of texts, to reconstruct television messages. Television, because it is popular, therefore becomes a force for popular resistance to dominant interests.

These audience studies and the theories they are generating offer a useful counterbalance to the flat assertion that messages produced by elites necessarily dominate social meaning-making processes. Nonetheless, the scope and character of audience power have not yet been delimited, and I believe they are as yet overstated.[2] It is clear that there are substantial limits to the polysemic potential of texts and of decodings. If television offered a true "semiotic democracy" (Fiske, 1987c, p. 236), we would have to assume either that television—with all the distortions described by the last 50 years of quantitative and critical analysts—is in fact an accurate producer of the popular interest or that it will soon reform itself to be such. This seems either too dark a description or too optimistic a forecast. The underlying agonistic theory common to British cultural studies, postmodern theory, and American rhetorical studies offers a more appropriate line of approach. We need to begin to describe the precise range of textual polysemy and the power held by the audience in its struggle with texts and message producers.

These limits ought to be found both in production conditions (Meehan, 1986) and in texts. As a rhetorical critic, I focus my attention on the latter, exploring, in a variety of ways, the communication event occasioned by the broadcast on November 11, 1985 of an episode of *Cagney & Lacey* concerning the topic of abortion. Because rhetorical criticism focuses on language usage as a means of distributing power among a particular group of agents who are uniquely situated in a communication process (e.g., McGee, 1982), this critique examines two particular audience members for the program, then the specific political codes made present in the message, and, finally, the historical occasion of the broadcast. While this case study leads to a focus on television, the implications extend to other national mass media as well.

THE POLYSEMOUS *CAGNEY & LACEY*

My own viewing of the abortion episode leads me to describe the central plot as follows: police detectives Cagney and Lacey help a pregnant woman (Mrs. Herrera) to enter an abortion clinic where pickets (led by Arlene Crenshaw) are blocking access. Lacey, married and pregnant, eagerly helps Mrs. Herrera, while Cagney, feeling conflicted, resists any assistance beyond that necessitated by her job. When the abortion clinic is bombed and a vagrant dies as a result, the detectives investigate and locate the bomber, who, in a climactic scene, threatens to blow up herself and the detectives. She gives up when confronted with the inconsistency of killing Lacey's "preborn" child for a Pro-life cause.[3]

Two viewers, selected from a larger project I am conducting, offer particularly interesting responses to the episode. The two were college students recruited through local-scale organizations active in the abortion controversy. They were asked to view the program and to respond, during commercial breaks and after the program ended, to my open-ended and nonjudgmental questions. These two college students and their responses are not presented because of their "typicality." I do not claim their responses are representative but rather that they are suggestive of new questions that must be asked in order to gain an accurate picture of the relative power of encoding and decoding as social processes. The first respondent, whom I call "Jack," was the leader of the student Pro-life group. A 21-year-old male, first exposed to the abortion issue through a required essay in a Catholic all-boys high school, Jack described himself as not being a particularly successful student and as having a life goal of becoming a major league baseball umpire. "Jill," a first year student, was the daughter of a feminist mother. Active in the student Pro-choice organization, her goal was to complete a doctorate. Neither of these two leaders of politically active groups had seen the episode previously, but both reported having heard about it and having talked about it in their organizations when the episode originally was broadcast. While Jill displayed more familiarity with the series, Jack showed more knowledge about the political preferences and activities of the actresses and producers and reported having read about the episode in newspapers and magazines.

At one important level, the 18 single-spaced pages of transcripts provided by these two opposed activists confirm the polysemy thesis. Their replies to my questions agreed less than 10% of the time. For example, when asked about the fairness of the presentation, Jill replied, "Yeah, I think it is fair," whereas Jack said, "I think it's really grossly unfair." Jill responded to Arlene Crenshaw by saying, "I don't like her. I don't respect her," whereas Jack listed her as his favorite character, noting that she was the "lone good-guy type of figure in the show." Similarly, Jill claimed that the value of "family" was "definitely portrayed as positive," whereas Jack concluded, "I don't think they take a very pro-family type response." Throughout their interviews, Jill and Jack provided virtually diametrically opposed opinions of the episode.

There were, nonetheless, important elements in their responses which lead me to suggest that the term "polyvalence" characterizes these differences better than does the term "polysemy." Polyvalence occurs when audience members share understandings of the denotations of a text but disagree about the valuation of those denotations to such a degree that they produce notably different interpretations. In this case, it is not a multiplicity or instability of textual meanings but rather a difference in audience evaluations of shared denotations that best accounts for the two viewers' discrepant interpretations. Careful listening and examination of the transcripts make it clear that neither Jill nor Jack misunderstood the program, and they did not decode the images and words as holding different denotations. Their plot summaries, although extremely rough, were not inconsistent. More important, perhaps, each advocate was able to predict what the other's response to the program would be. If we accept the premise that understanding is effectively assessed by the ability to predict another's interpretation, this is an important test that both pass. After claiming that the episode "presents both sides of the story," for example, Jill admitted that "I'm sure that a lot of Pro-life people would hate it because it ends up that they are criminals at the end." Jack shared the ability to reflect on how the text might be read by others with different values: "A lot of people . . . would say, 'oh, it's great, it's a fair portrayal, it presents our side very well and does a good job of the other one too,' whereas the Pro-lifers would say 'it's a terrible portrayal, it's absolutely biased against our side.'" On another occasion, in talking about his preference for Arlene Crenshaw as a character, he noted, "You know, obviously, coming from my point of view, I can see if I was [sic] pro-abortion, she'd be like the 'bad guy.'"

On a number of specific counts, it further becomes clear that both viewers shared a basic construction of the denotations of the text. Both described Cagney as the character "in the middle." Both cited the transformation of the lieutenant's attitudes. Both noted the poverty and minority status of Mrs. Herrera. Ultimately, in spite of their different attitudes toward the episode, there was nothing in their responses to suggest that they did not share a basic understanding of the story line or even of what the program was trying to convey.

This finding is consistent with other major audience studies. In David Morley's partial transcripts of interviews surrounding the program *Nationwide* (1980), I detect little fundamental inconsistency in the denotations processed by the viewers; instead it is the valuation of those denotations, and the attached connotations that viewers draw upon, which become important (see also Eco, 1979, pp. 54–56). The response of Morley's group members to an interview with Ralph Nader seems to be typical. Even groups which are opposed in their attitudes toward Nader, the program, and in their life conditions share a basic understanding of what the interview denoted. Likewise, in Radway's contrast of the professional critics and the Smithton readers (1984), it is not that the two sets of readings are inconsistent but simply that the critics devalue any patriarchal codings, whereas the Smithton women accept some of those codings as consistent with their values. The only instance in which true shifts in denotations are recorded, to my knowledge, is Elihu Katz and Tamar Liebes' study of Middle Eastern readers of *Dallas* (1984), and in this case it requires massive crosscultural differences and language shifts to produce such discrepant interpretations.

The emphasis on the polysemous quality of texts thus may be overdrawn. The claim perhaps needs to be scaled back to indicate that responses and interpretations are generally polyvalent, and texts themselves are occasionally or partially polysemic. It is not that texts routinely feature unstable denotation but that instability of connotation requires viewers to judge texts from their own value systems. Different respondents may similarly understand the messages that a text seeks to convey. They may, however, see the text as rhetorical—as urging positions upon them—and make their own selections among and evaluations of those persuasive messages. As I note in the conclusion, this will have profound implications for the practice of academic critical reading. For clarity, then, we might reserve the term "intertextual polysemy" to refer to the existence of variety in messages on mass communication channels, the terms "internally polysemous" or "open texts" for those discourses which truly offer unstable or internally contradictory meanings, and the term "polyvalence" to describe the fact that audiences routinely evaluate texts differently, assigning different value to different portions of a text and hence to the text itself. Such revisions imply the need to generate a more careful account of the actual social force of popular or mass communication. Such an endeavor begins with a more detailed exploration of audience interpretations.

AUDIENCES: GROUPS OF INDIVIDUALS

The claim that audiences have the ability to create their own empowering responses to mass mediated texts loses little of its force when it is acknowledged that the polysemic freeplay of discourse has been overestimated. Whether deriving from decoding processes related to denotation or connotation, critical audience studies have indicated fairly clearly that viewers can construct a variety of responses to any given mass mediated text. The central issue remains, however, to what extent do these responses constitute liberating pleasure and social empowerment? The situation of audiences as members of groups in a social process constructs some fundamental limits to these pleasures and powers which can now be explored.

The proposition that decoding a message always requires work is a fundamental postulate supporting the claim that audiences have control of the mass communication process. As Morley (1980, p. 10) puts it, "The production of a meaningful message in the TV discourse is always problematic 'work.'" The work receivers must do inserts them into a position of influence in relationship to the text. Such accounts, however, fail to note that decoding requires *differential* amounts of work for different audience groups. Jack's responses to *Cagney & Lacey* consumed more than twice the space and time of Jill's replies. Jill was positioned to give a reading of the text that was dominant or only slightly negotiated (e.g., she objected to the tokenizing of minorities in the program and the lack of women in the more powerful job hierarchies). Jack was required to provide a largely oppositional reading.

Not only did Jack's interpretation require more time and space, and visibly more effort (his nonverbal behavior was frequently tense and strained), it showed itself to be more incomplete and problematic in other ways. Frequently, Jack's responses departed from the program altogether to provide the background of a fairly extended Pro-life argument. In reacting to the abortion clinic's male physician, Jack cited the doctor's story about a 12-year-old girl who came in to get an abortion, arguing:

> . . . little does he tell them now, however, that it is easier for the younger, anywhere from a 12 to 18-year-old, statistically and medically, to bear children than it is for women who are over 25 or 30, only because it's like, their bodies are ripe and just developing, as opposed to either at the peak or really past that. See, they don't want to get into that; he just talks about how terrible it allegedly or supposedly is for the young women to have children. So it's the best thing to do, get them in there, you know, do the abortion, and get them out, no worries. Do they ever talk about post-abortion counseling that that doctor might do? . . . Are they willing to go so far as to say that he just does the abortion and have [sic] nothing more to do with her?

Jack thus worked very hard to oppose his own ideology to the program. At times this entailed distortions of the truth which were probably unintentional. For example, Jack's statistics are skewed. More important for Jack, at times he was simply unsuccessful at producing a consistent response. At several key points he was reduced to a position of virtual incoherence, and he indicated his frustration in nonverbal ways. For example, at one point he became trapped between his denial that normal Pro-life people are violent and his attempt to project how the network should portray abortion clinic bombers. He concluded:

> If I was [sic] nuts enough to bomb, I'd go about it real calmly, talk to them, and wait until they dig up some more information before I went, got overly nervous. I think they did a good job of portraying her as, well, see, she was involved in the sixties and seventies and all these demonstrations, the typical type. Why couldn't they portray, if they are going to, a bomber who is just an average everyday American? They did a good job of portraying her as an extreme fanatic. That is to say that, see, they're all like this. They're the type who did that and they'll do this again. It's rather illogical.

Jack was unable to come up with a consistent characterization of clinic bombers. He described them as "nuts" yet asked that they be portrayed as "an average everyday American," displaying his difficulty in putting together a response to the text that was persuasive (either to himself or to me). Jill did not show such strain in her interpretations.

Finally, Jill and Jack differed with regard to the chief tests they put to the text. For Jill, the recurrent test was "Is this realistic?" Accusing the text of committing errors, she argued that the portrayal of the Pro-life leaders and the bomber as women was inaccurate, but that Pro-lifers in fact generated violence, and so on. For Jack, the reality criterion emphasized motives rather than facts. His most frequent strategy was to talk about what the text omitted: the character of the fetus, the "ripeness" of young women, the poor quality of counseling the women received. For Jill, therefore, the negotiation process was simply one of relatively minor factual corrections. For Jack, the process was a matter of filling in major motivational absences in the text (see Sholle, 1988; Wander, 1984).

For Jack, in short, the work of interpreting the text and resisting its persuasive message was much more difficult than the accommodative response was for Jill. Although these differences may have been caused by factors other than their political positions (e.g., differential academic ability or familiarity with the series), they provide grounds for considering the important possibility that oppositional and negotiated readings require more work of viewers than do dominant readings. This possibility is reinforced as well by work with public speakers (Lucaites & Condit, 1986). Three factors give impact to the difference in audience work load: its silencing effects, its reduction of pleasure, and its code dependence.

The first consequence of the greater work load imposed on oppositionally situated audience groups is the tendency of such burdens to silence viewers. In its most stark form, this leads to turning off the television, a widespread phenomenon, especially among minority groups (Fiske, 1987c, p. 312; Morley, 1980, p. 135). If the particular range of television's textual polysemy excludes marginal group messages, and if oppositional reading requires comparatively oppressive quantities of work, then minority groups are indeed silenced, even as audiences, and therefore discriminated against in important ways.

Another consequence of this work load is disproportional pleasure for oppositional and dominant readers. As Fiske (1987c, p. 239) points out, it is clearly the case that viewers can take great pleasure in constructing oppositional readings, simply because of the human joy in constructing representations. Nonetheless, this does not mean that the pleasures of the text are fairly distributed. Jill indicated that she enjoyed the episode of *Cagney & Lacey* very much and that she found it "powerful," and her nonverbal response indicated a restful, enjoyable experience. Jack, on the other hand, clearly took some pleasure in his ability to argue against the text, but he also displayed clear signs of pain and struggle in that decoding. Jack's relative displeasure may be widely shared, given that even a popular program enlists only 20 million viewers out of a population of over 240 million and that most of those viewers are simultaneously engaged in other activities (Meyrowitz, 1985, p. 348). The disparity is made pernicious given that the most highly sought audiences have the characteristics of more elite groups: more money and hence more attractiveness to advertisers (Feur, 1984a, p. 26; Kerr, 1984, p. 68). Programs are tailored for the greater pleasure of a relative elite.

A similar disparity of pleasures in the mass publishing industry is suggested by Radway (1984, pp. 104, 165–167) when she reveals that the repressed pornography that producers of romance believe to be attractive to women may not actually be their primary interest and that an extremely different genre of stories might bring greater pleasures to these audiences. As Fiske (1987c, p. 66) notes, to be popular enough to gain economic rewards, mass media must attract a fairly large audience. That popularity, however, is only relative to other programming the producers are willing to construct. Hence, the trade-off among what marginal audience groups want, what other audience groups want, and what the producers are willing to give them as a compromise may still retain a great deal of control for producers and dominant groups.

Mass mediated texts might be viewed, therefore, not as giving the populace what they want but as compromises that give the relatively well-to-do more of what they want, bringing along as many economically marginal viewers as they comfortably can, within the limitations of the production teams' visions and values. If so, the differential availability of textual pleasures and the costs in pain become as important as any absolute statements about viewer abilities. It is not enough to argue that audiences can do the work to decode oppressive texts with some pleasure. We need to investigate how much more this costs them and how much more silencing of oppositional groups this engenders. In addition, we need to understand better the various conditions that best enable oppositional decoding.

A third consequence of the differential work load required of viewing groups provides further clues to the variability of audience experiences. Among oppositional readers of the *Cagney & Lacey* text, Jack was in a particularly empowered position. As a leader of a Pro-life group, he was experienced in producing Pro-life representations and had access to a large network of oppositional codes. This experience and access were evident throughout his interview (as in the instance where he used Pro-life rhetoric to point out gaps in the doctor's story). The utility of such experience and skill in helping viewers to produce self-satisfying decodings is echoed throughout the audience literature. Morley (1980, p. 141) especially notes the enhanced ability of shop stewards to produce oppositional codings more successfully than do rank and file union members. Importantly, most of the content-based audience research thus far taps into audiences where group leadership exists and where audience members have access to counter-rhetorics. Radway's study (1984) relies on a group centered on Dorothy Evans, who encodes negotiated readings, giving access to a resistive code to her group members. Linda Steiner's study (1988) relies similarly on a site, *Ms.* magazine, where oppositional rhetorics are provided.

In sum, the strongest evidence about the actualization of audiences' abilities to decode messages to their own advantage comes from studies that select audiences or conditions in which we would expect the receivers to be relatively advantaged as opponents to the message producers. Moreover, in cases with the weakest access to group organization, it also seems that oppositional interpretations are weaker. In his study of adolescent female responses to Madonna, for example, Fiske (1987a, p. 274; 1987c, p. 125) suggests that the young girls are only "struggling" to find counter-rhetorics. They experience, therefore, only limited success at resistance.

The commonalities in these studies suggest two conclusions. First, there is a need for research to assess the typicality of oppositional readings. The tendency to notice successful oppositional decodings may have led scholars to overplay the degree to which this denotes typical behavior. Correctives could come from comparing audiences with different access to oppositional codes on a particular topic and from studies of the relative degrees of oppositionality in typical decodings. Only if a strong and pervasive response to dominant messages can be demonstrated can we assert that the limited repertoire of mass mediated messages really coexists with a semiotic democracy.

Second, these commonalities also reestablish the importance of leadership and organized group interaction. Leadership always has been largely a matter of the ability to produce rhetorics that work for a group. While being human may mean having the ability to encode and decode texts (Burke, 1966), it is not the case that all human beings are equally skilled in responding to persuasive messages with countermessages. The masses may not be cultural dupes, but they are not necessarily skilled rhetors. Here, another fragment from the abortion communication event is instructive.

In interviews of abortion activists in California, Kristin Luker (1984, p. 111) noticed an interesting phenomenon. The women who became abortion activists reported one factor that led to replacing their guilt and negative feelings about abortions with active campaigning for a right to choose. It was not the experience of abortion per se; many of them had had abortions long before the change in their attitude. It was, they said, the ability of a few articulate rhetors that had been instrumental in helping them to resist the prior, dominant views. The presentation of different codings had helped them resist the dominant rhetorics. If popular media are read oppositionally only to the extent that countermedia exist to help audiences decode dominant messages, the mass media's role in social change processes may be extremely limited. In this case, Fiske (1987c, p. 326) is not wrong when he concludes that "resistive reading practices that assert the power of the subordinate in the process of representation and its subsequent pleasure pose a direct challenge to the power of capitalism to produce its subjects-in-ideology." It is simply that we do not yet know how widespread such resistive interpretive practices are or can be, given the more substantial obstacles outlined here. In contrast, we should weigh the power that these texts give to dominant audiences.

CODES AND THE PUBLIC

The disproportional viewing pleasures experienced by elite groups might present only a minor social problem if turning off the television set sufficiently closed down the influence of its texts. However, even in such relative silence, the television texts continue to go about constructing hegemony in important ways. This becomes evident if we shift our perspective so that the important audience for television is no longer individual viewers (even grouped by social interest) but "the public."

The term "public" is highly contested (Bitzer, 1987; Goodnight, 1987; Hauser, 1987; McGee, 1987). By "public" I mean those members of a nation-state who have had their interests articulated to a large enough mass of people to allow their preferred vocabulary legitimacy as a component in the formation of law and behavior. I suggest that television's political functions are not confined to its address to the pleasures of individuals. In addition, television "makes present" particular codings in the public space (Perelman & Olbrechts-Tyteca, 1971). Once such codings gain legitimacy they can be employed in forming public law, policy, and behavior. Even if they are not universally accepted, their presence gives them presumption (the right to participate in formulations, and even the need for others to take account of them in their policy formulations). Crucially, the upscale audience courted by television advertisers is also the group most likely to constitute the politically active public (e.g., "Young Blacks Have," 1987). Hence, television, or any mass medium, can do oppressive work solely by addressing the dominant audience that also constitutes the public.

It is because television "makes present in public" a vocabulary that prefers the dominant audience's interests that the dominant audience gets the most pleasure from television and that television actively promotes its interests. The fact that other groups can counter-read this discourse, and enjoy doing so, does not disrupt the direct functions of governance that television serves for dominant groups. A return to the case of the broadcast of abortion practices will explain this point more thoroughly.

Prime time television addressed the practice of abortion in clearly patterned ways. The very few, highly controversial programs concerning abortion in the sixties and early seventies occasioned sponsor withdrawal, boycotts of sponsors who did not withdraw, and extended editorial comment by opponents of legalized abortion (Condit, 1987). Probably as a consequence of this extra-popular control mechanism, a second round of abortion programs did not appear until the mid-eighties, more than a decade after abortion had been legalized through the actions of state legislators and the Supreme Court. For many years, television producers were dissuaded from making present the practice of abortion. When abortion reappeared, it did so with a dominant-preferring code firmly, if cleverly, in place.

The evolution of prime time television's treatment of abortion between the years 1984 and 1988 was such that it began to include more problematic cases of abortion, and it featured distinctive types. Nonetheless, the main clump of programs between 1984 and 1986 constructed a limited repertoire of meanings.

Different viewers, with different viewing habits, may have found themselves introduced to abortion in the mass culture in one of three ways. For viewers who enjoyed "family" programs, *Call to Glory, Webster, Family, Dallas,* or *Magruder and Loud* provided episodes in which prominent female characters found themselves unintentionally pregnant, decided against having an abortion, and then were relieved of the consequences of that decision through miscarriage or the discovery that they were not pregnant after all. Fans of MTM productions, and their liberal values (Feuer, 1984b), would have been introduced to abortion in a different manner. On *Cagney & Lacey, Hill Street Blues,* and *St. Elsewhere,* professionals supported the choices of transitory female characters to have abortions, and confronted the violence of the Pro-life movement. Finally, viewers might have first encountered televised abortion in a more sharply conflicted manner through *Spenser for Hire, L.A. Law,* or the second episode of *St. Elsewhere.* In these programs, central women characters made highly contested choices to undergo abortions.

Prime time television thus introduced the public to the practice of abortion with a polysemic voice. The mass mediated *message* itself appeared to bring different textual resources to different audiences. As I have previously argued, however, this textual polysemy had very clear limits (Condit, 1987). Regardless of whether the program was primarily "pro" or "anti," abortion was portrayed as a morally problematic act that was, nonetheless, the woman's choice. Although female characters decided in favor of and against abortions in a wide variety of problem situations, the abortions presented in prime time were never those of women in optimal reproductive situations. Women in caring, financially secure marriages did not abort healthy fetuses. Moreover, the practicalities of abortion were absent. There was no direct mention of the problem of payment, the pain of the operation, or the real but difficult alternatives of adoption or contraception.

As a consequence, dominant group vocabularies and practices were normalized (Condit, 1990). Career women could get abortions and feel more comfortable with the practice, even though their role or obligation as mothers was not erased. This was both an attractive enactment of career women's own reproductive practices and a discursive instantiation of their "choices" in the public vocabulary. The power distributed through such reinforcement is immense; it is virtually the social glue that allows dominant groups to coordinate their efforts in a democracy and thereby maintain power. Moreover, the reinforcement shields dominant groups from understanding the ways that different conditions might make different practices necessary or right for others. In the face of such a public culture, it was relatively easy for the Reagan administration, in its second term, to withdraw virtually all indirect financial support of abortion *and* of family planning in both the national and international arenas.

In contrast, prime time television neither informed the poor about how to finance abortions nor told the young how to avoid needing them and why they might want to avoid such a need. No constructive efforts on their behalf provided useful information or created pleasurable self-validation for these other groups of women. Hence, even if other groups were active interpreters of these programs, in order to seek legitimacy or cultural sympathy for their own practices they would have had to do double work—deconstructing the dominant code and reconstructing their own. In addition, to effect favorable policies, marginal groups also would have had to make a public argument in some other, *less pleasurable* arena, counterposing their interests and vocabulary to this now-dominant vocabulary. Finally, even if they were able to present an equally attractive argument, they would still, at best, be able to win a compromise with this already legitimated dominant code (a position they might not have faced absent its broadcast).

In sum, television disseminates and legitimates, in a pleasurable fashion, a political vocabulary that favors certain interests and groups over others, even if by no other means than consolidating the dominant audience by giving presence to their codes. Given the interest of advertisers in dominant economic groups, the ability of marginal groups to break this grip seems particularly unlikely. Fiske's conclusion (1987c, p. 319) that homogenization will lead to the inclusion of these other groups presumes much about the demographics of television audiences that is yet to be established. It also rests on imprecise definitions of "the popular" which do not seem to distinguish who the dominant elites are (the rich or the middle and well-to-do working class [e.g., in automotive unions]?) and who the "resisting populace" might be (secretaries or the unemployed?). Further examination of that relationship will require more careful studies of the economic side of this question. If, however, maximal economic return can be purchased through appeal to dominant audiences, then the fact that programs also attract oppositional readers around the globe may be only of minimal importance. In short, the jury is still out on the "popularity" of the mass media.

A second political consequence of television's coding of abortion practices has to do with the dissemination of new information to individuals. It can be explored through a turn to the third component of rhetorical events.

OCCASIONS: HISTORICAL AGENTS

Historical agents are embedded in particular occasions with specific power relationships, communicated through ideologies. Recent interpretations of ideology have begun to explore its character as information (Foucault, 1972; Lyotard, 1984; Sholle, 1988). In place of the old "ideology versus science" equation, some analyses suggest that one of the primary ways that ideology functions is by making present or dominant certain pieces of information to certain audiences. On this account, one important function of the broadcast of the *Cagney & Lacey* abortion episode was the degree to which it gave access to new and useful information about the practice of abortion.

To make such an evaluation of the *Cagney & Lacey* episode requires an accounting of the historical situation and self-consciousness about criteria. In the mid-eighties, it was clear that the legality of abortion was widely shared knowledge. Less widely shared was information of many kinds: about the types of women who have abortion and their reasons, about the experience of the operation, about women's control over their sexuality and fertility, and perhaps about the character of the fetus. *Cagney & Lacey* distributed some of this information (especially about the wide variety of "good" women who had abortions) but not others (the character of the operation and of the fetus).

The social impact of the program was in part a matter of the particular information it disseminated to different groups, even to groups able to decode the program through their own value structures. Jack, for example, was forced by the program's presence to confront the fact of abortion's "so-called social acceptability by too many people." Television programs distribute varying sorts of information about abortion, even to viewers who wish to change that practice and who actively and negatively decode the program.

Evaluating the impact of *Cagney & Lacey* on this learning dimension might seem to imply survey research, but that approach is unlikely to be cost effective. Research in the "direct effects" tradition of rhetorical studies indicated the virtual impossibility of quantitatively tracking learning and persuasion impacts on large audiences (e.g., Baran & Davis, 1975). Most important, in historical studies, scholars can never go back and get the kind of data that would meet the tests of quantitative-style knowledge claims. Further, academics are rarely prescient enough to know what programming is important with enough lead time to prepare for such surveys. Knowledge claims thus must be critically based.

Historically based evaluations need to take into account a more sensitive gauge than has been applied previously (and this might well be the most important moral of Radway's work on romance novels). Rather than describing a text and its readings simply as good or bad, critics need to develop judgments of better and worse. From this perspective, *Cagney & Lacey* should be evaluated on comparative grounds. First, it should be placed as the earliest of the second wave of the televisualization of abortion. Second, it should be compared to other programs and entertainment media. On this scale, the episode was far more conservative in the amount of information it provided than *St. Elsewhere*, with its far greater detail about the experience and emotions of having an abortion and inclusion of the issue of contraception. However, it was far more informative than episodes such as *Webster* or *Call to Glory*, neither of which ever directly even named abortion as "the option" nor dealt with the consequences.

Such an evaluation process will lead not to a condemnation or simple praise of a program but to a calibrated understanding of the particular role it played in introducing certain limited pieces of information to different ranges of audiences at different times. Critical analysis should therefore, at least at times, be rhetorical; it should be tied to the particularity of occasions: specific audiences, with specific codes or knowledges, addressed by specific programs and episodes (McGee, 1982; Wichelns, 1972). Such an approach does not deny the wisdom of also exploring the intertextuality of programs, the stripped character of the viewing experience (Newcomb, 1984, p. 44), and the disengaged character of much viewing. It merely adds one additional vector to our understanding.

EVALUATION

After considering the historical moment, the public code constructed, and the range of audience readings, we might be in a position to provide an evaluation of *Cagney & Lacey*. I wish to turn that evaluation to the key criterion on which I see Fiske, Hall, Morley, Radway, and others (but probably not Newcomb) converging, that is, the judgment of a mass communication event based on its "resistance" to the dominant ideology. This judgmental criterion rests on the assumption that academics have a duty to the society that pays their salaries to try to produce a better world. This is a duty widely accepted for the ever more technically oriented scientists, although with admittedly different procedures. In the humanities and social sciences, however, the execution of that criterion is eternally and politically controversial, and that deters us from encouraging scholars in communication studies to undertake endeavors of a sort we virtually demand from scholars in natural studies. I nonetheless support such efforts.

For many years, critics interested in bringing about positive social changes assumed that the deconstruction of the dominant ideologies contained in popular and political texts was the best contribution toward human progress. This kind of criticism gradually became too predictable to suit the tastes of an academic machine that voraciously devours "new ideas" in preference to the good execution of old ones. Furthermore, at its worst, and too frequently, such criticism merely imposed the ideology/methodology of a particular political preference upon dominant texts, threatening to produce nothing but a blanket condemnation of the status quo rather than insight into how to improve society.

Today, with the rise of attention to audiences, such a textual approach has come under further attack. Fiske (1987c) (see also 1987b) writes, for example:

> Textual studies of television now have to stop treating it as a closed text, that is, as one where the dominant ideology exerts considerable, if not total, influence over its ideological structure and therefore over its reader. Analysis has to pay less attention to the textual strategies of preference or closure and more to the gaps and spaces that open up to meanings not preferred by the textual structure. (p. 64)

In placing enormous faith in the capacity of audiences to resist, however, a similar blindness may be on its way to being produced on the other side. We can endlessly generate studies that demonstrate that clever readers can take pleasure in reconstructing texts, but this does not certify that mass communication in general functions as a force for positive social change.

The assumption that pleasure liberates is too simplistic on a myriad of counts. To begin with, Fiske's argument (1987c, p. 19) is based on the premise that "Pleasure results from a particular relationship between meanings and power. Pleasure for the subordinate is produced by the assertion of one's social identity in resistance to, in independence of, or in negotiation with, the structure of domination." This is a flat assertion with no support. It is based on the claim that "escape" is always escape from the dominant ideologies' subjective positioning of the marginal person (p. 317). While Fiske documents that this kind of escape can and does sometimes occur, he does not demonstrate that it is the only or primary kind of pleasure to be gained from a text by a subordinate. There are a wide variety of pleasures; some of them are merely temporary escape from truly painful thoughts and activities, and these do not challenge the subjective identity television programs present. The most important of these pleasures is what Kenneth Burke (1969, p. 19) has called "identification." One can fully identify with the rich patrons of *Dynasty*, enjoying the vicarious experience of opulence, without building any oppositional identity. I have revelled in such play, the pleasure coming from a temporary "giving in" rather than from resistance. My female career-oriented students generally admit relishing the Cinderella myth offered by *An Officer and a Gentleman*. Such pleasurable identification does not require that we naively confuse reality and our own position (a different thesis which Fiske [1987c, pp. 44–47, 63–72] argues against forcefully and accurately). We know that we are not as rich as Krystal and will never be. Nonetheless, we can enjoy playing as if we were. This kind of pleasure offers only temporary escape.

I would not willingly deny any of us such pleasures. Human life is hard, under capitalism or any other system human beings have yet devised. Radway's Smithton readers need a pleasurable escape from their oppressive husbands and demanding children. However, we should be very cautious about our portrayal of such escape as liberating. Attention to the discrepancies between critical readings of television's embedding of subjects in patriarchy and those subjects' own readings (the opening of Radway's book) should not obscure the realization that both personal pleasure and collective domination can go on at the same time (the conclusion of Radway's book). We need to make a clear distinction between the personal or "private" experience of pleasure which temporarily liberates us from the painful conditions of our lives and the collectivized pleasures which, in the right historical conditions, may move us toward changing those conditions. Because of the character of the mass media, both are social pleasures, but *collectivized* (grouped, internally organized through communication production) action and pleasure are essential to social change. Alterations in subjectivity may indeed provide a first step in that latter process, but it is an extremely limited step, and it is not the case that all pleasurable readings produce such resisting subjectivities (Sholle, 1988, p. 33). Moreover, if the cost of mildly altered subjectivities is complacence, the potential for change may be offset. Television does not, therefore, simply offer "a set of forces for social change" (Fiske, 1987c, p. 326); television is engaged in a set of social forces within which actors may or may not promote social change.

To assess the social consequences of a mass communication event requires, consequently, that we dispense with the totalized concept of "resistance." It is not enough to describe a program or an interpretation of a program as oppositional. It is essential to describe what particular things are resisted and how that resistance occurs. In part, this requires taking more seriously the melding of liberal interest group theory and Marxism evident in Fiske's work (1987c, p. 16). Fiske's explicit political theory dismantles views of politics that portray it either as an even-handed barter between various interest groups (the classic liberal account) or as the dominance of a unified, all-powerful elite. Instead, he argues (1987c, p. 16), as do I (1990), that politics is a battle and barter among a wide range of groups, each of which is differently and unevenly empowered. Unfortunately, like most other audience theorists, Fiske does not carry this theory through into his analysis. Instead, he reduces the multiplicity of differently empowered groups to "the dominant" and "the resistant." Such a totalized concept of resistance from a system is at odds with a theory that posits a wide range of groups with a wide range of investments in the system they share. Given that perspective, for my interpretation of *Cagney & Lacey,* I offer the following evaluations.

From the perspective of women like Jill, the decisions by the production team headed by Barney Rosenzweig, which resulted in this particular treatment of abortion on prime time television, were mildly progressive. Jill's interpretation needs to be supplemented by that of other women, but for her the program portrayed powerful characterizations of "good" women having abortions and reaffirmed the evaluation that abortion was not a repudiation of familial love. Most important, it affirmed that even though abortion is the morally problematic termination of the potential of a growing creature's life, it is always the woman who must weigh the principles and factors involved to make the decision. This is perhaps surprisingly mild progressive ideological work for a production team that dealt in outstanding detail with the experience of rape and that treated the fallout of the AIDS crisis on single adults with gingerly directness. The program, however, was the leader of the second wave of telecasts and took a great deal of public criticism even for these steps. For Jill's group, it accomplished some important ideological work.

For women in poverty and women of color the program is more mixed. It explicitly affirmed the choices of a particular minority woman, but it did not deal with the ways in which poor women might fund abortion or contraception. It did not deal with the options provided by extended families or with the importance of motherhood in different cultures. It offered a sugary and unrealistic moral, "have an abortion so you can go to school and get off welfare," that may have appealed to latent racism in white audiences more than assisting poor women with real options. In the face of such silences, the Republican administration could continue its largely hidden work in pro-natalism by dismantling funding for family planning. From the perspective of these groups of viewers, this restricted presentation of abortion represents a serious political shortcoming of this episode.

The situation is much grimmer from Jack's perspective as a clearly marginal viewer of this text, and in many ways a person whom I sensed to be involved in popular culture (especially sports), but disempowered by the dominant political economy. I find it difficult to argue that Jack found his reading of this text, resistant and skilled as it was, to be either a predominantly pleasurable or liberating experience. Jack expressed the following general response to the program's significance: "I think it's a [sic] pretty much a devastating blow, not that it's totally going to stop the movement, but it set us back." For Jack, as for other relatively unempowered males, especially of Pro-life positions, *Cagney & Lacey* did not promote the social changes they preferred. Even their resistant readings left them with the feeling of oppression by the media.

Cagney & Lacey's broadcast about abortion broke new ideological ground, inserting new political codes into the public culture. It was thus a progressive but not radical text that tended to oppose the interests of marginally positioned traditional males. It favored the interests of career women but only marginally supported other groups of women.

I have, of course, stacked the deck here by probing readings that scramble the left's general presumption that marginal readers of texts are the potential source of liberation, the groups with whom we, as academics, ought to identify and praise. I have done so to heighten my point that "resistance" and the metaphor of a "dominant system" is a bad way to phrase what it is those interested in social change should praise. History creates "hegemonies," but hegemonies are not equivalent to dominant ideologies. A hegemony is a negotiation among elite and nonelite groups and therefore always contains interests of nonelite groups, though to a lesser degree. To resist the power of dominant groups may be safe, but to resist the hegemony that is constructed in negotiation with those groups is always also to resist what is partially of one's own interests. The totalizing concept of resistance should give way to the recognition and analysis of historically particular acts in order to bring about specific social changes. This shift will require academics to affirm particular goals rather than simply to critique that which is.

CONCLUSIONS

Recent reemphasis on the audience as an important component of what happens in the process of mass communicating is a useful redress of an old imbalance. We should avoid, however, totalizing the audience's abilities. The receiver's political power in mass mediated societies is dependent upon a complex balance of historically particular forces which include the relative abilities of popular groups and their access to oppositional codes, the work/pleasure ratio of the available range of the media's intertextual polysemy, the modifications programs make in the dominant code, and the degree of empowerment provided to dominant audiences.

To scholars, this balance of forces presents a series of challenges. There is a need to explore more precisely the relative decoding abilities of audiences and their access to counter-rhetorics. There is also a need to continue to explore what texts "make present," even without regard to their "seams," through careful historically grounded studies of the particular issue contents of television programming. There is, finally, a need to explore the "occasion" of a discourse in terms other than the family viewing context (contexts emphasized in Fiske [1987c, p. 239] and Morley [1986, p. 14]). Different families and different members of families are always embedded in larger political occasions that create collective experiences across family walls. Unless we ask about the particular contents of particular sets of programs, the relationship of those contents to the stasis of the issue for viewers and for the larger society at the time of broadcast, we will not be able to assess fully television's roles in the process of social change for its various constituencies.

There are additional implications for scholars as teachers. One of the primary ways through which we can bring about positive social change is through our teaching of undergraduates for whom our arcane battles about research protocols are rightfully boring and meaningless. For our students, decoding alternatives, through painful effort, can become pleasurable resources they can use throughout life. A perspective that emphasizes the receiver's placement within a complexly balanced process suggests the need to continue to use classrooms to teach students a range of decodings for possible texts, a project that may include increasing their ideological range (the ability to see *An Officer and a Gentleman* as *Cinderella*, Sonny Crocket as a 1980s John Wayne, *Dallas* as the costs inherent to capitalism). It might also include familiarizing students with the history of the various issue contents of the mass media. Studies of the participation of news and entertainment programming, in particular social movements and issues, might be added to genre studies and analyses of private audiences (e.g., Hallin, 1986; Rushing 1986a; 1986b).

As a whole, the effort to gain a more variegated picture of audiences is an important one. However, the tendency to isolate the audience from the communication process and then pronounce the social effects of mass communication based on the ability of some receivers to experience pleasure in producing oppositional decoding is undesirable. It simply repeats the error of message-dominated research which attempted to describe the mass media's influence solely by investigating texts (or, in other research strands, presumed intents of sources). Audience members are neither simply resistive nor dupes. They neither find television simply pleasurable, simply an escape, nor simply obnoxious and oppressive. The audience's variability is a consequence of the fact that humans, in their inherent character as audiences, are inevitably situated in a communication *system*, of which they are a part, and hence have some influence within, but by which they are also influenced. To study the role of that communication system in the processes that change our humanity and the system itself therefore requires a multiplicity of approaches to the critical analysis of the massive media.

Acknowledgments: The author thanks John Louis Lucaites for his useful insights and Lawrence Grossberg for continual challenges that helped to produce this essay.

NOTES

1. I am aware that to locate intent in television programs is a difficult matter because of the multiplicity of inputs into such productions. However, this multiplicity does not negate the fact that messages have sources and therefore some collection of intended meanings. To abrogate the use of the term simply because intent is complex would be to ignore an important component of the communication process.
2. Radway (1984; 1986) begins such a delimitation with regard to her case study of romance readers.
3. I choose the terms "Pro-life" and "Pro-choice" because they are the names employed by the members of the respective movements to define themselves.

REFERENCES

Baran, S. J., & Davis, D. K. (1975). The audience of public television: Did Watergate make a difference? *Central States Speech Journal, 26*, 93–98.
Bennett, T., & Woollacott, J. (1987). *Bond and beyond: The political career of a popular hero.* New York: Methuen.
Bitzer, L. F. (1987). Rhetorical public communication. *Critical Studies in Mass Communication, 4*, 425–428.
Burke, J., Wilson, H., & Agardy, S. (1983). *A Country Practice and the child audience—A case study.* Melbourne: Australian Broadcasting Tribunal.
Burke, K. (1966). Definition of man. In *Language as symbolic action* (pp. 3–24). Berkeley: University of California Press.
Burke, K. (1969). Identification. In *A rhetoric of motives* (pp. 55–59). Berkeley: University of California Press.
Condit, C. (1987). Abortion on television: The "system" and ideological production. *Journal of Communication Inquiry, 11*, 47–60.
Condit, C. (1990). *Decoding abortion rhetoric: Communicating social change.* Urbana: University of Illinois Press.
Eco, U. (1979). Denotation and connotation. In *A theory of semiotics* (pp. 54–57). Bloomington: Indiana University Press.
Feuer, J. (1984a). MTM enterprises: An overview. In J. Feuer, P. Kerr, & T. Vahimagi (Eds.), *MTM: "Quality television"* (pp. 1–31). London: British Film Institute.

Feuer, J. (1984b). The MTM style. In J. Feuer, P. Kerr, & T. Vahimagi (Eds.), *MTM: "Quality Television"* (pp. 32–60). London: British Film Institute.

Fiske, J. (1986). Television: Polysemy and popularity. *Critical Studies in Mass Communication, 3,* 391–408.

Fiske, J. (1987a). British cultural studies and television. In R. C. Allen (Ed.), *Channels of discourse* (pp. 254–289). Chapel Hill: University of North Carolina Press.

Fiske, J. (1987b). *Cagney and Lacey:* Reading character structurally and politically. *Communication, 9,* 399–426.

Fiske, J. (1987c). *Television culture.* New York: Methuen.

Foucault, M. (1972). *The archaeology of knowledge.* New York: Pantheon.

Goodnight, G. T. (1987). Public discourse. *Critical Studies in Mass Communication, 4,* 428–432.

Hall, S. (1980) Encoding/decoding. In S. Hall, D. Hobson, A. Lowe, & P. Willis (Eds.), *Culture, media, language* (pp. 128–138). London: Hutchinson.

Hallin, D. C. (1986). *The "uncensored war". The media and Vietnam.* New York: Oxford University Press.

Hauser, G. A. (1987). Features of the public sphere. *Critical Studies in Mass Communication, 4,* 437–441.

Hobson, D. (1982). *Crossroads: The drama of a soap opera.* London: Methuen.

Katz, E., & Liebes, T. (1984). Once upon a time in *Dallas. Intermedia, 12,* 28–32.

Kellner, D. (1982). TV, ideology, and emancipatory popular culture. In H. Newcomb (Ed.), *Television: The critical view* (3rd ed., pp. 386–421). New York: Oxford University Press.

Kerr, P. (1984). The making of (the) MTM (show). In J. Feuer, P. Kerr, & T. Vahimagi (Eds.), *MTM: "Quality television"* (pp. 61–98). London: British Film Institute.

Lucaites J., & Condit, C. (1986, November). *Equality in the martyrd black vision.* Paper presented at the meeting of the Speech Communication Association, Chicago.

Luker, K. (1984). *Abortion and the politics of motherhood.* Berkeley: University of California Press.

Lyotard, J. F. (1984). *The postmodern condition: A report on knowledge.* Minneapolis: University of Minnesota Press.

McGee, M. (1982). A materialist's conception of rhetoric. In R. E. McKerrow (Ed.), *Explorations in rhetoric* (pp. 23–48). Scott, Foresman and Company.

McGee, M. C. (1987). Power to (the people). *Critical Studies in Mass Communication, 4,* 432–437.

Meehan, E. R. (1986). Conceptualizing culture as commodity: The problem of television. *Critical Studies in Mass Communication, 3,* 448–457.

Meyrowitz, J. (1985). *No sense of place.* New York: Oxford University Press.

Morley, D. (1980). *The "Nationwide" audience: Structure and decoding.* London: British Film Institute.

Morley, D. (1986). *Family television: Cultural power and domestic leisure.* London: Comedia.

Newcomb, H. (1984). On the dialogic aspects of mass communication. *Critical Studies in Mass Communication, 1,* 34–50.

Palmer, P. (1986). *The lively audience: A study of children around the TV set.* Sydney: Allen & Unwin.

Perelman, P., & Olbrechts-Tyteca, L. (1971). *The new rhetoric: A treatise on argumentation.* Notre Dame: University of Notre Dame Press.

Radway, J. (1984). *Reading the romance: Woman, patriarchy, and popular literature*. Chapel Hill: University of North Carolina Press.

Radway, J. (1986). Identifying ideological seams: Mass culture, analytical method, and political practice. *Communication, 9*, 93–123.

Rushing, J. (1986a). Mythic evolution of "The new frontier" in mass mediated rhetoric. *Critical Studies in Mass Communication, 3*, 265–296.

Rushing, J. (1986b). Ronald Reagan's "Star Wars" address: Mythic containment of technical reasoning. *Quarterly Journal of Speech, 72*, 415–433.

Sholle, D. J. (1988). Critical studies: From the theory of ideology to power/knowledge. *Critical Studies in Mass Communication, 5*, 16–41.

Steiner, L. (1988). Oppositional decoding as an act of resistance. *Critical Studies in Mass Communication, 5*, 1–15.

Wander, P. (1984). The third persona: An ideological turn in rhetorical theory. *Central States Speech Journal, 35*, 197–216.

Wichelns, H. (1972). The literary criticism of oratory. In R. L. Scott & B. Brock (Eds.), *Methods of rhetorical criticism: A twentieth century perspective* (pp. 27–60). New York: Harper & Row.

Young blacks have higher voting rate than 18–24 whites. (1987, October 7). *The Champaign-Urbana News-Gazette*, p. A13.

18 The Domestic Economy of Television Viewing in Postwar America

LYNN SPIGEL

In 1952, the Western-Holly Company marketed a new design in domestic technology, the TV-stove. The oven included a window through which the housewife could watch her chicken roast. Above the oven window was a television screen which presented an even more spectacular sight. With the aid of this machine the housewife would be able to prepare her meal, but at the same time she could watch television. Although it was clearly an odd object, this TV-stove was not simply a historical fluke. Rather, its invention is a reminder of the concrete social, economic, and ideological conditions that made this contraption possible. Indeed, the TV-stove was a response to the conflation of labor and leisure time at home. If it now seems strange, this has as much to do with the way in which society has conceptualized work and leisure as it does with the machine's bizarre technological form.[1]

In this essay, I examine television viewing in terms of a history of ideas concerning gendered patterns of work and leisure in the home. Based on a study of popular media from the postwar era (especially middle class women's magazines), this essay considers how television was introduced to the American housewife. Television's innovation after World War II occasioned a multitude of responses and expectations voiced in films, magazines, newspapers, and on television itself. These popular discourses were replete with ambivalence about television's relationship to family life. As the TV-stove so dramatically suggests, there was a profound uncertainty about television's place and function in the home, an uncertainty that gave rise to a fierce debate on the cultural and social value of this new domestic object and entertainment form.

Indeed, as other historians have shown, this kind of ambivalence has characterized America's response to a host of household technologies, including television's most obvious predecessor, radio (Covert, 1984; Davis, 1965). In this respect, the popular debates about television should be seen not as an aberrant phenomenon but rather as a specific manifestation of a larger history of ideas about household technology, ideas which were firmly inscribed in

387

gendered patterns of labor and leisure in domestic space. It is these patterns, as they were described to the first wave of television viewers, that I consider in the following pages. To do so, I first briefly describe the historical roots of the domestic ideology and some theoretical questions to which they give rise.

GENDER, WORK, AND LEISURE

Since the nineteenth century, middle class ideals of domesticity had been predicated on divisions of leisure time and work time. This doctrine of two spheres represented human activity in spatial terms: the public world came to be conceived of as a place of productive labor, while the home was seen as a site of rejuvenation and consumption. By the 1920s, the public world was still a sphere of work, but it was also opened up to a host of commercial pleasures like movies and amusement parks that were incorporated into middle class family life styles. The ideal home, however, remained a place of revitalization and, with the expansion of convenience products that promised to reduce household chores, domesticity was even less associated with production.

As feminists have argued, this separation has served to justify the exploitation of the housewife whose work at home simply does not count. Along these lines, Nancy Folbre (1982) claims that classical economics considers women's work as voluntary labor and therefore outside the realm of exploitation. In addition, she argues, even Marxist critics neglect the issue of domestic exploitation since they assume that the labor theory of value can be applied only to efficiency-oriented production for the market and not to "inefficient" and "idiosyncratic" household chores.

But as feminist critics and historians have shown, the home is indeed a site of labor. Not only do women do physical chores, but also the basic relations of our economy and society are reproduced at home, including the literal reproduction of workers through child rearing labor. Once the home is considered as a work place, the divisions between public/work and domestic/leisure become less clear. The ways in which work and leisure are connected, however, remain a complex issue.

Henri Lefebvre's studies of everyday life offer ways to consider the general interrelations among work, leisure, and family life in modern society. In his foreword to the 1958 edition of *Critique de la Vie Quotidienne*, Lefebvre argues that:

> Leisure . . . cannot be separated from work. It is the same man who, after work, rests or relaxes or does whatever he chooses. Every day, at the same time, the worker leaves the factory, and the employee, the office. Every week, Saturday and Sunday are spent on leisure activities, with the same regularity as that of the weekdays' work. Thus we must think in terms of the unity "work-leisure," because that unity exists, and everyone tries to program his

own available time according to what his work is—and what it is not. (1958/1979, p. 136)

While Lefebvre concentrated on the "working man," the case of the housewife presents an even more pronounced example of the integration of work and leisure in everyday life.

In the absence of a thoroughgoing critique of the issues surrounding work and leisure, it has been difficult for television critics and historians to deal with the central importance of domestic labor for television spectatorship. Recent British ethnographic research suggests that men and women tend to use television according to their specific position within the distribution of leisure and labor activities inside and outside the home (Gray, 1987; Morley, 1986). In the American context, two of the most serious examinations come from Tania Modleski (1983) and Nick Browne (1984), who theorize the way television watching fits into a general pattern of everyday life where work and leisure are intertwined. Modleski suggests that the soap opera might be understood in terms of the "rhythms of reception," or the way women working at home relate to the text within a specific milieu of distraction: cleaning, cooking, child rearing, etc. Browne concentrates not on the individual text but rather on the entire television schedule, which he claims is ordered according to the logic of the workday of both men and women. As he writes, "the position of the programs in the television schedule reflects and is determined by the work-structured order of the real social world. The patterns of position and flow imply the question of who is home, and through complicated social relays and temporal mediations, link television to the modes, processes, and scheduling of production characteristic of the general population" (p. 176).

WOMEN'S MAGAZINES AND TELEVISION

The fluid interconnection between leisure and labor at home presents a context for exploring the ways women use and understand television programming in their daily lives. In the following pages, I focus on a moment in American history, specifically the years 1948–1955, when women were first learning how to accommodate television, both as a domestic object and as an entertainment form. During these years, more than half of all American households installed television, and the basic patterns of daytime television emerged as a distinct cultural form which entailed a particular set of female viewing practices. While most women might not have had the elaborate mechanism offered by the TV-stove, they were in the process of adapting themselves to—or else resisting—a new and curious entertainment machine.

How can we understand the way people integrated television into their lives some 30 years ago? How can we discover a history of everyday life that was not recorded by the people who lived it at the time? The women's home magazines I examine illuminate the reception of television as it was registered in popular media of the postwar period. These magazines included graphics, articles, cartoons, and illustrations depicting television's relationship to family life.[2] While they cannot tell us how television was actually received by people at the time, popular magazines do reveal an intertextual context through which people could make sense of television and its relation to their lives.

The debates about television drew upon and magnified the more general obsession with the reconstruction of family life and domestic ideals after World War II. The 1950s was a decade that placed an enormous amount of cultural capital in the ability to form a family and to live out a set of highly structured gender roles. Although people at the time might well have experienced and understood the constraining aspects of this domestic dream, it nevertheless was a consensus ideology, promising practical benefits like security and stability to people who had witnessed the shocks and social dislocations of the previous two decades. As Elaine Tyler May (1988) suggests, while people acknowledged the limitations of postwar domesticity, they nevertheless often spoke of their strong faith in the overall project of being in a family. In this social climate, television was typically welcomed as a catalyst for renewed familial values. Indeed, television, in many popular discussions, was depicted as a panacea for the broken homes and hearts of wartime life; not only was it shown to restore faith in family togetherness, but as the most sought-after appliance for sale in postwar America, it also renewed faith in the splendors of consumer capitalism. By the same token, however, television was also greeted in less euphoric terms, and as I have argued elsewhere (1988a; 1988b), the discourses on television typically expressed profound doubts about domesticity—especially, gender roles in the home.

Women's home magazines were the primary venue for this debate on television and the family. Yet, apart from the occasional reference, these magazines have been disregarded in television histories. Rather than focusing on the social and domestic context, broadcast history has continually framed its object of study around questions of industry, regulation, and technological invention: that is, around spheres where men have participated as executives, policy makers, and inventors. Women, on the other hand, are systematically marginalized in television history. According to the assumptions of our current historical paradigms, the woman is simply the receiver of the television text—the one to whom the advertiser promotes products. This is not to say industrial history necessarily fails to explain gender relations. Indeed, as other feminist critics have shown, the very notion of femininity itself is in part constructed through and by mass media images as they are produced by the "culture industries." But industrial history clearly needs to be supplemented by methods of investigation that will better illuminate women's subjective experiences and the way those experiences, in turn, might have affected industry output and policies.

By looking at women's magazines as a source of historical evidence, we find another story, one that tells us something (however partial and mediated) about the way women might have experienced the arrival of television in their own homes. These magazines, through their debates on television's place in the domestic sphere, provided women with opportunities to negotiate rules and practices for watching television at home. In addition, they addressed women not simply as passive consumers of promotional rhetoric but also as producers within the domestic sphere. In fact, even the television manufacturers, who used women's magazines to promote the sale of television sets, seem to have recognized this productive role. For, as I will show, rather than simply offering women the passive consumer luxury of total television pleasure, the manufacturers tailored their messages to the everyday concerns of the housewife; they typically acknowledged the conflicts between household chores and television leisure, and they offered their products as solutions to these conflicts.

In this sense, I emphasize the importance of looking at advertisements in relation to the wider media context in which they appear. A popular assumption in advertising history and theory is that ads are the voice of big industry, a voice that instills consumer fantasies into the minds of the masses. But advertising is not simply one voice; rather it is necessarily composed of multiple voices. Advertising adopts the voice of an imaginary consumer—it must speak from his or her point of view, even if that point of view is at odds with the immediate goals of the sales effort. In this respect, television advertisers did not simply promote ideas and values in the sense of an overwhelming "product propaganda." Rather, they followed certain *discursive rules* found in a media form that was popular with women since the nineteenth century. Advertisers often adjusted their sales messages to fit with the concerns voiced in women's magazines, and they also used conventions of language and representation that were typical of the magazines as a whole.

The common thread uniting the ads, editorial content, and pictorial representations was mode of address. The discourses of middle class women's magazines assumed, a priori, that women were housewives and that their interests necessarily revolved around cleaning, cooking, child rearing, and, less explicitly, love making. Indeed, even though the 1950s witnessed a dramatic rise in the female labor force—and, in particular, the number of married women taking jobs outside the home rose significantly (Chafe, 1972; Gatlin, 1987)—these magazines tacitly held to an outdated model of femininity, ignoring the fact that both working class and middle class women were dividing their time between the family work space and the public work space. In this sense, the conventions formed for viewing television arose in relation to this housewife figure; even if the actual reader was employed outside the domestic sphere, her leisure time was represented in terms of her household work. Representations of television continually presented women with a notion of spectatorship that was inextricably intertwined with their useful labor at home.

These magazines offered women instructions on how to cope with television, and they established a set of viewing practices based around the tenuous balance of labor and leisure at home. They told women of the utopian possibilities of fantasy and romantic transport that television might bring to their relatively "unglorious" lives as homemakers, but they also warned that television might wreak havoc on the home and therefore had to be carefully managed and skillfully controlled. Indeed, these magazines offered women an ambivalent picture of television; the television set appeared less as a simple consumer luxury than as a complex set of problems that called for women's rational decisions and careful examination. In the discussion below, I consider the industrial solution to the working/viewing continuum, then detail the concerns which circulated in magazines, and finally address some of the implications these popular discourses had for gender dynamics in general.

THE INDUSTRY'S IDEAL VIEWER

Unlike the many household appliances which, since the nineteenth century, have promised to simplify women's work, the television set threatened to disrupt the efficient functioning of the household. And while other home entertainment media such as the phonograph could be enjoyed while doing household tasks, pleasure in television appeared to be fundamentally incompatible with women's productive labor. As William Boddy (1979) argues, the broadcasting industry recognized this conflict when radio was first introduced to the public. But overcoming its initial reluctance, the industry successfully developed daytime radio in the 1930s, and by the 1940s housewives were a faithful audience for soap operas and advice programs.

During the postwar years, advertisers and networks once more viewed the daytime market with skepticism, fearing that their loyal radio audiences would not be able to make the transition to television. The industry assumed that, unlike radio, television might require the housewife's complete attention and thus disrupt her work in the home (Boddy, 1985). Indeed, while network prime time schedules were well worked out in 1948, both networks and advertisers were reluctant to feature regular daytime television programs.

The first network to offer a regular daytime schedule was DuMont, which began operations on its New York station WABD in November 1948. It seems likely that DuMont, which had severe problems competing with CBS and NBC, entered the daytime market to offset its economic losses in prime time during a period when even the major networks were losing money on television. Explaining the economic strategy behind the move into daytime, one DuMont executive claimed, "WABD is starting daytime programming because it is not economically feasible to do otherwise. Night time programming alone could not support radio, nor can it support television" ("DuMont Expansion," 1949, p. 23). In December 1949, DuMont offered a two-hour afternoon program to its nine affiliate stations, and it also made kinescopes available to its non-interconnected affiliates. DuMont director Commander Mortimer W. Loewi reasoned that the move into daytime would attract small ticket advertisers who wanted to buy "small segments of time at a low, daytime rate" ("Daytime Video," 1949, p. 3).

It was in 1951 that the major networks aggressively attempted to colonize the housewife's workday with advice programs, soap operas, and variety shows. One of the central reasons for the networks' move into daytime that year was the fact that prime time hours were fully booked by advertisers and that, by this point, there was more demand for television advertising in general. Daytime might have been more risky than prime time, but it had the advantage of being available—and at a cheaper network cost. Confident of its move into daytime, CBS claimed, "We aren't risking our reputation by predicting that daytime television will be a solid sell-out a year from today . . . and that once again there will be some sad advertisers who didn't read the tea leaves right" (*Sponsor*, 1951, p. 19). Alexander Stronach Jr., ABC vice president, was equally certain about the daytime market, and having just taken the plunge with the *Frances Langford-Don Ameche Show* (a variety program budgeted at the then steep $40,000 a week), Stronach told *Newsweek* (1951, p. 56), "It's a good thing electric dishwashers and washing machines were invented. The housewives will need them."

The networks' faith in daytime carried through to advertisers. In September 1951, the trade journal *Televiser* (p. 20) reported that "47 big advertisers have used daytime network television during the past season or are starting this Fall." Included were such well-known companies as American Home Products, Best Foods, Proctor and Gamble, General Foods, Hazel Bishop Lipsticks, Minute Maid, Hotpoint, and the woman's magazine *Ladies' Home Journal*.

But even after the networks and advertisers had put their faith in daytime programming, they had not resolved the conflict between women's work and television. The industry still needed to construct program types conducive to the activities of household work. The format that has received the most critical attention is the soap opera, which first came to network television in December, 1950. As Robert C. Allen (1985) demonstrates, early soap opera producers like Irna Philips of *Guiding Light* were skeptical of moving their shows from radio to television. By 1954, however, the Neilsen Company reported that the soaps had a substantial following; *Search For Tomorrow* was the second most popular daytime show, while *Guiding Light* was in fourth place. The early soaps, with their minimum of action and visual interest, allowed housewives to listen to dialogue while working in another room. Moreover, their segmented story lines (usually two a day), as well as their repetition and constant explanation of previous plots, allowed women to divide their attention between viewing and household work.

Another popular solution to the daytime dilemma was the segmented variety format which allowed women to enter and exit the text according to its discrete narrative units. One of DuMont's first programs, for example, was a shopping show (alternatively called *At Your Service* and *Shopper's Matinee*) which consisted of 21 entertainment segments, all revolving around different types of "women's issues." For instance, the "Bite Shop" presented fashion tips while "Kitchen Fare" gave culinary advice ("Daytime Video," 1949; "DuMont Daytime," 1949). While DuMont's program was short lived, the basic principles survived in the daytime shows at the major networks. Programs like *The Gary Moore Show* (CBS), *The Kate Smith Show* (NBC), *The Arthur Godfrey Show* (CBS) and *Home* (NBC) catered to housewife audiences with their segmented variety of entertainment and/or advice. Instituted in 1954 by NBC President Sylvester Pat Weaver (also responsible for the early morning *Today Show*), *Home* borrowed its narrative techniques from women's magazines with segments on gardening, child psychology, food, fashion, health, and interior decor. As *Newsweek* reported, "The program is planned to do for women on the screen what the women's magazines have long done in print" ("For the Girls," 1954, p. 92).

As NBC began to adapt narrative strategies from women's periodicals, it also initiated an advertising campaign that instructed housewives on ways to watch the new programs while doing household chores. In 1955, *Ladies' Home Journal* and *Good Housekeeping* carried ads for NBC's daytime lineup which suggested that not only the programs but also the scheduling of the programs would suit the content and organization of the housewife's day. The ads evoked a sense of fragmented leisure time and suggested that television viewing could be conducted in a state of distraction. But this was not the kind of critical contemplative distraction that Walter Benjamin (1936/1969) suggested in his seminal essay, "The Work of Art in the Age of Mechanical Reproduction." Rather, the ads implied that the housewife could accomplish her chores in a state of "utopian forgetfulness" as she moved freely between her work and the act of watching television.

One ad that is particularly striking in this regard includes a sketch of a housewife and her little daughter at the top of the page. Below this, the graphic layout is divided into eight boxes composed of television screens, each representing a different program in NBC's daytime lineup. The caption functions as the housewife's testimony to her distracted state. She asks, "Where Did the Morning Go ? The house is tidy . . . but it hasn't seemed like a terribly tiring morning. . . . I think I started ironing while I watched the *Sheila Graham Show*." The housewife goes on to register details of the programs, but she cannot with certainty account for her productive activities in the home. Furthermore, as the ad's layout suggests, the woman's daily activities are literally fragmented according to the pattern of the daytime television schedule, to the extent that her everyday experiences become imbricated in a kind of serial narrative. Most significantly, her child pictured at the top of the ad is depicted within the contours of a television screen so that the labor of child rearing is itself made part of the narrative pleasures offered by the NBC daytime lineup (*Ladies' Home Journal*, 1955, p. 130).

NEGOTIATING WITH THE IDEAL VIEWER

Although industry advertisements offered television as spiritual transportation for the housewife/spectator, popular media were not complicit with distraction as a remedy for the television/labor problem. Women's magazines warned of television's thoroughly negative effect on household chores and suggested that a careful management of domestic space might solve the problem. In 1950, *House Beautiful* warned of television: "It delivers about five times as much wallop as radio and requires in return five times as much attention. . . . It's impossible to get anything accomplished in the same room while it's on." The magazine offered a spatial solution, telling women "to get the darn thing out of the living room," and into the TV room, cellar, library, "or as a last resort stick it in the dining room" (Crosby, p. 125).

An ad for Drano *(American Home,* 1955a, p. 14) provided a solution to television's obstruction of household chores: The housewife is shown watching her afternoon soap opera, but this nonproductive activity is sanctioned only insofar as her servant does the housework. As the maid exclaims, "Shucks, I'll never know if she gets her man 'cause this is the day of the week I put Drano in all the drains!'" The Drano Company thus attempted to sell its product by giving women a glamorous vision of themselves enjoying an afternoon of television. But it could do so only by splitting the function of leisure and work across two representational figures: the lady of leisure and the domestic servant.

If the domestic servant was a fantasy solution to the conflict between work and television, the women's magazines suggested more practical ways to manage the problem. As *Better Homes and Gardens* suggested, the television set should be placed in an area where it could be viewed, "while you're doing things up in the kitchen" (Adams & Hungerford, 1949, p. 38). Similarly, *American Home* (1954, p. 39) told readers to put the television set in the kitchen so that "Mama sees her pet programs. . . ." Via such spatial remedies labor would not be affected by the leisure of viewing, nor would viewing be denied by household chores. In fact, household labor and television were continually condensed into one space designed to accommodate both activities. In one advertisement this labor-viewing condensation provided the basis of a joke. A graphic depicted a housewife tediously hanging her laundry on the outdoor clothesline. The drudgery of this work is miraculously solved as the housewife brings her laundry into her home and sits before her television set while letting the laundry dry on the antenna *(American Home,* 1955b, p. 138).

This spatial condensation of labor and viewing was part of a well-entrenched functionalist discourse. The home had to provide rooms that would allow for a practical orchestration of "modern living activities" which now included watching television. Functionalism was particularly useful for advertisers who used it to promote not just one household item but an entire product line. An ad for the Crane Company *(House Beautiful,* 1952a, p. 59) displayed its kitchen appliance ensemble, complete with ironing, laundering, and cooking facilities. Here the housewife could do multiple chores at once because all the fixtures were "matched together as a complete chore unit." One particularly attractive component of this "chore unit" was a television set built into the wall above the washer and dryer.

While spatial condensations of labor and leisure helped to soothe tensions about television's obstruction of household chores, other problems still existed. The magazines suggested that television would cause increasing work loads. Considering the cleanliness of the living room, *House Beautiful* told its readers: "Then the men move in for boxing, wrestling, basketball, hockey. They get excited. Ashes on the floor. Pretzel crumbs. Beer stains." The remedy was spatial: "Lots of sets after a few months have been moved into dens and recreation rooms" (Ward, 1948, p. 220).

In a slight twist of terms, the activity of eating was said to be moving out of the dining area and into the television-sitting area. Food stains on upholstery, floors, and other surfaces meant extra work for women. Vinyl upholstery, linoleum floors, tiling, and other spill-proof surfaces were recommended. In addition, the magazines showed women how to be gracious TV hostesses, always prepared to serve family and friends special TV treats. These snack-time chores created a lucrative market for manufacturers who offered a new breed of "made for TV objects" including TV trays, tables, china sets, and, in 1954, the TV dinner.

While magazines presented readers with a host of television-related tasks, they also suggested ways for housewives to ration their labor. Time-motion studies, which had been integral to the discourses of feminism and domestic science since the progressive era, were rigorously applied to the problem of increasing work loads. All unnecessary human movement which the television set might demand had to be minimized. Again, this called for a careful management of space. The magazines suggested that chairs and sofas be placed so that they need not be moved for watching television. Alternatively, furniture could be made mobile. By placing wheels on a couch, it was possible to exert minimal energy while converting a sitting space into a viewing space. More typically, the television was mobilized. Casters and lazy Susans were suggested for the heavy console models, but the ideal solution was the easy-to-handle portable set.

More radically, space between rooms could be made continuous in order to minimize the extra movements of household labor which the television set might demand. An ad for *House Beautiful* (1952b, p. 138) suggested a "continuity" of living, dining, and television areas wherein "a curved sofa and a folding screen mark off [the] television corner from the living and dining room." Via this carefully managed spatial continuum, "it takes no more than an extra ten steps or so to serve the TV fans."

Continuous space was also a response to a more general problem of television and family relationships. Popular women's magazines discussed television in the context of domestic ideals that can be traced back to the Victorian period—ideals that were organized around the often contradictory goals of family unity and gender/social hierarchies. By incorporating notions of gender and social place within its structural layout, the middle class homes of Victorian America intended to construct a classically balanced order where ideals of family unity and division were joined in a harmonious blend of formalized rules that governed the residents' behavior. While, for example, the back parlor provided for family bonding during leisure time pursuits, individual bedrooms ensured difference among men, women, and children who were expected to carry out their own essential functions in private spaces. In the twentieth century, and certainly in the postwar era, the ideals of unity and division still pertained—even if domestic architecture had gone through a number of drastic revisions.

Women's household work presented a special dilemma for the twin ideals of family unity and social divisions because household chores demanded a more fluid relation to space than that provided by the formalized settings of the Victorian ideal. This problem became particularly significant by the early decades of the twentieth century when middle class women became increasingly responsible for household chores due to a radical reduction in the number of domestic servants.[3] As Gwendolyn Wright (1981, p. 172) has observed, women were now often cut off from the family group as they worked in kitchens designed to resemble scientific laboratories and far removed from the family activities in the central living areas of the home. Architects did little to respond to the problem of female isolation but continued instead to build kitchens fully separated from communal living spaces, suggesting that labor-saving kitchen appliances would solve the servant shortage.

In the postwar era when the continuous spaces of ranch-style architecture became a cultural ideal, the small suburban home placed a greater emphasis on interaction among family members. The "open plan" of the postwar home eliminated some of the walls between the dining room, living room, and kitchen, and thus it was associated with a higher degree of family bonding and recreational activity. With the help of this new design for living, postwar Americans were meant to rediscover the domestic bonding and personal security that was threatened during wartime. The new "family togetherness" (a term first coined by *McCalls* in 1954) served as convenient spatial metaphor that offered a soothing alternative to the vast economic, residential, and social dislocations of the postwar world. As Roland Marchand (1982) argues, the ranch-style home and the values placed on domestic cohesion promised a last gasp at cultural "dominion" in a world increasingly structured by bureaucratic corporations and the anonymity of suburban landscapes. But even if the fantasy of dominion was a potent model of postwar experience, the new family home never functioned so idyllically in practice, nor was the domestic ideal itself so simple. Just as the Victorian idea of domesticity was rooted in a fundamental contradiction between family unity and social/sexual hierarchy, the postwar notion of family togetherness was itself based on rigid distinctions between gender lines and social function. The domestic architecture of the period is a testimony to this tenuous balance between unity and division. Even in the continuous ranch-style homes, space was often organized around the implicit differences in the everyday lives of men, women, and children. In the model homes of postwar suburbia, the woman's work area was still zoned off from the activity area, and the woman's role as homemaker still worked to separate her from the leisure activities of her family.

Women's magazines suggested intricately balanced spatial arrangements that would mediate the tensions between female integration and isolation. Here, television viewing became a special topic of consideration. *House Beautiful* placed a television set in its remodeled kitchen which combined "such varied functions as cooking, storage, laundry, flower arranging, dining, and TV viewing" (Conway, 1951, p. 121). In this case, as elsewhere, the call for functionalism was related to the woman's ability to work among a group engaged in leisure activities. A graphic showed a television placed in a "special area" devoted to "eating" and "relaxing," one "not shut off by a partition." In continuous space, "the worker . . . is always part of the group, can share in the conversation and fun while work is in progress."

While this example presents a harmonious solution, often the ideals of integration and isolation resulted in highly contradictory representations of domestic life. Typically, illustrations that depicted family groups watching television showed the housewife to be oddly disconnected from her family members who were huddled together in a semicircle pattern. Sentinnel Television organized its advertising campaign around this pictorial convention. One ad, for example, depicted a housewife holding a tray of beverages, standing off to the side of her family which was gathered around the television set *(Better Homes and Gardens*, 1952a, p. 144). Another ad showed a housewife cradling her baby in her arms and standing at a window, far away from the rest of her family which gathered around the Sentinnel console *(Better Homes and Gardens*, 1953, p. 169). In an ad for Magnavox Television, the housewife's chores separated her from her circle of friends. The ad was organized around a U-shaped sofa that provided a quite literal manifestation of the semicircle visual cliche *(House Beautiful*, 1948, p. 5). A group of adult couples sat on the sofa watching the new Magnavox set, but the hostess stood at the kitchen door, holding a tray of snacks. Spatially removed from the television viewers, the housewife appeared to be sneaking a look at the set as she went about her hostess chores.

This problem of female spatial isolation gave way to what I call a "corrective cycle of commodity purchases." An article in *American Home* about the joys of the electric dishwasher is typical here (Ramsay, 1949, p. 66). A graphic depicting a family gathered around the living room console included the caption, "No martyr banished to kitchen, she never misses television programs. Lunch, dinner dishes are in an electric dishwasher." An ad for Hotpoint dishwashers used the same discursive strategy *(House Beautiful*, 1950, p. 77). The illustration showed a wall of dishes that separated a housewife in the kitchen from her family which sat huddled around the television set in the living room. The caption read, "Please . . . Let Your Wife Come Out Into the Living Room! Don't let dirty dishes make your wife a kitchen exile! She loses the most precious hours of her life shut off from pleasures of the family circle by the never-ending chore of old-fashioned dishwashing!"

This ideal version of female integration in a unified family space was contested by the competing discourse on divided spaces. Distinctions between work and leisure space remained an important principle of household efficiency. The magazines argued that room dividers or separate television corners might help to sanction off the work place from the viewing place and thus allow housewives the luxury of privacy from the television crowd. General Electric used this notion of family division to support the sale of a second television *(Better Homes and Gardens*, 1955, p. 139). The ad depicted a harried housewife who was able to find peace on her new GE kitchen portable. As the split-screen design of the layout showed, Mother and Daughter were able to perform their household work as they watched a cooking show, while Dad enjoyed total passive relaxation as he watched a football game on the living room console.

TELEVISION, GENDER, AND DOMESTIC POWER

The bifurcation of sexual roles, of male (leisure) and female (productive) activities served as an occasion for a full consideration of power dynamics between men and women in the home. Typically, the magazines extended their categories of feminine and masculine viewing practices into representations of the body. For men, television viewing was most often depicted in terms of a posture of repose. Men were typically shown to be sprawled out on easy chairs as they watched the set. Remote controls allowed the father to watch in undisturbed passive comfort. In many ways, this representation of the male body was based on Victorian notions of rejuvenation for the working man. Relaxation was condoned for men because it served a revitalizing function, preparing them for the struggles of the work-a-day world. But for women the passive calm of television viewing was simply more problematic. Although women were shown to relax in the home, as I have shown, the female body watching television was often engaged in productive activities.

Sometimes, representations of married couples became excessively literal about the gendered patterns of television leisure. When the Cleavelander Company advertised its new "T-Vue" chair, it told consumers "Once you sink into the softness of Cleavelander's cloud-like contours, cares seem to float away . . ." *(House Beautiful*, 1954, p. 158). Thus, not only the body but also the spirit would be revitalized by the television chair. But this form of rejuvenation was markedly gendered. While the chair allowed the father "to stretch out with his feet on the ottoman," the mother's television leisure was nevertheless productive. For as the caption stated, "Mother likes to gently rock as she sews." An advertisement for Airfoam furniture cushions used a similar discursive strategy *(Better Homes and Gardens*, 1952b, p. 177). The graphic showed a husband dozing in his foam rubber cushioned chair as he sits before a television set. Meanwhile, his wife clears away his snack. The text read, "Man's pleasure is the body coddling comfort" of the cushioned chair while "Woman's treasure is a home lovely to look at, easy to keep perfectly tidy and neat," with cushioning that "never needs fluffing."

In such cases, the man's pleasure in television is associated with passive relaxation. But for women pleasure is derived through the aesthetics of a well-kept home and labor-saving devices which promise to rationalize the extra labor that television brings to domestic space. Although on one level these representations are compatible with traditional gender roles, subtle reversals of power ran through the magazines as a whole. Even if there was a certain degree of privilege attached to man's position of total relaxation—his right to rule from the easy chair throne—this power was in no way absolute, nor was it stable. Instead, it seems to me, the most striking thing about this gendered representation of the body is that it was at odds with the normative conception of masculinity and femininity. Whereas Western society associates activity with maleness, representations of television attributed this trait to women. Conversely, the notion of feminine passivity was transferred over to the man of the house.[4]

Indeed, it might be concluded that the cultural ideals which demanded that women be shown as productive workers also had the peculiar side effect of "feminizing" the father. As Andreas Huyssen (1986, p. 47) argues, this notion of feminization has been a motif in the discourse on mass culture since the nineteenth century. "Mass culture," Huyssen claims, "is somehow associated with women while real, authentic culture remains the prerogative of men." Indeed, mass culture has repeatedly been figured in terms of patriarchal ideas of femininity and represented in tropes of passivity, consumption, penetration, and addiction. In this way, it threatens the very foundations of so-called "authentic" or high culture that is represented in terms of masculine tropes of activity, productivity, and knowledge.

In 1941, this gendered conception of mass culture reached a dramatic pitch when Philip Wylie wrote his classic misogynist text, *Generation of Vipers*, which was reprinted 16 times. In this book, Wylie connected the discourse on mass culture and women to broadcasting. In general, Wylie argued, women had somehow joined in a conspiracy with big industry and, with the aid of advanced technology, had supplanted the need for men altogether. Women, along with the technocratic world, had stripped men of their masculine privilege and turned them into cowering sissies. In his most bitter chapter entitled "Common Women," Wylie argued that women had somehow gained control of the airwaves. Women, he suggested, made radio listening into a passive activity which threatened manhood and, in fact, civilization. As Wylie (pp. 214–215) wrote,

> The radio is mom's final tool, for it stamps everybody who listens with the matriarchal brand. . . . Just as Goebbels has revealed what can be done with such a mass-stamping of the public psyche in his nation, so our land is a living representation of the same fact worked out in matriarchal sentimentality, goo, slop, hidden cruelty, and the foreshadow of national death.

In the annotated notes of the 1955 edition, Wylie (pp. 213–214) updated these fears, claiming that television would soon take the place of radio and turn men into female-dominated dupes. Women, he wrote, "will not rest until every electronic moment has been bought to sell suds and every program censored to the last decibel and syllable according to her self-adulation—along with that (to the degree the mom-indoctrinated pops are permitted access to the dials) of her de-sexed, de-souled, de-cerebrated mate." Although Wylie's rhetoric might seem to be the product of a fevered mind, this basic blend of misogyny and technophobia was common to representations of television and everyday life in the postwar period.

Men's magazines offered tongue-in-cheek versions of the situation, showing how television had turned men into passive homebodies. The fashionable men's magazine *Esquire* and the working man's magazine *Popular Science* presented ironic views of the male sloth. In 1951, for example, *Esquire* (p. 10) showed the stereotypical husband relaxing with his shoes off, beer in hand, smiling idiotically while seated before a television set. Two years later, the same magazine referred to television fans as "televidiots" (O'Brien, p. 24).

If these magazines provided a humorous look at the man of leisure, they also offered alternatives. In very much the same way that Victorians like Catherine Beecher sought to elevate the woman by making her the center of domestic affairs, the men's magazines suggested that fathers could regain their authority through increased participation in family life. As early as 1940, Sydnie Greenbie called for the reinstitution of manhood in his book titled *Leisure for Living*. Greenbie reasoned that the popular figure of the male "boob" could be counteracted if the father cultivated his mechanical skills. As he wrote (p. 210), "At last man has found something more in keeping with his nature, the workshop, with its lathe and mechanical saws, something he has kept as yet his own against the predacious female. . . . And [it becomes] more natural . . . for the man to be a homemaker as well as the woman."

After the war, this reintegration of the father became a popular ideal.[5] As *Esquire* told its male readers, "your place, Mister, is in the home, too, and if you'll make a few thoughtful improvements to it, you'll build yourself a happier, more comfortable, less backbreaking world . . ." ("Home is for Husbands," 1951, p. 88). From this perspective, the men's magazines suggested ways for fathers to take an active and productive attitude in relation to television. Even if men were passive spectators, when not watching they could learn to repair the set or else produce television carts, built-ins, and stylish cabinets. Articles with step-by-step instructions were circulated in *Popular Science*, and the *Home Craftsman* even had a special "TV: Improve Your Home Show" column featuring a husband and wife, Thelma and Vince, and their adventures in home repairs.

Popular Science also suggested hobbies for men to use television in an active and productive way. The magazine ran several articles on a new fad—television photography. Men were shown how to take still pictures off their sets, and in 1950 the magazine even conducted a readership contest for prize winning photos that were published in the December issue ("From Readers' Albums," p. 166).

CONCLUSION

The gendered division of domestic labor and the complex relations of power entailed by it were thus shown to organize the experience of watching television. While these early representations cannot tell us how real people actually used television in their own homes, they do begin to reveal a set of discursive rules that were formed for thinking about television in the early period. They begin to disclose the social construction of television as it is rooted in a mode of thought based on categories of sexual difference.

Recent ethnographic studies conducted by David Morley (1986), Ann Gray (1987), James Lull (1988), and others reveal the continued impact of gender (and other social differences) on the ways families watch television. Gray's work on VCR usage among working class families in Britain especially highlights how gender-based ideas about domestic technology and productive labor in the home circumscribe women's use of the new machine. Such ethnographic work provides compelling evidence for the intricate relations of television and gender as they are experienced in the viewing situation.

For historians, questions about the television audience pose different problems and call for other methods. The reconstruction of viewing experiences at some point in the past is an elusive project. By its very nature, the history of spectatorship is a patchwork history, one that must draw together a number of approaches and perspectives in the hopes of achieving a partial picture of past experiences. The approach I have taken here provides insights into the way television viewing has been connected to larger patterns of family ideals and gender construction within our culture.

Women's magazines depicted a subtle interplay between labor and leisure at home, and they offered the postwar housewife ways to deal with television in her daily life. These popular discourses show that television was not simply promoted as a pleasure machine; rather, the media engaged women in a dialogue about the concrete problems television posed for productive labor in the home. If our culture has systematically relegated domestic leisure to the realm of nonproduction, these magazines reveal the tenuousness of such notions. Indeed, for the postwar housewife, television was not represented as a passive activity, but rather it was imbricated in a pattern of everyday life where work is never done.

NOTES

1. This stove was mentioned in *Sponsor* (1951, p. 119) and *Popular Science* (1952, p. 132). Interestingly, *Popular Science* did not discuss the television component of the stove as a vehicle for leisure but rather showed how "A housewife can follow telecast cooking instructions step-by-step on the TV set built into this electric oven." Perhaps in this way, this men's magazine allayed readers' fears that their wives would use the new technology for diversion as opposed to useful labor.

2. This essay is based on a sample that includes four of the leading middle class women's home magazines, *Better Homes and Gardens, American Home, Ladies' Home Journal*, and *House Beautiful*. I examined each of these magazines for its entire run of issues, 1948–1955. For purposes of comparison, I have also researched general magazines, men's magazines, and women's magazines aimed at a less affluent reader. For more on sources and method, see my dissertation (1988a).
3. I do not mean to ignore the fact that domestic servants were themselves detached from the family activities through the Victorian model of space and its elaborate separation of servant quarters from central living areas.
4. This is not to say that television was the only domestic machine to disrupt representations of gender. Roland Marchand (1985) claims that ads for radio sets and phonographs reversed pictorial conventions for the depiction of men and women. Ads traditionally showed husbands seated while wives perched on the arm of a chair or sofa. But Marchand finds that "in the presence of culturally uplifting [radio and phonograph] music, the woman more often gained the right of reposed concentration while the (more technologically inclined) man stood prepared to change the records or adjust the radio dials" (pp. 252–253). In the case of television, Marchand's analysis and interpretation do not seem to apply since men were often shown seated and unable or unwilling to control the technology.
5. The reasons for this warrant a book-length study. Some tentative explanations come from Marchand (1982), who argues that the waning of male authority in the public sphere of corporate life contributed to men's increased participation and "quests for dominion" in private life. However, I would add speculatively that the whole category of masculinity was being contested in this period. The "quests for dominion" were accompanied by an equally strong manifestation of their opposite. The down-trodden male heroes of film *noir* and the constant uncertainty about the sexual status of the "family man" in the melodramas and social problem films suggest that American culture was seeking to redefine sexual identity, or at least to give sexual identity meaning in a world where the gendered balance of social and economic power was undergoing change.

REFERENCES

Adams, W., & Hungerford, E. A. (1949, September). Television: Buying and installing is fun; These ideas will help. *Better Homes and Gardens*, pp. 38–39, 152–156, 158.

Allen, R. C. (1985) *Speaking of soap operas*. Chapel Hill: University of North Carolina Press.

American Home. (1954, December). p. 39.

American Home. (1955a, October). p. 14.

American Home. (1955b, May). p. 138.

Benjamin, W. (1969). The work of art in the age of mechanical reproduction. In H. Arendt (Ed.), *Illuminations* (pp. 217–252). New York: Shocken. (Original work published 1936)

Better Homes and Gardens. (1952a, December). p. 144.

Better Homes and Gardens. (1952b, October). p. 177.

Better Homes and Gardens. (1953, February). p. 169.

Better Homes and Gardens. (1955, October). p. 139.

Boddy, W. (1979). The rhetoric and economic roots of the American broadcasting industry. *Cinetracts*, 6(2), 37–54.

Boddy, W. (1985). "The shining centre of the home": Ontologies of television in the "golden age." In P. Drummand & R. Patterson (Eds.), *Television in transition* (pp. 125–133). London: British Film Institute.

Browne, N. (1984). The political economy of the television (super) text. *Quarterly Review of Film Studies*, 9(3), 175–182.

Chafe, W. (1972). *The American woman: Her changing social, economic, and political roles, 1920–1970.* London: Oxford University Press.

Conway, C. (1951, June). Remodeled thinking made over this kitchen. *House Beautiful*, pp. 121–122.

Covert, C.L. (1984). "We may hear too much": American sensibility and the response to radio, 1919–1924. In C. L. Covert & J. D. Stevens (Eds.), *Mass media between the wars: Perceptions of cultural tension, 1918–1941* (pp. 199–220). Syracuse: Syracuse University Press.

Crosby, J. (1950, February). What's television going to do to your life? *House Beautiful*, pp. 66–67, 125–126.

Davis, R. E. (1965). Response to innovation: A study of popular argument about new mass media (Doctoral dissertation, University of Iowa). *Dissertation Abstracts International, 26*, 6232.

Daytime video: Dumont plans afternoon programming. (1949, November 28). *Telecasting*, p. 3.

Dumont daytime "shoppers" series starts. (1949, December 12). *Telecasting*, p. 5.

Dumont expansion continues. (1949, April 12). *Radio Daily*, p. 23.

Esquire (1951, March), p. 10.

Folbre, N. (1982). Exploitation comes home: A critique of the marxist theory of family labour. *Cambridge Journal of Economics, 6*, 317–329.

For the girls at home. (1954, March 15). *Newsweek*, pp. 92–93.

From readers' albums of television photos. (1950, December). *Popular Science*, p. 166.

Gatlin, R. (1987). *American women since 1945*. Jackson: University of Mississippi Press.

Gray, A. (1987). Behind closed doors: Video recorders in the home. In H. Baehr & G. Dyer (Eds.), *Boxed in: Women and television* (pp. 38–54). New York: Pandora.

Greenbie, S. (1940). *Leisure for living.* New York: George W. Stewart.

Home is for husbands too. (1951, June). *Esquire*, pp. 88–91.

House Beautiful. (1948, November). p. 5.

House Beautiful. (1950, December). p. 77.

House Beautiful. (1952a, June). p. 59.

House Beautiful. (1952b, May). p. 138.

House Beautiful. (1954, November). p. 158.

Huyssen, A. (1986). *After the great divide: Modernism, mass culture, postmodernism.* Bloomington: Indiana University Press.

Ladies' Home Journal. (1955, April). p. 130.

Lefebvre, H. (1979). Work and leisure in daily life. In A. Mattelart & S. Siegelaub (Eds.), M. C. Axtmann (Trans.), *Communication and class struggle* (pp. 135–141). New York: International General. (Reprinted from *Critique de la Vie Quotidienne,* Forward, 1958)

Lull, J. (Ed.). (1988). *World families watching television.* Beverly Hills: Sage.

Marchand, R. (1982). Visions of classlessness, quests for dominion: American popular culture, 1945–1960. In R. H. Bremner & G. W. Reichard (Eds.), *Reshaping America: Society and institutions, 1945–1960* (pp. 163–190). Columbus: Ohio State University Press.

Marchand, R. (1985). *Advertising the American dream: Making way for modernity, 1920–1940.* Berkeley: University of California Press.

Modleski, T. (1983). The rhythms of reception: Daytime television and women's work. In E. A. Kaplan (Ed.), *Regarding television* (pp. 67–75). Los Angeles: University Publications of America.

Morley, D. (1986). *Family television: Cultural power and domestic leisure.* London: Comedia.

Newsweek. (1951, September 24). p. 56.

O'Brien, J. (1953, November). Offsides in sports. *Esquire*, pp. 24, 26.

Popular Science. (1952, May). p. 132.

Ramsay, E. (1949, September). How to stretch a day. *American Home*, pp. 66–67.

Spigel, L. (1988a). Installing the television set: The social construction of television's place in the American home, 1948–55 (Doctoral dissertation, University of California). *Dissertation Abstracts International, 49*, 2283A.

Spigel, L. (1988b). Installing the television set: Popular discourses on television and domestic space, 1948–55. *Camera Obscura, 16*, 11–47.

Sponsor. (1951, June 4), p. 19.

Televiser. (1951, September), p. 20.

Tyler May, E. (1988). *Homeward bound: American families in the cold war era.* New York: Basic Books.

Ward, W. W. (1948, October). Is it time to buy television? *House Beautiful*, pp. 169–173, 220–221, 224, 287.

Wright, G. (1981). *Building the dream: A social history of housing in America.* Cambridge: Massachusetts Institute of Technology Press.

Wylie, P. (1955). *Generation of vipers* (annotated ed.) New York: Holt, Rinehart and Winston.

Index